The American Political System
Introductory Readings

The American Political System
Introductory Readings

Richard E. Morgan
Bowdoin College

James E. Connor
Office of Economic Opportunity

HARCOURT BRACE JOVANOVICH, INC.
New York/Chicago/San Francisco/Atlanta

© 1971 by Harcourt Brace Jovanovich, Inc.

All rights reserved. No part of this publication may be reproduced or transmitted in any form or by any means, electronic or mechanical, including photocopy, recording, or any information storage and retrieval system, without permission in writing from the publisher.

ISBN: 0–15–502550–3

Library of Congress Catalog Card Number: 70–148842

Printed in the United States of America

Preface

The American Political System: Introductory Readings differs from most other books of readings designed for basic courses in American politics in that fewer authors are represented by longer selections. We are convinced that beginning undergraduates benefit more from the complete arguments of noted political scientists than from encapsulated "points of view." Thus, the decision to include complete readings of manageable length by well-known and widely respected authors was our first and most important guideline. The readings were chosen on the basis of intrinsic interest and central importance to the literature of political science, with emphasis on matters of vital contemporary concern. Since we have not imposed any restrictive framework, the book may be used in any American government course. At the end of each chapter we have provided annotated bibliographies of works readily available to the undergraduate.

We gratefully acknowledge the suggestions and criticisms of Milton C. Cummings, Jr., Theodore Lowi, Kenneth Prewitt, Douglas Rae, and Emmette S.

Redford. The book is distinctly improved by the extent to which we were able to follow their advice. At another level of obligation, we thank Eva Morgan and our good friends, Arthur Strimling and Elizabeth Hansot, without whose sustained encouragement work might never have begun.

RICHARD E. MORGAN
JAMES E. CONNOR

Contents

Preface   v
Introduction   1

1   The System at Its Outset   5

Seymour Martin Lipset, THE NEED FOR PAYOFF   7
William Nisbet Chambers, POLITICAL PARTIES IN THE NEW NATION   15
Suggestions for Further Reading   20

2   The Social Determinants of the System   23

Philip Selznick, LEGAL INSTITUTIONS AND SOCIAL CONTROLS   25
Nathan Glazer and Daniel P. Moynihan, BEYOND THE MELTING POT   33
Suggestions for Further Reading   53

CONTENTS

3 The Cultural and Ideological Determinants of the System   55

Robert D. Hess and Judith V. Torney, ATTACHMENT TO GOVERNMENT   57
Samuel H. Beer, LIBERALISM AND THE NATIONAL IDEA   66
Suggestions for Further Reading   78

4 Public Opinion and Political Parties   81

V. O. Key, Jr., PUBLIC OPINION AND DEMOCRATIC POLITICS   83
Angus Campbell, A CLASSIFICATION OF PRESIDENTIAL ELECTIONS   97
Walter Dean Burnham, PARTY SYSTEMS AND THE POLITICAL PROCESS   109
Suggestions for Further Reading   120

5 Interest Groups   123

Lester W. Milbrath, THE IMPACT OF LOBBYING ON GOVERNMENTAL DECISIONS   126
Theodore Lowi, GROUPS AND THE PROBLEM OF GOVERNING   139
Suggestions for Further Reading   149

6 The Congress   151

Nelson W. Polsby, THE INSTITUTIONALIZATION OF THE U. S. HOUSE OF REPRESENTATIVES   153
Richard F. Fenno, Jr., THE HOUSE APPROPRIATIONS COMMITTEE AS A POLITICAL SYSTEM: THE PROBLEM OF INTEGRATION   174
Samuel P. Huntington, CONGRESSIONAL RESPONSES IN THE TWENTIETH CENTURY   196
Suggestions for Further Reading   220

7 The Presidency   223

Richard E. Neustadt, THE PRESIDENCY AT MID-CENTURY   224
Fred I. Greenstein, THE PSYCHOLOGICAL FUNCTIONS OF THE PRESIDENCY FOR CITIZENS   259
Suggestions for Further Reading   267

Contents

8 The Bureaucracy — 269

James Q. Wilson, THE BUREAUCRACY PROBLEM — 271
Herbert Kaufman, ADMINISTRATIVE DECENTRALIZATION AND POLITICAL POWER — 277
Suggestions for Further Reading — 290

9 The Supreme Court — 293

Archibald Cox, THE REFORM OF THE CRIMINAL PROCESS — 295
Alexander M. Bickel, CURBING THE UNION — 308
Suggestions for Further Reading — 321

10 Intergovernmental Relations — 323

Morton Grodzins, SHARING OF FUNCTIONS: THE "NATIONAL" POLICE SYSTEM — 325
Mark DeWolfe Howe, FEDERALISM AND CIVIL RIGHTS — 341
Suggestions for Further Reading — 351

11 Local and State Governments — 353

Robert Wood, THE AMERICAN MINIATURE — 356
James E. Connor and Richard E. Morgan, THE GOVERNOR AND THE EXECUTIVE ESTABLISHMENT — 367
Suggestions for Further Reading — 373

12 The Urban Crisis — 375

Daniel J. Elazar, ARE WE A NATION OF CITIES? — 377
James Q. Wilson, THE MAYORS VS. THE CITIES — 392
Suggestions for Further Reading — 403

13 The Eruption of Violence — 405

Edward C. Banfield, RIOTING MAINLY FOR FUN AND PROFIT — 407
Richard Maxwell Brown, THE AMERICAN VIGILANTE TRADITION — 427
Suggestions for Further Reading — 439

14 The Battle over Foreign Policy 441

Roger Hilsman, IMPROVING THE POLICY "MACHINERY" 444
The Senate Foreign Relations Committee, FOR AN INCREASED
   CONGRESSIONAL ROLE IN FOREIGN POLICY MAKING 455
John P. Roche, CAN A FREE SOCIETY FIGHT A LIMITED WAR? 461
Ronald Steel, THE CASE FOR RETRENCHMENT 470
Suggestions for Further Reading 480

The American Political System
Introductory Readings

Introduction

THE EDITORS OF COLLECTIONS OF READINGS have an obligation to provide some justification for them to students who have been required to buy them. Justifications can be of two sorts: a collection can be said either to provide brief snippets of "sources" and "great books," or to present in convenient form some distinguished articles that originally appeared in journals and were thus inaccessible to a large number of beginning students. The increasing sophistication of political scientists and of undergraduates is, happily, reducing the need for the first sort of reader; snippets are out! This volume is of the second sort: entire articles and major parts of books are reproduced, and while most footnotes and other purely scholarly apparatus have been deleted, the editors have otherwise intruded little into the works they present.

But the productivity of political scientists over the past decade has created difficulties for those who would assemble this type of collection. There are so many themes in the literature that anyone's favorite thirty pieces might, when put between covers, appear utterly unrelated; yet if one states a single theme and insists on articles that precisely complement it, too many good pieces are left out and too many important aspects of the political process are left untreated. We have sought a middle way. While we have not restricted ourselves to a single theme, we do wish to alert students to several leitmotifs that run through at least some of the superficially dissimilar writings we have chosen to present here. Not all the selections relate to these themes, and some may even illustrate counter-themes. But these themes were important in our thinking as selections were made, and the reader should be aware of them.

One theme is the increasing centralization of governmental power in America; by this we mean that the national and state governments have been steadily moving into areas that had previously been considered local. A second theme is the increasing domination of the American political system by nongovernmental institutions (corporations, unions, civil rights groups, and so on) that are national in scope and in impact. A third theme is our growing tendency as citizens to think in national terms and identify less with our towns and counties. A fourth is the growth of executive power as opposed to that of popular assemblies (Congress, legislatures, town councils). A fifth is the way in which the dissatisfaction of America's "marginal citizens" may be imperiling the stability of the system. A sixth is the growing tendency in America to regard basic social problems as easily soluble by the government ("If we can put a man on the moon, surely we can . . ."), and the poisonous disillusionment that results when this is shown to be untrue.

No single factor can adequately explain all these trends. Certainly, the rapidly increasing complexity of a post-industrial society is an important consideration. Problems become translated into technical terms and are then the province of those relative few who possess technical competence and who are typically concentrated in national or at least large institutions. In addition, geographical mobility and electronic communication have eroded localism and quickened expectations among blacks and young people. Village and regional identifications made in quieter and slower-moving times are obliterated by mass migration from rural to urban areas, by the daily rush of commuters across city, county, and even state lines, by the career patterns of the highly educated, and by the nightly barrage of "broadcast journalism." Events are no longer heavily insulated by space and time. The righteous (or merely petulant) anger of a handful of people in one part of the nation is immediately conveyed to the nation as a whole and is perceived by large parts of the nation as a "problem" that somehow must be "solved" for the good of the whole.

There are, of course, many more things going on in the American political system than are described by the six themes we have mentioned, and many of these other phenomena are reflected in the articles that follow. The themes merely suggest particularly important points to which many of the articles speak. If borne in mind as the student works through the book, they will alert him to relationships between the selections that might otherwise have escaped his notice.

In organizing the materials, we have proceeded in a quite traditional and, we hope, sensible fashion. Chapter 1, on the American system at its outset, is followed by two chapters on the social and attitudinal bases of the contemporary system. Chapters 4 and 5 deal with informal political institutions—political parties and interest groups. Chapters 6–9 treat the

Introduction

major components of the federal government—the Congress, the Presidency, the bureaucracy, and the Supreme Court. Chapter 10 deals with intergovernmental relations and Chapter 11 with state and local governments. Chapters 12, 13, and 14 deal with matters that are presently the subjects of intense debate—the ills of the cities, the resort to violence as a political technique, and the future of American foreign policy.

1 The system at its outset

WHATEVER THE REALITIES OF AMERICAN POLITICS TODAY, at its inception and in its early decades our system was highly decentralized. Ratification of the national Constitution was very much in doubt in a number of ex-colonies, such as Virginia, New York, and Massachusetts. Secretary of the Treasury Hamilton's efforts to secure the financial power of the federal government were bitterly resisted in the name of freedom from centralized tyranny. Jefferson's frequently portrayed achievements in centralizing power through party building and congressional leadership were, as James S. Young has pointed out,[1] tenuous and transient. The most important single fact about American politics during the formative period was the deeply ingrained resistance of the provinces to the fledging national government.

To say that the Jeffersonians spoke for the small farmer and the frontier and that the Federalists spoke for urban merchants and landed wealth does communicate *something* about the politics of that time. And if one has a taste for unrefined economic determinism, Charles Beard's interpretation of the period is always available—that is, those who stood to profit directly from the new national government supported it, and vice versa. Such single-factored explanations do have value; they may serve to focus scholarly attention on previously ignored relationships and thus give rise to a whole new wave of research and productive controversy. However, a balanced

---

[1] James S. Young, *The Washington Community* (New York: Columbia University Press, 1966).

understanding of the multiple centrifugal forces that operated in the developing American polity requires subtler categories.

In *The First New Nation,* Seymour Martin Lipset examined the American formative period from a new perspective—using the concepts developed by political scientists and sociologists to describe the dynamics of political development in the post–World War II "new nations." Drawing heavily on the functionalist thought of Max Weber and Talcott Parsons, these investigators had sought to identify the universal problems that vex developing political orders, and then to describe the institutions that deal with these problems in particular systems. With them, Lipset argues in the selection reprinted here that newly formed political institutions must quickly establish their legitimacy in the eyes of the subject population. The institutions created by the Constitution of 1787 passed through precisely such a crisis of legitimacy. Lipset sees the financial programs of Hamilton as efforts to achieve legitimacy by tying the interests of propertied persons ("influentials" in their states and localities) to the national government. Despite Hamilton's efforts, decentralization persisted as the dominant force in American politics, but its most disastrous potential consequence, the breakdown of the new constitutional order, was averted.

The fragmented character of early political parties has been vividly described by William Nisbet Chambers in *Political Parties in the New Nation,* a selection from which is reprinted here. Chambers, in addition to describing the politics of sectionalism, points out the obvious geographical and technical factors that limited national communications and the strength of the individualistic ideology that permeated the society. Political parties in the last decade of the eighteenth century were characterized by shifting coalitions that were dominated by local notables loosely organized into caucuses and cabals. It was excruciatingly difficult to assert the leadership necessary to create a coalition for electing a President, or to enable a President once in office to marshal support for his policies among congressmen and senators, even those of his own party.

There is little in the Lipset or the Chambers articles that explicitly contradicts earlier analyses of the formative period, but their recasting of the familiar battles in terms of centralized power versus persistent centrifugal forces expands our understanding and puts us in a far better position to make sense of such later developments as the decline of presidential power under Madison, Monroe, and Adams.

◘ The Need for Payoff

SEYMOUR MARTIN LIPSET

All claims to a legitimate title to rule in new states must ultimately win acceptance through demonstrating effectiveness. The loyalty of the different groups to the system must be won through developing in them the conviction that this system is the best—or at least an excellent—way to accomplish their objectives. And even claims to legitimacy of a supernatural sort, such as "the gift of grace," are subjected on the part of the populace to a highly pragmatic test—that is, what is the payoff? For new states today, demonstrating effectiveness means one thing: economic development. Given the "revolution of rising expectations" that has swept the emerging nations, need for payoff in terms of economic goods and living standards is more important than ever.

As most new states lack the traditional means for rapid economic growth, they have been led in recent years to introduce large-scale government planning and direct state intervention. Although such efforts concur with the socialist ideology, the desire to use the state to direct and speed up the processes of economic growth has deeper roots than ideological conviction. It rests upon the dual necessity to demonstrate effectiveness to the various groups within the polity, and to display national competence to the outside world. To a considerable degree the leaders seek development as part of their more general effort to overcome feelings of national inferiority, particularly vis-à-vis the former metropolitan ruler.

Similar processes were at work in the United States, even though after the Revolution many leaders, particularly Jefferson, opposed any aid to manufacturing or commerce. As one economic historian has put it:

American industrial consciousness . . . received much of its early stimulus from the political storm and stress which preceded and led to the winning of independence. . . . American industrial consciousness grew out of the broad wave of political and economic resentment against England, but was mainly directed almost from the start toward the transfer of English skill and technique to this country. By 1830, it had succeeded, and American technology and industrial organization were by then comparable to those of England.

Pressure to develop domestic manufacturing followed shortly on the first effort at a national government, since the depression

FROM pp. 45–60 of *The First New Nation* by Seymour Martin Lipset, © 1963 by Seymour Martin Lipset, Basic Books, Inc., Publishers, New York. Reprinted by permission of Basic Books, Inc., and Heinemann Educational Books Ltd.

which intervened between 1783 and 1787 produced a reawakening of manufacturing zeal. Patriotism . . . provided the impetus to it, while there was also a better appreciation of the fact that English superiority in technique could be overcome only by borrowing it. The new wave of industrial agitation rose to a rapid climax in the first years of the federal government. Manufactures, like the Constitution, were expected to strengthen the country and help it achieve true independence.

Even Jefferson, the enthusiastic supporter of the physiocratic doctrine that agriculture was the only source of true wealth, felt compelled, when President, to modify his former objections to manufacturing. "As early as 1805 . . . [he] complained that his former views had been misunderstood. They were intended to apply only to the great cities of Europe and not to this country at the present time."

In fact, in this period prior to the War of 1812, the Federalists and Republicans appear to have supported government aid to industrialization when in office, and to have pointed up some of its adverse effects when in opposition. The Republicans defended Jefferson's Embargo on the grounds that:

It must be truly gratifying to every true American to witness the rapid introduction and progress of manufacturing establishments in the various parts of the United States. The Federalists . . . attacked the Embargo . . . from every angle. It was ruining the state's wealth, destroying agriculture and commerce to the advantage of manufactures, building up an aristocracy [and] corrupting the moral life. . . .

In evaluating early American economic development, it should be recognized that there was *a great deal of government intervention and even public investment in the economy so as to develop industry and commerce.* As Carter Goodrich has pointed out in discussing such activities:

The closest modern analogy, indeed, is to be found in the current projects of so-called underdeveloped countries. . . . So much, indeed, was done by public initiative that the distinguished economic historian, G. S. Callender, declared that this country was at the time an early and leading example of the "modern tendency to extend the activity of the state into industry."

On a national level, efforts were made—stimulated by Albert Gallatin, Jefferson's Secretary of the Treasury—to foster direct federal support for companies building new transportation facilities; but with some minor exceptions, these proposals, though advocated by Jefferson and Monroe, failed. The most important federal measures directly supporting economic growth took the form of investment in the Bank of the United States and, more important, protective tariffs to encourage domestic industry against products manufactured in England.

The failure of the effort to involve the federal government directly in economic activities did not reflect the strength of business opposition or of *laissez-faire* beliefs. "States' rights, state and sectional interests, and a belief in the capacities of the several states seem to have played the decisive role in the downfall of national planning. By contrast business enterprise offered far less formidable competition." As a consequence, most governmental efforts occurred at the state level, and many states felt it proper and necessary to use public funds to develop transportation facilities, banking, manufactures, and the like.

State intervention on behalf of economic growth took various forms, sometimes regulative, as in the setting up of inspection standards, and sometimes directly encouraging, as in financial assistance from lotteries or in the form of bounties. A third method was the franchise, which amounted to a monopoly that protected a company from competition during its early growth. And not unimportant in many states was direct government investment in, or outright ownership of, various companies whose development was deemed necessary for economic growth or the public welfare.

The system of public inspection "set up categories of goods which could not be sold and thus placed in a privileged position those the state judged fit." The government relaxed its laws against gambling to sanction lotteries, the proceeds of which were used to finance various state projects such as the building of bridges and roads, paper mills and glasshouses. The bounty was used to some extent by the states to encourage individual enterprises, though this technique fell into disuse in the early part of the nineteenth century.

The granting of franchises was particularly important in the construction of bridges, aqueducts, and mills, all of which interfered in some way with public waterways and fishing rights. The building of dams flooded adjacent lands and diverted water from natural channels.

Without the states' tolerance, builders faced unlimited responsibility for damages. To encourage industry, the government generously dealt out such franchises. . . . All franchises included an element of privilege, permitting to a few, as special assistance in a worthwhile enterprise, what was forbidden to all.

While applying the techniques of inspection, lotteries, bounties, and franchises, the states soon found the granting of charters to new corporations the most successful means of promoting economic development, for the "coercive power of assessment . . . gave the corporation a more efficient fund-raising mechanism." Consequently, the states' most important promotional policy became that of chartering business corporations. "After . . . [the Revolution] charter policy gradually established itself as one of the primary concerns of American state governments and expanded steadily through the pre-Civil War epoch."

The granting of bank charters was closely linked with developments in transportation. "This was due to an established legislative practice which frequently incorporated into bank charters requirements for assisting specified transportation companies. Such assistance usually took the form of stock subscriptions, loans, or outright grants of money."

Most of the early corporations were for religious or charitable organizations or for road, bridge, canal, bank and insurance companies. . . . In all some 557 manufacturing companies were incorporated in eight states between 1800 and 1823, Massachusetts and New York being far in the lead. . . . Before 1860 nearly all the states had general incorporation statutes.

Direct government financing of economic activities which required large sums of capital occurred in many states. During the first thirty or forty years of the nineteenth century, the states created a funded debt of more than two hundred million dollars, "a larger debt than that created by any government for purely industrial purposes." Internal improvements, particularly turnpikes and canals, constituted the most general area of direct state intervention. Virginia, Maryland, New York, Pennsylvania, Massachusetts, South Carolina, Georgia, Kentucky, Tennessee, Indiana, Illinois, and Michigan were among the states which used their financial resources for such purposes. Railroads also were built with government support in many states. And many banks were formed with governmental help. "Almost from the first introduction of banks into this country, it became a common practice for the State governments to invest revenue in bank stock."

In Pennsylvania, a state under one-party Democratic control for the first thirty-five years of the nineteenth century, there was considerable direct government intervention in the form of public ownership of transportation facilities and banks. The state encouraged the growth of credit facilities by investing heavily in bank stocks between 1800 and 1815. Similarly, a number of turnpike, canal, and navigation companies were owned jointly by the state and private investors. With the coming of railroads, Pennsylvania added railway stock to the list of companies in which it had investments. Local governments, counties, and cities invested even more heavily than did the state in such businesses. "Total municipal and county investments between 1840 and 1853 were estimated at fourteen million dollars—over twice the state investment at its 1843 peak." Direct public ownership occurred as well in many of these areas. Thus Pennsylvania built and owned the first railways along the main line.

For the first forty years of Pennsylvania's existence as a state within the Union, there was little argument over the propriety or even necessity of direct state participation in ownership as a means of facilitating economic development. In effect, as in many contemporary new nations, Pennsylvania and other American states followed a policy of government investment in areas basic to economic growth where private efforts seemed inadequate. The *doctrine of "laissez-faire" became dominant only after the growth of large corporations and private investment funds reduced the pressures for public funds.*

. . .

Local governments, especially cities, also played a major role in fostering economic development. To elaborate further on their activities is not necessary here. It may be noted, however, that Cincinnati owned a major railroad, while

The Need for Payoff

Baltimore was an extremely important investor in the Baltimore and Ohio and other lines. In New York State 315 municipalities were involved in the construction of railroad lines. In Pennsylvania, cities and counties contributed far more to railway construction than did the state. "The major portion of the stock issued by Missouri's state-aided railroads in the 1850's was sold to counties and municipalities."

The story of state and local investment in early economic development in the United States clearly justifies the conclusion that government in this period played a role corresponding to that envisaged in most new nations today. The need for large sums of investment capital in a new and as yet undeveloped economy could only be met domestically from government sources. And given the commitment and need of new states to develop economically, the American political leaders found the arguments to justify state intervention, even if they were different from those popular today. A reviewer of various recent works by economic historians dealing with economic development on the state and local level summarizes the conclusions to be drawn from these studies:

[These studies suggest] a new view of American capitalism in its formative years. . . . [T]he elected official replaced the individual enterpriser as the key figure in the release of capitalist energy; the public treasury, rather than private saving, became the major source of venture capital; and community purpose outweighed personal ambition in the selection of large goals for local economies. "Mixed" enterprise was the customary organization for important innovations, and government everywhere undertook the role put on it by the people, that of planner, promoter, investor, and regulator.

Rapid economic growth during this formative period in our economy benefited not only from assistance by the states themselves, but perhaps even more from the massive foreign capital furnished the new nation by outside investors, particularly British. There is a definite parallel between the dependence of contemporary new nations on external funds and the conditions which facilitated development here:[2]

[2] "By 1805 the coupons paid through Barings [Bros., London] represented a nominal capital of £5,747,283. This sum included, besides the unpaid debt of the United States abroad, at least seven million dollars in the stock of the First Bank of the United States. As the debt, foreign and domestic, was paid off British holdings diminished. The extinction of the Bank in 1811 and the War of 1812 reduced to £1,500,000 the amount upon which Barings paid dividends. . . .

"A more progressive movement set in after the war. In 1817 and 1818 temporary loans of bullion were made to the Second Bank of the United States. They became the basis of a permanent investment in the stock of that institution which in 1820 amounted to nearly three million dollars. Another million was added to this amount by 1828, and the total was doubled during the next three years. Out of 300,000 shares in private hands in July, 1831, 79,159 were held abroad by 466 shareholders. . . . Meanwhile part of the American public debt had returned abroad. Fourteen million dollars of it were owned by British investors in 1828, five millions by other European creditors." Leland Hamilton Jenks, *The Migration of British Capital to 1875* (New York: Alfred A. Knopf, 1927), p. 66.

England was the principal source of loans to American enterprise, both directly . . . through the purchase by Englishmen of stock in American banks or railways, as well as indirectly through the purchase by English investors of American State bonds, the proceeds of which in large measure were employed in the furtherance of "internal improvements."

The dependence of American expansion on foreign capital was to be seen in all areas of economic development: trade, internal improvements, banking, agriculture, and industry. Jenks has summarized the story:

[The wholesale merchants of the Yankee drygoods houses, who handled the import trade at the Atlantic ports in the antebellum period] could not trade adequately with their own capital. The[se] Yankee firms depended to a large extent in their buying upon credits which came, directly or indirectly, from such firms as Barings themselves.
. . . promoter-politicians, who perceived the advantages, whether public or private, which could accrue from the building of highways, canals and railroads, turned to foreign capital, filtered thru the public treasuries for support. . . . State-owned and state-constructed, the Erie Canal was financed by the issue of New York state bonds. Something over seven million dollars' worth were sold between 1817 and 1825, and they passed almost at once into the hands of Englishmen.
Before 1836 over ninety million dollars had been invested in canals and railways in the North, of which more than half was a charge upon public credit. The bulk of this capital had been procured from England.
. . . British capital which promoted transportation and westward expansion indirectly financed industry as well. American merchants and banks could draw credits for objects unspecified, and these were available in the United States for the expansion of industry. . . . *It will not be far wrong to estimate the total quantity of British capital invested in the United States during the thirties as approximately equal to the indebtedness incurred by the several states.*

It should be noted that the willingness of English holders of capital to invest heavily in American economic development was not unrelated to the governmental policies which fostered the growth of industry. Government sponsorship was fostered by the need for large sums of capital, since both domestic and foreign investors were often not willing to expend the large sums necessary for speculative and unknown ventures in distant lands.

The only securities that could do this were public securities, or the securities of corporations which were guaranteed or assisted by the government. . . . Accordingly, we find that English foreign investments in the early part of the nineteenth century were made chiefly in public securities. The stock and bonds of private corporations formed in foreign countries, unless endorsed by the government, played but a very small part on the London stock market until after the middle of the century.

And the legislation which gave corporations various governmental protections, referred to earlier, fostered the trans-Atlantic migration of capital.

The Need for Payoff

[T]he fact that the privileges of incorporation were much more easily acquired in America than in England in the first half of the [nineteenth] century gave certain types of American industry readier access to nonindustrial savings and indeed, it was sometimes said, gave them readier access even to English "blind capital" than English industrialists themselves enjoyed.

But if the activities of state governments and foreign investors contributed to economic growth, the rapidity of that development must also be credited to a particularly productive, symbiotic relationship between economic growth and the American value system. The existence of a set of values that enshrined "the good life" as one of hard, continuous work, frugality, self-disciplined living, and individual initiative provided the necessary ideological framework for making use of foreign capital for long-range industrial development.[3] Also, the weakness of aristocratic traditions meant that the United States was free to develop a dominant economic class of merchants and manufacturers whose passion for the accumulation of wealth was unfettered by values that deprecated hard work and the concentration of capital. The rationale for concentrating national resources and energies on such pursuits violated the anti-urban, agrarian utopia of the Jeffersonians, but it was defended on nationalistic grounds. The prospect of spiritual and economic domination at the hands of European manufacturers was viewed as especially degrading since this group was presided over by a "devilish class of aristocrats" to whom were attributed all kinds of corruptions, from immoral leisure to extravagance and intellectual cunning:

Convinced, on the whole, of an identity between moral and material progress, these industrialists, while not averse to profits, were conscious of making a patriotic contribution and of trying to establish a pattern in manufacturing for the nation. . . .

The rising tide of nationalism stimulated by the American Revolution and the War of 1812 made it popular to justify American manufacturing on the ground of economic independence. Such pleas for a national economic independence, however, usually pointed to the horrifying alternative of a moral and spiritual as well as economic prostration at the feet of the manufacturers of Europe. Though these public pronouncements may have functioned consciously as convenient rationalizations of economic interest . . . the same ideas appeared again and again in their private letters and journals, when they had no need for propaganda. To them European manufacturing on the whole, not only seemed degrading to character; it was presided over by a devilish class of aristocrats. . . .

Belief in the existence of a conspiratorial European devil led also to the patriotic contrast of honestly made American manufactures with reputedly fraudulent European goods.

---

[3] These two factors, the Protestant Ethic and foreign investment, can be viewed as functional substitutes for present day socialist ideology and foreign aid. Incidentally, it is becoming increasingly common to see Marxism, Communism, or Socialism fulfilling in the twentieth century what the Protestant Ethic did for Western Europe and North America in the eighteenth and nineteenth centuries—that is, fostering motivation for work and economic development.

Foreign visitors to the United States were struck, from its earliest days, with the greater emphasis on materialism here, on economic gain, as contrasted to that present in Europe, including even Britain. A detailed analysis of the writings of English travelers in America from the end of the Revolution to the age of Jackson sums up the evidence:

At this period, the Americans already had the reputation for being a money-loving and money-getting people. So universal was this belief that it is with surprise that we see any denial of it. . . . [T]he enterprise of the Americans could not be charitably attributed to a dread of future want, nor did it seem to most Englishmen that they were consciously actuated by a "desire to obtain distinction by means of wealth." . . . Flint said that it was security of property and the high profits on capital that tended to promote this disposition. Fowler attributed the eagerness to accumulate to the fact that in the absence of titles and all acknowledged distinctions in rank, wealth constituted the primary basis of contrast between individuals. At any rate, this trait became to foreigners an integral part of the American nature.

Given the absence of a traditional aristocratic class, and the withdrawal into Canada of many of those who most sympathized with such a societal model, the entrepreneur became a cultural hero—and rapid growth followed. Canada, on the other hand, though possessing many of the same material conditions as the United States, did not develop as rapidly or as strongly. The combination of foreign rule and a different class model apparently had negative effects on its potentialities for development. And the new states of nineteenth century Latin America, led by traditional Catholic oligarchies drawn mainly from the landed aristocracy, were even more backward economically. They retained many of the pre-industrial values of the Iberian Peninsula. Latin America lacked a dynamic business class, a Protestant work ethos, and an ideological commitment to economic modernization.

The emergence of a functioning polity in the first half-century of American independence was accompanied by rapid economic growth and territorial expansion.

The United States gradually acquired legitimacy as a result of being *effective*. There was no question that the new nation worked, that its economy had "taken off," to use Walt Rostow's image. Henry Adams, in his great history of the early years of the republic, saw these economic developments as crucial in guaranteeing the survival of the country as a viable unit:

The results of the sixteen years [1800–1816], considered only in the economical development of the Union, were decisive. Although population increased more rapidly than was usual in human experience, wealth accumulated faster. . . .

These sixteen years set at rest the natural doubts that had attended the nation's birth. . . . Every serious difficulty which seemed alarming to the people of the Union in 1800 had been removed or sunk from notice in 1816. . . . This result was not the only or even the chief proof that economical progress was to be at least as rapid in the future. . . . The continent lay before them, like an uncovered ore-bed. They could see, and they even could calculate with reasonable accuracy the wealth it could be made to yield.

It is important to recognize that a basic condition for acquiring legitimacy in a new state is effectiveness, particularly in the economic sphere. In return for support, the populace demands from its leaders rewards, some symbolic in content, such as national heroes and prestige, and others, perhaps more important, of a tangible nature. This is true today; it was true in America a hundred and fifty years ago. As Denis Brogan has well said:

The first and almost the last rule is that the rulers must deliver the goods, that they must share some of the winnings of the game with their clients, with the great mass of the American people, and that these winnings must be absolutely more than any rival system can plausibly promise. I have used the word "clients" advisedly, for the rulers of America have not the advantage of some of their European brethren, the advantage of a patina of age.

Political Parties in the New Nation

WILLIAM NISBET CHAMBERS

Political practices in the early states were . . . generally loose and subject to change without notice. Like any people undertaking self-government, Americans faced three crucial problems of political functioning. These were the conduct of nominations for office; the conduct of elections; and management in government or policymaking—and in the early states with their circumscribed executives, policy was made largely by legislation. These tasks were performed in a medley of non-party ways.

Nominating procedures, by narrowing the range of candidates for any given office, may provide manageable choices for voters. Most rudimentary among early American practices was the procedure of self-announced candidacies or, less directly, "nominations" by letters in local newspapers. This latter practice was followed particularly in the South, where announcements or letters frequently came after private discussions or tacit agreements among leading

FROM *Political Parties in the New Nation* by William Nisbet Chambers, pp. 21–27. Copyright © 1963 by Oxford University Press, Inc. Reprinted by permission.

planters in the locality. In the Middle Atlantic and to some degree in the New England sections, the absence or more rapid decline of cohesive social elites prompted more advanced procedures. In colonial times a common method was selection by secret "parlor caucuses," or "garret caucuses" like the ones Tom Dawes arranged in Boston. During the Revolution, nominations often came from larger caucuses, societies like the Sons of Liberty, or the committees of correspondence; and by the 1780's local caucuses lost their secret, private character and became public, with local nominations also often falling into the hands of ward or township meetings open to all voters. Presumably a gain for emergent democracy, this latter practice may also have marked a setback for order. In a few states, the mid-1780's also saw the emergence of ephemeral county conventions. These early conventions, another step toward democratization, were, however, very irregular in their operation and in drawing representatives from townships or election districts. Called *ad hoc* by caucuses, town meetings, or coteries of leaders, they had no continuing life from election to election. Leaders would often revise the slates named by the conventions, putting forth carefully devised "mixed tickets," which included popular nominees of rival conventions; and convention decisions were not binding on anyone. Frequently, rejected hopefuls would offer themselves as candidates on their own. By and large, the flaccidity of the early, non-party conventions was due to the fact that they generally had no continuing machinery available to mobilize voters for their selections. In this respect they were weaker than many caucuses.

In comparison with nominations for local office, nominations of candidates for governor or other statewide offices posed a thornier problem. Efforts toward state meetings or conventions foundered on the difficulties of distance, rough roads, and expense. The issue was thus often left to correspondence among local leaders or semi-regularized local committees, or (particularly in the South) in the hands of courthouse juntos. Eventually, well after the end of the Revolutionary War, a partial solution was found in caucuses of like-minded members of the state legislatures. Yet at the beginning such caucuses remained loose and uncertain. They were often attended by leaders who were not legislative members as well as those who were, and were called before some elections and not before others.

The conduct of elections, critical in giving voters a voice in public policy, was also variable. In many cases in the early years there was little campaigning, and candidates were local "notables," prestigious and well-known figures in their communities, who simply "stood" for election more often than they "ran." Efforts to woo voters did lead to "treating," however, and Washington was not the only candidate to indulge in it, despite criticism of the practice. Addresses to meetings of voters, or "speakings," were also occasionally resorted to, though few candidates went so far as Madison did when his nose got frostbitten. In Pennsylvania, prompt naturalization of immigrants who could then be herded to the polls, and the practice of "repeating," or voting the same individual several times in an election, gave evidence of an early sophisticated (if seamy) style in politics.

In New York, early rival houses set a pattern for later cliques by simply marching their tenants to the polls and by seeking to mobilize the less dependent voters of New York City by public appeals. Mobilization in rougher wards was often reinforced by local "bruisers." More in accord with democratic ideals, freely formed but short-lived organized groups, like the Associators in Pennsylvania in the mid-1770's or the grandly-named Society for the Preservation of Liberty in Virginia in the mid-1780's, resolved to support only candidates whose views they approved. The political press also stepped up appeals to public opinion on behalf of candidates.

Early American political leaders clearly showed far more ingenuity than naïveté. They had seen the need for concentrating votes on a single candidate or slate if they were to win, grasped the tool of association, invented devices of backdoor politicking—which offered lessons for later bosses and machines—and developed engines of propaganda. Yet as candidates were cast up and stood or ran for office, they presented no party or other labels to clarify their identity to the voters, for, in a personal politics, candidacies were also personal or sponsored by cliques or factions, and methods were irregular and erratic. Furthermore, clique or factional associations were often partially hidden or subject to change from election to election, and there was little or no machinery to polarize, mobilize, or stabilize public opinion over the years. In short, the new nation still lacked the rudimentary co-ordination that political parties can bring to provide clarity and continuity in nominations and elections.

Considering American experience down to the adoption of the new Constitution in 1789, it is possible to note several immediate reasons why this was so. By and large they lay in certain conditions which came out of the colonial past, conditions whose effects still persisted in some degree through the 1780's even though the acids of the Revolutionary era were gradually dissolving them. Not only was there no national political crucible in colonial times to precipitate a national politics, but in the long years of colonial rule there had been few elective offices to fill in the provinces, little patronage to stimulate party development, and comparatively few voters, despite early grants of suffrage—and what voters there were often had to travel to distant polling places, where their vote was not secret, to participate in infrequent elections. Furthermore, despite the emerging fluidity and free individualism of the new American society, colonial gradations of social dominance and subordination remained at certain points, and men at the higher levels of social position were accustomed to winning compliance from men at lower levels. Different regions exhibited different patterns of such notables and deference to them: in New England, the Congregational clergy and old families; in New York, the Hudson River magnates, frequently with New York City mercantile connections; in the South, the great planters. Whatever their basis, however, such patterns had a limiting effect on the development of parties as a product of mass or popular politics. The liberal effervescence that followed the Revolution ate away at social hierarchy and habits of deference to "the few and the great," as it also promoted the extension of voting rights. Yet even in this situation the formation of parties required new skills in popular leadership, and such skills necessarily emerged slowly. Finally, there were continuing obstacles to the minimal necessities of association: communication and assembly. In western Pennsylvania, for example, poor roads and postal facilities, the absence of newspapers in the earliest years, and a paucity of natural social gatherings worked against political association; and these disadvantages were only gradually offset by increases in the number and popularity of churches, taverns, court sessions, and militia musters as opportunities for meeting or assembly. Communication and face-to-face meeting between people living in different states were still more difficult when, for example, a trip from Philadelphia to Charleston, South Carolina, might take two weeks.

Yet probably the greatest obstacles to party development remained the refractory individualism and pluralism of the society and general attitudes which were inimical to party alignment. Many individuals resisted being herded; states and state leaders stressed their special identities and interests; and heterogeneities, from regionalism to economic variety to religion, tossed up a multiplicity of opinions and interests. Although this very individualism and pluralism were eventually to stimulate the resort to party coordination, it was no easy matter to harness them at the outset. The bonds of party support could be established only by devising intricate agreements which would join together broad pluralistic combinations—all in the face of doubts about the legitimacy of party combinations as such.

In the legislative process, where the outcome of policy decisions was determined, politics also proceeded in pre-party ways. Central control at some times or in some states contrasted with free-style fragmentation in others. In Massachusetts after 1776, close association in the Boston caucus under the adept organizer and propagandist Sam Adams marked early paths to control by the caucus; but this power was limited and soon balanced by Shaysites and the varied thrusts of free-lance individual members of the assembly. In Maryland, legislative control remained in the hands of the planter junto, with members drawn from the state's leading "Fifty Families" repeatedly returned to office while mercantile Baltimore was nearly unrepresented. Continuing power for the Tidewater planter faction in South Carolina depended on gross under-representation in the assembly for middle- and back-country elements. In Rhode Island, where the dominant force in the late 1780's was a so-called country faction—which actually enlisted as many or more merchant investors in state-debt securities as it did plain farmers—a caucus of this faction met nights, reviewed proposed legislation, and the next day marshalled its assembly members accordingly. In New York, the Clinton clique cozened allies and watchfully served a sufficient diversity of interests by special legislation to undercut rivals. In Connecticut, an involved combination of four factions was held together by shared interests and loose personal ties among a few leaders, who parceled out the benefits of politics. In Pennsylvania, the infant state parties jockeyed in the assembly, but the helter-skelter of interests between and within parties became more and more difficult to sort out. In Virginia, a politics of notables and personal followings was given some direction by the influence of Patrick Henry as governor, but legislative decision-making remained individualistic, sometimes sectionally influenced, and fluid. In New Jersey, fragmented representation of diverse interests prompted an extremely free-style, unstructured politics, with few significant or divisive issues.

In early American state politics as a whole it is possible to distinguish four types of political formation: factions, cliques, juntos, and caucuses. Generally a faction appeared as a portion of an electorate, political elite, or legislature whose adherents were engaged in parallel action or co-ordination of some consistency but limited durability in conflict with other portions. A clique, most readily seen in the notable-family "connexions" in New York, was a factional group whose relationships depended upon a family, a commanding individual, or a close coterie of personal associates: generally the demise or retirement of the focal person led to the collapse of the clique. A junto, as the term was used most commonly in the South to apply to statehouse or courthouse groups, was a small, often secret, dominant factional formation at a center of government, which might or might not act for a larger social stratum. A caucus was generally the co-ordinating nucleus of a larger faction or alignment of interests, or sometimes merely a temporary, *ad hoc* assemblage. None of these formations took on the stature of parties. It is in this sense of hinging on factionlike formations that we may speak of early American politics as "faction politics," using the term "faction" to include lesser but similar groups such as cliques, juntos, and caucuses. Such politics depended heavily on personalities and personal ties, and was subject to abrupt, kaleidoscopic change.

From the point of view of clarity or order of democratic functioning, faction politics had little to offer to the new American nation. Control by social elites or hidden juntos tended, by its very nature, to thwart popular participation or influence over policy. The confusion of individualistic, factional, or clique patterns of legislative policy-making, on the other hand, made the realities of the legislative process virtually invisible or nearly incomprehensible to the voters. Even when the process was visible, the absence of stable party or factional designations in elections made it extremely difficult for voters to hold representatives responsible for their acts. Legislative decision-making was often only tenuously oriented to divisions outside the assemblies, while blocs, alliances, or cabals formed and dissolved almost independently in the assemblies themselves; and thus, voters were baffled by frequent discontinuities from election to election or by the smudging of choice on issues in a given election. Links between the electorate on the one hand and government policy on the other remained uncertain. Insofar as democracy may hinge on an orderly choice in elections which has some effect in government, faction politics failed. It was inherently unable to provide voters with reasonably clear, continuing, and effective alternatives.

The result, even in a nation that was broadly "republican" in character and generating a "democratic" climate, was an advantage in power for certain elements in the society. Thus planter, mercantile, or similar groups with access to influence, inside information, and the levers of authority were able to "work" the system more advantageously than plain men or less favored groups, such as the nation's broad ranks of small-freehold farmers. The common run of men were thwarted by the looseness, semi-invisibility, disorder, personal ties, and confusion of faction, and popular impact on policymaking was limited accordingly. . . .

SUGGESTIONS FOR FURTHER READING

Studies of the foundation and early development of America's formal governmental institutions, of course, abound. Perhaps the best short book on the Constitutional Convention is Max Farrand's *The Framing of the Constitution of the United States* (New Haven, Conn.: Yale University Press, 1913). Paul Eidelberg's *The Philosophy of the American Constitution* (New York: Free Press, 1968) is a very helpful work that covers the same ground as Farrand's book and reemphasizes the commitment of the framers of the Constitution to a theory of mixed government (qualified democracy). Among American historians, one should consult Richard Hofstadter for analyses of the origins and development of American parties in *The American Political Tradition* (New York: Knopf, 1948) and *The Idea of a Party System* (Berkeley, Calif.: University of California Press, 1969). Dixon Ryan Fox's *The Decline of Aristocracy in the Politics of New York, 1801–1840* is a minor classic. First published in 1919, it is available now, edited by Robert V. Remini, in Harper Torchbooks (New York: 1965). Also useful are Bernard Bailyn's *The Origins of American Politics* (New York: Knopf, 1968) and Joseph Charles' *The Origins of the American Party System* (New York: Harper & Row, 1961).

For monographic studies on early parties, see Jackson T. Main, *The Social Structure of Revolutionary America* (Princeton, N. J.: Princeton University Press, 1965); Shaw Livermore, *The Twilight of Federalism: The Disintegration of the Federalist Party, 1815–1830* (Princeton, N. J.: Princeton University Press, 1962); and Manning J. Dauer, *The Adams Federalists* (Baltimore: Johns Hopkins Press, 1968). For discussions of early Republicans, see Alfred F. Young, *The Democratic-Republicans of New York: The Origins, 1763–1797* (Chapel Hill, N. C.: University of North Carolina Press, 1967); Noble E. Cunningham, *The Jeffersonian Republicans: The Formation of Party Organization, 1789–1801* (Chapel Hill, N. C.: University of North Carolina Press, 1957); and N. K. Risjord, *The Old Republicans: Southern Conservatism in the Age of Jefferson* (New York: Columbia University Press, 1965).

Still valuable on the entire early period of American political development is Leonard D. White's magisterial trilogy: *The Federalists, The Jeffersonians,* and *The Jacksonians* (New York: Macmillan, 1948-54).

Richard L. Merritt's *Symbols of American Community, 1735-1775* (New Haven, Conn.: Yale University Press, 1965) is a fascinating attempt to apply a quantitative method developed by contemporary political scientists—content analysis of the press—to early American materials.

2 The social determinants of the system

ANTHROPOLOGISTS TELL US that a human culture is a seamless web—that what happens in one sector will affect other sectors. Thus the distinctions that academic analysts have drawn between the economic system, the social system, and the political system are to a considerable extent arbitrary.

These distinctions have nevertheless been drawn, because it is necessary for social scientists to deal with intellectually manageable parcels of closely related phenomena. On occasion, particularly vigorous thinkers such as Oswald Spengler, Arnold Toynbee, and Talcott Parsons have attempted to encompass whole civilizations or all human behavior. The results of their labors have been fascinating, but their economic theory has often been disappointing to economists, their history to historians, and so on down the professional line. It appears that the human experience in its entirety cannot be dealt with systematically; to try to do so is to run a high risk of lapsing into superficiality or of abstracting to the point of obscurity and irrelevance. The cultural webs are so extensive that one can only hope to become moderately familiar with parts of them. But of their interrelated character there can be no doubt, and it is the purpose of this chapter to emphasize these interrelations.

Politics is crucially affected by social patterns, and political institutions are molded by social forces that at first glance may seem quite remote from elections, bill drafting, and other recognizable political activities. If the student of American politics is determined to discover why something is the way it is, he may find partial answers in the regional loyalties, occupational groupings, or ethnic identifications that characterize American society. We stress the phrase "partial answers"; numerous intervening variables (such as accidents of personality and the international environment) also affect the configuration of a political system. But when we perceive a change in the social system, we should be alerted to expect a concomitant change in the political system—even if we cannot predict precisely the form it will take or when it will occur.

In the selections that follow, two sociologists and a political scientist examine the relationship between political patterns and social variables in America.

Philip Selznick regards the decline of small-town America and the rise of an urbanized mass society as the efficient causes of the vast increase in the activities of government. Much necessary social control that was previously achieved informally through families and voluntary associations must now be accomplished by governments, at one level or another. Thus, power that was once dispersed throughout society has become concentrated (or centralized) in public officials.

The selection from *Beyond the Melting Pot*, by Nathan Glazer and Daniel Patrick Moynihan, is a case study of the impact of a particular social variable on a particular part of the American system. The authors focus on New York City and on ethnicity as a politically potent social force. Rather than finding a great deal of change, they are impressed by the somewhat unexpected continuities. Individual ethnic allegiances have not eroded as rapidly as the simple melting-pot theory would lead us to suppose. "Irishness" and "Jewishness," for example, persist as politically relevant identifications long after the ghettos have been handed over to new tenants. The Glazer-Moynihan research is an excellent reminder that in a period of very visible change, such as we are passing through today, it is easy to forget that some important factors that shape our politics remain persistently stable. John V. Lindsay forgot this in New York City in 1968 and early 1969, and felt the full fury of the "old ethnics" who perceived him as one who had sold out their interests to the new Negro and Puerto Rican arrivals. Only intensive and elaborately financed campaigning in Brooklyn, the Bronx, and especially in Queens saved the mayor on election day.

◻ Legal Institutions and Social Control

PHILIP SELZNICK

Paralleling every major legal concern is a much larger and more finely textured system of codes and relationships. Interests of personality are recognized and protected in many areas of the law, yet how little we really depend on law for the day-by-day comfort we gain from orderly arrangements that save us from embarrassment, unwanted intrusions, or worse. The law of contracts facilitates and protects concerted activity, but the bonds of organization rest far more on practical and informal reciprocity and interdependence than they do on the availability of formal sanctions. Society is still held together by self-help and not by the intervention of legal agencies. Claims of right are asserted, adjudicated, and enforced for the most part outside the formal legal system.

Having said this much, I must hasten to add that there is considerable variation, at different times and places, and in different sectors of society and law, in the effectiveness of self-help and in reliance on legal controls. It is here, at the point of variation, that real inquiry begins.

I

The evolution of modern society is marked by two master trends that have brought with them decisive changes in social control and in the role of law. The first of these trends is often referred to as the drift toward mass society. The second and closely related master trend is the increasing bureaucratization and centralization of industrial society.

There is a cruel contrast in these twin lines of evolution. In a mass society there is more freedom, more participation, more mobility, more equality. On the other hand, the bureaucratic trend creates a world of complex organizations, of more formalized controls, of centralized power, of individual helplessness and dependency. Yet both trends have the same source—the creation of an industrial society that imposes a remorseless logic on every human community that comes within its sway.

In contemporary social science there is much interest in studying the effects

FROM Philip Selznick, "Legal Institutions and Social Control," *Vanderbilt Law Review*, Vol. 17, No. 1 (December 1963), pp. 79–90.

of industrialization on the non-Western world. These societies, rapidly emerging out of a preindustrial past, are breaking the bonds of tradition, family, and locality. Reaching out for modern technology and its fruits, they are indeed experiencing great strains. To a certain extent, the history of industrialization in Europe and the United States is being recapitulated. All this is of great importance and eminently worth pursuing. On the other hand, I venture to suggest that we have not yet fully absorbed the significance for *our own* institutions of the industrial and urban revoluion.

For a long time, our society has had much to cushion it against the full impact of modernization. Until quite recently we continued to have a fairly strong rural and small-town counterweight. Our large immigrant population had its own resources of social organization. Political, economic, and cultural diversity set limits to change and helped give men roots. The inertia of tradition could sustain for generations a sense of identity and of moral continuity.

The loosening of social bonds, and the concomitant weakening of non-legal controls, is manifest in many ways. The most important, of course, is the decline of kinship as the major unit of social organization and therefore of social control. That the functions of the family have changed in recent history is a familiar sociological tale. What was once an enterprise and a nuclear community, a unit of production and an indispensable alliance against a forbidding external world, has now become a more specialized and limited institution. What it can do for its members, and what it may ask of them, have both been radically curtailed.

This is not to say that the family is unimportant. Of course it is still the chief source of personal gratification, the main agency for socializing the young, the true staff of life for most men and women. But the family has become a significantly weaker reed, both for the individual and for society. After all, we are not speaking here of complete social breakdown but of shifts that markedly aggravate our problems of social control. We still ask much of the family, but we have not fully recognized that its resources as an institution, its tools for doing the job, have become more and more limited.

As I see it, we are not dealing primarily with moral atrophy, the corrosion of personal values. If that exists, it is a symptom and not a cause. The main reasons for the waning role of the family in social control are practical and stem from larger changes in our economic life. The truth is that discipline in the family is less effective today because its practical significance in the routines of life has sharply declined. In an important but limited sense, it is no longer needed. When the family is really a going concern, and the activities of its members must be coordinated, if not for production then at least as a condition of survival, the need for discipline is apparent. Authority makes sense to the individual because it is justified by urgent necessity. Moreover, the family member is heavily dependent on this small social world and its resources. Given such a setting, it is easy for appropriate moral sentiments to be created and sustained.

Let us remember that for the most part society must rely on the willing acceptance of discipline. Without consent, discipline may be enforced, but that is always less effective and has heavy costs. Now what is the foundation of this consent? It may be that some societies have won consent to authority by creating an irresistible cake of custom, a communicated sense of what is right and wrong, respectable and disreputable. I suspect that this sort of thing is greatly exaggerated. The natural habitat of the human being is a world of opportunity and constraint, of alternatives set by the practical exigenices of making a living and winning self-esteem. Customs are enforced, not abstractly and mechanically, but in the course of giving guidance to activities that make sense in their own terms. When the activities no longer make sense, we can expect social codes and symbols to attenuate and lose their force.

That the adolescent needs discipline in his own psychic interests I do not doubt. That society would be better off if the family could exercise more effective control may also be true. But such a function cannot be simply "assigned" to the family. It will not be performed at the desired levels if it does not flow naturally out of the requirements of everyday life.

The weakening of the family as an agency of social control is only a phase, although a major one, of the broader trend toward a looser, less disciplined social order. Thus another feature of our society is the steady decline of *fixed status* as a vehicle of social control. For today's Americans, of all groups and classes, status-seeking is a sign of a society on the move. It is a good guess that many fewer people today than two generations ago "know their place" and limit their actions and their aspirations accordingly. We sometimes forget, I think, how much even our own society has depended on the proprieties of status, on the giving and receiving of deference. Perhaps most important, we have counted on a large amount of voluntary segregation, so that the more privileged and the better integrated member of the community might live out his respectable life without being much affected by his more vulgar fellow citizens.

This comfortable scheme of things already seems unreal. It will soon be gone forever. The dispossessed are knocking at the door. They are making their presence known, refusing to accept the rightness of middle-class values, appealing to a broader sense of justice. The revolution of rising expectations is far from restricted to the underdeveloped countries. On the contrary, it is no less important right here.

One way of observing the breakdown of group barriers is to take note of the spread of working-class patterns of dress and leisure-time activity among middle-class children. In our open, fluid society, styles do not flow only from the top down. They also move up from below. The result is a cultural diffusion that adds little to the stability of community life. We have created a society that makes these things possible and even inevitable. This we have done for good and sufficient reasons, but we must be ready to pay the price.

It seems obvious to me that we are in no position to deplore this waning of non-legal controls. Dedicated as we are to personal autonomy and well-being, we cannot very well yearn for the submergence of the individual in family or community. We expect and value his self-assertion; we shall honor in due course his new claims of right. Committed as we are to political freedom and legal equality, we cannot fail to accept the social transformations born in part of those ideals. Perhaps it is not logically necessary that political freedom be translated into social opportunity, or that legal equality produce a social leveling. But our political and legal concepts have, for better or worse, been hooked on to large-scale industry, the mass market, and mass communications. Together they create a revolutionary thrust that loosens and tears the social fabric.

The changes to which I have referred must inevitably increase the burdens of our legal institutions. If society cannot depend on an informal, autonomous, self-regulating, person-centered order for the maintenance of social control, it will turn to more explicitly organized agencies and to more powerful instruments of surveillance and regulation. Not only the police, but the schools, social work agencies, and perhaps other institutions, will be called upon to serve the needs of social control.

Traditionally, the formal agencies of control have been relatively weak. Their resources were limited, their techniques crude. Their effect on the life of the community was softened by a recognition of their own dependence on the people around them and by the continuity of the official and the ordinary citizen. The cop on the beat belonged to the community and he manifested his membership in dress and demeanor. Are we not already describing things remembered, a fading era?

The combination of social demand and technical competence will, in the not too distant future, create far more effective agencies of legal control. They will be more efficient and more honest, more isolated from the community and less dependent on it. They will be expert monitors of the round of life and will naturally tend to move from partial to total surveillance. Perhaps most important, the new agencies will have absorbed a prophylactic orientation, a doctrine of prevention to supplement repression.

When coercive authority enlarges its competence and adopts new, more positive goals, we have an obligation to sit up and take notice. The chief barrier to unbearable despotism has always been the limited competence of the ruler. It is one thing to have the ideology of autocracy, and its trappings; it is another to have the means to put it into practice. Thirty years ago Charles Merriam could write of the "poverty of power"—the "wide gap between the apparent omnipotence of authority and the actual operation of power, between the iron fist of force and its incidence upon human flesh and feeling." This is still very largely true. But is it not the deeper lesson of our century that effective, total power *can* be mustered and sustained, if not forever, then at least long enough to exact a memorable toll in suffering and degradation?

When an institution has low capabilities, it tends to conserve its strength, to be passive rather than active. It waits for things to happen, to make themselves visible. Increase its capabilities and a subtle transformation may occur. Now the agency can exercise more initiative and reach out to deal with potential trouble.

Such a prospect raises very real questions regarding the security of citizens who occasionally run afoul of the law.

As agencies of control become more rational and efficient, we may well hope for more searching study of how our institutions actually operate and what values lie half-hidden in accustomed practice, in administrative use and wont, in the traditional way of doing things. For example, how much do we depend on the policeman's role as a kind of magistrate, a dispenser of rough and ready justice as he exercises discretion in the streets? What will happen to this role in the motorized and mechanized elite corps of the future?

The ideal of equal justice seems to require that all offenders be treated alike. Yet there is evidence that the police routinely attempt to distinguish, especially among juveniles, the apparently casual offender from the committed delinquent. Lawyers and other social scientists may see in this a violation of even-handed justice. And indeed this is so, especially where racial and class bias are operative. But when confronted with these facts I am moved to ask: If the law is administered with prudence, does this not require some differential treatment at the first point of contact and not only after judgment, when ultimate disposition is made? Do we need or want agencies of control so efficient and so impartial that every actual offender has an equal chance of being known and processed? In considering this point we should bear in mind that offenses of all kinds are probably very much more numerous in fact than in record.

. . .

It is still true that legal policy, like any other, needs effective social supports. The more sensitive the policy, the more readily subject it is to distortion, and the more urgent are these supports. Some laws, as we know, are self-administering, because they stimulate and channel private initiative. Historically our system has depended on that, but the more we ask of the law the more often shall we find that this private initiative is lacking or ineffective. A recent study of National Labor Relations Board cases involving union members who lost their jobs because of union discrimination touches on this problem. The workers were interviewed and a full story of the context of the case, including what happened after the NLRB decision, was obtained. The results are illuminating. When the worker is a lone individual who has run afoul of union rules or otherwise given offense, the NLRB proceeding may be better than nothing, but on the whole it is quite ineffective. The worker has a hard time pursuing his case and faces an even rougher time if he is rehired. The law, as administered, offers little to the isolated individual confronted with great organizational power. On the other hand, in those cases where the member belonged to a faction, and thus had group support both during the litigation and after it, he fared rather well. In that setting, as in many others, a non-legal, autonomous order lends its strength to the law.

For many purposes, we are not going to be able to depend on this prior social organization, this force in being, this socially given capability of implementing legal norms. The legal order of the future will strive to develop the conditions of its own effectiveness. This suggests, again, more emphasis on the organizational side of things. In addition to new, more or less distinctively legal institutions, such as the juvenile court and the public defender, we should expect that other parts of government, and some private associations as well, will play a part in adding to the resources of the legal order. The coordination of these activities and agencies, within the framework of a unitary legal system, will stretch the minds and perhaps try the souls of legal analysts.

For example, how deep is our commitment to the adversary principle in the administration of justice? Is that principle fully compatible with new modes of adjudication and control? How much variation in the adversary idea is acceptable? How far should it be built into administrative structure and process? It seems clear that this hallowed if sometimes embattled procedural canon needs a great deal more study to assess its relevance for the legal system of the future.

Another problem is the emergence of new bodies of law, founded in dimly understood principles, confused by the *ad hoc* character of our legislation and case law. Have we been witnesses to the development of a law of welfare whose concepts and doctrines, including implications for procedure, need explication? What is the relation between this emergent branch of law, if it is one, to the rest of the system, especially the law of crimes? Is contemporary legal scholarship prepared to do the job of cutting across old categories and creating new ones? These things are suggested, not by an abstract concern for doctrinal clarity or symmetry, but by the compelling pressures of the living law, the law in action.

II

Earlier I suggested that we must accept a secular trend toward the waning of non-legal social control. To the sociologist, this is a phase of the drift toward mass society. I have also suggested that, at the same time, legal agencies of control will have increased responsibilities thrust upon them.

There is another and rather different part of this picture to which I should like to call attention. I refer to the growth of the large-scale organization as the representative institution of modern life. In industry, government, education, medicine, philanthropy—you name it!—the principle of rational coordination, the bureaucratic principle, holds sway. Self-perpetuating leadership and centralized authority are fixed stars in our firmament. In these areas there is no waning of social control. Quite the contrary. But is it *non-legal* control? That question might provoke a prolonged debate.

In an important sense, we are of course speaking of the private sector of economy and society. On the other hand, many observers have noted a blurring of the public and the private. A striking feature of this development is the *convergence* of governmental and non-governmental forms of organization and modes of action. A great deal of government activity is similar to that carried on by private groups. Government today includes many activities and agencies that have little to do with the distinctive functions of the sovereign and to which, therefore, the traditional logic of public law may not properly apply. At the same time, discussions of the modern corporation and trade union have increasingly stressed their "quasi-public" status. It is asked quite seriously whether such institutions are really so different from large public enterprises or service agencies.

Furthermore, and perhaps more important, a kind of legality seems to develop within these large enterprises. In both public and private bureaucracies, authority and rule-making tend to take on the impersonality, the objectivity, and the rationality of a legal system. The elaboration of formal rules creates expectations regarding the consistency and fairness of official action. In modern management there is an inner dynamic tending toward a progressive reduction in the arbitrariness of decision-making. In ever-wider areas of administration there is a demand that decisions be made in the light of general principles.

We are coming to see the private association as a group organized for defined and public ends—public, that is, from the standpoint of the group itself rather than the general community. Known and acknowledged purposes provide the basis of adherence and discipline. Given such ends, rational criteria may be developed to assess the means used to attain them. Thus membership in an association is a way of participating in a system of rationally coordinated activities. Objective and impersonal standards, determined by the requirements of that system, may be invoked for the assessment and control of organizational members. The members in turn may claim the protection of those same rational criteria.

It is this commitment of professional management to an atmosphere of legality—a commitment derived more from the necessities of modern enterprise than from good will or ideology—that underlies the widespread acceptance of private bigness as compatible with freedom. In our society the fear of corporate power has eased considerably. Criticism is muted in temper, reformist in intent. I believe that this is mainly due to the growing conviction that the large corporation is not necessarily a "rough beast." It is obscurely understood that the enterprise is enmeshed in circumstances that brake its power and create, indeed, a corporate conscience.

What and where is the corporate conscience? The corporate conscience is the internally accepted system of fair dealing, of respect for personal rights, of authority constituted and justified by rational necessity in the light of public ends. In a familiar phrase, it is corporate "due process."

This emerging ethic has its chief source in the practical necessities of industrial management. We see a convergence of three major tendencies in the institutional history of the firm:

1. The growing importance of impersonal procedures in the conduct of the enterprise—something I have already noted;

2. the recognition of "human relations" as a critical factor in management,

especially the significance of respect and status-protection for employee morale; and

3. the widespread adaptation of management to the power of trade unionism and the creation thereby of systematic procedures for the formulation and redress of grievances.

To say that a corporate conscience exists is not to say that we can rely on it. In questions of power and justice, we do not rely upon the individual conscience either. Our legal and political system necessarily postulates the existence of evil, especially the danger that some merely human form, believing itself free of error, will attempt to match its claimed perfection with unlimited power. Because of that risk, we cannot rely upon good will, personal or institutional.

We should distinguish, however, what we can rely upon from what we can aspire to. The ethic of rational coordination provides the foundation for new expectations, new claims of right, new legal controls. The existence of internal order within the enterprise validates external control and, at the same time, makes it feasible. It is just because fairness is already institutionalized to a large extent in the private sphere that an appeal to the larger political community, to the legal order, is warranted. The firmer the sense of legitimate expectation, the more likely it is that there will be an appeal beyond the immediate setting. Moreover, if a quasi-legal system of fair dealing already exists, there is some assurance that the routine case will be handled satisfactorily. Therefore, enforcement of exceptional claims for redress of grievances becomes feasible.

I take the view that, in the evolving law of private associations, we are responding to opportunities rather than resisting oppression. I do not say that private power is not abused, but the really important fact is that we now have the possibility, a product of modern history, of extending the ideals of due process to private associations. This might always have been a worthy objective, but the development of an inner order within the modern enterprise brings that objective into close accord with what historical reality makes possible.

These reflections suggest that we take a long, leisurely look at the so-called "limits of effective legal action." Can we assume fixed legal resources? What if changing institutions, both inside and outside the legal sphere, offer new opportunities for enriching the sense of justice? The answer may require a radical revision of that hard-nosed legal philosophy which celebrates the settlement of disputes and the curbing of irresponsible conduct. Today the law is summoned to fulfill aspirations, not merely to meet the minimal needs of social order. The business of taking that truth seriously may occupy us for some years to come.

▣ Beyond the Melting Pot

NATHAN GLAZER AND DANIEL P. MOYNIHAN

The idea of the melting pot is as old as the Republic. "I could point out to you a family," wrote the naturalized New Yorker, M-G. Jean de Crèvecoeur, in 1782,

whose grandfather was an Englishman, whose wife was Dutch, whose son married a French woman, and whose present four sons have now four wives of different nations. *He* is an American, who leaving behind him all his ancient prejudices and manners, receives new ones from the new mode of life he has embraced. . . . Here individuals of all nations are melted into a new race of men. . . ."

It was an idea close to the heart of the American self-image. But as a century passed, and the number of individuals and nations involved grew, the confidence that they could be fused together waned, and so also the conviction that it would be a good thing if they were to be. In 1882 the Chinese were excluded, and the first general immigration law was enacted. In a steady succession thereafter, new and more selective barriers were raised until, by the National Origins Act of 1924, the nation formally adopted the policy of using immigration to reinforce, rather than further to dilute, the racial stock of the early America.

This latter process was well underway, had become in ways inexorable, when Israel Zangwill's play *The Melting Pot* was first performed in 1908. The play (quite a bad one) was an instant success. It ran for months on Broadway; its title was seized upon as a concise evocation of a profoundly significant American fact.

Behold David Quixano, the Russian Jewish immigrant—a "pogrom orphan" —escaped to New York City, exulting in the glory of his new country:

. . . America is God's Crucible, the great Melting Pot where all the races of Europe are melting and reforming! Here you stand, good folk, think I, when I see them at Ellis Island, here you stand in your fifty groups with your fifty languages and histories, and your fifty blood hatreds and rivalries, but you won't be long like that brothers, for these are the fires of God you've come to—these are the fires of God. A fig for your feuds and vendettas! German and Frenchman, Irishman and Englishman, Jews and Russians—into the Crucible with you all! God is making the American.

. . .

FROM Nathan Glazer and Daniel P. Moynihan, *Beyond the Melting Pot,* pp. 288–315, by permission of the M.I.T. Press, Cambridge, Massachusetts. Copyright © 1963 by The Massachusetts Institute of Technology and the President and Fellows of Harvard College.

... The real American has not yet arrived. He is only in the Crucible, I tell you—he will be the fusion of all the races, the coming superman.

Yet looking back, it is possible to speculate that the response to *The Melting Pot* was as much one of relief as of affirmation: more a matter of reassurance that what had already taken place would turn out all right, rather than encouragement to carry on in the same direction.

Zangwill's hero throws himself into the amalgam process with the utmost energy; by curtainfall he has written his American symphony and won his Muscovite aristocrat: almost all concerned have been reconciled to the homogeneous future. Yet the play seems but little involved with American reality. It is a drama about Jewish separatism and Russian anti-Semitism, with a German concertmaster and an Irish maid thrown in for comic relief. Both protagonists are New Model Europeans of the time. Free thinkers and revolutionaries, it was doubtless in the power of such to merge. But neither of these doctrines was dominant among the ethnic groups of New York City in the 1900's, and in significant ways this became less so as time passed. Individuals, in very considerable numbers to be sure, broke out of their mold, but the groups remained. The experience of Zangwill's hero and heroine was *not* general. The point about the melting pot is that it did not happen.

Significantly, Zangwill was himself much involved in one of the more significant deterrents to the melting pot process. He was a Zionist. He gave more and more of his energy to this cause as time passed, and retreated from his earlier position on racial and religious mixture. Only eight years after the opening of *The Melting Pot* he was writing "It was vain for Paul to declare that there should be neither Jew nor Greek. Nature will return even if driven out with a pitchfork, still more if driven out with a dogma."

We may argue whether it was "nature" that returned to frustrate continually the imminent creation of a single American nationality. The fact is that in every generation, throughout the history of the American republic, the merging of the varying streams of population differentiated from one another by origin, religion, outlook has seemed to lie just ahead—a generation, perhaps, in the future. This continual deferral of the final smelting of the different ingredients (or at least the different white ingredients) into a seamless national web as is to be found in the major national states of Europe suggests that we must search for some systematic and general causes for this American pattern of subnationalities; that it is not the temporary upsetting inflow of new and unassimilated immigrants that creates a pattern of ethnic groups within the nation, but rather some central tendency in the national ethos which structures people, whether those coming in afresh or the descendants of those who have been here for generations, into groups of different status and character.

It is striking that in 1963, almost forty years after mass immigration from Europe to this country ended, the ethnic pattern is still so strong in New York City. It is true we can point to specific causes that have served to maintain the pattern. But we know that it was not created by the great new migrations of Southern Negroes and Puerto Ricans into the city; nor by the "new" immigration, which added the great communities of East European Jews and Italians to the city; it was not even created by the great migration of Irish and Germans in the 1840's. Even in the 1830's, while the migration from Europe was still mild, and still consisted for the most part of English-speaking groups, one still finds in the politics of New York State, and of the city, the strong impress of group differentiation. In a fascinating study of the politics of the Jacksonian period in New York State, Lee Benson concludes: "At least since the 1820's, when manhood suffrage became widespread, ethnic and religious differences have tended to be *relatively* the most widespread sources of political differences."

There were ways of making distinctions among Welshmen and Englishmen, Yorkers and New Englanders, long before people speaking strange tongues and practicing strange religions came upon the scene. The group-forming characteristics of American social life—more concretely, the general expectation among those of new and old groups that group membership is significant and formative for opinion and behavior—are as old as the city. The tendency is fixed deep in American life generally; the specific pattern of ethnic differentiation, however, in every generation is created by specific events.

We can distinguish four major events or processes that have structured this pattern in New York during the past generation and whose effects will remain to maintain this pattern for some time to come—to be replaced by others we can scarcely now discern. These four formative events are the following:

First, the shaping of the Jewish community under the impact of the Nazi persecution of the Jews in Europe and the establishment of the state of Israel; second, the parallel, if less marked, shaping of a Catholic community by the reemergence of the Catholic school controversy; third, the migration of Southern Negroes to New York following World War I and continuing through the fifties; fourth, the influx of Puerto Ricans during the fifteen years following World War II.

THE JEWS

Developments within the Jewish community have had the most immediate significance. A fourth of the city is Jewish; very much more than a fourth of its wealth, energy, talent, and style is derived from the Jews. Over the past thirty years this community has undergone profound emotional experiences, centered almost entirely on the fact of Jewishness, has been measurably strengthened by immigration, and has become involved in vast Zionist enterprises, the rationale of which is exclusively Jewish. There are two aspects of these developments as they affect melting pot tendencies, one negative, the other positive.

The negative aspect has prevented a change that might otherwise have occurred. Prior to the 1930's Jews contributed significantly to the ethnic pattern of New York politics by virtue of their radicalism. This kept them apart from the Catholic establishment in the Democratic party and the Protestant regime within the Republican party but did give them a distinct role of their own. At the time of *The Melting Pot* there were, to be sure, a great many Democratic and Republican Jewish merchants and businessmen. Most East Side Jews probably voted the Tammany ticket. But indigenous Jewish politics, the politics of the *Jewish Daily Forward,* of the Workmen's Circle, and the needle-trades unions were predominantly socialist. The Russian Revolution, in which Russian Jews played a prominent role, had a strong attraction for a small but important number of their kinsmen in New York. It would appear, for example, that during the 1930's most Communist party members in New York City were Jewish. It must be stressed that the vast majority of New York Jews had nothing whatever to do with Communism. Some of the strongest centers of anti-Communist activity were and are to be found within the New York Jewish community. Nonetheless there was an ethnic cast to this form of political radicalism in New York, as there had been to the earlier Socialist movement.

Both Socialism and Communism are now considerably diminished and both have lost almost entirely any ethnic base. But just at the moment when the last distinctly Jewish political activity might have disappeared, a transcendent Jewish political interest was created by the ghastly persecutions of the Nazis, the vast dislocations of World War II, and the establishment of the State of Israel. These were matters that no Jew or Christian could ignore. They were equally matters about which little could be done except through politics. From the beginnings of the Zionist movement a certain number of New York Jews have been involved on that account with the high politics of the nation. Since the mid-1930's, however, this involvement has reached deeper and deeper into the New York Jewish community. They are the one group in the city (apart from the white Protestant financial establishment) of which it may fairly be said that among the leadership echelons there is a lively, active, and effective interest in who will be the next U. S. Secretary of State but one . . . or two, or three.

In a positive sense, events of the Nazi era and its aftermath have produced an intense group consciousness among New York Jews that binds together persons of widely disparate situations and beliefs. A pronounced religious revival has occurred. Among those without formal religious ties there is a heightened sense of the defensive importance of organized Jewish activity. Among intellectuals, the feeling of Jewishness is never far from the surface.

Now, as in the past, the Jewish community in New York is the one most actively committed to the principles of racial integration and group tolerance. But open housing is something different from the melting pot. There is no reason to think that any considerable portion of the Jewish community of New York ever subscribed to Israel Zangwill's vision of a nonreligious, intermarried, homogeneous population, but it surely does not do so today. To the contrary, much of the visible activity of the community is aimed in directions that will intensify Jewish identity: Jewish elementary and secondary schools, Jewish colleges and universities, Jewish periodicals, Jewish investments in Israel, and the like. In the meantime, Jewish politicians make more (or at least not less) of the "Jewish" vote.

This is not to say the Jewish community of New York has been *created* or *maintained* by these events of the thirties or forties: that would be too narrow a view of Jewish history, and would ignore the group-making characteristics of American civilization. But the Jewish community was *shaped* by these events. Moving rapidly from working-class to middle-class occupations and styles of life, many alternative courses of development were possible. Within the frame set by these large social movements, the historical drama shaped a community intensely conscious of its Jewishness. Religion plays in many ways the smallest part of the story of American Jews. In New York City in particular the religious definition of the group explains least. Here the formal religious groups are weakest, the degree of affiliation to synagogues and temples smallest. In a city with 2,000,000 Jews, Jews need make no excuses to explain Jewishness and Jewish interests. On the one hand, there is the social and economic structure of the community; on the other, ideologies and emotions molded by the specific history of recent decades. Together they have shaped a community that itself shapes New York and will for generations to come.

THE CATHOLICS

Outwardly, events since World War I have brought Catholics, notably the Irish Catholics, ever closer to the centers of power and doctrine in American life. But following a pattern common in human affairs, the process of closing the gap has heightened resentment, among some at all events, that a gap should exist. Here, as in much else concerning this general subject, it is hardly possible to isolate New York events from those of the nation generally, but because New York tends to be the center of Catholic thinking and publishing, the distinction is not crucial. The great division between the Catholic Church and the leftist and liberal groups in the city during the period from the Spanish Civil War to the era of McCarthy has been narrowed, with most elements of city politics converging on center positions. However issues of church–state relations have become considerably more difficult, and the issue of government aid to Catholic schools has become acute.

Controversy over church–state relations is nothing new to the American Catholic Church. What is new, however, and what is increasingly avowed, is the extent to which the current controversy derives from Catholic–Jewish disagreements rather than from traditional Catholic–Protestant differences. Relations between the two latter groups have steadily improved: to the point that after three centuries of separation Catholics in the 1960's began increasingly to talk of the prospects of reestablishing Christian unity. In general (there are, of course, many individual exceptions) the dominant view within Protestant and Catholic circles is that the United States is and ought to be a Christian commonwealth, to the point at very least of proclaiming "In God We Trust" on the currency and celebrating Christmas in the public schools. However, as this *rapprochement* has proceeded, within the Jewish community a contrary view has arisen which asserts that the separation of church and state ought to be even more complete than it has been, and that the "Post-Protestant era" means Post-Christian as well, insofar as government relations with religion are concerned.

The most dramatic episode of this development was the decision of the United States Supreme Court on June 25, 1962, that the recitation of an official prayer in the New York school system was unconstitutional. The case was brought by five parents of children in the public schools of the New York City suburb of New Hyde Park. Two of the parents were Jewish, one a member of the Ethical Culture Society, one a Unitarian, and one a nonbeliever. Before it concluded, however, the principal protagonists of the Catholic–Jewish controversy in New York City were involved. The attorney for the Archdiocese of New York, for example, argued in the Supreme Court for a group of parents who supported the prayer. The response to the decision could hardly have been more diametrical. Cardinal Spellman declared, "I am shocked and frightened. . . ." The New York Board of Rabbis, on the other hand, hailed the decision:

The recitation of prayers in the public schools, which is tantamount to the teaching of prayer, is not in conformity with the spirit of the American concept of the separation of church and state. All the religious groups in this country will best advance their respective faiths by adherence to this principle.

The American Jewish Committee, the American Jewish Congress, and the Anti-Defamation League of B'nai B'rith strongly supported the Court. Only among the Orthodox was there mild disagreement with the Supreme Court decision.

Although the argument could certainly be made that the American Catholic Church ought to be the first to object to the spectacle of civil servants composing government prayers, and although many Catholic commentators noted that the decision strengthened the case for private Church-sponsored schools, the general Catholic reaction was most hostile. The Jesuit publication *America,* in an editorial "To Our Jewish Friends," declared that Jewish efforts to assert an ever more strict separation of church and state were painting the Jewish community into a corner, where it would be isolated from the rest of Americans.

Significantly, Protestant reaction to the decision was mixed. The Brooklyn *Tablet* took the cue, stating that the crucial question raised by the decision was

What are the Protestants going to do about it? For, although this is a national problem, it is particularly a Protestant problem, given the large Protestant enrollment in the public schools. Catholics have been fighting long—and sometimes alone—against the Church–State extremists. May we count on Protestants to supply more leadership in this case? If so, we pledge our support to join efforts against the common enemy: secularism.

The subject of aid to Catholic schools is only one aspect of the more general issue of church–state relations, and here again the ethnic composition of New York City tends to produce the same alignment of opposing groups. There are elements within the Jewish community, again the Orthodox, that favor public assistance for religious schools, but the dominant view is opposed. In 1961 the New York Republican party at the state level made a tentative move toward the Catholic position by proposing a Constitutional amendment that would have permitted state construction loans to private institutions of higher learning, sectarian as well as secular. Opposition from Jewish (as well as some Protestant) groups was pronounced, and the measure was beaten at the polls.

The situation developing in this area could soberly be termed dangerous. An element of interfaith competition has entered the controversy. As the costs of education mount, it becomes increasingly difficult to maintain the quality of the education provided by private schools deprived of public assistance. It is not uncommon to hear it stated in Catholic circles that the results of national scholarship competitions already point to the weakness of Catholic education in fields such as the physical sciences. The specter is raised that a parochial education will involve sacrifice for the students as well as for their parents.

There is understandably much resentment within Catholic educational circles at the relative crudity of most such observations. At the same time this resentment is often accompanied by an unmistakable withdrawal. In a thoughtful address calling for more meticulous assessment of the qualities of Catholic education, Bishop McEntegart of the Diocese of Brooklyn went on to state that "Judgment on the effectiveness of an educational system should be something more profound and more subtle than counting heads of so-called intellectuals who happen to be named in Who's Who or the 'Social Register.'"

Whether the course of the controversy will lead Catholics further into separatist views of this kind is not clear. But it is abundantly evident that so long as Catholics maintain a separate education system and the rest of the community refuses to help support it by tax funds or tax relief, a basic divisive issue will exist. This will be an ethnic issue in measure that the Catholic community continues to include the bulk of the Irish, Italian, and Polish population in the city, at least the bulk of those affiliated with organizations taking a position on the issue. If, as may very well happen, the Catholics abandon elementary and even secondary education to concentrate on their colleges and universities, the larger issue of church–state relations will no doubt subside.

But it is not the single issue of school aid, no matter how important and long-lived it is, that alone shapes the polarization between the Jewish and the emerging Catholic community. There have been other issues in the past—for example, the struggle over the legitimacy of city hospitals giving advice on birth control, which put Jews and liberal Protestants on one side and Catholics on the other. There are the recurrent disputes over government censorship of books and movies and magazines that have become freer and freer in their handling of sex and sexual perversion. This again ranges Jewish and Protestant supporters of the widest possible freedom of speech against Catholics who are more anxious about the impact of such material on young people and family life. One can see emerging such issues as the rigid state laws on divorce and abortion.

Many of these issues involve Catholic *religious* doctrine. But there exists here a situation that is broader than a conflict over doctrines and the degree to which government should recognize them. What is involved is the emergence of two subcultures, two value systems, shaped and defined certainly in part by religious practice and experience and organization but by now supported by the existence of two communities. If the bishops and the rabbis were to disappear tomorrow, the subcultures and subcommunities would remain. One is secular in its attitudes, liberal in its outlook on sexual life and divorce, positive about science and social science. The other is religious in its outlook, resists the growing liberalization in sexual mores and its reflection in cultural and family life, feels strongly the tension between moral values and modern science and technology. The conflict may be seen in many ways—not least in the fact that the new disciplines such as psychoanalysis, particularly in New York, are so largely staffed by Jews.

Thus a Jewish ethos and a Catholic ethos emerge: they are more strongly affected by a specific religious doctrine in the Catholic case than in the Jewish, but neither is purely the expression of the spirit of a religion. Each is the result of the interplay of religion, ethnic group, American setting, and specific issues. The important fact is that the differences in values and attitudes between the two groups do not, in general, become smaller with time. On the contrary: there is probably a wider gap between Jews and Catholics in New York today than in the days of Al Smith.

NEGROES AND PUERTO RICANS

A close examination of Catholic–Jewish relations will reveal some of the tendency of ethnic relations in New York to be a form of class relations as well. However, the tendency is unmistakably clear with regard to the Negroes and Puerto Ricans. Some 22 per cent of the population of the city is now Negro or Puerto Rican, and the proportion will increase. (Thirty-six per cent of the births in 1961 were Negro or Puerto Rican.) To a degree that cannot fail to startle anyone who encounters the reality for the first time, the overwhelming portion of both groups constitutes a submerged, exploited, and very possibly permanent proletariat.

New York is properly regarded as the wealthiest city in the nation. Its more affluent suburbs enjoy some of the highest standards of living on earth. In the city itself white-collar wages are high, and skilled labor through aggressive trade union activity has obtained almost unprecedented standards. Bricklayers earn $5.35 an hour, plus 52¢ for pension, vacation, and insurance benefits. Electricians have a nominal twenty-five hour week and a base pay of $4.96 an hour plus fringe benefits. But amidst such plenty, unbelievable squalor persists: the line of demarcation is a color line in the case of Negroes, a less definite but equally real ethnic line in the case of Puerto Ricans.

The relationship between the rise of the Negro–Puerto Rican labor supply and the decline of industrial wages is unmistakable. In 1950 there were 246,000 Puerto Ricans in the city. By 1960 this number had increased by two and one-half times to 613,000, or 8 per cent. In 1950 the average hourly earnings of manufacturing production workers in New York City ranked tenth in the nation. By 1960 they ranked thirtieth. In the same period comparable wages in Birmingham, Alabama, rose from thirty-third to tenth. In 1959 median family income for Puerto Ricans was $3,811 as against $6,091 for all the city's families (and $8,052 for suburbs of Westchester). In 1962 average weekly earnings of manufacturing production workers were 19 per cent higher in Birmingham than in New York City, 15 per cent higher in New Orleans, and almost 10 per cent higher in the nation as a whole.

These economic conditions vastly reinforce the ethnic distinctions that serve to separate the Negro community and the Puerto Rican community from the rest of the city. The Negro separation is strengthened by the fact that the colored community is on the whole Protestant, and much of its leadership comes from Protestant clergy. Thus the Negroes provide the missing element of the Protestant–Catholic–Jew triad.

Housing segregation, otherwise an intolerable offense to the persons affected, serves nonetheless to ensure the Negroes a share of seats on the City Council and in the State Legislature and Congress. This power, as well as their voting power generally, has brought Negro political leaders to positions of considerable prominence. Following the 1961 mayoralty election, Mayor Wagner appointed the talented Harlem leader, J. Raymond Jones, as a political secretary through whom he would deal with all the Democratic party organizations of the city. Puerto Ricans have only begun to make their influence felt, but they are clearly on the way to doing so.

Their fate gives them an interest in the same issues: the housing of the poor in a city of perpetual housing shortage; the raising of the wages of the poorly paid service semiskilled occupations in which most of them work; the development of new approaches to raising motivation and capacity by means of education and training in the depressed areas of the city. They live adjacent to each other in vast neighborhoods. And they cooperate on many specific issues—for example, in fighting urban renewal programs that would displace them. But there are deeply felt differences between them. The more Americanized group is also more deeply marked by color. The furtive hope of the new group that it may move ahead as other immigrants have without the barrier of color, and the powerful links of language and culture that mark off the Puerto Ricans, suggest that, despite the fact that the two groups increasingly comprise the proletariat of the city, their history will be distinct.

Thus the cast of major characters for the next decades is complete: the Jews; the Catholics, subdivided at least into Irish and Italian components; the Negroes; the Puerto Ricans; and, of course, the white Anglo-Saxon Protestants. These latter, ranging from the Rockefeller brothers to reform district leaders in the Democratic party are, man for man, among the most influential and powerful persons in the city, and will continue to play a conspicuous and creative role in almost every aspect of the life of the metropolis.

THE ROLE OF POLITICS

The large movements of history and people which tend to reinforce the role of the ethnic groups in the city have been accompanied by new developments in political life which similarly strengthen ethnic identities. This is a complicated matter, but we can point to a number of elements. First, there is some tendency (encouraged by the development of genuine ethnic-class combinations) to substitute ethnic issues in politics for class issues. Second, there has been a decline in the vigor and creativity of politics in New York City, which seems to make New York politicians prefer to deal in terms of premelting pot verities rather than to cope with the chaotic present. Third, the development of public opinion polling would seem to have significantly strengthened the historic tendency of New York political parties to occupy the same middle ground on substantive issues, and indirectly has the effect of strengthening the ethnic component in political campaigns. As competing parties and factions use substantially the same polling techniques, they get substantially the same information about the likes and dislikes of the electorate. Hence they tend to adopt similar positions on political issues. (In much the same way, the development of marketing survey techniques in business has produced standardized commercial products such as cigarettes, automobiles, detergents, and so forth.) For the time being at least, this seems to have increased the importance of racial and ethnic distinctions that, like advertising, can still create distinctions in appearance even if little or none exist in fact. Everything we say in this field is highly speculative, but the impression that the political patterns of the city strengthen the roles of ethnic groups is overwhelming.

It is not easy to illustrate the substitution of ethnic appeals for class appeals. To the extent it occurs, those involved would hope to conceal it, always assuming the practice is deliberate. The basic fact is that for the first half of the twentieth century New York was a center of political radicalism. Faced with fierce opposition, some at least of the left wing discovered that their best tactic was to couch class appeals in ethnic terms. In such manner Vito Marcantonio, a notorious fellow traveler, flourished in the United States Congress as an Italian representative of the Italians and Puerto Ricans of East Harlem. In response to such tactics, the traditional parties have themselves employed the ethnic shorthand to deal with what are essentially class problems. Thus much was made in terms of its ethnic significance of the appointment of a Puerto Rican as a City Commissioner responsible for the relocation of families affected by urban renewal projects, but behind this significance was the more basic one that the slum-dwelling proletariat of the city was being given some control over its housing. In much the same way the balanced ticket makes it possible to offer a slate of candidates ranging across the social spectrum—rich man, poor man, beggar man, thief—but to do so in terms of the ethnic groups represented rather than the classes. In a democratic culture that has never much liked to identify individuals in terms of social classes, and does so less in the aftermath of the radical 1930's and 1940's, the ethnic shorthand is a considerable advantage.

This is of course possible only because of the splintering of traditional economic classes along ethnic lines, which tends to create class-ethnic combinations that have considerable significance at the present time in New York. The sharp division and increasing conflict between the well-paid Jewish cutters in the International Ladies' Garment Workers' Union and the low-paid Negro and Puerto Rican majority in the union have been widely publicized. One Negro cutter hailed the union before the State Commission for Human Rights and obtained a favorable decision. Similar distinctions between skilled and unskilled workers are common enough throughout the trade unions of the city. At a higher level, not dissimilar patterns can be found among the large law firms and banks, where Protestant–Catholic–Jew distinctions exist and are important, even if somewhat less so than in past times.

From time to time the most significant issues of class relations assume ethnic form. Reform movements in New York City politics have invariably been class movements as well. Citing a study of Theodore Lowi, showing that reform in New York City has always meant a change in the class and ethnic background of top city appointees, James Q. Wilson summarized the phenomenon as follows:

> The three "reform" mayors preceding Wagner favored upper-middle-class Yankee Protestants six to one over the Irish as appointees. Almost 40 per cent of the appointees of Seth Low were listed in the Social Register. Further, all four reform mayors—Low, Mitchel, La Guardia, and Wagner—have appointed a much larger percentage of Jews to their cabinets than their regular organization predecessors.

In fact, of course, the problem posed by the amateur Democrats is not simply one of ethnic succession. Militant reform leaders in Manhattan get angry when they hear this "explanation" of their motives, for they reject the idea that ethnicity or religion ought to be considered at all in politics. Although most amateur Democrats are either Jewish or Anglo-Saxon and practically none are Catholic, it is not their entry into politics so much as it is their desire to see a certain political ethic (which middle-class Jews and Yankees happen to share) implemented in local politics.

The 1961 Democratic primary fight, which ended with the defeat of Carmine DeSapio and the regular Democratic organization, was a mixture of class and ethnic conflict that produced the utmost bitterness. In the mayoralty election that followed, the Democratic State Chairman, Michael H. Prendergast, in an unprecedented move, came out in support of an independent candidate, a conservative Italian Catholic, Lawrence E. Gerosa, against Mayor Wagner, who was running for reelection with the support of the middle-class reform elements within the Democratic party. In a bitter *cri de coeur,* almost inevitably his last statement as an acknowledged political leader, Prendergast lashed out at what he regarded as a leftwing conspiracy to take over the Democratic party and merge it with the Liberal party of David Dubinsky and Alex Rose, in the process excluding the traditional Catholic leadership of the city democracy. He declared:

The New York Post lays the whole plot bare in a signed column entitled "One Big Party?" in its September 27 issue. Every Democrat should read it. "The first prerequisite of the new coalition," James A. Wechsler writes, "is that Mayor Wagner win the election." He goes on to say that the new "troops" which Messrs. Dubinsky and Rose will bring to this alliance will have to fight a "rear-guard action" on the part of "Catholics of Irish descent" who, Mr. Wechsler declares, "take their temporal guidance from Patrick Scanlan and his Brooklyn Tablet propaganda sheet."

. . .

It's time to call a spade a spade. The party of Al Smith's time was big enough for Democrats of all descent. The Democratic party of today is big enough for Americans of every race, creed, color or national origin.

Although much larger issues were at stake, it was natural enough for a traditionalist in politics such as Prendergast to describe the conflict in ethnic terms. And in justice it must be said that the ethnic elements of the controversy were probably much more significant than Prendergast's opponents would likely admit.

Apart from the reform movement represented by the Committee for Democratic Voters (which has yet to wield any decisive power over city- or statewide political nominations), the level of political creativity in New York politics has not been high over the past several decades. The almost pathetic tendency to follow established patterns has been reinforced by the growing practice of nominating sons and grandsons of prominent public persons. The cast of such men as Roosevelt, Rockefeller, Harriman, Wagner, and Morgenthau seems almost bent on recreating the gaslight era. In this context the balanced ticket and the balanced distribution of patronage along ethnic lines have assumed an almost fervid sanctity—to the point indeed of caricature, as in the 1961 mayoralty contest in which the Republican team of Lefkowitz, Gilhooley, and Fino faced Democrats Wagner, Screvane, and Beame, the latter victors in a primary contest with Levitt, Mackell, and Di Fede. It will be noted that each ticket consisted of a Jew, an Italian Catholic, and an Irish Catholic, or German-Irish Catholic in the case of Wagner.

The development of polling techniques has greatly facilitated the calculations—and perhaps also the illusions—that go into the construction of a balanced ticket. It should be noted that these techniques would apply equally well, or badly, to all manner of social and economic classifications, but that so far it is the ethnic information that has attracted the interest of the political leaders and persons of influence in politics. Here, for example, is the key passage of the poll on the basis of which Robert M. Morgenthau was nominated as the Democratic candidate for governor in 1962:

> The optimum way to look at the anatomy of the New York State electorate is to take three symbolic races for Governor and two for the Senate and compare them group by group. The three we will select for Governor are Screvane, Morgenthau, and Burke.[1] We select these because each represents a different fundamental assumption. Screvane makes sense as a candidate, if the election should be cast in terms of an extension of the Wagner–Rockefeller fight. This could have the advantage of potentially firming up a strong New York City vote, where, in fact, the election must be won by the Democrats. On the other hand, a Rockefeller–Screvane battle would make it more difficult to cast the election in national terms of Rockefeller vs. Kennedy, which, as we shall also see, is a critical dimension to pursue.
>
> A Morgenthau–Rockefeller race is run mainly because it represents meeting the Rockefeller–Javits ticket on its own grounds of maximum strength: among Jewish and liberal-minded voters, especially in New York City. Morgenthau is the kind of name that stands with Lehman, and, as we shall see, has undoubted appeal with Jewish voters. The question of running a moderately liberal Jewish candidate for Governor is whether this would in turn lose the Democrats some conservative Catholic voters who are not enchanted with Rockefeller and Javits to begin with, but who might normally vote Republican.
>
> The third tack that might be taken on the Governorship is to put up an outstanding Irish Catholic candidate on the assumption that with liberal Republicans Rockefeller and Javits running, the Catholic vote can be moved appreciably over to the Democratic column, especially in view of Rockefeller's divorce as a silent but powerful issue. Here, Court of Appeals Judge Adrian Burke, who far outstripped the statewide ticket in 1954, might be considered typical of this type of candidate.
>
> Let us then look at each of these alternatives and see how the pattern of the vote varies by each. For it is certain that the key Democratic decision in 1962 must be over the candidate for Governor first, and then followed by the candidate for U. S.

---

[1] Paul R. Screvane, President of the City Council, an Italian Catholic; Robert M. Morgenthau, United States Attorney for the Southern District of New York, a Jew; Adrian P. Burke, Judge of the Court of Appeals, an Irish Catholic.

TABLE 1 Key Group Breakdowns.*

	Democratic candidates for governor pitted against Rockefeller			Democratic candidates for U. S. Senate against Javits	
Statewide	Screvane 47%	Burke 43%	Morgenthau 49%	Bunche 47%	Murrow 46%
By Area					
New York City (43%)	61	54	61	57	55
Suburbs (16%)	41	41	43	42	40
Upstate (41%)	35	35	40	40	40
By Occupation					
Business and Professional (14%)	35	22	30	57	33
White collar (19%)	36	44	51	50	44
Sales and service (8%)	49	49	54	42	42
Labor (34%)	56	53	57	34	52
Small business, shopkeeper (5%)	38	41	41	42	36
Retired and other (13%)	39	30	39	52	43
By Ethnic Groups					
White U.S.A. (29%)	35	37	36	36	40
Irish (9%)	44	49	44	48	36
English-Scotch (7%)	42	26	33	34	34
German (16%)	29	34	39	42	41
Italian (13%)	59	53	53	45	55
By Religion and Race					
White Protestant (37%)	27	27	29	35	32
White Catholic (37%)	51	54	51	42	48
White Jewish (18%)	70	56	82	71	61
Negro (8%)	70	55	68	93	74
Sex by Age					
Men (49%)	47	40	48	47	43
21–34 (15%)	42	39	40	43	34
35–49 (16%)	53	39	54	43	54
50 and over (18%)	48	43	51	55	42
Women (51%)	47	48	50	47	49
21–34 (15%)	56	56	58	55	45
35–49 (18%)	50	52	59	53	58
50 and over (18%)	39	35	36	37	41
By Union Membership					
Union member (25%)	66	61	65	49	57
Union family (11%)	56	59	57	52	47
Nonunion (64%)	38	35	42	45	40
By Income Groups					
Upper middle (22%)	33	20	32	40	27
Lower middle (64%)	47	47	52	45	48
Low (14%)	63	61	62	66	61

* Each figure gives the percentage of total vote that the proposed candidate received in the specified category. Thus, 35 per cent of the business and professional vote were recorded as saying they would vote for Screvane against Rockefeller.

Beyond the Melting Pot

Senate. We also include the breakdowns by key groups for Bunche and Murrow against Javits.[2]

Here some fascinating and revealing patterns emerge which point the way sharply toward the kind of choice the Democrats can make optimally in their selection of Gubernatorial and Senatorial candidates for 1962 in New York:

—By area, it appears that the recent Democratic gains in the suburbs are quite solid, and a range of from 40 to 43 per cent of the vote seems wholly obtainable.

—By race and religion, we find equally revealing results. The Protestant vote is as low as it was for Kennedy in 1960, when the religious issue was running strong.

—By contrast, the Catholic vote remains relatively stable, with a slight play for Burke above the rest, and with Bunche and Murrow showing some weaknesses here. (The relative percentages, however, for a James A. Farley[3] race against Javits show Farley with 30 per cent Protestant, a relatively lower standing; 58 per cent of the Catholics, a very good showing, but with only 36 per cent of the Jewish vote, a very poor result; and 67 per cent of the Negro vote, only a fair showing).

The really volatile votes in this election clearly are going to be the Jewish and Negro votes. The Jewish vote ranges from a low of 56 per cent (for Burke); 61 per cent for Murrow (against Javits); 70 per cent for Screvane (against Rockefeller); a very good 71 per cent for Bunche (against Javits); and a thumping 82 per cent for Morgenthau (against Rockefeller). Here the conclusion is perfectly obvious: by running a Lehman type of Jewish candidate against Rockefeller, the Jewish vote can be anchored well up into the high 70's and even into the 80's. By running an Irish Catholic candidate against Rockefeller, the Jewish vote comes tumbling precipitously down into the 50's. What is more, with Javits on the ticket, with strong appeal among Jews, any weakness among Jews with the Gubernatorial candidate, and the defection of the Jewish vote can be large enough to reduce the city vote to disastrously low proportions for the Democrats.

The Negro vote is only slightly less volatile. It ranges from a low of 55 per cent (for Burke, again); to 68 per cent for Morgenthau, not too good (an indication that Negroes will not automatically vote for a Jewish candidate, there being friction between the two groups); 70 per cent for Screvane (who carried over some of the strong Wagner appeal among Negroes); 74 per cent for Murrow, a good showing; and an incredibly high 93 per cent for Bunche.

Observation: The conclusion for Governor seems self-evident from these results. A candidate who would run in the Wagner image, such as Screvane, would poll a powerful New York City vote, but would fade more upstate and would not pull in a full measure of the Jewish swing vote. An Irish Catholic candidate would not do appreciably better than Screvane upstate (a pattern that has been repeated throughout New York's modern political history, with Kennedy the sole exception in 1960), but with good appeal in the suburbs, yet with a disas-

---

[2] Ralph J. Bunche, United Nations official, a Negro; Edward R. Murrow, Director, United States Information Agency, a white Protestant; Jacob K. Javits, United States Senator, a Jew.
[3] James A. Farley, former Postmaster General, an Irish Catholic.

trous showing among Jews and Negroes in New York City. A Lehman-type Jewish candidate, such as Morgenthau, by contrast, would appeal to a number of Protestants upstate (as, indeed, Lehman always did in his runs), would hold well in the suburbs, and could bring in solidly the pivotal Jewish vote in New York City.

The first choice must be a Jewish candidate for Governor of the highest caliber (sic).

There are two things to note about this poll. In the first place, the New York Jews did *not* vote solidly for Morgenthau, who lost by half a million votes. A week before the election Morgenthau headquarters received a report that a follow-up poll showed that 50 per cent of New York City Jews who had voted for the Democratic candidate Averell Harriman in 1958 were undecided about voting for Morgenthau four years later. An analysis of the vote cast in predominately Jewish election districts shows that Rockefeller significantly improved his performance over 1958, when he had run against Averell Harriman, another white Protestant. In important areas such as Long Beach, Rockefeller went from 37.2 per cent in 1958 to 62.7 per cent in 1962, which is sufficient evidence that a Jewish name alone does not pull many votes. It could also confirm the pre-election fears of the Democrats that the notoriety of their search for a "Lehman type of Jewish candidate" had produced a strong resentment within the Jewish community. The following are returns from predominantly Jewish districts:

TABLE 2

	Rockefeller			Javits		
	1962	1958	Dif.	1962	1956	Dif.
New York City						
Bronx A.D. 2, School 90	27.2	20.5	+6.7	41.9	19.2	+22.7
3	21.6	18.7	+2.9	44.0	17.5	+26.5
5	26.4	19.8	+6.6	39.9	21.4	+18.5
Queens A.D. 7, School 164	43.8	36.5	+7.3	66.5	32.0	+34.5
Suburbs						
Jericho (part)	50.7	34.4	+16.3	60.7	36.1	+24.6
Long Beach (part)	62.7	37.2	+25.5	66.2	34.3	+31.9
Harrison (part)	71.3	69.6	+1.7	71.4	64.6	+6.8
New Rochelle, Ward 4	57.8	58.8	−1.0	57.1	55.8	+1.3

These returns, which are typical enough, reveal an important fact about ethnic voting. Class interests and geographical location are the dominant influences in voting behavior, whatever the ethnic group involved. In urban, Democratic Bronx, the great majority of Jews vote Democratic. In suburban, Republican Westchester, the next county, the great majority of Jews vote Republican. But within that over-all pattern a definite ethnic swing does occur. Thus Rockefeller got barely a fifth of the vote in the third Assembly district of Democratic Bronx, while he got almost three-quarters in Harrison in Republican Westchester, *but he improved his performance in both areas* despite the fact that his 1962 plurality was lower, statewide, than 1948. Similarly, Rockefeller got as little as 8.8 per cent of the vote in the predominately Negro third ward of Democratic Albany, and as much as 76 per cent in upper-middle-class, Republican Rye in Westchester, but generally speaking, Rockefeller appears to have lost Negro votes in 1962 over 1958.

A second point to note is that while the poll provided detailed information on the response to the various potential candidates classified by sex, occupational status, and similar characteristics of the persons interviewed, the candidates proposed were all essentially ethnic prototypes, and the responses analyzed in the commentary were those on the ethnic line. These are terms, howsoever misleading, which are familiar to New York politics, and with which New York politicians prefer to deal.

THE FUTURE

We have tried to show how deeply the pattern of ethnicity is impressed on the life of the city. Ethnicity is more than an influence on events; it is commonly the source of events. Social and political institutions do not merely respond to ethnic interests; a great number of institutions exist for the specific purpose of serving ethnic interests. This in turn tends to perpetuate them. In many ways, the atmosphere of New York City is hospitable to ethnic groupings: it recognizes them, and rewards them, and to that extent encourages them.

This is not to say that no individual group will disappear. This, on the contrary, is a recurring phenomenon. The disappearance of the Germans is a particularly revealing case.

In terms of size or the achievements of its members, the Germans ought certainly to be included among the principal ethnic groups of the city. It never quite as numerous as the Irish, they were indisputably the second largest group in the late nineteenth century, accounting for perhaps a third of the population and enjoying the highest reputation. But today, while German influence is to be seen in virtually every aspect of the city's life, the Germans *as a group* are vanished. No appeals are made to the German vote, there are no German politicians in the sense that there are Irish or Italian politicians, there are in fact few Germans in political life and, generally speaking, no German component in the structure of the ethnic interests of the city.

The logical explanation of this development, in terms of the presumed course of American social evolution, is simply that the Germans have been "assimilated" by the Anglo-Saxon center. To some extent this has happened. The German immigrants of the nineteenth century were certainly much closer to the old Americans than were the Irish who arrived in the same period. Many were Protestants, many were skilled workers or even members of the professions, and their level of education in general was high. Despite the language difference, they did not seem nearly so alien to the New York mercantile establishment as did the Irish. At the time of their arrival German sympathies were high in New York. (George Templeton Strong was violent in his support of doughty Prussia in its struggle with imperial, tyrannical France.) All of this greatly facilitated German assimilation.

In any event, there were obstacles to the Germans' becoming a distinct ethnic bloc. Each of the five groups we have discussed arrived with a high degree of homogeneity: in matters of education, skills, and religion the members of the group were for the most part alike. This homogeneity, as we have tried to show, invested ethnicity with meaning and importance that it would not otherwise have had. But this was not so with the Germans, who were split between Catholics and Protestants, liberals and conservatives, craftsmen and businessmen and laborers. They reflected, as it were, an entire modern society, not simply an element of one. The only things all had in common were the outward manifestations of German culture: language for a generation or two, and after that a fondness for certain types of food and drink and a consciousness of the German fatherland. This was a powerful enough bond and would very likely be visible today, except for the impact of the World Wars. The Germanophobia of America during the First World War is, of course, notorious. It had limits in New York where, for instance, German was *not* driven from the public school curriculum, but the attraction of things German was marred. This period was followed, in hardly more than a decade, by the Nazi era, during which German fascism made its appearance in Jewish New York, with what results one can imagine. The German American Bund was never a major force in the city, but it did exist. The revulsion against Nazism extended indiscriminately to things German. Thereafter, German Americans, as shocked by the Nazis as any, were disinclined to make overmuch of their national origins.

Even so, it is not clear that consciousness of German nationality has entirely ceased to exist among German-Americans in the city, or elsewhere. There is evidence that for many it has simply been submerged. In New York City, which ought logically to be producing a series of Italian and Jewish mayors, the political phenomenon of the postwar period has been Robert F. Wagner.

It is even possible that the future will see a certain resurgence of German identity in New York, although we expect it will be mild. The enemy of two world wars has become an increasingly powerful and important ally in the Cold War. Berlin has become a symbol of resistance to totalitarianism; Germany has become an integral part of the New Europe. Significantly, the German-Americans of the city have recently begun an annual Steuben Day Parade, adding for the politicians of the city yet another command performance at an ethnic outing.

Despite this mild German resurgence, it is a good general rule that except where color is involved as well the specifically *national* aspect of most ethnic groups rarely survives the third generation in any significant terms. The intermarriage which de Crèvecoeur described continues apace, so that even the strongest national traditions are steadily diluted. The groups do not disappear, however, because of their *religious* aspect which serves as the basis of a subcommunity, and a subculture. Doctrines and practices are modified to some extent to conform to an American norm, but a distinctive set of values is nurtured in the social groupings defined by religious affiliation. This is quite contrary to early expectations. It appeared to de Crèvecoeur, for example, that religious as well as national identity was being melted into one by the process of mixed neighborhoods and marriage:

... This mixed neighborhood will exhibit a strange religious medley, that will be neither pure Catholicism nor pure Calvinism. A very perceptible indifference even in the first generation, will become apparent; and it may happen that the daughter of the Catholic will marry the son of the seceder, and settle by themselves at a distance from their parents. What religious education will they give their children? A very imperfect one. If there happens to be in the neighborhood any place of worship, we will suppose a Quaker's meeting; rather than not shew their fine clothes, they will go to it, and some of them may attach themselves to that society. Others will remain in a perfect state of indifference; the children of these zealous parents will not be able to tell what their religious principles are, and their grandchildren still less.

Thus all sects are mixed as well as all nations; thus religious indifference is imperceptibly disseminated from one end of the continent to the other; which is at present one of the strongest characteristics of the Americans.

If this was the case in the late eighteenth century, it is no longer. Religious identities are strongly held by New Yorkers, and Americans generally, and they are for the most part transmitted by blood line from the original immigrant group. A great deal of intermarriage occurs among nationality groups of the three great religious groups, of the kind Ruby Jo Kennedy described in New Haven, Connecticut, under the general term of the Triple Melting Pot, but this does not weaken religious identity. When marriages occur between different religions, often one is dominant, and the result among the children is not indifference, but an increase in the numbers of one of the groups.

Religion and race seem to define the major groups into which American society is evolving as the specifically national aspect of ethnicity declines. In our large American cities, four major groups emerge: Catholics, Jews, white Protestants, and Negroes, each making up the city in different proportions. This evolution is by no means complete. And yet we can discern that the next stage of the evolution of the immigrant groups will involve a Catholic group in which the distinctions between Irish, Italian, Polish, and German Catholic are steadily reduced by intermarriage; a Jewish group, in which the line between East European, German, and Near Eastern Jews is already weak; the Negro group; and a white Protestant group, which adds to its Anglo-Saxon and Dutch old-stock elements German and Scandinavian Protestants, as well as, more typically, the white Protestant immigrants to the city from the interior.

The white Protestants are a distinct ethnic group in New York, one that has probably passed its low point and will now begin to grow in numbers and probably also in influence. It has its special occupations, with the customary freemasonry. This involves the banks, corporation front offices, educational and philanthropic institutions, and the law offices who serve them. It has its own social world (epitomized by, but by no means confined to, the *Social Register*), its own churches, schools, voluntary organizations and all the varied institutions of a New York minority. These are accompanied by the characteristic styles in food, clothing, and drink, special family patterns, special psychological problems and ailments. For a long while political conservatism, as well as social aloofness, tended to keep the white Protestants out of the main stream of New York politics, much in the way that political radicalism tended to isolate the Jews in the early parts of the century. Theodore Roosevelt, when cautioned that none of his friends would touch New York politics, had a point in replying that it must follow that none of his friends were members of the governing classes.

There has been a resurgence of liberalism within the white Protestant group, in part based on its growth through vigorous young migrants from outside the city, who are conspicuous in the communications industry, law firms, and corporation offices of New York. These are the young people that supported Adlai Stevenson and helped lead and staff the Democratic reform movement. The influence of the white Protestant group on this city, it appears, must now grow as its numbers grow.

In this large array of the four major religio-racial groups, where do the Puerto Ricans stand? Ultimately perhaps they are to be absorbed into the Catholic group. But that is a long time away. The Puerto Ricans are separated from the Catholics as well as the Negroes by color and culture. One cannot even guess how this large element will ultimately relate itself to the other elements of the city; perhaps it will serve, in line with its own nature and genius, to soften the sharp lines that divide them.

Protestants will enjoy immunities in politics even in New York. When the Irish era came to an end in the Brooklyn Democratic party in 1961, Joseph T. Sharkey was succeeded by a troika (as it was called) of an Irish Catholic, a Jew, and a Negro Protestant. The last was a distinguished clergyman, who was at the same time head of the New York City Council of Protestant Churches. It would have been unlikely for a rabbi, unheard of for a priest, to hold such a position.

Religion and race define the next stage in the evolution of the American peoples. But the American nationality is still forming: its processes are mysterious, and the final form, if there is ever to be a final form, is as yet unknown.

SUGGESTIONS FOR FURTHER READING

The literature of political sociology has grown rapidly in the past fifteen years. An early work recently reprinted in the United States, by the English sociologist T. H. Marshall, *Class, Citizenship and Social Development* (Garden City, N. Y.: Doubleday, 1964), is an excellent introduction to the interrelation of social and political variables.

Preeminent among American political sociologists are Talcott Parsons, *The Social System* (New York: Free Press, 1951), Robert Merton, *Social Theory and Social Structure* (New York: Free Press, 1956), and Edward A. Shils, *The Torment of Secrecy* (New York: Free Press, 1956). Seymour Martin Lipset also belongs on this list, and in addition to the work excerpted in Chapter 1 students might examine *Political Man* (Garden City, N. Y.: Doubleday, 1960), *Revolution and Counterrevolution* (New York: Basic Books, 1968), and *Politics and the Social Sciences* (New York: Oxford University Press, 1969).

Also useful on recent patterns of social change are Daniel Bell, *The End of Ideology: On the Exhaustion of Political Ideas in the Fifties* (New York: Free Press, 1960), and Bell's edited volume *The Radical Right* (Garden City, N. Y.: Doubleday, 1963). For a review and critique of the literature, see Robert A. Nisbet, *Social Change and History: Aspects of the Western Theory of Development* (New York: Oxford University Press, 1969).

On the decline of the frontier and the famous "Turner thesis," a new set of appraisals has appeared under the editorship of Richard Hofstadter and Seymour Martin Lipset: *Turner and the Sociology of the Frontier* (New York: Basic Books, 1968). Particularly good on the interrelations of religion and politics are Joseph Gusfield, *Symbolic Crusade: Status Politics and the American Temperance Movement* (Urbana, Ill.: University of Illinois Press, 1963), and Gerhard Lenski, *The Religious Factor* (Garden City, N. Y.: Doubleday, 1961).

Journals such as the *American Sociological Review, American Journal of Sociology,* and *Social Forces* are likely vehicles for articles in this area.

3 The cultural and ideological determinants of the system

IN ADDITION TO ITS SOCIAL DETERMINANTS, the American political system is shaped by (1) ingrained political predispositions of the people and (2) political doctrines espoused by their leaders.

Contemporary political science has been making substantial progress in the study of political predispositions. In the early 1960's, scholars concerned with comparing quite diverse polities (for example, emerging systems such as Burma with modern systems such as Great Britain) developed the concept of "political culture." In the words of Almond and Verba, the principal architects of the concept, a population is distinguished by "specifically political orientations—attitudes towards the political system and its various parts, and attitudes towards the role of the self in the system." [1] Almond and Powell [2] developed further the argument that a prerequisite for certain political forms—most notably the pluralist democracy of the Anglo-American sort—is the presence within the population of a certain constellation of attitudes.

Spinning off from this concept of political culture was that of political socialization—based on a simple but fruitful analogy drawn from anthropology. It is fundamental anthropological theory that any culture is undergirded by attitudes and expectations that must be transmitted inter-

---

[1] Gabriel Almond and Sidney Verba, *The Civic Culture* (Princeton, N. J.: Princeton University Press, 1963), p. 13.
[2] Gabriel Almond and G. Bingham Powell, Jr., *Comparative Politics* (Boston: Little, Brown, 1966).

generationally if the culture is to survive. And it is possible to identify the agents that transmit particular attitudes—those that "socialize" the young and equip them to function in society. In the same way, political scientists should be able to ascertain precisely how political learning, or political socialization, takes place in any national or tribal setting. What is learned? When is it learned? How is it learned (from the family, from school, from peer groups, from the mass media)? Finally, what changes are taking place in the patterns of political socialization over time?

This last question is crucial. If the system is in part a function of attitudes and expectations about politics, it would follow that when change does take place in the process of political socialization (for example, when the family fails to instill respect for certain types of public authority), this change will sooner or later result in altered political behavior.

Of course there is a provisional character to this argument. Research into political socialization in America is only in its early stages, and it is neither wise nor fair to expect any confident predictions about what changes are taking place in the process or what consequences are likely to follow for the system as a whole. Nonetheless, some interesting and suggestive findings are being made, and perhaps the most provocative publication to date is *The Development of Political Attitudes* by Robert D. Hess and Judith V. Torney. A selection from that book is presented here. Building on the work of Fred I. Greenstein[3] and Easton and Dennis,[4] Hess and Torney argue that the first political identifications of children are with national objects and that these early identifications are unlikely to be greatly altered in the later development of the personality. Since there are no systematic studies of the past American generations, it is difficult to argue that any change is reflected by the Hess-Torney data. But if we can rely even a bit on traditional historical research (based on what persons in the past wrote about themselves), local and state identifications used to be considerably more prominent than they are today. If the direction of change in basic political predispositions is toward positive national identifications (perhaps because of the development of mass media over the past thirty years), an important decentralizing force in the American system is abating. Political consciousness is becoming more national, and the electronic media provide continual nationwide stimulation for it.

The study of American political ideas (that is, of articulated doctrines) is now somewhat out of fashion among political scientists. This kind of question is often raised: "Will reading what John Locke said about the good state explain how the federal government functioned during Johnson's presidency? If not, what good is it?" But enthusiasm for the obvious and measurable often leads us to overlook the elusive and tenuous relationships that exist between doctrine and behavior. Suppose one asked a different question: "Would the American system have developed in the way

[3] *Children and Politics* (New Haven, Conn.: Yale University Press, 1965).
[4] David Easton and Jack Dennis, "The Child's Acquisition of Regime Norms: Political Efficacy," *American Political Science Review,* Vol. 61, No. 1 (March 1967), pp. 25–38.

it did had Thomas Hobbes been avidly read by our early political elite in place of John Locke?" Put this way, the importance of doctrines becomes clear.

Samuel H. Beer's essay, "Liberalism and the National Idea," is an example of generalizing about doctrine at its best. Arguing that a national ideal and a provincial ideal contended for the loyalty of Americans during the nineteenth and early twentieth centuries, Beer concludes that the national ideal has in our time been fused with social-welfare liberalism. Antiprovincial liberals have set the tone for both the federal service and the intellectual community for most of the time since 1933, and they have created a climate and a set of justifications for a vast expansion of national —or central—political power.

Attachment to Government

ROBERT D. HESS AND JUDITH V. TORNEY

CONCEPT OF THE SYSTEM

It is difficult for a child to comprehend a complex political institution. Although there are symbols of Congress, the Supreme Court, and other institutions of government, these are not used with the same frequency and ritual as the flag and pledge of allegiance are used as symbols of the nation. It seems likely that complex social and political systems are initially conceptualized as *persons* to whom the child can relate. Through attachments to these persons, the individual becomes related to the system. In short, to the child, the government is a man who lives in Washington, while Congress is a lot of men who help the President. During the developmental period when a child begins to build a positive regard for institutions and becomes subject to their sanctions, complex social systems must be represented by personal figures who can act as sanctioning agents and objects of attachment.

. . .

The second- or third-grade child's image of government is largely confined to persons. In interviews, these young children referred to government as "the

FROM Robert D. Hess and Judith V. Torney, *The Development of Political Attitudes in Children* (Chicago: Aldine Publishing Company, 1967), pp. 32–45; copyright © 1967 by Robert D. Hess and Judith V. Torney.

THE CULTURAL AND IDEOLOGICAL DETERMINANTS

man who signs the checks," "the state and city governments are different men, but they both are governments," or "the government is a nice man." On a pretest questionnaire, 60 per cent of a group of fourth-graders expressed agreement with the statement, "The government is a man."

Data from a question asking children to select the two pictures that "showed best what the government is" are presented in Table 1. Pictures of President

TABLE 1 Changes by Grade in Choice of "The Best Picture of Government." (Children were asked to choose two alternatives.)*

Grade level	N	Policeman	George Washington	Uncle Sam	Voting	Supreme Court
2	1,619	8.2%	39.4%	15.6%	4.3%	4.5%
3	1,662	4.1	26.8	19.0	8.4	6.4
4	1,726	5.7	14.2	18.0	10.8	10.2
5	1,789	2.7	6.9	19.4	19.2	16.8
6	1,740	2.4	4.9	16.8	28.0	16.8
7	1,714	3.0	3.4	18.3	39.4	13.5
8	1,689	1.7	1.7	16.4	46.8	15.9
Teachers	390	1.3	1.3	4.6	71.8	12.8

Grade level	Capitol	Congress	Flag	Statue of Liberty	President	Don't know
2	13.6%	13.6%	5.9%	12.1%	46.2%	15.7%
3	16.1	12.9	16.5	14.3	46.8	12.9
4	16.6	29.0	13.3	12.9	37.2	13.2
5	11.6	49.0	11.6	11.2	38.5	4.9
6	9.9	49.7	11.4	17.1	30.3	4.7
7	9.4	44.2	12.8	18.6	27.9	3.0
8	6.9	49.1	11.8	19.6	22.9	1.5
Teachers	5.1	71.0	6.2	8.5	15.1	.2

NOTES Item: Here are some pictures that show what our government is. Pick the *two* pictures that show best what our government is.
Significance unit: 3%.
* Percentages do not always sum to 200 per cent for any grade because some children chose only one alternative or chose "I don't know."

Kennedy and George Washington were chosen by 46 per cent and 39 per cent respectively of the second-graders. For older children, choices of these personal figures, particulary Washington, dropped off sharply. *Congress and voting*, which represent government as an institution and a process, were chosen by less than 10 per cent of the second-graders. Eighth-graders (between 45 and

Attachment to Government

50 per cent) found these impersonal aspects of government to be more appropriate symbols. This approached the 72 per cent choice by teachers. Selection of Congress increased at an earlier grade-level than did voting. This suggests that the conceptualization of government is tied to personal figures for young children, then to institutions, and finally to political processes for older children.

Parallel developmental trends occur in the child's conception of the origin of laws and governmental administration. As children grow older, they come to believe that Congress is more important in law-making than the President. In the second grade, 76 per cent chose the President and 5 per cent the Congress

TABLE 2   Changes by Grade in Perception of Source of Laws.

Grade level	N	Congress makes laws	President makes laws	Supreme Court makes laws	Don't know
2	1,627	4.8%	75.6%	11.5%	8.2%
3	1,648	11.4	66.1	17.0	5.5
4	1,723	27.5	44.1	21.1	7.3
5	1,793	57.4	19.4	19.8	3.4
6	1,743	65.1	13.2	18.3	3.4
7	1,712	72.1	8.9	16.4	2.6
8	1,690	85.3	5.4	7.9	1.4
Teachers	384	96.4	.5	3.1	*

NOTES Item: Who makes the laws? Put an X next to the [picture of the] *one* who does most to make laws.
Significance unit: 3%.
* No d.k. alternative.

when asked "Who makes the laws?" By eighth grade, 85 per cent chose the Congress and only 5 per cent the President. The most striking change occurred between grades four and five (Table 2). Younger children were also more likely to say that "the President runs the country" (Table 3).

Unlike the marked shift with age on the item dealing with *legislative* functions (Table 2), the response to questions about the *administrative* functions of Congress and the President (Table 3) remained relatively constant; a differentiation with increasing age does occur in the children's conceptions, and they tend to see the administrative functions as divided between the President and the Congress. At grade eight, 58 per cent believed that the President ran the country.

A Young Child's Image of the National Government Is Confined Mainly to the President. He is the figure about whom children believe they know most. They reported seeing him on television, and 95 per cent of the second-grade children

THE CULTURAL AND IDEOLOGICAL DETERMINANTS

TABLE 3 Changes by Grade in Perception of "Who Runs the Country."

Grade level	N	Congress runs country	President runs country	Supreme Court runs country	Don't know
2	1,627	3.9%	86.3%	3.3%	6.5%
3	1,662	6.7	85.4	3.1	4.7
4	1,725	13.2	77.0	3.4	6.5
5	1,796	20.0	71.8	3.8	4.3
6	1,744	24.9	66.2	4.5	4.4
7	1,711	27.8	64.0	5.3	2.9
8	1,683	35.1	58.4	3.6	2.9
Teachers	383	61.4	35.8	3.0	*

NOTES Item: Who does the most to run the country? Put an X in the box next to the [picture of the] *one* who does most to run the country.
Significance unit: 3%.
* No d.k. alternative.

knew his name. The President is a source of national pride, and is seen as serving a vital function in protecting and representing the nation and watching over its administration. The following excerpts from an interview with a third-grade boy, the son of a teacher, give a fairly representative impression of the younger children's image of the President, although these responses are more complete and articulate than those of most subjects this age.

"Have you ever seen the President?"
"I've seen him on television, and heard him on the radio, and seen him in newspapers."
"What does the President do?"
"He runs the country, he decides the decisions that we should try to get out of, and he goes to meetings and tries to make peace and things like that."
"When you say he runs the country, what do you mean?"
"Well, he's just about the boss of everything. . . ."
"And what kind of person do you think he is?"
"Well, usually he's an honest one."
"Anything else?"
"Well, loyal and usually is pretty smart."
"Usually, but not always?"
"Well, they're all smart, but they aren't exactly perfect [pause] . . . most of them are."
"Who pays him?"
"Well, gee, I don't know if anybody pays him, he probably doesn't get too much money for the job—I don't even know if he gets any money."
"Why would he take the job?"
"Well, he loves his country and he wants this country to live in peace."

The President is not a noble, salient figure to all children. For some he is visible but apparently not very important. Bobby, a fourth-grade boy, shows something less than enthusiasm in his comments about the President:

"Bobby, have you seen the President on TV?"
"Yes."
"What kind of things does the President do in his job?"
"Well, he goes on trips, and . . . I don't know."
"What does he do when he goes on these trips?"
"I dunno . . . he has speeches and all that stuff."
"Have you seen him make speeches on TV?"
"Yes."
"What does he talk about?"
"I dunno . . . Ma always watches it."

The Child Subsequently Develops a More Impersonal and Institutionalized Conception of the Government. Interviews provide clues to the development of this view. Responses such as the following are given by older children: "The government is made up of representatives that the people elect," or "The government is just an organization that the people formed to rule themselves." Instead of focusing on one person, these children emphasized a group of persons elected by the citizens. Perceiving government as synonymous with the President is a simple way for young children to organize perceptions of the political world. The school is important in fostering the more refined, complex picture of government which develops later. Our evidence indicates, however, that schools put equal and concurrent emphasis upon the President and Congress. . . .

The importance of the President in young children's conceptualization of government is not determined primarily by classroom learning but by the child's tendency to focus upon a personal representative of the system. . . . The child is not conceptually ready to understand the government as an abstract institutionalized entity, and he transfers the approach to personalized authority which has been useful to him in coping with other social systems (such as the school). This pattern of induction to systems through personal authority is applicable to a range of other social systems. The small child's view of the medical profession centers around the doctor, the nurse, and the specifics of his interaction with them; his image of the church is initially one of human and super-human figures; his understanding of the school is not concerned with policy, finance, or administration, but with the teacher and the principal.

CONCEPT OF THE CITIZEN'S ROLE

The initial conception of a "good citizen" is largely one of the "good person." Interview responses suggest that second- and third-grade children made little distinction between a good person and a good citizen. They stressed the image of general goodness, although concern with the country was of some importance. An interview excerpt from a conversation with the fourth-grade son of working-class parents illustrates this point:

"Well, what is a good citizen?"
"A person whose house is clean and who is polite."

A second example is from a fourth-grade, working-class child:

"How could a citizen help his country?"
"Well, follow the laws, don't get in accidents, and do practically everything as hard as he can."

Children in this study chose from seven alternatives the two which they believed characterized the good child citizen and the good adult citizen. Seventy-four per cent of second- and third-grade children reported that the "boy who helps others" is the best citizen. Choices of personally oriented alternatives declined with age for both child and adult citizen, to be replaced by a conception of the citizen in more specifically political terms—voting (for the adult citizen) and showing interest in government. . . . The absence of distinctions between personal goodness and politically oriented citizenship exemplifies the low level of differentiation in children's thinking, the assimilation of the political world to personal experiences, and the transfer of rules from the personal to the political realm. . . .

THE CHILD'S RELATIONSHIP TO THE SYSTEM

The child's first relationship with his government is with the President, whom he sees in highly positive terms. This indicates his basic trust in the benevolence of government. Young children relate to the President as they do to figures they know personally, expressing strong emotional attachment to him and expecting protection from him. They believe that the President is intimately involved not only in momentous decisions concerning the fate of the country but also in more mundane decisions that affect them and their neighborhood: how much meat will cost, whether people must remain in jail or be freed, what the traffic laws are. A strong sense of trust is evident in their responses; they think that the President is personally responsive to children's wishes and believe that they could even go to the White House and talk to him.

The child's conception of the President's concern for the individual is also indicated by responses to the item, "If you write to the President, does he care what you think?" . . . Seventy-five per cent of second-grade children felt that the President would care about their ideas if they wrote to him. The mean response to this item declined, but eighth-graders also believed that the President would pay considerable attention to their opinions.

Young children also believe that the President personally would help them if they needed it. . . . The average second-grade child in the sample reported that the President would be nearly as helpful to him if he were in trouble as the policeman or his father. For students in grade eight, the mean score for these figures diverged; the President was rated similarly to impersonal and distant agencies such as the Supreme Court and government. The child's early approach to the system is highly personal; he expects from personal representatives of the political system the same help and nurturance he receives from his parents.

In one pilot study the percentage of children choosing the alternative, "The President is about the best person in the world," declined from approximately 52 per cent at grade two to 10 per cent at grade eight. This illustrates the charismatic quality in second-graders' relationships to the President. . . . Davies, in analyzing charisma in the 1952 campaign, suggested that it was the result of insecurity generated either by unstable upbringing or by situations of national crises. We have suggested that idealization of the President as an authority figure is a technique children utilize in dealing with feelings of vulnerability and powerlessness. . . .

Since government is perceived as personally responsive to the individual, the second- or third-grade child might be expected to be attached to the President in the same manner he is attached to his father; indeed, a positive feeling was reflected in ratings of the President as a personal favorite. . . . The age trends and relative positions of father and President on these ratings resembled those on the item dealing with helpfulness. Expressions of this type of emotional attachment to the President declined most rapidly between grades two and five.

Although the senator would be appropriate as a personal link between the child and the system, children do not develop a high level of regard for him. At all grade levels, the senator was rated below all other figures in willingness to help. He was also less well-liked than the President. Interviews indicated that children know little about the senator; references to his function were vague—". . . to help the President when he asks them."

The Senate and senators are not clearly etched in the child's image of political institutions. A fifth-grade boy described a senator as ". . . a man in the House of Representatives that's gone up so far he's become a senator so he can run against the Vice-President. Only the senator and Vice-President can run for President."

An eighth-grade girl also shows a good bit of misinformation about the role of senator:

"What's their job—the Senate and the House of Representatives?"
"Well, I think . . . I don't know, but my opinion is that they have more part

of the government than anyone else because that's where most of the bills originate . . . and the laws."

"What's the difference between the House of Representatives and the Senate?"

"Well, isn't the Senate Democratic and the House of Representatives Republican? I mean . . . ah .. . . . what do I mean? Democrats and Republicans, that's right . . . I'm not sure."

"How does a senator get to be a senator?"

"Well, he's probably a member of the Senate first and then they would vote a . . . a senator . . . oh, wait . . . he's elected by the state which he represents."

There were many children, of course, who have more information about the Senate and about the role of senator. There was little evidence, however, that individual senators, as persons, are salient in the child's mind. This may be because of the lack of visibility and publicity given to senators in the public press and, apparently, in classroom instruction. It may also derive from the number of persons in the Senate, resulting in a diffusion of individual importance in the child's view. It also seems possible that the executive and administrative functions are more visible, more dramatic, and more easily presented to children, while the significance of senators often gets lost in the teaching process.

The reciprocal nature of children's attachments is illustrated by children's expectation that the President would be concerned with their welfare: they reciprocate by extending loyalty and affection. This is the essence of a role relationship, one of the most basic personal attachments: protection reciprocated by love.[1] The recognition of these personal feelings toward the President contributes to an understanding of the strength of early attachment and its implications for the stability of the political system.

As Children Grow Older They Learn to Distinguish between the Personal Characteristics of the President and the Abilities He Needs to Perform His Job. They like him less as a person but have more respect for his executive abilities. Interviews indicated that children often saw the President's most important duty as being an administrator of the country, making decisions which affect the nation and the world. Mean ratings of the President on these aspects of performance classified him as knowing more and working harder than most people, always a leader, making important decisions all the time. These ratings were reasonably constant from the fourth through eighth grade, and ratings of his decision-making role increased. . . . Teachers and eighth-graders differed only slightly.

The policeman and father were rated lower than the President on all of these attributes. Apparently, leadership, working hard, being knowledgeable, and making decisions are defined, even by younger children, as Presidential

---

[1] The extent to which adults also feel personally close to the President is documented by reactions to President Kennedy's assassination. Greenstein reported that college students compared the event to deaths within their immediate group. [See Fred I. Greenstein, *Children and Politics* (New Haven, Conn.: Yale University Press, 1965).]

qualities. These characteristics clearly differentiate his role from that of other authority figures. With increasing age, children see the President as one whose abilities are appropriate to the demands of his office and whose behavior is shaped by these demands, rather than as a personal authority directly related to the child.

The average senator was rated as much less responsive than the President. This suggests that the relationship existing between the child and the President is possible because the President's name and face are known. Children's relationships with him are comparable to *para-social* interactions that television audiences experience with performers. . . . This intimacy and perceived reciprocity of relationship is based upon the existence of a living, visible person—President Kennedy for these children—not a composite figure such as Average U. S. Senator. The clearest distinction children make in judging responsiveness is between the figures in their immediate environment (father and policeman) and those who are not known personally (institutions, senator). The President, for second- and third-graders, is intermediate to this dichotomy. The relationship with him is para-social. Older children perceive the President as a distant figure similar to the senator, Supreme Court, and the government.

The Older Child Perceives Institutions of Government as Powerful and Infallible. At the same time that the child forms opinions about the President's role qualities apart from his personal attractiveness, he becomes aware of institutions of government which do not have personal representatives and which are competent in performing leadership and decision-making functions. These institutions are regarded by older children as more dependable than the President. For example, at the later grades the Supreme Court and the government are regarded as more knowledgeable and less likely to make mistakes than the President. . . . These institutions and the President are perceived as fairly equally important in making decisions by seventh- and eighth-graders. . . . In contrast to perceptions of the President, children do not perceive these impersonal institutions to be highly protective or helpful. . . . In summary, eighth-graders distinguish between persons and institutions that are highly knowledgeable and make many important decisions (President, government, Supreme Court), and figures who are not noted for either superior knowledge or decision-making (senator, father, policeman).

The infallibility of figures and institutions is a particularly important aspect of children's perceptions. At later grades, all personal authority figures were judged more fallible than institutions; this suggests that institutionalized role, independent of an individual's whim, is perceived as more legitimate. Early belief in the benign qualities of political authority sets a level of expectations that is never completely abandoned.

◻ Liberalism and the National Idea

SAMUEL H. BEER

A FEW YEARS AGO, WHILE PREPARING A TALK ON LIBERALISM, I thought I would look back before the 1930's in order to see what leading figures in our past had taken the term to mean. To my surprise, I found that they almost never used it. I turned, for instance, to Herbert Croly, who, as author of *The Promise of American Life* and founder of *The New Republic,* could surely be regarded as one of the principal voices of liberalism in this century. Only very occasionally in that book, which was written between 1905 and 1909, did he use the term "liberal" or "liberalism." No more frequently he spoke of conservatism, and then only as one of two extremes, of which the other was radicalism.

Similarly, in political controversies before Croly's time, generic terms—such as "progressive" and "democratic"—were used in addition to party labels to designate important viewpoints. But "liberal" was not among them. Nor did contemporaries in these contests use the liberal-vs.-conservative formula to describe their confrontations. This is not to say that the terms are never found in American political discourse. Among the educated, who were in touch with politics abroad, "liberal" and "liberalism" were sometimes used. In this way one can account for occasional uses, as when Orestes Brownson for a few years called himself a liberal. This does not change the main point: that "liberal" and "liberalism" were used hardly at all in American political debate in the eighteenth, nineteenth, and early twentieth centuries. Then, suddenly, in the first years of the Presidency of Franklin Roosevelt, they were widely adopted by editorial writers, politicians, and the articulate public in general to identify a major position in American politics, namely the outlook of the New Deal.

In politics words are cheap and this striking innovation in political terminology could have been merely verbal. In fact, the New Deal brought into existence not only a new alignment of social forces and a new balance between the parties, but also a new outlook on public policy. Between that outlook and elements of our political past, there are, of course, many continuities, stretching back through movements of progressive and democratic reform even to

FROM Samuel H. Beer, "Liberalism and the National Idea," in Robert A. Goldwin, ed., *Left, Right, and Center,* © 1965 by Rand McNally and Company, Chicago, pp. 142–69.

Liberalism and the National Idea

Jefferson and his "cherishment of the people." The novelty in the New Deal that needs emphasis is precisely the union of this tradition of democratic reform with what I shall call the national idea.

My central point is not merely the familiar observation that the party of Jefferson took over the old Hamiltonian advocacy of strong central government. The national idea is not only a view of American federalism, but also a principle of public policy. As a principle of public policy, it is a doctrine of what today is commonly called "nation-building." Its imperative is to use the power of the nation as a whole not only to promote social improvement and individual excellence, but also to make the nation more solidary, more cohesive, more interdependent in its growing diversity: in short, to make the nation more of a nation. Thus, American liberalism descends from and builds upon old traditions of democratic reformism, but also joins to them a powerful thrust toward national integration.

This view of the origin and twofold nature of American liberalism derives mainly from Croly's interpretation of our political history in his *Promise of American Life*. Following his suggestive account, I should like first to review the role of the national idea in American party politics and then, in some rather more speculative pages, develop the meaning of the national idea and relate it to the new era of public policy which we have entered with the Kennedy and Johnson Administrations. Throughout I shall confine myself to attitudes toward domestic affairs in order to avoid undue complexity.

I

Croly's *Promise* was written at a time when "the social problem" was making its first hard impact on our politics and in much that he said there he laid out the path that liberalism was to take a generation later. At the same time, he could look back over a field of vision that had not yet been obscured by the liberal–conservative realignment of ideas, social forces, and political parties. What he saw was an enduring tension between "the principle of nationality" and "the principle of democracy." Originating in the clash of ideas between Hamilton and Jefferson, this opposition, he believed, had lasted into his own day. His effort was to find a conception that reconciled the two ideas, suitably reinterpreted to fit the facts of the twentieth century.

If we look at the past from the perspective of the democratic idea (in his usage), we may indeed find confrontations similar to one important aspect of the present liberal–conservative conflict. Charles A. Beard, for instance, gave us a reading along these lines. In his view, our politics in the earliest days of the Republic revovled around the clash of economic interest groups: broadly, a coalition of owners of large property against a coalition of owners of small or no property. A rough, very rough, parallel with the liberal–conservative alignment of recent years can be granted and thus Jefferson made the ultimate author of the New Deal and Hamilton of its opposition.

But when we look at these early contests from the perspective of the national idea, the lineage is reversed. The modern liberal, as a champion of strong and active central government in the service of nation-wide purposes, becomes the heir of Hamilton, while the modern conservative, as the opponent of centralization and friend of states rights and localism, represents the Jeffersonian tradition. In short, even if we grant a certain continuity between modern liberalism and Jeffersonian democracy, the total configuration is strikingly different: the powerful strain of Hamiltonian nationalism in the liberal tendency separates it fundamentally from the Jeffersonians.

For the sake of clarity, I will state the point with some exaggeration. For the greater part of our history and well into the present century, the main division of political forces consisted of the following: (1) on the one hand, a national party, tending toward elitism, *viz.*, the Federalists, the Whigs, and then the Republicans; (2) on the other hand, an anti-national or "provincial" party[1] tending to be "democratic," *viz.*, the Jeffersonian Republican and then the Democratic Party. Granting the continuity between the elitist–democratic division and one aspect of our present conservative–liberal split, my object here is to emphasize that during our first century and more the issue of overwhelming importance was the national question. The conflict of classes was, and always has been, mild in comparison with such conflicts in other countries of the Western world. The national question, however, precipitated the one instance of large-scale armed subversion in our history.

The National Idea vs. States Sovereignty

As an issue of political conflict, this question had two main aspects, relating, first, to a theory of the Constitution, and, second, to a view of public policy. As a theory of the Constitution, the national idea was opposed by the compact or state sovereignty theory. According to the latter, the Union was established by agreement among the thirteen states, which had previously been independent, sovereign political entities. In the Constitution, rather as in a treaty among separate nations, they agreed to give up certain powers to the Federal government. Federal power thus was derivative from state power and one might well feel that the states were, and continued to be, the fundamental political communities. From this theory, it also was plausibly inferred that the states had the right to interpret the compact and, if necessary, to nullify an unconstitu-

---

[1] I take the adjective from Albert Beveridge who, in his biography of John Marshall, described how in the 1790's the political parties arose, "one standing for the National and the other for the Provincial idea."

tional act, to interpose their power to prevent its execution and in the final resort to secede from the Union.

According to the national theory, on the other hand, the Union was brought into existence not by independent states, but by the people as a whole; "we, the people," as it says in the Preamble, formed the Union. As a community of individuals, not a combination of states, we constitute the nation. From this national community the authority of the states, as of the Federal government, is derivative. Nor is it simply the state governments, but the people of any state themselves who derive their authority from the nation. This national community is our essential form of political existence and to it we owe our primary allegiance. "The Union," said Lincoln, "and not themselves [*i.e.*, the states] separately, produced their independence and their liberty. . . . The Union gave each of them whatever of independence or liberty it has. The Union is older than any of the States, and, in fact, it created them as States." According to this view, of course, no state could secede or nullify or interpose, since it had been given no such authority by the nation.

On balance, the national theory is the better account of the state of mind and will of the American people at the time of the foundation of the Republic. Yet, unfortunately, the compact theory was also supported by considerable evidence, including interpretations rendered by leading men among the Fathers themselves. Nor did the words of the Constitution itself clear up the ambiguity. From the start, in other words, there existed in our conception of nationhood a deep and tragic flaw. As a result, the United States for many generations struggled with a severe problem of national identity. One can, of course, find instances when both theories of the Union were used as mere rationalizations for economic or social interest. This should not, however, obscure the real motivational force of the underlying values that were at issue. The Civil War sprang not only from a conflict of economic and social interests, but also, as Hans Kohn has said, from a conflict of American nationalism with "another nascent true nationalism."

Given this ambiguity in American political culture, it was natural that our early party divisions should center on the national question. The purpose of the national party was, in the first place, to defend in word and deed the national ideal of the Union. But the national party did not simply defend a view of the Constitution and American federalism. It also made the national idea into a view of public policy. This was the view not only that the American people were one nation, but also that they ought over time to become more of a nation. In its various incarnations, the national party was, to use Croly's awkward phrase, the "nationalizing" party. In Hamilton's opinion, according to Croly, the central government was to be used "not merely to maintain the Constitution, but to promote the national interest and to consolidate the national organization," a policy which implied "an active interference with the national course of American economic and political business and its regulation and guidance in the national direction." In spite of many setbacks and the great crisis of the 1860's, this purpose was more and more fulfilled. "The organic growth [of the United States]," said Elihu Root, in 1913, "which must ultimately determine the form of institutions, has been away from a mere union of states towards the union of individuals in the relation of national citizenship."

In opposition to Hamiltonian nationalism and elitism, Croly set Jeffersonian democracy. In it he found not only the political doctrine of "trust the people," but also an economic doctrine of "extreme individualism." "The people" were the best safeguard against authoritarianism in government and at the same time entirely capable of taking care of themselves individually. These beliefs led to the Jeffersonian conclusion that "good government, particularly on the part of Federal officials, consisted, apart from routine business, in letting things alone." This "old fatal policy of drift" meant that in our history one result of Jeffersonian democracy was to promote "a system of unrestricted individual aggrandizement and collective irresponsibility."

From Jefferson to F.D.R.

In what way does the national–provincial distinction relate to the liberal–conservative division and the positions of the two major parties in recent decades? Clearly, in the present-day meanings of the terms, Jefferson was no more a liberal than Hamilton a conservative. This is not to say, however, that the national question became irrelevant when the rise of the "social problem" brought forward the issues that ultimately produced the New Deal. For not the least remarkable aspect of that turning point was the exchange of policies, indeed of long-held principles, on this vital question by the Democratic and Republican parties. The Democratic party—more precisely, its liberal section—became the bearer of the national idea, while the conservative wing of the Republicans became the champions of the provincial idea.

We are now so accustomed to thinking of the Democrats as the "nationalizing" party that we may well forget how radically contrary this tendency is to what that party stood for through most of its history. Again Croly's reading in *The Promise of American Life* is instructive. Reviewing Democratic advocacy of the "old fatal policy of drift" in general, and of such heresies in particular as "nullification, squatter sovereignty, secession, free silver and occasional projects of repudiation," he found that in all our history no "measure of legislation expressive of a progressive national idea can be attributed to the Democratic party." That party, he concluded, "cannot become the party of national responsibility without being faithless to its own creed." It was, of course, to the Republicans, as restored to their "historic position and purpose" by Theodore Roosevelt, that he looked for "vigorous national action" to deal with the social problem.

This was not an idle hope. It was surely a shorter step to the New Deal from the New Nationalism than from Wilson's New Freedom—at any rate, before the New Freedom in office had absorbed the main substance of the first Roosevelt's program. Perhaps after the era of Harding and Coolidge it was too late for the Republicans again to return to their "historic position and purpose." Still, one is tempted to speculate what would have happened if Al Smith had won in 1928 and Hoover had taken office in 1932 free of the obligation to defend the policies that had led to collapse.

Perhaps it was an historical accident. In any event it fell to the second Roosevelt, no small student and admirer of his cousin, to restore the national idea. His measures had definite "class" overtones that give them a distant, but discernible affinity with the Jeffersonian "cherishment of the people." Yet we miss a major dimension of the New Deal and of the liberalism it propagated if we confine our attention to its bearing on the economic interests of various social strata.

In dealing with economic concentration and deprivation, the New Deal and its successors created a new balance of power and a new level of security. By these measures, beneficiary groups, such as industrial labor and recent immigrants, also won a degree of acceptance in the national consciousness and in every-day social and economic intercourse that they had never previously enjoyed. American liberalism acted as a "nationalizing" force not only in the sense that it centralized governmental power, using the authority of the national government to deal with problems that had previously been left to state or local government, or had not been dealt with at all. It was also "nationalizing" in the sense that it integrated into the national community groups which had previously been marginal or excluded. Through the new doctrine and force of liberalism, the national idea worked to integrate the pluralism of the twentieth century as it had once countered the territorial sectionalism of the nineteenth.

Of this liberal achievement the Democratic party became the principal instrument. The result was an imbalance in our party system which persists to this day. For most of our history, each of the two main parties has had a mixed character, its outlook combining a major strength, moral and electoral, with a major weakness. A national party suffering from elitism has faced a democratic party put at a disadvantage by its provincialism. Not surprisingly in this country, the democratic party has shown greater longevity, so that the political party founded by Jefferson today may claim to be the oldest in the world.

Still, an opposition has been able to survive for long periods, even when burdened with a more or less ill-disguised distrust of the people. The essential electoral condition of its survival, however, has been an adherence to the national idea. When the Federalists weakened in this faith, they lost their coherence and their following and deservedly sank into nullity. Likewise, when the Whigs, for all their talk of Union, burked the problem of slavery as a national problem, they rightly went into decline. Similarly, when in the past generation the Republicans joined to their elitism the old provincial causes of the Democrats, they too lost support and fell into the position of the minority party. More recently, in the 1964 presidential campaign, pursuing this fatal course in the name of conservatism, they reduced themselves to such a position of impotence as to raise fears for the future of our two-party system. For at the same time, the Democrats, among whom the liberals were stronger than ever, retained in modern form important elements of their Jeffersonian heritage and also continued their adherence to the national idea. Croly's hope for a party that was at once national and democratic had been fulfilled, although hardly in the way that he had expected.

II

Today the national idea is in no danger from the grosser forms of menace that threatened it a hundred years ago. Yet as a theory of American federalism which provides an approach to constitutional interpretation and, even more important, sustains a state of mind, it still needs emphasis. When Southern Senators, or Barry Goldwater, explicitly advocate the compact theory, we need not be greatly disturbed. But was it only a lapse when President Eisenhower in 1952, having declared that the "Federal Government did not create the States," went on to claim that "the States created the Federal Government"?

Today the national idea is, first of all, a perspective for viewing and judging the relations of the Federal and the state governments. People sometimes slip into the habit of speaking as if there were something inherently preferable about state or local government in contrast with Federal. And indeed if the states were the primary political communities, that would be true. But since the nation is our essential form of political existence, such preference as flows from the structure of authority favors the activity of what Daniel Webster called the "general government" as against the provincial governments. The point is relevant to the assertion that state and local governments are "closer" to the people. If, as the national theory teaches, one means by "the people" the basic political community, the nation as a whole, then certainly the "general government" is "closer" to this community than are the lesser governments whose contacts with it are partial and separated.

Similarly, from the perspective of the national theory, one will not necessarily be alarmed if the state governments decline in power and scope of activity in relation to the general government. From the viewpoint of the national theory, it is legitimate and logical that as the process of integration of the national community goes forward, the content of the common good, with whose promotion the central government is charged, should likewise develop. This is not to say that the national theory must imply the ultimate demise of the states. On the contrary, there are excellent practical reasons why they should flourish, especially in the context of cooperative federalism and new forms of regional cooperation. The merit of the national theory is to help us see that the considerations sustaining and defining a role for the states are almost entirely practical in character, not constitutional. In essence, this was also the view of Hamilton, Marshall, and the men "who 'put across' the Constitution and who set the national government going." For in their opinion, according to E. S. Corwin, "the national government . . . is under no constitutional compulsion, either in the selection of means whereby to make its powers effective or in the selection of objects to be attained by their exercise, to take account of the coexistence of the states or to concern itself to preserve any particular relationship of power between itself and the states."

Croly and the National Purpose

But the national idea is more than a theory of constitutional interpretation. It also sustains a dynamic perspective on public policy and national development. In the first place, it favors the process of *governmental unification* which has been a principal theme of our political history. By governmental unification I mean what is often called "centralization," "consolidation," or, in Croly's terms, the "nationalization" of governmental functions. The national idea, however, does not legitimate governmental unification simply for its own sake. There is some end or purpose to which it is instrumental and in the light of which one may judge in what specific ways and at what pace unification should proceed. In one phase of his thought, Croly clearly drew this distinction by making democracy itself this purpose.

To Croly, as to many other political theorists, the term "democracy" is less a concept of analysis than a stimulus to speculation. One need not agree with all his uses of the word to find his speculation interesting. Certainly, he did not confine the meaning of democracy to a conception of authority, a definition of how power ought to be distributed in the polity. To him it meant not only popular sovereignty, but also the end for which power was to be exerted. Yet he was not content with the Jeffersonian ideal of "equal rights for all and special privileges for none" as a definition of this end. For in this ideal he found that "extreme individualism" which, in the course of economic development, had produced the "social problem." Indeed, in rejecting this doctrine Croly asserts that the national government must "discriminate" constructively "among the various prevailing ways of exercising individual rights" for the sake of certain results. These results consisted in the first place in "social improvement," meaning action to promote "a constantly higher standard of living" and, more positively, "to guarantee to every male adult a certain minimum of economic power and responsibility." In this branch of Croly's approach to the "social problem," it is fair to see his anticipation of the main theme of New Deal liberalism, its use of national power for economic balance and security.

Even more interesting to us today, however, is Croly's conception of the other element in the democratic purpose in the twentieth century. This was to use the powers of the nation to promote "the increase of American individuality." Indeed, to this problem of raising the standards and stimulating the pursuit of "individual distinction," Croly gives far more attention than he does to the material problems of the economy. He thunders at the American's faith in mere good intentions and his lack of moral and intellectual discipline. "In all civilized communities," he wrote, "the great individualizing force is the resolute, efficient, and intense pursuit of special ideals, standards, and occupations." In this emphasis one finds vivid anticipation of that "pursuit of excellence" which, beginning with the Kennedy Administration, has increasingly formed the theme of some of the more original programs of the national government.

For Croly, then, the national purpose, as he saw it in his time, was to use "the democratic organization for the joint benefit of individual distinction and social improvement." This dual purpose was to legitimate and guide the process of governmental unification and the exercise of power by the national government. Similarly, if we look at the development of Federal programs in very recent years, it is possible and instructive to discern in them this same twofold purpose. Plainly enough, there is in the Kennedy-Johnson effort a massive stratum of New Deal liberalism. I am thinking not only of the development of basic statutes, such as the wage-hour and social security laws, but also new programs using familiar means, such as the Appalachia program. Contrasting with this old stratum of public policy is a new layer. Typical and most important is the series of programs involving education. Looking at the problems that confronted President Kennedy just after his inauguration, Theodore H. White put first "the unbelievable problems of education and knowledge." Going over the main Kennedy programs a while back I counted fully a third that made education in some form a central element. And, it hardly need be said, the priority given education has only increased under President Johnson, who indeed is reported to have said that "the answer for all our national problems comes down to one single word: education."

The use of labels is of no great moment. But it is worth seeing where there is continuity and discontinuity between these new departures in public policy and the pattern of New Deal liberalism. There is continuity in the vigorous use of the powers of the national government. These measures are a further step in governmental unification. In particular, the growing programs of Federal aid to education mark a large advance in the process of unification which the New Deal itself greatly forwarded. In other respects, however, there are contrasts. Above all, where New Deal liberalism sought to achieve its effects by alterations in structure, especially economic stucture, the new programs operate rather through improvements in the intellectual capacities of individuals—and not only intellectual, but also moral capacities, insofar as education develops powers of discipline, self-reliance, and independent choice. This difference in the tactics of reform implies also a difference in analysis. In place of that tinge of economic determinism which colored New Deal liberalism, this new liberalism, while as strongly national as the old, puts much greater emphasis on cultural factors.

Public policy, it hardly needs to be said, cannot be neatly and exclusively sorted out into a few simple categories. The erratic pressures, *ad hoc* responses, bureaucratic snarls, legislative compromises, and all the vast complexity of our society and its government mean that no descriptive scheme can do more than indicate general tendencies. Granting this obvious qualification, one can still outline the broad meaning that these tendencies have, given the national idea today. This is: that the process of governmental unification goes forward guided by a national purpose that can still be accurately stated in Croly's words: "the joint benefit of individual distinction and social improvement." Yet there is, I believe, a major dimension of the national idea of which this discussion has not yet taken account.

Toward National Integration

Throughout *The Promise of American Life* Croly presents "the principle of nationality" as on a par with "the principle of democracy." To say, however, that the national idea means merely that unification should be used to promote democratization is to make the national subordinate to the democratic idea. One cannot feel that this is fair to Croly's meaning. The "principle of nationality" clearly means more than that a strong central government is acting to promote "the joint benefit of individual distinction and social improvement." It means further that a process of national integration is being carried on in which the community is being made more of a community.

National government and national community, like the processes of unification and integration from which they emerge, are interdependent. At the moment, however, I wish to direct attention to the national community as something distinguishable from government. For this community and the process of integration by which it develops are surely much harder to observe and analyze than the national government and its growth. Yet it hardly need be said that all that furious activity and mighty agglomeration of power at the center has little point apart from the quality of life it promotes in the nation.

No national community, especially if it is a free nation, will embrace the whole of an individual's life. Outside these national bonds will remain not only the activities of many groups, but also the ultimate privacy of the individual. Yet community in the form of nationality can be a principal means of moral fulfillment.

By community I mean, to begin with, an emotional fact: a massive background feeling of "belongingness" and identification. This emotional aspect of American nationality is not usually in the front of our consciousness. But from time to time, in moments of ritual or crisis or reflection—or perhaps simply when we travel around the country or return home from abroad—it comes sharply forward, showing its power. We perceive then a force that continually, although imperceptibly, conditions our attitudes and behavior. We recognize that, apart from the *private* emotions which we share with family, friends, and other limited groups, we are joined with a vast national community by a distinctive kind of emotional tie: by *public* joy, grief, pride, anger, envy, fear, hope, and so on. Few Americans who watched the funeral of President Kennedy will doubt this fact. His family and personal friends had their private grief. Throughout the world people could respond to certain universal human themes, such as the tragedy of a gallant and youthful leader struck down senselessly at the height of his powers and promise. But for Americans there was a special experience: emotions of grief, anger, fear, and loss that only members of this national community could feel.

People who constitute a community in some basic sense share a common life. This common life consists, in one respect, of certain resemblances, certain conformities. In this sense, one may speak of an American consensus—a pattern of values and beliefs generally pervading the nation—or perhaps even of an American national character. These shared cultural objects, constituting resemblances among the members of the community, are a source of solidarity.

It is usually these resemblances that are analyzed by students of nations and their development. Exculsively to emphasize resemblance, however, is misleading, for there is another equally important aspect of community, *viz.*, the fact that relations among members are complementary. Croly suggested this aspect when he spoke of the national community as "a socially constructive drama." Durkheim referred to the "division of labor" and in a memorable passage described the mutual identification that results from its complementary diversities. "The image of the one who completes us," he wrote,

becomes inseparable from ours, not only because it is frequently associated with ours, but particularly because it is the natural complement of it. It thus becomes an integral and permanent part of our conscience, to such a point that we can no longer separate ourselves from it and seek to increase its force.

Here Durkheim is speaking of face-to-face communities in which the members are directly and visibly in contact with one another. His insight, however, directs attention to similar complementary relations in a large-scale community, such as a nation, in which a widely shared image of interlocking roles or types likewise enhances solidarity. This is, I think, our commonsense perception of the matter. If we reflect on the object of our national loyalty, one aspect is no doubt certain general ideas. With its political and non-political elements, this consensus, although rough and ready and far from lucidly systematic, is vitally important to the maintenance of the governmental and social systems. Yet the object toward which our national feelings are directed obviously includes far more. It is more concrete and richly varied, more historical and less ideological.

It is a common life, consisting not only of similarities, but also diversities. In other words, our attachment to the nation does not proceed simply from our resemblances—the American consensus or "way of life." The social context with which we identify as members of the nation also includes a pattern of complex, varied, and highly differentiated attitudes and behavior.

Along with the more familiar factor of *consensual cohesion,* this *functional cohesion* is a major source of the stability of American institutions. Consensus is, of course, important and students of American government and society are right to be much occupied with identifying a body of values and beliefs that members of the national community generally share. Yet this consensus on generalities may sometimes be a thin and insufficient foundation for toleration and support between persons or groups. In such situations, it is helpful to see that a further force for stability may be provided by the more particularistic bonds of functional cohesion.

National integration in this twofold meaning is a principal purpose of governmental unification. To say, however, that the thrust of the national idea is in this sense "to make the nation more of a nation" is to attribute to it no new significance. From the start this was one of its goals and effects. If, for instance, the Whig policy of internal improvements had been realized, our common life as a nation could not have failed to be enriched and strengthened. To stress this old significance here is important in order to make clear that the national idea means something more than mere centralization of power. As the principle of community, it provides, along with the democratic idea, one of the standards by which governmental unification can be justified and by which it should be controlled and guided.

The National Idea and Civil Rights

The national idea has persisted throughout our history. It has always confronted opposition, and this tension has constituted one of the major axes of our political life. Its friends have not always cherished "the people" or professed sensitivity to the grievances of the poor. At different times they have called themselves Federalists, Whigs, and Republicans. Beginning in the 1930's, the Democrats, or more precisely the liberal Democrats, became the principal bearers of the national idea. The liberalism brought into existence by the New Deal consisted of a combination of the national idea and the democratic idea which was unique in our history, although in broad outline it had been anticipated by Herbert Croly. Looked at from the democratic perspective (in Croly's meaning), it aims at the "joint benefit" of social improvement and individual distinction. Yet these same programs also serve the national idea by providing means and enhancing capacities for extending and deepening community.

At present, the civil rights programs are without doubt the most important example of this old effort to make the nation more of a nation. According to some historic conceptions of liberalism, it is a proper and decent solution for a minority if it is given the opportunity to live unto itself in such a way that it may enjoy and develop its own way of life—a status comparable, for instance, to that of the French-speaking people of Canada. American liberalism, however, rejects such solutions along with the doctrine of "separate but equal" and, as a force influencing both Negroes and whites, compels us toward integration. This new stage in American nation-building is surely one of the most ambitious, difficult, and characteristic undertakings into which the national idea has led us.

SUGGESTIONS FOR FURTHER READING

Serious study in the areas of political culture and ideas is impossible without some knowledge of American history. There are many fine texts available, but none better for a quick review than Allan Nevins and Henry Steele Commager, *A Short History of the United States* (New York: Modern Library, 1945), and John M. Blum et al., *The National Experience*, 2nd ed. (New York: Harcourt Brace Jovanovich, 1968).

On the subject of political socialization, a useful review of the early literature can be found in Herbert Hyman's *Political Socialization* (New York: Free Press, 1969). Two perceptive, seminal studies published in the 1960's are Fred I. Greenstein's *Children and Politics* (New Haven, Conn.: Yale University Press, 1965), and Orville G. Brim's and Stanton Wheeler's *Socialization After Childhood: Two Essays* (New York: Wiley, 1966). In recent years the *American Political Science Review* has carried a number of articles dealing with aspects of the socialization process. A good summary of recent literature can be found in Richard E. Dawson and Kenneth Prewitt, *Political Socialization* (Boston: Little, Brown, 1969). Perhaps the best work to date is Jack Dennis and David Easton, *Children in the Political System: Origins of Political Legitimacy* (New York: McGraw-Hill, 1969). In the field of child psychology there is a work of general interest on the cognitive development of children by the French psychologist Jean Piaget entitled *The Psychology of Intelligence* (London: Routledge & Kegan Paul, 1947).

Several interesting works have appeared on the implications of communications theory for the study of politics. See Richard F. Fagen, *Politics and Communication* (Boston: Little, Brown, 1966), and Murray Edelman, *The Symbolic Uses of Politics* (Urbana, Ill.: University of Illinois Press, 1967).

The standard texts on American political ideas are Ralph Gabriel's *The Course of American Democratic Thought* (New York: Ronald, 1940); Alpheus

Suggestions for Further Reading

T. Mason's *Security Through Freedom* (Ithaca, N. Y.: Cornell University Press, 1955); and David W. Minar's *Ideas and Politics: The American Experience* (London: Dorsey Press, 1964). One should not ignore Vernon L. Parrington's *Main Currents in American Thought* (New York: Harcourt Brace Jovanovich, 1927–30); Henry Steele Commager's informal sequel, *The American Mind* (New Haven, Conn.: Yale University Press, 1950), and Lloyd A. Free and Hadley Cantril's *Political Beliefs of Americans: A Study of Public Opinion* (New Brunswick, N. J.: Rutgers University Press, 1967).

Periodicals such as the *Journal of American History* and the *Yale Review* often carry articles dealing with American political ideas, as do regional and specialized publications such as the *New England Quarterly* and the *William and Mary Quarterly*.

4 Public opinion and political parties

STUDENTS OFTEN EXPERIENCE AN INITIAL DIFFICULTY in distinguishing between political ideas (articulated doctrine), political culture (basic predispositions), and public opinion. As we saw in the preceding chapter, "political culture" involves underlying and intergenerationally transmitted attitudes about how politics should be conducted, and "political ideas" connotes fairly systematic expressions on eternal questions such as the purposes of the state or man's potential for self-government. "Public opinion," as defined by one of its most acute students, the late V. O. Key, Jr., involves "those views on issues of public policy which those in power find it prudent from time to time to take into account." Put somewhat differently, public opinion consists of views held by numbers of people on matters of pressing public consequence—what "those out there" feel about issues on which a decision has been or is going to be made.

The study of public opinion has undergone a revolution over the past fifty years. At the turn of the century there was a pervasive and naive faith in public opinion as a motor force for "good government." A cardinal doctrine of both Populist and Progressive teaching was that the people should more directly and continuously participate in governmental decision-making. Wise and responsible policies would be the result. This position rested on the assumption that "the people" usually had a well-shaped and coherent "opinion" on significant issues—or at least a small number of opposing positions that would allow for head-counting and majority rule. If this was not so, it was because of inadequate education or the machinations of those evildoers, "the interests," who gulled and lulled the citizens into acceptance of predatory and dishonest practices.

The first statement of what is today the prevailing view of public opinion did not come from a political scientist but from that durable journalistic commentator Walter Lippmann. Lippmann's *Public Opinion*,[1] first published in 1922, reflected the author's own disillusionment with the Populist-Progressive optimism of the years before 1914, and he did a mighty job of debunking the "good government" view of public opinion. Lippmann argued that most Americans have very little time for politics or interest in it. They are preoccupied with earning a living, raising their families, and seizing opportunities for recreation in the few free hours they have available. To expect such private people, even those with excellent educational equipment, to inform themselves carefully concerning the relative merits of sewers versus subways (or of guns versus butter) is expecting too much of the poor creatures.

And even if people were prepared to devote themselves to the study of civic issues, the information available to them is not very good. Newspapers and journals of opinion have been supplemented (or perhaps supplanted) by radio and television since Lippmann wrote his book, but there is good reason to believe that while the media have made us more worldly, they still fall far short of providing the sorts of information necessary for independent judgment on complex issues. Lippmann further suggested that since ordinary citizens cannot in the nature of things think carefully about politics, they operate in terms of great myths (for example, American democratic virtue as opposed to European aristocratic degeneracy) which by their very sweeping character distort or obscure reality.

On the basis of this characterization, Lippmann concluded that government should be directed by a carefully recruited class of men whose talents and training have equipped them to understand affairs of state and to take responsible action. This governing group would be ultimately but not immediately responsible to the mass electorate.[2]

Many political scientists, while granting that Lippmann's pessimistic analysis has been borne out by recent survey research, have moved to somewhat different conclusions. What Lippmann forgot, they suggest, is the elaborate structure of political parties and interest groups in America. The groups to which an individual belongs and the political party with which he identifies provide him with "privileged" information—information evaluated and organized in terms of the goals of the group. The individual cannot make himself an expert on a wide range of civic issues, but it is quite possible for him to belong to or sympathize with a variety of voluntary associations that supply him with trusted "positions" on issues. In addition, party identification in America has a certain minimal policy content. Individuals identify with the past records of particular Presidents or presidential aspirants, and hope for future triumphs with similar people. Interest groups and political parties provide networks of highly informed elites

---

[1] (New York: Free Press, 1965).
[2] See Lippmann's *The Public Philosophy* (Boston: Little, Brown, 1955).

through which the more politically attentive individuals express needs or demands to those in positions of governmental power and "provide" opinions to their followers.

V. O. Key, Jr., concluded his own study of public opinion with an optimism that contrasted sharply with Lippmann's pessimism.

The critical element for the health of a democratic order consists in the beliefs, standards, and competence of those who constitute the influentials, the opinion-leaders, the political activists in the order. That group, as has been made plain, refuses to define itself with any great clarity in the American system: yet analysis after analysis points to its existence. If a democracy tends toward indecision, decay, and disaster, the responsibility rests here, not in the mass of the people.

Thus we are not faced with a choice between presuming that the citizen is omnicompetent and presuming that the citizen is an irrational beast and the Republic is doomed.

In the selections that follow, Key discusses the importance of elites in the process of opinion formation, and Angus Campbell describes how the labels "Democrat" and "Republican" perform a structuring function in our politics. The final selection, by Walter Dean Burnham, shifts the focus from parties as national labels back to parties as discrete organizations—or, in Key's terms, as a set of interrelated elites. Noting that party organizations have been a major decentralizing force in American politics—reflecting deep-seated localism and regionalism—Burnham goes on to note a decline in the importance of party organizations in the policy-making process, and suggests that the party as a decentralizing force may become less and less a part of American politics in the future.

▣ Public Opinion and Democratic Politics

V. O. KEY, JR.

The exploration of public [opinion] is a pursuit of endless fascination—and frustration. Depiction of the distribution of opinions within the public, identification of the qualities of opinion, isolation of the odd and of the obvious correlates of opinion, and ascertainment of the modes of opinion formation are pur-

FROM *Public Opinion and American Democracy*, pp. 535–58, by V. O. Key, Jr. Copyright © 1961 by V. O. Key, Jr. Reprinted by permission of Alfred A. Knopf, Inc.

suits that excite human curiosity. Yet these endeavors are bootless unless the findings about the preferences, aspirations, and prejudices of the public can be connected with the workings of the governmental system. The nature of that connection has been suggested by the examination of the channels by which governments become aware of public sentiment and the institutions through which opinion finds more or less formal expression.

When all these linkages are treated, the place of public opinion in government has still not been adequately portrayed. The problem of opinion and government needs to be viewed in an even broader context. Consideration of the role of public opinion drives the observer to the more fundamental question of how it is that democratic governments manage to operate at all. Despite endless speculation on that problem, perplexities still exist about what critical circumstances, beliefs, outlooks, faiths, and conditions are conducive to the maintenance of regimes under which public opinion is controlling, at least in principle, and is, in fact, highly influential.

1. A MISSING PIECE OF THE PUZZLE

Though the preceding analyses did not uncover the secret of the conditions precedent to the practice of democratic politics, they pointed to a major piece of the puzzle that was missing as we sought to assemble the elements that go into the construction of a democratic regime. The significance of that missing piece may be made apparent in an indirect manner. In an earlier day public opinion seemed to be pictured as a mysterious vapor that emanated from the undifferentiated citizenry and in some way or another enveloped the apparatus of government to bring it into conformity with the public will. These weird conceptions . . . passed out of style as the technique of the sample survey permitted the determination, with some accuracy, of the distribution of opinions within the population. Vast areas of ignorance remain in our information about people's opinions and aspirations; nevertheless, a far more revealing map of the gross topography of public opinion can now be drawn than could have been a quarter of a century ago.

Despite their power as instruments for the observation of mass opinion, sampling procedures do not bring within their range elements of the political system basic for the understanding of the role of mass opinion within the system. Repeatedly, as we have sought to explain particular distributions, movements, and qualities of mass opinion, we have had to go beyond the survey data and make assumptions and estimates about the role and behavior of that thin stratum of persons referred to variously as the political elite, the political activists, the leadership echelons, or the influentials. In the normal operation of surveys designed to obtain tests of mass sentiment, so few persons from this activist stratum fall into the sample that they cannot well be differentiated, even in a static description, from those persons less involved politically. The data tell us almost nothing about the dynamic relations between the upper layer of activists and mass opinion. The missing piece of our puzzle is this elite element of the opinion system. That these political influentials both affect mass opinion and are conditioned in their behavior by it is obvious. Yet systematic knowledge of the composition, distribution in the social structure, and patterns of behavior of this sector of the political system remains far from satisfactory.

The longer one frets with the puzzle of how democratic regimes manage to function, the more plausible it appears that a substantial part of the explanation is to be found in the motives that actuate the leadership echelon, the values that it holds, in the rules of the political game to which it adheres, in the expectations which it entertains about its own status in society, and perhaps in some of the objective circumstances, both material and institutional, in which it functions. Focus of attention on this sector of the opinion system contrasts with the more usual quest for the qualities of the people that may be thought to make democratic practices feasible. That focus does not deny the importance of mass attitudes. It rather emphasizes that the pieces of the puzzle are different in form and function, and that for the existence of a democratic opinion-oriented system each piece must possess the characteristics necessary for it to fit together with the others in a working whole. The superimposition over a people habituated to tyranny of a leadership imbued with democratic ideals probably would not create a viable democratic order.

Values and Motives of the Activist Subculture. The traits and characteristics of political activists assume importance in the light of a theory about why the leadership and governing levels in any society behave as they do. That theory amounts to the proposition that these political actors constitute in effect a subculture with its own peculiar set of norms of behavior, motives, and approved standards. Processes of indoctrination internalize such norms among those who are born to or climb to positions of power and leadership; they serve as standards of action, which are reinforced by a social discipline among the political activists. In some regimes the standards of the ruling groups prescribe practices of firmness toward the governed who are regarded as menials with no rights; they deserve no more than the rough and arbitrary treatment they receive. The rules of the game may prescribe that the proper practice for rulers is to maximize their own advantage as well as the correlative deprivations of the ruled. The ignorant, the poor, and the incompetent may be seen as entitled to what they get, which is very little. Or the rules of the game of a regime may mitigate the harshness of these outlooks by a compassionate attitude toward the wretched masses who cannot help themselves. Hence, we may have little fathers of the people. The point is that the politically active classes may develop characteristic norms and practices that tend to guide their behavior. In a loose sense these may be the norms of a subculture, that of the specialists in politics and government. Beliefs generally accepted among these persons tend to establish habits and patterns of behavior with considerable power of self-maintenance or persistence through time.

While the ruling classes of a democratic order are in a way invisible because of the vagueness of the lines defining the influentials and the relative ease of entry to their ranks, it is plain that the modal norms and standards of a democratic elite have their peculiarities. Not all persons in leadership echelons have precisely the same basic beliefs; some may even regard the people as a beast. Yet a fairly high concentration prevails around the modal beliefs, even though the definition of those beliefs must be imprecise. Fundamental is a regard for public opinion, a belief that in some way or another it should prevail. Even those who cynically humbug the people make a great show of deference to the populace. The basic doctrine goes further to include a sense of trusteeship for the people generally and an adherence to the basic doctrine that collective efforts should be dedicated to the promotion of mass gains rather than of narrow class advantage; elite elements tethered to narrow group interest have no slack for maneuver to accommodate themselves to mass aspirations. Ultimate expression of these faiths comes in the willingness to abide by the outcome of popular elections. The growth of leadership structures with beliefs including these broad articles of faith is probably accomplished only over a considerable period of time, and then only under auspicious circumstances.

If an elite is not to monopolize power and thereby to bring an end to democratic practices, its rules of the game must include restraints in the exploitation of public opinion. Dimly perceptible are rules of etiquette that limit the kinds of appeals to public opinion that may be properly made. If it is assumed that the public is manipulable at the hands of unscrupulous leadership (as it is under some conditions), the maintenance of a democratic order requires the inculcation in leadership elements of a taboo against appeals that would endanger the existence of democratic practices. Inflammation of the sentiments of a sector of the public disposed to exert the tyranny of an intolerant majority (or minority) would be a means of destruction of a democratic order. Or by the exploitation of latent differences and conflicts within the citizenry it may at times be possible to paralyze a regime as intense hatreds among classes of people come to dominate public affairs. Or by encouraging unrealistic expectations among the people a clique of politicians may rise to power, a position to be kept by repression as disillusionment sets in. In an experienced democracy such tactics may be "unfair" competition among members of the politically active class. In short, certain restraints on political competition help keep competition within tolerable limits. The observation of a few American political campaigns might lead one to the conclusion that there are no restraints on politicians as they attempt to humbug the people. Even so, admonitions ever recur against arousing class against class, against stirring the animosities of religious groups, and against demagoguery in its more extreme forms. American politicians manifest considerable restraint in this regard when they are tested against the standards of behavior of politicians of most of those regimes that have failed in the attempt to establish or maintain democratic practices.

The norms of the practice of politics in an order that has regard for public opinion include broad rules of etiquette governing relations among the activists, as well as rules governing the relations of activists with the public. Those rules, in their fundamental effect, assure the existence of a minority among the political activists; if those who control government can suppress opposition activists, an instrument essential for the formation and expression of public opinion is destroyed. A body of customs that amounts to a policy of "live and let live" must prevail. In constitutional democracies some of these rules are crystallized into fundamental law in guarantees such as those of freedom of speech, freedom of press, and the right to appeal to the electorate for power. Relevant also are procedures for the protection of property rights; a political opposition may be destroyed by expropriation as well as by execution. While such rules extend in their application to the entire population, one of their major functions is to prevent politicians from putting each other into jail or from destroying each other in the ordinary course of their competitive endeavors. All these elements of the rules of the game gain strength, not from their statement in the statues and codes, but from their incorporation into the norms that guide the behavior of the political activists.

Form and Structure. Certain broad structural or organizational characteristics may need to be maintained among the activists of a democratic order if they are to perform their functions in the system. Fundamental is the absence of sufficient cohesion among the activists to unite them into a single group dedicated to the management of public affairs and public opinion. Solidification of the elite by definition forecloses opportunity for public choice among alternative governing groups and also destroys the mechanism for the unfettered expression of public opinion or of the opinions of the many subpublics. Maintenance of division and competition among political activists requires the kinds of etiquette that have been mentioned to govern their relations among themselves. Those rules, though, do not create the cleavages among the activists. Competitive segments of the leadership echelons normally have their roots in interests or opinion blocs within society. A degree of social diversity thus may be, if not a prerequisite, at least helpful in the construction of a leadership appropriate for a democratic regime. A series of independent social bases provide the foundations for a political elite difficult to bring to the state of unification that either prevents the rise of democratic processes or converts them into sham rituals.

At a more earthy level, maintenance of a multiplicity of centers of leadership and political activism requires arrangements by which men may gain a livelihood despite the fact that they are out of power. Consider the consequences for the structure of opinion leadership of a socioeconomic system in which those skilled in the arts of governance have open to them no way of obtaining a livelihood save by the exercise of those skills. In the United States the high incidence of lawyers among the politically influential provides a base of economic independence; the defeated politician can always find a few clients. Extensive reliance on part-time, amateur politicians in representative bodies and in many governing commissions has assured an economic cushion for many political activists. The custom of making many such offices economically unattractive has, in effect, required that they be filled by persons with an economic base independent of the public treasury. Opinion leaders and managers often find economic independence in posts with business associations and other voluntary societies. Communications enterprises, important in the operation of democracies, gain independence from government by their commercial position. The structure of government itself, through its many independent units and agencies, assures havens of some security for spokesmen for a variety of viewpoints. All this may boil down to the contention that development and maintenance of the type of leadership essential for the operation of a democratic political order is facilitated by the existence of a social system of some complexity with many centers that have some autonomy and economic independence. Perhaps a safer formulation would be that societies that do not meet these requisites may encounter difficult problems in the support of a fractionalized stratum of political activists; they need to construct functional equivalents of the means we have been describing to assure the maintenance of competing centers of leadership.

When we viewed from another angle, these comments about the utility of independent foundations for competing sectors of the political elite relate to the more general proposition that regimes deferential to public opinion may best flourish when the deprivations contingent upon the loss of an election are limited. The structure of government itself may also contribute to that loss limitation. In federal regimes and in regimes with extensive devolution to elective local governmental authorities the prospect of loss of a national election may be faced with some equanimity, for the national minority may retain its position in many subordinate units of the nation and remain in a measure undisturbed by the alternations of control within the nation as a whole. The same function of loss limitation may be served by constitutional and customary expectations that limit the permissible range of governmental action.

Another characteristic may be mentioned as one that, if not a prerequisite to government by public opinion, may profoundly affect the nature of a democratic order. This is the distribution through the social structure of those persons highly active in politics. By various analyses, none founded on completely satisfactory data, we have shown that in the United States the political activists —if we define the term broadly—are scattered through the socio-economic hierarchy. The upper-income and occupational groups, to be sure, contribute disproportionately; nevertheless, individuals of high political participation are sprinkled throughout the lesser occupational strata. Contrast the circumstances when the highly active political stratum coincides with the high socio-economic stratum. Conceivably the winning of consent and the creation of a sense of political participation and of sharing in public affairs may be far simpler when political activists of some degree are spread through all social strata. The alternative circumstance may induce an insensitivity to mass opinion, a special reliance on mass communications, and a sharpened sense of cleavage and separatism within the political order. The contention made here amounts to more than the axiom that democracies can exist only in societies that possess a well-developed middle class. In a modern industrial society with universal suffrage the chances are that a considerable sprinkling of political activists needs to exist in groups below the "middle class," however that term of vague referent may be defined. The correct general proposition may be that the operation of democratic processes may be facilitated by the distribution of persons participating in the order through all strata of the electorate. When the belief that democracy depended upon the middle class flourished, a comparatively narrow suffrage prevailed.

Allied with these questions is the matter of access to the wider circles of political leadership and of the recruitment and indoctrination of these political activists. Relative ease of access to the arena of active politics may be a preventive of the rise of intransigent blocs of opinion managed by those denied participation in the regularized processes of politics. In a sense, ease of access is a necessary consequence of the existence of a somewhat fragmented stratum of political activists. Systems built on rigid class lines or on the dominance of clusters of families may be especially prone to the exclusion of those not to the proper status born—or married. Yet ease of access does not alone suffice. It must be accompanied by means, either deliberate or informal, for the indoctrination of those admitted in the special mores and customs of the activist elements of the polity. Otherwise, ease of access may only facilitate the depredations of those alienated from the values of the political order. By their nature democratic political systems have large opportunity—if there is the necessary will—to extend widely opportunities for political participation in lesser capacities and thereby to sift out those capable of achieving access to the more restricted circles of influentials. Whether the builders of political orders ever set about deliberately and systematically to tackle such problems of recruitment and indoctrination may be doubtful. Those problems may be solved, when they are solved, by the unconscious and unwilled processes of evolutionary adaptation of social systems.

This discussion in terms of leadership echelons, political activists, or elites falls painfully on the ears of democratic romantics. The mystique of democracy has in it no place for ruling classes. As perhaps with all powerful systems of faith, it is vague on the operating details. Yet by their nature governing systems, be they democratic or not, involve a division of social labor. Once that axiom is accepted, the comprehension of democratic practices requires a search for the peculiar characteristics of the political influentials in such an order, for the special conditions under which they work, and for the means by which the people keep them in check. The vagueness of the mystique of democracy is matched by the intricacy of its operating practices. If it is true that those who rule tend sooner or later to prove themselves enemies of the rights of man—and there is something to be said for the validity of this proposition—then any system that restrains that tendency however slightly can excite only awe.

2. MASS OPINION: VARIATIONS IN NATURE AND FUNCTION

The demarcation between the political activists and the "mass" must be regarded as a zone of gray rather than as a sharp line, but we may make a distinction between the two types of people with respect to their roles in a system in which public opinion conditions governmental action. The assumption of the preceding paragraphs has been that political activists must possess certain modal characteristics if a political system is to be a viable democracy. Without an imposing foundation of empirical data, an attempt was made to specify some of these characteristics of the activist stratum. Presumably the mass of the people must also possess attitudes and behavioral tendencies congenial to the necessities of a democratic order. That assumption involves us in a process of some circularity, for it has been repeatedly noted that the political activists may shape the opinions of the rest of the people. If the activists control, there is no need to consider mass opinion. Yet the remolding of popular attitudes is not the work of a day; they have a considerable viscosity. Hence, it is permissible to speak of the mass of the people as independent in their characteristics of the activist stratum and as one of the elements that combine with appropriate types of leadership behavior to create a functioning system. Specification of what modal qualities or attitudes should characterize the mass of the people if a society is to have a working democracy presents its difficulties. Although the survey data tell us a great deal about mass opinion, the available materials still leave wide gaps in the information relevant to the broad question that concerns us at the moment. Nevertheless, from what is known and surmised about mass opinion, we may grope toward an identification of those characteristics that may make it compatible with the practice of democracy.

Differentiations within the Public: Clues to Democratic Capabilities. Students of public opinion quickly learn that it is not illuminating to speak of "the public." In their biological characteristics men are animals of endless diversity; in their political behavior they may be equally varied. To bring that diversity within our comprehension, students of public opinion often attempt broad classifications of the citizenry. Thus, we have differentiations according to kinds of participation in political matters, ranging from the sector of the public with a continuing interest in public affairs and an inclination to write their congressman at the drop of a hat to those persons who pay virtually no attention to politics and rarely bother even to vote. The relevance of such categories at this point lies in the possibility that they may provide clues as we search for those qualities of outlook and behavior of the mass of the people or of large sectors of the public that are congenial to the workings of a democratic order—that help make possible the existence of a regime in which public opinion plays a role.

A recurring classification is that of the attentive public (or publics) and the inattentive public. So crude a statement conceals a variety in the objects as well as in the degrees of attention. Our data have identified, for example, variations in attention to presidential campaigns. Some people—nearly 10 per cent—do not follow even presidential campaigns through any of the media, while at the opposite end of the scale are others who follow the campaigns through all the media and entertain a deep concern about their outcome.

Doubtless those who manifest high interest in campaigns also maintain a continuing interest in the flow of action between campaigns. Their focus of attention on the stream of events certainly has its consequences at the next election, not only in their votes but in their influence on the less attentive to whom they communicate their views. Beyond this audience with its focus of attention on a range of political events generally, there exists a complex population of special publics whose attention center more or less continuously on specific governmental agencies or fields of policy. We lack surveys to define the dimensions of these publics, the objects of their attention, or the extent to which they overlap. Nevertheless, some types of such publics can be indicated. The most obvious attentive publics consist of those with a direct concern in particular policies or actions. That concern may rest, though not necessarily, on an economic self-interest. In any case, these special publics extend considerably beyond the leaders and spokesmen of formalized organizations. For example, farmers make up an attentive public; to be sure, not all farmers earn a place in that public, but the better-informed and more alert of them center attention on farm policy and its administrators, and have their views both solicited and taken into account by officialdom. Or consider the old folks. With both the leisure and the motivation of interest, many of them have a familiarity with policies and practices with respect to benefits for the aged as well as an eager eye for helpful new proposals. Congressmen are likely to hear from them.

Veterans constitute another attentive public whose attention seems to be especially capable of producing a feedback into the halls of government. Another attentive public keeps a continuing watch over policy toward education: teachers' associations and PTA's are the more prominent spokesmen for this public, but many (sometimes, one suspects, too many) people consider themselves to be experts on education and do not hesitate to give confident vent to their assured views. One could identify for almost every governmental function comparable attentive publics varying both in size and in the intensity of their concern. Not all such publics are motivated by a direct self-interest. Consider the public attentive to foreign policy. Sprinkled over the land are societies, associations, circles, and study groups whose members give attention to international affairs, entertain visiting ambassadors, advise both the government and their fellow citizens on recondite issues of foreign policy, and look down generally on those clods among their fellow men who do not pay heed to the really important questions of this world.

Another type of attentive public, probably of special influence, consists of professional groups. Professions develop their own codes of ethics as well as their standards of practice. Members of the professions who deviate from the norms of their group may be cold-shouldered by their brethren and under some circumstances even deprived of the right to earn a livelihood by the practice of their trade. Members of the professions who occupy official positions carry on their functions under the scrutiny of the nongovernmental members of the profession and are thus subjected to the gaze of an attentive public equipped with standards of appraisal of some precision. Consider the relations between the bench and the bar. Judges may have the last word with attorneys who practice before them, but they are not unmindful of the expectations of the bar generally. Their work is open to the criticism of their professional peers. Engineers are equipped with greater technical precision than lawyers but with a less compelling system of professional ethics. Nevertheless, engineers in public posts, when they botch a job, incur the disapproval of the attentive public of engineers. Medical men in public posts are not beyond the pull of their professional norms even as they develop public policy on medical care. Among persons engaged in general administration professional norms seem to be in the process of development, and these group standards emerge from an attentive public which is largely, but not entirely, intragovernmental.

This kind of differentiation between the attentive and nonattentive public is a commonplace of speculation about the place of the citizenry in a democracy. It is often accompanied by attempts to estimate the proportions of the public that share varying degrees and kinds of attentiveness, estimates often unsupported by the data of observation. But surely the highly attentive and active public of which we have been speaking constitutes normally no more than 10 to 15 per cent of the adult population, although at times of crisis far higher proportions may focus their attention on particular actions of government.

The reason, though, for the introduction here of the question of political differentiations among people was the hope that it might suggest popular characteristics conducive to, if not essential for, the existence of democratic practices. Obviously the highly attentive publics, as they monitor the actions of government and let their judgments be known, play a critical role in assuring a degree of responsiveness of government to nongovernmental opinion. For these publics to perform that function, though, an understanding and acceptance of their role must prevail among many people. The belief must exist that it is the public's business to engage in such activities of surveillance and criticism of government. Societies have existed and do exist in which there is a radically different role system; it may be improper for private persons to concern themselves with the business of officials. For lack of adequate comparative data, it is difficult to make vivid the significance of behaviors we regard as commonplace. It is sufficient to note that there is nothing in human nature to assure that the attentive publics will act as they do. Development of understandings of roles and of appropriate behaviors among large numbers of people requires considerable time and a good deal of trial and error; this is one reason why democracies are not created by decree but, rather, evolve.

Attentiveness with its correlative behaviors will wane unless it is associated with a belief that watchfulness and articulateness ultimately have some bearing on what government does or does not do. That belief can be engendered only if it has some foundation in reality. In turn, that reality depends upon the outlooks of those persons who constitute the highly activist element—the officials, the occupants of points of nongovernmental power, the persons who may next occupy points of private and public power. That is, each of the elements of the political system must have characteristics that make it possible for them to fit together. Thus, democratic politicians defer to expressions of opinion. They listen with patience to the crackpot and even maintain their composure in the face of unfair and uninformed criticism—especially when it comes from an influential constitutent. In all this there is a core of genuine concern about public opinion even though impracticable and intemperate expressions of opinion may be greeted with a ceremonial courtesy devoid of substantive deference. All these observations may amount to is the contention that if a democracy is to exist, the belief must be widespread that public opinion, at least in the long run, affects the course of public action. In a technical sense that belief may be a myth, an article of faith, yet its maintenance requires that it possess a degree of validity. It seems even that those clerics who most successfully perpetuate their myths are those who can turn up a miracle for their communicants now and then.

Political involvement is another type of differentiation among the citizenry that may provide clues to those characteristics of people which are congenial to the workings of a democracy. Variations in the degree of psychological "care" and "interest" in campaigns have served as a crude but useful index for many of our analyses. Almost by definition there must exist a fairly widespread psychological involvement in political affairs if a society is to operate by democratic procedures. Involvement probably carries with it at least a degree of attention to political affairs. Yet as we move from the most highly attentive and most highly involved sector of society, involvement may take on rather special dimensions. A substantial proportion of the citizenry may not belong to the highly attentive sector of the public of which we have spoken but may pay a routine heed to politics, may "care" about how elections come out, and may have an "interest" in campaigns. This involvement tends to carry with it some sense of sharing in the political process, some belief that participation makes a difference, some faith in the reality of the dogmas of democracy. Yet the activities associated with this sense of involvement are of a different order from those of the highly attentive publics whose members may be especially well informed and fairly closely in touch with political processes.

The psychological involvement of a substantial sector of the populace represents, of course, an acquired cultural characteristic. It takes some learning and habituation for a people to acquire a sense of participation, a sense of sharing in a political order. Yet this sense of involvement may be of prime significance. It is basic for any popular participation in governmental processes. Beyond this, the sense of involvement may be a fundamental means by which discontents and ambitions and desires are steered into constitutional channels. Earlier we identified even in the American system blocs of opinion of high intensity that were associated with low involvement, with a low sense of political efficacy, and with low levels of political participation. Groups of persons not involved in democratic processes but possessed of intense discontents may occur in any order. The practical question is how large such blocs of sentiment need to be and what circumstances need to exist for them to become destructive of the normal democratic processes.

• • •

3. INTERACTION AND DISCRETION

Analytically it is useful to conceive of the structure of a democratic order as consisting of the political activists and the mass of people. Yet this differentiation becomes deceptive unless it is kept in mind that the democratic activists consist of people arranged along a spectrum of political participation and involvement, ranging from those in the highest posts of official leadership to the amateurs who become sufficiently interested to try to round up a few votes for their favorite in the presidential campaign. In the preceding discussion we sought to isolate some of the characteristics of both activists and mass that appear to be compatible with, if not essential for, the operation of a democratic order, thus setting up a static picture of two broad political strata. It is in the dynamics of the system, the interactions between these strata, that the import of public opinion in democratic orders becomes manifest. Between the activists and the mass there exists a system of communication and interplay so complex as to defy simple description; yet identification of a few major features of that system may aid in our construction of a general conception of democratic processes.

Opinion Dikes. In the interactions between democratic leadership echelons and the mass of people some insight comes from the conception of public opinion as a system of dikes which channel public action or which fix a range of discretion within which government may act or within which debate at official levels may proceed. This conception avoids the error of personifying "public opinion" as an entity that exercises initiative and in some way functions as an operating organism to translate its purposes into governmental action.

In one of their aspects the dikes of opinion have a substantive nature in that they define areas within which day-to-day debate about the course of specific action may occur. Some types of legislative proposal, given the content of general opinion, can scarcely expect to attract serious attention. They depart too far from the general understandings of what is proper. A scheme for public ownership of the automobile industry, for example, would probably be regarded as so far outside the area of legitimate public action that not even the industry would become greatly concerned. On the other hand, other types of questions arise within areas of what we have called permissive consensus. A widespread, if not a unanimous, sentiment prevails that supports action toward some general objective, such as the care of the ill or the mitigation of the economic hazards of the individual. Probably quite commonly mass opinion of a permissive character tends to develop in advance of governmental action in many areas of domestic policy. That opinion grows out of public discussion against the background of the modal aspirations and values of people generally. As it takes shape, the time becomes ripe for action that will be generally acceptable or may even arouse popular acclaim for its authors.

The qualities of this substantive opinion doubtless differ widely from issue to issue and from person to person. On some issues opinion may be oriented favorably toward broadly defined objectives; on others, perhaps extremely few, opinion may become focused on sharply defined proposals. On any issue the more alert and informed persons may have fairly well-formed opinions about sharply defined issues; others may have broad preferences—for example, something ought to be done for the farmers but not too much.

Opinion dikes may bear on the manner as well as on the substance of action. And it may be that in a democratic order those opinions that control or guide the mode of action may be of special importance as substantive action moves into areas where it encounters formidable opposition. Action taken in a seemingly fair and equitable manner may be acceptable, but arbitrary action to the same effect may be regarded as intolerable. The procedural content of American public opinion has been little explored. The division of opinion and the spontaneous comment on the proposition that government employees accused of communism ought to be fired even though the charge is not proved suggest that notions of fair play may be widely held within the population. Doubtless other procedural notions have wide popular acceptance that could be demonstrated by survey methods.

The idea of public opinion as forming a system of dikes which channel action yields a different conception of the place of public opinion than does the notion of a government by public opinion as one in which by some mysterious means a referendum occurs on every major issue. In the former conception the articulation between government and opinion is relatively loose. Parallelism between action and opinion tends not to be precise in matters of detail; it prevails rather with respect to broad purpose. And in the correlation of purpose and action time lags may occur between the crystallization of a sense of mass purpose and its fulfillment in public action. Yet in the long run majority purpose and public action tend to be brought into harmony.

Modifications of the Opinion Context. The content of mass opinion changes through time; it is perhaps in such alterations that the power of mass opinion is made manifest. Though changes in opinion content occur continuously, at some moments combinations of events, imaginative leadership, and action induce relatively rapid and marked changes in popular preferences and expectations. These episodes may bring new opinion orientations, which in turn become rather rigid elements of the pattern of popular attitudes.

The movement of opinions and the expectations that accompanied the fulfillment of the program of the New Deal illustrate well the process of change and its consequences for governmental action. A spirited leadership with programs of action deviating markedly from past practice won approval and generated a new set of popular expectations about governmental action. The "power" of public opinion manifested itself in a negative way. Those candidates and leaders tainted with the suspicion that they wanted to turn the clock back had hard sledding for years. Until they could make a show of acceptance of changes they could not capture control of the government. Thus, through elections opinion ratified past reforms by its rejection of those who appeared to be at odds with the new balance of public sentiment.

Similarly, in the area of foreign policy World War II brought with it a reorientation of the context of public opinion, which became more supportive of involvement in international politics. Probably the body of popular opinion in this area has a less solid base and a less constricting effect upon public action than does opinion on domestic welfare policy. The radically changed position of the United States in world affairs creates new problems not only for a government that rests on public opinion, but also for those who seek to inform and to lead that opinion. The conduct of domestic debates over foreign policy carries hazards for external policy. On the other hand, repression of debate results in a failure to inform the people of incompetence in the conduct of foreign affairs.

Mass opinions, aspirations, and expectations change as the political system moves through time. It is in this moving situation that the power of mass opinion makes itself manifest in its interactions with democratic leadership—chiefly in its rejection of leadership factions whose outlook lags notably behind or strikes out markedly ahead of the moving average of opinion. Those who wish to turn the clock back, to reverse decisions already rooted in popular acceptance, gradually learn their lesson as they meet rebuff after rebuff. Those too far ahead of opinion, though they may contribute to the forces impelling alteration of the opinion context, likewise find themselves rejected. Deviants from dominant opinion, though, play a critical role in the preservation of the vitality of a democratic order as they urge alterations and modifications better to achieve the aspirations of men. Hence the fundamental significance of freedom of speech and agitation. Those activists closest to the core of power may hesitate to assume the risks of political entrepreneurship, but others, with less to lose, may by their efforts gradually make the endeavor that is not "practical politics" today feasible tomorrow.

• • •

The argument amounts essentially to the position that the masses do not corrupt themselves; if they are corrupt, they have been corrupted. If this hypothesis has a substantial strain of validity, the critical element for the health of a democratic order consists in the beliefs, standards, and competence of those who constitute the influentials, the opinion-leaders, the political activists in the order. That group, as has been made plain, refuses to define itself with great clarity in the American system; yet analysis after analysis points to its existence. If a democracy tends toward indecision, decay, and disaster, the responsibility rests here, not in the mass of the people.[1]

A Classification of Presidential Elections

ANGUS CAMPBELL

In some way each election is unique. New candidates, contemporary issues, the changing tides of domestic and international affairs—all these contribute to its individuality. Election rules do not differ significantly from year to year, but each election has its own characteristics, and to the voter who focuses on detail rather than generality each election seems like a new experience. We must assume, however, that with all their idiosyncrasies, elections do have common attributes and that these may be used to develop a descriptive model of all presidential elections. We propose to draw on the theory of the flow of the vote which we have presented in the preceding chapters as a basis for a classification of presidential elections.

Our basic assumption is that the standing commitments of the electorate define the "normal" division of the vote, and that fluctuations from this normal

FROM Angus Campbell, Philip E. Converse, Warren E. Miller, and Donald E. Stokes, *Elections and the Political Order* (New York: Wiley, 1966), pp. 63–77. Reprinted by permission of John Wiley & Sons, Inc.

[1] This analysis and its implications should be pondered well by those young gentlemen in whose education the Republic has invested considerable sums.

vote result from short-term forces which become important in specific elections. Depending on whether the movement of the vote results in the election of the candidate of the majority or the minority party, and on whether this movement is associated with a basic shift in long-term partisan attachments, each election can be classified as maintaining, deviating, or realigning.[1] We will draw on the four elections for which we have survey data to illustrate these classifications and will refer, but less confidently, to earlier elections in American history for further documentation.

MAINTAINING ELECTIONS

In a maintaining election the pattern of partisan attachments prevailing in the preceding period persists, and the majority party wins the Presidency. If the short-term forces are weak, the total turnout will be relatively low, and the partisan division of the vote will approximate the normal vote. If the short-term forces are strong, the turnout will be high, and the vote will typically swing away from the normal level to the advantage of one or the other candidate. If the short-term forces are advantageous to the majority party, its candidate will receive a higher than normal proportion of the vote. If they are disadvantageous, he will receive less of the vote than normal but may still win the election.

Most presidential elections during the last hundred years have been maintaining elections. If we assume that during the period immediately following the Civil War the majority of the electorate was Republican in its partisan sympathies, that this majority declined to something near an even balance during the 1876–1892 period and was revitalized in 1896, we may conclude that the numerous Republican victories down through the 1920's fall in this category. More recently, the later Roosevelt elections maintained a Democratic majority which had been established in the New Deal elections of the early thirties. Of the elections within the scope of our research program, two may be classified as maintaining. The elections of 1948 and 1960 differed greatly in important respects, but they both returned the candidate of the majority party to the White House.

The 1948 Election. The most striking feature of the presidential election in 1948 was the extraordinarily low turnout, only 51.5 per cent of the total citizenry. This was the smallest presidential vote since the establishment of the two-party system, except for the two elections immediately following the advent of women's suffrage. It was obviously a year in which the electorate was not greatly moved

---

[1] The reader will recognize that this classification is an extension of V. O. Key's theory of critical elections. See V. O. Key, Jr., "A Theory of Critical Elections," *Journal of Politics*, 17, 3–18 (February 1955).

A Classification of Presidential Elections 99

by the circumstances, issues, or personalities of the moment; . . . Mr. Truman was elected with slightly less than half the popular vote. Mr. Dewey received 45 per cent of the vote, and the remaining portion was divided between Thurmond (States' Rights Democrats) and Wallace (Progressives).

Our understanding of the nature of the presidential elections leads us to expect that the vote in an election with an abnormally low turnout will demonstrate the following characteristics:

1. The dropout of voters will be sharpest among those members of the electorate who are least strongly party-identified, that is, the Independents and weak identifiers. The strong identifiers will be sustained by the high level of political involvement associated with their party identification.

2. Among the strong party identifiers defections to the opposite party, resulting primarily from idiosyncratic influences, will be few in number and will balance between the two parties. The absence of short-term forces, which produces the low turnout, also removes the stimulus to defection from accustomed party loyalties.

3. Among the weak party identifiers there will also be idiosyncratic defections, more numerous than among strong identifiers but balanced between the two parties.

4. Those Independents who vote will divide their vote equally between the competing parties.

5. The partisan division of the total vote will approximate the "normal vote" determined by the standing strength of the competing parties at the time.

We see in Figure 1 the extent to which our data regarding the vote in 1948 conformed to these expectations. Unfortunately we did not measure party identification in our 1948 survey, and we must draw on data from our 1952 survey to construct this figure. We asked the respondents in our 1952 survey to recall their vote in 1948, and we can combine this statement with their party identification as stated in 1952.[2] When this is done we find that our expectations are

[2] This substitution of data gathered in 1952 for data which should ideally have been recorded at the time of the 1948 election involves us in two assumptions, neither of which is above criticism. In taking the 1952 statement of party identification in place of a 1948 statement, we are assuming that none of our respondents changed his identification during this period. We know this is not entirely true, although our evidence gives some assurance that such changes are infrequent. More serious is the acceptance of our respondents' recall of their 1948 vote four years after the event. We know there is a tendency for reminiscent reports of earlier voting decisions to overstate the vote of the candidate who won the election, and we find some indication of this "bandwagon" inflation in the present case. The 1952 sample reported having given Dewey only 42 per cent of the vote, when in fact he received 45 per cent. This discrepancy is not large but it is sufficient to distort Figure 1 slightly. We also know that errors of recall are most likely to occur among those people whose interest in the event being recalled is the weakest. Consequently we would expect the distortions of reported 1948 vote to occur primarily among the weakly identified and Independent voters rather than among the strong identifiers. As we see in Figure 1, it is precisely these groups which depart moderately from our expectations.

FIGURE 1 The Vote of Partisan Groups in 1948. (The data in this figure are based on recalled 1948 votes given by the respondents of the Survey Research Center's 1952 election study. Votes for Wallace and Thurmond are grouped with the Democratic votes.)

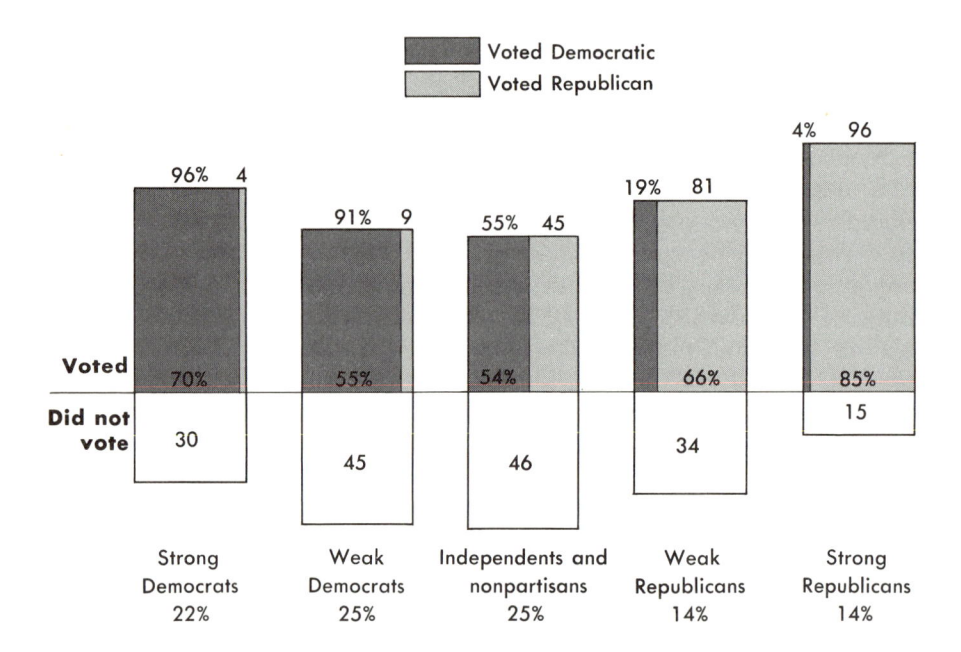

generally supported, the deviations apparently being related to the inadequacies of our reports based on memory. The configuration of turnout is as anticipated, and the sharpness of the drop in turnout of the weakly identified groups is especially impressive when compared with the slope of turnout in the higher turnout elections which followed 1948. The strong identifiers did indeed adhere to their parties, although it is noteworthy that the 4 per cent of defections on both sides is perceptibly higher than we find among strong Republican partisans in the Eisenhower elections when the short-term advantages of the Republican Party eliminated even the infrequent idiosyncratic defections. Defections were more numerous among the weak identifiers, as predicted, although much less frequent than in the elections which followed. The balance of these defections was not as close as expected, there being a larger proportion of weak Republicans reporting voting Democratic than weak Democrats reporting voting Republican.[3] The Independent voters split their votes in about an even division, with a slight inclination toward the Democratic candidate. Both of these minor discrepancies

[3] Because the total number of weak Republicans is much smaller than that of weak Democrats the actual number of transfers in one direction or the other is about equal.

appear to reflect the Democratic bias in the recall of the 1948 vote by respondents who were questioned in 1952.

Although it would appear from Figure 1 that the Democratic vote in 1948 exceeded normal expectations, this is entirely a function of the overstatement of the Democratic vote by our 1952 respondents. If we consider the actual election statistics and assume that those voters who supported Thurmond or Wallace were largely Democrats, we find that the combination of their votes and those for Mr. Truman approximates the proportion of the total vote which we take to represent the "normal" Democratic strength. The minority party was not able to swing the Independent vote or capture any advantage from defecting voters in 1948, and the majority party was maintained in power.

The 1960 Election. The Democratic Party was still the majority party in 1960, and it elected its presidential candidate. The election was thus also a maintaining election, although it differed substantially from the election of 1948. The characteristics of this election are discussed in detail in the ensuing chapter; we need only note two distinguishing attributes, the high turnout and the great discrepancy between the vote of the Democratic candidate and the vote for the congressional candidates who ran with him. It is obvious from these characteristics of the vote that short-term forces played a much stronger role in 1960 than they had in 1948. The general level of voter stimulation was high, as demonstrated by expressions of interest in our interviews as well as by the election statistics. The partisan direction of these forces is indicated by the fact that Mr. Kennedy failed by several percentage points to achieve the normal expectation of a Democratic presidential candidate.

When we compare Figure 2, showing the voting record of the partisan groups in 1960, with Figure 1, in which comparable data from 1948 are presented, we see first, the source of the substantial increase in turnout, and second, the location of the swing away from the normal vote toward the Republican candidate. It is clear that although all the party identification groups increased their turnout from the abnormally low levels of 1948, the increment was proportionately smallest in the strongly partisan groups and greatest in those groups with the weakest party commitment.[4] It is also apparent that it was the weakly identified Democrats who were most susceptible to the impact of short-term forces in 1960. The Independent vote was split about equally between the two candidates. The total movement away from the normal vote was not large (as we shall see the movement in 1952 was much larger), but it very nearly cost the Democratic Party the Presidency.

[4] The reported turnout in our 1960 study was somewhat inflated by the fact that our 1960 sample was based primarily on the survivors of a panel which had been selected in 1956. The losses from this panel over the four-year interval were somewhat larger among the uninvolved members of the sample than they were among the involved, resulting in an upward bias in the proportion of self-reported voters in 1960.

FIGURE 2   The Vote of Partisan Groups in 1960.

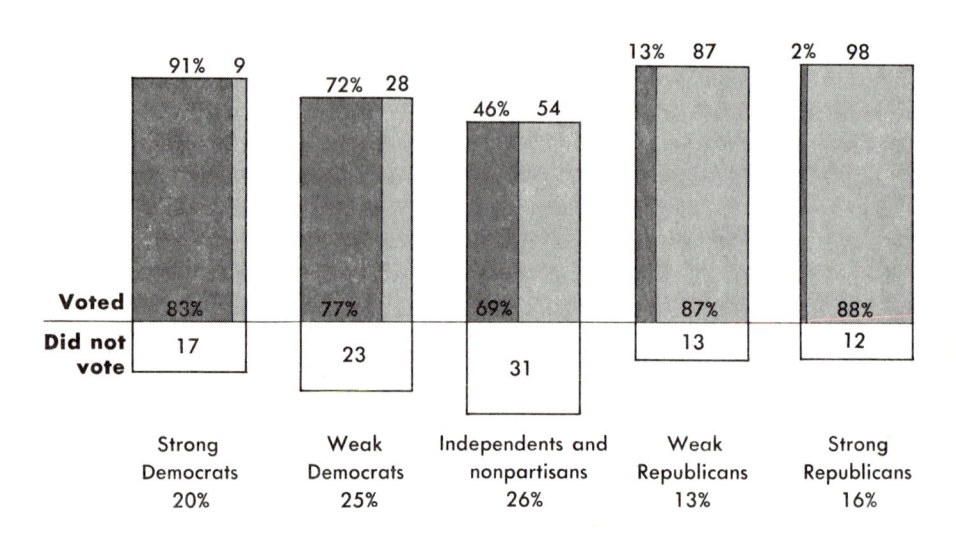

	Strong Democrats 20%	Weak Democrats 25%	Independents and nonpartisans 26%	Weak Republicans 13%	Strong Republicans 16%
Voted Democratic / Republican	91% / 9	72% / 28	46% / 54	13% / 87	2% / 98
Voted	83%	77%	69%	87%	88%
Did not vote	17	23	31	13	12

DEVIATING ELECTIONS

In a deviating election the basic division of party loyalties is not seriously disturbed, but the influence of short-term forces on the vote is such that it brings about the defeat of the majority party. After the specific circumstances that deflected the vote from what we would expect on the basis of party disappear from the scene, the political balance returns to a level which more closely reflects the underlying division of partisan attachments. A deviating election is thus a temporary reversal which occurs during a period when one or the other party holds a clear advantage in the long-term preferences of the electorate.

The election of Woodrow Wilson in 1916 is an obvious example of a deviating election. There seems little doubt that during the period of the Wilson elections the electorate was predominantly Republican. Wilson attained the White House in 1912 with a minority (42 per cent) of the total vote, as Roosevelt and Taft split the Republican Party. His incumbency and the public emotion aroused by the darkening shadow of the First World War apparently provided the additional votes he needed in 1916 to reach the narrow plurality that he achieved over his Republican opponent. According to Key, the Democratic gains of 1961 were due principally to "a short-term desertion of the Republican Party by classes of British origin and orientation." The temporary character of the

A Classification of Presidential Elections

Democratic victory began to become apparent in the 1918 elections when the Republican Party won control of both the Senate and the House of Representatives. In 1920 and the two following elections, the minority status of the Democratic Party was again convincingly demonstrated.

A similar situation occurred forty years later when, during a period of Democratic ascendancy, the Republican Party nominated General Dwight D. Eisenhower as its presidential candidate. These two elections fell within the coverage of our research program, and we can consider them in the light of our extensive survey data.

The 1952 Election. In November 1952, 62.7 per cent of the adult citizenry went to the polls, an increase of some 27 per cent over the total turnout four years earlier. They made the event further memorable by overturning a Democratic Administration which had been in office for twenty years, the longest unbroken period of party supremacy since the Republican Administrations of Lincoln and his successors. Mr. Eisenhower received over 55 per cent of the popular vote, and the Republican Party won both houses of Congress. This dramatic increase in turnout and the shift in the vote are illustrated in Figure 3.

The essential fact which emerges from Figure 3 is that in 1952 the number of people in the electorate who identified themselves as Democrats outnumbered those who called themselves Republicans by a ratio of three to two, and that the

FIGURE 3 The Vote of Partisan Groups in 1952.

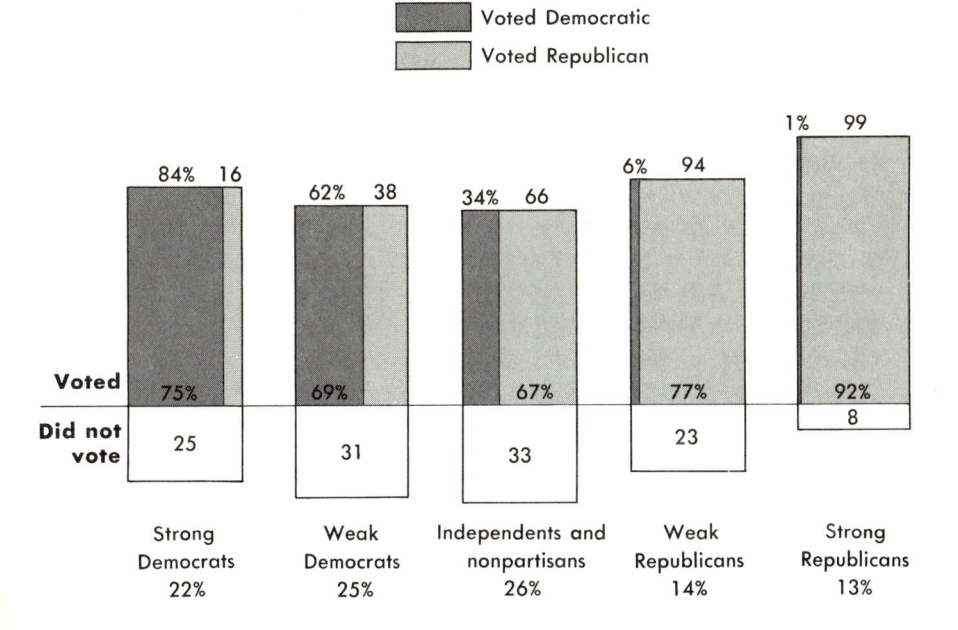

	Strong Democrats 22%	Weak Democrats 25%	Independents and nonpartisans 26%	Weak Republicans 14%	Strong Republicans 13%
Voted Democratic	84%	62%	34%	6%	1%
Voted Republican	16	38	66	94	99
Voted	75%	69%	67%	77%	92%
Did not vote	25	31	33	23	8

Eisenhower majority was assembled within this distribution without basically changing it. The impact of the combination of political forces which were important in 1952 was felt throughout the spectrum of party identification. . . . Normal Republicans held solidly to their party with only minor defections, even among those who called themselves "weak Republicans." A clear majority of the Independent voters supported Mr. Eisenhower, and serious inroads were made among those groups who ordinarily voted Democratic. The political circumstances of the moment were very unfavorable to the Democratic Party and resulted in its defeat, but they did not alter the underlying majority which it held in the standing partisan commitments of the electorate.

The Republican victory in 1952 was accomplished by a temporary movement of normal Democrats and nonpartisans toward the Republican candidate. The extent to which this was a movement toward the candidate and not toward the party is dramatically demonstrated by the high rate of ticket-splitting reported by these voters. Three out of five of those Democrats and Independents who voted for Mr. Eisenhower in 1952 were not willing to support the rest of the Republican slate. Subsequent events, beginning with the 1954 election when the Democratic Party again took both houses of Congress, made it clear that the election of 1952 deviated from normal expectations during a period of Democratic majority.

The 1956 Election. Mr. Eisenhower was re-elected to the Presidency in 1956 with a slightly higher majority (57 per cent) than he had received four years earlier. The distribution of party identification was almost precisely the same as it had been in 1952, and the contribution of the various party groups to Mr. Eisenhower's total vote closely resembled that of the previous election. This small increment in his support appeared to come largely from those voters who had no consistent partisan identification.[5] (See Figure 4.) The separation which the voters made between Mr. Eisenhower and the Republican ticket was clearly demonstrated as the Democratic candidates won both houses of Congress, the first time since 1848 that a split of this kind had occurred. This was accomplished by an even larger proportion of ticket-splitting by Democrats and Independents than was observed in 1952. Three out of four of these people who voted for Mr. Eisenhower rejected the party whose ticket he headed.

This increasing discrepancy between the vote for Mr. Eisenhower and the

---

[5] We find it especially interesting that the swing of the Independent vote to Eisenhower was larger in 1956 than it had been in 1952. Although we expect the nonpartisan voter to be more easily moved by short-term political forces than voters whose loyalties hold them to their party, it is also true that the nonpartisans are less involved in politics and less alert to political stimulation. Their votes are more likely to be influenced by experiences and events of an idiosyncratic character than are those of the voters who are concerned with political affairs. Apparently it took four years for the Eisenhower appeal to have its full impact on these relatively inattentive nonpartisan voters. We are reminded of our earlier finding that the preferences for Eisenhower among the even less involved nonvoters was very much greater in 1956 than they had been in 1952. . . .

A Classification of Presidential Elections 105

FIGURE 4 The Vote of Partisan Groups in 1956.

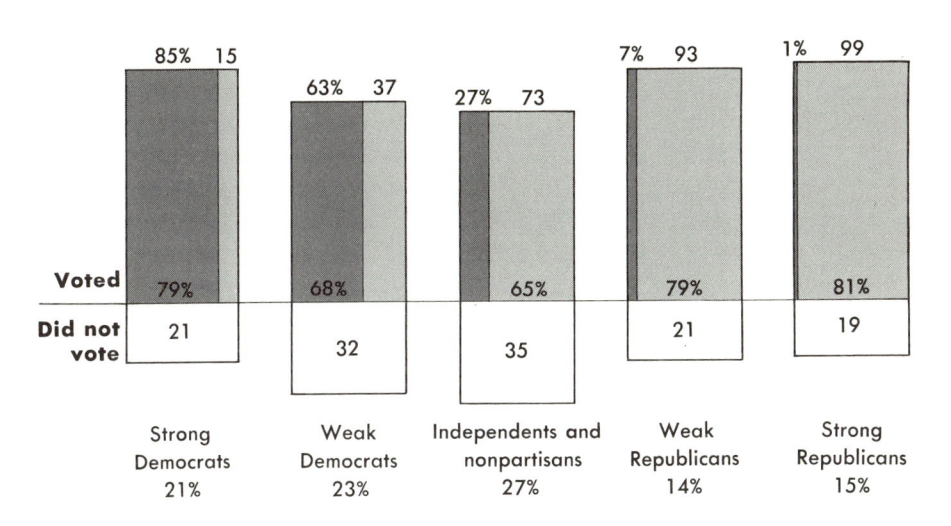

	Strong Democrats 21%	Weak Democrats 23%	Independents and nonpartisans 27%	Weak Republicans 14%	Strong Republicans 15%
Voted Democratic / Voted Republican	85% / 15	63% / 37	27% / 73	7% / 93	1% / 99
Voted	79%	68%	65%	79%	81%
Did not vote	21	32	35	21	19

vote for his fellow candidates foreshadowed the failure of the Republican Party to bring about a basic shift of party loyalties during the Eisenhower years. The congressional elections of 1958, in which the Democratic Party won 58 per cent of the popular vote, made the Republican weakness apparent. As the Eisenhower period drew to a close, it became clear that Mr. Eisenhower had attracted a tremendous personal following in his two elections, but his administration had not produced a significant realignment in the distribution of partisan attachments. The Democratic Party remained the majority party and in 1960, when the Eisenhower appeal was no longer a factor, it was reinstated in power.

The two Eisenhower elections were deviating elections; our survey data from 1952 and 1956 may provide a key to an understanding of the other elections of this type that have occurred in American history. The most striking fact about the flow of the vote in the 1952 election (and again in 1956) was the universality with which the various segments of the electorate moved toward the Republican candidate. It was not a situation in which some groups became more Republican than they had been in 1948 but were offset by other groups moving in the other direction. There was virtually no occupational, religious, regional, or other subdivision of the electorate which did not vote more strongly Republican in 1952 than it had in 1948.

The second impressive fact about these two elections was the relative insignificance of policy issues in the minds of the voters. There were no great questions of policy which the public saw as dividing the two parties. In 1952 the voters were thinking about the "mess in Washington," the stalemate in Korea, and General Eisenhower's heroic image. In 1956 they were no longer concerned with the Truman Administration or the Korean situation, but they were even more devoted to Mr. Eisenhower than they had been in 1952. It would appear that the flow of the vote from the Democratic majorities of the previous twenty years to the Republican victories in the 1950's was a response to short-term forces which had little policy content and did not set interest group against interest group, class against class, or region against region.

It is our belief that it is this absence of great ideological issues which provides the basic quality of these deviating elections. Professor Charles Sellers concludes from his application of these concepts to the full range of presidential elections since 1789 that the "essential ingredient" of such elections is the presence of a "popular hero" candidate. He points out that all the presidential elections displaying some aspects of temporary surge featured a military hero, Eisenhower, Harrison, Washington, Grant, Taylor, and Jackson.[6] The fact that so many of these elections have been dominated by persons of military background dramatizes their lack of ideological content. If Mr. Eisenhower may be taken as an example, the public image of these gentlemen has little to do with great issues of public policy. With certain notable exceptions, which we will consider shortly, the dramatic swings of turnout and partisanship during the last hundred years do not give the impression of an aroused electorate taking sides in a great debate on national policy. On the contrary, these swings in the vote appear to grow out of some immediate circumstance which is exploited by a candidate blessed with unusual personal appeal. Public interest in these events and persons is translated into political action, with a movement toward the party which happens to be in position to profit from the situation. The movement is unidirectional because the circumstances which produce it are not seen as favorable by one section of the electorate and unfavorable by another. They tend rather to create a generally positive or negative attitude throughout the electorate, resulting in the almost universal type of shift which we observed in 1952. The movement is temporary because the circumstances and personalities with which it is associated pass from the scene without having introduced a new dimension of party position around which the electorate might become realigned.

REALIGNING ELECTIONS

Key has pointed out that there is a third type of election, characterized by the appearance of "a more or less durable realignment" of party loyalties. In such a

---

[6] Sellers classifies the 1916 election as a realigning election; we include it with the deviating elections.

realigning election, popular feeling associated with politics is sufficiently intense that the basic partisan commitments of a portion of the electorate change, and a new party balance is created. Such shifts are infrequent. As Key observes, every election has the effect of creating lasting party loyalties in some individual voters, but it is "not often that the number so affected is so great as to create a sharp realignment."

Realigning elections have historically been associated with great national crises. The emergence of the Republican Party and its subsequent domination of national politics were the direct outgrowth of the great debate over slavery and the ultimate issue of secession. The election of 1896 divided the country again as the East and Midwest overcame the Populist challenge of the South and West. According to Key, "The Democratic defeat was so demoralizing and so thorough that the party made little headway in regrouping its forces until 1916." It might be argued that the Democratic Party did not in fact hold a clear majority of the electorate at the time of the Cleveland elections, but the election statistics make it clear that whatever hold it did have on the voters was greatly weakened after 1896.

The most dramatic reversal of party alignments in this century was associated with the Great Depression of the 1930's. The economic disater which befell the nation during the Hoover Administration so discredited the Republican Party that it fell from its impressive majorities of the 1920's to a series of defeats, which in 1936 reached overwhelming dimensions. These defeats were more than temporary departures from a continuing division of underlying party strength. There is little doubt that large numbers of people who had been voting Republican or had previously not voted at all, especially among the younger age groups and those social and economic classes hardest hit by the Depression, were converted to the Democratic Party during this period. The program of welfare legislation of the New Deal and the extraordinary personality of its major exponent, Franklin D. Roosevelt, brought about a profound realignment of party strength which has endured in large part up to the present time.

Key has pointed out that the shift toward the Democratic Party which occurred in the early 1930's was anticipated in the New England area in the 1928 election. It is difficult to ascertain whether the changes in these successive election years were actually part of the same movement. Since the shifts in New England were highly correlated with the proportions of Catholic voters in the communities studied, it would not be unreasonable to attribute them to the presence of Governor Alfred E. Smith at the head of the Democratic ticket in 1928. Had the Depression not intervened, the New England vote might have returned to its pre-1928 levels in the 1932 election. It may be recalled, however, that the Smith candidacy had not only a religious aspect but a class quality as well. It may well be that New England voters, having moved into the Democratic ranks in 1928 for reasons having to do with both religious and economic considerations, found it easy to remain there in 1932 when economic questions became compellingly important.

It is worth noting that the nationwide shift toward the Democratic Party during the 1930's was not fully accomplished in a single election. Although Mr. Roosevelt's margin of victory in 1932 was large (59 per cent of the two-party vote), it was not until 1936 that the Democratic wave reached its peak. The long-entrenched Republican sympathies of the electorate may not have given way easily in the early years of the Depression. Had not Mr. Roosevelt and his New Deal won the confidence of many of these people during his first administration—or even his second—there might have been a return to earlier party lines similar to that which occurred in 1920. From this point of view we may do well to speak of a realigning electoral era rather than a realigning election.

The total redistribution of party attachments in such an era does not necessarily result from a unilateral movement toward the advantaged party. The far-reaching impact of the crises which produce these alignments is likely to produce movements in both directions as individual voters find their new positions in the party conflict. It is also likely to increase the political polarization of important segments of the electorate, usually along sectional or class lines. We know that this happened during the 1930's as the Depression and the New Deal moved working-class people and certain minority groups toward a closer identification with the Democratic Party and middle-class people toward the Republican Party. Which party gains more from this sort of reshuffling depends on the relative size of the groups affected and the solidarity with which their membership moves.

The fact that the different regional and class divisions of the electorate become associated with the competing parties helps the shifting of loyalties develop into a lasting realignment. When an entire group polarizes around a new political standard, the pressures associated with group membership tend to hold the individual members to the group norm. Attitudes having the strength of group support are likely to be more stable than those which are merely individual. The development of the Solid South after the period of Reconstruction, when the expression of Republican sympathies became tantamount to sectional treason, is an illuminating case in point.

We may note finally that in contrast to those elections in which deviations from the normal vote were only temporary, the realigning elections have not been dominated by presidential candidates who came into office on a wave of great personal popularity. It is significant that neither Lincoln, McKinley, nor F. D. Roosevelt was a military figure, and none of them possessed any extraordinary personal appeal at the time he first took office. The quality which did distinguish the elections in which they came to power was the presence of a great national crisis, leading to a conflict regarding governmental policies and the association of the two major parties with relatively clearly contrasting programs for its solution. In some degree national politics during these realigning periods took on an ideological character. The flow of the vote was not a temporary reaction to a heroic figure or a passing embarrassment of the party in power; it reflected a reorientation of basic party attachments brought about during critical periods in the nation's history.

CONCLUSION

The ultimate significance of an election victory or defeat is often difficult to assess at the time. The immediate implications for the contending candidates are apparent, but the fuller meaning of the vote may not become clear until the succeeding elections have given a perspective within which it may be judged. The basic element in the long-term trend of the vote is the underlying division of party loyalties. If a substantial majority of the electorate are held by long-established commitments to one or another of the competing parties, the vote will oscillate from election to election around this party balance. If the circumstances in a particular election excite the electorate sufficiently, the oscillation may be large enough to dislodge the majority party temporarily from power. If the circumstances are so drastic as to force a new orientation of party positions, a period of realignment of partisan attachments may be induced, and a new balance of party strength created.

Party Systems and the Political Process

WALTER DEAN BURNHAM

The more deeply one reflects on the characteristic properties of political parties in the American party system of today, the more exceptional these parties seem to become by comparative standards. American mass-mobilization parties are the oldest such phenomena in the modern world. After an impressive trial run which extended from the 1790's to about 1820, they emerged as full-grown, recognizably modern structures by 1840—at least thirty years before the development of the first stable mass parties in Britain. During the enormously creative period ex-

FROM Walter Dean Burnham, "Party Systems and the Political Process," in William Nisbet Chambers and Walter Dean Burnham, eds., *The American Party Systems: Stages of Political Development*, pp. 277–87 and 305–07. Copyright © 1967 by Oxford University Press, Inc. Reprinted by permission.

tending roughly from the establishment of state nominating conventions in the 1820's to the creation of the Democratic National Committee in 1848, the party system took on a recognizably modern shape. But once that era had passed, very few major changes in organization occurred until the replacement of the convention by the direct primary during the years 1900–1915, and very few have taken place since.

No "branch" or "indirect caucus" types of party organization—still less "cell" or "militia" types—have been able, for example, to establish themselves in the American context.[1] Recruitment of elective elites remains closely associated, especially for the more important offices and in the larger states, with the candidates' wealth or access to large campaign contributions.[2] To this day the financing of the parties themselves remains to a substantial degree in the hands of those relatively few individuals and groups who make large donations; it does not rest on any stable mass base. This is, of course, but one reflection of the failure of European concepts or practices of party membership or organization to develop with democratization in the United States. Typically the American party is composed of an inner circle of office-holding and office-seeking cadres together with their personal supporters and a limited number of professional party workers. This structure has been decentralized but probably not significantly broadened under the direct primary system. Outside this circle lies the mass of party identifiers, only a tiny fraction of whom are involved in any more extensive partisan activity than voting every two or four years. Still further outside is the extraordinarily large part of the potential electorate which is not politically involved at all.[3]

All of the available evidence suggests that the American party systems, viewed comparatively, have exhibited an arrested development which stands in particularly striking contrast to the extraordinary dynamism of the nation's socioeconomic system.[4] This arrested development is visible both organizationally and functionally. There are at least four broad functions which are performed by fully developed democratic parties. The first of these is a nation-building, integrative, or . . . "constituent" function. This involves the regularized amalgamation and priority ordering of conflicting regional, ethno-cultural, group, or class interests through the mechanisms of the political party. In modern politics, broad acceptance of the legitimacy of the political regime as a whole depends in large measure on the successful performance of this function. Second, political

[1] For a useful typology of modern party organizations, see Maurice Duverger, *Political Parties* (New York, 1954), 1–60. A discussion in terms of the American party system of the present is found in Frank J. Sorauf, *Political Parties in the American System* (Boston, 1964), esp. 38–58, 153–69.
[2] This is especially the case at the crucial nominating stage. See Alexander Heard, *The Costs of Democracy* (Chapel Hill, 1960), 34–5, 318–43.
[3] Walter Dean Burnham, "The Changing Shape of the American Political Universe," *American Political Science Review*, LIX (1965), 7–28.
[4] This peculiarly nondevelopmental aspect of American party development has also been noted by Robert A. Dahl (ed.), *Political Oppositions in Western Democracies* (New Haven, 1966), 34–69.

parties carry out an office-filling function; orderly and democratic procedures are prescribed for elite recruitment to a limited number of elective and appointive positions. Third, parties perform a function of political education or political socialization for their mass clienteles. In its most developed form, this function is carried out through a network of party-controlled structures of education and media, with the intent of producing a more or less coherent frame of political reference among those clienteles. Fourth, major parties may perform a policy-making function. This involves not only the capture of office, but the capture of the policy-making machinery of government for programmatic purposes.

While the American parties have historically engaged in political education to some extent, and have occasionally been genuine policy-making vehicles, their involvement with such functions has been limited. Particularly in our own century, American political parties have been largely restricted in functional scope to the realm of the constituent and to the tasks of filling political offices. So far as the function of political education is concerned, indeed, there is evidence that during the nineteenth century the parties were engaged in propaganda and political-socialization activities on a scale which knows no parallel today. This intense activity seems to have been closely related to the quasi-monopoly which election campaigns and the partisan press of that period had on entertainment prior to the development of other mass media, and also to the relatively extreme frequency of elections and variability in election dates which existed prior to about 1880.[5] But as the party press faded out of the picture toward the end of the nineteenth century, as elections became concentrated in November and terms of office were lengthened, and as non-political mass media undermined the salience of the political campaign as a species of entertainment, the educative functions performed earlier by the parties tended to atrophy. American parties during the twentieth century have not been organized to provide political education or indoctrination for their clienteles on a month-in-month-out basis. Such an effort would require, in all probability, stable dues-paying memberships and the development of permanent ancillary party agencies for reaching a mass clientele whether or not an election was pending.

Similarly, the norm in American politics has been that the major parties lack the internal cohesion and organizational capacity to perform policy-making functions systematically or over a long term. In Great Britain, down through Lord Palmerston's time, majorities in the House of Commons—like those of the House of Representatives today—tended to be complex mixes of party and coalitional elements. Only after the sequential development of mass party organization following the Reform Bill of 1867 did the party whips in Britain become more than intelligence agents and persuaders for the leadership. In the United States, on the other hand, the development of mass parties in the 1830's destroyed the basis for consolidated party leadership which had existed during the time

[5] An illuminating discussion of the exacerbating effects of perpetual electioneering on antebellum politics is found in Roy F. Nichols, *The Disruption of American Democracy* (New York, 1948), 5–7.

of the first party system, permanently activated the cleavage between executive and legislature, and gave an enormous impetus to the decentralizing influence of federalism.[6] Since then, American parties have performed the policy-making function only very infrequently—as a rule, only in situations marked by unusual social and political tension. . . .

The history of American party development, taken as a whole, suggests that every major upsurge of democratization has led to a dispersion rather than a concentration of political power in the policy-making arena. In this the United States has been quite exceptional. Students of comparative party organizations and their development have often argued that mass-based parties develop in an industrial era in order to array on a broad scale the power of numbers against the power of wealth, interest, and social position enjoyed by existing elites. Concentration of organization and decision-making authority is essential to this end. Were this argument to be accepted as a binding generalization about party development in advanced societies, we should be confronted with an intriguing paradox suggested by the late Morton Grodzins: that American parties may actually be anti-parties.[7]

But this is not the end of analysis; it is merely a beginning. To make such an assumption is not only to take sides immediately in a substantive dispute with strong normative overtones, it is to plunge into a sea of analytical difficulties. It presupposes that there is, or more precisely ought to be, a clear-cut European confrontation between Left and Right in this country. It presupposes, moreover, that the cultural differences between the middle and working classes must necessarily dominate our domestic politics, and thus receive concrete expression in terms of party organization and evolution. But why should these differences receive such expression if they have not been dominant in the political culture? Nothing, indeed, is clearer than that the two major American parties are and always have been overwhelmingly middle-class in organization, values, and goals. From a European point of view, they can hardly fail to appear as exquisitely old-fashioned, as nineteenth-century anachronisms. Yet they have not only survived, they have totally dominated the American electoral scene—and at no time more completely than during the past generation. If parties seeking to organize the lower strata of American society along collectivist lines have been so evanescent, if the two major components of the system have so feebly performed the educative and policy-making functions, the reason for this must lie not only in our dispersive political institutions but more fundamentally within the American political culture itself.

Of all theses regarding that culture, the one which has the greatest explanatory power is the theory of the liberal tradition in America which has been

---

[6] Wilfred E. Binkley, *President and Congress* (New York, 1962), 83–104. . . .
[7] Morton Grodzins, "American Political Parties and the American System," *Western Political Quarterly*, XIII (1960), 974–98.

developed by Louis Hartz.[8] According to this analysis, the United States is a fragment of Europe, which was detached at a bourgeois point in history and subsequently developed a nearly monolithic, absolutist commitment to the values of individualist liberalism. These values, for most Americans at most times, have been so pervasive and have been so feebly challenged from within that they have tended to assume some of the properties of natural law in the American mind. Absolutist individualism has, of course, been buttressed both by the frontier experience and by the enormous relative affluence which most of the population has enjoyed throughout the country's history.[9] But the quite differing political experiences of other societies which have been relatively prosperous, or which have passed through a frontier stage, suggest the importance of the liberal cultural monolith in shaping the course of American political development.

Economic and social development consequently took place under very different political conditions than in Europe, other fragment cultures, or the modernizing states of the third world. During an initial period in which there was inadequate capital which was both private and internally generated, governments at all levels played a major promotional role, especially but by no means exclusively in the fields of transportation and finance. This period was comparatively short, however, and was supplanted by an era in which an adequate supply of domestic take-off capital in private hands and a widely accepted economic theory of laissez-faire combined to restrict governmental intervention in the private sector. This arrangement, in its turn, survived with little effective challenge until the corporate world of private enterprise had clearly lost its capacity to regulate the development of the American economy without incurring ruinous social costs. But from beginning to end—from the age of neo-mercantilism down to the modern welfare-warfare state—the overwhelming value consensus in this field has been in favor of maximum private enterprise and minimum intervention by public authority. Neither the New Deal nor the post–New Deal periods can be adequately understood unless it is appreciated that this has remained official doctrine. Controversies over public involvement in the American economy have essentially tended to be differences, based on interest and ideology, over what "minimum intervention" ought to be at any given time.[10] Under such conditions there is hardly room for political parties to undertake sustained policy-making or government-control functions even if their leaders were for some reason inclined to make the attempt. Nor would such an attempt be likely to take place, since such control functions have not been considered necessary by any significant part of the population.

But this hardly means that there have been no political conflicts—or even

---

[8] Louis Hartz, *The Liberal Tradition in America* (New York, 1955), and Hartz, *The Founding of New Societies* (New York, 1964), 1–122.
[9] David M. Potter, *People of Plenty: Economic Abundance and the American Character* (Chicago, 1954).
[10] Andrew Shonfield, *Modern Capitalism* (New York, 1965), 298–329.

that there have been no significant elements of class conflicts—in our history. Still less does it mean that the party system itself has played an insignificant role in that history. To be sure, it may be argued that its role has been peripheral and institutionally supportive of the American consensus concerning the primacy of the private sector in economic affairs. But there are other, and extremely important, dimensions of conflict which must be considered. Lee Benson is clearly right in his argument that the very consensus on economic and other fundamentals in the United States has produced not a lack of political cleavages, but a striking variety of them.[11] If the political culture and the party system have given only limited expression to vertical divisions within American society, they have accommodated an enormous variety of horizontal cleavages. Of these, three have been of paramount importance in our political history and, as the 1960 and 1964 elections have demonstrated, remain vital factors in American party politics to the present day.

1. The Clash of Sectional Subcultures. The literature which emphasizes and documents the vital historical importance of cultural and economic divergences along sectional lines is enormous. It may be enough here to mark the role of mass party politics in contributing to the full articulation of these cleavages. A student of the Missouri Compromise has pointed out that if the intense struggle in Congress over its terms had resulted in civil war, the war would have been fought out in the halls of Congress itself, with the rest of the country looking on in some amazement.[12] If a vastly different public reaction to its repeal was manifested a generation later, one can hardly doubt that the development of a mass-based party system, and the mobilization of mass opinion which accompanied it, bore much of the responsibility for the difference. In particular, the more Americans of the New England and Southern subcultures came to learn about each other's social values and political goals, the more pronounced their hostility toward each other grew. A strong argument can be made for the proposition that the Civil War was far more directly the product of the expansion of public political consciousness which is inherent in the dynamics of democratic development than of any economic causes.

The twofold decision of the period from 1861 to 1877—first to keep the South in the Union by force, and then to permit it to reassert substantially complete autonomy in its political affairs—enormously increased the need for the components of the party system to place major emphasis on integrative activities and functions. It is enough to recall that the influence of sectional cleavages was overwhelmingly dominant in American political history from 1854 to 1932, or to note the evidences of the age-old antipathy between the New England and white Southern subcultures which emerged in the massive voter shifts of the 1964 election. The South over the past century has influenced

---

[11] Lee Benson, *The Concept of Jacksonian Democracy* (Princeton, 1961), 272–7.
[12] Glover Moore, *The Missouri Controversy, 1819–21* (Lexington, Ky., 1953), 175.

American politics in ways not dissimilar to the influence of Quebec in Canada or of Ireland in the United Kingdom in the years from 1870 to 1922. The massive influence of that deviant subculture upon national party politics and policy outputs has scarcely run its course a century after Appomattox.

2. *The Clash between "Community" and "Society."* This cleavage, like the sectionalism with which it has some relationship on the national level, can in a sense be traced back to the controversies between the Hamiltonians and the Virginia agrarian school in the infancy of the republic. But it becomes particularly significant in the industrializing and post-industrializing eras of our history.... Between 1880 and 1920 a substantial portion of our industrializing elites and their supporters were pitted against the parties themselves. Whatever may have been the parties' contributions to centralized policy-formation prior to the industrial takeover, after the end of Reconstruction the parties became bulwarks of localist resistance to the forced-draft change initiated by cosmopolitan elites. Thus was born a tradition of hostility to the political party as such, with an associated theme which emphasized that political centralization at any level in the system required the displacement rather than the further development of the political party as an instrument of popular government. This anti-partisan tradition of the Progressive Era, and the power shifts which developed from it at the local level, were both in profound harmony with the dominant function of the alignment system of 1896 to 1932: the insulation of industrial elites from the threat of effective, popularly based "counterrevolution." The persistence of this tradition and its consequences has undoubtedly made a significant contribution to the truncating of American party development during this century.

Viewed somewhat more broadly, this local–cosmopolitan cleavage may also be related to a larger regional phenomenon in post–Civil War America. This is the ongoing conflict between the Northeastern metropole on one hand and the Southern and Western regions, which stood in a quasicolonial relationship to the metropole, on the other.[13] William Jennings Bryan, as H. L. Mencken sarcastically noted, was the political evangelist of white Anglo-Saxon provincial "locals" who were in revolt against "their betters"—by which Mencken meant metropole cosmopolitans like himself.[14] After the shattering blow which fell upon the Democratic party in the Northeast during the 1890's, the Democratic party became to a substantial extent the party of the "locals" or the community-oriented, while the G.O.P.—especially in its Bull Moose wing—tended to become the dominant partisan vehicle of the "cosmopolitans" or the society-oriented.[15] This helped, no doubt, to reinforce the persistent Republican charge, which was re-

---

[13] An excellent statement of the case from a self-consciously colonial point of view is Walter Prescott Webb, *Divided We Stand* (New York, 1937).
[14] H. L. Mencken, "In Memoriam: W. J. B.," in Alistair Cooke (ed.), *The Vintage Mencken* (New York, 1959), 161–7.
[15] The *locus classicus* here, on the level of the Progressive intellectual, is surely Herbert Croly, *The Promise of American Life* (New York, 1909).

iterated down through the 1930's, that the Democratic party was incompetent to govern in an industrial society. Many of the urban "locals"—the working-class elements who were deliberately bypassed by Progressive-era reform in local government—supported this Republican position, at least at the presidential level, by their votes. That they did so probably reflects their memory of the "Democratic depression" of 1893–97, as well as their ethno-cultural hostility to the Bryan crusade and its clienteles. It is possible that this support may also have been a manifestation of "working-class imperialism" akin to the support which Disraeli and his Conservative party successors enjoyed in England during the last third of the nineteenth century. By the beginning decades of the twentieth century the differential in economic development between the Northeast and the rest of the country had become enormous; to a greater or lesser extent most politically active groups in the metropole shared in its relative affluence.

Nor has intersectional antagonism disappeared as a force in contemporary American politics since, even though regional differentials in economic development have been severely eroded since World War II. While the terms of the political discourse involved have shifted beyond recognition, at the bottom of this antagonism may well be an ongoing "community" resistance—which still tends to be geographically concentrated—to massive, centrally directed social change. It seems reasonable to suppose that both the growth of a doctrinaire Right and the contemporary conflicts between the executive and Congress can be at least partially explained in terms of this community-society continuum.

3. *The Clash of Ethno-Cultural Groups.* It is by now axiomatic that the diversity of ethnic origins in the American melting pot has been basic to American political alignments since the creation of the first party system in the 1790's. There appears to be a curiously circular relationship between ethnic diversity and the limited role which class alignments have played in the history of American politics. On one hand, as Benson argues, the American liberal value consensus on such fundamentals as economic and church–state relationships helped make possible a full articulation of ethno-cultural antagonisms in party politics at a remarkably early date.[16] On the other hand, however, the very existence of ethnic fragmentation—especially after the "new immigration" of 1882–1914 added novel elements to the American melting pot—severely inhibited the formation even of mass trade unions, and was instrumental in preventing the emergence of socialism as a major political force.

In the Northeast, for example, lines of class and ethnic division tended to coincide during and after the era of industrialization. Most of the middle classes in such centers as New York, Boston, and Philadelphia were of old-stock Protestant background, while many of the working-class elements were relatively recent arrivals with wholly different cultural traditions. But if class and ethnic lines tended to coincide in the conurbations, the lower classes were also enor-

---

[16] Benson, *The Concept of Jacksonian Democracy*, 165–207.

mously internally fragmented along ethnic lines. Some groups, such as the Jews of Manhattan and the Germans of Milwaukee, had cultural traditions which favored the growth of socialist movements among them.[17] Groups such as these, coupled with certain radical native-stock farm elements in the colonial regions of the country, gave the American Socialist party most of such vitality as it possessed at its apogee around 1912. But most of the "new immigrant" groups came from a European stratum, the peasantry, which had no counterpart in the social experience of most other Americans. Such groups required the most extensive acculturation simply to come to terms with urban-industrial existence as such, much less to enter the party system as relatively independent actors.

It is hardly surprising, consequently, that the typical American form of urban political organization during and after the industrializing era was the non-programmatic, patronage-fueled urban machine rather than the disciplined, programmatic Leftist party of the type which was emerging in European conurbations during the same historical period. As Robert K. Merton's pioneering analysis has made clear, the urban machine developed as an unofficial means of concentrating political power in an official context of power dispersion.[18] Its functions, at least on the latent level, were overwhelmingly integrative. For the lower strata, in return for their votes, it provided a considerable measure of primitive welfare functions, personalized help for individuals caught up in the toils of the law, and political socialization. For business elements it provided a helpful structure of centralized decision-making in areas of vital concern to them. Of the classical urban political machine it may be said, first, that it provided services for which there was a persistent social demand and which no other institution was capable of providing; and second, that the extraordinary fragmentation and lack of acculturation among its mass clientele ensured its preoccupation with ethnic-coalition politics to the virtual exclusion of class politics.

Here, as elsewhere in the study of American political cleavages and organizational structures, there appears to be an inverse relationship between the integrative or "constituent" functions of parties and their policy-making or government-control functions. If the social context in which a two-party system operates is extensively fragmented along regional, ethnic, and other lines, its major components will tend to be overwhelmingly concerned with coalition-building and internal conflict management. The need to unite for electoral purposes presupposes a corresponding need to generate consensus at whatever level such consensus can be found. Surely, at the primordial level, the American liberal consensus in its various nuances provides a framework for party action. Yet this essentially middle-class frame of reference and the feebleness of social solidarities

---

[17] See e.g. Lawrence Fuchs, *The Political Behavior of American Jews* (Glencoe, 1956). To this day Jewish voters are very atypically Democratic (or "Leftist") at levels of socio-economic status where substantial Republican strength is normally encountered in other population groups. Angus Campbell *et al.*, *The American Voter* (New York, 1960), 302, 306.

[18] Robert K. Merton, *Social Theory and Social Structure* (Glencoe, 1957), 72–82.

above the level of the primordial have worked together throughout our history to exclude programmatic politics—or programmatic parties—from the mainstream of American political development. More than a decade ago Samuel Lubell argued that the major task of American politics was that of building a nation out of a congeries of regions and peoples.[19] So long as that task remains unfinished, there is little reason to suppose that our major parties will break out of the mold in which they were cast during the generative years of the second party system.

. . .

[In addition, our party system may be] undergoing extensive atrophy because so many of its functions are being performed by other agencies. At the bottom of such a development are certain rather obvious but momentous changes in American life. In the first place, a continually increasing majority of the active American electorate has moved above the poverty line. Most of this electorate is no longer bound to party through the time-honored links of patronage and the machine. Indeed, for a large number of people, politics appears to have the character of an item of luxury consumption in competition with other such items, an indoor sport involving a host of discrete players rather than the teams of old. Connected with this tendency toward depoliticization is clearly a second factor: the extraordinarily complex and technical character of many key political issues as these become translated into concrete proposals for action and policy decisions. In such an intricate political environment, partisan cues to the public are perhaps less relevant than in an age of fewer and broader political issues. In a sense, this may be considered to involve an extension of the principles of civil service to the substance of policy: as there is said to be no Democratic or Republican way to run an agency, so it often appears—whether accurately or not—that there is no Democratic or Republican way to solve highly complex policy problems.

The third and most significant of all these changes has been the international emergence of the United States as an *imperium* in fact, if not in rhetoric or intent. This development has many profound implications for the subordinate role of the political party in the broader decision-making system. Two of these raise particularly serious questions of relevance. In the first place, as is well known, in the United States the making of foreign-policy and military decisions is the province of a bipartisan elite drawn from the executive establishment and from private industry. It is not the province of the political parties, and it is not normally capable of being structured into a cluster of issues on which the parties are opposed and between which the voters can choose. Since these decisions involve the expenditure of between three-fifths and three-quarters of the current federal administrative budget, depending upon which items are included, it is not inaccurate to say that most of the present-day activities of the federal govern-

---

[19] Samuel Lubell, *The Future of American Politics* (New York, 1952), 245–61; and Lubell, *White and Black* (New York, 1964), 153–74.

ment lie quite outside of areas in which parties can make any positive contributions to the political system. Second, the compartmentalization between foreign defense policies and domestic affairs which used to exist has increasingly dissolved since World War II. The nonpartisan military–foreign affairs sector has come more and more to infiltrate the world of domestic politics and nominally domestic or private activities. Since this growing sector involves areas far removed indeed in complexity and remoteness from the lives of the voters, and consequently tends to escape even the forms of democratic control, its infiltration of the domestic scene suggests a growing restriction of the scope of effective party activity even there.

At the outset it was argued that this country has had a common middle-class, liberal political culture. Even though the absolutism of its assumptions has been brought into serious question in recent decades, the social center of gravity of the active electorate and the structure and financing of our parties have produced elective and appointive elites who have tended not to question the postulates of our traditional liberal absolutism. As the American cultural fragment has rejoined the world, it has been confronted by the most serious challenges to both the relevance and validity of the economic and poiltical values which had so often been assumed to be "givens" in this country. What are the implications of this for the future of American party politics?

On the whole, the outlook is not reassuring. The socialist phase of historical development, and thus of party organization and development, is clearly a thing of the past all over the Western world. Whether for good or for ill, it was a phase through which American party organization never passed. Largely as a consequence of the failure of collectively based vehicles of mass political mobilization to develop here, American major parties have never performed most of the ranges of educative or policy-making functions in any sustained or systematic way. They are most unlikely to begin doing so now. Moreover, as we have indicated, there are large and rapidly growing areas of contemporary public policy from which they—and hence the public at large—have been effectively excluded.

It would clearly be a radical oversimplification, of course, to assert that the parties have been reduced solely to the office-filling function. There is, for example, no hard evidence that the parties have lost their constituent function. . . . Nor—as any examination of congressional roll calls in recent years makes clear —can it be said that policy differences between Republicans and Democrats are unimportant, much less that such differences do not exist. In the aftermath of the election of 1964, it would be particularly misleading to discount overmuch the very great salience which the political party continues to display in American political life. All that is suggested here is that the relative weight of nonpartisan factors at the top decision-making levels of the American political system has increased substantially over the past generation, and that, granted the massive scope of American involvement in the rest of the world alone, these factors will probably continue to grow in importance. Partisan politics, in such a case, will tend to be confined to a narrowing—though not necessarily unimportant—range of activity.

In politics, as in architecture, form follows function. In an affluent, corporate, technologically complex America, an America whose national policy processes seem likely to be increasingly dominated by its external commitments, it may be asked what functions will be left for political parties to perform? The answer to this question is not at all clear. What does seem clear is that—in the future as in the recent past—the functions which the parties perform and the forms which they assume will be determined by the emergent needs of the broader social and political system, and not by the parties themselves.

SUGGESTIONS FOR FURTHER READING

A quite useful introduction to the development and techniques of the study of public opinion is Bernard Berelson and Morris Janowitz, *Reader in Public Opinion and Communication* (New York: Free Press, 1966); still useful is Herbert H. Hyman, *Survey Design and Analysis* (New York: Free Press, 1955). Excellent recent studies of the state of survey research techniques are John P. Robinson et al., *Measure of Political Attitudes* (Ann Arbor, Mich.: University of Michigan Institute for Social Research, 1968), and Charles H. Backstrom and Gerald D. Hursh, *Survey Research* (Evanston, Ill.: Northwestern University Press, 1963). The principal journal in this area is the *Public Opinion Quarterly*.

On American political parties the work of V. O. Key, Jr., is still preeminent. His *Southern Politics* (New York: Random House, 1965), originally published in 1949, stimulated much new work. The same is true of Key's *American State Politics* (New York: Knopf, 1956).

Some useful recent studies are Samuel Eldersveld's *Political Parties* (Chicago: Rand McNally, 1964) and Frank Sorauf's *Party Politics in America* (Boston: Little, Brown, 1968).

An interesting review of the work and opinions of political scientists is Judson L. James's *American Political Parties* (New York: Pegasus, 1969). Wilfred E. Binkley's *American Political Parties: Their Natural History* (New York: Knopf, 1962) remains the best short summary of party development.

The literature on electoral behavior is one of the richest in political science. The basic book remains Angus Campbell, Philip E. Converse, Warren E. Miller, and Donald E. Stokes, *The American Voter* (New York: Wiley, 1960); their collection, *Elections and the Political Order* (New York: Wiley, 1966), is also useful. Recent works that follow through on the achievement of the Campbell group include V. O. Key, Jr., and Milton C. Cummings, Jr., *The Responsible Electorate: Rationality in Presidential Voting, 1936–60* (Cambridge, Mass.: Harvard University Press, 1966), Donald R. Matthews and James W. Prothro,

Suggestions for Further Reading

Negroes and the New Southern Politics (New York: Harcourt Brace Jovanovich, 1966), and Gerald M. Pomper, *Elections in America: Control and Influence in Democratic Politics* (New York: Dodd, Mead, 1968).

Students should also take note of works on political participation and individual awareness of political efficacy; see Lester W. Milbrath, *Political Participation: How and Why Do People Get Involved in Politics?* (Chicago: Rand McNally, 1965), and Robert E. Lane, *Political Ideology* (New York: Free Press, 1962).

The *American Poiltical Science Review,* the *Journal of Politics,* and the *Midwest Journal of Political Science* are good sources for articles.

Finally, students might wish to examine Fred I. Greenstein's recent *Personality to Politics* (Chicago: Markham, 1969), an attempt to give coherence to the study of the relationship between the two.

5 Interest groups

IT UNDERSTATES THE POINT to say that much can be learned about American politics by studying the activities of interest groups. In fact, a good rule of political analysis is that whatever the issue that interests you—civil rights, water pollution, welfare—you cannot hope to understand how public policy is made unless you know what groups are active in the area and what they are doing.

Over the past forty years political scientists have devoted a great deal of time and resources to interest-group analysis, and this scholarly investment was necessary to compensate for a previous overconcentration on formal institutions and legal rules. Today we are so accustomed to thinking of interest groups as an important part of the political process that we should note that the first serious (that is, non-muckraking) study of the subject appeared only in 1908. This was Arthur F. Bentley's *The Process of Government*,[1] and its brilliantly suggestive quality stimulated a number of group-focused works in the interwar years.[2] However, it was with the publication in 1951 of David B. Truman's *The Governmental Process*[3] that group analysis came of age. Truman supplied a broader definition of the

---

[1] (Chicago: University of Chicago Press, 1908).
[2] Among the best were E. Pendleton Herring's *Group Representation Before Congress* (Baltimore: Johns Hopkins Press, 1929); Peter F. Odegard's *Pressure Politics: The Story of the Anti-Saloon League* (New York: Columbia University Press, 1928); and E. E. Schattschneider's *Politics, Pressures and the Tariff* (Englewood Cliffs, N. J.: Prentice-Hall, 1937).
[3] (New York: Knopf, 1951).

term "interest group" than had previous writers: "any group that, on the basis of one or more shared attitudes, makes certain claims upon other groups in the society for the establishment, maintenance, or enhancement of forms of behavior that are implied by the shared attitudes."[4] This definition broadened the field of investigation to include not only formal organizations but informal groups (for example, "China lobby" or "the country club crowd") and even governmental agencies when they are engaged in getting some other governmental actors to behave in a desired fashion. And Truman marshaled such a wealth of illustrative material as to stamp the pervasiveness and importance of interest groups indelibly on the consciousness of his colleagues.

We are all familiar with the more dramatic episodes of group influence, such as the National Rifle Association's opposition to gun control in the late 1960's and the American Medical Association's opposition to Medicare in the early 1960's. What is more important is the day-in-day-out communication between those who *rule* and those who serve as spokesmen for the various narrow concerns of those who *are ruled*. This continuing communication process is the subject of Lester W. Milbrath's careful, empirical study *The Washington Lobbyists*,[5] a major chapter of which appears as the first selection in this chapter.

But the decades of work by political scientists on interest groups produced something more than a description of the complicated ways in which groups are involved in public decision-making. A fair reading of the interest-group literature will reveal that political scientists, on the whole, have come to regard the involvement of private interests in the governmental process as good. They have been moving from a description of reality to a qualified endorsement of it. Groups, they have suggested, compete to influence governmental decisions, and they operate at many different points and levels in the governmental structure. The effects of this are to disperse and check public power, to broaden the base of political participation, and to supplement electoral politics. This formula calls to mind James Madison's classic *Federalist* Number Ten, and not without reason. Like Madison, modern political scientists regard the operations of large numbers of groups as a check against tyranny; if governmental power were concentrated in a single center, or even in a few centers, what would prevent these centers from coming under the domination of a narrow range of interests? This democracy-through-group-competition argument is generally attributed to Truman's *The Governmental Process*, but a close reading of that work reveals a number of amendments and qualifications that the author found it necessary to introduce.

First, there is the tendency for groups to be oligarchic. In even the most informal grouping, an "active minority" usually emerges, because of the continuing necessity of relatively informed choice. If the group is to function effectively in the political arena, someone has to be in a position to make decisions and to commit the group's resources—often in a hurry.

[4] *Ibid.*, p. 33.
[5] (Chicago: Rand McNally, 1963).

There simply is not enough time to hold meetings and to allow for time-consuming negotiations within the group. In highly organized groups, the professionals in the secretariat of the organization conduct all the business; they are in touch with allied interests; and they understand and handle the problems of the group in a way that members, who give only sporadic attention to group affairs, cannot. This active minority usually has the knowledge and skills necessary for group action. By the nature of their full-time positions or their willingness to do the dirty work of fund-raising and management, they become the principal decision-makers for the group.[6]

Second, there are many sectors of the American political system, at national, state, and local levels, where group competition never has existed or has broken down. In many instances we find single groups dominating whole areas of governmental activity. Douglass Cater, who observed this phenomenon at the national level in his deft little book *Power in Washington*,[7] called attention to "private subgovernments," or pockets of single-interest-group domination. Similarly, Robert Dahl, in *Who Governs?*,[8] his now classic study of the structure of political power in New Haven, Connecticut, portrayed a local setting in which influence over civic affairs, while not residing in any one group, was monopolized by particular groups in particular issue arenas. While there was no predominant oligarchy, neither was there much competition. Such multiple oligarchies produce decentralization to the extent that the dominant groups will protect their own fiefs, thereby fragmenting their influence, but they also constitute subcenters (or nodules) of unopposed power.

Third, Truman makes it quite clear that the resources for group combat are unequally distributed through the society. While it is intellectually slipshod to talk about an American "establishment," it is equally wrong to portray the system as tending toward an equilibrium in which a claim that is effectively advanced evokes an effective response. Some groups (those with money, talent, and high social status) win frequently, and other groups (those with the reverse attributes) lose frequently. But one-time losers can become winners, as happened in the past with labor groups and is happening today with Negro groups (although the process is painfully slow).

Fourth, and not greatly stressed by Truman, are the changes that are occurring in the structures of political interest groups as a result of changes in the social and economic environment. Put simply, large bureaucratic enterprises are responding to the needs of a suburban, highly mobile society and availing themselves of new techniques of communication and information manipulation; they are becoming the characteristic form of organization in America.[9] This does not mean that *all* groups will achieve the scale

---

[6] A useful supplement to Truman on this point is Mancur Olsen's *The Logic of Collective Action* (Cambridge, Mass.: Harvard University Press, 1965).
[7] (New York, Knopf, 1964).
[8] (New Haven, Conn.: Yale University Press, 1961).
[9] Excellent on this point is John Kenneth Galbraith, *The New Industrial State* (Boston: Houghton Mifflin, 1967).

of DuPont or the AFL–CIO or the American Bar Association. Most politically active groups will continue to be small and local. But it is now clear that while they will continue to exist, the myriad of small local groups will become less and less crucial in affecting the course of American public policy. Certainly there will always be local choices which local groups will influence; yet, with the most important allocations of public resources being made increasingly in Washington and in state capitals, the future would appear to belong to groups with national or regional bases and capacities for action. Big, centralized government and big, centralized groups reinforce one another.

While all these developments are consistent with the expectations of Truman and earlier group theorists, they are only now becoming apparent, and this had led to an assault on the conventional wisdom concerning the beneficent functions performed by interest groups. A number of political scientists have begun to question the propriety of extensive group involvement in the policy-making process, and to call for more government and less "bargaining" or "cooperating" by public officials. No one has argued this anti-pluralist position more persuasively than Theodore Lowi, whose warning on the dangers of group takeovers and decentralization is the second selection in this chapter.

The Impact of Lobbying on Governmental Decisions

LESTER W. MILBRATH

Perhaps the most difficult question about lobbying is that of the extent of its influence or impact on governmental decisions. No one has a definitive answer to that question. Yet an understanding of the influence of lobbying is essential to a full perspective on the topic. This study was not designed to measure the impact of lobbying and can offer only partial answers. Still, quite a number of observable facts contribute some enlightenment. Some have been alluded to previously. In this chapter, all findings relevant to the impact of lobbying will be reviewed to provide as broad a perspective as possible.

Inquiring about the influence of lobbying is not the same as inquiring about the influence of pressure groups. Admittedly, the factors are highly related, but they are not identical. Some lobbying is carried out on behalf of individuals or

FROM Lester W. Milbrath, *The Washington Lobbyists,* © 1963 by Rand McNally and Company, Chicago, pp. 328–58.

corporations as well as groups. On the other hand, some of the influence of pressure groups is not exerted through lobbying (using a special envoy at the seat of government) or lobbyists. It will not be necessary to maintain a clear distinction between lobbying and pressure groups, but the reader should be aware that the primary purpose of this chapter is to evaluate the influence of lobbying, not that of pressure groups.

SOME CHARACTERISTICS OF INFLUENCE

... Influence is not an absolute quantity of which an individual or an institution has a certain measurable amount. One can speak about influence in comparative terms (e.g., A has more influence than B) but even that can be done only with reference to a given issue or decision (B may have more influence than A on another decision). Influence, then, varies with the decisional setting, the roles of the actors, the diligence with which goals are pursued, and the tactics employed, as well as with the assets available to each contestant.

Second, influence does not automatically make itself felt; it must be exerted. Moreover, exertion entails some costs (time, money, attention, etc.) on the part of the influencer. The costs of exerting influence must be weighed relative to the value of the anticipated reward. ... Influence [has been viewed] as analogous to money; it is a scarce resource which can be saved, invested, and spent. Some political actors have more influence assets than others, but assets must be carefully managed to avoid influence bankruptcy. It is "rational" for political actors to try to maximize their influence just as it is "rational" for economic actors to maximize their monetary assets or gains.

Third, political influence is necessarily focused on the decisional processes of authoritative decision-makers (government officials). Influence can be achieved only by affecting the perceptions of officials (short of replacing one official by another), and it must be conveyed via some kind of communication.

The perceptions of the policy process held by the official decision-makers and the values they try to achieve are of central importance. The problems involved in measuring the perceptions and values of officials, even assuming they would remain constant enough to be measured, are so great that one can make only very general statements. Some generalizations [may be] made ... : (1) The basic goal of officials is to maintain and enhance their position; achieving a "good record" is usually essential to that. (2) Assuming position can be maintained, officials tend to decide policy questions in accordance with their political philosophy. (3) Motivations of friendship, having a good time, making money, and so forth will generally be of lesser importance than the first two.

One could push to a more abstract analysis of influence by dealing with such questions as free will versus determinism, but that would take us far afield. In the other direction, one could press for a more specific level of analysis, but that would require dealing with many specific issues and actors and would not readily lead to a general understanding of the process.

Because influence takes place only in the decisional process of human beings, it is extremely difficult to measure. Most humans could not report accurately, even if they sincerely desired to, the proportionate weight they assign to various influences as they make a decision. Influence is generally measured by some less direct method. . . . Three general ways to measure influence have been widely used: measuring attributed influence, measuring changes in opinions, and measuring interaction between actors. This study contains only measures of attributed influence and some measures of interaction between lobbyists and officials.

In this discussion of the influence of lobbying, three kinds of evidence relevant to the point will be presented. First is an analysis and pinpointing of where and how influence can be exerted; some supposed methods of influence fall by the wayside because they are too difficult or too costly to employ. For example, it is virtually impossible to steal or buy governmental decisions of any consequence in Washington. In seeking points at which influence may be exerted, it is relevant to examine the factors that officials consider as they make their decisions. Second is an analysis of lobbyists' evaluations of their personal success and the success of their organization and their selections of the most effective lobby organization in Washington; these are taken as partial evidence of attributed influence. Third, the influence of lobbying is compared to other forces also attempting to influence policy. Some lobbying cancels out other lobbying because groups oppose one another; some lobbying is simply overwhelmed by the power of non-lobbying forces.

FACTORS CONSIDERED BY OFFICIALS WHEN MAKING DECISIONS

. . . The pre-eminent motivation to maintain or enhance one's position is probably characteristic of both elected and appointed officials. However, for elected officials, it is oriented toward pleasing constituents; whereas for appointed officials, it probably is oriented toward following the directions of and attempting to please elected officials. This study has no data relevant to the latter generalization.

Congressional respondents were asked the following question:

Whenever a person must decide how he will vote on an issue or a bill, he must take several factors into account, such as: the wishes of his constituents, the views of interest groups, the recommendations of his colleagues and friends, and his personal feelings. Which of these kinds of factors are uppermost in your mind as you arrive at your decisions?

The Impact of Lobbying on Governmental Decisions

Members gave complicated and varied answers reflecting different backgrounds and different situations. Before discussing each factor more fully, some quotations from members will point up the complexity of the interrelationships:

> That is the sixty-four-dollar question to ask a member of Congress. I think it varies. If it is a question which affects the national security, why I invariably vote the way the best information for me indicates I should vote regardless of the constituents.

> I take them all into account, but I almost always vote the way I personally decide. I don't make this decision naïvely, by the way. My own view is that it is good politics to take a personal position, and that is the way representative government should function. However, it is not as simple and clear-cut as that. Many times you may see an issue very clearly at the beginning of a session, and you know how you are going to stand on that issue, but by the time you get to the end of the session, it may become confused because there are so many compromises and changes. You wonder if the problem is being evaded and how you should really stand on it. . . . I would say by and large I have a view of my own before I am approached by an interest group. The lobbyist may bring me the first information on a "cat and dog bill"; those are bills without much consequence for the public. I don't remember a time when a position I had was changed by a contact. I do recall making at least one recognizable mistake each year I have been in Congress. The only one that ever upset me was one time when I voted on both sides of an issue; I voted for the bill and then voted to sustain the President's veto. I tried to explain it to the people in the next campaign and discovered it had no effect on my election; since then I haven't been too worried about making a mistake once in a while.

> You haven't listed the most important one—that is, the merits of the legislation. There is an interaction in the mind of the legislator which considers all those factors. The attitude of every member is influenced by his over-all background and the nature of his constituency. Members are either born economizers or born spenders, and this is influenced by the nature of his constituency. Most members are more or less predisposed toward an issue before they get to it. We take a pretty common sense approach to the views of interest groups: Are they selfish or unselfish? How does opinion run in one's district? Is there undue advocacy or undue advantage? How the views are presented is a lesser factor but still a factor.

> Your first claim is to your district or you won't be here next time. Second comes the desires of the President; I am his leader in the House, and I wouldn't desert the President or the aims of the administration unless there were a mighty weighty reason. I am a member of the team, and this is uppermost in my mind on most questions. I don't take the views of interest groups too seriously. Actually, I don't get too much pressure; I have a very good district in that respect. Maybe it is because I have been here thirty years; they know what to expect. Either they have confidence that I will do the right thing, or they figure it is hopeless—either way I don't get a lot of letters.

> The number one factor is that you make sure it doesn't adversely affect the people you represent. If it doesn't hurt your people or you feel it might be good for them,

INTEREST GROUPS 130

you also try to weigh the public or the national interest and try to decide what the legislation will do over a long pull. If you decide it is a good bill and it is lasting, why this is a very persuasive factor in one's decision. What your colleagues think about an issue or a bill doesn't enter into your decision. All of these people have their own problems, and just because one guy is in favor of a bill doesn't mean you should be. He may have different problems with his constituency. What shall it profiteth a man if he vote to save the country and lose his own seat? . . . I do discuss certain problems with other members; these are men I have come to know and trust over the years.

It can be seen from the quotations that the wishes of a member's constituents are an omnipresent factor, and, in a broad sense, they are decisive. The desires of constituents might be conceived of as boundaries beyond which a member dare not step without suffering dire consequences. These boundaries might be very wide on certain questions and very narrow on others. If a constituency is vitally interested in a question—for example that of segregation (for a southern district)—the boundaries are very tight, and the representative can take only one action if he hopes to be re-elected. The folkways of the Congress recognize these restrictions, and a member who breaks with the leadership to please his constituency on such a tight matter will be forgiven. If a constituency is not so vitally interested, the boundaries are broader, and on some questions there are no boundaries at all. Lobbying has greater opportunities for influence when the constituency is not very interested and the decision-maker has greater decision latitude. If the constituents are interested and aware, their desires are undoubtedly the most important factor. A congressman put it this way:

Well, of course the views of the constituents are always uppermost in the politician's mind. We jokingly make a distinction between a politician and a statesman, but we are all politicians, too. As statesmen, we are delegated to represent not only the views of our constituents but also their best interests. If we could count on the people being properly informed, well then, their views would be all that is necessary, but unfortunately that cannot always be counted on. When you come up here they expect you to study and advise them, and I try to do so. I lead them a little bit, but in the end, their views tend to be uppermost.

A clerk for a congressional committee said:

If I had to select one as the most important day-in-and-day-out, I would say it is the appraisal of the member of what his constituents think. He may not know what his constituents think; he has no really good measure; but it is what he thinks they think that is important. Even if he believes his constituency is not too interested in a bill, he may try to parlay his vote on that bill into an advantage for him in his constituency on some other kind of issue. Ninety-nine per cent of the money spent on lobbying falls short because it ignores that fact. . . . To the extent lobbying can influence public opinion, it has some impact because voter reaction is the most important thing in Congress.

Most lobbyists also recognize the predominating influence of voter desires:

> Most of what happens in the legislative area is at least 80 per cent determined on the day of election; in addition, much of the legislative activity throughout a session of Congress is actually a setting of the stage for the next election. It is impossible for a lobbyist "to make a silk purse out of a sow's ear." . . . You do not change a member of Congress by buying him or browbeating him or otherwise attempting to change him.

The smart lobbyist tries to demonstrate to a member that following a particular course of action will help him in his constituency. The member usually listens attentively to such information, but he also learns that he must view claims of constituency support with some skepticism. Reliable information about constituent desires is difficult to obtain. The leaders of large membership organizations generally claim that they speak for all their members, but this is a claim they can hardly substantiate.

> You can't be a public official without having considerable knowledge in your own right, and you learn to discount what these groups say. I come from a farm district, and it makes a difference if the Farm Bureau is for or against a piece of legislation. But I have learned that the top people in these organizations often have views that are different from their members down below who are my constituents; therefore, I discount what they say a little.

Following constituent desires too closely can be harmful in certain cases. Constituents generally do not and cannot follow the development of information and arguments on an issue. The complexion of the issue may change, and the available alternatives may shift to such an extent that constituent desires provide little or no guidance. Many members also take the traditional Burkean perspective that constituents really elect a man's judgment and that it is proper to vote according to their own judgment even if it goes against the desires of the constituents. Members report that they feel compelled on occasion to vote against their constituents, especially if they believe it is for the good of the country:

> It so happens that practically all of my votes are the way that the prevailing opinion is in my district. This is probably because my own philosophy of government is the same as that of the people in my district. However, there are times when we differ, and in such cases I vote the way my best judgment indicates. In the long run, this is in the interests of the people, and they do have an opportunity to express approval or disapproval at the next election. The Lend-Lease and defense acts early in World War II were opposed by 75 per cent of the people in my district; yet I voted for every one of them and in so doing I was performing my representative function.

> There are two types of issues. When it doesn't involve a profound decision or doesn't strongly affect the government or there will be no great disparity in cost, I

give the weight to what the people feel strongly about. There are other kinds of decisions that are weighty and will affect the security or solvency of the country. On those kind your own convictions are dominant. The people are very understanding even if you go against their wishes. If you frankly tell them that it wasn't wise for the country, they are not going to turn against you. You can try to educate them, but generally you can't make them change their mind. They may still be against you, but they will realize there are two sides to the question, and they will not turn against you.

If boundaries set by the constituents on an issue have left some decision latitude to the member, the next most important factor is likely to be his personal convictions about the issue. Most members have a long-established political philosophy which guides their decisions. Through their political philosophy they "know" what is good and bad for the country and the people. Furthermore, a man who has served in public office for some time has had to take a stand on most issues in the past. A prior stand tends to freeze his current position. A change from a past position can easily be interpreted as a tacit admission that the prior position was incorrect or possibly that undue influence was used.

. . .

It is important to keep in mind that simple "yeas" or "nays" are not the only alternatives open to a member when an issue is up for decision. A wide range of actions is possible—from campaigning on the issue, to mere voting, to abstaining. [One writer has] diagrammed nine alternative positions that a member might take on an issue. Most lobbying effort, then, is aimed not at conversion but at activating the favorable member or at least at ensuring that he remains committed and votes "correctly."

Every public official is interested in making a "good record." A "good record" is instrumental in maintaining and enhancing his position. It brings increased influence, which is important to all public officials. Further, when an official pursues policies that fulfill his political philosophy, he thinks that he is making a "good record"; this is important in satisfying his ego needs (his conception of himself). But no public official can make a "good record" by himself. He must have the cooperation of other officials. To obtain this cooperation, he must be prepared to bargain and must learn to play as a "member of the team." Former Speaker Rayburn is reputed to have said, "The way to get along is to go along."

The organization of a majority to get a bill passed requires some minimum amount of discipline and compromise. Once the "team" position on a given piece of legislation has emerged, the pressures for the members of the team to "go along" become rather intense. Failure to "go along" lowers one's standing within the team and lessens one's chances for advancement in the system; it may even result in negative sanctions such as withdrawal of campaign support or loss of preferred committee assignments, although Congress is generally reluctant to apply such severe sanctions. The major penalty for not playing as a member of the team is loss of reputation or standing, which provide influence or power. Certain members can be characterized as very powerful; their power generally derives from the respect they have gained from their fellow members as they have played by the rules on the team over the years. A non-team player never gains that respect and influence.

When a member's political party holds the Presidency, his team grows to include the presidential office and even the executive departments. His leader becomes the President, and much of the policy initiative flows from that quarter. Presidential and departmental recommendations become important influences on his voting decisions. These recommendations are backed by superior information and research as well as all of the influences associated with the team effort.

Officials cannot avoid making decisions though they generally must make them on the basis of somewhat imperfect information. To fill the gap, they usually welcome or actively seek out information. The need for facts provides lobbyists with their best opportunity to influence decisions. But even here, lobbyists must compete with many other sources of information and advice. Information and recommendations of colleagues are very important in this process. Officials are inclined to accept information and advice from a colleague if they respect his integrity and wisdom and believe that he has superior knowledge. The complexity of modern legislation and the norms of the institution encourage members to develop knowledge in depth in only a few legislative subjects. In subjects about which they are not so well informed, members lean heavily on committee recommendations or on the advice of a member of the relevant committee.

Informal circles of friends with similar political philosophies spring up in Congress. Information on forthcoming developments is exchanged within them. Respect for one another's specialties within such a circle can be so great that the recommendation of the specialist in a certain policy area can determine the votes of the entire friendship circle. One lobbyist said that at the time when he was a member of Congress he belonged to a circle of friends with similar political philosophies. Each member of the group served on a different committee, and they met weekly at lunch to report to one another on developments in their respective committees. Asked if he accepted the recommendations of his colleagues without further investigation, the respondent rocked back in his chair, thought for a full minute, and then said quite decisively, "Yes, by God, I did."

Staff assistants to decision-makers also exercise an important influence on the information and advice accepted by officials. Staffs not only process incoming information, they also take the initiative in digging out information. Staff persons are appointed by their superiors and are supposed to be alter egos for them, but since staff members are individuals, they may have some political convictions which intrude into the performance of their tasks. It is impossible to say with any precision how much decision-makers lean on their staffs; some are probably much more dependent than others. Dependence on staff recommendations probably increases if decisions involve technical or specialized questions and as decision-makers become more rushed.

Since officials have several alternative sources for information and advice, it is difficult to measure how effective lobbyist messages are. . . . Officials do attend to lobbying information; they welcome it even if they do not feel very dependent on it. A rough indication of the value decision-makers place upon messages from lobbyists also can be derived from answers to the question of how often decision-makers come to lobbyists for information and advice.

The table shows how often lobbyists have been solicited for their views and

TABLE 1 Decision-Makers' Solicitation of Policy Views from Lobbyists.

Type of Views Solicited	Never	2 times a year or less	3–10 times a year	11–25 times a year	On-going activity	No response	Total
None	24%						24
Inquiry confined to organizational views or information		13	25	15	8		61
Wide range of issues		2	2	3	3		10
Confidential conversations					3		3
No response		1	1			14	16
Total	24	16	28	18	14	14	114

the kind of views sought. Twenty-four per cent report that they have never been solicited; 44 per cent say it has happened no more than ten times a year; 18 per cent say it occurred eleven to twenty-five times a year; and 14 per cent say it has been continual. Most lobbyists report that communications initiated by decision-makers are confined to requests for information to which the lobby organization has unique access or to views on issues on which the organization has strong and established opinions. A prime aim of most lobbyists is to develop confidential relationships with decision-makers which will provide regular opportunities to exert influence. These data suggest that no more than 10 per cent of the lobbyists achieve this with even one official; only 9 per cent are consulted frequently on a wide range of policy issues. There is no evidence in this table that lobbying messages are widely sought after by decision-makers.

The representatives of large organizations with considerable power at the polls, such as labor and farm groups, report being solicited for their views more often than other lobbyists. This again reflects the power of the constituents; the stand of an organization with power at the polls may be important information when an official is making a decision. Organizational executives and officers who are the spokesmen for their organizations are solicited more often for their views than lobbyists in other roles. Lawyers in private practice are seldom solicited. Lobbyists who have previously had confidential relationships with decision-makers tend to carry part of that confidence over to their new role; former office-holders, those with Hill experience, and those who are very active in groups, tend to be solicited more frequently. Political activity also seems to be rewarded by increased solicitation of one's views; political contributors, especially political fund-raisers, are solicited more than those who do not so participate.

These data do not precisely indicate the extent to which lobbyists are heard. However, where lobby groups have useful information, it is heeded; and when their stand has important political implications, it is heeded. But we must also say that many lobby messages fall on deaf ears. Decision-makers occasionally seek information and advice from lobbyists, but very few of these interchanges are on a confidential and wide-ranging basis. Very few lobbyists report, and none of the congressional respondents report, having such confidential relationships.

Looking back now on the factors that decision-makers consider as they make their decisions, we can more clearly evaluate the range of lobbying influence by inquiring into the probability that lobbying or lobbyists can affect these factors. Lobbyists and lobby groups have a very limited ability to control the selection of officials or to affect the likelihood that an official can keep or enhance his position. . . . Lobbyists and lobby groups are reluctant to become involved in partisan politics. They also find it difficult and very expensive to try to manipulate public opinion; many of them have great difficulty manipulating even the opinion of their own membership. This is not the same as saying that groups have little influence on politics; they obviously do have considerable influence; however, the influence of groups is derived from the fact that members of groups are citizens and the political system is designed to respond to the influence of their votes.

In similar vein, lobbyists and the leaders of lobby groups cannot, by themselves, make an official look good or bad. They have little to say about whether an official makes a "good record" or not. They can, of course, offer support to or oppose an official, and that may have some little impact on his public image; but they do not have votes on bills that they can use to bargain with officials in the way officials bargain for one another's votes. They are not members of the team and do not have team norms and sanctions to use to control the behavior of officials. They have little or no success in changing the political philosophies of officials. Even their impact from supplying information and suggested policy alternatives to officials is diluted by the many alternative sources officials have for information and ideas.

The kinds of rewards and punishments that lobbyists are in the best position to offer have relatively low priority for the officials. It has been shown that entertainment and parties are not even considered a reward by most officials. Favors and bribes are not highly valued and are considered very dangerous by both officials and lobbyists. Lobbyists do have a kind of nuisance impact. They can make life somewhat unpleasant for officials who do not go along with them: It is embarrassing to vote against someone who is watching; it is difficult to vote against a group that has sent six thousand letters; it is hard not to listen to someone who is very persistent; it is hard to stand up to scorn by the public media. On small matters these nuisance factors may have considerable impact; they may even be decisive; but on matters of large public import such factors are rarely, if ever, of any great importance.

It has been suggested that the impact of lobbying on governmental decisions varies with the nature of the issue. On broad political issues commanding considerable public attention, the major determinant is the desire of the public. Lobbyists can do very little to affect the outcome, though they may influence the details of the bill or the specific language of small sections. If the legislation is specialized and affects only a small segment of the population, lobbyists are more likely to play a larger role. A member of the Ways and Means Committee of the House told a story about representatives of two large whiskey distilleries who came before the committee to argue about when the tax on whiskey should become due and payable. Each was seeking a competitive advantage over the other. There was no governmental or public interest to be served or disserved. The issue received no attention in the press. The committee listened quietly to the pleas from both sides and then made its decision (handed down its judgment). Lobbying may have been important on this bill, but was the bill really important?[1]

. . .

THE BALANCE OF POWER IN LOBBYING

An important factor attenuating the impact of lobbying on governmental decisions is the fact that nearly every vigorous push in one direction stimulates an opponent or coalition of opponents to push in the opposite direction. This natural self-balancing factor comes into play so often that it almost amounts to a law. The great numbers of lobbyists in Washington may actually be a blessing instead of a threat to the governmental system. When groups push on both sides

---

[1] [One writer], speaking of his own study of pressure groups, said, "In a nutshell, the study suggests (to me, at any rate) that the influence of private groups is greatest when, from the standpoint of democratic values, it matters least whether it is great or small."

of an issue, officials can more freely exercise their judgment than when the groups push on only one side.

The theory that countervailing power will cancel out some of the one-sided strength and evil effects of lobbying is an old one in Washington and is criticized vigorously by some persons. One criticism is that certain interests, such as consumers, have no one to represent them and that, therefore, any pressure against the welfare of these weakly organized interests is not resisted adequately. Although there is some truth to that criticism, the point is often overstressed. From time to time, consumer representatives are placed on boards and other decision-making bodies. More important, consumers, and any other poorly organized group, have a voice through constituent pressures and the vote. In addition, it is common for one of the organized interests to have an interest coinciding with unorganized interests. For example, in the struggle over the tariff, the direct interest of the consumer is in free trade; the goods he purchases will be cheaper. Every time tariff decisions must be made, some organized interests lobby vigorously in favor of free trade.

A more telling criticism of the theory of countervailing power is that there is some danger that such an overwhelming coalition of groups may be organized on one side of an issue that the beneficial effect of competition may be outweighed by the irresistible force of combination. This criticism can be overemphasized, too. If an overwhelming combination of powerful groups were on one side of an issue, the public would probably also favor that side of the issue. In such a case, the outcome would be completely in accord with our beliefs about how the political process should work. If the public were not behind the coalition of groups, the decision-makers would have sufficient public support to decide without being irresistibly influenced by the coalition.

When thinking about the theory of countervailing power, it is important not to think of decision-makers as inanimate objects which are manipulated by group pressures. Officials have beliefs and values of their own which are important guides to their decisions. The group or coalition with the greatest numbers, or the most money, or the loudest noise will not necessarily prevail, especially if their prevailing is not in the public or national interest. As we saw above, the pressures of groups are but one of the factors considered by decision-makers— and by no means the most important one.

Another false notion in thinking about the impact of lobbying is the condemnation of all pressure as bad. It is a fact that life, especially organized community life, does not exist without pressure of one kind or another. Pressure is effective when it is backed by sanctions. The sanction with the greatest impact on the public official is the decision of the voters to support him or not. Every vote is a unit of pressure on a representative. Every communication from a constituent to his representative is a pressure. Our political system was designed to register those pressures, and we consider it proper when public officials respond to them.

All other forms of pressure derive meaning only as they are converted into voter pressure. If a lobby group can use money and other resources to convince the body politic that a certain policy should be followed, that conviction will be registered in pressure at the polls, and it will be proper for the system to respond to that pressure. We would not, in fact, want public officials who were insensitive to pressures at the polls. The only feasible and legitimate way to counteract political pressures is to form opposing groups and to try to convince the public that the original pressure group is wrong. If a group can sway the body politic, that is exactly what our system responds to and should reward.

• • •

THE CONTRIBUTIONS OF LOBBYING

Eckstein raises the most fundamental question about lobbying and pressure groups: "What contributions do pressure groups make to the political system as a whole, and do these contributions tend to make the system more or less viable (stable and effective)? Are their consequences 'dysfunctional' or 'eufunctional' for the larger systems in which they operate?"[2] Though this study focuses on lobbying rather than pressure groups, the question is essentially the same; however, the contribution of these data to an answer is relatively limited.

In this context it is relevant to point out again that lobbying is inevitable and is likely to grow in scope. One lobbyist says it is analogous to automobile drivers: there are a few bad drivers, but people continue to drive, and more cars are added to the road each year. Lobbying is protected by the First Amendment to the Constitution, and government officials are not disposed to hamper its growth or activities.

Granted the inevitability of lobbying, what are its positive contributions to the political process? Lobbyists provide information and other sevices which are welcomed by governmental decision-makers. These services are costly and somewhat wasteful; the public or the consumer pays for them ultimately; congressional officials even claim they could function quite adequately without them. In another sense, however, they are indispensable. If information from lobbyists and lobby groups was, for some reason, unavailable to government officials, they would be largely dependent on their own staff for information and ideas. Since the Congress is reluctant to staff itself adequately, it would have to turn primarily to the Executive for information. This would create an even futher imbalance between Congress and the Executive in policy-making. More important, cutting off lobbying communications would eliminate a valuable, even indispensable, source of creativity. There is no assurance that government institutions can turn up all the possible alternative solutions to policy problems. A decision-maker who has his mind made up may well have to have new points of view forcefully thrust upon him before he can perceive and

[2] [Harry Eckstein, *Pressure Group Politics* (Stanford, Calif.: Stanford University Press, 1960), p. 152.]

accept them. The clash of viewpoints between contesting groups is not only informative; it also is creative. Formerly unperceived alternatives may arise from the challenge to previously accepted possibilities.

Eckstein . . . suggests that lobby groups perform two other indispensable functions in the political system: integration and disjunction. Officials must know very specifically what the effects of a given policy will be and how citizens will react to that policy. Lobby groups and lobbyists define opinion for government with a sense of reality and specificity which political parties, the mass media, opinion polls, and staff assistants seldom, if ever, can achieve. Aggregating and defining specialized opinions have both integrative and disjunctive aspects. The function is integrative in that persons with special interests or problems need group action to aggregate their views and communicate the positions to officials. The aggregation process requires some compromise on the part of group members and therefore is integrative. Group opinion is a more manageable consideration for officials than scattered individual opinions.

Specialized opinion is disjunctive as well, in that it encourages multiple group demands. Political parties (especially in a two-party system) strive for a very broad integration in order to win elections. That kind of integration can be achieved only by reaching a very low and vague denominator which may not be very functional for making policy. If special interests were confined to vague representation through political parties, they might begin to feel alienated from a political system which persistently distorts their goals. Affording disparate interests special representation through their own lobby group probably contributes to the stability of the system. There is reason to suppose, then, that the policy-making system produces wiser or more intelligent decisions and functions with more stability than might be the case if lobby groups and lobbyists were not present. If we had no lobby groups and lobbyists we would probably have to invent them to improve the functioning of the system.

Groups and the Problem of Governing

THEODORE LOWI

Americans are by tradition, habit, culture, and ideology fearful of power. Yet they see power only in certain places and not in others. They are prepared to

FROM Theodore Lowi, "Decentralization—To Whom? For What?" *Midway,* Vol. 9, No. 3 (Winter 1969), pp. 45–57. © 1969 The University of Chicago Press.

defend themselves against certain kinds of power, but against other kinds of power they provide themselves with no safeguards whatsoever. The primary source of power to Americans—and therefore the direction against which they orient their safeguards—is the state. For more than a century after its founding, the Constitution of the United States was written and interpreted so as to prevent as effectively as possible the development of a strong state. The very word itself tended to be replaced with such euphemisms as "government," "the public sector," and so on, as if to avoid development of undue respect toward *l'état*.

Eventually *l'état* did expand, so that by the middle of the twentieth century the "public sector" equaled in proportionate size that of any of the western European and Commonwealth democracies. But even after the expansion the Americans never ceased worrying about it. Each stage in government expansion came only after lengthy and elaborate constitutional debates in Congress and in the courts. Moreover, each expansion of government power was accompanied by expansions in the mechanisms of representation. The first expansions of Federal power, between 1888 and 1892 and between 1910 and 1914, were accompanied by spectacular social movements—populism and progressivism—each of which was strongly oriented toward enhanced representation. Their goals included congressional reform, direct election of senators, reform in methods of nominating candidates for public office, adoption of the "secret ballot," and so on. Further expansions of government before and during the period of Woodrow Wilson were accompanied by further dramatic reforms in Congress, amending the Constitution to admit female suffrage, drastic reforms in the system of balloting, and major reforms in the structure of local government. During the Roosevelt period, the doctrine of "interest representation" became a dominating force in American political thought. The corporativistic structure of the famous National Recovery Administration (NRA) is but one small example of the effort of political leaders to extend representation as a safeguard against the extension of the state. Since Roosevelt, the expansion of the state has been regular rather than by revolution; and since that time, the expansion of representative devices has been equally regular. Interest representation continues to be seriously demanded in the United States even as demands for it are declining in Europe. Significant advances have been made in suffrage and in methods of nomination. Even more significant reforms have taken place in methods of apportioning population in election districts.

But the state has not merely expanded. The expansion has taken on newer forms that may not be met at all by expansion of the mechanisms of representation. Americans, for example, always look with some consternation upon the Western European democracies because of the degree to which central state administration enters into private processes. The decrees and prefects in France, the aristocratic civil servant governing by discretion in England, the aloof civil servant governing by routine in Germany, the apolitical bureaucracies with their benevolent ombudsman in Sweden all seem too heavy-handed. *Etatism* has negative connotations in the United States because it means administrative intervention. Administration has inevitably and unavoidably expanded in the United States, and it has excited all sorts of efforts to "solve the problem."

The latest cry is for decentralization. Related cries are for "interest representation" and "cooperation" and "partnership" and "creative federalism" by the old left, and for "participatory democracy" and "community action" by the new. All of these cries are related in that their aim is for some means of conserving the creative and directive power of the state without losing the grip of localized popular control on that power. Since these cries are inappropriate, all reforms responding to them are self-defeating.

Resistance to the development of centralized and bureaucratized administrative structures in the public sector is a policy upon which most American liberals tend to agree with American conservatives. There has been an almost permanent consensus among political leaders in the United States in favor of expanding the state while dreading expansion of centralized and formal administrative intervention in private affairs. American trade unions have consistently throughout modern history opposed federal intervention in collective bargaining, once the collective bargaining process was established. Farmers have been traditionally in favor of state intervention, but only on the basis of various forms of "cooperation." Most of the new Great Society programs have resulted at one and the same time in a large net expansion of state power and an incredibly intense effort to avoid giving the impression that there has been a net increase in bureaucratic power.

This concern for administrative power in the public sector has been matched by a singular lack of concern for the same thing in the private sector. There may be a large body of criticism concerning the over-centralization of capitalist wealth. There may be widespread recognition that some safeguards must be erected against this kind of "economic power." However, criticisms are rarely directed to the extent to which the "private sector" is now governed by an administrative state.

The rise of the private administrative state began early and has been dramatic. For example, in less than half a century, between 1900 and 1950, administrative employees in the United States increased from below 6 per cent to nearly 25 per cent of all industrial employees. These rates are comparable to those of Great Britain and Sweden. According to Reinhard Bendix, the rate of increase has been lower in Germany (from 5 per cent to nearly 12 per cent), and considerably lower in France (a static level of about 12 per cent). The latter two cases are particularly significant, because these two countries are known to have had the largest and most authoritative state apparatus. This suggests that the quantum of administrative need is about the same in all industrial states. The bureaucratization of the private sector is less understood in the United States, but its existence and its influence on private life are impossible to deny. Many an American giant corporation had a five-year plan before the concept was invented in the Soviet Union. As of 1956 white-collar workers in the Untied States outnumbered blue-collar workers, suggesting the extent to which work and workers have been reduced to shuffling papers, handling routines, and supervising the conduct of others.

A more direct view of private life in modern industrial society is the trade association. It is a slightly extreme case of the typical. Thus it is a good introduction into the realities of politics after decentralization.

The trade association is basically an administrative structure whose quintessential mission in life is to regularize relations among potential competitors in the same industry, trade, or economic sector. In history and in theory, the law of the commercial marketplace is competition. The trade association seeks to replace this with an administrative process.

Trade associations have been widely misunderstood, much to their own advantage in public relations. Social scientists tend to treat them as a form of "interest group" or "pressure group," suggesting that the trade association is primarily a category of political activity. Within this rubric the trade association is merely a means of efficient representation of certain economic interests. This means of course that the trade association is a good thing insofar as there are always several trade associations each representing other economic interests. Under such conditions no concern need be given to life within any of the respective associations.

It is true that Washington and every state capital and city hall abound with trade associations and their political representatives, the lobbyists. However, political activity is only marginal and occasional with any trade association. In the first place, there are thousands of issues being faced by the legislatures of the country in any given year, and only a very few of these issues will be salient to any one trade association. On public housing, for example, the National Association of Home Builders is intensely active; but new public housing legislation is not even an annual affair. In the second place, political activity is a functional specialization inside each major trade association. This responsibility is turned over to one bureau among many bureaus inside the association. The other bureaus are meanwhile intensively active making their respective contributions to the other administrative responsibilities of the association. These responsibilities include research and development or subsidies therefor, information on pricing and costs, market research, joint advertising campaigns and other promotions, collection and dissemination of political information, and information regarding civic duties.

The population of trade associations began to mushroom in the late nineteenth century and was given special impetus during and after World War I. From a few guilds and rate bureaus as late as 1850, the trade association effort to formalize economic relations expanded until, by 1940, when an official census was taken, there were at least 12,000 national, state, and local trade associations. Over a quarter of these were national or international in scope. No recent census has been taken, but there is no reason to expect that the number or importance of trade associations has declined. It is probable that no production or service facility in the nation exists without a trade association to serve it by controlling the behavior of its members. Single businesses of more than modest size usually find it desirable to belong to several such associations.

If trade associations are not primarily political but administrative animals, neither are they the mere expressions of centralized and oligopolized economic sectors. The fact is that the more decentralized and potentially competitive sectors and industries need the trade associations and their administrative functions most of all. Where the number of firms is greater, the fear of competition is stronger; the need for research and marketing information is greater; the need for systems of recruiting trained personnel and sharing the results of research and technological advances is far greater. Such services are often provided from within by the giant corporations, but they must be provided solely by trade associations among the smaller operations. Thus, many of the most famous American trade associations serve highly decentralized economic sectors. Examples include the National Association of Real Estate Boards, the National Association of Retail Druggists, and the American Medical Association.

But life in industrial society is not administered only by trade associations. There are at least three categories of groups not, strictly speaking, trade associations that perform most of the functions of a trade association. The first of these is the "peak association." The second, and a formidable type indeed, is the organization of agricultural commodities. The third, of course, is the trade union.

The peak association is a group formed primarily by other groups and associations which join together in order to cooperate on a front larger than an individual trade or sector, yet far narrower than a whole class. Robert Brady reports on the same phenomenon in many countries, in particular the *Spitzenverbande* in Germany. Probably the best-known European example was the pre-Vichy French Confédération générale de la production française. In the United States the National Association of Manufacturers is probably the best-known example. The American Farm Bureau Federation is another. Each has a large staff in Washington, the NAM has still another large staff in New York, and the AFBF has an impressive staff in every agricultural state in the country. Their research and educational services are impressive. The AFBF offers various types of insurance along with its other services. The United States Chamber of Commerce is another example, and there are nearly four thousand local chambers which perform admirably as peak associations for city and regional groups.

Every major commodity in the United States is represented by a commodity organization. These range from immense and aged groups, such as those organized around cotton, tobacco, and wool interests, to very narrow groups, such as one organized by the cranberry growers. Each of these groups is deeply involved in politics, because agriculture is highly politicized. But most of the year's reality for all these commodity groups is administrative. They not only must keep their members informed of the complex price system in agriculture but are deeply involved in the actual implementation of federal and state agriculture programs.

The trade union in the United States was almost self-consciously modeled after business associations. The founder of modern unionism, Samuel Gompers, was considered a success largely because he espoused the principle of "business unionism" against the alternatives of class solidarity and political action. Unions act politically from time to time, and unions do compete in the labor market in a political process called collective bargaining. But collective bargaining is itself highly bureaucratized, involving elaborate studies of business profits, national economic conditions, prospects for gains outside the wages area ("fringe benefits"), and problems of jurisdiction. Moreover, most of the year union staffs are busy administering the labor-management contract, not bargaining or campaigning for it. Still other union responsibilities, most particularly job classification, must be bureaucratized if they are to succeed.

The trade association and related types of groups became a factor of still greater importance in the economy of the United States because of the antitrust laws. Certain kinds of direct business cooperation and coordination were considered to be illegal restraints upon trade. Trusts were clearly illegal. Pools and market-sharing devices were highly vulnerable to civil and criminal prosecution. Any consolidation that involved a potential competitor was illegal. Private contracts to stabilize markets, even if not illegal, were almost completely unenforceable in the courts. In contrast, the trade association was a structure against which Americans had no particular defenses. Cooperation for advertising, exchange of information, collaborative research, standardization of sizes and grades, and campaigns to discourage "cutthroat competition" all seemed far enough removed from the problem of excessive economic power or the ideal of the free and unencumbered market. Some associations—for example, the Linseed Crushers' Council and the American Hardwood Manufacturers' Association—have been successfully prosecuted for coercing their members or helping members conspire to influence prices directly; but as time passed, the trade associations have become more and more legitimate. This is the basis for practices of today and begins to suggest why decentralization means delegation of power to these groups.

These are the primary types of interest groups in the country, but they are by no means the only ones. There are multitudes of noneconomic groups—special interest and general interests groups—and being less economic in interest makes them no less oligarchic in internal structure. To stress this character of the organization of private interest groups as strongly as possible, Grant McConnell prefers to refer to them as "private governments." This aspect of life is as true of local health and welfare councils as it is of the National Association of Manufacturers. It is as true of the League of Women Voters as it is of the local commerce and industry association. Groups are run by the few on behalf of the many, and the richer and larger the group the more staff it will have to assume organizational responsibilities. Newer groups, although less bureaucratized, tend to be extremely oligarchic. Many such groups are no more than the leader, a small cadre, and a collection of affiliates of varying degrees of affiliation.

The phenomenon of the formally organized group is a distinguishing mark of modernity. This means also that the administration of social relationships is also a prime condition of modern life. If one defines administration properly—as a relatively formal means of social control through the use of the most rational possible ordering of means to ends—it is obvious that modern men prefer administration, for they are constantly in search of rational controls, on human as well as physical environments. All of this must mean increases in routine, in hierarchy, in oligarchy, in inequality. The phenomenon of the organized group is also a mark of what social scientists call the pluralist system, another mark of modernity. It is true that groups introduce an important element of competition into large-scale society. It is true that groups can interact with each other in a manner which increases the dynamism of such a society. However, it romanticizes the notion to pretend that life inside established groups is egalitarian, flexible—in a word, democratic. Leading contemporary students of groups such as David B. Truman, as well as such predecessors as Robert Michels, look at the constitution and the myths of groups and provide for them such appellations as "the iron law of oligarchy" (Michels) and "the democratic mold" (Truman).

GROUPS AND THE PROBLEM OF GOVERNING

Parallel to the development of formal groups was the increased recognition of such groups as legitimate units of representation. As syndicalism and corporatism were making their mark in Europe, so pluralism, interest representation, and more contemporary variants were gaining ground in the United States. The precedents were established by government cooperation with trade associations and commodity associations beginning in the late nineteenth century. Formal cooperation spread to other types of groups and became more and more systematic as more and more interest groups established themselves on a national scale. The Department of Commerce considered trade associations indispensable in the collection of business statistics. Agencies in the Department of Agriculture had been working for a long time directly with a rather large number of commodity associations and the local "farm bureaus" of the young Chamber of Commerce. Eventually it became government policy to encourage groups in areas where no such groups existed. The Departments of Commerce and Agriculture were instrumental, for example, in the creation of the Chamber of Commerce and the American Farm Bureau Federation, respectively. Various kinds of employer and employee associations were encouraged and brought into the interior processes of government as a fundamental part of war mobilization after 1914. But the zenith of popularity for business and nonbusiness groups in the eyes of government came not during war or during reactionary Republican administrations but during the height of the Roosevelt administration. The essential instrument of New Deal industrial planning was the National Industrial Recovery Act of 1933 and its administrative apparatus, the National Recovery Administration. In good corporativistic fashion, NRA worked through the activities of officially recognized trade organizations. Each sector and service industry and agricultural commodity organized into governing committees of trade association representatives. These representatives developed elaborate codes of fair competition—dealing with prices, wages, exchanges, health conditions, and so on—and, once approved, these codes were officially promulgated as federal law.

The NRA was eventually declared unconstitutional as an excessive delegation of law-making power to private groups and government agencies. However, the practice of government controls in cooperation with trade associations did not end; it simply became somewhat less formal and explicit. At present, the Federal Trade Commission could not carry on its business without the regular cooperation of the trade associations and other interest groups. The Interstate Commerce Commission depends almost totally upon the information and administration of the associations of railroads to achieve any regulation at all in the railroad industry. Almost the same pattern of government-supported self-government by trade association is true in the more ancient trade of shipping and the more recently developed airline industry. The vital role of the commodity associations in the administration of agricultural policy has been identified. In other fields, such as coal mining, insurance rate regulation, the export trade, space industries, and defense research and development, the official role of trade associations is somewhat more difficult to assess exactly, but their importance in each of these fields is undoubtedly the same.

The official and semiofficial role of the well-organized groups in government in the past half-century merely proves their legitimacy. Their actual scope and significance in American life are far greater. The stamp of governmental legitimacy has had the effect of blinding the American citizen to the real extent to which his life is being controlled irresponsibly. To anyone with any juridical concerns at all, the trade association represents a dilemma, because it is an exercise in control against which there is no regular defense governed by law. This is also true of the trade union. In more subtle forms it is also true of many noneconomic groups. When a person with an LL.B. degree is denied membership in a state bar association on the grounds that he refuses to reveal his political activities, he has no recourse as a citizen although the denial results in a severe deprivation. When a person with an M.D. degree is denied membership in a state medical society solely on the grounds that he is black, he too has no recourse in the courts. When a minority member of a trade union seeks to organize a competing union in the shop, he is very likely to run afoul of prohibitions against such a thing in legislation enacted and supported even by liberals.

Due to some colossal misunderstanding or misplacement of liberal sympathies, the most poetic and sympathetic defenses of groups and their official and semiofficial access have come from liberals whose concerns are otherwise for equality and justice. Treating groups as mere interest groups—and disregarding the degree of internal and administrative control of the members—political scientists tend to elevate such associations to an essentially democratic form. When the economist and philosopher-prince John Kenneth Galbraith created the economic model called "countervailing power," he elevated the trade association to a general principle of virtue, so precious in our society that he could propose that "support of countervailing power has become in modern times a major peacetime function of the Federal government."

These considerations have almost everything to do with any realistic evaluation of the drive for decentralization. If one sincerely wishes to implement such a goal, he is faced with two possibilities—and two only. One possibility for decentralization is the absence of government altogether, in the spirit of *laissez faire*. But in our day and age, and to the very ones who cry for decentralization, this solution is not acceptable, for it appears to mean abdication to all sorts of forces which have already come to be considered evil. The only other possible way of implementing the notions of decentralization is to use direct and positive government involvement on the basis of *delegation of power*. This is undoubtedly what most of the decentralization campaigners have in mind. But this leads precisely to the group domination and the oligarchic pattern of control which have already been described.

When a government program is deliberately and carefully decentralized, it begins with a grant of power and responsibility to an administrative agency. This is called "enabling legislation." This enabling legislation leads to a decentralization through what is called "delegation of power." The delegating authority—Congress at the national level—must carefully avoid accompanying that delegation of power with any clear standards of guidance in law. If such clear standards were present in the law, Congress would in effect be giving with one hand what it takes back with the other, and that would not be considered sincere decentralization. This is because clear standards at law limit the discretion of the administrator, and the ultimate choices which guide conduct would then be left with the decisions made by congressional authority and the presidential authorities at the center.

Delegation of power, and decentralization by this process, is the very jurisprudence of the modern liberal state: Give the agency and its agents sufficient discretion by keeping the rules of law broad and permissive so that agencies can enter into a true policy-making relationship with their clientele. True decentralization would then be consonant with liberal belief in the pluralistic process of bargaining. This is seriously the process of decentralization as it is widely described in the professional literature and as it is understood by the campaigners for real decentralization. The traditional notion of rule of law has in effect been replaced by a rule of bargaining. The rule of bargaining is in turn justified in the name of representation, decentralization, and participatory democracy.

But can we ennoble such practices by calling them true representation or effective participatory democracy or applying to them any other halo-laden words in the democratic lexicon? When the law passed and promulgated at the center sets no central directions, all the advantages in eventual implementation rest with those elements of the community which are best organized and most sensitive to what is going on. That in turn obviously means the trade associations and all their organized cousins. Sometimes a government program sets out deliberately to create new groups in order to equalize the access a bit. This was done in the War on Poverty, but it was not new there, for it had been done many years ago with the Chamber of Commerce and the American Farm Bureau Federation. In any of those cases the effort to create the new groups to improve "countervailing power" affects the political situation mainly on the first round of organization, if at all. That is to say, once new groups have been formed, they take on all the oligarchic trappings of previously organized groups, and the character of true representation in the society has hardly been affected at all.

Decentralization through delegation of power to lower levels, therefore, almost always results in unequal access and group domination of the public situation. However, the situation is far worse when these arrangements for access are formalized. This is true in the case of the War on Poverty as in the case of COMSAT. It is also true of agriculture policy-making vis-à-vis the commodity organizations. It is incredible that this pattern of policy-making could ever be supported by any person sincerely espousing the values of true representation and true political equality. Formal recognition of groups and their representatives for purposes of such participatory democracy converts each of the groups so honored into official components of government. Such recognition converts what is already an oligarchic situation into an involuntary situation. One of the saving characteristics of oligarchy in groups is that a person may have alternative group memberships and therefore may choose among them. This may even give him a kind of consumer influence over the activities and policies of each of the groups. But when groups are officially recognized for purposes of being included in the interior processes of policy-making, the virtues of multiple membership pass out of existence.

Thus, public recognition of a private group gives that group an involuntary character and increases the degree to which persons are subject to hierarchy, and even at that price does not increase the sum total of real representation. Whether the recognition is formal or merely clear and *de facto,* social control by irresponsible processes is the result. The notion of the "voluntary association" becomes more and more an absurdity. On the South Side of Chicago there is a group called the Blackstone Rangers. The group is feared by many because it forces teen-agers to be members. However, the [distinction] between the Blackstone Rangers and some other local groups participating in the War on Poverty or some educational program becomes less and less easy to make as that group becomes more and more the officially recognized channel of access to public policy-making. The Blackstone Ranger organizer may say, "Join our organization or I will beat your head in." But how different is this from the community organizer who says, "Join our organization or you will have very little say in community policy-making"?

Increasing demands in the country for decentralization are a reflection of increasing distrust of public programs. But direct response to those pleas through *apparent* decentralization—by further spreading the pattern of devolving programs upon organized interest groups—is a complete misunderstanding of the nature of the demand and of the nature of the problem. Decentralizing in these terms and along these lines as a response to the present crisis of public authority in the United States is comparable to the practice of bleeding in medieval medicine. For the physician the only answer to noxious blood was its elimination, at the very time when the patient could hardly spare any blood of whatever character. Further decentralization at the federal level at a time when so much power has already devolved upon private structures is an almost certain way of perpetuating the very crisis decentralization is supposed to cure.

Thus, the real question was never one of centralization versus decentralization. Decentralization was always a question of to whom and for what. Decentralization through delegation of power merely meant conversion from government control to a far more irresponsible and enigmatic and unpredictable group control. The only apparent way out of the present crisis is not to yield directly to private claims but quite independently to determine the clear injustices and inequities that are involved and to exercise control over them through clear laws that do not depend upon the good wishes or the participatory practices of any of the subjects of those laws. If such laws were for a time properly and vigorously administered by duly constituted governmental administrative bodies— and this has not happened for many years—one might at some point thereafter anticipate a proper and effective decentralization. Until such time as true federal power and a clear national commitment to racial equality and economic equity have been established beyond doubt, decentralization is abdication.

SUGGESTIONS FOR FURTHER READING

In searching out materials on interest-group activity, the student should be aware of the richness of "traditional" historical and biographical materials, in which interest groups often figure prominently; see, for instance, Glyndon G.

Van Deusen, *Thurlow Weed, Wizard of the Lobby* (Boston: Little, Brown, 1947).

Interesting recent additions to the literature on interest groups include Raymond A. Bauer, Ithiel de Sola Pool, and Lewis Anthony Dexter, *American Business and Public Policy* (New York: Atherton Press, 1963); Harmon Zeigler and Michael Baer, *Lobbying: Interaction and Influence in American State Legislatures* (Belmont, Calif.: Wadsworth, 1969); and Lewis Anthony Dexter, *How Organizations Are Represented in Washington* (Indianapolis, Ind.: Bobbs-Merrill, 1969).

Another elegant warning of the dangers of unfettered group competition is Grant McConnell, *Private Power and American Democracy* (New York: Knopf, 1966).

Excellent among older studies are Earl Latham, *The Group Basis of Politics* (Ithaca, N. Y.: Cornell University Press, 1952), and Oliver Gorceau, *The Political Life of the American Medical Association* (Cambridge, Mass.: Harvard University Press, 1941). The latter can be usefully compared with Harry Eckstein, *Pressure Group Politics: The Case of the British Medical Association* (Stanford, Calif.: Stanford University Press, 1960).

The most interesting recent contribution to interest-group theory is Mancur L. Olson, Jr., *The Logic of Collective Action: Public Goods and the Theory of Groups* (Cambridge, Mass.: Harvard University Press, 1965), and excellent collections of readings are Robert H. Salisbury, ed., *Interest Group Politics in America* (New York: Harper & Row, 1970), and Betty H. Zisk, ed., *American Political Interest Groups: Readings in Theory and Research* (Belmont, Calif.: Wadsworth, 1969).

6 The congress

FROM ITS INCEPTION the Congress has been a major decentralizing force in American politics. The dual constitutional requirements of shared powers and state-based constituencies were consciously aimed at circumscribing the powers of the central executive by granting institutional recognition to local interests. In recent years several changes have been wrought in this system. Increasingly, Senators are becoming national figures with concerns and ambitions of national scope. Some breakdown of localism is apparent among younger liberal members of the House in the Democratic Study Group. Nevertheless, the local character of Congress still predominates and is a constant source of wonder to those who view it from the perspective of unitary parliamentary states such as Great Britain.

The maintenance of localist tendencies, however, is not the only characteristic that distinguishes the American Congress from other legislative bodies. To an extent unparalleled in Western democracies, Congress has retained a considerable measure of power vis-à-vis the executive. The frequency and ease with which, regardless of party alignments, one house or another rejects crucial items in a President's domestic program testify to the continued power of the legislature.

The three selections in this chapter illustrate different facets of the relationship between the decentralized character of Congress and the nature of its power. Nelson W. Polsby focuses on the process by which the House of Representatives emerged as a distinct political institution within the broader confines of the American political system. He identifies three factors as crucial in this process: (1) boundary establishment, in which the career patterns of House members and leaders diverge from others in the political and social system; (2) increasing complexity and specialization in the internal structure and operations of the House; and (3) the shift from particularistic to universalistic decision-making—that is, the creation of procedural norms for settling internal House matters. The data presented in each of these areas clearly indicate the trend toward institutionalization. Distinct career patterns for members and leaders of the House have developed and are easily distinguishable from those for other actors in the political arena. Moreover, the internal organization of the House has grown increasingly complex. An array of specialized committees and subcommittees now dominates the legislative process. Finally, decision-making in two important areas has become virtually automatic and universal: Committee chairmen are almost invariably selected on the basis of seniority, and contested elections are regularly settled on the merits of the claims rather than on blatant partisan advantage.

Polsby goes on to argue that institutionalization has preserved the power of the House in the political system while at the same time enhancing the decentralized character of the body itself. The contemporary House encompasses a multitude of locally based and relatively autonomous legislators who function through the committee system as specialists in different public policy areas. Their expertise and continuity in office have enabled the House to continue to exert influence across the whole range of government activity, a situation that markedly differentiates it from the more centralized but less influential legislatures of other nations.

The strikingly original and detailed study by Richard F. Fenno, Jr., of the Appropriations Committee gives us a view of the House of Representatives at its basic operating level. Like Polsby, Fenno acknowledges the importance of specialization; it is, he claims, one of the "most compelling" norms of the Committee. But a gaggle of specialists does not *per se* constitute an effective body, and Fenno's major contribution is in identifying the unwritten goals and norms that serve to integrate the Committee internally and to make it an extremely influential organ within the House.

Through a number of processes, then, the Congress has managed to retain a measure of power within the political system. It has done so, however, at considerable cost to itself. In the third article in this chapter, "Congressional Responses in the Twentieth Century," Samuel P. Huntington sets forth the terms of the trade-off. Using data similar to Polsby's but adopting a different perspective, Huntington demonstrates the growing unrepresentativeness of Congress and argues that in a democracy the authority of unrepresentative institutions dwindles. Congressmen differ significantly in a number of important demographic characteristics from other national leaders. It is a question not merely of distinct career lines but of such factors as family background, mobility, and prior professional experience. The profiles of Congressmen simply do not match those of the urbanized, post-industrial citizen they represent. Furthermore, congressional procedures are ill-suited to deal with the complex worlds of electronic weaponry, sudden technological change, and complicated social, economic, and environmental problems that require rapid and flexible responses. The price of maintaining congressional power, Huntington argues, has been the surrender of congressional *initiative* on the most important contemporary issues. Congress undoubtedly can affect the course of policy, but only negatively. It asserts its autonomy and influence by rejecting or delaying proposals rather than by initiating or fundamentally altering them, and thus it has forfeited its opportunity to play a major role in shaping American society in the last third of the twentieth century.

In the last section of his article, Huntington scrutinizes some of the prescriptions usually offered to restore the representative and vital character of the Congress. He reacts to these proposals with a considerable degree of skepticism, pointing out that a less decentralized, more responsive and representative Congress is likely to become an appendage of the executive, as have most other democratic legislatures. The dilemma Congress faces is that it cannot perform its legislative function without radically altering the basis of its power, and once that basis is gone it may become nothing more than a docile instrument of other governmental sectors. The nature of modern policy problems is such, Huntington suggests, that legislatures are no longer able to perform legislative functions. This does not mean, however, that they have simply become useless relics. The autonomy and decentralized character of Congress admirably suit it for an important and as yet formally unfilled role in the political system, that of overseer of the federal bureaucracy. Should the Congress accept in principle this role which it now plays in practice, it would assume a different yet at least equally important position within the American polity.

▫ The Institutionalization of the U. S. House of Representatives

NELSON W. POLSBY

Most people who study politics are in general agreement, it seems to me, on at least two propositions. First, we agree that for a political system to be viable, for it to succeed in performing tasks of authoritative resource allocation, problem solving, conflict settlement, and so on, in behalf of a population of any substantial size, it must be institutionalized. That is to say, organizations must be created

FROM Nelson W. Polsby, "The Institutionalization of the U. S. House of Representatives," *American Political Science Review*, Vol. 62, No. 2 (March 1968), pp. 144–68.

and sustained that are specialized to political activity. Otherwise, the political system is likely to be unstable, weak, and incapable of servicing the demands or protecting the interests of its constituent groups. Secondly, it is generally agreed that for a political system to be in some sense free and democratic, means must be found for institutionalizing representativeness with all the diversity that this implies, and for legitimizing yet at the same time containing political opposition within the system.[1]

Our growing interest in both of these propositions, and in the problems to which they point, can begin to suggest the importance of studying one of the very few extant examples of a highly specialized political institution which over the long run has succeeded in representing a large number of diverse constituents, and in legitimizing, expressing, and containing political opposition within a complex political system—namely, the U. S. House of Representatives.

The focus of my attention here will be first of all descriptive, drawing together disparate strands—some of which already exist in the literature—in an attempt to show in what sense we may regard the House as an institutionalized organ of government. Not all the necessary work has been done on this rather difficult descriptive problem, as I shall indicate. Secondly, I shall offer a number of speculative observations about causes, consequences, and possible lessons to be drawn from the institutionalization of the House.

. . .

For the purposes of this study, let us say that an institutionalized organization has three major characteristics: 1) it is relatively well-bounded, that is to say, differentiated from its environment. Its members are easily identifiable, it is relatively difficult to become a member, and its leaders are recruited principally from within the organization. 2) The organization is relatively complex, that is, its functions are internally separated on some regular and explicit basis, its parts are not wholly interchangeable, and for at least some important purposes, its parts are interdependent. There is a division of labor in which roles are specified, and there are widely shared expectations about the performance of roles. There are regularized patterns of recruitment to roles, and of movement from role to role. 3) Finally, the organization tends to use universalistic rather than particularistic criteria, and automatic rather than discretionary methods for conducting its internal business. Precedents and rules are followed; merit systems replace favoritism and nepotism; and impersonal codes supplant personal preferences as prescriptions for behavior.

---

[1] Robert A. Dahl speaks of "the three great milestones in the development of democratic institutions—the right to participate in governmental decisions by casting a vote, the right to be represented, and the right of an organized opposition to appeal for votes against the government in elections and in parliament." In enumerating these three great achievements of democratic government, Dahl also implies that they are embodied principally in three main institutions: parties, elections, and legislatures: Robert A. Dahl (ed.), *Political Oppositions in Western Democracies* (New Haven and London: Yale University Press, 1966), p. xi. . . .

Since we are studying a single institution, the repeated use of words like "relatively" and "tends" in the sentences above refers to a comparison of the House of Representatives with itself at different points in time. The descriptive statement: "The House of Representatives has become institutionalized over time" means, then, that over the life span of this institution, it has become perceptibly more bounded, more complex, and more universalistic and automatic in its internal decision making. But can we find measures which will capture enough of the meaning of the term "institutionalization" to warrant their use in an investigation of the process at work in the U. S. House of Representatives?

1. THE ESTABLISHMENT OF BOUNDARIES

One aspect of institutionalization is the differentiation of an organization from its environment. The establishment of boundaries in a political organization refers mostly to a channeling of career opportunities. In an undifferentiated organization, entry to and exit from membership are easy and frequent. Leaders emerge rapidly, lateral entry from outside to positions of leadership is quite common, and persistence of leadership over time is rare. As an organization institutionalizes, it stabilizes its membership, entry is more difficult, and turnover is less frequent. Its leadership professionalizes and persists. Recruitment to leaderhip is more likely to occur from within, and the apprenticeship period lengthens. Thus the organization establishes and "hardens" its outer boundaries.

Such measures as are available for the House of Representatives unmistakably show this process at work. In the 18th and 19th centuries, the turnover of Representatives at each election was enormous. Excluding the Congress of 1789, when of course everyone started new, turnover of House members exceeded fifty per cent in fifteen elections—the last of which was held in 1882. In the 20th century, the highest incidence of turnover (37.2 per cent—almost double the 20th-century median) occurred in the Roosevelt landslide of 1932—a figure exceeded forty-seven times—in other words almost all the time—in the 18th and 19th centuries. As . . . Figure 1 make[s] clear, there has been a distinct decline in the rate at which new members are introduced into the House. . . . Figure 2 make[s] a similar point with data that are partially independent; [it] show[s] that the overall stability of membership, as measured by the mean terms of members (total number of terms served divided by total number of Representatives) has been on the rise.

These [figures] provide a fairly good indication of what has happened over the years to rank-and-file members of the House. Another method of investigating the extent to which an institution has established boundaries is to consider its leaders, how they are recruited, what happens to them, and most particularly the extent to which the institution permits lateral entry to and exit from positions of leadership.

THE CONGRESS 156

The classic example of lateral movement—possibly the most impressive such record in American history—is of course contained in the kaleidoscopic career of Henry Clay, seventh Speaker of the House. Before his first election to the House, Clay had already served two terms in the Kentucky House of Representatives, and had been sent by the legislature to the U. S. Senate for two non-

FIGURE 1 The Establishment of Boundaries: Decline in Percentage of First-Term Members, U. S. House of Representatives, 1789–1965.

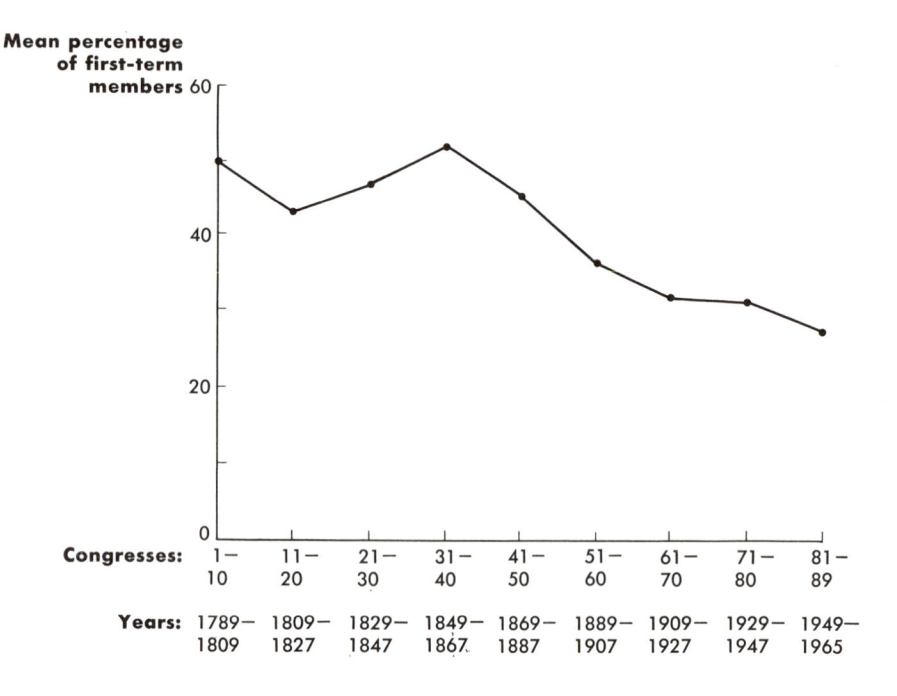

consecutive short terms. Instead of returning to the Senate in 1811, he ran for the Lexington seat in the U. S. House and was elected. He took his seat on March 4, 1811, and eight months later was elected Speaker at the age of 34. Three years later, he resigned and was appointed a commissioner to negotiate the Treaty of Ghent with Great Britain. The next year, he returned to Congress, where he was again promptly elected Speaker. In 1820 he resigned once again and left public office for two years. But in 1823 he returned to the House, served as Speaker two more terms, and then resigned again, to become Secretary of State in John Quincy Adams' cabinet. In 1831, Clay became a freshman Senator. He remained in the Senate until 1844, when he resigned his seat. Five years later he re-entered the Senate, this time remaining until his death in 1852. Three times (in 1824, 1832, 1844) he was a candidate for president.

Clay's career was remarkable, no doubt, even in a day and age when the boundaries of the House of Representatives were only lightly guarded and leadership in the House was relatively open to lateral entry. But the point to be emphasized here is that Clay's swift rise to the Speakership is only slightly atypical for the period before the turn of the 20th century.

FIGURE 2 The Establishment of Boundaries: Increase in Terms Served by Incumbent Members of the U. S. House of Representatives, 1789–1963.

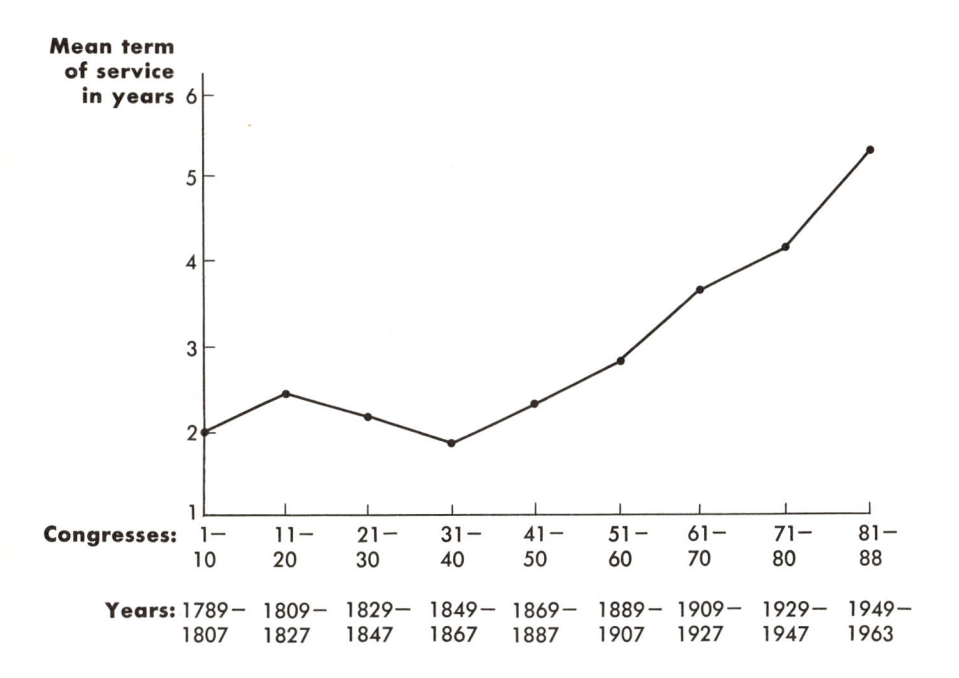

... There has been a change over time in the seniority of men selected for the Speakership. Before 1899, the mean years of service of members selected for the Speakership was six; after 1899, the mean rises steeply to twenty-six. Figure 3 and Table 1 summarize the gist of the finding in compact form.

Just as 19th-century Speakers arrived early at the pinnacle of House leadership, many left early as well and went on to other things: freshman Senators, state legislators, Cabinet members, and judges in the state courts. One became President of the U. S., one a Justice of the Supreme Court, one a Minister to Russia, one the Mayor of Auburn, New York, and one the Receiver-General of the Pennsylvania land office. Indeed, of the first twenty-seven men to be Speaker, during the first eight-six years of the Republic, *none* died while serving in the House of Representatives. In contrast, of the last ten Speakers, six died

FIGURE 3 The Establishment of Boundaries: Mean Years Served in Congress Before First Becoming Speaker (by Twenty-Year Intervals).

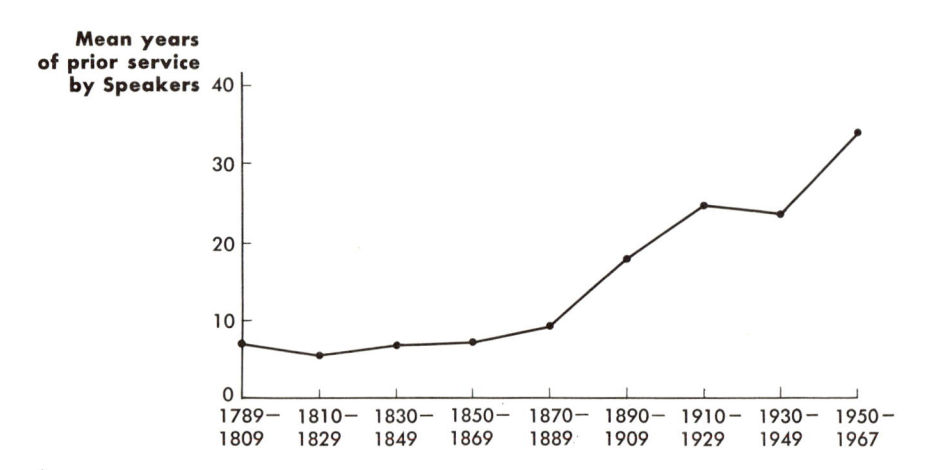

Mean years of prior service by Speakers

(Graph showing mean years of prior service by Speakers across twenty-year intervals from 1789–1809 to 1950–1967. Values remain low (around 5–10 years) from 1789 through 1889, then rise sharply: ~18 (1890–1909), ~25 (1910–1929), ~24 (1930–1949), ~34 (1950–1967).)

while serving, and of course one other sits in the House today. . . . Figure 4 give[s] the relevant information for all Speakers.

The importance of this information about Speakers' careers is that it gives a strong indication of the development of the Speakership as a singular occupational specialty. In earlier times, the Speakership seems to have been regarded as a position of political leadership capable of being interchanged with other, comparable positions of public responsibility—and indeed a high incidence of this sort of interchange is recorded in the careers of 19th-century Speakers. That this sort of interchange is most unusual today suggests—as do the other data presented in this section—that one important feature in the development of the U. S. House of Representatives has been its differentiation from other organizations in the political system, a stabilization of its membership, and a growing specialization of its leaders to leadership of the House as a separate career.

The development of a specifically House leadership, the increase in the over-

TABLE 1 The Establishment of Boundaries: Summary of Years Served in Congress Before First Selection as Speaker.

	Before 1899	1899 and after
8 years or less	25	0
9–14 years	8	0
15–20 years	0	2
21–28 years	0	10
	33 Speakers	12 Speakers

FIGURE 4 The Establishment of Boundaries: Emergence of Careers Specialized to House Leadership.

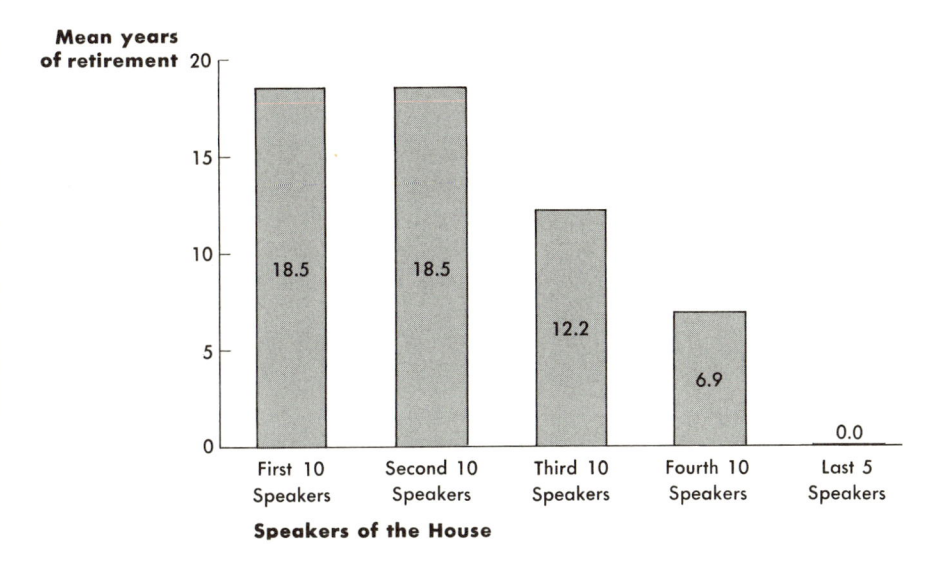

Mean years of retirement

Speakers of the House	Mean years of retirement
First 10 Speakers	18.5
Second 10 Speakers	18.5
Third 10 Speakers	12.2
Fourth 10 Speakers	6.9
Last 5 Speakers	0.0

all seniority of members, and the decrease in the influx of newcomers at any point in time have the effect not only of separating the House from other organizations in the political system, but also of facilitating the growth of stable ways of doing business within the institution, as we shall see shortly.

2. THE GROWTH OF INTERNAL COMPLEXITY

Simple operational indices of institutional complexity and universalistic-automated decision making are less easy to produce in neat and comparable time series. As for the growth of internal complexity, this is easy enough to establish impressionistically, but the most obvious quantitative measure presents a drastic problem of interpretation. The temptation is great to measure internal differentiation by simply counting the number of standing committees in each Congress. This would produce a curiously curvilinear result, because in 1946 the number of standing committees was reduced from 48 to 19, and the number has since crept up only as far as 20.

But the "streamlining," as it was called, of 1946 can hardly be said to have reduced the internal differentiation of the House. On the contrary, by explicitly delineating the legislative jurisdictions of the committees, by consolidating committees with parallel and overlapping functions, by assigning committees exclusive oversight responsibilities over agencies of the executive branch, and by providing committees with expanded staff aid, the 1946 reorganization contributed to, rather than detracted from, the reliance of the House upon committees in the conduct of its business. Thus the mute testimony of the sheer numbers of committees cannot be accepted as an appropriate index of internal complexity. I shall therefore attempt a more anecdotal accounting procedure.

Briefly, the growth of internal complexity can be shown in three ways: in the growth in the autonomy and importance of committees, in the growth of specialized agencies of party leadership, and in the general increase in the provision of various emoluments and auxiliary aids to members in the form of office space, salaries, allowances, staff aid, and committee staffs.

A wholly satisfactory account of the historical development of the House committee system does not exist. But perhaps I can swiftly sketch in a number of plausible conclusions from the literature.

From the perspective of the present-day United States, the use of standing committees by Congress is scarcely a controversial issue.[2] Yet, in the beginning the House relied only very slightly upon standing committees. Instead of the present-day system, where bills are introduced in great profusion and automatically shunted to one or another of the committees whose jurisdictions are set forth in the rules, the practice in the first and early Congresses was for subjects to be debated initially in the whole House and general principles settled upon, before they were parceled out for further action—fact-finding, detailed consideration or the proposal of a bill—to any one of four possible locations: an officer in the Executive Branch, a Committee of the Whole, a Select Committee formed *ad hoc* for the reception of a particular subject, or a standing committee. Generally, one of the alternatives to standing committees was used.

Of the First Congress, Harlow writes:

The outstanding feature of procedure in the House was the important part played by the Committee of the Whole. Much of the business in the House of Delegates of Virginia was transacted in that way, and the Virginians were influential enough to impose their methods upon the federal House. . . . It was in Committee of the Whole that Congress worked out the first tariff bill, and also the main outlines of such important measures as the laws organizing the executive departments. After the general principles were once determined, select committees would be appointed to work out the details, and to frame bills in accordance with the decision already agreed upon in Committee of the Whole. Considerable work was done by these select committees, especially after the first session.

[2] It certainly is, on the other hand, in the present-day United Kingdom, where purely legislative committees are regarded as a threat to the cohesion of the national political parties because they would give the parliamentary parties special instruments with which they could develop independent policy judgments and expertise and exercise oversight over an executive which is, after all, not formally constituted as an entity separate from Parliament. Thus committees can be construed as fundamentally inimical to unified Cabinet government. . . .

And Alexander says:

> In the early history of the House the select committee . . . was used exclusively for the consideration of bills, resolutions, and other legislative matters. As business increased and kindred subjects became scattered, however, a tendency to concentrate inaugurated a system of standing committees. It rooted itself slowly. There was an evident distrust of the centralizing influence of permanent bodies. Besides, it took important business from the many and gave it to a few, one standing committee of three or five members often taking the place of half a dozen select committees.

It is difficult to disentangle the early growth of the standing committee system from concurrent developments in the party system. For as Alexander Hamilton took control of the administration of George Washington, and extended his influence toward men of like mind in Congress, the third alternative to standing committees—reference to a member of the Executive Branch—became an important device of the Federalist majority in the House.

By the winter of 1790 [Harlow writes] Hamilton was attracting attention because of his influence over Congress. . . . His ready intelligence grasped the truth at once that Jefferson spent more than ten years learning: that not even the Constitution of the United States could keep apart two such inseparable factors in government as executive and legislature.

In the first two Congresses Hamilton is said to have used the Federalist caucus to guide debate in the Committee of the Whole, and also to have arranged for key financial measures to be referred directly to himself for detailed drafting. This practice led, in the Second Congress, to sharp clashes with followers of Jefferson, who

made it perfectly clear that if they should ever get the upper hand in Congress, they would make short work of Hamilton, and restore to the House what they considered to be its constitutional authority over finance.

The Republicans did in fact gain the upper hand in the Third Congress (elected in 1792) and they restored detailed power over finances to the Committee of the Whole. This did not work satisfactorily, however, and in the Fourth Congress a Committee on Ways and Means was formed. Harlow says:

> The appointment of . . . standing committees, particularly . . . Ways and Means, was in a way a manifestation of the Republican theory of government. From their point of view, the members of the House, as the direct representatives of the voters, ought to be the mainspring of the whole system. Hitherto, the Federalists had sold their birthright by permitting the executive to take a more active part in the government than was warranted by the Constitution. The Republicans now planned to bring about the proper balance between the different branches, by broadening at

once the scope of the operations of the House, and restricting the executive. It was the better to enable the House to take its assigned part that the new type of organization was worked out. Just as the heads of departments were looked upon as agents of the executive, so the committees would be considered as the agents of the House.

During the presidency of Thomas Jefferson, committtees were constituted and employed as agents of the President's faction in Congress which was in most matters actively led by the President himself. Binkley says:

. . . When the House of Representatives had elected its Speaker and the committee chairmen had been appointed it was apparent to the discerning that lieutenants of the President had not appointed them, but his wishes, confidentially expressed, had determined them just as surely as if he had formally and publicly nominated them. Here was the fulfillment of Marshall's prediction that Jefferson would "embody himself in the House of Representatives."

There is, however, some doubt as to Jefferson's absolute mastery over committee appointments, since it is also reported that Speaker Macon was extremely important in constituting the committees, and, in particular, in keeping John Randolph on as chairman of the Ways and Means Committee for some time after Randolph had repeatedly and violently broken with the Jefferson administration.

Recently the suggestion has been made that the direct evidence is slight and contradictory that political parties in Congress went through rapid organization and differentiation in the earliest years of the Republic. This revisionist interpretation lays greater stress upon boarding house cliques, more or less sectional and more or less ideologically factional in their composition, as the heretofore neglected building blocks out of which the more conventionally partisan Congressional politics of the Jacksonian era eventually grew.

But even revisionists concede to Jefferson a large influence over Congressional politics; the conventional accounts of the growth of the committee system are pretty much undisturbed by their critique. In essence, by the early years of the 19th century, the House committee system had passed through two distinct phases: the no-committee, Hamiltonian era, in which little or no internal differentiation within the institution was visible; and a Jeffersonian phase, in which factional alignments had begun to develop—these were exploited by the brilliant and incessant maneuverings of the President himself, who selected his lieutenants and confidants from the ranks of Congress *ad hoc,* as political requirements and opportunities dictated. During this period a small number of standing committees existed, but were not heavily relied upon. Their jurisdictions were not so securely fixed that the Speaker could not instead appoint select committees to deal with business that ought to have been sent to them.

The advent of Henry Clay and the victory of the War Hawk faction in the elections of 1810 brought the committee system to its third phase. Clay for the first time used the Speaker's prerogative of appointment of members to committees independently of Presidential designs. There is some question whether Clay's appointment policies were calculated to further his policy preferences or merely his popularity (and hence his Presidential ambitions) within the factionally divided house, but there seems no reason to doubt that Clay won for the Speakership a new measure of independence as a power base in the American political system. Under Clay five House committees were constituted to oversee expenditures in executive departments, the first major institutionalization of the Congressional function of oversight. William N. Chambers writes:

[By] 1814 the committee system had become the dominant force in the chamber. Thus effective power was exercised not by the President, as had been the case with Jefferson, but by factional Congressional leaders working through the speakership, the caucus, and the committees.

For the next 100 years the committee system waxed and waned more or less according to the ways in which committees were employed by the party or faction that dominated the House and elected the Speaker. Figures from the latter decades of the 19th century testify amply to the leeway afforded Speakers—especially new ones—in constituting committees regardless of their prior composition. In part, it was Speaker Cannon's increasing use of this prerogative in an attempt to keep control of his fragmenting party that triggered the revolt against his Speakership in 1910–11, and that led to the establishment of the committee system as we know it today.

Under the fourth, decentralized, phase of the committee system, committees have won solid institutionalized independence from party leaders both inside and outside Congress. Their jurisdictions are fixed in the rules; their composition is largely determined and their leadership entirely determined by the automatic operation of seniority. Their work is increasingly technical and specialized, and the way in which they organize internally to do their work is entirely at their own discretion. Committees nowadays have developed an independent sovereignty of their own, subject only to very infrequent reversals and modifications of their powers by House party leaders backed by large and insistent majorities.

To a degree, the development over the last sixty years of an increasingly complex machinery of party leadership within the House cross-cuts and attenuates the independent power of committees. Earlier, the leading faction in the House elected the Speaker and the Speaker in turn distributed the chairmanships of key committees to his principal allies and opponents. Thus the work of the House was centralized to the extent that the leading faction in the House was centralized. But differences of opinion are not uncommon among qualified observers. The Jeffersonian era, for example, is widely regarded as a high point of centralization during the 19th century. Harlow reports:

From 1801 to 1808 the floor leader was distinctly the lieutenant of the executive. William B. Giles, who was actually referred to as "the premier, or prime minister,"

Caesar A. Rodney, John Randolph of Roanoke, and Wilson Cary Nicholas all held that honorable position at one time or another. It was their duty to look after party interests in the House, and in particular to carry out the commands of the President. The status of these men was different from that of the floor leader of today. . . . They were presidential agents, appointed by the executive, and dismissed at his pleasure.

But another observer, a Federalist congressman quoted by Noble Cunningham, suggests that the Jeffersonian group was not at all times well organized:

The ruling faction in the legislature have not yet been able to understand each other. . . . There evidently appears much rivalry and jealousy among the leaders. S[amuel] Smith thinks his experience and great address ought to give him a preponderance in all their measures, whilst Nicholson evidently looks upon these pretensions of his colleague with contempt, and Giles thinks the first representative of the Ancient Dominion ought certainly on all important occasions to take the lead, and Johnny Randolph is perfectly astonished that his great abilities should be overlooked. There is likewise a great number of other persons who are impatient of control and disposed to revolt at any attempts at discipline.

This certainly squares with the reports of Jefferson's own continued attempts, also revealed in his letters, to recruit men to the House with whom he could work.

Despite Jefferson's difficulties, he was the most consistently successful of all the 19th-century Presidents in "embodying himself in the House of Representatives." After Jefferson, the Speaker became a power in his own right; not infrequently he was a candidate for the Presidency himself, and the House was more or less organized around his, rather than the President's, political interests. There was no formal position of majority leader; the leading spokesman for the majority party on the floor was identified by personal qualities of leadership and by the favor of the Speaker (or in the Jeffersonian era, of the President) rather than by his institutional position.

Later, however, the chairman of the Ways and Means Committee—a key post reserved for the chief lieutenant of the Speaker—became *de facto* floor leader, a natural consequence of his responsibilities in managing the tariff bills that were so important in 19th-century congressional politics. Occasionally the chairman of the Committee on Appropriations was the *de facto* leader, especially during periods of war mobilization, when the power of the House in the political system was coextensive with the power of the purse. In the last part of the 19th century, however, the Committee on Appropriations was temporarily dismantled, and the chairman of Ways and Means Committee began to receive the formal designation as party leader.

The high point of the Ways and Means chairman's power came in the aftermath of the 1910 revolt against the Speaker. The power of committee appointments was for Democrats lodged in the Ways and Means Committee. Chairman

Oscar Underwood, in cooperation with President Wilson, for a time (1911–1915) eclipsed the Speaker and the committee chairmen by operating the majority party by caucus.

But Underwood's successor as Chairman of Ways and Means, Claude Kitchin (majority leader 1915–1919), disapproved of Wilson's war policies; this made it cumbersome and impractical for the leader of the majority on the floor and in caucus to hold this job by virtue of what was becoming an automatic succession through seniority to the chairmanship of Ways and Means. A separation of the two roles was effected after the Democrats became the minority in 1919. Ever since then, the majority leader's job has existed as a full-time position; the incumbent now holds a nominal, junior committee post but he rarely attends committee meetings. At the same time, the majority leader has become less of a President's man, and the caucus is now dormant as an instrument of party leadership— although it now sometimes becomes a vehicle, especially at the opening of Congress, for the expression of widespread dissatisfaction by rank-and-file House members. Thus, while binding votes on policy matters have not been put through the caucus by party leaders, the Republican caucus has three times in recent years deposed party leaders and the Democratic caucus has deprived three of its members of their committee seniority.

Formally designated party whips are, like the differentiated post of majority leaders, an innovation principally of the 20th century. The first whips date back to just before the turn of the century. In the early years, the designation seems to have been quite informal, and it is only recently that an elaborate whip system, with numerous deputies, a small staff, and formal procedures for canvassing members, has been established by both parties in the House.

Thus, we can draw a contrast between the practices of recent and earlier years with respect to formal party leaders other than the Speaker:

1. Floor leaders in the 20th century are officially designated; in the 19th, they were often informally designated, indefinite, shifting or even competitive, and based on such factors as personal prestige, speaking ability, or Presidential favor.

2. Floor leaders in recent years are separated from the committee system and elected by party members; earlier they were prominent committee chairmen who were given their posts by the Speaker, sometimes as a side-payment in the formation of a coalition to elect the Speaker.

3. Floor leaders today rely upon whip systems; before 1897 there were no formally designated whips.

A third indicator of the growth of internal organization is the growth of resources assigned to internal House management, measured in terms of personnel, facilities, and money. Visitors to Washington are not likely to forget the sight of the five large office buildings, three of them belonging to the House, that flank the Capitol. The oldest of these on the House side was built just after the turn of the century, in 1909, when a great many other of our indices show significant changes.

Reliable figures, past or present, on personnel assigned to the House are impossible to come by; but it is unlikely that a commentator today would agree with the observer early in this century who said:

It is somewhat singular that Congress is one of the few legislative bodies that attempts to do its work almost entirely without expert assistance—without the aid of parliamentary counsel, without bill drafting and revising machinery and without legislative and reference agencies, and until now it has shown little inclination to regard with favor proposals looking toward the introduction of such agencies.

Indeed, the only major contemporary study we have of congressional staff speaks of present "tendencies toward overexpansion of the congressional staff," and says that "Three-fourths of the committee aides interviewed" thought that professional staffs of committtees were sufficiently large to handle their present work load.

Needless to say, that work load has grown, and, though it is impossible to say precisely by how much, congressional staffs have grown as well. This is roughly reflected in figures that are more or less comparable over time on that portion of the legislative budget assigned to the House. These figures show the expected increases. However, except for the jump between 1945 and 1946, reflecting the new provisions for staff aid of the Legislative Reorganization Act, the changes in these figures over time are not as abrupt as is the case with other of our time series. . . . So we must regard this indicator as weak, but nevertheless pointing in the expected direction.

3. FROM PARTICULARISTIC AND DISCRETIONARY TO UNIVERSALISTIC AND AUTOMATED DECISION MAKING

The best evidence we have of a shift away from discretionary and toward automatic decision making is the growth of seniority as a criterion determining committee rank and the growth of the practice of deciding contested elections to the House strictly on the merits.

The literature on seniority presents a welter of conflicting testimony. Some commentators date the seniority system from 1910; others say that seniority as a criterion for determining the committee rank of members was in use well before. Woodrow Wilson's classic account of *Congressional Government* in 1884 pays tribute both to the independence of the committees and their chairman and to the absolute discretion of the Speaker in the committee appointment process. It is clear that the Speaker has no such power today. In another paper my colleagues and I present a detailed preliminary tabulation and discussion on the extent to which seniority in its contemporary meaning was followed in the selection of committee chairmen in the most recent 40 Congresses. The central finding for our present purposes (summarized in Table 2 and Figure 5) is that the seniority

TABLE 2 The Growth of Universalism: Violations of Seniority in the Appointment of Committee Chairmen, U. S. House of Representatives, 1881–1963.

Percentage of committees on which the chairman was not selected by seniority (averaged by decades)

Congress:	47–51	52–56	57–61	62–66
Years:	1881–89	1891–99	1901–09	1911–19
Average: Violations of seniority	60.4%	49.4%	19%	30.8%
Congress:	67–71	72–76	77–81	82–88
Years:	1921–29	1931–39	1941–49	1951–63
Average: Violations	26%	23%	14%	.7%

system—an automatic, universally applied, nondiscretionary method of selection—is now always used, but that formerly the process by which chairmen were selected was highly and later partially discretionary.

The figures for before 1911 can be interpreted as indicating the use of the Speaker's discretion in the appointment of committee chairmen. After 1911, when committee appointment powers are vested in committees on committees, the figures principally reflect the growth of the norm that no one man should serve as chairman of more than one committee. Congressmen often sat on a large number of committees, and senior men rose to the top of more than one committee, but allowed less senior men to take the chair, much as the custom presently is in the U. S. Senate. After 1946, when the number of committees was drastically reduced, this practice died out, and a strictly automated system of seniority has asserted itself.

The settlement of contested elections on some basis other than the merits seems in earlier years to have been a common phenomenon. . . .

A journalist writing at the beginning of the 20th century summarizes the situation as he had encountered it over a twenty-year period:

> It may be said . . . that there is no fairness whatever exercised in . . . contests for seats, especially where the majority needs the vote for party purposes. Hundreds of men have lost their seats in Congress, to which they were justly entitled upon all

FIGURE 5 The Growth of Universalism: Decline in Violations of Seniority, Committee Chairmen, U. S. House of Representatives, 1881–1963.

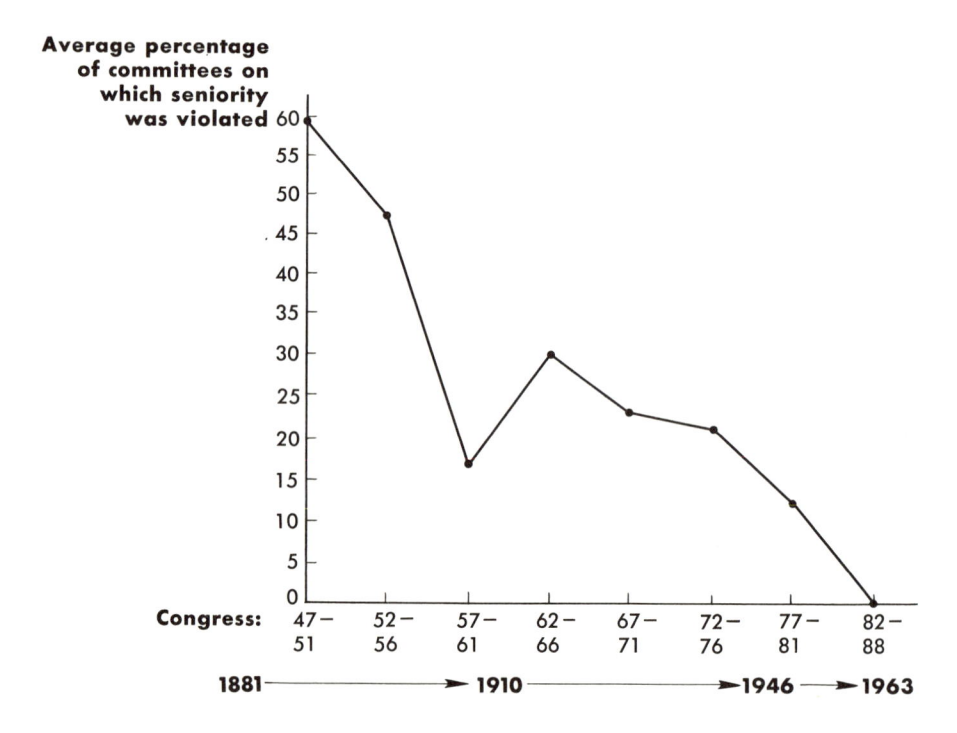

fair, reasonable, and legal grounds, and others put in their places for purely partisan reasons. This has always been so and doubtless will continue so. . . .

In fact, it has not continued so; nowadays, contested elections are settled with much more regard to due process and the merits of the case than was true throughout the 19th century. By 1926, a minority member of the Committee on Elections No. 1 could say:

In the eight years I have served on Elections Committees and six years upon this Committee, I have never seen partisanship creep into that Committee but one time. There has not been any partisanship in the Committee since the distinguished gentleman from Utah became Chairman of that Committee. A Democrat was seated the last time over a Republican by this Committee, and every member of the Committee voted to seat that Democrat.

This quotation suggests a method by which the development of universalistic criteria for settling contested House elections can be monitored, namely, measuring the extent to which party lines are breached in committee reports and in voting on the floor in contest cases. I have made no such study, but on the basis of the accumulated weight of contemporary reports such as I have been quoting,

The Institutionalization of the U. S. House of Representatives 169

I predict that a time series would show strict party voting in the 19th century, switching to unanimity or near-unanimity, in most cases, from the early years of the 20th century onward.

Attempts to establish legal precedents for the settlement of contested elections date from the recommendations of the Ames Committee in 1791. In 1798 a law was enacted prescribing a uniform mode of taking testimony and for compelling the attendance of witnesses. This law was required to be renewed in each Congress and was allowed to lapse in 1804. Bills embodying similar laws were proposed in 1805, 1806, 1810, 1813, and 1830. Not until 1851 was such a law passed, which provided for the gathering of testimony forming the bases of the proofs of each contestant's claim, but not for rules concerning other aspects of contested elections. More significant, however, was a clause permitting the House to set the law aside in whole or in part in specific cases, which apparently the House availed itself of with some regularity in the 19th century. With a few modifications this law is still in effect.

The absolute number of contests shows a decrease in recent decades, as does the number of contests in relation to the number of seats. This suggests that the practice of instigating contests for frivolous reasons has passed into history; contemporary House procedures no longer hold out the hope of success for such contests. . . . Figure 6 give[s] the figures, by decades.

FIGURE 6 The Growth of Universalism: Contested Elections in the House by Decades, 1789–1964.

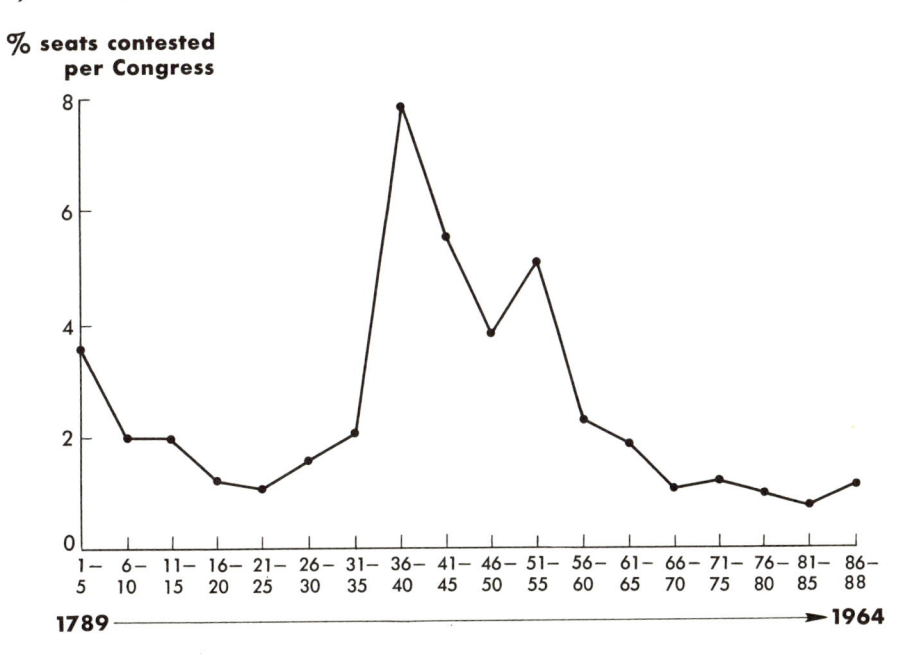

There is today, certainly, no wholesale stealing of seats. If any bias exists in the system, it probably favors the protection of incumbents irrespective of party, and hence (we may surmise not incidentally) the protection of the boundaries of the organization.

4. CAUSES, CONSEQUENCES, CONCLUSIONS

It seems reasonable to conclude that one of the main long-run changes in the U. S. House of Representatives has been toward greater institutionalization. Knowing this, we may wish to ask, at a minimum, three questions: What caused it? What follows from it? What can this case tell us about the process in general? It is not from lack of space alone that our answers to each of these questions will be brief and highly speculative.

Not much, for example, is known about the causes of institutionalization. The best theoretical guess in the literature is probably Durkheim's: "The division of labor varies in direct ratio with the volume and density of societies, and, if it progresses in a continuous manner in the course of social development, it is because societies become regularly denser and generally more voluminous." "Density" in at least some sense is capable of being operationalized and measured separately from its institutional consequences. For present purposes, the proposition can probably be rendered as follows: As the responsibilities of the national government grew, as a larger proportion of the national economy was affected by decisions taken at the center, the agencies of the national government institutionalized. Another, complementary, translation of the density theorem would be that as organizations grow in size, they tend to develop internally in ways predicted by the theory of institutionalization. Size and increasing workload seem to me in principle measurable phenomena. Size alone, in fact, seems almost too easy. Until a deliberative body has some minimum amount of work to do, the necessity for interaction among its members remains slight, and, having no purpose, coordination by means of a division of labor, rules and regulations, precedents and so on, seems unlikely to develop. So a somewhat more complicated formula has to be worked out, perhaps relating the size of an organization to the amount of work it performs (e.g., number of work-days per year, number of full-time as opposed to nominal members, number of items considered, number of reports rendered) before the strength of "density" and "volume" can be tested as causes of the process of institutionalization.

A discussion of the consequences of the House's institutionalization must be equally tentative. It is hard—indeed for the contemporary observer, impossible—to shake the conviction that the House's institutional structure does matter greatly in the production of political outcomes. A recent popular account begins:

A United States Congressman has two principal functions: to make laws and to keep laws from being made. The first of these he and his colleagues perform only with sweat, patience and a remarkable skill in the handling of creaking machinery; but the second they perform daily, with ease and infinite variety.

No observer who focuses upon policy results, or who cares about the outputs of the American legislative process, fails to note the "complicated forms and diversified structure" which "confuse the vision, and conceal the system which underlies its composition." All this is such settled knowledge that it seems unnecessary to mention it here. Still, it is important to stress that the very features of the House which casual observers and freshman legislators find most obstrusive are principal consequences of (among other things) the process we have been describing.

It is, however, not merely the complexity or the venerability of the machinery that they notice. These, in our discussion so far, have been treated as defining characteristics rather than consequences of institutionalization. What puzzles and irks the outside observer is a partial displacement of goals, and a focus of resources upon internal processes at the expense of external demands, that come as a consequence of institutionalization. This process of displacement is, of course, well known to social theory in other settings. A closer look at the general character of this displacement is bound to suggest a number of additional consequences.

For example, representatives may find that the process of institutionalization has increased their incentives to stay within the system. For them, the displacement of resources transforms the organization from a convenient instrument for the pursuit of social policies into an end value itself, a prime source of gratification, of status and power.

The increasing complexity of the division of labor presents an opportunity for individual Representatives to specialize and thereby enormously increase their influence upon a narrow range of policy outcomes in the political system at large. Considered separately, the phenomenon of specialization may strike the superficial observer as productive of narrow-minded drones. But the total impact of a cadre of specialists operating over the entire spectrum of public policies is a formidable asset for a political institution; and it has undoubtedly enabled the House to retain a measure of autonomy and influence that is quite exceptional for a 20th-century legislature.

Institutionalization has, in the House, on the whole meant the decentralization of power. This has created a great many important and interesting jobs within the House, and thus increased the attractiveness of service therein as a career. Proposed reforms of Congress which seek to move toward a recentralization of Congressional power rarely consider this fact. But it is at least possible that some moves to restore discretion to the Speaker, or to centralized party agencies outside Congress, would reduce the effectiveness of Congress far below the level anticipated, because the House would come to be less valued in and of itself, its division of labor would provide less of a power base for subject matter specialists, and the incentives to stay within the organization would sharply decline.

Thus we can argue that, along with the more obvious effects of institutionalization, the process has also served to increase the power of the House within the political system and to spread somewhat more widely incentives for legislators to participate actively in policy making.

A final possible consequence of institutionalization can be suggested: that the process tends to promote professional norms of conduct among participants. Indeed, something like these norms are built into the definition of institutionalization by some commentators. But the built-in norms typically mentioned in discussions of "organization men" have to do with the segmental, ritualized interaction that characterizes organizations coordinated by hierarchical means; slightly different predictions about norms would have to be made for more decentralized, more egalitarian institutionalized legislative bodies.

In fact, there is coming to be a sizeable body of literature about the norms of professional legislative conduct. Time and again, the norms of predictability, courtesy, and reciprocity are offered by professional legislators as central to the rules of the legislative game. Thus, we can suggest a hypothesis that the extent to which these norms are widely applied in a legislative body is a direct function of that body's structural institutionalization. Appropriate tests can be made cross-sectionally, by comparing contemporary legislatures that vary with respect to boundary-maintenance, internal complexity, and universalistic-automated internal decision making. Historically, less satisfactory tests are possible, since a number of vagaries enter into the determination of what is recorded and what is not, and since antecedent factors may account for both structural and normative institutionalization. This makes it hard to estimate the dispersion and importance of norms of conduct.

Nevertheless, the history of the House does suggest that there has been a growth in the rather tame virtues of reciprocity, courtesy, and predictability in legislative life since the turn of the century. Clem Miller describes human relations in the House of today:

One's overwhelming first impression as a member of Congress is the aura of friendliness that surrounds the life of a congressman. No wonder that "few die and none resign." Almost everyone is unfailingly polite and courteous. Window washers, clerks, senators—it cuts all ways. We live in a cocoon of good feeling. . . .

No doubt there are breaches in the fabric of good fellowship, mostly unpublicized, but the student of Congress cannot refrain even so from comparing of this testimony with the following sampling of 19th-century congressional conduct:

Upon resuming his seat, after having replied to a severe personal arraignment of Henry Clay, former Speaker White, without the slightest warning, received a blow in the face. In the fight that followed a pistol was discharged wounding an officer of the police. John Bell, the distinguished Speaker and statesman, had a similar experience in Committee of the Whole (1838). The fisticuffs became so violent that even the Chair would not quell it. Later in the day both parties apologized and "made their submissions." On February 6, 1845, Edward J. Black, of Georgia, "crossed over from his seat, and, coming within the bar behind Joshua R. Giddings as he was speaking, made a pass at the back of his head with a cane. William H. Hammett, of Mississippi, threw his arms round Black and bore him off as he would a woman from a fire. . . ."

When Reuben M. Whitney was before a committee of investigation in 1837, Bailie Peyton, of Tennessee, taking offense at one of his answers, threatened him fiercely, and when he rose to claim the committee's protection, Mr. Peyton, with due and appropriate profanity, shouted: "You shan't say one word while you are in this room; if you do I will put you to death." The chairman, Henry A. Wise, added: "Yes; this insolence is insufferable." As both these gentlemen were armed with deadly weapons, the witness could hardly be blamed for not wanting to testify before the committee again.

"These were not pleasant days," writes Thomas B. Reed. "Men were not nice in their treatment of each other."

Indeed they were not: 19th-century accounts of Congressional behavior abound in passages like these. There is the consternation of members who put up with the presence on the floor of John Randolph's hunting dogs. There is the famous scene on May 22, 1851, when Representative Preston Brooks of South Carolina entered the U. S. Senate and beat Senator Charles Sumner senseless with a cane, and the record contains accounts of more than one such occasion:

When Matthew Lyon, of Kentucky, spat in his face, [Roger] Griswold [of Connecticut, a member 1795–1805] stiffened his arm to strike, but remembering where he was, he coolly wiped his cheek. But after the House by its vote failed to expel Lyon, he "beat him with great violence," says a contemporary chronicle, "using a strong walking-stick."

With all the ill will that the heat of battle sometimes generates currently, the House has long since left behind the era of guns and dogs, canings and fisticuffs, that occupied so much of the 19th-century scene. No doubt this reflects general changes in manners and morals, but it also reflects a growth in the value of the House as an institution capable of claiming the loyalty and good behavior of its members. The best test of the hypothesis, to be sure, remains the cross-sectional one. If American state legislatures, for example, can be found to differ significantly with respect to structural institutionalization, they may also be found to vary concomitantly with respect to the application of the norms of professional legislative life.

Finally, the study of the institutionalization of the House affords us a perspective from which to comment upon the process in general. First, as to its reversibility. Many of our indicators show a substantial decay in the institutional structure of the House in the period surrounding the Civil War. In sheer numbers, the House declined from 237 members in the Congress of 1859 to 178 in the Congress of 1861; not until a decade later did the House regain its former strength. Frivolous contests for seats reached a height in this period, and our rank-and-file boundary measures reflect decay as well. It may be true, and it is certainly amusing, that the strength of the British Admiralty grows as the number of ships declines; but that this illustrates an inflexibly narcissistic law of institutional growth may be doubted. As institutions grow, our expectations about the displacement of resources inward do give us warrant to predict that they will resist decay, but the indications of curvilinearity in our present findings give us ample warning that institutions are also continuously subject to environmental influence and their power to modify and channel that influence is bound to be less than all-encompassing.

Some of our indicators give conditional support for a "take-off" theory of modernization. If one of the stigmata of the take-off to modernity is the rapid development of universalistic, bounded, complex institutional forms, the data presented here lend this theory some plausibility. The "big bang" seems to come in the 1890–1910 period, on at least some of the measures.

In conclusion, these findings suggest that increasing hierarchical structure is not a necessary feature of the institutionalization process. Organizations other than bureaucracies, it seems clear, also are capable of having natural histories which increase their viability in the modern world without forcing them into uniformly centralized patterns of authority.

▢ The House Appropriations Committee as a Political System: The Problem of Integration

RICHARD F. FENNO, JR.

Studies of Congress by political scientists have produced a time-tested consensus on the very considerable power and autonomy of Congressional committees. Because of these two related characteristics, it makes empirical and analytical sense to treat the Congressional committee as a discrete unit for analysis. This paper conceives of the committee as a political system (or, more accurately,

FROM Richard F. Fenno, Jr., "The House Appropriations Committee as a Political System: The Problem of Integration," *American Political Science Review*, Vol. 56, No. 2 (June 1962), pp. 310–24.

as a political subsystem) faced with a number of basic problems which it must solve in order to achieve its goals and maintain itself. Generally speaking these functional problems pertain to the environmental and the internal relations of the committee. This study is concerned almost exclusively with the internal problems of the committee and particularly with the problem of self-integration. It describes how one congressional committee—the Committee on Appropriations of the House of Representatives—has dealt with this problem in the period 1947–1961. Its purpose is to add to our understanding of appropriations politics in Congress and to suggest the usefulness of this type of analysis for studying the activities of any congressional committee.

The necessity for integration in any social system arises from the differentiation among its various elements. Most importantly there is a differentiation among subgroups and among individual positions, together with the roles that flow therefrom. A committee faces the problem, how shall these diverse elements be made to mesh together or function in support of one another? No political system (or subsystem) is perfectly integrated; yet no political system can survive without some minimum degree of integration among its differentiated parts. Committee integration is defined as the degree to which there is a working together or a meshing together or mutual support among its role and subgroups. Conversely, it is also defined as the degree to which a committee is able to minimize conflict among its roles and its subgroups, by heading off or resolving the conflicts that arise. A concomitant of integration is the existence of a fairly consistent set of norms, widely agreed upon and widely followed by the members. Another concomitant of integration is the existence of control mechanisms (*i.e.*, socialization and sanctioning mechanisms) capable of maintaining reasonable conformity to norms. In other words the more highly integrated a committee, the smaller will be the gap between expected and actual behavior.

This study is concerned with integration both as a structural characteristic of, and as a functional problem for, the Appropriations Committee. First, certain basic characteristics of the Committee need description, to help explain the integration of its parts. Second comes a partial description of the degree to which and the ways in which the Committee achieves integration. No attempt is made to state this in quantitative terms, but the object is to examine the meshing together or the minimization of conflict among certain subgroups and among certain key roles. Also, important control mechanisms are described. The study concludes with some comments on the consequences of Committee integration for appropriations politics and on the usefulness of further Congressional committee analysis in terms of functional problems such as this one.

I

Five important characteristics of the Appropriations Committee which help explain Committee integration are (1) the existence of a well-articulated and deeply rooted consensus on Committee goals or tasks; (2) the nature of the Committee's subject matter; (3) the legislative orientation of its members; (4) the attractiveness of the Committee for its members; and (5) the stability of Committee membership.

Consensus. The Appropriations Committee sees its tasks as taking form within the broad guidelines set by its parent body, the House of Representatives. For it is the primary condition of the Committee's existence that it was created by the House for the purpose of assisting the House in the performance of House legislative tasks dealing with appropriations. Committee members agree that their fundamental duty is to serve the House in the manner and with the substantive results that the House prescribes. Given, however, the imprecision of House expectations and the permissiveness of House surveillance, the Committee must elaborate for itself a definition of tasks plus a supporting set of perceptions (of itself and of others) explicit enough to furnish day-to-day guidance.

The Committee's view begins with the preeminence of the House—often mistakenly attributed to the Constitution ("all bills for raising revenue," Art. I, sec. 7) but nevertheless firmly sanctioned by custom—in appropriations affairs.

It moves easily to the conviction that, as the efficient part of the House in this matter, the Constitution has endowed it with special obligations and special prerogatives. It ends in the view that the Committee on Appropriations, far from being merely one among many units in a complicated legislative-executive system, is the most important, most responsible unit in the whole appropriations process. Hand in hand with the consensus on their primacy goes a consensus that all of their House-prescribed tasks can be fulfilled by superimposing upon them one, single, paramount task—*to guard the Federal Treasury*. Committee members state their goals in the essentially negative terms of guardianship—screening requests for money, checking against ill-advised expenditures, and protecting the taxpayer's dollar. In the language of the Committee's official history, the job of each member is, "constantly and courageously to protect the Federal Treasury against thousands of appeals and imperative demands for unnecessary, unwise, and excessive expenditures."

To buttress its self-image as guardian of public funds the Committee elaborates a set of perceptions about other participants in the appropriations process to which most members hold most of the time. Each executive official, for example, is seen to be interested in the expansion of his own particular program. Each one asks, therefore, for more money than he really needs, in view of the total picture, to run an adequate program. This and other Committee perceptions —of the Budget Bureau, of the Senate, and of their fellow Representatives—help to shape and support the Committee members in their belief that most budget estimates can, should, and must be reduced and that, since no one else can be relied upon, the House Committee must do the job. To the consensus on the main task of protecting the Treasury is added, therefore, a consensus on the instrumental task of *cutting whatever budget estimates are submitted*.

As an immediate goal, Committee members agree that they must strike a highly critical, aggressive posture toward budget requests, and that they should, on principle, reduce them. In the words of the Committee's veterans: "There has never been a budget submitted to the Congress that couldn't be cut." "There isn't a budget that can't be cut 10 per cent immediately." "I've been on the Committee for 17 years. No subcommittee of which I have been a member has ever reported out a bill without a cut in the budget. I'm proud of that record." The aim of budget-cutting is strongly internalized for the Committee member. "It's a tradition in the Appropriations Committee to cut." "You're grounded in it. . . . It's ingrained in you from the time you get on the Committee." For the purposes of a larger study, the appropriations case histories of 37 executive bureaus have been examined for a 12-year period, 1947–1959. Of 443 separate bureau estimates, the Committee reduced 77.2 per cent (342) of them.

It is a mark of the intensity and self-consciousnes of the Committee consensus on budget-cutting that it is couched in a distinctive vocabulary. The workaday lingo of the Committee member is replete with negative verbs, undesirable objects of attention, and effective instruments of action. Agency budgets are said to be filled with "fat," "padding," "grease," "pork," "oleaginous substance," "water," "oil," "cushions," "avoirdupois," "waste tissue," and "soft spots." The action verbs most commonly used are "cut," "carve," "slice," "prune," "whittle," "squeeze," "wring," "trim," "lop off," "chop," "slash," "pare," "shave," "fry," and "whack." The tools of the trade are appropriately referred to as "knife," "blade," "meat axe," "scalpel," "meat cleaver," "hatchet," "shears," "wringer," and "fine-tooth comb." Members are hailed by their fellows as being "pretty sharp with the knife." Agencies may "have the meat axe thrown at them." Executives are urged to put their agencies "on a fat boy's diet." Budgets are praised when they are "cut to the bone." And members agree that "You can always get a little more fat out of a piece of pork if you fry it a little longer and a little harder."

To the major task of protecting the Treasury and the instrumental task of cutting budget estimates, each Committee member adds, usually by way of exception, a third task—*serving the constituency to which he owes his election*. This creates no problem for him when, as is sometimes the case, he can serve his district best by cutting the budget requests of a federal agency whose program is in conflict with the demands of his constituency. Normally, however, members find that their most common role-conflict is between a Committee-oriented budget-reducing role and a constituency-oriented budget-increasing role. Committee ideology resolves the conflict by assigning top, long-run priority to the budget-cutting task and making of the constituency service a permissible, short-run exception. No member is expected to commit electoral suicide; but no member is expected to allow his district's desire for federal funds to dominate his Committee behavior.

Subject Matter. Appropriations Committee integration is facilitated by the subject matter with which the group deals. The Committee makes decisions on the same controversial issues as do the committees handling substantive legislation. But a money decision—however vitally it affects national policy—is, or at least seems to be, less directly a policy decision. Since they deal immediately with dollars and cents, it is easy for the members to hold to the idea that they are not dealing with programmatic questions, that theirs is a "business" rather than a "policy" committee. The subject matter, furthermore, keeps Committee members relatively free agents, which promotes intra-Committee maneuvering and, hence, conflict avoidance. Members do not commit themselves to their constituents in terms of precise money amounts, and no dollar sum is sacred—it can always be adjusted without conceding that a principle has been breached. By contrast, members of committees dealing directly with controversial issues are often pressured into taking concrete stands on these issues; consequently, they may come to their committee work with fixed and hardened attitudes. This leads to unavoidable, head-on intra-committee conflict and renders integrative mechanisms relatively ineffective.

The fact of an annual appropriations process means the Committee members repeat the same operations with respect to the same subject matters year after year—and frequently more than once in a given year. Substantive and procedural repetition promotes familiarity with key problems and provides ample opportunity to test and confirm the most satisfactory methods of dealing with them. And the absolute necessity that appropriations bills do ultimately pass gives urgency to the search for such methods. Furthermore, the House rule that no member of the Committee can serve on another standing committee is a deterrent against a fragmentation of Committee member activity which could be a source of difficulty in holding the group together. If a committee has developed (as this one has) a number of norms designed to foster integration, repeated and concentrated exposure to them increases the likelihood that they will be understood, accepted, and followed.

Legislative Orientation. The recruitment of members for the Appropriations Committee produces a group of individuals with an orientation especially conducive to Committee integration. Those who make the selection pay special attention to the characteristics which Masters has described as those of the "responsible legislator"—approval of and conformity to the norms of the legislative process and of the House of Representatives.

Key selectors speak of wanting, for the Appropriations Committee, "the kind of man you can deal with" or "a fellow who is well-balanced and won't go off half-cocked on things." A Northern liberal Democrat felt that he had been chosen over eight competitors because, "I had made a lot of friends and was known as a nice guy"—especially, he noted, among Southern Congressmen. Another Democrat explained, "I got the blessing of the Speaker and the leadership. It's personal friendships. I had done a lot of things for them in the past, and when I went to them and asked them, they gave it to me." A Republican chosen for the Committee in his first term recalled,

The House Appropriations Committee as a Political System 179

The Chairman [Rep. Taber] I guess did some checking around in my area. After all, I was new and he didn't know me. People told me that they were called to see if I was—well, unstable or apt to go off on tangents . . . to see whether or not I had any preconceived notions about things and would not be flexible—whether I would oppose things even though it was obvious.

A key criterion in each of the cases mentioned with a demonstrable record of, or an assumed predisposition toward, legislative give-and-take.

The 106 Appropriations Committee members serving between 1947 and 1961 spent an average of 3–6 years on other House committees before coming to the Committee. Only 17 of the 106 were selected as first term Congressmen. A house apprenticeship (which Appropriations maintains more successfully than all committees save Ways and Means and Rules[1]) provides the time in which legislative reputations can be established by the member and an assessment of that reputation in terms of Appropriations Committee requirements can be made. Moreover, the mere fact that a member survives for a couple of terms is some indication of an electoral situation conducive to his "responsible" legislative behavior. The optimum bet for the Committee is a member from a sufficiently safe district to permit him freedom of maneuver inside the House without fear of reprisal at the polls.[2] The degree of responsiveness to House norms which the Committee selectors value may be the product of a safe district as well as an individual temperament.

Attractiveness. A fourth factor is the extraordinarily high degree of attractiveness which the Committee holds for its members—as measured by the low rate of departure from it. Committee members do not leave it for service on other committees. To the contrary, they are attracted to it from nearly every other committee.[3] Of the 106 members in the 1947–1961 period, only two men left the Committee voluntarily; and neither of them initiated the move.[4] Committee attractiveness is a measure of its capacity to satisfy individual member needs—for power, prestige, recognition, respect, self-esteem, friendship, etc. Such satisfaction in

---

[1] In the period from 1947 through 1950 (80th to 86th Congress), 79 separate appointments were made to the Appropriations Committee, with 14 going to freshmen. The Committee filled, in other words, 17.7 per cent of its vacancies with freshmen. The Rules Committee had 26 vacancies and selected no freshmen at all. The Ways and Means Committee had 36 vacancies and selected 2 freshmen (5.6 per cent). All other Committees had a higher percentage of freshmen appointments. Armed Services ranked fourth, with 45 vacancies and 12 freshmen appointed, for a percentage of 26.7. Foreign Affairs figures were 46 and 14, or 30.4 per cent; UnAmerican Activities figures were 22 and 7, or 31.8 per cent. . . .
[2] In the 1960 elections, 41 out of the current 50 members received more than 55.1 per cent of the vote in their districts. By a common definition, that is, only 9 of the 50 came from marginal districts.
[3] The 106 members came to Appropriations from every committee except Ways and Means.
[4] One was personally requested by the Speaker to move to Ways and Means. The other was chosen by a caucus of regional Congressmen to be his party's representative on the Rules Committee. Of the 21 members who were forced off the Committee for lack of seniority during a change in party control, or who were defeated for reelection and later returned, 20 sought to regain Committee membership at the earliest opportunity.

turn increases the likelihood that members will behave in such a way as to hold the group together.

The most frequently mentioned source of Committee attractiveness is its power—based on its control of financial resources. "Where the money is, that's where the power is," sums up the feeling of the members. They prize their ability to reward or punish so many other participants in the political process—executive officials, fellow Congressmen, constituents and other clientele groups. In the eyes of its own members, the Committee is either the most powerful in the House or it is on a par with Ways and Means, or less frequently, on a par with Ways and Means and Rules. The second important ingredient in member satisfaction is the government-wide scope of Committee activity. The ordinary Congressman may feel that he has too little knowledge of and too little control over his environment. Membership on this Committee compensates for this feeling of helplessness by the wider contacts, the greater amount of information, and the sense of being "in the middle of things" which are consequent, if not to subcommittee activity, at least to the full Committee's overview of the federal government.

Thirdly, Committee attractiveness is heightened by the group's recognizable and distinctive political style—one that is, moreover, highly valued in American political culture. The style is that of *hard work*; and the Committee's self-image is that of "the hardest working Committee in Congress." His willingness to work is the Committee member's badge of identification, and it is proudly worn. It colors his perceptions of others and their perceptions of him.[5] It is a cherished axiom of all members that, "This Committee is no place for a man who doesn't work. They have to be hard working. It's a way of life. It isn't just a job; it's a way of life."

The mere existence of some identifiable and valued style or "way of life" is a cohesive force for a group. But the particular style of hard work is one which increases group morale and group identification twice over. Hard work means a long, dull, and tedious application to detail, via the technique of "dig, dig, dig, day after day behind closed doors"—in an estimated 460 subcommittee and full committee meetings a year. And virtually all of these meetings are in executive session. By adopting the style of hard work, the Committee discourages highly individualized forms of legislative behavior, which could be disruptive within the Committee. It rewards its members with power, but it is power based rather on

---

[5] A sidelight on this attitude is displayed in a current feud between the House and Senate Appropriations Committees over the meeting place for their conference committees. The House Committee is trying to break the century-old custom that conferences to resolve differences on money bills are always held on the Senate side of the Capitol. House Committee members "complain that they often have to trudge back to the House two or three times to answer roll calls during a conference. They say they go over in a body to work, while Senators flit in and out. . . . The House Appropriations Committee feels that it does all the hard work listening to witnesses for months on each bill, only to have the Senate Committee sit as a court of appeals and, with little more than a cursory glance, restore most of the funds cut." . . .

work inside the Committee than on the political glamour of activities carried on in the limelight of the mass media. Prolonged daily work together encourages sentiments of mutual regard, sympathy, and solidarity. This *esprit* is, in turn, functional for integration on the Committee. A Republican leader summed up,

I think it's more closely knit than any other committee. Yet it's the biggest committee, and you'd think it would be the reverse. I know on my subcommittee, you sit together day after day. You get better acquainted. You have sympathy when other fellows go off to play golf. There's a lot of *esprit de corps* in the Committee.

The strong attraction which members have for the Committee increases the influence which the Committee and its norms exercise on all of them. It increases the susceptibility of the newcomer to Committee socialization and of the veteran to Committee sanctions applicable against deviant behavior.

Membership Stability. Members of the Appropriations Committee are strongly attracted to it; they also have, which bears out their selection as "responsible legislators," a strong attraction for a career in the House of Representatives. The 50 members on the Committee in 1961 had served an average of 13.1 years in the House. These twin attractions produce a noteworthy stability of Committee membership. In the period from the 80th to the 87th Congress, 35.7 per cent of the Committee's membership remained constant. That is to say, 15 of the 42 members on the Committee in March, 1947, were still on the Committee in March, 1961. The 50 members of the Committee in 1961 averaged 9.3 years of prior service on that Committee. In no single year during the last fourteen has the Committee had to absorb an influx of new members totalling more than one-quarter of its membership. At all times, in other words, at least three-fourths of the members have had previous Committee experience. This extraordinary stability of personnel extends into the staff as well. As of June 1961, its 15 professionals had served an average of 10.7 years with the Committee.

The opportunity exists, therefore, for the development of a stable leadership group, a set of traditional norms for the regulation of internal Committee behavior, and informal techniques of personal accommodation. Time is provided in which new members can learn and internalize Committee norms before they attain high seniority rankings. The Committee does not suffer from the potentially disruptive consequences of rapid changeovers in its leadership group, nor of sudden impositions of new sets of norms governing internal Committee behavior.

II

If one considers the main activity of a political system to be decision-making, the acid test of its internal integration is its capacity to make collective decisions without flying apart in the process. Analysis of Committee integration should focus directly, therefore, upon its subgroups and the roles of its members. Two kinds of subgroups are of central importance—subcommittees and majority or minority party groups. The roles which are most relevant derive from: (1) positions which each member holds by virtue of his subgroup attachments, *e.g.*, as subcommittee member, majority (or minority) party member; (2) positions which relate to full Committee membership, *e.g.*, Committee member, and the seniority rankings of veteran, man of moderate experience, and newcomer;[6] (3) positions which relate to both subgroup and full Committee membership, *e.g.*, Chairman of the Committee, ranking minority member of the Committee, subcommittee chairman, ranking subcommittee member. Clusters of norms state the expectations about subgroup and role behavior. The description which follows treats the ways in which these norms and their associated behaviors mesh and clash. It treats, also, the internal control mechanisms by which behavior is brought into reasonable conformity with expectations.

Subgroup Integration. The day-to-day work of the Committee is carried on in its subcommittees, each of which is given jurisdiction over a number of related governmental units. The number of subcommittees is determined by the Committee Chairman, and has varied recently from a low of 9 in 1949 to a high of 15 in 1959. The present total of 14 reflects, as always, a set of strategic and personal judgments by the Chairman balanced against the limitations placed on him by Committee tradition and member wishes. The Chairman also determines subcommittee jurisdiction, appoints subcommittee chairmen and selects the majority party members of each group. The ranking minority member of the Committee exercises similar control over subcommittee assignments on his side of the aisle.

Each subcommittee holds hearings on the budget estimates of the agencies assigned to it, meets in executive session to decide what figures and what language to recommend to the full Committee (to "mark up" the bill), defends its recommendations before the full Committee, writes the Committee's report to the House, dominates the debate on the floor, and bargains for the House in conference committee. Within its jurisdiction, each subcommittee functions independently of the others and guards its autonomy jealously. The Chairman and ranking minority member of the full Committee have, as we shall see, certain opportunities to oversee and dip into the operations of all subcommittees. But their intervention is expected to be minimal. Moreover, they themselves operate importantly within the subcommittee framework by sitting as chairman or ranking minority member of the subcommittee in which they are most interested. Each subcommittee, under the guidance of its chairman, transacts its business in considerable isolation from every other one. One subcommittee chairman exclaimed,

[6] "Newcomers" are defined as men who have served no more than two terms on the Committee. "Men of moderate experience" are those with 3–5 terms of service. "Veterans" are those who have 6 or more terms of Committee service.

Why, you'd be branded an impostor if you went into one of those other subcommittee meetings. The only time I go is by appointment, by arrangement with the chairman at a special time. I'm as much a stranger in another subcommittee as I would be in the legislative Committee on Post Office and Civil Service. Each one does its work apart from all others.

All members of all subcommittees are expected to behave in similar fashion in the role of subcommittee member. Three main norms define this role; to the extent that they are observed, they promote harmony and reduce conflict among subcommittees.[7] Subcommittee autonomy gives to the House norm of *specialization* an intensified application on the Appropriations Committee. Each member is expected to play the role of specialist in the activities on one subcommittee. He will sit on from one to four subcommittees, but normally will specialize in the work, or a portion of the work, of only one. Except for the Chairman, ranking minority member, and their confidants, a Committee member's time, energy, contacts, and experience are devoted to his subcommittees. Specialization is, therefore, among the earliest and most compelling of the Committee norms to which a newcomer is exposed. Within the Committee, respect, deference, and power are earned through subcommittee activity and hence, to a degree, through specialization. Specialization is valued further because it is well suited to the task of guarding the Treasury. Only by specializing, Committee members believe, can they unearth the volume of factual information necessary for the intelligent screening of budget requests. Since "the facts" are acquired only through industry an effective specialist will, perforce, adopt and promote the Committee's style of hard work.

Committee-wide acceptance of specialization is an integrative force in decision-making because it helps support a second norm—*reciprocity*. The stage at which a subcommittee makes its recommendations is a potential point of internal friction. Conflict among subcommittees (or between one subcommittee and the rest of the Committee) is minimized by the deference traditionally accorded to the recommendation of the subcommittee which has specialized in the area, has worked hard, and has "the facts." "It's a matter of 'You respect my work and I'll respect yours.'" "It's frowned upon if you offer an amendment in the full Committee if you aren't on the subcommittee. It's considered presumptuous to pose as an expert if you aren't on the subcommittee." Though records of full Committee decisions are not available, members agree that subcommittee recommendations are "very rarely changed," "almost always approved," "changed one time in fifty," "very seldom changed," etc.

No subcommittee is likely to keep the deference of the full Committee for

---

[7] A statement of expected behavior was taken to be a Committee norm when it was expressed by a substantial number of respondents (a dozen or so) who represented both parties, and varying degrees of experience. In nearly every case, moreover, no refutation of them was encountered, and ample confirmation of their existence can be found in the public record. Their articulation came most frequently from the veterans of the group.

long unless its recommendations have widespread support among its own members. To this end, a third norm—*subcommittee unity*—is expected to be observed by subcommittee members. Unity means a willingness to support (or not to oppose) the recommendations of one's own subcommittee. Reciprocity and unity are closely dependent upon one another. Reciprocity is difficult to maintain when subcommittees themselves are badly divided; and unity has little appeal unless reciprocity will subsequently be observed. The norm of reciprocity functions to minimize inter-subcommittee conflict. The norm of unity functions to minimize intra-subcommittee conflict. Both are deemed essential to subcommittee influence.

One payoff for the original selection of "responsible legislators" is their special willingness to compromise in pursuit of subcommittee unity. The impulse to this end is registered most strongly at the time when the subcommittee meets in executive session to mark up the bill. Two ranking minority members explained this aspect of markup procedure in their subcommittees:

If there's agreement, we go right along. If there's a lot of controversy we put the item aside and go on. Then, after a day or two, we may have a list of ten controversial items. We give and take and pound them down till we get agreement.

We have a unanimous agreement on everything. If a fellow enters an objection and we can't talk him out of it—and sometimes we can get him to go along—that's it. We put it in there.

Once the bargain is struck, the subcommittee is expected to "stick together."

It is, of course, easier to achieve unity among the five, seven, or nine members of a subcommittee than among the fifty members of the full Committee. But members are expected wherever possible to observe the norm of unity in the full Committee as well. That is, they should not only defer to the recommendations of the subcommittee involved, but they should support (or not oppose) that recommendation when it reaches the floor in the form of a Committee decision. On the floor, Committee members believe, their power and prestige depend largely on the degree to which the norms of reciprocity and unity continue to be observed. Members warn each other that if they go to the floor in disarray they will be "rolled," "jumped," or "run over" by the membership. It is a cardinal maxim among Committee members that "You can't turn an appropriations bill loose on the floor." Two senior subcommittee chairmen explain,

We iron out our differences in Committee. We argue it out and usually have a meeting of the minds, a composite view of the Committee. . . . If we went on the floor in wide disagreement, they would say, 'If you can't agree after listening to the testimony and discussing it, how can we understand it? We'll just vote on the basis of who we like the best.'

I tell them (the full Committee) we should have a united front. If there are any objections or changes, we ought to hear it now, and not wash our dirty linen out on the floor. If we don't have a bill that we can all agree on and support, we ought not to report it out. To do that is like throwing a piece of meat to a bunch of hungry animals.

One of the most functional Committee practices supporting the norm of unity is the tradition against minority reports in the subcommittee and in the full Committee. It is symptomatic of Committee integration that custom should proscribe the use of the most formal and irrevocable symbol of congressional committee disunity—the minority report. A few have been written—but only 9 out of a possible 141 during the 11 years, 1947–1957. That is to say, 95 per cent of all original appropriations bills in this period were reported out without dissent. The technique of "reserving" is the Committee member's equivalent for the registering of dissent. In subcommittee or Committee, when a member reserves, he goes on record informally by informing his colleagues that he reserves the right to disagree on a specified item later on in the proceedings. He may seek a change or support a change in that particular item in full Committee or on the floor. But he does not publicize his dissent. The subcommittee or the full Committee can then make an unopposed recommendation. The individual retains some freedom of maneuver without firm commitment. Often a member reserves on an appropriations item but takes no further action. A member explained how the procedure operates in subcommittee:

If there's something I feel too strongly about, and just can't go along, I'll say, 'Mr. Chairman, we can have a unanimous report, but I reserve the right to bring this up in full Committee. I feel duty bound to make a play for it and see if I can't sell it to the other members.' But if I don't say anything, or don't reserve this right, and then I bring it up in full Committee, they'll say, 'Who are you trying to embarrass? You're a member of the team, aren't you? That's not the way to get along.'

Disagreement cannot, of course, be eliminated from the Committee. But the Committee has accepted a method for ventilating it which produces a minimum of internal disruption. And members believe that the greater their internal unity, the greater the likelihood that their recommendations will pass the House.

The degree to which the role of the subcommittee member can be so played and subcommittee conflict thereby minimized depends upon the minimization of conflict between the majority and minority party subgroups. Nothing would be more disruptive to the Committee's work than bitter and extended partisan controversy. It is, therefore, important to Appropriations Committee integration that a fourth norm—*minimal partisanship*—should be observed by members of both party contingents. Nearly every respondent emphasized, with approval, that "very little" or "not much" partisanship prevailed on the Committee. One subcommittee chairman stated flatly, "My job is to keep down partisanship." A ranking minority member said, "You might think that we Republicans would defend the Administration and the budget, but we don't." Majority and minority party ratios are constant and do not change (*i.e.,* in 1958) to reflect changes in the strength of the controlling party. The Committee operates with a completely non-partisan professional staff, which does not change in tune with shifts in party control. Requests for studies by the Committee's investigating staff must be made by the Chairman and ranking minority member of the full Committee and by the Chairman and ranking minority member of the subcommittee involved. Subcommittees can produce recommendations without dissent and the full Committee can adopt reports without dissent precisely because party conflict is (during the period 1947–1961) the exception rather than the rule.

The Committee is in no sense immune from the temperature of party conflict, but it does have a relatively high specific heat. Intense party strife or a strongly taken presidential position will get reflected in subcommittee and in Committee recommendations. Sharp divisions in party policy were carried, with disruptive impact, into some areas of Committee activity during the 80th Congress and subsequently, by way of reaction, into the 81st Congress. During the Eisenhower years, extraordinary presidential pleas, especially concerning foreign aid, were given special heed by the Republican members of the Committee. Partisanship is normally generated from the environment and not from within the Committee's party groups. Partisanship is therefore, likely to be least evident in subcommittee activity, stronger in the full Committee, and most potent at the floor stage. Studies which have focussed on roll-call analysis have stressed the influence of party in legislative decision-making. In the appropriations process, at any rate, the floor stage probably represents party influence at its maximum. Our examination, by interview, of decision-making at the subcommittee and full Committee level would stress the influence of Committee-oriented norms—the strength of which tends to vary inversely with that of party bonds. In the secrecy and intimacy of the subcommittee and full Committee hearing rooms, the member finds it easy to compromise on questions of more or less, to take money from one program and give it to another and, in general, to avoid yes-or-no type party stands. These decisions, taken in response to the integrative norms of the Committee, are the most important ones in the entire appropriations process.

Role Integration. The roles of subcommittee member and party member are common to all.

Other more specific decision-making positions are allocated among the members. Different positions produce different roles, and in an integrated system, these too must fit together. Integration, in other words, must be achieved through the complementarity or reciprocity of roles as well as through a similarity of roles. This may mean a pattern in which expectations are so different that there is very little contact between individuals; or it may mean a pattern in which contacts require the working out of an involved system of exchange of obligations and rewards. In either case, the desired result is the minimization of conflict among prominent Committee roles. Two crucial instances of role reciprocity on the Committee involve the seniority positions of old-timer and newcomer and the

The House Appropriations Committee as a Political System

leadership positions of Chairman and ranking minority member, on both the full Committee and on each subcommittee.

The differentiation between senior and junior members is the broadest definition of who shall and who shall not actively participate in Committee decisions. Of a junior member, it will be said, "Oh, he doesn't count—what I mean is, he hasn't been on the Committee long enough." He is not expected to and ordinarily does not have much influence. His role is that of apprentice. He is expected to learn the business and the norms of the Committee by applying himself to its work. He is expected to acquiesce in an arrangement which gives most influence (except in affairs involving him locally) to the veterans of the group. Newcomers will be advised to "follow the chairman until you get your bearings. For the first two years, follow the chairman. He knows." "Work hard, keep quiet, and attend the Committee sessions. We don't want to listen to some new person coming in here." And newcomers perceive their role in identical terms: "You have to sit in the back seat and edge up little by little." "You just go to subcommittee meetings and assimilate the routine. The new members are made to feel welcome, but you have a lot of rope-learning to do before you carry much weight."

At every stage of Committee work, this differentiation prevails. There is remarkable agreement on the radically different sets of expectations involved. During the hearings, the view of the elders is that "Newcomers . . . don't know what the score is and they don't have enough information to ask intelligent questions." A newcomer described his behavior in typically similar terms: "I attended all the hearings and studied and collected information that I can use next year. I'm just marking time now." During the crucial subcommittee markup, the newcomer will have little opportunity to speak—save in local important matters. A subcommittee chairman stated the norm from his viewpoint this way: "When we get a compromise, nobody's going to break that up. If someone tries, we sit on him fast. We don't want young people who throw bricks or slow things down." And a newcomer reciprocated, describing his markup conduct: "I'm not provocative. I'm in there for information. They're the experts in the field. I go along." In full Committee, on the floor, and in conference committee, the Committee's senior members take the lead and the junior members are expected to follow. The apprentice role is common to all new members of the House. But it is wrong to assume that each Committee will give it the same emphasis. Some pay it scant heed. The Appropriations Committee makes it a cornerstone of its internal structure.

Among the Committee's veterans, the key roles are those of Committee Chairman and ranking minority member, and their counterparts in every subcommittee. It is a measure of Committee integration and the low degree of partisanship that considerable reciprocity obtains between these roles. Their partisan status nevertheless sets limits to the degree of possible integration. The Chairman is given certain authority which he and only he can exercise. But save in times of extreme party controversy, the expectation is that consultation and cooperation between the Chairman [and the] ranking minority member shall lubricate the Committee's entire work. For example, by Committee tradition, its Chairman and ranking minority member are both *ex officio* voting members of each subcommittee and of every conference committee. The two of them thus have joint access at every stage of the internal process. A subcommittee chairman, too, is expected to discuss matters of scheduling and agenda with his opposite minority number. He is expected to work with him during the markup session and to give him (and, normally, only him) an opportunity to read and comment on the subcommittee report. A ranking minority member described his subcommittee markup procedure approvingly:

Frequently the chairman has a figure which he states. Sometimes he will have no figure, and he'll turn to me and say, '————, what do you think?' Maybe I'll have a figure. It's a very flexible. Everyone has a chance to say what he thinks, and we'll move it around. Sometimes it takes a long time. . . . He's a rapid partisan on the floor, but he is a very fair man in the subcommittee.

Where influence is shared, an important exchange of rewards occurs. The chairman gains support for his leadership and the ranking minority member gains intra-Committee power. The Committee as a whole insures against the possibility of drastic change in its internal structure by giving to its key minority members a stake in its operation. Chairmen and ranking minority members will, in the course of time, exchange positions; and it is expected that such a switch will produce no form of retribution nor any drastic change in the functioning of the Committee. Reciprocity of roles, in this case, promotes continued integration. A ranking minority member testified to one successful arrangement when he took the floor in the 83d Congress to say:

The gentleman and I have been seesawing back and forth on this Committee for some time. He was chairman in the 80th Congress. I had the privilege of serving as chairman in the 81st and 72nd Congresses. Now he is back in the saddle. I can say that he has never failed to give me his utmost cooperation, and I have tried to give him the same cooperation during his service as chairman of this Committee. We seldom disagree, but we have found out that we can disagree without being disagreeable. Consequently, we have unusual harmony on this Committee.

Reciprocity between chairmen and ranking minority members on the Appropriations Committee is to some incalculable degree a function of the stability of membership which allows a pair of particular individuals to work out the kind of personal accommodation described above. The close working relationship of Clarence Cannon and John Taber, whose service on the Committee totals 68 years and who have been changing places as Chairman and ranking minority member for 19 years, highlights and sustains a pattern of majority–minority reciprocity throughout the group.

The House Appropriations Committee as a Political System

Internal Control Mechanisms. The expectations which apply to subcommittee, to party, to veterans and to newcomers, to chairmen and to ranking minority members prescribe highly integrative behaviors. We have concentrated on these expectations, and have both illustrated and assumed the close correlation between expected and actual behavior. This does not mean that all the norms of the Committee have been canvassed. Nor does it mean that deviation from the integrative norms does not occur. It does. From what can be gathered, however, from piecing together a study of the public record on appropriations from 1947 to 1961 with interview materials, the Committee has been markedly successful in maintaining a stable internal structure over time. As might be expected, therefore, changes and threats of change have been generated more from the environment—when outsiders consider the Committee as unresponsive—than from inside the subsystem itself. One source of internal stability, and an added reason for assuming a correlation between expected and actual behavior, is the existence of what appear to be reasonably effective internal control mechanisms. Two of these are the socialization processes applied to newcomers and the sanctioning mechanisms applicable to all Committee members.

Socialization is in part a training in perception. Before members of a group can be expected to behave in accordance with its norms, they must learn to see and interpret the world around them with reasonable similarity. The socialization of the Committee newcomer during his term or two of apprenticeship serves to bring his perceptions and his attitudes sufficiently into line with those of the other members to serve as a basis for Committee integration. The Committee, as we have seen, is chosen from Congressmen whose political flexibility connotes an aptitude for learning new lessons of power. Furthermore, the high degree of satisfaction of its members with the group increases their susceptibility to its processes of learning and training.

For example, one half of the Committee's Democrats are Northerners and Westerners from urban constituencies, whose voting records are just as "liberal" on behalf of domestic social welfare programs as non-Committee Democrats from like constituencies. They come to the Committee favorably disposed toward the high level of federal spending necessary to support such programs, and with no sense of urgency about the Committee's task of guarding the Treasury or reducing budget estimates. Given the criteria governing their selection, however, they come without rigid preconceptions and with a built-in responsiveness to the socialization processes of any legislative group of which they are members. It is crucial to Committee integration that they learn to temper their potentially disruptive welfare-state ideology with a conservative's concern for saving money. They must change their perceptions and attitudes sufficiently to view the Committee's tasks in nearly the same terms as their more conservative Southern Democratic and Republican colleagues. What their elders perceive as reality (*i.e.,* the disposition of executives to ask for more money than is necessary) they, too, must see as reality. A subcommittee chairman explained:

When you have sat on the Committee, you see that these bureaus are always asking for more money—always up, never down. They want to build up their organization. You reach the point—I have—where it sickens you, where you rebel against it. Year after year, they want more money. They say, 'Only $50,000 this year'; but you know the pattern. Next year they'll be back for $100,000, then $200,000. The younger members haven't been on the Committee long enough, haven't had the experience to know this.

The younger men, in this case the younger liberals, do learn from their Committee experience. Within one or two terms, they are differentiating between themselves and the "wild-eyed spenders" or the "free spenders" in the House. "Some of these guys would spend you through the roof," exclaimed one liberal of moderate seniority. Repeated exposure to Committee work and to fellow members has altered their perceptions and their attitudes in money matters. Half a dozen Northern Democrats of low or moderate seniority agreed with one of their number who said: "Yes, it's true. I can see it myself. I suppose I came here a flaming liberal; but as the years go by I get more conservative. You just hate like hell to spend all this money. . . . You come to the point where you say, 'By God, this is enough jobs.'" These men will remain more inclined toward spending than their Committee colleagues, but their perceptions and hence their attitudes have been brought close enough to the others to support a consensus on tasks. They are responsive to appeals on budget-cutting grounds that would not have registered earlier and which remain meaningless to liberals outside the Committee. In cases, therefore, where Committee selection does not and cannot initially produce individuals with a predisposition toward protecting the Treasury, the same result is achieved by socialization.

Socialization is a training in behavior as well as in perception. For the newcomer, conformity to norms in specific situations is insured through the appropriate application, by the committee veterans, of rewards and punishments. For the Committee member who serves his apprenticeship creditably, the passage of time holds the promise that he will inherit a position of influence. He may, as an incentive, be given some small reward early in his Committee career. One man, in his second year, had been assigned the task of specializing in one particular program. However narrow the scope of his specialization, it had placed him on the road to influence within the Committee. He explained with evident pleasure:

The first year, you let things go by. You can't participate. But you learn by watching the others operate. The next year, you know what you're interested in and when to step in. . . . For instance, I've become an expert on the ——— program. The chairman said to me, 'This is something you ought to get interested in.' I did; and now I'm the expert on the Committee. Whatever I say on that, the other members listen to me and do what I want.

At some later date, provided he continues to observe Committee norms, he will be granted additional influence, perhaps through a prominent floor role. A model Committee man of moderate seniority who had just attained to this stage of accomplishment, and who had suffered through several political campaigns back home fending off charges that he was a do-nothing Congressman, spoke about the rewards he was beginning to reap.

When you perform well on the floor when you bring out a bill, and Members know that you know the bill, you develop prestige with other Members of Congress. They come over and ask you what you think, because they know you've studied it. You begin to get a reputation beyond your subcommittee. And you get inner satisfaction, too. You don't feel that you're down here doing nothing.

The first taste of influence which comes to men on this Committee is compensation for the frustrations of apprenticeship. Committee integration in general, and the meshing of roles between elders and newcomers in particular, rests on the fact that conformity to role expectations over time does guarantee to the young positive rewards—the very kind of rewards of power, prestige, and personal satisfaction which led most of them to seek Committee membership in the first place.

The important function of apprenticeship is that it provides the necessary time during which socialization can go forward. And teaching proceeds with the aid of punishments as well as rewards. Should a new member inadvertently or deliberately run afoul of Committee norms during his apprenticeship, he will find himself confronted with negative sanctions ranging in subtlety from "jaundiced eyes" to a changed subcommittee assignment. Several members, for example, recalled their earliest encounter with the norm of unity and the tradition against minority reports. One remembered his attempt to file a minority report.

The Chairman was pretty upset about it. It's just a tradition, I guess, not to have minority reports. I didn't know it was a tradition. When I said I was going to write a minority report, some eyebrows were raised. The Chairman said it just wasn't the thing to do. Nothing more was said about it. But it wasn't a very popular thing to do, I guess.

He added that he had not filed one since.

Some younger members have congenital difficulty in observing the norms of the apprentice's role. In the 86th Congress, these types tended to come from the Republican minority. The minority newcomers (described by one of the men who selected them as "eight young, energetic, fighting conservatives") were a group of economy-minded individuals some of whom chafed against any barrier which kept them from immediate influence on Committee policy. Their reaction was quite different from that of the young Democrats, whose difficulty was in learning to become economy-minded, but who did not actively resent their lack of influence. One freshman, who felt that "The appropriations system is lousy, inadequate, and old fashioned," recalled that he had spoken out in full Committee against the recommendations of a subcommittee of which he was not a member.

Having failed, he continued to oppose the recommendation during floor debate. By speaking up, speaking in relation to the work of another subcommittee, and by opposing a Committee recommendation, he had violated the particular norms of his apprentice role as well of the generally applicable norms of reciprocity and unity. He explained what he had learned, but remained only partially socialized:

They want to wash their dirty linen in the Committee and they want no opposition afterward. They let me say my piece in Committee. . . . But I just couldn't keep quiet. I said some things on the floor, and I found out that's about all they would take. . . . If you don't get along with your Committee and have their support, you don't get anything accomplished around here. . . . I'm trying to be a loyal, cooperative member of the Committee. You hate to be a stinker; but I'm still picking at the little things because I can't work on the big things. There's nothing for the new men to do, so they have to find places to needle in order to take some part in it.

Another freshman, who had deliberately violated apprenticeship norms by trying to ask "as many questions as the Chairman" during subcommittee hearings, reported a story of unremitting counteraction against his deviation:

In the hearings, I have to wait sometimes nine or ten hours for a chance; and he hopes I'll get tired and stay home. I've had to wait till some pretty unreasonable hours. Once I've gotten the floor, though, I've been able to make a good case. Sometimes I've been the only person there. . . . He's all powerful. He's got all the power. He wouldn't think of taking me on a trip with him when he goes to hold hearings. Last year, he went to ———. He wouldn't give me a nudge there. And in the hearings, when I'm questioning a witness, he'll keep butting in so that my case won't appear to be too rosy.

Carried on over a period of two years, this behavior resulted in considerable personal friction between a Committee elder and the newcomer. Other members of his subcommittee pointedly gave him a great lack of support for his non-conformity. "They tried to slow him down and tone him down a little," not because he and his subcommittee chairman disagreed, but on the grounds that the Committee has developed accepted ways of disagreeing which minimize, rather than exacerbate, interpersonal friction.

One internal threat to Committee integration comes from new members who from untutored perceptions, from ignorance of norms, or from dissatisfaction with the apprentice role may not act in accordance with Committee expectations. The seriousness of this threat is minimized, however, by the fact that the deviant newcomer does not possess sufficient resources to affect adversely the operation of the system. Even if he does not respond immediately to the application of sanctions, he can be held in check and subjected to an extended and (given the frequency of interaction among members) intensive period of socialization. The success of Committee socialization is indicated by the fact that whereas wholesale criticism of Committee operations was frequently voiced among junior members, it had disappeared among the men of moderate experience. And what these middle seniority members now accept as the facts of Committee life, the veterans vigorously assert and defend as the essentials of a smoothly functioning system. Satisfaction with the Committee's internal structure increases with length of Committee service.

An important reason for changing member attitudes is that those who have attained leadership positions have learned, as newcomers characteristically have not, that their conformity to Committee norms is the ultimate source of their influence inside the group. Freshman members do not as readily perceive the degree to which interpersonal influence is rooted in obedience to group norms. They seem to convert their own sense of powerlessness into the view that the Committee's leaders possess, by virtue of their positions, arbitrary, absolute, and awesome power. Typically, they say: "If you're a subcommittee chairman, it's your Committee." "The Chairman runs the show. He gets what he wants. He decides what he wants and gets it through." Older members of the Committee, however, view the power of the leaders as a highly contingent and revocable grant, tendered by the Committee for so long and only so long as their leaders abide by Committee expectations. In commenting on internal influence, their typical reaction is: "Of course, the Committee wouldn't follow him if it didn't want to. He has a great deal of respect. He's an able man, a hard-working man." "He knows the bill backwards and forwards. He works hard, awfully hard, and the members know it." Committee leaders have an imposing set of formal prerogatives. But they can capitalize on them only if they command the respect, confidence and deference of their colleagues.

It is basic to Committee integration that members who have the greatest power to change the system evidence the least disposition to do so. Despite their institutional conservatism, however, Committee elders do occasionally violate the norms applicable to them and hence represent a potential threat to successful integration. Excessive deviation from Committee expectations by some leaders will bring counter-measures by other leaders. Thus, for example, the Chairman and his subcommittee chairmen exercise reciprocal controls over one another's behavior. The Chairman has the authority to appoint the chairman and members of each subcommittee and fix its jurisdiction. "He runs the Committee. He has a lot of power," agrees one subcommittee chairman. "But it's all done on the basis of personal friendship. If he tries to get too big, the members can whack him down by majority vote."

In the 84th Congress, Chairman Cannon attempted an unusually broad reorganization of subcommittee jurisdictions. The subcommittee chairman most adversely affected rallied his senior colleagues against the Chairman's action—on the ground that it was an excessive violation of role expectations and threatening to subcommittee autonomy. Faced with the prospect of a negative Committee vote, the chairman was forced to act in closer conformity to the expectations of the other leaders. As one participant described the episode,

Mr. Cannon, for reasons of his own, tried to bust up one of the subcommittees. We didn't like that. . . . He was breaking up the whole Committee. A couple of weeks later, a few of the senior members got together and worked out a compromise. By that time, he had seen a few things, so we went to him and talked to him and worked it out.

On the subcommittees, too, it is the veterans of both parties who will levy sanctions against an offending chairman. It is they who speak of "cutting down to size" and "trimming the whiskers" of leaders who become "too cocky," "too stubborn," or who "do things wrong too often." Committee integration is underwritten by the fact that no member high or low is permanently immune from the operation of its sanctioning mechanisms.

III

Data concerning internal committee activity can be organized and presented in various ways. One way is to use key functional problems like integration as the focal points for descriptive analysis. On the basis of our analysis (and without, for the time being, having devised any precise measure of integration), we are lead to the summary observation that the House Appropriations Committee appears to be a well integrated, if not an extremely well integrated committee. The question arises as to whether anything can be gained from this study other than a description of one property of one political subsystem. If it is reasonable to assume that the internal life of a congressional committee affects all legislative activity involving that committee, and if it is reasonable to assume that the analysis of a committee's internal relationships will produce useful knowledge about legislative behavior, some broader implications for this study are indicated.

In the first place, the success of the House Appropriations Committee in solving the problem of integration probably does have important consequences for the appropriations process. Some of the possible relationships can be stated as hypotheses and tested; others can be suggested as possible guides to understanding. All of them require further research. Of primary interest is the relationship between integration and the power of the Committee. There is little doubt about the fact of Committee power. Of the 443 separate case histories of bureau appropriations examined, the House accepted Committee recommendations in 387, or 87.4 per cent of them; and in 159, or 33.6 per cent of the cases, the House Committee's original recommendations on money amounts were the exact ones enacted into law. The hypothesis that the greater the degree of Committee unity the greater the probability that its recommendations will be accepted is being tested as part of a larger study. House Committee integration may be a key factor in producing House victories in conference committee. This relationship, too, might be tested. Integration appears to help provide the House conferees with a feeling of confidence and superiority which is one of their important advantages in the mix of psychological factors affecting conference deliberations.

Another suggested consequence of high integration is that party groups have a relatively small influence upon appropriations decisions. It suggests, too, that Committee-oriented behavior should be duly emphasized in any analysis of Congressional oversight of administrative activity by this Committee. Successful integration promotes the achievement of the Committee's goals, and doubtless helps account for the fairly consistent production of budget-cutting decisions. Another consequence will be found in the strategies adopted by people seeking favorable Committee decisions. For example, the characteristic lines of contact from executive officials to the Committee will run to the chairman and the ranking minority member (and to the professional staff man) of the single subcommittee handling their agency's appropriations. The ways in which the Committee achieves integration may even affect the success or failure of a bureau in getting its appropriations. Committee members, for instance, will react more favorably toward an administrator who conforms to their self-image of the hard-working master-of-detail than to one who does not—and Committee response to individual administrators bulks large in their determinations.

Finally, the internal integration of this Committee helps to explain the extraordinary stability, since 1920, of appropriations procedures—in the face of repeated proposals to change them through omnibus appropriations, legislative budgets, new budgetary forms, item veto, Treasury borrowing, etc. Integration is a stabilizing force, and the stability of the House Appropriations Committee has been a force for stabilization throughout the entire process. It was, for example, the disagreement between Cannon and Taber which led to the indecisiveness reflected in the short-lived experiment with a single appropriations bill. One need only examine the conditions most likely to decrease Committee integration to ascertain some of the critical factors for producing changes in the appropriations process. A description of integration is also an excellent base-line from which to analyze changes in internal structure.

All of these are speculative propositions which call for further research. But they suggest, as a second implication, that committee integration does have important consequences for legislative activity and, hence, that it is a key variable in the study of legislative politics. It would seem, therefore, to be a fruitful focal point for the study of other congressional committees.[8] Comparative committee analysis could usefully be devoted to (1) the factors which tend to increase or

[8] This view has been confirmed by the results of interviews conducted by the author with members of the House Committee on Education and Labor, together with an examination of that Committee's activity in one policy area. They indicate very significant contrasts between the internal structure of that Committee and the Appropriations Committee—contrasts which center around their comparative success in meeting the problem of integration. The House Committee on Education and Labor appears to be a poorly integrated committee. Its internal structure is characterized by a great deal of subgroup conflict, relatively little role reciprocity, and minimally effective internal control mechanisms. External concerns, like those of party, constituency, and clientele groups, are probably more effective in determining its decisions than is likely to be the case in a well integrated committee. . . .

decrease integration; (2) the degree to which integration is achieved; and (3) the consequences of varying degrees of integration for committee behavior and influence. If analyses of committee integration are of any value, they should encourage the analysis and the classification of congressional committees along functional lines. And they should lead to the discussion of interrelated problems of committee survival. Functional classifications of committees (*i.e.*, well or poorly integrated) derived from a large number of descriptive analyses of several functional problems, may prove helpful in constructing more general propositions about the legislative process.

Congressional Responses in the Twentieth Century

SAMUEL P. HUNTINGTON

Congress is a frequent source of anguish to both its friends and its foes. The critics point to its legislative failure. The function of a legislature, they argue, is to legislate, and Congress either does not legislate or legislates too little and too late. The intensity of their criticism varies inversely with the degree and despatch with which Congress approves the President's legislative proposals. When in 1963 the 88th Congress seemed to stymie the Kennedy legislative program, criticism rapidly mounted. "What kind of legislative body is it," asked Walter Lippmann, neatly summing up the prevailing exasperation, "that will not or cannot legislate?" When in 1964 the same 88th Congress passed the civil rights, tax, and other bills, criticism of Congress correspondingly subsided. Reacting differently to this familiar pattern, the friends of Congress lamented its acquiescence to presidential dictate. Since 1933, they said, the authority of the executive branch—President, administration, and bureaucracy—has waxed, while that of Congress has waned. They warned of the constitutional perils stemming from the permanent subordination of one branch of government to another. Thus, at the same time that it is an obstructive ogre to its enemies, Congress is also the declining despair of its friends. Can both images be true? In large part, they are. The loss of power by Congress, indeed, can be measured

FROM Samuel P. Huntington, "Congressional Responses in the Twentieth Century," in David B. Truman, ed., *The Congress and America's Future* (Englewood Cliffs, N. J.: Prentice-Hall, 1965), pp. 5–31.

by the extent to which congressional assertion coincides with congressional obstruction.

This paradox has been at the root of the "problem" of Congress since the early days of the New Deal. Vis-à-vis the Executive, Congress is an autonomous, legislative body. But apparently Congress can defend its autonomy only be refusing to legislate, and it can legislate only by surrendering its autonomy. When Congress balks, criticism rises, and the clamoring voices of reformers fill the air with demands for the "modernization" of the "antiquated procedures" of an "eighteenth-century" Congress so it can deal with "twentieth-century realities." The demands for reform serve as counters in the legislative game to get the President's measures through Congress. Independence thus provokes criticism; acquiescence brings approbation. If Congress legislates, it subordinates itself to the President; if it refuses to legislate, it alienates itself from public opinion. Congress can assert its power or it can pass laws; but it cannot do both.

LEGISLATIVE POWER AND INSTITUTIONAL CRISIS

The roots of this legislative dilemma lie in the changes in American society during the twentieth century. The twentieth century has seen: rapid urbanization and the beginnings of a post-industrial, technological society; the nationalization of social and economic problems and the concomitant growth of national organizations to deal with these problems; the increasing bureaucratization of social, economic, and governmental organizations; and the sustained high-level international involvement of the United States in world politics. These developments have generated new forces in American politics and initiated major changes in the distribution of power in American society. In particular, the twentieth century has witnessed the tremendous expansion of the responsibilities of the national government and the size of the national bureaucracy. In 1901, the national government had 351,798 employees or less than 1½ per cent of the national labor force. In 1962, it had 5,232,819 employees, constituting 7 per cent of the labor force. The expansion of the national government has been paralleled by the emergence of other large, national, bureaucratic organizations: manufacturing corporations, banks, insurance companies, labor unions, trade associations, farm organizations, newspaper chains, radio-TV networks. Each organization may have relatively specialized and concrete interests, but typically it functions on a national basis. Its headquarters are in New York or Washington; its operations are scattered across a dozen or more states. The emergence of these organizations truly constitutes, in Kenneth Boulding's expressive phrase, an "organizational revolution." The existence of this private "Establishment," more than anything else, distinguishes twentieth-century America from nineteenth-century America. The leaders of these organizations are the notables of American society: they are the prime wielders of social and economic power.

These momentous social changes have confronted Congress with an institutional "adaptation crisis." Such a crisis occurs when changes in the environment of a governmental institution force the institution either to alter its functions, affiliation, and modes of behavior, or to face decline, decay, and isolation. Crises usually occur when an institution loses its previous sources of support or fails to adapt itself to the rise of new social forces. Such a crisis, for instance, affected the Presidency in the second and third decades of the nineteenth century. Under the leadership of Henry Clay the focal center of power in the national government was in the House of Representatives; the congressional caucus dictated presidential nominations; popular interest in and support for the Presidency were minimal. The "Executive," Justice Story remarked in 1818, "has no longer a commanding influence. The House of Representatives has absorbed all the popular feelings and all the effective power of the country." The Presidency was on the verge of becoming a weak, secondary instrumental organ of government. It was rescued from this fate by the Jacksonian movement, which democratized the Presidency, broadened its basis of popular support, and restored it as the center of vitality and leadership in the national government. The House of Commons was faced with a somewhat similar crisis during the agitation preceding the first Reform Bill of 1832. New social groups were developing in England which were demanding admission to the political arena and the opportunity to share in political leadership. Broadening the constituency of the House of Commons and reforming the system of election enabled the House to revitalize itself and to continue as the principal locus of power in the British government.

In both these cases a governmental institution got a new lease on life, new vigor, new power, by embodying within itself dynamic, new social forces. When an institution fails to make such an alignment, it must either restrict its own authority or submit to a limitation upon its authority imposed from outside. Thus in 1910, when the House of Lords refused to approve Lloyd George's budget, it was first compelled by governmental pressure, popular opinion, and the threat of the creation of new peers to acquiesce in the budget and then through a similar process to acquiesce in the curtailment of its own power to obstruct legislation approved by the Commons. In this case the effort to block legislation approved by the dominant forces in the political community resulted in a permanent diminution of the authority of the offending institution. A somewhat similar crisis developed with respect to the Supreme Court in the 1930's. Here again a less popular body attempted to veto the actions of more popular bodies. In three years the Court invalidated twelve acts of Congress. Inevitably this precipitated vigorous criticism and demands for reform, culminating in Roosevelt's court reorganization proposal in February of 1937. The alternatives confronting the Court were relatively clear-cut: it could "reform" or be "reformed." In "the switch in time that saved nine," it chose the former

Congressional Responses in the Twentieth Century

course, signaling its change by approving the National Labor Relations Act in April 1937 and the Social Security Act in May. With this switch, support for the reorganization of the Court drained away. The result was, in the words of Justice Jackson, "a failure of the reform forces and a victory of the reform."

Each of these four institutional crises arose from the failure of a governmental institution to adjust to social change and the rise of new viewpoints, new needs, and new political forces. Congress's legislative dilemma and loss of power stem from the nature of its over-all institutional response to the changes in American society. This response involves three major aspects of Congress as an institution: its affiliations, its structure, and its functions. During the twentieth century Congress has insulated itself from the new political forces which social change has generated and which are, in turn, generating more change. Hence the leadership of Congress has lacked the incentive to take the legislative initiative in handling emerging national problems. Within Congress power has become dispersed among many officials, committees, and subcommittees. Hence the central leadership of Congress has lacked the ability to establish national legislative priorities. As a result, the legislative function of Congress has declined in importance, while the growth of the federal bureaucracy has made the administrative overseeing function of Congress more important. These three tendencies—toward insulation, dispersion, and oversight—have dominated the evolution of Congress during the twentieth century.

AFFILIATIONS: INSULATION FROM POWER

Perhaps the single most important trend in congressional evolution during the twentieth century has been the growing insulation of Congress from other social groups and political institutions. In 1900 no gap existed between congressmen and the other leaders of American society and politics. Half a century later the changes in American society, on the one hand, and the institutional evolution of Congress, on the other, had produced a marked gap between congressional leaders and the bureaucratically oriented leadership of the executive branch and of the Establishment. The growth of this gap can be seen in seven trends in congressional evolution.

1. *Increasing Tenure of Office.* In the nineteenth century few congressmen stayed in Congress very long. During the twentieth century the average tenure of congressmen has inexorably lengthened. In 1900 only 9 per cent of the members of the House of Representatives had served five terms or more and less than 1 per cent had served ten terms or more. In 1957, 45 per cent of the House had served five terms or more and 14 per cent ten terms or more. In 1897, for each representative who had served ten terms or more in the House, there were 34 representatives who had served two terms or less. In 1961, for each ten-

termer there were only 1.6 representatives who had served two terms or less. In the middle of the nineteenth century, only about half the representatives in any one Congress had served in a previous Congress, and only about one-third of the senators had been elected to the Senate more than once. By 1961 close to 90 per cent of the House were veterans, and almost two-thirds of the senators were beyond their first term. The biennial infusion of new blood had reached an all-time low.

TABLE 1 Veteran Congressmen in Congress.

Congress	Date	Representatives elected to House more than once	Senators elected to Senate more than once
42nd	1871	53%	32%
50th	1887	63	45
64th	1915	74	47
74th	1935	77	54
87th	1961	87	66

2. *The Increasingly Important Role of Seniority.* Increasing tenure of congressmen is closely linked to increasingly rigid adherence to the practices of seniority. The longer men stay in Congress, the more likely they are to see virtue in seniority. Conversely, the more important seniority is, the greater is the constituent appeal of men who have been long in office. The current rigid system of seniority in *both* houses of Congress is a product of the twentieth century.

In the nineteenth century seniority was far more significant in the Senate than in the House. Since the middle of that century apparently only in five instances—the last in 1925—has the chairmanship of a Senate committee been denied to the most senior member of the committee. In the House, on the other hand, the Speaker early received the power to appoint committees and to designate their chairmen. During the nineteenth century Speakers made much of this power. Committee appointment and the selection of chairmen were involved political processes, in which the Speaker carefully balanced factors of seniority, geography, expertise, and policy viewpoint in making his choices. Not infrequently prolonged bargaining would result as the Speaker traded committee positions for legislative commitments. Commenting on James G. Blaine's efforts at committee construction in the early 1870's, one member of his family wrote that Blaine "left for New York on Wednesday. He had cotton and wool manufacturers to meet in Boston, and, over and above all, pressure to resist or permit. As fast as he gets his committees arranged, just so fast some after consideration comes up which overtopples the whole list like a row of bricks." Only with the drastic curtailment of the powers of the Speaker in 1910 and 1911 did the seniority system in the House assume the inflexible pattern which it has today. Only twice since the 1910 revolt—once in 1915 and once in 1921—has seniority been neglected in the choice of committee chairmen.

3. *Extended Tenure: A Prerequisite for Leadership.* Before 1896 Speakers, at the time of their first election, averaged only seven years' tenure in the House. Since 1896 Speakers have averaged twenty-two years of House service at their first election. In 1811 and in 1859 Henry Clay and William Pennington were elected Speaker when they first entered the House. In 1807 Thomas Jefferson arranged for the election of his friend, William C. Nicholas, to the House and then for his immediate selection by the party caucus as floor leader. Such an intrusion of leadership from outside would now be unthinkable. Today the Speaker and other leaders of the House and, to a lesser degree, the leaders of the Senate are legislative veterans of long standing. In 1961 fifty-seven House leaders averaged twenty years of service in the House and thirty-four Senate leaders sixteen years of serivce in the Senate. The top House leaders (Speaker, floor leaders, chairmen and ranking minority members of Ways and Means, Appropriations, and Rules Committees) averaged thirty-one years in the House and nineteen years in leadership positions. The top Senate leaders (President *pro tem.*, floor leaders, chairmen and ranking minority members of Finance, Foreign Relations, and Appropriations Committees) averaged twenty years in the Senate and nine years in leadership positions. Between 1948 and 1961 the average tenure of top leaders increased by two years in the House and by three years in the Senate. Increasing tenure means increasing age. In the nineteenth century the leaders of Congress were often in their thirties. Clay was thirty-four when he became Speaker in 1811; Hunter, thirty when he became Speaker in 1839; White, thirty-six at his accession to the Speakership in 1841; and Ore, thirty-five when he became Speaker, Martin sixty-three, and McCormack seventy-one.

4. *Leadership within Congress: A One-Way Street.* Normally in American life becoming a leader in one institution opens up leadership possibilities in other institutions: corporation presidents head civic agencies or become cabinet officers; foundation and university executives move into government; leading lawyers and bankers take over industrial corporations. The greater one's prestige, authority, and accomplishments within one organization, the easier it is to move to other and better posts in other organizations. Such, however, is not the case with Congress. Leadership in the House of Representatives leads nowhere except to leadership in the House of Representatives. To a lesser degree, the same is true of the Senate. The successful House or Senate leader has to identify himself completely with his institution, its mores, traditions, and ways of behavior. "The very ingredients which make you a powerful House leader," one representative

has commented, "are the ones which keep you from being a public leader."[1] Representatives typically confront a "fourth-term crisis": if they wish to run for higher office—for governor or senator—they must usually do so by the beginning of their fourth term in the House. If they stay in the House for four or more terms, they in effect choose to make a career in the House and to forswear the other electoral possibilities of American politics. Leadership in the Senate is not as exclusive a commitment as it is in the House. But despite such notable exceptions as Taft and Johnson, the most influential men in the Senate have typically been those who have looked with disdain upon the prospect of being anything but a United States Senator. Even someone with the high talent and broad ambition of Lyndon Johnson could not escape this exclusive embrace during his years as majority leader. In the words of Theodore H. White, the Senate, for Johnson, was "faith, calling, club, habit, relaxation, devotion, hobby, and love." Over the years it became "almost a monomania with him, his private life itself." Such "monomania" is normally the prerequisite for Senate leadership. It is also normally an insurmountable barrier, psychologically and politically, to leadership anywhere outside the Senate.

5. *The Decline of Personnel Interchange between Congress and the Administration.* Movement of leaders in recent years between the great national institutions of "The Establishment" and the top positions in the administration has been frequent, easy, and natural. This pattern of lateral entry distinguishes the American executive branch from the governments of most other modern societies. The circulation of individuals between leadership positions in governmental and private institutions eases the strains between political and private leadership and performs a unifying function comparable to that which common class origins perform in Great Britain or common membership in the Communist Party does in the Soviet Union.

The frequent movement of individuals between administration and establishment contrasts sharply with the virtual absence of such movement between Congress and the administration or between Congress and the establishment. The gap between congressional leadership and administration leadership has increased sharply during this century. Seniority makes it virtually impossible for administration leaders to become leaders of Congress and makes it unlikely that leaders of Congress will want to become leaders of the administration. The separation of powers has become the insulation of leaders. Between 1861 and 1896, 37 per cent of the people appointed to posts in the President's cabinet had served in the House or Senate. Between 1897 and 1940, 19 per cent of the Cabinet positions were filled by former congressmen or senators. Between 1941 and 1963, only 15 per cent of the cabinet posts were so filled. Former congressmen received only 4 per cent of over 1,000 appointments of political executives

---

[1] Quoted in Charles L. Clapp, *The Congressman: His Work as He Sees It* (Washington: Brookings Institution, 1963), p. 21.

made during the Roosevelt, Truman, Eisenhower, and Kennedy Administrations. In 1963, apart from the President and Vice-President, only one of the top seventy-five leaders of the Kennedy Administration (Secretary of the Interior Udall) had served in Congress.

Movement from the administration to leadership positions in Congress is almost equally rare. In 1963 only one of eighty-one congressional leaders (Senator Anderson) had previously served in the President's Cabinet. Those members of the administration who do move on to Congress are typically those who have come to the administration from state and local politics rather than from the great national institutions. Few congressmen and even fewer congressional leaders move from Congress to positions of leadership in national private organizations, and relatively few leaders of these organizations move on to Congress. Successful men who have come to the top in business, law, or education naturally hesitate to shift to another world in which they would have to start all over again at the bottom. In some cases, undoubtedly, Establishment leaders also consider legislative office simply beneath them.

6. *The Social Origins and Careers of Congressmen.* Congressmen are much more likely to come from rural and small-town backgrounds than are administration and establishment leaders. A majority of the senators holding office between 1947 and 1957 were born in rural areas; 64 per cent of the 1959 senators were raised in rural areas or in small towns, and only 19 per cent in metropolitan centers. In contrast, 52 per cent of the presidents of the largest industrial corporations grew up in metropolitan centers, as did a large proportion of the political executives appointed during the Roosevelt, Truman, Eisenhower, and Kennedy Administrations. The contrast in origins is reflected in fathers' occupations. In the 1950s, the proportion of farmer fathers among senators (32 per cent) was more than twice as high as it was among administration leaders (13 per cent) and business leaders (9 to 15 per cent).

Of perhaps greater significance is the difference in geographical mobility between congressmen and private and public executives. Forty-one per cent of the 1959 senators, but only 12 per cent of the 1959 corporation presidents, were currently residing in their original hometowns. Seventy per cent of the presidents had moved 100 miles or more from their hometowns but only 29 per cent of the senators had done so. In 1963, over one-third (37 per cent) of the top leaders of Congress but only 11 per cent of administration leaders were still living in their places of birth. Seventy-seven per cent of the congressional leaders were living in their states of birth, while 70 per cent of the administration leaders had moved out of their states of birth. Sixty-one per cent of administration leaders and 73 per cent of political executives had moved from one region of the country to another, but only 19 per cent of congressional leaders had similar mobility.

During the course of this century the career patterns of congressmen and of executive leaders have diverged. At an earlier period both leaderships had ex-

TABLE 2   Geographical Mobility of National Leaders.

	Congressional leaders (1963) N: 81	Administration leaders (1963) N: 74	Political executives (1959) N: 1,865	Business leaders (1952) N: 8,300
None	37%	11%	14%	40%
Intrastate	40	19		
Interstate, intraregion	5	9	10	15
Interregion	19	61	73	45
International	0	0	3	0

tensive experience in local and state politics. In 1903 about one-half of executive leaders and three-quarters of congressional leaders had held office in state or local government. In 1963 the congressional pattern had not changed significantly, with 64 per cent of the congressional leaders having held state or

TABLE 3   Experience of National Political Leaders in State and Local Government.

Offices held	Congressional leaders 1903	Congressional leaders 1963	Administration leaders 1903	Administration leaders 1963
Any state or local office	75%	64%	49%	17%
Elective local office	55	46	22	5
State legislature	47	30	17	3
Appointive state office	12	10	20	7
Governor	16	9	5	4

local office. The proportion of executive leaders with this experience, however, had dropped drastically. The congressional leaders of 1963, moreover, were more often professional politicians than the congressional leaders of 1903: in 1903 only 5 per cent of the congressional leaders had no major occupation outside politics, while in 1963, 22 per cent of the congressional leaders had spent almost all their lives in electoral politics.

The typical congressman may have gone away to college, but he then returned to his home state to pursue an electoral career, working his way up through local office, the state legislature, and eventually to Congress. The typical political executive, on the other hand, like the typical corporation executive, went away to college and then did not return home but instead pursued a career in a metropolitan center or worked in one or more national organizations with frequent changes of residence. As a result, political executives have become divorced from state and local politics, just as the congressional leaders have become isolated from national organizations. Congressional leaders, in short, come up through a "local politics" line while executives move up through a "national organization" line.

The differences in geographical mobility and career patterns reflect two different styles of life which cut across the usual occupational groupings. Businessmen, lawyers, and bankers are found in both Congress and the administration. But those in Congress are likely to be small businessmen, small-town lawyers, and small-town bankers. Among the sixty-six lawyers in the Senate in 1963, for instance, only two—Joseph Clark and Clifford Case—had been "prominent corporation counsel[s]" before going into politics. Administration leaders, in contrast, are far more likely to be affiliated with large national industrial corporations, with Wall Street or State Street law firms, and with New York banks.

7. *The Provincialism of Congressmen.* The absence of mobility between Congress and the executive branch and the differing backgrounds of the leaders of the two branches of government stimulate different policy attitudes. Congressmen tend to be oriented toward local needs and small-town ways of thought. The leaders of the administration and of the great private national institutions are more likely to think in national terms. Analyzing consensus-building on foreign aid, James N. Rosenau concluded that congressmen typically had "segmental" orientations while other national leaders had "continental" orientations. The segmentally oriented leaders "give highest priority to the subnational units which they head or represent" and are "not prepared to admit a discrepancy between" the national welfare and "their subnational concerns." The congressman is part of a local consensus of local politicians, local businessmen, local bankers, local trade union leaders, and local newspaper editors who constitute the opinion-making elite of their districts. As Senator Richard Neuberger noted: "If there is one maxim which seems to prevail among many members of our national legislature, it is that local matters must come first and global problems a poor second—that is, if the member of Congress is to survive politically." As a result, the members of Congress are "isolated" from other national leaders. At gatherings of national leaders, "members of Congress seem more conspicuous by their absence than by their presence." One piece of evidence is fairly conclusive: of 623 national opinion-makers who attended ten American Assembly sessions between 1956 and 1960, only nine (1.4 per cent) were members of Congress!

The differences in attitude between segmentally oriented congressmen and the other, continentally oriented national leaders are particularly marked in those areas of foreign policy (such as foreign aid) which involve the commitment of tangible resources for intangible ends. But they may also exist in domestic policy. The approaches of senators and corporation presidents to economic issues, Andrew Hacker found, are rooted in "disparate images of society." Senators are provincially oriented; corporation presidents "mertopolitan" in their thinking. Senators may be sympathetic to business, but they think of business in small-town, small-business terms. They may attempt to accommodate themselves to the needs of the national corporations, but basically "they are faced with a power they do not really understand and with demands about whose legitimacy they are uneasy." As a result, Hacker suggests, "serious tensions exist between our major political and economic institutions . . . . There is, at base, a real lack of understanding and a failure of communication between the two elites."

"Segmental" or "provincial" attitudes are undoubtedly stronger in the House than they are in the Senate. But they also exist in the Senate. Despite the increased unity of the country caused by mass communications and the growth of "national as distinguished from local or sectional industry," the Senate, according to an admiring portraitist, "is if anything progressively less national in its approach to most affairs" and "is increasingly engaged upon the protection of what is primarily local or sectional in economic life."

Old ideas, old values, old beliefs die hard in Congress. The structure of Congress encourages their perpetuation. The newcomer to Congress is repeatedly warned that "to get along he must go along." To go along means to adjust to the prevailing mores and attitudes of the Inner Club. The more the young congressman desires a career in the House or Senate, the more readily he makes the necessary adjustments. The country at large has become urban, suburban, and metropolitan. Its economic, social, educational, and technological activities are increasingly performed by huge national bureaucratic organizations. But on Capitol Hill the nineteenth-century ethos of the small town, the independent farmer, and the small businessman is still entrenched behind the institutional defenses which have developed in this century to insulate Congress from the new America.

The executive branch has thus grown in power vis-à-vis Congress for precisely the same reason that the House of Representatives grew in power vis-à-vis the Executive in the second and third decades of the nineteenth century. It has become more powerful because it has become more representative. Congress has lost power because it has had two defects as a representative body. One, relatively minor and in part easily remedied, deals with the representation of people as individuals; the other, more serious and perhaps beyond remedy, concerns the representation of organized groups and interests.

Congress was originally designed to represent individuals in the House and governmental units—the states—in the Senate. In the course of time the significance of the states as organized interests declined, and popular election of senators was introduced. In effect, both senators and representatives now represent relatively arbitrarily-defined territorial collections of individuals. This system of individual representation suffers from two inequities. First, of course, is the constitutional equal representation of states in the Senate irrespective of population. Second, in the House, congressional districts vary widely in size and may also be gerrymandered to benefit one party or group of voters. The net effect of these practices in recent years has been to place the urban and, even more importantly, the suburban voter at a disadvantage vis-à-vis the rural and small-town voter. In due course, however, the Supreme Court decision in *Wesberry* v. *Sanders* in February 1964 will correct much of this discrepancy.

The second and more significant deficiency of Congress as a representative body concerns its insulation from the interests which have emerged in the twentieth century's "organizational revolution." How can national institutions be represented in a locally elected legislature? In the absence of any easy answer to this question, the administration has tended to emerge as the natural point of access to the government for these national organizations and the place where their interests and viewpoints are brought into the policy-making process. In effect, the American system of government is moving toward a three-way system of representation. Particular territorial interests are represented in Congress; particular functional interests are represented in the administration; and the national interest is represented territorially and functionally in the Presidency.

Every four years the American people choose a President, but they elect an administration. In this century the administration has acquired many of the traditional characteristics of a representative body that Congress has tended to lose. The Jacksonian principle of "rotation in office" and the classic concept of the Cincinnatus-like statesman are far more relevant now to the administration than they are to Congress. Administration officials, unlike congressmen, are more frequently mobile amateurs in government than career professionals in politics. The patterns of power in Congress are rigid. The patterns of power in the administration are flexible. The administration is thus a far more sensitive register of changing currents of opinion than is Congress. A continuous adjustment of power and authority takes place within each administration; major changes in the distribution of power take place at every change of administration. The Truman Administration represented one combination of men, interests, and experience, the Eisenhower Administration another, and the Kennedy Administration yet a third. Each time a new President takes office, the executive branch is invigorated in the same way that the House of Representatives was invigorated by Henry Clay and his western congressmen in 1811. A thousand new officials descend on Washington, coming fresh from the people, representing the diverse forces behind the new President, and bringing with them new demands, new ideas, and new power. Here truly is representative government along classic lines and of a sort which Congress has not known for decades. One key to the "decline" of Congress lies in the defects of Congress as a representative body.

STRUCTURE: THE DISPERSION OF POWER IN CONGRESS

The influence of Congress in our political system thus varies directly with its ties to the more dynamic and dominant groups in society. The power of Congress also varies directly, however, with the centralization of power in Congress. The corollary of these propositions is likewise true: centralization of authority within Congress usually goes with close connections between congressional leadership and major external forces and groups. The power of the House of Representatives was at a peak in the second decade of the nineteenth century, when power was centralized in the Speaker and when Henry Clay and his associates represented the dynamic new forces of trans-Appalachian nationalism. Another peak in the power of the House came during Reconstruction, when power was centralized in Speaker Colfax and the Joint Committee on Reconstruction as spokesmen for triumphant northern Radicalism. A third peak in the power of the House came between 1890 and 1910, when the authority of the Speaker reached its height and Speakers Reed and Cannon reflected the newly established forces of nationalist conservatism. The peak in Senate power came during the post-Reconstruction period of the 1870's and 1880's. Within Congress, power was centralized in the senatorial leaders who represented the booming forces of the rising industrial capitalism and the new party machines. These were the years, as Wilfred Binkley put it, of "the Hegemony of the Senate."

Since its first years, the twentieth century has seen no comparable centralization of power in Congress. Instead, the dominant tendency has been toward the dispersion of power. This leaves Congress only partially equipped to deal with the problems of modern society. In general, the complex modern environment requires in social and political institutions *both* a high degree of specialization and a high degree of centralized authority to coordinate and to integrate the activities of the specialized units. Specialization of function and centralization of authority have been the dominant trends of twentieth-century institutional development. Congress, however, has adjusted only half-way. Through its committees and subcommittees it has provided effectively for specialization, much more effectively, indeed, than the national legislature of any other country. But it has failed to combine increasing specialization of function with increasing centralization of authority. Instead the central leadership in Congress has been weakened, and as a result Congress lacks the central authority to integrate its specialized bodies. In a "rational" bureaucracy authority varies inversely with specialization. Within Congress authority usually varies directly with specialization.

The authority of the specialist is a distinctive feature of congressional behavior. "Specialization" is a key norm in both House and Senate. The man who makes a career in the House, one congressman has observed "is primarily a worker, a specialist, and a craftsman—someone who will concentrate his energies in a particular field and gain prestige and influence in that." "The members who are most successful," another congressman concurred, "are those who pick a specialty or an area and become real experts in it." The emphasis on specialization as a norm, of course, complements the importance of the committee as an institution. It also leads to a great stress on reciprocity. In a bureaucracy, specialized units compete with each other for the support of less specialized officials. In Congress, however, reciprocity among specialists replaces coordination by generalists. When a committee bill comes to the floor, the non-specialists in that subject acquiesce in its passage with the unspoken but complete understanding that they will receive similar treatment. "The traditional deference to the authority of one of its committees overwhelms the main body," one congressman has observed. "The whole fabric of Congress is based on committee expertise. . . ." Reciprocity thus substitutes for centralization and confirms the diffusion of power among the committees.

The current phase of dispersed power in Congress dates from the second decade of this century. The turning point in the House came with the revolt against Speaker Cannon in 1910, the removal of the Speaker from the Rules Committee, and the loss by the Speaker of his power to appoint standing committees. For a brief period, from 1911 to 1915, much of the Speaker's former power was assumed by Oscar Underwood in his capacities as majority floor leader and chairman of the Ways and Means Committee. In 1915, however, Underwood was elected to the Senate, and the dispersion of power which had begun with the overthrow of the Speaker rapidly accelerated.

During the first years of the Wilson Administration, authority in the Senate was concentrated in the floor leader, John Worth Kern, a junior senator first elected to the Senate in 1910. Under his leadership the seniority system was bypassed, and the Senate played an active and creative role in the remarkable legislative achievements of the Sixty-third Congress. Conceivably the long-entrenched position of seniority could have been broken at this point. "If the rule of 'seniority' was not destroyed in 1913," says Claude G. Bowers, "it was so badly shattered that it easily could have been given the finishing stroke." Kern, however, was defeated for re-election in 1916, seniority was restored to its earlier position of eminence, and the power which Kern had temporarily centralized was again dispersed.

Thus since 1910 in the House and since 1915 in the Senate the overall tendency has been toward the weakening of central leadership and the strengthening of the committees. The restoration of seniority in the Senate and its development and rigidification in the House have contributed directly to this end. So also have most of the "reforms" which have been made in the procedures of Congress. "Since 1910," the historian of the House has observed, "the leadership of the House has been in commission. . . . The net effect of the various changes of the last thirty-five years in the power structure of the House of Representatives has been to diffuse the leadership, and to disperse its risks, among a numerous body of leaders." The Budget and Accounting Act of 1921 strengthened the Appropriations Committees by giving them exclusive authority to report appropriations, but its primary effects were felt in the executive branch with the creation of the Bureau of the Budget. During the 1920s power was further dispersed among the Speaker, floor leaders, Rules, Appropriations, Ways and Means chairmen, and caucus chairman. In the following decade political development also contributed to the diffusion of influence when the conservative majority on the Rules Committee broke with the administration in 1937.

The dispersion of power to the committees of Congress was intensified by the Legislative Reorganization Act of 1946. In essence, this act was a "Committee reorganization act" making the committees stronger and more effective. The reduction in the number of standing committees from eighty-one to thirty-four increased the importance of the committee chairmanships. Committee consolidation led to the proliferation of subcommittees, now estimated to number over two hundred and fifty. Thus the functions of integration and coordination which, if performed at all, would previously have been performed by the central leadership of the two houses, have now devolved on the leadership of the standing committees. Before the reorganization, for instance, committee jurisdictions frequently overlapped, and the presiding officers of the House and Senate could often influence the fate of a bill by exercising their discretion in referring it to committee. While jurisdictional uncertainties have not been totally eliminated, the discretion of the presiding officers has been drastically curtailed. The committee chairman, on the other hand, can often influence the fate of legislation by manipulating the subcommittee structure of the committee and by exercising his discretion in referring bills to subcommittees. Similarly, the intention of the framers of the Reorganization Act to reduce, if not to eliminate, the use of special committees has had the effect of restricting the freedom of action of the central leadership in the two houses at the same time that it confirms the authority of the standing committees in their respective jurisdictions. The Reorganization Act also bolstered the committees by significantly expanding their staffs and by specifically authorizing them to exercise legislative overseeing functions with respect to the administrative agencies in their field of responsibility.

The Act included few provisions strengthening the central leadership of Congress. Those which it did include usually have not operated succesfully. A proposal for party policy committees in each house was defeated in the House of Representatives. The Senate subsequently authorized party policy committees in the Senate, but they have not been active or influential enough to affect the legislative process significantly. The Act's provision for a Joint Committee on the Budget which would set an appropriations ceiling by February 15th of each year was implemented twice and then abandoned. In 1950 the Appropriations Committees reported a consolidated supply bill which cut the presidential estimates by two billion dollars and was approved by Congress two months before the approval of the individual supply bills of 1949. Specialized interests within Congress, however, objected strenuously to this procedure, and it has not been attempted again. The net effect of the Reorganization Act was thus to further the dispersion of power, to strengthen and to institutionalize committee authority, and to circumscribe still more the influence of the central leadership.

In the years after the Legislative Reorganization Act, the issues which earlier had divided the central leadership and committee chairmen reappeared in each committee in struggles between committee chairmen and subcommittees. The chairmen attempted to maintain their own control and flexibility over the number, nature, staff, membership, and leadership of their subcommittees. Several of the most assertive chairmen either prevented the creation of subcommittees or created numbered subcommittees without distinct legislative jurisdictions, thereby reserving to themselves the assignment of legislation to the subcommittees. Those who wished to limit the power of the chairman, on the other hand, often invoked seniority as the rule to be followed in designating subcommittee chairmen. In 1961 thirty-one of the thirty-six standing committees of the House and Senate had subcommittees and in twenty-four the subcommittees had fixed jurisdictions and significant autonomy, thus playing a major role in the legislative process. In many committees the subcommittees go their independent way, jealously guarding their autonomy and prerogatives against other subcommittees and their own committee chairman. "Given an active subcommittee chairman working in a specialized field with a staff of his own," one congressional staff member observes, "the parent committee can do no more than change the grammar of a subcommittee report." Specialization of function and dispersion of power, which once worked to the benefit of the committee chairmen, now work against them.

The Speaker and the majority floor leaders are, of course, the most powerful men in Congress, but their power is not markedly greater than that of many other congressional leaders. In 1959, for instance, thirteen of nineteen committee chairmen broke with the Speaker to support the Landrum-Griffin bill. "This graphically illustrated the locus of power in the House," one congressman commented. "The Speaker, unable to deliver votes, was revealed in outline against the chairmen. This fact was not lost on Democratic Members." The power base of the central leaders has tended to atrophy, caught between the expansion of presidential authority and influence, on the one hand, and the institutionalization of committee authority, on the other.

At times individual central leaders have built up impressive networks of personal influence. These, however, have been individual, not institutional, phenomena. The ascendency of Rayburn and Johnson during the 1950s, for instance, tended to obscure the difference between personal influence and institutional authority. With the departure of the Texas coalition their personal networks collapsed. "Rayburn's personal power and prestige," observed Representative Richard Bolling, "made the institution *appear* to work. When Rayburn died, the thing just fell apart." Similarly, Johnson's effectiveness as Senate leader, in the words of one of his assistants, was "overwhelmingly a matter of personal influence. By all accounts, Johnson was the most personal among recent leaders in his approach. For years it was said that he talked to every Democratic senator every day. Persuasion ranged from the awesome pyrotechnics known as 'Treatment A' to the apparently casual but always purposeful exchange as he roamed the floor and the cloakroom." When Johnson's successor was accused of failing to provide the necesary leadership to the Senate, he defended himself on the grounds that he was Mansfield and not Johnson. His definition of the leader's role was largely negative: "I am neither a circus ringmaster, the master of ceremonies of a Senate nightclub, a tamer of Senate lions, or a wheeler and dealer . . . ." The majority leadership role was uninstitutionalized and the kindly, gentlemanly, easygoing qualities which Mansfield had had as Senator from Montana were not changed when he became majority leader. The power of the President has been institutionalized; the powers of the congressional committees and their chairmen have been institutionalized; but the power of the central leaders of Congress remains personal, *ad hoc,* and transitory.

FUNCTION: THE SHIFT TO OVERSIGHT

The insulation of Congress from external social forces and the dispersion of power within Congress have stimulated significant changes in the functions of Congress. The congressional role in legislation has largely been reduced to delay and amendment; congressional activity in overseeing administration has expanded and diversified. During the nineteenth century Congress frequently took the legislative initiative in dealing with major national problems. Even when the original proposal came from the President, Congress usually played an active and positive role in reshaping the proposal into law. "The predominant and controlling force, the centre and source of all motive and of all regulative power," Woodrow Wilson observed in 1885, "is Congress. . . . The legislature is the aggressive spirit." Since 1933, however, the initiative in formulating legislation, in assigning legislative priorities, in arousing support for legislation, and in determining the final content of the legislation enacted has clearly shifted to the executive branch. All three elements of the executive branch—President, administration, and bureaucracy—have gained legislative functions at the expense of Congress. Today's "aggressive spirit" is clearly the executive branch.

In 1908, it is reported, the Senate, in high dudgeon at the effrontery of the Secretary of the Interior, returned to him the draft of a bill which he had proposed, resolving to refuse any further communications from executive officers unless they were transmitted by the President himself. Now, however, congressmen expect the executive departments to present them with bills. Eighty per cent of the bills enacted into law, one congressman has estimated, originate in the executive branch. Indeed, in most instances congressmen do not admit a responsibility to take legislative action except in response to executive requests. Congress, as one senator has complained, "has surrendered its rightful place in the leadership in the lawmaking process to the White House. No longer is Congress the source of major legislation. It now merely filters legislative proposals from the President, straining out some and reluctantly letting others pass through. These days no one expects Congress to devise the important bills." The President now determines the legislative agenda of Congress almost as thoroughly as the British Cabinet sets the legislative agenda of Parliament. The institutionalization of this role was one of the more significant developments in presidential–congressional relations after World War II.

Congress has conceded not only the initiative in originating legislation but—and perhaps inevitably as the result of losing the initiative—it has also lost the dominant influence it once had in shaping the final content of legislation. Between 1882 and 1909 Congress had a preponderant influence in shaping the content of sixteen (55 per cent) out of twenty-nine major laws enacted during those years. It had a preponderant influence over seventeen (46 per cent) of thirty-seven major laws passed between 1910 and 1932. During the constitutional revolution of the New Deal, however, its influence declined markedly: only two (8 per cent) of twenty-four major laws passed between 1933 and 1940 were primarily the work of Congress. Certainly its record after World War II was little better. The loss of congressional control over the substance of policy is most marked, of course, in the area of national defense and foreign policy. At one time Congress did not hesitate to legislate the size and weapons of the armed forces. Now this power—to raise and support armies, to provide and maintain a navy—is firmly in the hands of the executive. Is Congress, one congressional committee asked plaintively in 1962, to play simply "the passive role of supine acquiescence" in executive programs or is it to be "an active participant in the determination of the direction of our defense policy?" The committee, however, already knew the answer:

> To any student of government, it is eminently clear that the role of the Congress in determining national policy, defense or otherwise, has deteriorated over the years. More and more the role of Congress has come to be that of a sometimes querulous but essentially kindly uncle who complains while furiously puffing on his pipe but who finally, as everyone expects, gives in and hands over the allowance, grants the permission, or raises his hand in blessing, and then returns to the rocking chair for another year of somnolence broken only by an occasional anxious glance down the avenue and a muttered doubt as to whether he had done the right thing.

In domestic legislation Congress's influence is undoubtedly greater, but even here its primary impact is on the timing and details of legislation, not on the subjects and content of legislation.

The decline in the legislative role of Congress has been accompanied by an increase in its administrative role. The modern state differs from the liberal state of the eighteenth and nineteenth centuries in terms of the greater control it exercises over society and the increase in the size, functions, and importance of its bureaucracy. Needed in the modern state are means to control, check, supplement, stimulate, and ameliorate this bureaucracy. The institutions and techniques available for this task vary from country to country: the Scandinavian countries have their *Ombudsmen;* Communist countries use party bureaucracy to check state bureaucracy. In the United States, Congress has come to play a major, if not the major, role in this regard. Indeed, many of the innovations in Congress in recent years have strengthened its control over the administrative process of the executive branch. Congressional committees responded with alacrity to the mandate of the 1946 Reorganization Act that they "exercise continuous watchfulness" over the administration of laws. Congressional investigations of the bureaucracy have multiplied: each Congress during the period between 1950 and 1962 conducted more investigations than were conducted by *all* the Congresses during the nineteenth century. Other mechanisms of committee control, such as the legislative veto and committee clearance of administrative decisions, have been increasingly employed. "Not legislation but control of administration," as Galloway remarks, "is becoming the primary function of the modern Congress." In discharging this function, congressmen uncover waste and abuse, push particular projects and innovations, highlight inconsistencies, correct injustices, and compel exposition and defense of bureaucratic decisions.

In performing these activities, Congress is acting where it is most competent to act: it is dealing with particulars, not general policies. Unlike legislating, these concerns are perfectly compatible with the current patterns of insulation and dispersion. Committee specialization and committee power enhance rather than detract from the effectiveness of the committees as administrative overseers. In addition, as the great organized interests of society come to be represented more directly in the bureaucracy and administration, the role of Congress as representative of individual citizens becomes all the more important. The congressman more often serves their interests by representing them in the administrative process than in the legislative process. As has been recognized many times, the actual work of congressmen, in practice if not in theory, is directed toward mediation between constituents and government agencies. "The most pressing day-to-day demands for the time of Senators and Congressmen," Hubert Humphrey has written, "are not directly linked to legislative tasks. They come from constituents." One representative has estimated that half of his own time and two-thirds of that of his staff are devoted to constituent service. This appears to be average. In performing these services congressmen are both representing their constituents where they need to be represented and checking upon and ameliorating the impact of the federal bureaucracy. Constituent service and legislative oversight are two sides of the same coin. Increasingly divorced from the principal organized social forces of society, Congress has come to play a more and more significant role as spokesman for the interests of unorganized individuals.

ADAPTATION OR REFORM

Insulation has made Congress unwilling to initiate laws. Dispersion has made Congress unable to aggregate individual bills into a coherent legislative program. Constituent service and administrative overseeing have eaten into the time and energy which congressmen give legislative matters. Congress is thus left in its legislative dilemma where the assertion of power is almost equivalent to the obstruction of action. What then are the possibilities for institutional adaptation or institutional reform?

Living with the Dilemma. Conceivably neither adaptation nor reform is necessary. The present distribution of power and functions could continue indefinitely. Instead of escaping from its dilemma, Congress could learn to live with it. In each of the four institutional crises mentioned earlier, the issue of institutional adaptation came to a head over one issue: the presidential election of 1824, the House of Commons Reform Bill of 1832, the Lloyd George budget of 1910, and the Supreme Court reorganization plan of 1937. The adaptation crisis of Congress differs in that to date a constitutional crisis between the executive branch and Congress has been avoided. Congress has procrastinated, obstructed, and watered down executive legislative proposals, but it has also come close to the point where it no longer dares openly to veto them. Thus the challenge which Congress poses to the executive branch is less blatant and dramatic, but in many ways more complex, ambiguous, and irritating, than the challenge which the Lords posed to Asquith or the Supreme Court to Roosevelt. If Congress uses its powers to delay and to amend with prudence and circumspection, there is no necessary reason why it should not retain them for the indefinite future. In this case, the legislative process in the national government would continually appear to be on the verge of stalemate and breakdown which never quite materialize. The supporters of Congress would continue to bemoan its decline at the same time that its critics would continue to denounce its obstructionism. The system would work so long as Congress stretched but did not exhaust the patience of the executive branch and public. If Congress, however, did reject a major administration measure, like tax reduction or civil rights, the issue would be joined, the country would be thrown into a constitutional crisis, and the executive branch would mobilize its forces for a showdown over the authority of Congress to veto legislation.

Reform Versus Adaptation: Restructuring Power. The resumption by Congress of an active, positive role in the legislative process would require a drastic restructuring of power relationships, including reversal of the tendencies toward insulation, dispersion, and oversight. Fundamental "reforms" would thus be required. To date two general types of proposals have been advanced for the structural reform of Congress. Ironically, however, neither set of proposals is likely, if enacted, to achieve the results which its principal proponents desire. One set of reformers, "democratizers" like Senator Clark, attack the power of the Senate "Establishment" or "Inner Club" and urge an equalizing of power among congressmen so that a majority of each house can work its will. These reformers stand four-square in the Norris tradition. Dissolution of the Senate "Establishment" and other measures of democratization, however, would disperse power among still more people, multiply the opportunities for minority veto (by extending them to more minorities), and thus make timely legislative action still more difficult. The "party reformers" such as Profesor James M. Burns, on the other hand, place their reliance on presidential leadership and urge the strengthening of the party organization in Congress to insure support by his own party for the President's measures. In actuality, however, the centralization of power within Congress in party committees and leadership bodies would also increase the power of Congress. It would tend to reconstitute Congress as an effective legislative body, deprive the President of his monopoly of the "national interest," and force him to come to terms with the centralized congressional leadership, much as Theodore Roosevelt had to come to terms with Speaker Cannon. Instead of strengthening presidential leadership, the proposals of the party reformers would weaken it.

The dispersion of power in Congress has created a situation in which the internal problem of Congress is not dictatorship but oligarchy. The only effective alternative to oligarchy is centralized authority. Oligarchies, however, are unlikely to reform themselves. In most political systems centralized power is a necessary although not sufficient condition for reform and adaptation to environmental change. At present the central leaders of Congress are, with rare exceptions, products of and closely identified with the committee oligarchy. Reform of Congress would depend upon the central leaders' breaking with the oligarchy, mobilizing majorities from younger and less influential congressmen, and employing these majorities to expand and to institutionalize their own power.

Centralization of power within Congress would also, in some measure, help solve the problem of insulation. Some of Congress's insulation has been defensive in nature, a compensation for its declining role in the legislative process as well as a cause of that decline. Seniority, which is largely responsible for the insulation, is a symptom of more basic institutional needs and fears. Greater authority for the central leaders of Congress would necessarily involve a modification of the seniority system. Conversely, in the absence of strong central leadership, recourse to seniority is virtually inevitable. Election of committee chairmen by the committees themselves, by party caucuses, or by each house would stimulate antagonisms among members and multiply the opportunities for outside forces from the executive branch or from interest groups to influence the proceedings. Selection by seniority is, in effect, selection by heredity: power goes not to the oldest son of the king but to the oldest child of the institution. It protects Congress against divisive and external influences. It does this, however, through a purely arbitrary method which offers no assurance that the distribution of authority in the Congress will bear any relation to the distribution of opinion in the country, in the rest of the government, or within Congress itself. It purchases institutional integrity at a high price in terms of institutional isolation. The nineteenth-century assignment of committee positions and chairmanships by the Speaker, on the other hand, permitted flexibility and a balancing of viewpoints from within and without the House. External influences, however nefarious (as the earlier remark about Blaine suggests they might be at times), all came to bear on the Speaker, and yet the authority which he possessed enabled him to play a creative political role in balancing these external influences against the claims and viewpoints arising from within the House and against his own personal and policy preferences. The process by which the Speaker selected committee chairmen was not too different from the process by which a President selects a cabinet, and it resembled rather closely the process by which a British Prime Minister appoints a ministry from among his colleagues in Parliament. The resumption of this power by the Speaker in the House and its acquisition by the majority leader in the Senate would restore to Congress a more positive role in the legislative process and strengthen it vis-à-vis the executive branch. Paradoxically, however, the most ardent congressional critics of executive power are also the most strenuous opponents of centralized power in Congress.

Congressional insulation may also be weakened in other ways. The decline in mobility between congressional leadership positions and administration leadership positions has been counterbalanced, in some measure, by the rise of the Senate as a source of Presidents. This is due to several causes. The almost insoluble problems confronting state governments tarnish the glamor and limit the tenure of their governors. The nationalization of communications has helped senators play a role in the news media which is exceeded only by the President. In addition, senators, unlike governors, can usually claim some familiarity with the overriding problems of domestic and foreign policy.

Senatorial insulation may also be weakened to the extent that individuals who have made their reputations on the national scene find it feasible and desirable to run for the Senate. It is normally assumed that too much attention to national problems and too much neglect of state and constituency issues complicate election or reelection to the Senate. Lucas, McFarland, George, and Connally are cited as cases in point. Given the nationalization of communications, however, a political leader may be able to develop greater appeal in a local area by action on the national level than by action on the local level.

Salinger's California and Robert Kennedy's New York Senate candidacies could mark the beginning of a new trend in American politics. It is effective testimonial to the extent to which the President dominates the national scene and the national scene dominates the news that in 1964 Robert Kennedy would probably have been the strongest candidate in any one of a dozen northeastern industrial states.

Recruitment of senators from the national scene rather than from local politics would significantly narrow the gap between Congress and the other elements of national leadership. The "local politics" ladder to the Senate would be replaced or supplemented by a "national politics" line in which mobile individuals might move from the Establishment to the administration to the Senate. This would be one important step toward breaking congressional insulation. The end of insulation, however, would only occur if at a later date these same individuals could freely move back from the Senate to the administration. Mobility between Congress and the administration similar to that which now exists between the establishment and the administration would bring about drastic changes in American politics, not the least of which would be a great increase in the attractiveness of running for Congress. Opening up this possibility, however, depends upon the modification of seniority, and that, in turn, depends upon the centralization of power in Congress.

Adaptation and Reform: Redefining Function. A politically easier, although psychologically more difficult, way out of Congress's dilemma involves not the reversal but the intensification of the recent trends of congressional evolution. Congress is in a legislative dilemma because opinion conceives of it as a legislature. If it gave up the effort to play even a delaying role in the legislative process, it could, quite conceivably, play a much more positive and influential role in the political system as a whole. Representative assemblies have not always been legislatures. They had their origins in medieval times and as courts and as councils. An assembly need not legislate to exist and to be important. Indeed, some would argue that assemblies should not legislate. "[A] numerous assembly," John Stuart Mill contended, "is as little fitted for the direct business of legislation as for that of administration." Representative assemblies acquired their legislative functions in the seventeenth and eighteenth centuries; there is no necessary reason why liberty, democracy, or constitutional government depends upon their exercising those functions in the twentieth century. Legislation has become much too complex politically to be effectively handled by a representative assembly. The primary work of legislation must be done, and increasingly is being done, by the three "houses" of the executive branch: the bureaucracy, the administration, and the President.

Far more important than the preservation of Congress as a legislative institution is the preservation of Congress as an autonomous institution. When the performance of one function becomes "dysfunctional" to the workings of an institution, the sensible course is to abandon it for other functions. In the 1930s the Supreme Court forced to surrender its function of disallowing national and state social legislation. Since then it has wielded its veto on federal legislation only rarely and with the greatest of discretion. This loss of power, however, has been more than compensated for by its new role in protecting civil rights and civil liberties against state action. This is a role which neither its supporters nor its opponents in the 1930s would have thought possible. In effect, the Court is using the great conservative weapon of the 1930s to promote the great liberal ends of the 1960s. Such is the way skillful leaders and great institutions adapt to changing circumstances.

The redefinition of Congress's functions away from legislation would involve, in the first instance, a restriction of the power of Congress to delay indefinitely presidential legislative requests. Constitutionally, Congress would still retain its authority to approve legislation. Practically, Congress could, as Walter Lippmann and others have suggested, bind itself to approve or disapprove urgent Presidential proposals within a time limit of, say, three or six months. If thus compelled to choose openly, Congress, it may be supposed, would almost invariably approve Presidential requests. Its veto power would become a reserve power like that of the Supreme Court if not like that of the British Crown. On these "urgent" measures it would perform a legitimizing function rather than a legislative function. At the same time, the requirement that Congress pass or reject presidential requests would also presumably induce executive leaders to consult with congressional leaders in drafting such legislation. Congress would also, of course, continue to amend and to vote freely on "non-urgent" executive requests.

Explicit acceptance of the idea that legislation was not its primary function would, in large part, simply be recognition of the direction which change has already been taking. It would legitimize and expand the functions of constituent service and administrative oversight which, in practice, already constitute the principal work of most congressmen. Increasingly isolated as it is from the dominant social forces in society, Congress would capitalize on its position as the representative of the unorganized interests of individuals. It would become a proponent of popular demands against the bureaucracy rather than the opponent of popular demands for legislation. It would thus continue to play a major although different role in the constitutional system of checks and balances.

A recent survey of the functioning of legislative bodies in forty-one countries concludes that parliaments are in general losing their initiative and power in legislation. At the same time, however, they are gaining power in the "control of government activity." Most legislatures, however, are much less autonomous and powerful than Congress. Congress has lost less power over legislation and gained more power over administration than other parliaments. It is precisely this fact which gives rise to its legislative dilemma. If Congress can generate the leadership and the will to make the drastic changes required to reverse the trends toward insulation, dispersion, and overseeing, it could still resume a positive role in the legislative process. If this is impossible, an alternative path is to abandon the legislative effort and to focus upon those functions of constituent service and bureaucratic control which insulation and dispersion do enable it to play in the national government.

SUGGESTIONS FOR FURTHER READING

A remarkable older work on the Congress is Robert Luce, *Legislative Assemblies* (Boston: Houghton Mifflin, 1924). Two books of the past decade that stand out clearly are David B. Truman, *The Congressional Party* (New York: Wiley, 1960), and Richard F. Fenno, Jr., *The Power of the Purse* (Boston: Little, Brown, 1966).

The American Political Science Association's Study of Congress Project has recently begun to bear fruit; see Lewis A. Froman, Jr., *The Congressional Process: Strategies, Rules, and Procedures* (Boston: Little, Brown, 1967), Randall B. Ripley, *Majority Party Leadership in Congress* (Boston: Little, Brown, 1969), and John S. Saloma III, *Congress and the New Politics* (Boston: Little, Brown, 1969).

A good summary of the congressional roll-call studies thus far is W. Wayne Shannon, *Party, Constituency, and Congressional Voting: A Study of Legislative Behavior in the United States House of Representatives* (Baton Rouge, La.: Louisiana State University Press, 1968).

Interesting works on legislative behavior in general, not only the national Congress, are: James David Barber, *The Lawmakers: Recruitment and Adaptation to Legislative Life* (New Haven, Conn.: Yale University Press, 1965); Malcolm E. Jewell and Samuel C. Patterson, *The Legislative Process in the United States* (New York: Random House, 1966); John C. Wahlke, Heinz Eulau, William Buchanan, and LeRoy C. Ferguson, *The Legislative System* (New York: Wiley, 1962); and Samuel C. Patterson, ed., *American Legislative Behavior* (Princeton, N.J.: Van Nostrand, 1968).

Useful case studies are: Stephen K. Bailey, *Congress Makes a Law* (New York: Columbia University Press, 1950); Fred W. Riggs, *Pressures on Congress: A Study of the Repeal of Chinese Exclusion* (New York: Columbia University Press, 1950); and H. Douglas Price, "Race, Religion, and the Rules Committee: The Kennedy Aid-to-Education Bills," in Alan F. Westin, ed., *The Uses of Power* (New York: Harcourt Brace Jovanovich, 1962).

On the "overseeing" role of Congress, see Joseph P. Harris, *Congressional Control of Administration* (Washington, D. C.: Brookings Institution, 1964).

On the House of Representatives, see especially Robert Peabody and Nelson W. Polsby, eds., *New Perspectives on the House of Representatives,*

2nd ed. (Chicago: Rand McNally, 1969). On leadership in the Senate, Rowland Evans and Robert Novak's *Lyndon B. Johnson: The Exercise of Power* (New York: New American Library, 1968) is extraordinarily perceptive.

Indispensable for continuing, serious study of Congress is the *Congressional Quarterly Weekly Reports*.

7 The presidency

ONE OF THE ANOMALIES OF POLITICAL SCIENCE is that the Presidency, the most important, most visible, and most discussed office in the national government, is the least studied. In recent years some journalistic impressions and a few memoirs have appeared, but the number of good analytical books and articles on the office can almost literally be counted on the fingers of one hand. This lack of careful study is surprising if only because we are a nation of inveterate President-watchers. The press and television seriously report the President's preferences in food and books; tailors comment on the style of his clothes and columnists on the style of his politics. And yet, for all this literature, we really know remarkably little about the institution of the Presidency.

Part of the reason for this lack of knowledge is the inaccessibility and secrecy of the White House. The visiting political scientist is a fixture on Capitol Hill. When he is not prowling about the corridors arranging interviews, he may be busily scrutinizing congressional records trying to uncover subtle but significant patterns in voting. The West Wing of the White House, on the other hand, has barely enough room for the presidential staff. The men who occupy positions at the very center of national affairs work in shoebox-sized offices. When political scientists enter these precincts, most of them do so as presidential employees, not as scholars.

The difficulties of gaining access to the Presidency are compounded by our predilections. So much time is spent on assessing the performances of particular Presidents that we rarely get around to generalizing about the institution of the Presidency. The Congress and the Supreme Court are clearly identifiable social structures affected by, but distinct from, the individuals who may ornament them for a time. The Presidency, however, is all too easily equated with the man of the moment—an Eisenhower, a

Kennedy, a Johnson, or a Nixon. As a result, the institution itself—the set of precedents, roles, expectations, and constraints that define the presidential task—has received short shrift.

The two articles presented in this chapter have been selected because they go well beyond a discussion of individual Presidents and into an examination of the institution itself.

Written in 1956, Richard E. Neustadt's essay on "The Presidency at Mid-Century" has worn very well. Neustadt's portrait of a President surrounded by a complex of pressures, demands, and obligations that shape and limit his power is still the most vivid and accurate brief description of the Chief Executive's role. Neustadt views the Presidency from the inside, from the perspective of the President himself. Seen from that point of view, the office is at once far more vulnerable and yet far more central to the system than a simple constitutional description might suggest.

Fred I. Greenstein's approach differs markedly from Neustadt's. In his analysis of "The Psychological Functions of the Presidency for Citizens," Greenstein stands well back from the Presidency and describes the strength and the sources of the psychological bonds between the Chief Executive and the populace. By doing so, he helps to clarify the critical unifying function that the Presidency performs in the American system—a function with importance far beyond the "good" or "bad" decisions of particular Presidents.

The Presidency at Mid-Century

RICHARD E. NEUSTADT

There are many way to look at the American Presidency. It can be done in terms juridical or biographical, political or managerial: the office viewed primarily as a compendium of precedents, a succession of personalities, a fulcrum for party politics, a focus for administrative management. This essay denies the relevance of none of these approaches and makes use, incidentally, of them all, but aims at observation from a rather different point of view. This is an effort to look at the Presidency *operationally*, in working terms, as an instrument of governance in the middle years of the twentieth century; as man-in-office, that is to say, in a time of continuing "cold war," spiralling atomic discovery

FROM Richard E. Neustadt, "The Presidency at Mid-Century." Reprinted with permission from a symposium, The Presidential Office, appearing in *Law and Contemporary Problems*, Vol. 21, No. 4 (Autumn 1956), pp. 609–45, published by the Duke University School of Law, Durham, North Carolina. Copyright, 1956, by Duke University.

(and vulnerability), stablized "big government," and stalemated partisan alignment—the *policy* environment capsuled by Clinton Rossiter as "new economy" and "new internationalism"; the *political* environment billed by Samuel Lubell as "politics of twilight."

This calls for an examination of the President at work within the Presidency in a setting bounded on the one hand by the final phases of the last World War and on the other by the unknowns of the next decade—the setting for Harry S. Truman's term in office and for Dwight D. Eisenhower's up to the fall of 1956. Given that contemporary focus, there is less need for emphasis on presidential tasks, per se, than on the means and methods of performance; the theme, here, is less "what" than "how." The modern Presidency's powers and responsibilities—the "what," that is to say—are widely known, however we may differ on their import for our form of government, and anyone in doubt has only to review numerous recent writings in the field. But the "how" is relatively unexplored terrain for which there are no ready references outside the realm of selective particulars in press reports, case studies, memoirs, and the like. Granting the President his modern "roles," how does the work get done? What are his means? How may these be employed? Under what limitations? At what cost? With what effect? In what degree sufficient to the Presidency's purposes?

These are the central questions I should like to pose—to pose, note, not to "answer." The search for answers is a task I am prepared, at this writing, to acknowledge as ambition, not accomplishment.

.   .   .

There is, though, a prerequisite: If one would focus on the doing of the presidential job, one needs a characterization of the job, as such, that lends itself to operational appraisal; a characterization that defines what need be done in terms approaching those in which the doer does it. For working purposes, the President is never "many men," but one; the Presidency, as an instrument of government, is indivisible; the White House has no separate rooms for the "Chief Legislator," "Chief of Party," "Chief Administrator," *et al.* Observations on the doing of the job must build upon a statement of what exists to be done in terms other than these.

Hence, having stressed an emphasis on means and advertised its claims, I must begin where everyone begins, with a review of presidential powers—a review of the Presidency's place, that is to say, in the contemporary governmental scene.

2. THE PRESIDENCY IN GOVERNMENT

"His is the vital place of action in the system," wrote Woodrow Wilson of the President toward the close of TR's term. And this, a new discovery for Wilson's generation, is now, at mid-century, a matter of course. Presidential leadership is now a matter of routine to a degree quite unknown before the Second World War. If the President remains at liberty, in Wilson's phrase, "to be as big a man as he can," the obverse holds no longer: he *cannot* be as small as he might choose.

Once, TR daringly assumed the "steward's" role in the emergency created by the great coal strike of 1902; the Railway Labor Act and the Taft-Hartley Act now make such interventions mandatory upon Presidents. Once, FDR dramatically asserted personal responsibility for gauging and guiding the American economy; now, the Employment Act binds his successors to that task. Wilson and FDR became chief spokesmen, leading actors on a world stage at the height of war; now UN membership, far-flung alliances, the facts of power, prescribe that role continuously in times termed "peace." Through both World Wars, our Presidents grappled experimentally with an emergency-created need to "integrate" foreign and military and domestic policies; the National Security Act now takes that need for granted as a constant of our times. FDR and Truman made themselves responsible for the development and first use of atomic weapons; the Atomic Energy Act now puts a comparable burden on the back of every President. In instance after instance, the one-time personal initiatives, innovations of this century's "strong" Presidents, have now been set by statutes as requirements of office. And what has escaped statutory recognition has mostly been absorbed into presidential "common law," confirmed by custom, no less binding: the unrehearsed press conference, for example, or the personally presented legislative program.

The "vital place of action" has been rendered permanent; the *forms* of leadership fixed in the cumulative image of *ad hoc* assertions under Wilson and the two Roosevelts; past precedents of personality and crisis absorbed into the Government's continuing routines. For the executive establishment and for the Congress, both, the Presidency has become the regular, accustomed source of all major initiatives: supplier of both general plans and detailed programs: articulator of the forward course in every sphere of policy encompassed by contemporary government. Bold or bland, aggressive or conciliatory, massive or minimal, as the case may be, the lead is his.

Thus, we have made a matter of routine the President's responsibility to take the policy lead. And at the same time, we have institutionalized, in marked degree, the exercise of that responsibility. President and Presidency are synonymous no longer; the office now comprises an officialdom twelve-hundred strong. For almost every phase of policy development, there is now institutional machinery engaged in preparations on the President's behalf: for the financial and administrative work plan of the Government, the Budget Bureau; for the administration's legislative program, the White House counsel and the Budget's clearance organization; for programming in economic and social spheres, the Council of Economic Advisers (and to some degree the cabinet, Eisenhower-style); in foreign and military fields, the National Security Council; in spheres of domestic preparedness, the Office of Defense Mobilization; these pieces of machinery, among others, each built around a program-making task, all lumped together, formally, under the rubric, "The Executive Office of the President," an institutional conception and a statutory entity less than two decades old.

These are significant developments, this rendering routine, this institutionalizing of the initiative. They give the Presidency nowadays a different look than it has worn before, an aspect permanently "positive." But the reality behind that look was not just conjured up by statutes or by staffing. These, rather, are *responses* to the impacts of external circumstance upon our form of government; not causes but effects.

Actually or potentially, the Presidency has always been—at least since Jackson's time—a unique point of intersection for three lines of leadership responsibility: "executive" and partisan and national. The mandates of our Constitution, the structure of our political parties, the nature of the President's electorate, fused long ago to draw these lines together *at that point and there alone:* The Presidency at once the sole nationally elective office,[1] independently responsible to a unique constituency; sole centralizing stake of power, source of control, in each party (as a glance at either party out of power shows); sole organ of foreign relations and military command; sole object of the "take care" clause and the veto power; and with all this, sole crown-like symbol of the Union.

By Wilson's time, that combination, in the context of world power stakes and status, had brought a fourth line of leadership into play, a line of leadership abroad, its only point of intersection with the other three the White House, once again. Since then, there have been revolutionary changes in the world and in American society and in the character of government's commitments toward both; changes productive of fast-rising expectations and requirements for leadership transmitted toward the Presidency along each line—four streams of action impulses and obligations converging on the President, whoever he may be, their volume and their rate of flow varying with events, a source which never, nowadays, runs dry.

The contemporary President, in short, has *four constituencies,* each with distinctive expectations of him and demands upon him. One of these is his "government" constituency, comprising the great group of public officers—congressional as well as executive—who cannot do their own official jobs without some measure of performance on his part. A second is his "partisan" constituency, comprising at once his own party's congressional delegation, and its organization leaders, workers, even voters, all those whose political fortunes, interests, sentiments, are tied, in some degree, to his performance. A third is his "national" constituency, comprising all those individuals and groups among Americans who look to him, especially when crises come, for an embodiment and an expression of government's relationship to its citizenry, for a response

---

[1] Discounting the Vice Presidency, which I am prepared to do.

to their needs, purposes, endeavors. And fourth, is his "overseas" constituency, comprising not alone the officers of foreign governments, but the political oppositions, the opinion molders, even the plain citizens to some degree, in every country where our power, policies, or postures have imposed themselves upon domestic politics.

In respect to the first three of these constituencies, membership is not a mutually exclusive matter. A number of American officials—among them cabinet officers and congressmen—are members of all three. And most Americans hold membership in two, as at once partisans and citizens. But whatever its effects on individual or group behavior, multiple membership does not preclude distinctly differentiated sets of Presidency-oriented expectations and demands, identifiable with each constituency, arising in the circumstances of mid-century from the pervasive needs of each for governmental action.

In these terms, it appears no accident that at a time when stakes of government are high for all the President's constituents, to him has passed, routinely, the continuing initiative in government. That role is both assured him and required of him by the very uniqueness of his place at the only point of intersection, the sole juncture, of those four lines of leadership responsibility and the constituencies they represent.

Yet, the demands and expectations pressing in upon the President propel him not alone toward enunciation, but delivery. Executive officials want decisions, Congressmen want proposals, partisans want power, citizens want substance, friends abroad want steadiness and insight and assistance on their terms—all these as shorthand statements of complex material and psychological desires. These things are wanted *done;* given our Constitution and our politics, that means done by, or through, or with assistance from, or acquiescence of, the President. The very factors that contribute to his unique opportunities—and routinized responsibilities—as an initiator, make him essential also as protector, energizer, implementor, of initiatives once taken. His special place in government requires of him, indeed, thrusts upon him, a unique responsibility—and opportunity—to oversee and assure execution.

But while responsibility for the initiative has now been routinized and even institutionalized, authority to implement the courses set remains fragmented in our system. In most respects and for most purposes, the President lacks any solid base of assured, institutionalized support to carry through the measures he proposes. His four constituencies are capable of constant pressure, but not of reliable response to downward leads. The "executive" is not a unity with a firm command-and-subordination structure, nor is the Government, nor is the political party, in Congress or out, nor is the nation, nor the alliance system overseas. All these are feudalities in power terms; pluralistic structures every one of them. Our Constitution, our political system, our symbolism, and our history make certain that the President alone assumes, in form, the leadership of each; and guarantee, no less, that he will not have systematic, unified, assured support from any. Indeed, precisely the conditions vesting him alone with leadership responsibility for all prevent the rendering of any one of them into tight-welded followings. The constitutional separation of powers—really, of institutions sharing powers—the federal separations of sovereignty, hence politics, the geographic separations of electorates, these and their consequences at once have helped the Presidency to its special place and hindered the creation of a strong supporting base. And, at a time when the executive establishment has grown too vast for personal surveillance, when Congress is controlled in form by narrow, shifting partisan majorities, in fact by factional coalition, weighted against the President's electorate, the hindrances are bound to be enhanced. Ours is that sort of time.

This does not mean that Presidents are powerless; far from it. Their four-way leadership position gives them vantage points aplenty for exerting strength in Government, in party, in the country, and abroad; collectively, by all odds, an array of strong points quite unmatched by any other single power-holder in our system. It does mean, though, that presidential power must be exercised *ad hoc*, through the employment of whatever sources of support, whatever transient advantages can be found and put together, case by case. It means the President can never choose a policy with certainty that it will be approximated in reality or that he will not have it to unmake or make again. It means he cannot, as he pleases, moderate, adjust, or set aside the rival, overlapping, often contradictory claims of his constituencies. *He has no option but to act, at once, as agent of them all, for their conjunction in his person is the keystone of his potency;* none is dispensable, hence the demands of none are automatically disposable at his convenience. Events, not his free choices, regulate their pressures and condition his response.

Dilemmas, consequently, are the Presidency's daily bread. The President must now initiate specific policies and programs for all fields of federal action; he has become the focus for all forward planning in our system; whatever leads the Government and country and his party (and indeed, the opposition, also) are to have, will stem from him. Yet, not his preferences only, but events in an inordinately complex world, not his reasoning alone, but his constituencies' felt requirements, contradictory as they may be, mold his determinations, limit his choices, force his hand. What he initiates he must attempt to implement. He must try so to manage the executive establishment, and Congress, and his party oligarchs, and the other party's also, and "public opinion," and overseas support, that the essential things get done—so far at least as government can do them—to keep administration reasonably competent, the country reasonably prosperous, the cold war reasonably cold, and his party in the White House; objectives which will seem to him synonymous (no President in memory . . . has ever thought his policies could best be carried forward by the other party's men). Yet, none of these agencies of action, of execution, are subject to his management by fiat; not even those closest to home, his own administration, his own party, are constructed to provide him with assured support. Rarely can he order, mostly must he persuade. And even were his controls taut and sharp, there would remain, of course, those agencies beyond his power to command, events.

No doubt, in times of great emergency, sharp crisis seen and felt as such throughout the country, the Presidency's measure of assured support from public, party, and administration tends to increase dramatically, if temporarily, while "politics as usual" abates, at least until the sharpness wanes; witness the situation circa 1942. But it is characteristic of our circumstances at mid-century—in all the years since the Second World War—that while our Government's responsibilities retain a trace of every prior crisis, no comparable sense of national emergency pervades our politics. If this is an "era of permanent crisis," it is one in which Presidents must manage without benefit of crisis consensus.

Given the underlying situation here described, the balance of this paper is, perforce, a study of dilemmas; dilemmas nurtured by disparities between the Presidency's obligation to initiate and its capacity to achieve, the one nailed down, the other relatively tenuous, both bound to be so by the nature of our institutional adjustment, up to now, to the complexities of governing this country at mid-century.

What, currently, is the American Presidency? A cat on a hot tin roof.

3. THE PRESIDENT IN THE PRESIDENCY

So far in this discussion, "President" and "Presidency" have been used almost interchangeably; the man and his office equated in an effort at capsule characterization. But since it is our purpose to appraise the man *in* office, the *President* at work, we must now differentiate between the individual and his official tasks, between the work done by the White House occupant and that performed by others in his name.

What does the President, himself, contribute to the conduct of the Presidency? What, in an office now so institutionalized that it encompasses six hundred "professional" aides, has he, himself, to do? What, in a government of vast and complicated undertakings, in a substantive environment demanding every sort of expertise, can there be *left* for him to do? To put the case in current terms, what is there that no "chief of staff" can do without him?

There are two ways to approach answers to these questions. One is to abstract the person of the President from office at a given point in time; the other is to note what occupies his working day when he is on the scene. Both methods, it appears, produce equivalent results, as may be seen by trying them in turn.

The Eisenhower illnesses provide us with illustrations ready-made for speculation on the Presidency *sans* the President, to wit: Three days after his heart attack, Cairo announced its arms deal with the Czechs, thereby upsetting the whole power balance in the Middle East.[2] By all accounts, this action, far-reaching in implications, did not catch the State Department unawares. For months, American diplomacy had sought to head it off. Once it occurred, however, we confined ourselves for a long period to verbal protests and to indecisive consultations. There were no prompt moves made either to force reversal or to take countermeasures of decisive sort. Some persons outside Government have speculated that had Mr. Truman then been President, the Sixth Fleet might have steamed to the Aegean with orders to halt shipments of Czech arms by sea or air. One wonders if in office his response would have been so Draconian. One can be sure, however, that had he, like his successor, then been hospitalized, critically ill, under a regiment of absolute quiet, no orders of this sort would have gone to the Navy. (Indeed, in the far starker, more extreme, hence simpler instance of Korea, can one imagine Louis Johnson taking Dean Acheson's view on anybody's say-so but the President's?)

This is not to suggest that Eisenhower, healthy, would have approved—much less been urged to sanction—any forcible reaction to the Czech–Egyptian deal; it seems unlikely on the public record, though one cannot know for certain from outside. Nor is it implied that some such response should have been attempted; policy is not the issue here. What *is* suggested, here, is that the option was not open to our Government because the President himself was not available to choose. It is suggested that the risk of action, the onus of decision, in this case could have been shouldered only by the President, by him or not at all; *the Presidency's functioning dependent on his individual performance as maker of the residual choices no one else will make.*

Turn now to Eisenhower's second illness for a moment. Three weeks after last June's ileitis operation, while he was still recovering at Gettysburg—allowed to work, by press reports, but one hour a day—the House of Representatives rejected the School Construction Assistance Bill, thereby seeming to terminate all chances of substantial federal aid to education in the current presidential term.[3] The bill was lost in circumstances complicated partly by its contact with the segregation issue, partly by its Democratic sponsors' preferences for certain sums and formulae unlike those forwarded from the Republican administration. And on the latter ground, or nearly so, a number of Republicans seem to have justified "nay" votes. But Eisenhower's actions and pronouncements over three years' time had long made it appear he strongly wanted some measure of aid to education by 1956. Indeed, this bill, reportedly, might not have reached the floor save for the Democratic leaders' understanding that he was in earnest and would not let his House Republicans forget it. Yet, when the ultimate test came, he was not there to remind them.

---

[2] The President was taken ill on September 24, 1955; the Egyptian–Czech agreement was announced on September 27.
[3] Surgery was performed on June 9, 1956. The final House votes on the School Aid Bill (H.R. 7535) came on July 5.

To quote the correspondent of the New York Times:

> There is hardly an observer in Washington who doubts that a personal appeal from a healthy Dwight Eisenhower—or even some last-minute personal letters from Gettysburg—would have changed enough Republican votes to make the difference.

Perhaps, of course, the President in full health would have foregone that appeal. We do not know his private views upon the final bill in terms either of substance or of Senate tactics. We do not know what private tallies were run or what was reasoned from them; the problem, after all, was scarcely his alone, for party lines broke sharply on both sides of the aisle. But whatever he might have done, if well, he *could not* act, one may believe, when ill. Were this conceived a proper matter for the patient and as such worth exclusion of all else, an hour's working day scarcely suffices for the requisite persuasive phone calls to the Hill or for the substitute of letter writing (in the circumstances only done convincingly longhand). And in this case, if Eisenhower could not institute his own appeals, no one could make them for him. The option of a final presidential exhoration is not open to the White House save as the man himself can serve; *the Presidency's functioning dependent on his personal performance as persuader of those otherwise indifferent or unmoved.*

There are numbers of other illness illustrations, but these suffice to make the point: the President's own specialties within the Presidency, the contributions none can make without him, consist of acts of choice and of persuasion; choices not in foreign policy alone, but in all spheres of action and of men as well as measures; persuasion not only of Congressmen, but of administrative officers and politicians, of private interests and "the public" generally, of foreign governments and their publics; choice and persuasion exercised, in short, throughout the range of problems and of persons covered by his four constituencies.

These things are his to do because he is the sole, accountable human embodiment of an office which, in turn, is uniquely the center of responsibility and motive-power in our system. No President, of course, takes to himself more than a fraction of the choices, efforts at persuasion, made on his authority and in his name. But beyond a certain point—a point, of course, that varies case by case—choice-making and persuasion become personalized, of necessity, because his aides and auditors insist that it be so; because no one will accept others' choices, because no one will heed others' persuasions, because no others dare or care to run his risks on their discretion or their risks on his authority. Beyond another point—which may or may not coincide—persuasive acts and choices become ripe for his personal attention as a matter of desirability in his own interest, because his personal perceptions of that interest are ultimately untransferable; because save second-hand, by empathy, not even Harry Hopkins, Sherman Adams, can know fully what it feels like to sit where he sits (endowed with his intelligence, his temperament) at the solitary juncture of his four constituencies, "President of the United States"—hence, no one else can bring to bear precisely his own "feel" for risks to him, to the totality of his unique position, inherent in alternatives of doing and not doing.

If a look at the Presidency without a working President shows choices and persuasion at the man's own occupation, that impression cannot be strengthened by a glance at what takes up his time when on the job. Nowadays, the normal presidential working week revolves around a series of fixed sessions: one set meeting apiece with the National Security Council, and the cabinet, and (when Congress is on hand) the legislative leaders,[4] and the press, each preceded and followed by appropriate staff briefings, consultations; one set appointment apiece with the Secretary of State, the Secretary of Defense, the Chairman of the Joint Chiefs of Staff, and (an Eisenhower innovation, now suspended) the Chairman of the Council of Economic Advisers. Truman had, besides, a daily morning conference with his principal staff aides to make *ad hoc* assignments and receive routine reports; such sessions Sherman Adams has conducted under Eisenhower.

When one includes the chores of getting ready, cleaning up, these regularly scheduled consultations pre-empt a substantial portion of the President's own working hours, week by week. In the case of a President like Eisenhower, who finds these mechanisms to his taste and uses them to the exclusion of much else, that share of hours occupied mounts high. And what is the object of this outlay of his time? Such sessions serve, in part, as occasions for others to put their concerns, their views before him; partly as occasions for him to impress his personality and attitudes *on* others. Which of these parts has major place will vary with each sort of session, influenced by subject matter, membership, and *his* proclivities. But whatever their variation, the components are the same: one part material for choice-making, the other part the stuff of personal persuasion.

As for the balance of the presidential working week, the bulk of it is turned to comparable account; the documents signed, the persons seen, the places filled, the arguments resolved, the messages sent, the speeches made, the ceremonies held, all these are characteristically acts of choice or efforts at persuasion, often both at once—even the formal ceremonials contributing a portion of his power to persuade, even their performance contingent on his choice.

The preoccupations of the presidential week will vary with the seasons of the presidential year, from budget and message seasons in the fall, through early, middle, and late stages of the legislative season, through the rush of adjournment and enrollments, to that precious period, the post-adjournment lull (if any), season for recovery and repairs, and so to fall again—a round, successively, of planning to decision, campaigning to compromise, recuperating to resumption; a peacetime rhythm set primarily to legislative tasks but liable constantly to interruptions on account of mishaps and emergencies in operating

---

[4] With the Senate and House leadership, that is to say, of the President's own party, whether in the majority or not.

spheres. Inevitably, presidential choices, efforts at persuasion, reflect in their intensities, their objects, and their scope these swings of emphasis throughout the year. And even more may they reflect swings in the cycle of the presidential term, from early groping through a first consolidation and a forward push up to the test at midterm, then regrouping and a second forward effort dwindling toward hiatus in the final year. But whatever their application in a given context, choice-making and persuasion remain the components of the President's own work; comprising what he does himself, both on the insistence of others and at his own inner promptings.

These are, in short, his means; the means by which he, personally, exercises influence within his office and upon the course of government; the means by which he makes his own mark on the tasks of office sketched in part 2, above. As such, these "means" are not for him mere instruments employed at will to carry out those tasks. Rather they are the concrete manifestations of the tasks themselves, applying to him personally; the work he has to do, no act of will required. In literary terms, one may say that he sets the tone, provides the lead in government by choosing and persuading. In operating terms, though, one must put it in reverse: that acts of choice and of persuasion cumulated over time produce an ultimate effect of tone and lead which may or may not correspond to any prior blueprint, purpose, or intentions. Such is the consequence of disentangling the President from the Presidency.

That ultimate resultant labelled "leadership" will be compounded of two types of actions by the President: those he may reach for in his own discretion and those thrust on him of necessity; the one type, opportunities, the other, compulsions. And, as the compound will be viewed by his constituents and history, more than these enter in; the multifarious things done or left undone by others in his name, or the Government's, and happenings beyond the Government's discretion, plain events.

No President is free to concentrate upon his opportunities at the expense of his compulsions; he can but hope to find room for the things he may do amidst all things he must. Nor is he free to wave away those other actors on the scene; he can but hope to channel and deflect their impacts on his audience. To the extent he wants to make his own will dominate the conduct of his office, his regime, he has no recourse but to choices and persuasion exercised within these narrow limits. The purposeful President, his face set against drift (and any President, these days, will so regard himself), is thus confronted by an operating problem of immense complexity and large proportions, or more precisely by two problems tightly linked: Given those limits and in furtherance of his own purposes, how is he to maximize the efficiency of his choice-making? How maximize the efficacy of his power to persuade?

The proportions and complexities of these two connected problems it now becomes our object to explore.

4. THE FREEDOM TO CHOOSE

If Presidents were free to choose the matters they made choices on, their problems of choice-making would be relatively simplified; but Presidents are not. The flow of issues they must face cannot be turned off like a water tap; to know that, one has but to note its sources.

Why do men in government and politics (and in the country and the world) bring issues to a President, invoke his act of choice? To amplify the foregoing analysis, it may be said that they do so for one, or another, or all of three reasons. First, there are matters that by law or custom require some sort of personal performance on his part, his signature, his presence, or his voice. Second, there are matters on which others, theoretically competent to act, want the loan of his potency or the cover of his prestige, his impetus behind their preferences, his brand on their performance. Third, there are the matters he himself wants made his own, that on his own initiative he has marked "count me in," matters on which he exercises the discretion we have already discussed. And in the circumstances of mid-century, no President will lack for quantities of matters of each sort.

In the first of these three categories, volume is adjustable, at least to a degree. A President who does not like to sign his name hundreds of times a day, can ease that chore somewhat, by turning over to department heads his formal exercise of statutory powers; so Eisenhower has done in some routine instances. A President who dislikes handshaking *ad infinitum* may find excuses for curtailment of big White House social functions, as FDR did with the war and Truman with repairs and Eisenhower with his heart attacks. But such adjustments are mere nibbles at the fringes; they may save time or energy but not the mind and heart. No President can delegate the formal exercise of constitutional prerogatives, and it is from those that the greatest number of tough, touchy signatures derive. No President can be excused from all political speech-making, disaster visiting, fireside chatting, dignitary dealing, least of all from the big ones, sources of greatest strain.

As for the second category, the most a President seriously can hope to do is slow the rate of flow, shut out the marginal case. He may pound tables at associates, demanding that they mind their business on their own responsibility; he may set obstacle courses for them to run, complete with committees, secretariats, and Sherman Adamses—and still there will be persons, plenty of them, spurred by their convictions or their fears, their sense of others' power or of their own insufficiency, who press on him the matters in their bailiwicks, or in their neighbors'. . . .

There remains the third category, where interventions come at *his* initiative. There, he has the option, theoretically, of moving not at all. But this is fatal; also quite impracticable. No doubt, some Presidents may relish, others shy away from forcing matters into their own hands. No doubt, each will evolve some special preferences according to his particular competences, interests. But every President will find some issues that he wants to seize and ride—Truman on Point Four, Eisenhower on Atoms for Peace—and each will find a plenitude he feels *impelled* to take upon himself. . . .

Since acts of choice are often negative, there are, of course, more instances of such "enforced" discretion than will appear in current press reports: Eisenhower choosing time and again . . . *not* to blast McCarthy; Truman choosing—as he sometimes did—not to leap, guns blazings, into loyalty cases that aroused his ire; so forth, *ad infinitum*. The "I don't know about that" in press conference is deceptive, as a guide to presidential doings. In most such cases, this would remain the expedient response, assuming he did know. Yet every President, one may suppose, will now go out of office wishing that in some respects he had pushed further still, discretion *un*enforced, toward taking over at times and in places where contemporary happenings did not push him.

. . . No President finds pleasure in waiting upon "messes" for his cue to intervene. But none can be sure, either, that initiatives of others will suffice to flash a warning to him in good time. There is an obverse of the second category named above: those issues men bring to the President out of their fears, uncertainties, are matched by those kept from him out of confidence, or cussedness, or independent power (even ignorance). . . . The Wage Board's public members, circa 1952, surely were guilty of too broad a view of their role and too narrow a conception of the Government's, in rendering their famous Steel decision without sounding out the White House. For other illustrations one can point, as always, to the classic record of the Corps of Engineers or to the Pentagon's routines for waging internecine warfare. Far from reducing his discretionary range, a President is bound to end by wishing he could widen it.

But time stands in his way. He cannot afford to do nothing at his own discretion; but neither can he manage to do everything. Priority of place on his choice-making production line belongs of sheer necessity to matters with *deadlines* attached. And in most days of his working week, most seasons of his year, a President has quite enough of these to drain his energy, crowd his attention regardless of all else. It is not "policy" but pressure that determines what comes first.

What makes a "deadline"? For one thing, constitutional or statutory obligations: the President must send his annual messages to Congress, must sign or veto its enactments. Or, for another, items on political agendas all across the country: the nomination and election contests over offices, both partisan and public, the distribution of the patronage, the management of national conventions and campaigns. Or, for a third, turns of events in diplomacy or war: the approach to the "summit" spurring a disarmament departure, "open skies"; the outbreak in Korea forcing a new Formosan policy. Or, for a fourth, "outside" events at home: a sharpened economic trend (whether up or down), a dragged-out strike, a natural disaster, a race riot; not necessarily the great things only but the small-with-bite, as when a Texas waitress would not serve the Indian Ambassador. Or, finally, for a fifth, such operational disorders in administration, day by day, as dot the preceding pages—plus, of course, their congressional counterparts. Dates-certain make for deadlines, so does heat; dates generated by our laws, our politics, and our diplomacy; heat generated by events impacting on the needs and expectations of presidential constituents. Singly or together—though most readily inflammable combined—dates and heat start the fires burning underneath the White House.

The President, of course, has influence on deadline-making and unmaking, but only to a limited degree. He sets or evades dates when he voluntarily decides upon a message or a meeting or a speech. He turns heat on when he permits himself to arouse expectations, as Eisenhower did in his press conferences before Geneva. He turns heat aside, if not off, when he finds plausible grounds, proper-looking means for "further study," as was done so notably in 1953. But these are marginal endeavors relative to the totality of dates and heat potentially imposed upon him from outside. And even these are usually reactions or responses to pressures not intrinsically his own. For the most part, even deadlines self-imposed are only nominally self-engendered. Save in rare instances, a mid-century President, however talented, simply has not time to man both ends of the choice-generating process.

The result is to put him in a paradoxical position anent the whole discretionary range of his choice-making. To reach out and take over *before* the dates are nigh or the heat on—publicly at least—can be crucially useful in his interest; yet, he always has to deal first with deadlines already at his desk. As has been said above, he cannot count on the initiatives of others to spur him into interventions timely in *his* terms; yet he is poorly placed to be his own self-starter. He needs to be an actor, yet he is pre-eminently a reactor, forced to be so by the nature of his work and its priorities. Since Eisenhower made Atoms for Peace his response to the heat expressed by cries for "candor" and to the dates required for a UN presentation in 1953, one may suppose he has not been entirely happy with its slowness to get off the ground. One may suppose, besides, that had he arrogated to himself all implementing choices and given them first call upon his time, the matter might have moved a little faster. Similarly, in the case of Truman and Point Four: had he, not State and Budget, implemented his inaugural's fourth point and made of this his first priority (as it never was for them), the sixteen months after his 1949 inauguration might have produced more results than one meager piece of legislation newly on the books. But whatever these Presidents might have done differently or "better" than they actually did, one thing they could *not* do: accord that hypothetical priority in terms of their own time.

Washington correspondents frequently complain that Eisenhower talks a better line than his administration takes; that he proposes better than his own regime disposes. Complaints of the same sort were made in Truman's time, oftener than not by the same correspondents. And these complaints—along with the realities behind them—symptomize the underlying problem here described. For in a time of routinized responsibility to take the policy lead, a President himself will have few deadlines more compelling than those clustering around the choice of measures to *propose,* of policies to *state.* Except, perhaps, in general war or comparable emergency, these gain and take his time more surely and more regularly than the general run of operating choices bound to follow in their wake. . . .

Ideally, a President concerned for the efficiency of his own choice-making in furtherance of his own purposes as *he* conceives them, should have free rein in choosing what to choose—and when—within the range of matters subject to his choice at his discretion. In practice, though, that is precisely what he *cannot* have. His discretionary range, while not a sham, is nowhere near as open as the term implies. Only his compulsions are potentially unbounded; his opportunities are always limited. Ideals apart, he is in no position to do more than seek some finite widening of those confines; he has no chance to break them down. But paradoxically, the only practical direction which his search can take —given the conditions here described—is toward some means of putting pressure on himself, *of imposing new deadlines on himself,* to come to grips with those things he would want to make his own if only he had time to contemplate the world about him, interfering at his leisure. And it is ironic that the very measures that a President may take to spare himself for "bigger things" by staffing out the "small," tend to work in the opposite direction. Of this, more later.

The limitations upon "what" and "when" which so restrict freedom of choice are reinforced by certain other limits of a different sort; limits on the substance of alternatives in choices actually made. The President's discretion is restricted by these limits also; they, too, are features of his landscape subject to some rearrangement but beyond his power to remove. What are these limitations on alternatives? Mainly three: limits of presentation, of substantive complexity, and of effectuation, each term loosely descriptive of a whole array of complications worth a chapter to themselves, though necessarily denied it here.

By "presentation" is meant time, form, and manner in which issues reach a President for his determination. If his desk is where the buck stops, as Truman liked to say, by the same token, it is the *last* stop on the line. Most matters reach him at a late stage of their evolution into issues calling for his choice; and many when they reach him warrant action fast. Wherever they occur, lateness and urgency—singly or combined—are bound to narrow options and to curtail chances for fresh looks or second thoughts. As for the *form* which issues take, the *context* of their presentation to a President, his settling of a budget sum, or phrasing of a speech, or soothing of a legislator, each in its own terms may mean disposal of an issue multi-faceted in terms of but one facet, thereby foreclosing options anent others. There is no counting the occasions on which Presidents have backed themselves—or been backed—into corners by this route. Moreover, those who brief a President, who can appeal to him, who can argue before him, have interests of their own which grow remote from his with every increment of organizational distance, institutional independence. Rarely will they see an issue wholly in his terms; oftener in some hybrid of his and theirs, sometimes in theirs alone. And Presidents are no less vulnerable than others (rather more so, in the circumstances) to the lure of wrong answers rightly put.

A tracing out of many of the illustrations posed above would show the workings of these presentation limits; signs of their presence are, of course, no novelty to readers of the *New York Times*. Nothing is intrinsically new about them nowadays, nor anything particularly obscure, though they are none the easier for being old and obvious. But when it comes to limits raised by substantive complexity, the case is rather different. Though not by any means a mid-century invention unknown to earlier times, the magnitude (and durability) of complications in the substance of issues with which Presidents must deal, these days, is greater in degree, to some extent in kind, than we have known before.

Take the question of the military budget which has haunted Eisenhower as it haunted Truman. That budget represents more than half the dollars of federal outlay year by year, four-fifths of the persons on all federal payrolls, half the Government's civilian personnel. It represents a mainstay of deterrence and recourse in the cold war, a bed-rock stabilizer in the national economy. Its annual determination raises issues of strategy, of economics, politics, administration, and (emphatically) technology; none of which are really manageable in annual or financial terms (the limit of form, again); none of which are really soluble by reference to anybody's certain knowledge, for nothing is certain save uncertainty in these spheres. To estimate what the American economy can "stand" is not to answer what Congress and interest groups will "take" (or what would be required to equate the two). To estimate what new weapons may do is not to answer what may be demanded of them, or opposed to them, years hence. To estimate the Russians' *capabilities* is not to answer what are their *intentions*.

Yet, on some sorts of "answers" to these questions must military budgets now be built. And limited in terms of what is knowable, a President has no recourse but to select among the "guesstimates" of others—or to compound a compromise among them—by way of searching for his answer-substitutes. In such a search, the signs most readily discerned are bound to be those rendered most concrete by visibility, or pressure, or personal proclivities, or "common sense." No doubt a President needs better signposts in times of cold war, technological revolution; but given the uncertainties these generate, whence are such signs to come?

Parenthetically, it may be said that whatever the answer to that question, the "experts" are unlikely candidates. For if the real technicians see far more than a President can see, the record up to now suggests that they, least of all, show a capacity to ask themselves, out of their expertise, the questions pertinent to him; to translate their vision (and language) into his terms. Shifting the illustration, one thinks in this connection of an aspect of the thermonuclear "crash-program" controversy during 1949, as rendered by the transcript in the Oppenheimer case: that for weeks AEC's consulting scientists debated what the President should do in terms rendered obsolete, for him, by the mere fact of their debate.

Finally, there is the problem of effectuation, the third of the stated factors limiting alternatives in choice. How is a President to make "no" stick; to translate "yes" into performance, actuality? He is not bound to make each choice dependent on his response to these questions, but in the normal course he cannot fail to ask them and to give the answers weight. When Truman chose intervention in Korea, it happened that the necessary military means lay near at hand across the Sea of Japan; a factor, surely, in his choice. The obverse holds, of course, for our passivity in the last days of Dien Bienphu; the means that *were* at hand were scarcely suited to the circumstance. But to cite instances of capability in military terms is to belittle the complexity of the how-to-do-it factor; in other terms, there are few choices blessed by aspects so nearly absolute or so readily calculable. Mostly the problem for the President is both more tenuous and more complex in character: how far can he hope to carry matters by persuading those whom he cannot command to do those things he lacks capacity to compel?

"I sit here all day," Truman used to remark, "trying to persuade people to do the things they ought to have sense enough to do without my persuading them." And on each posed alternative, in every act of choice, the question becomes whether to that workload he should add one thing more; with what prospect, at what risk. That question asked and answered may suffice to cancel options of all sorts; the President's choice-making ultimately interlocking with his power to persuade.

5. THE POWER TO PERSUADE

Concrete acts of choice engender concrete efforts at persuasion. Persuasion of whom? In general, of the President's constituencies, any or all as the case may be. In particular, of those who do the daily chores of governing this country: administrators, Congressmen, and organization politicians. To these one might add certain foreign notables and private persons prominent at home, on whom the Government depends for something in particular, a boost, a service, or a sacrifice; but since such dependence is *ad hoc*, intermittent, their case can be ignored for present purposes.

In the main, day by day, it is the public officers and party politicians whom a President must reach to get his choices rendered into government performance. He may move toward them indirectly through public or interest-group opinion, sometimes his only routes, but they remain his objects because they, not the "public," do the close work; his preferences conditioned on their doing. To influence these men at work, he has at his disposal a quantity of instruments

—refined and crude in varying degree—derived from his prerogatives of office as filtered through his personality.

Those instruments of influence, tools of persuasion, are common knowledge, no mystery about them and none pretended here: There is the aura of his office, coupled to the impact of his person and prestige, such as they may be. There are the varied forms of help, concrete and psychological, that Congressmen want from the White House in dealing, as they must, with the executive establishment. There are, in turn, the various assistances desired by executive officialdom in dealing with the Congress. There are also the loyalties, varying in depth, of administrators to their chief, of party members to the boss, of Congressmen (and citizens) to the head of State and Government. In party terms, there are, at once, supplies of federal patronage, such as it is, a presidential record which no party nowadays can shake, the prospect of a renewed candidacy (for first termers, anyway), and—save for Democrats, perhaps—a constantly replenished campaign chest, centrally controlled. These things, among others, are available to Presidents for use, reversibly, as carrots and as sticks in aid of their persuasion.

This listing has a formidable ring. In theory, it deserves it. For if a President could bring to bear that whole array effectively and all at once upon a given point, one may presume he would be irresistible. But practically speaking, such conjunctions are not easily arranged; far from it. Oftener than not, one or another of these tools will turn out ineffective of itself or in the hands of its prospective user, unsuited to use, by him, in any combination of resources he contrives. Why should this be so? What dulls their cutting edge and limits their employment? These questions become our immediate concern. Full answers would run far beyond the compass of this essay; no more can be attempted here than a suggestion of some factors that seem specially significant in the contemporary setting.

First among these factors—in order of discussion, not importance—is the uncertainty of a President's own hold upon his instruments of influence. They may attach to his office but can slip away from *him*. One doubts that at any time since 1935, or thereabouts, and not often before, have Presidents got half the mileage out of patorange the textbooks advertise. One doubts that Eisenhower can be sure from day to day of his control over the stockpile of administrative actions sought by Congressmen. Most of these, certainly, are not under his sole lock and key. Others than he have the arts of persuasion to practice, and keys of their own. The story is told that a powerful House Democrat was traded off the same dam twice; once in Truman's time and once in Eisenhower's. If so, the Budget Bureau ought to be commended for its careful husbanding of presidential trading-stock. But such care is by no means universal in this Government (not even in the Budget). Moreover, a supply of trading-stock may prove insufficient just when the need is greatest. Appetites are insatiable and fears short-lived; a situation summed up in the phrase "What have you done for me lately," as amplified by "or *to* me."

In addition, sources of supplies to aid persuasion on one front may be endangered by the very effort at persuasion on another. A great share of a President's potential trading-stock with Congress is actually in the hands of the executive departments: jobs, expertise, publicity, administrative actions of all sorts. No less a share of his potential leverage with the departments is actually in the hands of his congressional supporters: protection or defense, consideration or support, in every sort of legislative situation. Too many sticks applied too often on the Hill may tend to uproot the supply of carrots growing there for use downtown, and vice versa.

A second factor is the tendency of certain presidential tools to cut in opposite directions, thereby impairing their simultaneous employment. It is not easy for a President to combine partisan approaches with attempts to crystallize support around the symbol of his office. He courts trouble when he tells his party's Congressmen that his proposals will help them at the polls and simultaneously exhorts the other party's men to do their patriotic duty by their President. He courts trouble when he tries to draw upon the loyalties of subordinate officials and at the same time offers up their kind as human sacrifices on the altar, say, of adequate appropriations for their work. Such troubles come in infinite varieties; in every instance, they will tend to limit hypothetical effectiveness of each paired instrument. To say this is not to suggest, of course, that all these troubles are escapable. Carrying water on both shoulders—plus, perhaps, in both hands, also strapped around the waist—is frequently imperative for Presidents, a natural resultant of their four-way leadership position. But the complications are no less for often being unavoidable. So Truman found on many memorable occasions and even Eisenhower, now and then, especially in those first years of turmoil over "cleaning out the Communists" and Senator McCarthy.

A third factor complicating the persuasion process can be stated, most simply, as general dissatisfaction with the product to be "sold." It is difficult, in other words, to press a course of action intrinsically lacking much appeal to *any* of the persons whose support is being sought. Instruments of influence, however handled, are poor substitutes for genuine enthusiasm on the part of somebody among the movers and shakers in the case. And if the substitution must be made, as not infrequently occurs, the limits on the efficacy of persuasive tools will tend to be severe. . . . In the complex struggle over foreign aid in the 1956 session of Congress, . . . Eisenhower pitted his own personal prestige, plus other sorts of pressure, against the disappointments, disenchantments, irritations, and forebodings which had penetrated every corner of both Houses. The result was a sharp check to the President—how serious in program terms one cannot know from the outside—a check administered, moreover, by traditional supporters of his course among the Democrats, together with a great proportion of *his* party's membership, election year or no. It is quite conceivable, in all the circumstances, that another President, in another year, might have done worse. But why did this President in this year not do better?

No doubt, his ileitis operation and its aftermath blunted Eisenhower's own persuasive influence at a crucial time.[5] Perhaps there were things poorly done or left undone at other times as well. But however healthy and adroit he might have been last summer, there are no indications—not, anyway, of public record—that by then his persuasion could have bettered the result in any *marked* degree. For the great lack, apparently, was not of influence in mechanistic terms, but of program in substantive respects. A sense of changing world relationships pervaded the debates, providing ammunition for old enemies of Mutual Security and worries for old friends. Yet, the administration's program appeared cast from the same mold as all its predecessors back to 1951, when the world wore a very different look. And Eisenhower's troubles in July seem, by hindsight, an inevitable outcome of his choices in December; the efficacy of persuasive instruments conditioned, in their turn, upon the exercise—and limits—of choice-making.

Alongside these three factors there is need to place a fourth, which looms at least as large under mid-century conditions: the factor of too many things at once, as represented, classically, by FDR's fight for reorganization powers amidst controversy over his "court-packing" plan. In that instance, Roosevelt was criticized for moving for his management reform at a time when his influence was mortgaged to another cause. Perhaps he had an option then—though that can be debated—but not so his successors. In 1956, in a relatively quiet time at home and abroad, the Eisenhower influence has been demanded in three closely spaced, competing, legislative fights of first importance to his regime—farm, education, foreign aid—to say nothing of those headed off, like tax reduction, or of the many other issues on which White House labels were affixed to controversial aspects: Hells Canyon, highway aid, social security amendments, the civil rights commission, and numbers more. In Truman's time, the list was often longer, the controversial aspects sharper, the presidential temperature higher, and, besides, in many of his years, such legislative struggles were accompanied by operational involvements—military, diplomatic, economic, or administrative —also calling his persuasion into play on a grand scale.

A President's tools of persuasion are put under great strains when used on many projects simultaneously. Look at the tools themselves, and that becomes quite obvious. Yet, such use is the normal practice, nowadays; often mandatory, always wanted. No more as persuaders than as choice-makers are contemporary Presidents at liberty, discretion unconfined, to choose the "what" and "when" of their endeavors to persuade.

Four factors have been named, so far, as limiting the efficacy of persuasive instruments. But there remains a fifth, a factor so important as to dominate the rest, continually affecting the dimensions of all four. This is the element of

---

[5] Eisenhower was hospitalized on June 8, 1956, and did not return to the White House until July 16. In the interim, the Mutual Security authorization went through floor debate in House and Senate, through conference, and on to signature, $800 million short of his request; the following appropriation, completed after his return to Washington, fell $300 million shorter still.

"setting" in persuasion, a matter not of instruments, as such, but of the *background* against which they are employed. As a rough rule, it may be said that for a fraction of the persons on whom Presidents depend, continuing exposure to the White House and its occupant provides a background favoring—though not, of course, determining—effective exercise of presidential influence upon them. The bigger the "staff system," the smaller the fraction; but even an open door could not enlarge it into a preponderance. For most officials, both public and partisan, a favorable background will be differently derived. Derived from what? To this we may now turn.

In the case of executive officials, all sorts of variables of time, place, situation, substance, tend to affect actual responses to a particular pressure from the President. But there would seem to be one variable always present, always influential: their own instinctive estimate of his prestige with Congress, his potency on Capitol Hill. This may not square with visions conjured up by the tag "Chief Executive"; it is, however, entirely natural. For Congress, day in and day out, means life or death to programs, institutions, personnel. Putting the matter in its crudest terms (and thus rather larger than life): if Presidents can make much difference in these respects, either way, their own officialdom will be well disposed toward their wishes; if not, so much the worse for them; many a bureaucrat, like many a Congressman, was there before and will be after.

Of course, such bureaucratic estimates of presidential prowess will vary from time to time. George Kennan once remarked that diplomats must rethink foreign policy each morning; so bureaucrats must reappraise their attitudes toward a President, and so they do, day after day. Such estimates will vary, also, from place to place. The weaker an agency, in terms of institutional entrenchment, program support, the more its officials will tend to view the President as a resource, no matter what the state of his congressional relations; thus Labor is traditionally a "tame" department. And every agency, however "strong," will make its calculations with reference, mainly, to those elements in Congress and those issues before Congress that affect it the most; even as between Army and Air the President is not appraised alike.

This does not mean that there is any one-to-one relationship between a President's congressional prestige and agency compliance with his wishes—though sometimes, certainly, the correlation is that close—but rather that a favorable background for persuasive efforts at his end of Pennsylvania Avenue is markedly dependent, over time, upon his prestige at the other end, with Congress. And in precisely the same sense—no more, no less—a favorable background for persuasion of the Congress is provided by his prestige with the country. As in the bureaucratic case, Senators and Congressmen differently situated, institutionally and electorally, will not see that matter all alike; place, time, party, and electorate make for differing appraisals, though by no means along strict party lines: witness Republican and Democratic attitudes in the Eighty-fourth Congress. No more than with the bureaucrats are estimates of this sort to be taken as controlling the congressional response in given instances of presidential pressure, but there can be no doubt that they contribute most significantly to the background against which such pressure is applied.

As for a President's own party's politicians outside Congress, they are quite comparably circumstanced, with the important qualification that at certain moments in the cycle of his term, their own enforced commitment to his record and his name may enhance their responsiveness regardless of his momentary popular prestige; a qualification applicable, equally, to certain of their brethren on the Hill.

In short, the President's persuasive power with those who do the daily chores of governing, is influenced by a sort of *progression of prestige,* a sequence culminating in the regard of the "general public," the country-at-large. Woodrow Wilson once wrote, in an academic vein, that a President "may be both the leader of his party and the leader of the nation or he may be one or the other." Whatever the case fifty years ago, no such option is open to him now. He must endeavor to lead "party" (for which read public officers as well), since "nation" does not run the government machine, cannot itself effectuate his choices. But if he is to manage those who make the wheels go 'round, he needs public opinion at his back, must seek consensus as his context for persuasion. And in that dual compulsion lies the *ultimate dilemma* of the presidential operation at mid-century.

How describe this dilemma? One may begin by pointing to the sources of that popular prestige which so affects the President's own power to persuade. His general public—in our terms, national and partisan constituencies combined—actually comprises a diversity of presidential publics, their expectations nurtured variously by claims on him as "government," by respect for his office, or by ties to his personality: "interest" publics, "capacity" publics, and "personal" publics, each subdivided many times, all linked by the crisscrossing lines of overlapping membership, collectively encompassing the country, or that part of it which cares about the President.

His national prestige, therefore—which Congressmen and politicians watch and weigh—is simply the net balance of favorable response these many groups, in sum, accord their varied images of him (a matter always to be gauged, not scientifically determined, the result influenced, of course, by the affiliation of the gauger). Those images and the responses to them are not static; they can and do vary over time. And what are the determinants of variation? Happenings, mainly, or the appearance of happenings, ascribable—or anyway ascribed—to him: the reward or frustration of a bread-and-butter want, an ethical attitude, a psychological identification; to such as these his publics will react wherever and in whatever degree they see his office or his person as the cause. Inevitably, every concrete choice he makes, both positive and negative, and every effort at persuasion will set off some reactions of the sort, and not all of one kind; if somebody is pleased, then someone else is bound to be offended.

For the President to give offense is to risk blurring his own image in the eyes of those offended, hence to risk lowering their favorable response to him.

But on a maximum of such response, as aggregated all across the country, must he depend for the effectuation of his choices. And on choice-making he depends for the impression of his person on the product of his office. But the conduct of office is liable to require policy initiatives in all directions, not as free will, but as constituency pressures and events decree. Hence, acts of choice and of persuasion become mandatory, inescapable. Yet, they are bound to give offense.

This, then, is the ultimate dilemma, the vicious circle Presidents must tread by virtue of their unique placement in our system, the personal equivalent for them, as individuals, of that disparity which haunts their office, routinely responsible for programming without assured support to carry through. No President, of course, is wholly helpless in this situation. He gains from office when he enters it a sizable initial fund of favorable response; if he is fortunate enough to be an Eisenhower, he brings still more *to* office. Once installed, his actions bring him gains as well as losses. Approbation, no less than offense, is bound to follow, from some quarter, everything he does or fails to do. And nobody in government is better placed than he to focus public interest and attention where he wants it, to foster certain images, obscuring others, to make desired happenings occur, to give events a nudge.

These are not insignificant resources. Particularly in a time of sharp emergency—which a preponderance of publics see or can be made to see as such—their use with skill, accompanied by luck, should help a President to break out of that circle altogether, in a fashion advantageous to his person and his cause; enabling him to gain from what he does far more by way of favorable response than negative reaction. For such a time, a crisis-time, tends to put premiums on affirmative action, to make the very act of doing almost its own reward, not doing almost its own penalty; so Hoover found to his discomfiture and Roosevelt to his taste a quarter-century ago. Of course, if circumstances are precisely opposite and times all peace and quiet, the outcome may be no less advantageous for a President; so Coolidge made a virtue of *not* doing and was well rewarded for it.

But our situation at mid-century fits neither of these models; the years since the Second World War have neither been perceived, widely, as crisis-times, nor have they been, in fact, peace-times in any familiar sense. And nowadays, the things that Presidents must do and those they may be called upon to do expose them regularly to the penalties of *both* such times with no assurance that they can gain the rewards of either. These days, both doing and not doing give offense in indeterminate proportion to offsetting approbation, almost all actions now *tend* to produce a negative reaction more concrete than favorable response. Both forms of action are abrasive; from neither can our Presidents now *count* upon a bonus of response. Yet, they are constantly impelled to actions of both sorts and so it has to be, these days, their preferences notwithstanding.

Consider what a President must do in times we now call "peace": keep taxes relatively high, armed forces relatively large, the budget "swollen," the bureaucracy "outsize"; inject himself into labor disputes just when tempers grow highest, into defense of overseas constituents just when they seem, at home, most irritating or unwise. And so the list goes on. Consider, also, what a President now may be called upon to do: intervene with arms in Korea, Indo-China; intervene with counsel in Southern school segregation; back the Benson plan for aid to farmers; endorse the Hobby plan for aid to schools; accept the Rockefeller plan for aid abroad; impose the New York Bar committee plan for personnel security; keep Nixon or take Herter; choose silence on McCarthy or attack; these among others. Such "musts" and "mays," as manifested in his acts of doing or not doing, are bound to outrage some among his publics (and anger may last long), to be accepted grudgingly by many as unpleasant facts of life, to warm the hearts of an uncertain number whose warmth may be short-lived. Whichever way he acts, his penalties may outrun his rewards in prestige terms. And rarely can he calculate with certainty, in advance, the net balance either way. Yet act he must.

By virtue of his unique place in government, a President gains unequalled opportunities to mold the images his publics have of him. But, for these opportunities, he pays a heavy price. Even for Eisenhower, immune, so far, to many of the payments levied on his predecessors, there is now the real price his illnesses exact: the issue of his health in the 1956 campaign; an issue taking its dimensions from the nature of his office at mid-century.

This observation instantly suggests a qualification upon everything that has been said so far: the ultimate dilemma for a President—and with it all the intermediate dilemmas here described—takes shape and form, in actuality, from the particulars of his own personality and of the situations he confronts throughout his term. This paper has presented up to now an outline, in the abstract, of the operating burdens thrust on Presidents, in general. Now, before we can consider what, if anything, ought to be done in consequence, we need note how these burdens, these dilemmas, have been manifested in real-life and what the real-life men in office have made of them, each in his way and time. That becomes necessarily a first step toward conclusion.

6. PERSONALITIES AND SITUATIONS

Two men have held the Presidency at mid-century, Truman and Eisenhower. While Franklin Roosevelt's shadow is upon them and their office, he is not counted of their number because he served in different times, faced different partisan and governmental situations; only from 1938 to 1941 had he a foretaste of the situations scheduled for his final term. For present purposes, Truman and Eisenhower stand alone.

In some respects, their personalities and circumstances are more similar than either might admit. Their likenesses of personality have been canvassed with dash and perceptivity by Richard Rovere . . . ; there is no need to retrace all his ground. Suffice it to say here that both appear to have displayed in office an optimistic faith in progress, a confident, uncynical approach, no less sustaining and heart-warming for being late Victorian. So far, the White House at mid-century has been home to men formed, essentially, before the First World War, the Great Depression. No mid-century man, product of the Second World War and of the Great Prosperity, has yet lived in the place; for that there is, perhaps, some reason to be grateful.

Their situations, too, are much alike in numerous respects, those respects which give unity to times here termed "mid-century." Truman and Eisenhower, both, have had to deal with cold war and a full employment mandate; with inflation and recession, high taxes and high debt; with large armed forces, entangling alliances, atomic power, and "brush" warfare; with a bureaucracy two million strong; with a deeply split congressional party, sometimes in the minority, rarely more than nominally a majority; with notable discrepancies between each party's presidential and congressional electorates; with crises and with politics-as-usual combined.

These similarities of situation are accompanied by certain likenesses in approach, also. Both Presidents have been men rather narrowly acquainted outside their own professions, tending to rely for stimulation, counsel, and advice primarily on their official associates; neither has had anything like FDR's acquaintance, nationwide. Moreover, both have tended to put special credence in successful products of an idealized career line other than their own: military men in Truman's case; business men in Eisenhower's. To these and others among their subordinates both Presidents have delegated vastly, though in different spheres, and both have seemed to take ideas and issues as they come; to see what reaches them, often with sharpness and great common sense, but not to reach out constantly in restless search; displaying, so it seems, neither the intellectual's disquiet nor FDR's pervasive curiosity.

These similarities, of person, situation, and approach may well appear, historically, no less significant than many of the differences between their Presidencies. But if we are to set their own reactions in the office against our generalized discussion, differences become our main concern. In what do these consist? In respect to personality, of course, the public record is replete with information, not all of it informative, which scarcely needs rephrasing in this paper. It is enough, here, to identify those facets seemingly of special influence upon the styles of these two men as presidential operators: Eisenhower temperamentally a mediator, Truman disposed to put his head down and charge; Truman the politician, professional thick-skinned and relatively acclimated to abuse, save of his family, as against Eisenhower, the Supreme Commander, thin-skinned, apparently, and touchy at barbed questioning of his official conduct. These things, quite clearly, have affected and have differentiated *style*.

Yet, style in the abstract helps us very little; what counts, for present purposes, is application in the situations faced by these two Presidents, as actually experienced and met by each in turn. How differentiate their situations and responses? By focusing upon three crucial, common, interrelated aspects of their Presidencies: initial unpreparedness, pressure of events, and portions of prestige.

First is the matter of unpreparedness. Both men came to office inexperienced but ignorant of different things in differing degrees. Truman had been ten years in Washington, not close to the White House, not part of the executive establishment, but thoroughly accustomed to the search for and the uses of elective office; knowledgeable in the whole milieu of politics and in the power game, at least as played on the Hill; knowledgeable also, in a senatorial way, anent the divisive home-front issues of the past decade bound to project themselves into his Presidency; yet, almost wholly uninformed in the strategic spheres of foreign policy and military operations, his first concerns on taking office. At every point, the Eisenhower contrast is both plain and sharp. And when one notes their early opportunities for learning on the job, contrasts again are clear. Eisenhower, had, at least, the warm-up of campaign and preinaugural; Truman had two hours. Truman, on the other hand, inherited a going concern, albeit not of his contriving; Eisenhower had to build a new regime from scratch out of a party twenty years in opposition to the White House, its legislative oligarchy recently opposed to *him*. Yet, he did fall heir to a relatively stable home economy, a relatively viable position abroad, while Truman was confronted at the outset by immediate and drastic consequences of the shift from total war to general "peace."

This brings us to the matter of events, their tempo, and their context, not only at the start but throughout all the years of these two Presidents. Waves of inflation and industrial unrest, threats to the welfare-state, Soviet expansionism and intransigence and armament, European weakness, Chinese collapse, the aftermath of Alger Hiss, the outbreak in Korea and its consequences—these, among others, were themes sounded harshly and insistently in Truman's years; evoking a long line of *overt* events, almost all of them intense in pressure for affirmative, abrasive action, many of them thoroughly devisive in their social and political results. In Eisenhower's term, thus far (the early fall of 1956), some of these themes have been submerged, or nearly so; the rest have been productive of a lesser number of such overt events and at longer intervals.

To be sure, Eisenhower's years have not been without incident. The worst of McCarthy, the imminence of Bricker, the fall of farm income, the risks of renewed war in the Far East, the death of the European Defense Community, threats in the Middle East, convulsions in North Africa; these and others and, besides, those steps toward the future: in great power relationships, the coming of "competitive coexistence"; in their defense, the integration of tactical atomic weapons; in social policy at home, the Supreme Court decision on desegregation; and in home industry, the turn toward automation. Yet, unlike Truman's time, there have been virtually no national emergencies as a result of strikes, no spiralling price upswings (and only the mildest of recessions off the farm), no frontal assaults on the Roosevelt revolution, no *new* spy scares, no imminent collapses in Europe, no Americans fighting in Asia, no overt threats or acts of force from Moscow. Stalin, after all, turned ugly in Truman's first year; he died in Eisenhower's. And without these, the din of Truman's time has been muted indeed, for in his day, these made the greatest noise.

This does not mean the one man's problems of choice-making and persuasion were *intrinsically* much "harder" than the other's. That is a judgment the historians will have to render in due course; contemporary evidence appears to cut both ways. When Truman came to office, the New Deal inheritance remained to be secured; by Eisenhower's time, that had been done, the argument pushed to another level, the *Fair* Deal in dispute but the hallmarks of Roosevelt's revolution well entrenched: witness social security. Clearly, this eases Eisenhower's situation relative to Truman's. On the other hand, it seems less difficult, in terms both intellectual and political, to counter Stalin than to coexist with his successors. Building "situations of strength" in the face of intransigence and military threat is bound to be more concrete, more congenial, hence more manageable than using them, renewing them once built; especially when guns and money turn out insufficient, of themselves, as maintenance materials, and when the purpose loses shape, specific or short-run. Korea interrupted Truman's regime in preliminary grapplings with that harder task, and programs then frozen in a military guise have yet to be thawed out. But long before Eisenhower came to office, it appeared clear that should the Soviets, someday, mellow their manners, if not aims, our Government would be hard put to fashion adequate response.

Still, if one cannot strike a balance of intrinsic hardship in the troubles which events decreed for Truman and for Eisenhower, one can note certain things about the *context* of events which rendered Truman's handling of his troubles relatively harder. On the one hand, it happened in his time, as against Eisenhower's, that a lesser number of events had government and public impacts gradual, postponable, or transient: contrast Korea with Indo-China; the Steel dispute of 1952 with that of 1956, the rise of "neutralism" with the fall of dollar balances. On the other hand, it is distinctly different to respond to events as "Fair Dealer" than as "dynamic conservative"; different in terms of ideological commitment; different in terms of attitude about the Presidency's four constituencies, their diverse and conflicting expectations; differences only of degree, perhaps, but no less definite for that. So many things might Truman not have done, or held himself above, or dissociated himself from, had he been leader of the Eisenhower coalition instead of heir to Roosevelt's (and had he not been Truman, matters might have gone still otherwise; style counts in application).

Obviously there are connecting links between these two aspects of the context of events in Truman's time and in his later years, both are related to another: by June of 1950, this country to all public appearances, was launched upon a period of relative tranquility, assured, it seemed, by nice adjustments between the not-too-heavy burdens of a stabilized world leadership and the growing pleasures of a resurgent, expanding home economy; a period of calm protected, also, by the tranquilizing stand-off between reformism represented at the White House and conservatism dominant in Congress. After two decades of depression, World War, post-war readjustments, there we were, millions of us, savoring another gilded age. Then Korea and its prolongation and its side effects blasted the happy scene, upsetting expectations on every hand. With Eisenhower's advent and Korean truce, the happy prospects were revived; by this he has gained greatly. Meanwhile, in proportion, Truman took the rap.

This raises the whole question of prestige, the third of those situational matters requiring review. Truman, of course, gained what he had to start with from his office, not his person. He suffered always from the prestige handicap of "daring," as an unknown and a commoner, to fill the regal shoes of FDR, a handicap increased, at first, by images of a lost little man, which his own "moon and stars" remarks did nothing to reduce. Those early images were to be overlaid in time, especially in 1948, but the more positive impressions which then took their place were of the sort, mostly, to blur at once with any undesired happenings, and these, perforce, were plentiful for many of his publics. In terms of the uncertainties of public prestige for a mid-century President as characterized above (part 5), the Truman case is classic to the point of caricature. As the enormous variations in his Gallup polls suggest, he sometimes seemed assured a net balance of negative reaction no matter what he did or failed to do.

With Eisenhower, it has all been otherwise; almost the opposite at every point. Throughout his term, his own progression of prestige has culminated, constantly, in an extraordinary popular response. It may be that his images, like Truman's, have been changing over time; that he is now more nearly "grandfather" than a "crusader" to his publics; so Louis Harris suggests. But, if so, there has seemed to be no diminution of response, at least up to the start of the 1956 campaign. For evidence, one need but note the polls, or trace the *tactics* and the *expressed* views (which is not to say votes) of his congressional opponents on both sides of the aisle as good a rough gauge of his popular prestige as once of Truman's. Eisenhower, therefore, has enjoyed at all times what was rarely Truman's lot: a hospitable climate for the making of those choices that impose the greatest strain upon the power to persuade.

And yet it has been Truman, far more typically than Eisenhower, who made that sort of choice, this past decade, interjecting the divisive issue, imposing the stiff commitment, calling for the drastic action by administration, Congress, party, and the country; Truman with his fluctuating, always limited prestige, which he endangered in the very act of drawing on it; not Eisenhower with his vast supply which has yet to be plumbed, much less drawn down. Truman treated prestige as a weapon to be brandished; Eisenhower treats it as an asset to be preserved. Yet we may not assume that either of them thought he had an option. For Truman seems to have regarded advocacy as *the* obligation of his office; while Eisenhower, seemingly, acts in the conviction that beneficence is its own reward.

No matter what his thoughts, of course, events and their context narrowed Truman's option; this we have seen above. But where he did have leeway, his concept of his role disparaged an interpolation of the prestige factor into choice. In all that he has said and written on the Presidency, his emphasis always is on its constitutional and statutory obligations; the duty to decide, the responsibility to state; the initiative primary, implementation secondary; the *focus* on choice-making, not effectuation. "The President's got to set the sights," he once remarked. "What the country needed in every field . . . was up to me to say . . . and if Congress wouldn't respond, well, I'd have done all I could in a straightforward way." And this seems to have been not posture, but precept, allowing little room for concern over personal prestige. What we have termed his ultimate dilemma never seemed to faze this President; indeed, he never would have granted its existence in our terms. In his own outlook, he resolved it without having to acknowledge it, by ignoring the dimension he could do the least about.

Events in another context have been easier on Eisenhower; to that degree, his option has been greater. But one gains the impression from outside that he attributes much of the eased pressure of events to his prestige, per se. To be, becomes then, a great act of doing in itself; to do, or not to do, must be adjudged in its relationship to being, to those images which calm and quiet by the very fact of their existence. Of course, great prestige from the start permits considerable flexibility; this standard—if it is the standard—does not call for frozen immobility, assuming such were feasible these days, which it is not; rather, what seems to be at stake is a fixed attitude that in so far as possible, things others might have done—not all, but many things—should not be done, or done a different way: so with overt approaches to the Congress; hassles in the executive, disputes in the party, wrangles in the country, crises abroad. Save in extremity, the calming images must not be blurred. And up to now, this standard (if it is the standard) must seem practical and workable to its adherents. In 1954, McCarthy hangs himself; in 1955, a Democratic Congress remains reasonable; in 1956, the Congress does no less than usual in an election year, while a steel strike evaporates without emergency; and so it goes. This Presidency, up to now, belies its supposed ultimate dilemma, for where—save in two illnesses by act of God—are the hard enforced acts of doing and not doing which may evoke more negative reaction than favorable response? Apparently, they have been calmed away. To all appearances, indeed, beneficence *is* its own reward.

These observations are by way of a trial balance on the operational approaches of two Presidents. A "trial" is all that can be offered here. History permits of no more now, particularly in Eisenhower's instance; also, an observership conducted inside one administration, not the other, puts comparison in double jeopardy. Moreover, in a perfectly objective sense, the value of comparison is jeopardized as well by the disparate tenures of Truman and of Eisenhower. The Truman style which we remember now, the Truman staff which is familiar in our recollections, date at the earliest from 1947. In Eisenhower's case, the comparable date might be, say, January 1954. A good eight months, or more, of Truman's term in 1948, again in 1952, were lost for forwarding policy endeavors by virtue of election-year uncertainties, preoccupations. A comparable pause in Eisenhower's term would date from the early spring of 1956. And in the four preceding months, of course, he was either hospitalized or convalescent. We are comparing, then, one man's activities in office during four and two-thirds years with another's during twenty months, at most. Even if one assumes that the Eisenhower regime might have tended less than Truman's to suspend its forward planning long before the election, the ileitis operation helps redress the balance. The shortness of the working term for a new President, discounting both his first year(s) and his last, does not get from our literature the notice it deserves. But note it here we must; for as applied in these two instances, it limits the utility of our comparison.

Still, such as it is, we have run a trial balance. What does it show? It indicates, at first glance, that one of these Presidents worked at his tasks as though they posed no "ultimate dilemma," while the other has managed in a fashion to dissipate it, up to now. These findings do not signify that the dilemma, as abstractly stated, lacks reality, in the concrete. Truman may have ignored it, but it haunted his Presidency none the less and manifested itself, at the last, in Eisenhower's election. As for the latter, history will have the final word about beneficence; the record yet is incomplete. Besides, we have no precedents since Washington, if then, for so remarkable a showing of popular prestige diffused so widely, for so long. National heroes do not come a dime-a-dozen; the hero in our momentary concord of events remains unique, by definition. One may expect the cardinal dilemmas of the Presidency in our time to re-enter the White House upon its next change of occupant, if not, indeed, before.

What then is to be learned from our trial balance? Essentially that every President will meet and measure those dilemmas according to the dictates of his situation, his personality. It is a good and necessary thing that this be so. Had Truman seen his problems in what seem to be his successor's terms, it well might have destroyed him as an integrated individual, the task beyond his powers, in his circumstances, to perform; but had he seen things so he would not have been Truman. And on the other hand, had Eisenhower willingly aroused the sort of criticism taken by his predecessor, one wonders what would have become of him; but had he done so, he would never have been Eisenhower. It follows, therefore, that whatever we conceive to help our Presidents shoulder their burdens at mid-century, we must be wary of diminishing their freedom to define those burdens after their own fashion, in their situations as they see them, each in his turn and time. That freedom is already tightly circumscribed by laws and institutions and constituency expectations. No need for students and observers to make the crowding worse.

7. PROSPECTS AND PROPOSALS

"Mid-century" will not endure forever. If the cold war holds its present course and if our national economy continues, generally, to climb, we may face six, eight, even ten years, perhaps more, that will bear an affinity, in presidential terms, to the decade just past. Beyond another decade, though, our population, science, and resources, our industrial development, urbanization, regional realignments, will have brought us to such a point that even if affairs abroad held constant—which they cannot do—what has been described here may be wholly out of date. Even a decade may turn out too long a period to bracket as a portion of "our times." But there is likelihood, at least, that the next two, perhaps three, presidential terms will have much in common with the three since the Second World War.

How then might the next few Presidents be helped to ease the likely operating problems of the office? The answer, plainly, is that nothing fundamental can be done to help them. Nothing short of really revolutionary party centralization bids fair to eliminate that basic and dilemma-nurturing disparity between the Presidency's obligation to initiate and its capacity to achieve. Of course, were our parties fully nationalized and centralized, the party oligarchs might well command the capacity and would tend to assume the obligation, relieving the Presidency, as such, both of burdens and of unique place. But it has been six years now since a committee of the American Political Science Association summoned the revolution to commence, and I am prepared to predict that our parties will endure, for one more decade anyway, substantially unnationalized as in the last.

Barring fundamentals, one can try to nibble at the fringes of the Presidency's problems via piecemeal structural reforms. But those a President might find most fun cannot be had, as a practical matter: witness the item veto. And those most certain to affect him for the worse are only too likely to be thrust upon him: as now we have the two-term amendment and still might find ourselves some day with Bricker's or with Mundt's. As for the many proposed statutory changes which fit neither of these two extremes, opinions differ; their proponents, though, would be well advised to reflect upon Rossiter's admonition: "Leave Your Presidency Alone." In my own view, that caution makes great sense and applies equally to all proposals of a structural and statutory sort. For all of them—all, anyway, of which I am aware—incur a common risk: that they will produce *wayward side-effects,* however unintended by their sponsors, which may make matters worse, or at least put new problems in the place of old. Even the twentieth amendment, widely heralded as an essential modernization, made matters difficult for Eisenhower his first year, and scarcely would have aided FDR, and easily might have been ruinous in Lincoln's time, the

The Presidency at Mid-Century

classic case of grave emergency it is intended to relieve. This is not to suggest we should repeal the "Lame Duck" amendment, or even alter its required starting-dates for the congressional and presidential terms; the point, rather, is that if so logical and seemingly so slight a change produces wayward side-effects, it might be well to avoid others more complex or more obscure.

Some risks, of course, accompany all change; this is no argument for never changing anything. But when one can foresee a wayward consequence, however unintended by proponents, then is the time, it seems to me, to move on their proposals very cautiously indeed. . . . Of course, if one's concern is less with easing operational dilemmas than with checking arbitrary power, the matter wears a wholly different look. But if the Presidency now is dangerously powerful, this essay's premises and argument are all awry.

In terms of easing burdens, hence of strengthening the President, by means externally imposed, there is but one proposal that in all good conscience I could urge without equivocation, a proposal once made (but not patented) by a former Roosevelt aide: to guarantee new Presidents a solid partisan majority in both Houses of Congress, composed of men dependent on the President's own electorate. But in the circumstances of mid-century, this, above all, is never to be guaranteed; indeed it is not even to be hoped for.

Where does this leave us then? It leaves us with the Presidents themselves, with what they might do for themselves in their own self-defense, within the confines and environs of their office.

To make suggestions to them, without knowing them or their specific situations, imposes certain limitations on would-be suggestors, one limit above all: that each suggestion be adaptable for use by an incumbent, whatever his work-habits and his style; that each be usable by men so various in those respects as Eisenhower, Truman, FDR. Truman's White House rather resembled a senatorial establishment, writ large: the staff informal, almost family-like, assignments shifting casually among jacks-of-all-trades, organization plastic, hierarchy slight, and anything liable to be mulled over with the President. Eisenhower, one supposes, could not have abided it. But no more could Truman have abided —much less politically afforded—the military sort of staff system as adapted and on display in Eisenhower's White House. Yet this is the way Eisenhower works and that was the way Truman worked and the next President may want to work like one, or the other, or like neither. There is no point in urging upon any of them a suggestion he could not adopt without foregoing his accustomed way of work.

. . . Our need is for things Presidents might do to help themselves, on their initiative, at their discretion. Suggestions that seem reasonably practicable for a man of military background, entrenched behind the paraphernalia of elaborate staff, are likely to be usable, as well, by those schooled in more fluid, personalized, working-ways of civil government and politics, whence one supposes the next Presidents will come. But having so delimited the field of search, what remains to be found? In such a narrow ground, what is there to discover that may help a President resolve—or live with—his dilemmas? Tentatively, I would hazard the following response.

First, the fewer a President's illusions about the limitations on his power stakes and status in our system, the better his performance on the job. The more nearly he sees his power problem as I have endeavored to describe it here, the greater his chance to master his circumstances or at least hinder them from overwhelming him. Of course, a man wants the illusions that sustain him at his work, and if he needs to look upon the world in terms other than jungle, then so he must. It might help, though, if Presidents who felt impelled to find identification with a forerunner, would look to Lincoln, not as myth or symbol, but as man-in-office. For in their wartime crises, FDR and Wilson seem more removed from our mid-century state than Lincoln does, despite the fact of war. In its operational dilemmas, his was a very modern Presidency, contrasts notwithstanding. And should they seek such parallels, I suggest that the image of his operating burdens and his power problem, rather than, say, Washington's (or Jackson's or a Roosevelt's), be graven on the minds of our next Presidents.

Second, of all the self-perceptions that can help a President, nothing helps so much as an awareness of his absolutely unique place—of his aloneness at the only juncture of his four constituencies—and an alertness, consequently, to the fact that he can count on no one else in Government to sense his interests in precisely his own terms. To stress the "team" and teamwork is a fine thing for morale and useful, too, in binding others to one's cause. But any President who regards the blithe spirit all-for-one-and-one-for-all as a reality which may assume full right-and-title to his interests is assured disenchantment and distortion of his aims.

It follows that he needs to widen, so far as he can, the confines of his own freedom to choose what he himself would think he were well advised to make choices on and undertake persuasion on and when. As we have seen, he cannot hope to widen these confines more than a little; how might even that little be accomplished? On the one hand, I would suggest, by rendering the regular assistance he receives more representative of the totality of his constituencies; on the other hand, by building into government and his own staff the sorts of competitions which will create "deadlines" for him at times and on issues useful in his terms.

Perhaps we do not recognize sufficiently the deep distortions, in constituency terms, of staff assistance now officially available to a President. Without exception, his department heads and institutional staff aides are tightly linked to, actually are part of, his "government" constituency. The same thing can be said for his legislative leaders and for such White House aides as he may draw from agency or congressional sources to help with liaison in both directions. Many of these people also represent, in varying degree, some portions of his "partisan" constituency; so, of course, does the National Committee Chairman, whose office is more or less part of presidential staff facilities. And all of them can claim to be in some sense representative of "national" constituency as well. But taking them together as a collectivity, their representative character is decidedly different than his own; greatly overweighing the governmental element, especially its executive side, while relatively slighting partisan, underweighing national, and virtually ignoring overseas components. Even in the White House staff, none but the Press Secretary is free of institutionalized routines which pull particularly in the government direction (perhaps explaining why that post becomes so powerful when manned by a superb technician).

To compensate for these distortions, Presidents must break out of their official families and so they do, with ceremonials and visitors, with trips and tête-à-têtes, with consultations and with confidants, each in his fashion. But I submit that these are frail reliances which need the utmost buttressing by Presidents themselves in conscious, purposeful awareness of official insufficiencies. And not the means but that awareness becomes crucial in this case; if that be strong enough, the man makes his own means. His aides, of course, can help and so they will, provided his insistence is incessant, but their reach is no *substitute* for his, nor their awareness either.

As for the matter of "created deadlines, this was a specialty with FDR which, suitably adapted, I commend to his successors. Roosevelt is commonly supposed a "poor" administrator; lines of authority confused, the same assignments in the hands of numerous subordinates, doors opening and closing unpredictably, nobody knowing everything of anybody's business and everybody horning in on everything. Yet with all this and *by* it, he kept in his own hands more power of judgment and decision than most Presidents before or since. In the administration of the Presidency, what could be more important? This is not to suggest that future Presidents should try to play by ear, *ad hoc*, in Roosevelt's special way. They cannot if they would—nor could he either, at the end—for government has grown too big, its scope too broad, their own responsibilities too routinized, their office far too institutionalized. What is suggested, rather, is a search for substitutes compatible with their more complex circumstances. The building-in of competition seems to me the key.

Without attempting an exhaustive exploration, let me mention two means by which competitive relations might be fostered: namely appointments and reorganizations. The President who wishes to enhance his prospects for free choices in an area of policy will do well to arrange that opposed attitudes in country or in Congress, or in his own mind, are represented among appointees charged institutionally with its consideration *and* administration. By "represented" is meant not in form alone, but in a balance that suffices to force underlying issues on the table, up the line, and in good time, without exhausting institutional support for a decision *either* way. Thus, Eisenhower seems to run tremendous risks of foreclosed freedom in the sphere of foreign aid, when all the posts of massive institutional power are held by men reportedly conservative in view, with "balance" furnished mainly by a brace of White House aides.

One sympathizes with the wish of both Roosevelt's successors to avoid such unseemly public struggles as were carried on from inside his regime. But foreclosed freedom can be harder on a President than struggling subordinates. Indeed, unless they are sufficiently well-matched to carry controversies to the press, he loses one among the early warning signals built-in-competitions can provide. If he is lucky and adroit and granted a respectful opposition, perhaps he can hold down the public outcries though he keep his fighters matched, and can devise internal signals as a substitute. But if, to keep the public peace, he rigs fights overmuch, he pays an exorbitant price, or so it seems to me. Indeed, under the circumstances of mid-century, an outward look of total harmony in a regime might well be taken as itself a warning sign.

As for reorganization, it is obviously useful, often essential, as a supplement to the appointive power in building or in equalizing institutionalized competitions. There is one disability, however: my colleague, Wallace Sayre, has propounded the sound "law" that any benefits of a reorganization are immediate, while disadvantages are cumulative over time. To this I would append the simple corollary that as for a President's own freedom, gains are short-range, risks long-run. And this applies with greater force the closer one approaches his own person. The moral appears plain. It cannot be enough to reorganize, one must keep on with it. In their relations to each other and the President, his official associates need stirring up; not with such frequency that they shrink into immobility, but just enough so that they are never absolutely confident in unchecked judgment of their chief's own judgment, or of their colleagues' either.

With that I would conclude. These several imprecise suggestions of what Presidents might do in their own self-defense are neither very bold nor very new; assuredly, they are neither my own last testament nor anybody's. In that regard, one final word: if we, as citizens, cannot rescue our Presidents from their dilemmas but must leave them to help themselves as best they can, there is one thing that we, as students and observers, might do to render their self-help a little easier. We might take more care in the future than sometimes in the past, lest we foster stereotypes and expectations not within their capacities or even their own interests to fulfill.

In the two decades since the report of the President's Committee on Administrative Management, great numbers of experts, in universities and out, have been hard at work seeking solutions for the managerial dilemmas of the federal government. And whether the focus be on budgeting, on organization, or on personnel—in order of prevailing fashion, then to now—the outcome tends to be the same: "The President, himself, must take command."

Faster than perhaps we realize, the frame of reference underlying such investigations, such solutions, becomes popularized (and oversimplified), eventuating in those plain truths nobody learns but everybody knows: "The President, of course! As in business, so in government; the title is the same and so should be the function." Perhaps it would not be amiss to remind the managerial enthusiasts of Woodrow Wilson's wise prognosis half a century ago:

". . . as the business of government becomes more and more complex and extended . . . the President is becoming more and more a political and less an executive officer . . . incumbents will come more and more [to be] directors of affairs and leaders of the nation—men of counsel and of the sort of action that makes for enlightenment."

For so it has turned out; these and not management are the great objects of their work and sources of their troubles at mid-century.

▢ The Psychological Functions of the Presidency for Citizens

FRED I. GREENSTEIN

When we speak of "presidential power" in anything beyond the strictly legal meaning of the phrase we are addressing ourselves to a phenomenon which involves more than the Chief Executive. "Speaking of power and the powerful is," as Lasswell puts it, "an ellipsis. . . . Power is an interpersonal situation; those who hold power are empowered. They depend upon and continue only so long as there is a continuing stream of empowering responses. . . . [P]ower is not a brick that can be lugged from place to place, but a process that vanishes when the supporting responses cease." Therefore, an understanding of the power of the President calls for insight into both presidential action and the reactions of others to him.

In recent years we have begun to get increasingly precise accounts of the political behavior of public officials and of citizens. Unfortunately, we are not very well informed about the complex connections between the official and citizen levels of the political system, although the evidence necessary to remedy this deficiency has begun to be available. For example, we can now

FROM Fred I. Greenstein, "The Psychological Functions of the Presidency for Citizens," in Elmer Cornwall, ed., *The American Presidency* (Chicago: Scott, Foresman, 1966), pp. 31–36. Reprinted by permission of the author. Slightly revised by the author in September 1970 to take into account fluctuations in presidential popularity since the original publication.

provisionally chart certain of the characteristics of public dispositions toward the President.

We may begin considering the nature of public orientations toward the President by noting what seems to be a paradox. For the great bulk of the electorate in the United States (and in other countries, as well) most of what goes on in public life seems to be of very little interest and to recieve meager attention. This includes a large proportion of the politically significant day-to-day activities of the President. Public indifference to politics has been documented in endless ways by the public opinion pollsters. For example, 80 per cent of the electorate does not regularly engage in political conversations, and 90 per cent fails to write public officials. A great many citizens are without many of the elementary items of political information which would seem necessary for minimally thoughtful political participation. (Forty-five per cent do not know the number of Senators from each state, 53 per cent do not know the term in office of a member of the House of Representatives, and so forth.) Yet, in spite of this evident indifference toward the sphere of society in which the President is a key actor, under some circumstances—notably following the death in office of a President—the Chief Executive becomes the object of extraordinary outbursts of deeply felt and widely shared emotion. The magnitude of response on such an occasion seems far to exceed what might have been expected from the prior attitudes and behavior of citizens.

The profound nature of public reactions to a presidential death was extensively documented in a national survey conducted immediately after President Kennedy's assassination. A large majority of the respondents (79 per cent) report that their immediate and "deeply felt" reaction was to think of the President's death as "the loss of someone very close and dear." Half of the national sample acknowledged having wept, many reported such symptoms as loss of appetite (43 per cent), insomnia (48 per cent), general feelings of nervousness and tension (68 per cent). Throughout the weekend following the assassination, people were unable or unwilling to carry on their normal activities. "The average adult spent eight hours on Friday, ten hours on Saturday, eight hours on Sunday and another eight hours on Monday" attending to television and radio reports of the assassination and its aftermath.

Some of this distress was certainly a result of the violent nature of the President's death and some certainly was reaction to President Kennedy's personal characteristics—especially his youth. Historical evidence makes it clear, however, that the main stimulus for the flood of spontaneous feelings was that *the President* had died. When Franklin Roosevelt, a much older man, died in office of natural causes, there was a wave of public reaction which in most respects seems to have been identical to the response to Kennedy's death. There are similar reports of reaction to every presidential death in office since that of Lincoln. Note, for example, the following reports of reaction to the death of Warren Harding (who is scarcely remembered as a strong or impressive President).

The Psychological Functions of the Presidency for Citizens

People in the streets around Times Square could hardly believe the news. A man in evening dress said, "It can't be true." There was a steady stream of telephone calls to newspaper offices by persons seeking to verify the news.

Taxicab drivers, waiters, conductors, and people in all walks of life . . . echoed the same comment. "Why did not the doctors prepare the people for this sad announcement?"

Meyer London, Socialist Congressman: "Oh, what a calamity. This is a tremendous shock. . . . Politics are now forgotten in the love all factions had for him as a man."

August 10, 1923, was the official day of mourning. All public activity was suspended for that day; banks, stores, theaters, and movie houses were closed. At noon, the entire nation observed two minutes' silence in honor of the dead President.

The deaths of other public figures—political leaders, ex-Presidents, religious leaders, entertainment celebrities—do not produce a comparable response, except in very specialized segments of the population.

This preliminary statement of the paradox has already suggested one of the sources at our disposal for characterizing public dispositions toward the President—research on public opinion among members of the adult population. We also may draw upon two further sources of insight into the matter—a recent body of investigations into children's orientations toward political authority, and an interesting, if uneven, collection of psychiatric case materials which have accumulated over the years on the responses by individuals in psychotherapy to public officials such as the President. The findings in these three bodies of literature complement each other and will provide us with the basis for several speculative concluding observations about the psychological functions of the Presidency for citizens.

SURVEY RESEARCH FINDINGS ON ADULT ORIENTATIONS TOWARD THE PRESIDENT

One of the things the polls have made clear is that the President is the best known political figure in the United States. Indeed, he probably is the best known individual in the nation. As we have already seen, surveys consistently show how little general awareness there is of many of the most highly publicized objects in the political environment. A good half (or more) of the electorate is typically unable to name—or even to recognize the names of—such leading figures as cabinet secretaries, governors of major states, etc. In September 1963, less than a year before he received the Republican presidential nomination, Barry Goldwater was unknown to a full 42 per cent of a Gallup poll national sample. Virtually all politicians are less well known than a variety of mass entertainment figures (motion picture stars, television celebrities, athletes), many of whom are familiar to 90 per cent or more of the public.

But virtually everyone (95 per cent) knows who the President is. For some Americans, the President provides virtually the sole cognitive link to the political system, a fact which is certainly not unrelated to the consistent ability of twentieth century Presidents to be reelected.

A second poll finding is that high public officials are greatly respected in American society. Americans commonly express dislike and distrust of "politicians." But when they are asked to rank occupations according to their "general standing," they regularly place such roles as Supreme Court Justice, Governor, and Senator at the top of their rankings, ahead of even the most prestigious civilian role (which happens to be that of physician). Curiously, during the long history of occupational prestige studies the Presidency appears not to have been included until the 1966 mid-term Congressional election survey of the University of Michigan Survey Research Center, which posed the following question:

We're interested in learning what kind of work Americans respect most highly. Which of these occupations do you respect the most?

The card handed to respondents included "United States Senator, bishop or other church official, general or admiral, famous doctor, Justice of the U.S. Supreme Court, atomic scientist, professor at a large university, President of the United States, well-known athlete, president of a large corporation like General Motors, and Governor of your state." Somewhat more than half of the respondents listed President of the United States as their first choice; the next most prestigious category, "famous doctor," was mentioned by only about 15 per cent of the respondents.

A third poll finding is that most incumbent Presidents on most occasions have received a good bit more approval than disapproval from the electorate. In the case of four of the six Presidents who have held office since national opinion polls were first conducted—Roosevelt, Eisenhower, Kennedy, and Nixon as of September 1970—the regular Gallup poll assessments of "how good a job the President is doing" have never found more people disapproving than approving. Of the two Presidents who did not consistently receive the approval of a plurality of the public, Truman had the most persistent difficulties. He began office with the highest favorable rating ever recorded by the Gallup poll (87 per cent), but at one point registered the record low of 27 per cent. Truman was disapproved of by a plurality of those polled in twenty-five of the forty-three surveys conducted during his term of office and, after the first three surveys conducted during the Korean conflict, consistently had more disapprovals than approvals for the remainder of his term (October 1950 through January 1953). Johnson's popularity began high when he succeeded Kennedy and stayed high through his election in his own right, slowly eroding from percentages in the 60's in 1965 to the 50's and then the 40's in 1966. In August 1967—as the Vietnam conflict ground on—he finally slipped to the point of greater disapproval than approval. All told, Johnson was disapproved of in twelve of the monthly Gallup polls conducted during his term, but he was approved of in fifty-six polls and retired from office with a modest surplus of approval over disapproval. In both Truman's and Johnson's case prolonged, inconclusive limited war in Asia was the most consistent correlate of low popularity.

Fourth, we may note the consistent readiness of citizens to come to the President's support in times of crisis, particularly international crisis. While assessments of the President's performance are generally more positive than negative, his public esteem does fluctuate. Very often the increases in presidential popularity follow fast upon some major presidential action. When the decision was made to resist the Communist invasion of South Korea, President Truman's popularity rose—within the period of a single month—from 37 per cent approve–45 per cent disapprove, to 46 per cent approve–45 per cent disapprove. Eisenhower's popularity rose from 67 per cent to 75 per cent during the month of the Suez crisis, from 52 per cent to 58 per cent after sending the marines to Lebanon, in 1958. Roosevelt's popularity rose from 72 to 84 per cent after Pearl Harbor. Even international actions which informed observers view as unsuccessful have led to increased presidential popularity. Eisenhower's popularity went up by 6 percentage points after the U-2 incident and the collapse of the summit meetings; Kennedy's by 10 points after the Bay of Pigs Invasion. A rally-around-the-President effect also typically takes place just after his election or reelection, indicating that there is a substance to the familiar metaphor which sees public office as a "mantle"—that is, a cloak or covering which affects one's appearance. For example, John F. Kennedy had the support of only a fraction of one per cent more than half of the electorate in November 1960. By the time of his inauguration, two months later, he appeared worthy of approval to 69 per cent of the electorate.[1]

Finally, there is evidence that citizens perceive and judge the President largely in personal terms, that is, on the basis of what he is rather than what he stands for. In early 1948 a three-state sample of voters who had indicated their preferred presidential candidate were asked: "What are the qualities that you think would make him the best man (for President)?" References to personal qualities exceeded ideological references by more than fourfold. When people were asked during the Eisenhower years to indicate what they liked or disliked about the President they most commonly referred to aspects of his personal image—for example, his conscientiousness, his warmth or coldness, his physical vigor, his sincerity and integrity, his religious background and practice. There were also references to his policy positions and his leadership skill (a characteristic standing somewhere between personal image and policy position),

---

[1] A number of studies have shown the almost self-conscious process through which many of a presidential candidate's erstwhile opponents "improve" their opinion of him after his election. . . . The main exception seems to have been 1964, when Johnson's popularity did not rise in the first postelection poll, possibly because it already had been at a quite high level before the election and possibly because of the unusual amount of personal abuse in the campaign.

but together these were less frequent than statements about his personal qualities. Comparable evidence is available on public perceptions of Kennedy and Nixon in the 1960 campaign. For both there were substantially fewer references to policy commitments than references to the man.

In summary, the surveys show that the President is almost universally known, standing out with far greater clarity than other actors on the political scene; his role seems to be highly respected; his personal popularity fluctuates, but tends generally to be high; support for him increases when he takes decisive action, particularly actions which commit the nation in the international arena; he is perceived and judged to a considerable extent in personal terms.

RESEARCH ON CHILDREN'S ORIENTATIONS TOWARD THE PRESIDENT

Research into "political socialization" (the study of how and when political behavior enters into the individual's life cycle) shows that the President normally is the first public official of whom children become aware. By the age of nine (and evidently earlier) virtually every child knows the name of the incumbent President. Children of this age resemble the least informed members of the adult population in that they know very little else about government and politics. They *do,* however, already share the adult conception of high political roles as being very important. Nine-year-olds, when asked to rank occupations in terms of their importance, place the President at the top of their rankings, well above, for example, physicians, school teachers, and clergymen. In addition, young children perceive of the President in an overwhelmingly positive fashion, thinking of him as a benevolent, helpful individual. We encounter statements such as the following in children's descriptions of the President:

"The President is doing a very good job of helping people to be safe." "The President . . . takes care of the U.S." "The President has the right to stop bad things before they start."

It has been argued that children's early conceptions of the presidential role provide them with "perceptual filters," which shape their later learning about politics; the positive nature of these early conceptions contributes to a generally positive orientation toward the political system and encourages assumptions about the importance of the presidency in relation to other political institutions (e.g., Congress). Whether or not this argument can be supported, the emphasis on the President in children's early political learning is a further indication of the conspicuousness of the Chief Executive in the political system into which the child is in the process of being inducted.

PSYCHIATRIC REPORTS ABOUT THE DEEPER MEANINGS OF THE PRESIDENT

Among the most fascinating, controversial, and pervasively influential intellectual currents of the twentieth century are the hypotheses about mental functioning which stem from the psychiatric work of Sigmund Freud in turn-of-the-century Vienna. In caricatured simplification, Freud's conception of the psyche is one which places a great emphasis on the role of unconscious processes. The mind, in this view (which underlies much of contemporary psychiatry), tends to thrust out of consciousness that which is distasteful—for example, memories of emotionally painful childhood experiences and various unacceptable impulses, many of which are sexual or aggressive. But what is so repressed strives to reassert itself, appearing in a variety of disguises—in dreams, neurotic symptoms, and as latent meaning underlying much of the manifest content of everyday life. A good bit of the repressed content of mental activity, the psychoanalytic argument runs, is related to and results from early childhood experiences with parental authority. The reassertion of these impulses (which typically involve ambivalent needs to be dominated or protected by and to rebel against one's parents) takes a number of forms, one of which includes the symbolic equation of public authorities (Presidents, Kings, etc.) with the earlier private authorities of one's childhood.

Space forbids even a roughly satisfactory exposition of this line of thought and the questions which have been raised about it. But we may suggest two reasons for taking account of it in attempting to understand public dispositions to the President. First, psychiatric thinking is especially designed to deal with seeming paradoxes of the sort described at the beginning of this essay, in which an emotional reaction to some stimulus (in this case, the death in office of a President) far exceeds what might have been expected from the prior surface manifestations of the individual. In such instances the psychiatric thinker expects to find that the object of the response has unconscious meanings of which the respondent is not aware. Secondly, psychiatric theory of the sort we have been discussing is based on a particularly interesting, if controversial kind of evidence—the behavior of individuals who have been studied in the prolonged, intensive, and intimate interview situations known as psychotherapy. Even if one does not subscribe to the theory of psychoanalysis, reports of what occurs in the analytic situation provide observational data which require explanation. And there happen to be a number of such reports, especially on the occasion of presidential deaths in office, which are relevant to our discussion. For example, when President Roosevelt died a number of psychoanalysts reported that their patients responded to his death in ways which indicated that they symbolically equated the President with one or both of their parents. There is at least one report by an analyst who found similar associations among his patients under the less extreme circumstances of the national election campaigns of 1948, 1952, and 1956. And there are psychiatric reports of similar symbolic associations with President Kennedy, both before and after his assassination. Little is known, however, about the frequency with which such linkage occurs among psychiatric patients, much less in the general population. Nor do we have a clear indication of the variation in form that a linkage of this sort might take from individual to individual. More research needs to be done in this borderline area between political science and psychiatry as well as along the more traditional lines of charting the nature of people's more conscious and explicit orientations toward the President and his office.

PSYCHOLOGICAL FUNCTIONS OF THE PRESIDENCY

Using the three classes of research findings noted above as points of departure, we may now indicate a number of ways in which citizens seem to make psychological use of their Chief Executive. First, the existence of this highly publicized national figure who combines the roles of political leader and head of state *simplifies perception* of government and politics. Just as the mid-twentieth century President provides the central source of initiative and energy in the actual governmental policy-making process, he also serves as the main cognitive "handle" for providing busy citizens with some sense of what their government is doing. For some citizens, as we have seen, he is virtually the only vehicle for following government and politics, and for children he serves, if unwittingly, as an instrument of civic learning.

Secondly, the President provides citizens with an *outlet for emotional expression*. In addition to the obvious uses to which he is put in connection with partisan politics, we may note all of his ceremonial duties and the publicized aspects of his (and his family's) private life. Here, presumably, we have an equivalent to the more dignified displays of symbolic activity associated elsewhere in the world with monarchs. This aspect of the presidency probably engages the attention and interest of more segments of the population than do the activities of the nation's other highly publicized celebrities—the film stars and the like.

The previous point about the cross-cutting nature of interest in the President suggests another of his functions for citizens—he evidently may serve as a *symbol of unity*. The public reaction to a presidential death provides a rather grim instance of the unifying power of the presidency. Although there were differences from group to group in society in the intensity of response to the assassination, the overwhelming impression is of the homogeneity of public opinion. Regret at President Kennedy's death was shared by such diverse segments of the population as pro-Kennedy Northern Negroes and anti-Kennedy Southern whites. Another instance which we have already noted is the tendency of citizens to rally to the support of their President when he takes action in time of international crisis. Under those circumstances when he represents the nation against an international adversary it may well be that the President serves still another function, that of providing citizens with a *vicarious means of taking political action*. Apart from whatever attachments there may be to the President at the deeper "psychiatric" levels of the personality, it seems quite likely that during international (and possibly some internal) crises, numerous people find themselves "identifying" with the President at least in the superficial fashion in which we find ourselves taking the part of the hero of a motion picture or novel. To the degree that the President's actions are effective, citizens who identify themselves with him may experience heightened feelings of strength—of being in a world which is not completely dependent upon external circumstances and events.

Finally, whether or not one psychically takes the part of the President, it is clear that the President serves as a reassuring *symbol of social stability*. For many people, one of the most disturbing aspects of President Kennedy's assassination was the implication that went with it of lack of control—of possible national and international disorder. Here, in effect, was the direct opposite of the situation in which the President increases the citizen's sense of power and security by acting decisively and effectively in the international arena. It is a great parody of the complex, sprawling, uncoordinated nature of the political system to think in terms of a ship of state, sailing on, with the President firmly at the rudder. But it is a comfort to be able to think in these terms, and the perceptually simple, easily personified nature of the presidential role probably enables a good many people to do precisely this.

SUGGESTIONS FOR FURTHER READING

Perhaps the best single volume on the contemporary presidency is Richard E. Neustadt's *Presidential Power* (New York: Wiley, 1960). A number of historical and biographical works are valuable—for example, James M. Burns, *Roosevelt: The Lion and the Fox* (New York: Harcourt Brace Jovanovich, 1956), and Wilfred E. Brinkley, *President and Congress* (New York: Random House, 1962). Louis Koenig's *The Chief Executive* (New York: Harcourt Brace Jovanovich, 1964) is a political scientist's very useful overview of the institutionalized Presidency.

On the "public law of the presidency," Edward S. Corwin's *The President: Office and Powers* (New York: New York University Press, 1957) is the standard work, along with Glendon G. Schubert's *The Presidency in the Courts* (Ann Arbor, Mich.: University of Minnesota Press, 1957).

Among the biographical studies, particularly useful are Arthur M. Schlesinger, Jr., *A Thousand Days* (Boston: Houghton Mifflin, 1965), Robert Sherwood, *Roosevelt and Hopkins* (New York: Harper & Row, 1950), and the three available volumes of Schlesinger's *The Age of Roosevelt* series: *The Crisis of the Old Order: 1919–1933, The Coming of the New Deal,* and *The Politics of Upheaval* (Boston: Houghton Mifflin, 1957–60). Excellent short studies are John Morton Blum's *The Republican Roosevelt* (Cambridge, Mass.: Harvard University Press, 1954), and his *Woodrow Wilson and the Politics of Morality* (Boston: Little, Brown, 1956).

Interesting specialized studies are Richard Longaker, *The Presidency and Individual Liberties* (Ithaca, N. Y.: Cornell University Press, 1961), and Ruth P. Morgan, *The President and Civil Rights* (New York: St. Martin's Press, 1970).

More specialized treatments include Elmer Cornwell, *Presidential Leadership of Public Opinion* (Bloomington, Ind.: Indiana University Press, 1965), and Richard F. Fenno, Jr., *The President's Cabinet: An Analysis in the Period from Wilson to Eisenhower* (Cambridge, Mass.: Harvard University Press, 1959). An excellent case study is Grant McConnell, *Steel and the Presidency, 1962* (New York: W. Norton, 1963); a good reader is Donald Bruce Johnson and Jack L. Walker, *The Dynamics of the American Presidency* (New York: Wiley, 1964); and a good short text is Dorothy B. James, *The Contemporary Presidency* (New York: Pegasus, 1969).

An excellent collection of materials on the men around the President is Thomas E. Cronin and Sanford Greenberg, eds., *The Presidential Advisory System* (New York: Harper & Row, 1969).

8 The bureaucracy

GROSS CHANGES IN MAGNITUDE are not always the most significant indicators of social change, but there is no gainsaying the importance of the growth of the federal bureaucracy since the turn of the century and especially since Franklin Delano Roosevelt's accession to the Presidency. In 1900 the federal government employed 208,000 people; today it employs more than 2.5 million. Federal government expenditures in 1900 were less than $600 million, and the largest single item in that year was the payment of pensions. The 1971 budget called for expenditures of more than $200 billion in areas ranging from adult education to zinc price stabilization; although defense expenditures consumed the largest single part of the 1969 budget, nearly $60 billion was spent on old-age benefits, welfare, and other socially oriented programs. Dollar figures for various years are not entirely comparable, of course, but the growing number of federal employees, the magnitude of the resources at their disposal, and the scope of their concerns all indicate the emergence of a major centralizing force in the American political system: the bureaucracy.

The anatomy of this sprawling administrative apparatus is a subject for basic texts, not for a collection of analytical writings. Moreover, the growth of the bureaucracy has given rise to a number of excellent studies of administrative behavior, which are summarized in recent texts by March and Simon[1] and by Presthus.[2] Although such matters are of interest to

---

[1] J. G. March and H. A. Simon, *Organizations* (New York: Wiley, 1958).
[2] R. V. Presthus, *The Organizational Society* (New York: Knopf, 1962).

all serious students of politics, we are concerned here only with the consequences of bureaucratic growth for the distribution of power within the political system as a whole. To what extent do bureaucracies "naturally" contribute to the centralization of power? How can they be made into more effective social instruments? What are the prospects for the decentralization ("de-bureaucratization") of certain governmental functions?

The articles in this chapter are unusual in that they approach these problems with a measure of historical and analytical detachment rather than with the pomposity and didacticism that marked the earlier writings of civil service reformers or with the shrill moral outrage that characterizes the work of a more recent generation of neopopulists who appear to have discovered, as if for the first time, the limitations and faults of formal organizations and institutions.

In his essay on "The Bureaucratic Problem," James Q. Wilson argues that much of the dissatisfaction and disillusionment with bureaucracies results from lack of appreciation of their institutional limitations. He points to the qualities of accountability, equity, efficiency, responsiveness, and fiscal integrity, all of which have been advanced as goals for the bureaucracy, and demonstrates that these are often incompatible, if not mutually exclusive, aims. In addition to this confusion of aims, Wilson notes the tendency to exaggerate the bureaucracy's ability to deal with social and political problems. Lack of money is often the least of the difficulties. Far more important, he claims, is the absolute lack of qualified people to administer present and proposed programs. This lack, combined with the difficulty of defining precisely the potential objectives sought from programs, reduces the bureaucracy's potential for resolving many of the problems that are now most vexing to American society.

Herbert Kaufman's timely and perceptive article on "Administrative Decentralization and Political Power" places in historical perspective much of the current discussion about decentralizing bureaucracy. Kaufman identifies a cyclical pattern in values and attitudes toward governmental structure. The three elements of the pattern—representativeness, politically neutral competence, and executive leadership—are always present in administrative patterns, but the balance among them has varied over time. The dynamic relationship among the three elements results from the actions of groups that are attached to one or the other of the values currently being de-emphasized. Much of the present dissatisfaction, Kaufman argues, can be traced to the triumph of previous approaches and to the concomitant disaffection of groups that neither share the values of nor derive benefits from those approaches.

The recent eruption of anti-bureaucratic rhetoric, which in some cases amounts to a romantic elevation of the neighborhood over all other administrative units, should not be taken too seriously. Kaufman admits that "some modifications" in the direction of decentralization are likely to occur; however, it is equally likely that these modifications will themselves produce dissatisfactions which, within a short time, will move us into the next phase of the cycle.

◻ The Bureaucracy Problem

JAMES Q. WILSON

The federal bureaucracy, whose growth and problems were once only the concern of the Right, has now become a major concern of the Left, the Center, and almost all points in between. Conservatives once feared that a powerful bureaucracy would work a social revolution. The Left now fears this same bureaucracy is working a conservative reaction. And the Center fears that the bureaucracy isn't working at all.

Increasing federal power has always been seen by conservatives in terms of increasing *bureaucratic* power. If greater federal power merely meant, say, greater uniformity in government regulations—standardized trucking regulations, for example, or uniform professional licensing practices—a substantial segment of American businessmen would probably be pleased. But growing federal power means increased discretion vested in appointive officials whose behavior can neither be anticipated nor controlled. The behavior of state and local bureaucrats, by contrast, can often be anticipated *because* it can be controlled by businessmen and others.

Knowing this, liberals have always resolved most questions in favor of enhancing federal power. The "hacks" running local administrative agencies were too often, in liberal eyes, the agents of local political and economic forces—businessmen, party bosses, organized professions, and the like. A federal bureaucrat, because he was responsible to a national power center and to a single President elected by a nationwide constituency, could not so easily be bought off by local vested interests; in addition, he would take his policy guidance from a President elected by a process that gave heavy weight to the votes of urban, labor, and minority groups. The New Deal bureaucrats, especially those appointed to the new, "emergency" agencies, were expected by liberals to be free to chart a radically new program and to be competent to direct its implementation.

It was an understandable illusion. It frequently appears in history in the hopes of otherwise intelligent and far-sighted men. Henry II thought his clerks and scribes would help him subdue England's feudal barons; how was he to know that in time they would become the agents of Parliamentary authority directed at stripping the king of his prerogatives? And how were Parliament and its Cabinet ministers, in turn, to know that eventually these permanent undersecretaries would become an almost self-governing class whose day-to-day

FROM James Q. Wilson, "The Bureaucracy Problem," *The Public Interest*, No. 6 (Winter 1967), pp. 3–9. © National Affairs, Inc., 1967. Reprinted by permission of the author.

behavior would become virtually immune to scrutiny or control? Marxists thought that Soviet bureaucrats would work for the people, despite the fact that Max Weber had pointed out why one could be almost certain they would work mostly for themselves. It is ironic that among today's members of the "New Left," the "Leninist problem"—i.e., the problem of over-organization and of self-perpetuating administrative power—should become a major preoccupation.

This apparent agreement among polemicists of the Right and Left that there is a bureaucracy problem accounts, one suspects, for the fact that non-bureaucratic solutions to contemporary problems seem to command support from both groups. The negative income tax as a strategy for dealing with poverty is endorsed by economists of such different persuasions as Milton Friedman and James Tobin, and has received favorable consideration among members of both the Goldwater brain trust and the Students for a Democratic Society. Though the interests of the two groups are somewhat divergent, one common element is a desire to scuttle the social workers and the public welfare bureaucracy, who are usually portrayed as prying busybodies with pursed lips and steel-rimmed glasses ordering midnight bedchecks in public housing projects. (Police officers who complain that television makes them look like fools in the eyes of their children will know just what the social workers are going through.)

Now that everybody seems to agree that we ought to do something about the problem of bureaucracy, one might suppose that something would get done. Perhaps a grand reorganization, accompanied by lots of "systems analysis," "citizen participation," "creative federalism," and "interdepartmental co-ordination." Merely to state this prospect is to deny it.

There is not one bureaucracy problem, there are several, and the solution to each is in some degree incompatible with the solution to every other. First, there is the problem of accountability or control—getting the bureaucracy to serve agreed-on national goals. Second is the problem of equity—getting bureaucrats to treat like cases alike and on the basis of clear rules, known in advance. Third is the problem of efficiency—maximizing output for a given expenditure, or minimizing expenditures for a given output. Fourth is the problem of responsiveness—inducing bureaucrats to meet, with alacrity and compassion, those cases which can never be brought under a single national rule and which, by common human standards of justice or benevolence, seem to require that an exception be made or a rule stretched. Fifth is the problem of fiscal integrity—properly spending and accounting for public money.

Each of these problems mobilizes a somewhat different segment of the public. The problem of power is the unending preoccupation of the President and his staff, especially during the first years of an administration. Equity concerns the lawyers and the courts, though increasingly the Supreme Court seems to act as if it thinks its job is to help set national goals as a kind of auxiliary White House. Efficiency has traditionally been the concern of businessmen who thought, mistakenly, that an efficient government was one that didn't

The Bureaucracy Problem

spend very much money. (Of late, efficiency has come to have a broader and more accurate meaning as an optimal relationship between objectives and resources. Robert McNamara has shown that an "efficient" Department of Defense costs a lot more money than an "inefficient" one; his disciples are now carrying the message to all parts of a skeptical federal establishment.) Responsiveness has been the concern of individual citizens and of their political representatives, usually out of wholly proper motives, but sometimes out of corrupt ones. Congress, especially, has tried to retain some power over the bureaucracy by intervening on behalf of tens of thousands of immigrants, widows, businessmen, and mothers-of-soldiers, hoping that the collective effect of many individual interventions would be a bureaucracy that, on large matters as well as small, would do Congress's will. (Since Congress only occasionally has a clear will, this strategy only works occasionally.) Finally, fiscal integrity—especially its absence—is the concern of the political "outs" who want to get in and thus it becomes the concern of "ins" who want to keep them out.

Obviously the more a bureaucracy is responsive to its clients—whether those clients are organized by radicals into Mothers for Adequate Welfare or represented by Congressmen anxious to please constituents—the less it can be accountable to presidential directives. Similarly, the more equity, the less responsiveness. And a preoccupation with fiscal integrity can make the kind of program budgeting required by enthusiasts of efficiency difficult, if not impossible.

Indeed, of all the groups interested in bureaucracy, those concerned with fiscal integrity usually play the winning hand. To be efficient, one must have clearly stated goals, but goals are often hard to state at all, much less clearly. To be responsive, one must be willing to run risks, and the career civil service is not ordinarily attractive to people with a taste for risk. Equity is an abstraction, of concern for the most part only to people who haven't been given any. Accountability is "politics," and the bureaucracy itself is the first to resist that (unless, of course, it is the kind of politics that produces pay raises and greater job security). But an absence of fiscal integrity is welfare chiseling, sweetheart deals, windfall profits, conflict of interest, malfeasance in high places—in short, corruption. Everybody recognizes *that* when he sees it, and none but a few misguided academics have anything good to say about it. As a result, fiscal scandal typically becomes the standard by which a bureaucracy is judged (the FBI is good because it hasn't had any, the Internal Revenue Service is bad because it has) and thus the all-consuming fear of responsible executives.

If it is this hard to make up one's mind about how one wants the bureaucracy to behave, one might be forgiven if one threw up one's hands and let nature take its course. Though it may come to that in the end, it is possible—and important—to begin with a resolution to face the issue squarely and try to think through the choices. Facing the issue means admitting what, in our zeal for new programs, we usually ignore: *There are inherent limits to what can be accomplished by large hierarchical organizations.*

The opposite view is more often in vogue. If enough people don't like something, it becomes a problem; if the intellectuals agree with them, it becomes a crisis; any crisis must be solved; if it must be solved, then it can be solved—and creating a new organization is the way to do it. If the organization fails to solve the problem (and when the problem is a fundamental one, it will almost surely fail), then the reason is "politics," or "mismanagement," or "incompetent people," or "meddling," or "socialism," or "inertia."

Some problems cannot be solved and some government functions cannot, in principle, be done well. Notwithstanding, the effort must often be made. The rule of reason should be to try to do as few undoable things as possible. It is regrettable, for example, that any country must have a foreign office, since none can have a good one. The reason is simple: it is literally impossible to have a "policy" with respect to *all* relevant matters concerning *all* foreign countries, much less a consistent and reasonable policy. And the difficulty increases with the square of the number of countries, and probably with the cube of the speed of communications. The problem long ago became insoluble and any sensible Secretary of State will cease trying to solve it. He will divide his time instead between *ad hoc* responses to the crisis of the moment and appearances on Meet the Press.

The answer is not, it must be emphasized, one of simply finding good people, though it is at least that. Most professors don't think much of the State Department, but it is by no means clear that a department made up only of professors would be any better, and some reason to believe that it would be worse. One reason is that bringing in "good outsiders," especially good outsiders from universities, means bringing in men with little experience in dealing with the substantive problem but many large ideas about how to approach problems "in general." General ideas, no matter how soundly based in history or social science, rarely tell one what to do tomorrow about the visit from the foreign trade mission from Ruritania or the questions from the congressional appropriations subcommittee.

Another reason is that good people are in very short supply, even assuming we knew how to recognize them. Some things literally cannot be done—or cannot be done well—because there is no one available to do them who knows how. *The supply of able, experienced executives is not increasing nearly as fast as the number of problems being addressed by public policy.* All the fellowships, internships, and "mid-career training programs" in the world aren't likely to increase that supply very much, simply because the essential qualities for an executive—judgment about men and events, a facility for making good guesses, a sensitivity to political realities, and an ability to motivate others—are things which, if they can be taught at all, cannot be taught systematically or to more than a handful of apprentices at one time.

This constraint deserves emphasis, for it is rarely recognized as a constraint at all. Anyone who opposed a bold new program on the grounds that there was nobody around able to run it would be accused of being a pettifogger at best and a reactionary do-nothing at worst. Everywhere except in government, it seems, the scarcity of talent is accepted as a fact of life. Nobody (or almost nobody) thinks seriously of setting up a great new university overnight, because anybody familiar with the university business knows that, for almost any professorship one would want to fill, there are rarely more than five (if that) really top-flight people in the country, and they are all quite happy—and certainly well-paid—right where they are. Lots of new business ideas don't become profit-making realities because good business executives are both hard to find and expensive to hire. The government—at least publicly—seems to act as if the supply of able political executives were infinitely elastic, though people setting up new agencies will often admit privately that they are so frustrated and appalled by the shortage of talent that the only wonder is why disaster is so long in coming. Much would be gained if this constraint were mentioned to Congress *before* the bill is passed and the hopes aroused, instead of being mentioned afterward as an excuse for failure or as a reason why higher pay scales for public servants are an urgent necessity. "Talent Is Scarcer Than Money" should be the motto of the Budget Bureau.

If administrative feasibility is such a critical issue, what can be done about it? Not a great deal. If the bureaucracy problem is a major reason why so many programs are in trouble, it is also a reason why the problem itself cannot be "solved." But it can be mitigated—though not usually through the kinds of expedients we are fond of trying: Hoover Commissions, management studies, expensive consultants, co-ordinating committees, "czars," and the like. The only point at which very much leverage can be gained on the problem *is when we decide what it is we are trying to accomplish*. When we define our goals, we are implicitly deciding how much, or how little, of a bureaucracy problem we are going to have. A program with clear objectives, clearly stated, is a program with a fighting chance of coping with each of the many aspects of the bureaucracy problem. Controlling an agency is easier when you know what you want. Equity is more likely to be assured when over-all objectives can be stated, at least in part, in general rules to which people in and out of the agency are asked to conform. Efficiency is made possible when you know what you are buying with your money. Responsiveness is never easy or wholly desirable; if every person were treated in accordance with his special needs, there would be no program at all. (The only system that meets the responsiveness problem squarely is the free market.) But at least with clear objectives we would know what we are giving up in those cases when responsiveness seems necessary, and thus we would be able to decide how much we are willing to tolerate. And fiscal integrity is just as easy to insure in a system with clear objectives as in one with fuzzy ones; in the former case, moreover, we are less likely to judge success simply in terms of avoiding scandal. We might even be willing to accept a little looseness if we knew what we were getting for it.

The rejoinder to this argument is that there are many government functions which, by their nature, can never have clear objectives. I hope I have made it obvious by now that I am aware of that. We can't stop dealing with foreign nations just because we don't know what we want; after all, they may know what *they* want, and we had better find out. My argument is advanced, not as a panacea—there is no way to avoid the problem of administration—but as a guide to choice in those cases where choice is open to us, and as a criterion by which to evaluate proposals for coping with the bureaucracy problem.

Dealing with poverty—at least in part—by giving people money seems like an obvious strategy. Governments are very good at taking money from one person and giving it to another; the goals are not particularly difficult to state; measures are available to evaluate how well we are doing in achieving a predetermined income distribution. There may be many things wrong with this approach, but administrative difficulty is not one of them. And yet, paradoxically, it is the last approach we will probably try. We will try everything else first—case work, counseling, remedial education, community action, federally-financed mass protests to end "alienation," etc. And whatever else might be said in their favor, the likelihood of smooth administration and ample talent can hardly be included.

Both the White House and the Congress seem eager to do something about the bureaucracy problem. All too often, however, the problem is described in terms of "digesting" the "glut" of new federal programs—as if solving administrative difficulties had something in common with treating heartburn. Perhaps those seriously concerned with this issue will put themselves on notice that they ought not to begin with the pain and reach for some administrative bicarbonate of soda; they ought instead to begin with what was swallowed and ask whether an emetic is necessary. *Coping with the bureaucracy problem is inseparable from rethinking the objectives of the programs in question.* Administrative reshuffling, budgetary cuts (or budgetary increases), and congressional investigation of lower-level boondoggling will not suffice and are likely, unless there are some happy accidents, to make matters worse. Thinking clearly about goals is a tough assignment for a political system that has been held together in great part by compromise, ambiguity, and contradiction. And if a choice must be made, any reasonable person would, I think, prefer the system to the clarity. But now that we have decided to intervene in such a wide range of human affairs, perhaps we ought to reassess that particular trade-off.

◻ Administrative Decentralization and Political Power

HERBERT KAUFMAN

Curious as it may seem today, bureaucrats in the '30's were regarded by many as heroes in the struggles for a better social order. As late as 1945, Paul Appleby, a prominent New Deal official, felt impelled to dedicate a book to "Bill Bureaucrat," and much of the literature of professional academic public administration had a confident, approving, consensual tone.

By the mid-50's it was possible to discern emerging conflicts of doctrine and practice among those who previously applauded and defended bureaucrats. A major shift of outlook and values in governmental design seemed to be taking place.

It was not the first such shift to occur in our history. On the contrary, the administrative history of our governmental machinery can be construed as a succession of shifts of this kind, each brought about by a change in emphasis among three values: representativeness, politically neutral competence, and executive leadership. None of these values was ever totally neglected in any of our past modifications of governmental design, but each enjoyed greater emphasis than the others in different periods.

Thus, for example, our earliest political institutions at all levels can be interpreted as reactions against executive dominance in the colonial era. Later on, extreme reliance was placed on representative mechanisms, which made the post-Revolutionary years an interval of great power for legislatures and elective officials and of comparative weakness for executives in most jurisdictions. By the middle of the 19th century, however, legislative supremacy, the long ballot, and the spoils system resulted in widespread disillusionment with our political institutions, which in turn gave impetus to efforts to take administration out of politics by lodging it in independent boards and commissions and by introducing the merit system to break the hold of parties on the bureaucracies. But the fragmentation of government reduced both efficiency and representativeness, and the search for unification led to the popularly elected chief executives; the 20th century was marked by a rapid growth in their powers.

This is not to say the values are pursued abstractly, as ends in themselves, or

FROM Herbert Kaufman, "Administrative Decentralization and Political Power," *Political Administration Review,* Vol. 29, No. 1 (January–February 1969).

that there is universal agreement on which should be emphasized at any given time. On the contrary, different segments of the population feel differentially disadvantaged by the governmental machinery in operation at any given moment, and agitate for structural changes to improve their position—i.e., to increase their influence—in the system. Discontent on the part of various groups is thus the dynamic force that motivates the quest for new forms. Some groups feel resentful because they consider themselves inadequately represented; some feel frustrated because, though they are influential in forming policy, the policy decisions seem to be dissipated by the political biases or the technical incompetence of the public bureaucracies; some feel thwarted by lack of leadership to weld the numerous parts of government into a coherent, unified team that can get things done. At different points in time, enough people (not necessarily a numerical majority) will be persuaded by one or another of these discontents to support remedial action—increased representativeness, better and politically neutral bureaucracies, or stronger chief executives as the case may be. But emphasis on one remedy over a prolonged period merely accumulates the other discontents until new remedies gain enough support to be put into effect, and no totally stable solution has yet been devised. So the constant shift in emphasis goes on.

No matter how vigorous the pursuit of any one value at any given time, the other two are never obliterated. And no matter how determined the quest for any one value, it is never realized as fully as its most extreme advocates would like. Even after a century of efforts to strengthen neutral competence and executive leadership, partisan influence still retains great vitality and executive institutions at all levels of government are still remarkably fragmented. And after a century of denigration of "politics," politicians, and "special interests," representativeness is still a powerful force in American government. But in that century of building professional bureaucracies and executive capacities for leadership, the need for new modes of representation designed to keep pace with new economic, social, and political developments did not arouse equal concern. Partly for this reason, and partly because the burgeoning of large-scale organizations in every area of life contributes to the sensation of individual helplessness, recent years have witnessed an upsurge of a sense of alienation on the part of many people, to a feeling that they as individuals cannot effectively register their own preferences on the decisions emanating from the organs of government. These people have begun to demand redress of the balance among the three values, with special attention to the deficiencies in representativeness.

CURRENT DISSATISFACTION

America is not wanting in arrangements for representation. More than half a million public offices are still elective. Legislatures and individual legislators retain immense powers, and do not hesitate to wield them liberally. Parties are still strong and attentive to the claims of many constituencies. Interest groups are numerous and press their demands through myriad channels. The mass media serve as watchdogs of governmental operations. Administrative agencies incorporate manifold procedures for representation into their decision-making processes, including quasi-judicial and quasi-legislative hearings, representative or bipartisan administrative boards, and advisory bodies. Opportunities for participation in political decisions are plentiful. Why, then, is there dissatisfaction with these arrangements?

Fundamentally, because substantial (though minority) segments of the population apparently believe the political, economic, and social systems have not delivered to them fair—even minimally fair—shares of the system's benefits and rewards, and because they think they cannot win their appropriate shares in those benefits and rewards through the political institutions of the country as these are now constituted. These people are not mollified by assurances that the characteristics of the system thwarting them also thwart selfish and extremist interests; it appears to them that only the powerful get attention, and that the already powerful are helped by the system to deny influence to all who now lack it. Thus, the system itself, and not just evil men who abuse it, is discredited.

At least three characteristics of the system contribute heavily to this impression on the part of the deprived: first, existing representative organs are capable of giving only quite general mandates to administrative agencies, yet it is in the day-to-day decisions and actions of officials and employees in the lower levels that individual citizens perceive the policies. There are often gross discrepancies between the promise of the programs (as construed by the populace to be served) and performance—sometimes because the expectations of the populace are unrealistically optimistic, sometimes because programs are impeded by difficulties that could not be foreseen, and sometimes because bureaucracies are too bound by habit or timidity to alter their customary behavior in any but the most modest ways.

Second, the pluralistic nature of the political system provides abundant opportunities for vetoes by opponents of change. Each proposed innovation must run a gamut of obstacles, and ends as a product of bargains and compromises. So change usually comes slowly, by small advances, in bits and pieces. Those who regard particular problems as requiring urgent, immediate action are prone to condemn a system that behaves so "sluggishly."

Third, the scale of organization in our society has grown so large that only through large-scale organization does it seem possible to have a significant impact. This impression alone is enough to make individual people feel helplessly overwhelmed by huge, impersonal machines indifferent to their uniqueness and their humanity. In addition, however, some interests—notably those of Negroes and of youth—have recently begun to develop the organizational skills to mobilize their political resources only to find that it takes time to build channels of access to political structures. Rather than wait for admission to these structures—where, incidentally, they are likely to encounter larger, more experienced, well-entrenched organizations opposed to them—these groups, while continuing to strive for recognition in the older institutions, have adopted a strategy of deriding those institutions and seeking to build new ones in which they can have greater, perhaps dominant, influence.

Thus, the plenitude of traditional modes of representation no longer suffices; the existing methods do not adequately accommodate many of the demands upon them. Just as the adaptation of governmental design during the past century has gravitated toward furnishing expertise and leadership, so it is now under pressure from several quarters to accord a greater role to representativeness.

INCREASING REPRESENTATIVENESS THROUGH ADMINISTRATIVE CHANGE

The quest for representativeness in this generation centers primarily on administrative agencies. Since administrative agencies have grown dramatically in size, function, and authority in the middle third of this century, this is hardly surprising. Chief executives, legislatures, and courts make more decisions of *sweeping* effect, but the agencies make a far greater number of decisions affecting individual citizens in *intimate* ways. In them lies the source of much present unrest; in them, therefore, the remedies are sought.

One type of proposal for making administrative agencies more representative is traditional in character: situating spokesmen for the interests affected in strategic positions within the organizations. Often, this means nothing more than filling vacancies on existing boards and commissions with appointees enjoying the confidence of, or perhaps even chosen by, those interests. In the case of the controversial police review boards, it involves injecting into administrative structures new bodies, dominated by ethnic minority groups or their friends, to survey and constrain bureaucratic behavior. Architecturally, such plans do not require drastic modifications of existing organizations, and their objectives could probably be met by changes in personnel at high organizational levels.

More unorthodox, but swiftly gaining acceptance, is the concept of a centralized governmental complaint bureau, clothed with legal powers of investigation, to look into citizen complaints against administrative agencies and to correct inequities and abuses—the office of "ombudsman." Once, it was chiefly through his representative in the appropriate legislative body, or through the local unit of his political party, that a citizen of modest status and means petitioned for a remedy of a grievance. But professionalization of administration and the insulation of bureaucrats from party politics have reduced the ability of the parties to be of real help, and the constituencies of legislators have grown so large that they rarely intervene in more than a *pro forma* fashion on behalf of most individual constituents. Today, some observers contend that only a specialized, full-time official, wise in the ways of bureaucracy, having a vested interest in correcting its errors, and supported by adequate staff and authority, can perform this function effectively; apparently, it takes a bureaucrat to control a bureaucrat. Advocates of this proposed new agency defend it on the grounds that it would constitute a channel of representation for people who now have no satisfactory alternative.

The most sweeping expression of the unrest over lack of representativeness is the growing demand for extreme administrative decentralization, frequently coupled with insistence on local clientele domination of the decentralized organizations. Dramatic manifestations of this movement occurred in the antipoverty program and in education.

In the antipoverty program the original legislation included a provision that community action be "developed, conducted, and administered with maximum feasible participation of residents of the areas and members of the groups served." Initially by interpretation of the Office of Economic Opportunity, and later by statute, the provision was construed to mean that community action boards should try to allot some of their chairs to the poor, so that the poor would have a voice in the highest policy councils of the community programs. Whatever the original intent of the drafters of the phrase (about which there is some disagreement), it has come to mean the program is to be run in substantial degree *by* the poor, not merely *for* the poor.

In public education the new trend is exemplified by recent events in New York City. During 1967, demands for decentralization of the municipal school system gathered force swiftly: Leaders in the state legislature urged it. Three separate public reports recommended it in the strongest possible terms. The mayor endorsed the principle unequivocally. When concrete proposals were introduced into the legislature the following year, however, vehement opposition from the teachers' union, the school administrators' association, and the City Board of Education resulted in modification of many of the provisions the objectors found unacceptable. The measure ultimately enacted emerged weaker than the plans favored by the advocates of decentralization, but it was a major step in their direction; the thrust toward decentralization and neighborhood control of schools was slowed but not stopped, and resistance, however determined and forceful, seemed destined to give way over a broad front.

The outcry has not been limited to the war on poverty and to education. It was taken up in public housing when the Secretary of Housing and Urban Development unveiled a program to modernize low-rent projects that included an augmented role for tenants in their operation. At a meeting of the American Institute of Planners, a dissenting group, calling itself Planners for Equal Opportunity, demanded a larger place for the poor in city planning, and exhorted its members to engage in "advocate planning," which is to say expert counsel for neighborhood associations unhappy with official plans for renewal in their areas. New York City recently began experimenting with a process of "affiliating" its public hospitals with voluntary hospitals that would be responsible for their administration, a plan that would presumably include lay boards representing the community served by each institution, and its Police Department is cooperating with experimental community security patrols of locally recruited young people. Similarly, a neighborhood council in Washington, D. C., "asked for more citizen control over police, either in the form of local police aides or resurrection of the auxiliary police force used here in World War II." The American Assembly, assessing the role of law in a changing society, called for development of "rapid procedures at the neighborhood level . . . to adjudicate disputes over simple transactions." In response to the Poor People's Campaign in Washington, "Five agencies—Health, Education and Welfare, Agriculture, Labor, Housing and Urban Development and the Office of Economic Opportunity—said they would review their plans to involve poor people themselves in local decisions affecting welfare, food, employment, housing and other antipoverty programs."

The movement is not confined to public agencies; it reaches into colleges and universities, where students, often by direct action, have been asserting a claim to participation in the policies of these institutions—one activist reportedly going so far as to predict that American universities will soon resemble Latin American institutions, in which students hire and fire professors and determine the curricula. A sociologist recently suggested establishment of closed-circuit television stations in which the neighborhood listeners might control programming. In the Roman Catholic Archdiocese of New York, a committee of priests presented a petition to the archbishop-designate requesting, among other things, a voice in the selection of auxiliary bishops and other high officials, and establishment of a Pastoral Council of priests, nuns, and laymen to be consulted in advance on projected programs and budgets, a request to which he partially acceded on taking office. Later, priests formed a national organization, the National Federation of Priests Councils, to seek a stronger voice in church affairs. In Washington, D. C., classes at a high school were suspended in the face of a boycott by students demanding " a real say on what goes on inside the school."

But it is in the government sphere that the tendency has been winning widest endorsement. Indeed, some of our general forms of government, as well as specific agencies, have come under attack. The president of the American Political Science Association, for example, in his 1967 presidential address, raised questions about the compatibility of large units of government—national, state, and urban—with the principles of democracy. Searching for a unit large enough to avoid triviality yet "small enough so that citizens can participate extensively," he suggested 50,000 to 200,000 as the optimum size range for democratic city governments. Moreover, he concluded that even in polities of this size, "participation is reduced for most people to nothing more than voting in elections," and he therefore commended experimentation to decentralize power and authority still further in order to discover viable "smaller units within which citizens can from time to time formulate and express their desires, consult with officials, and in some cases participate even more fully in decisions."

Similarly, the Advisory Commission on Intergovernmental Relations in Washington, at almost the same time, was recommending that "Neighborhood initiative and self-respect be fostered by authorizing counties and large cities to establish, and at their discretion to abolish, neighborhood subunits endowed with limited powers of taxation and local self-government." At Ithaca, N.Y., the Office of Regional Resources and Development concluded that larger metropolitan centers should be decentralized because they have reached a point at which "it is almost impossible to deal with human problems on a human scale," and called for investigation of strategies for more effective use of cities with 50,000 to 500,000 residents—proposals that won the editorial plaudits of *The Washington Post*.

A meeting of Americans for Democratic Action was warned by Daniel P. Moynihan, an outspoken liberal, that "Liberals must divest themselves of the notion that the nation, especially the cities of the nation, can be run from agencies in Washington." Senator Robert F. Kennedy, campaigning for the Democratic presidential nomination in Los Angeles, promised audiences a revolution in the distribution of political power that would, among other things, reduce the authority of the federal bureaucracy in Washington. "I want," he said, "the control over your destinies to be decided by the people in Watts, not by those of us who are in Washington." Richard M. Nixon similarly urged the federal government to relinquish some of its powers to state and local governments, voluntary associations, and individuals, saying, "One reason people are shouting so loudly today is that it's far from where they are to where the power is," and that power should be brought closer to them rather than exercised from remote centers. In important respects, the Heller-Pechman plan rests partly on the premise that federal surpluses should be shared with states and cities in time of peace because they can be more effectively spent by the smaller units of government than by Washington directly.

In short, "decentralization" of administration is in the air everywhere. While it is sometimes defended on grounds of efficiency, it is more frequently justified in terms of effective popular participation in government. Reformers of earlier generations succeeded in raising the level of expertise and professionalism in the bureaucracies, and to a lesser extent, in improving capacity of chief executives to control the administrative arms of government. Now, people are once again turning their attention to representativeness, and are trying to elevate it to a more prominent place in the governmental scheme of things.

THE CONTINUING SEARCH FOR LEADERSHIP

Public bureaucracies are under fire not only from critics outside the machinery of government, but also from inside. Chief executives who once championed measures to insulate the bureaucracies from partisan politics as steps toward enlarging their own control over administrative agencies discovered that these measures did not make the agencies more responsive to executive direction; rather, they increased agency independence. This independence, in turn, makes it difficult for the executives to secure enthusiastic adoption of new approaches to social problems; money pumped into new programs administered by established agencies tends to be used more for intensification of traditional ways of operating than for inventive departures from familiar patterns. Furthermore, it results in massive problems of coordination of effort, and even in dissipation of energies in interbureau rivalries. Consequently, just as segments of the public are upset by the alleged unresponsiveness of administration to their demands, so chief executives have been increasingly concerned about the unresponsiveness of agencies to their leadership.

We may therefore look forward to new waves of administrative reorganization proposals. One principal thrust of the movement will, as in the past, be toward rationalizing, enlarging, and strengthening the executive-office staffs of the heads of governmental units at all levels, and toward building up the staffs of the administrators who report directly to the heads. More and more, chief executives will reach out for new devices to coordinate policy decisions, to work up fresh programs to deal with emergent problems, and to maintain the momentum of innovations adopted. Executive offices will be redesigned; the U. S. Bureau of the Budget, for example, has only recently undergone a major reorganization. New vigor will be applied to the exploration of "superdepartments," with the Department of Defense as a prototype; Mayor Lindsay, for instance, has expended much political capital on introducing this concept into the government of New York City. Programming-planning-budgeting systems, in many variants, will continue to spread. There will be a new burst of literature calling attention to the relative powerlessness of our highest public executives.

Another stream of recommendations will urge strengthening executive leadership through what its advocates will call "decentralization," but which, in fact, is better characterized as organization by area as opposed to the present almost exclusive organization by functional departments and bureaus. The justification for it will be couched in terms of efficiency—the need to speed decisions in the field without referral to headquarters and without loss of coordination among field personnel in different bureaus. The consequences will extend further, however, because areal officers in the field would give top executives lines of communication and control alternative to existing functional channels, thus actually strengthening central authority. At the federal level, this will mean renewed attempts to set up much stronger regional representatives of the heads of cabinet departments than any we have had in the past. It will also mean intensified efforts to establish regional presidential representatives in the field. Similarly, we may anticipate governors and their department heads will follow the same strategies with respect to regions within the states. At the local level, Mayor Lindsay has already sought—with very limited success—to win approval for "little city halls" throughout New York. Distinctively American versions of the European prefect may yet make an appearance.

In short, dissatisfaction with public bureaucracies will furnish ammunition for the defenders of executive leadership as well as for the proponents of increased representation of the consumers of public services. The bureaucracies will be pressed from both above and below.

CONFLICT AND COALITION

Sources of Conflict

It has long been recognized that much public policy is shaped largely by clusters of bureaus, their organized clienteles, and legislative committees and legislators specializing in each public function—health, education, welfare, etc. The arguments for strengthening chief executives and their department heads vis-à-vis the clusters are based chiefly on the need to offset the resulting fragmentation of government by introducing sufficient central direction to unify the policies and administration of these separate centers of power. The arguments for new modes of participation by the public in these centers rest on the conviction that hitherto excluded and unorganized interests have little to say about decisions that affect them profoundly. But it is most unlikely that the arguments of either kind will be warmly received by those already in key positions in each decision center.

They will resist not simply out of abstract jealousy of their own power or stubborn unwillingness to share their influence with each other, though these motives will doubtless not be absent. They will oppose because, in addition, the proposed reforms threaten those values which present arrangements protect. Bureau chiefs and the organized bureaucracies perceive intervention by political executives as the intrusion of partisan politics into fields from which doctrine has for many years held that politics should be excluded; they see jeopardy for the competence nurtured so carefully and painfully against political distortion or extinction. Similarly, opening the system to lay members of local communities looks like a negation of the expertise built up by the specialist. Legislators regard strong regional officials responsive to chief executives and their cabinets as executive attempts to invade legislative districts and usurp the representative function of legislative bodies. In like fashion, local control of administrative programs could conceivably weaken the representative basis of legislative institutions, a development that men of goodwill may fear for quite public-spirited reasons.

So the champions of executive leadership and the evangelists of expanded representativeness have many obstacles to overcome before they have their respective ways. For example, Congress has been cautious about presidential recommendations of added funds and personnel for the heads of cabinet departments, and has always looked with suspicion on so relatively innocuous an innovation as field offices for the Bureau of the Budget. The Office of Economic Opportunity in the Executive Office of the President always operated chiefly through established bureaus and engaged in independent administration only in limited ways; gradually, through delegation, it has been relinquishing its control over programs to the bureaus and the future of even those few programs it manages directly is uncertain. Moreover, its community-action program aroused resentment among both congressmen and local executives, to whom the action agencies appeared as springboards for political rivals; consequently, legislation in 1967 authorized greater control of the agencies by local governments. In New York City, the mayor's "little city halls," which he presented as a device for bringing the people and their government closer together, were soundly defeated by a City Council (dominated by the opposite party) denouncing the plan as a strategy for establishing political clubhouses throughout the city at public expense. And, when the plan for school decentralization appeared, the largest teachers' union and the Board of Education—which not long before had been at each other's throats in labor disputes—each took a similar firm stand against it. In Board-sponsored experiments with community control of schools in Harlem and in Brooklyn, the community leaders and the head of the same teachers' union engaged in acrimonious battles with each other. The reformers are not having an easy time of it.

A Coalition of Executives

To advance their cause, troubled chief executives at all levels, all suffering similar frustrations, could conceivably make common cause with one another. Thus, the President may well find it strategically advantageous to build closer ties with governors and big-city mayors than was ever the case before. Congress would find it more uncomfortable to resist presidential demands for creation of strong field representatives with jurisdiction over bureau field personnel if state and local officials in their own home areas support the demands than if the President alone advances them. And these state and local officials may be receptive to such an association because the fragmentation of the system is as vexing to them as it is to the President himself.

Gubernatorial and big-city mayoral vexations spring from three sources. First, procedures in many intergovernmental programs are irritatingly slow; it often takes months—sometimes more than a year, in fact—to get decisions on projects and financing from federal agencies, partly because so much business is referred to Washington for approval. To be sure, state and municipal executives have no wish to speed negative decisions on their requests, but hanging decisions are even worse; they can neither plan programs nor try to get the decisions reversed. They can only wait while dangerous pressures build up in their jurisdictions, and whole networks of interrelated programs are slowed or brought to a halt.

Second, procedures are often labyrinthine and uncoordinated, so that it takes specialists to keep track of terminal dates, filing of applications for renewal of grants, compliance with accounting requirements, meshing of separate grants in individual projects, and explanations of variations in allowances (such as differences in relocation allowances for businesses and individual tenants moved for highway construction on the one hand and urban renewal on the other), that bewilder and annoy the public. These intricacies almost paralyze action at the grassroots, and divert needed manpower from substantive program operations to administrative routine.

Third, federal grants for very specific purposes encourage a tendency toward what the 1955 Commission on Intergovernmental Relations referred to as "a more or less independent government of their own" on the part of functional specialists at all levels of government who are only nominally under the control of their respective chief executives. In point of fact, the chief executives are apparently reduced in many instances to virtually ceremonial ratification of the intergovernmental arrangements worked out by such specialists, and to the most superficial oversight of the administration of the arrangements.

So governors and big-city mayors have reason to applaud the introduction of federal regional officers with authority to rationalize the actions of federal field personnel in the bureaus. For reasons of their own, they may well find the "prefectoral" pattern of organization, which, as we have seen, will suggest itself ever more insistently to the President, coincides with their own preferences.

This congruence of presidential, gubernatorial, and mayoral interests is not entirely speculative; indications of it have already appeared. Late in 1966, for example, President Johnson sent to a number of his top officials a memorandum directing that federal assistance programs

be worked out and planned in a cooperative spirit with those chief officials of State, county and local governments who are answerable to the citizens. To the fullest practical extent, I want you to take steps to afford representatives of the Chief Executives of State and local governments the opportunity to advise and consult in the development and execution of programs which directly affect the conduct of State and local affairs.

A few months later, to implement the President's memorandum, the Bureau of the Budget issued a circular spelling out procedures for consultation, and identifying as one of its central policies the requirement that "The central coordinating role of heads of State and local governments, including their role of initiating and developing State and local programs, will be supported and strengthened." Meanwhile, former Florida Governor Farris Bryant, director of the Office of Emergency Planning in the Executive Office of the President, was leading teams of federal officials to 40 state capitals for discussions with governors and other state administrators; Vice President Humphrey was conducting a program of visits and discussions with mayors, county officers, and other local executives; and the President was formulating and announcing a plan to assign each member of his cabinet responsibility for liaison with four or five states, "with instructions to maintain personal contact between the Governors and the White

House." And in early 1968, the Advisory Commission on Intergovernmental Relations recommended that:

1. Coordination of Federal grant programs being administered by a variety of Federal departments and agencies be strengthened through the Executive Office of the President;
2. The authority to review and approve plans developed as a condition of Federal formula-type grants to State and local governments be decentralized to Federal regional offices and wide variations in boundaries of Federal administrative regions be reduced.

An alliance of public chief executives is already taking shape.

The Confluence of Representativeness and Leadership

At the same time, groups clamoring for local control of administrative programs, confronted with the suspicion and resentment of bureaucracies and their legislative and interest-group allies, will probably discover that they get their most sympathetic hearings from chief executives, especially from big-city mayors. For such groups can provide the executive with the counterweights to the bureaucracies: they constitute an alternative channel of information about administrative performance, reducing executive dependence on the bureaucracies on the one hand and on the mass media (with their bias toward the sensational) on the other. The groups are a constituency that can be mobilized to help exert leverage on bureaucracies resistant to executive leadership. They furnish a direct conduit to localities from the executive mansions. They can serve as the nuclei of discrete, executive-oriented campaign organizations. Chief executives probably could not create the groups if they set out deliberately to do so, but it would be surprising if they did not eventually perceive the advantages of collaborating with them now that a variety of complaints has brought the

It will be an uneasy, mutually wary relationship. To neighborhood and community associations, the paradox of turning to remote chief executives in a quest for local control will be disturbing. To chief executives, the risk of opening a Pandora's box and releasing uncontrollable disintegrative forces will give pause. Yet each can gain so much from an alliance with the other that it is hard to avoid the feeling [that] the attractions will overcome the anxieties. I do not mean to imply the alliance will be formal or structured. I mean only to suggest each side will turn to the other as appropriate occasions arise, and that the occasions will arise with increasing frequency in the years ahead. In this way, the new voices of representatives and the more familiar voices of executive leadership will be joined in a common challenge to those who speak for neutral competence and for older institutions of representation.

THE SUBSEQUENT PHASE OF THE CYCLE

So it seems reasonable to anticipate that "decentralization" of two types will indeed occur: concessions will be made to the demands for greater local influence on public programs, and there will be some headway toward establishing territorial officers with at least limited authority over field personnel of the functional bureaus.

It will not take long for the price of these changes to make itself felt. Decentralization will soon be followed by disparities in practice among the numerous small units, brought on by differences in human and financial resources, that will engender demands for central intervention to restore equality and balance and concerted action; the factors underlying the movement toward metropolitan units of government and toward conditional federal grants-in-aid will, in other words, reassert themselves. Decentralization will stand in the way of other goals, such as school integration (as did "states' rights" doctrines in other times). It will give rise to competition among the units that will be disastrous for many of them, which will find it more difficult to attract talent and money than others that start from a more advantageous position. In some units, strong factions may well succeed in reviving a new spoils system, thus lowering the quality of some vital services. Decentralization of public administration will not necessarily be accompanied by decentralization of the other institutions with which public units deal, such as unions of public employees, so that the local units may find themselves at a serious disadvantage in negotiations and unable to resist the pressures of special interests. Economies of scale, which are admittedly overstated very frequently, nevertheless do exist, and the multiplication of overhead costs in local units will divert some resources from substantive programs to administrative housekeeping. Initially, all these costs will be regarded by those concerned with representativeness as well worth paying, but the accumulation of such grievances over time will inspire a clamor for unification and consolidation.

Similarly, area officials reporting directly to chief executives will soon develop autonomous bases of political power in the regions to which they are assigned. Rapid rotation from area to area will help to reduce their independence, but the rate of rotation will decline because each new assignment will necessitate a period of familiarization with the new territory during which actions and decisions are held in abeyance, and because local interests, having established comparatively stable relationships with their regional officers, will protest and resist frequent transfers. As the regional officers get more and more involved in regional complexes, they will become more and more ambassadors from the regions to the chief executives instead of the executives' men in the regions. Regional differences and competition will become sources of irritation and controversy. Moreover, regional posts may become convenient and effective springboards to elective office. At first these dangers will seem remote and therefore less important than the immediate gains, but time is likely to reverse the balance.

So the wave of reform after the one now in progress will rally under a banner of earlier days: Take administration out of politics and politics out of administration. Disappointed partisans of the current movement on behalf of representativeness, having won some of their points, will acquiesce in the efforts of a new generation of idealists to elevate the quality, the consistency, the impartiality, the morale, and the devotion to duty of bureaucrats by strengthening and broadening central control and supervision. Chief executives anxious to regain command of the administrative field forces in each of their regions will rediscover the virtues of strong central direction of those forces by functional administrative agencies whose chiefs identify with the executives, and whose standards can be applied even-handedly everywhere. From above and below, to escape the distortions of purpose inflicted by the vigorous factional politics of localities and regions (as they once sought to free themselves from the toils of self-seeking factions in state and congressional district politics), the apostles of good government will turn back to insulating the bureaucracies against such political heat. The neutrality and independence of the civil service will again be extolled.

It should not be inferred that the process is fruitless because the succession of values is repetitive. Wheels turning on their own axes do advance. Each time the balance among the values is redressed, only to require redress again, some new accommodation among the myriad interests in the society is reached.

Precisely what shape the subsequent resurgence of neutral competence will take in the years beyond, it is impossible to prophesy now. But if the hypothesized cycle of values is at all valid, then strange as it may seem to this generation of reformers, innovators of tomorrow will defend many of the very institutions (as transformed in the course of current controversies) under attack today. And many a forgotten tome and obscure article on public administration, long gathering dust on unpatronized shelves and in unopened files, will be resurrected and praised for its prescience, only to subside again into temporary limbo when another turn of the wheel ends its brief moment of revived relevance.

SUGGESTIONS FOR FURTHER READING

Numerous texts on public administration are available; see, for instance, Herbert A. Simon, Donald W. Smithburg, and Victor A. Thompson, *Public Administration* (New York: Knopf, 1950), and John M. Pfiffner and Robert Presthus, *Public Administration*, 5th ed. (New York: Ronald, 1967).

A collection of case studies that is still useful is Harold Stein, ed., *Public Administration and Policy Development* (New York: Harcourt Brace Jovanovich, 1951).

Valuable analytical and critical works are: Charles Lindblom, *The Policy-Making Process* (Englewood Cliffs, N. J.: Prentice-Hall, 1968), David T. Stanley, *The Higher Civil Service: An Evaluation of Federal Personnel Practices* (Washington, D. C.: Brookings Institution, 1964), Emmette S. Redford, *Democracy in the Administrative State* (New York: Oxford University Press, 1969), Marver Bernstein, *The Job of the Federal Executive* (Washington, D. C.: Brookings Institution, 1958), Francis E. Rourke, *Bureaucracy, Politics, and Public Policy* (Boston: Little, Brown, 1969), and Norton E. Long, *The Polity* (Chicago: Rand McNally, 1962).

Other works focusing on the politics of bureaucracies are: Ira Sharkonsky, *Public Administration: Policy-Making in Government Agencies* (Chicago: Markham, 1970), Peter Woll, *American Bureaucracy* (New York: Norton, 1963), and Aaron Wildavsky, *The Politics of the Budgetary Process* (Boston: Little, Brown, 1964).

An excellent book of readings is Francis E. Rourke, ed., *Bureaucratic Power in National Politics* (Boston: Little, Brown, 1965).

On the regulatory commissions, Emmette S. Redford's *The Regulatory Process* (Austin, Tex.: University of Texas Press, 1969) is particularly good. Foster S. Dulles's *The Civil Rights Commission* (East Lansing, Mich.: Michigan State University Press, 1968) provides a history that makes clear the difficulties of government by commission. Two noteworthy recent studies of policy making by the executive branch are James L. Sundquist, *Politics and Policy* (Washington, D. C.: Brookings Institution, 1968), and Charles L. Schultz, *The Politics and Economics of Public Spending* (Washington, D. C.: Brookings Institution, 1968). A more specific study, on the administration of the Economic Opportunity Act of 1964, is Daniel P. Moynihan's *Maximum Feasible Misunderstanding* (New York: Free Press, 1969).

On organization theory, see James G. March and Herbert A. Simon, *Organizations* (New York: Wiley, 1965); James G. March, ed., *A Handbook of Organizations* (Chicago: Rand McNally, 1965); and Herbert A. Simon, *Administrative Behavior* (New York: Free Press, 1957).

The principal journal in this area is the *Public Administration Review*.

9 The supreme court

Now that Earl Warren has stepped down as chief justice, many observers think that the Supreme Court is at a turning point, that it is about to enter a new phase both in doctrine and in style. Thus, it is particularly appropriate to reflect on the impact of the Warren Court on our political system.

The Supreme Court of the 1950's and 1960's innovated in many different areas: it checked the worst excesses of anti-Communist witch-hunting; it opened the door to major legislative reapportionment; it triggered the Negro revolution; it attempted to cope with problems of religion and the public order which had been festering for a hundred years; it was a defender of free expression; and it focused national attention on inequities in our system of criminal justice. Much has been written about the Court's work in all the areas, and much more will be written in the future. But one quite fundamental aspect of the work of the Warren Court has not been sufficiently emphasized. In each of the policy areas in which the Court acted decisively, the effect of its decisions was to replace sets of differing local rules and customs with uniform national rules. The practical consequence of this activism is more federal governmental regulation of American life. As Theodore Lowi put it, "A strong and clear ruling is an act of centralization by the Supreme Court." [1]

In the matter of legal equality of the races, after its 1954 decision in

---

[1] Theodore Lowi, *The End of Liberalism* (New York: Norton, 1969), p. 302.

Brown v. Board of Education[2] the Court proceeded to hack away local restrictions on use by nonwhites of all sorts of public facilities. In recent years a body of judge-made criteria for desegregation of schools has been developed and supplemented by the school desegregation guidelines drawn up by the Department of Health, Education, and Welfare. In this important sense the Court has indeed become a national school board. Furthermore, in recent decisions[3] the Court has interpreted the Thirteenth and Fourteenth Amendments in a broad fashion that suggests that racial discrimination is forbidden not only when carried on by agencies of the state, but also when practiced (in certain forms) by private persons. To the extent that the traditional doctrine (that the post–Civil War amendments speak only to government and not to persons) is jettisoned, a substantial limitation on the central rule-making power of the Court is eliminated. It is open to the Justices to propagate national constitutional standards of private conduct in race relations.

After refusing for decades to take up the matter, the Court in 1961[4] launched an effort to establish a national standard of fair representation. The one-man-one-vote formula the Court developed in the case of a federal congressional district[5] has in successive decisions been held to apply to any government of general jurisdiction.[6] This clearly includes cities and counties, and there is some indication that special-purpose authorities (for example, school districts) may be constitutionally constrained in the ways they arrange their elections.[7]

In the area of criminal justice, the Justices have accumulated an almost breathtaking record of replacing local customs and usages with national rules. In 1962 the Court held that the federal rule on the exclusion of illegally obtained evidence at trials applied to the states;[8] in 1963 a uniform rule requiring state-appointed counsel in all serious criminal cases was announced;[9] in 1964 the federal constitutional privilege against self-incrimination was applied to the states;[10] and in a series of decisions involving the Fourth Amendment's guarantee against "unreasonable searches and seizures," rules have been enunciated that govern the searching, stopping, frisking, bugging, and wiretapping of criminal suspects.[11]

And when the Warren Court found no specific provision of the Constitution that applied to the situations under consideration, the Justices occasionally fell back on the general spirit of the document or on the due-process clauses of the Fifth and Fourteenth Amendments in order to create

---

[2] 347 U.S. 483 (1954).
[3] Reitman v. Mulkey, 387 U.S. 369 (1967); Jones v. Mayer, 392 U.S. 409 (1968); and Kyles v. Paul, —— U.S. —— (1969).
[4] Baker v. Carr, 369 U.S. 186 (1962).
[5] Reynolds v. Sims, 377 U.S. 533 (1964).
[6] Duseh v. Davis, 387 U.S. 112 (1967).
[7] Kramer v. Union Free School District No. 15, 395 U.S. 621 (1969).
[8] Mapp v. Ohio, 367 U.S. 643 (1961).
[9] Gideon v. Wainwright, 372 U.S. 335 (1963).
[10] Malloy v. Hogan, 378 U.S. 1 (1964).
[11] See especially Terry v. Ohio, 392 U.S. 1 (1968).

national standards. Thus, a Connecticut statute prohibiting the use of contraceptive devices was struck down as an invasion of privacy, and local disorderly conduct and vagrancy ordinances have been called into question on the grounds that they subject conduct that is by nature noncriminal to criminal penalties.[12]

Of course, this activism brought on waves of criticism, and it may be that the Court will tend less toward centralization under Chief Justice Warren Burger. But the work of the Warren Court captured the imagination and won the approval of large numbers of important American opinion-makers; one political scientist has gone so far as to propose a general reform of our system toward a "juridical democracy" in which government decisions generally would be better rationalized and more principled, after the manner of courts.[13] It is extremely unlikely that there will be much reversal of the work of the Warren years.

In the two selections that follow, former Solicitor-General Archibald Cox discusses the Court's work in the area of criminal defendants' rights, and Alexander M. Bickel describes part of the "states' rights" counterattack against the nationalizing decisions of the Warren Court.

The Reform of the Criminal Process

ARCHIBALD COX

A decade ago the Supreme Court began the widespread reform of criminal procedure in both the State and federal courts. Federal prosecutions are subject to its general supervisory authority, which extends to all matters of procedure and evidence not governed by specific legislation. State prosecutions, however, lie beyond the supervisory power, for in this area the States are sovereign—subject only to constitutional limitations. The States' administration of criminal law is many, many times more important than any federal jurisdiction, for the States are charged with preserving public order and maintaining the security of persons, property, and normal commercial transactions. If the Supreme Court

FROM Archibald Cox, *The Warren Court* (Cambridge, Mass.: Harvard University Press, 1968), pp. 71–91. Copyright, 1968, by the President and Fellows of Harvard College. Reprinted by permission of the publishers.
[12] Griswold v. Connecticut, 381 U.S. 479 (1965).
[13] Lowi, *op. cit.*, pp. 287–314.

was to influence these major aspects of the administration of criminal justice in State tribunals, it would have to act through constitutional law.

The vehicle became the Fourteenth Amendment's command that—

No state shall . . . deprive any person of life, liberty, or property, without due process of law . . .

The amendment had long been used to condemn a few extraordinary excesses in State procedure, but the settled view, as expressed by Justice Cardozo in *Palko* v. *Connecticut*,[1] was that the amendment did not enforce upon the States the relatively specific guarantees of the federal Bill of Rights, such as the necessity for indictment by a grand jury, trial by petit jury, and the prohibition against double jeopardy. Rather the amendment protected rights on the "different plane of social and moral values" which might be described as "the very essence of a scheme of ordered liberty" and "so rooted in the traditions and conscience of our people as to be ranked as fundamental." The formula proved flexible enough for progressively tightening the constitutional rules applicable to State procedure and this has been one vehicle of reform, but it implied a theory of federalism that restricted the Supreme Court's role in favor of vesting responsibility and discretion in the States.

The thrust of the doctrinal changes, therefore, centered upon repudiation of the *Palko* doctrine. In 1947 Justice Black's famous dissent in *Adamson* v. *California*[2] argued that *Palko* was wrong and that the Fourteenth Amendment did indeed take up and apply to the States each of the relatively specific guarantees of the federal Bill of Rights. He based his argument partly on a reading of history and partly on the thesis that the judges could find closer guidance in the words of the Constitution than in roaming through individual notions of ordered liberty. Justice Black's view has never commanded an open majority of the justices, but enough of them to hold the balance of power have gone part way by espousing a doctrine of selective incorporation under which individual provisions of the Bill of Rights are held to be incorporated into the Fourteenth Amendment.[3] The cynically minded might suggest that the doctrine of selective incorporation is only a Khrushchevian device for effectuating the Black position a slice at a time: thus far its exponents have not found a provision that should not be selectively incorporated. The theory, taken at face value, lacks even the historical warrant that Justice Black could assemble, and it does little to avoid the vagaries of individual judgment beyond channeling them into the process of selection. Whatever its defects as constitutional theory, however, selective incorporation has been a second important vehicle for the reform of criminal law.

[1] 302 U.S. 319 (1937).
[2] 332 U.S. 46, 68 (1947).
[3] See, e.g., Malloy v. Hogan, 378 U.S. 1 (1964).

The third vehicle is the expansion of the requirements of the Bill of Rights as applied to both State and federal prosecutions.

II

The catalog of changes wrought by these doctrinal instruments would be too familiar for review if it were not for the impact that is achieved by looking simultaneously at the total body of reforms.

Throughout our constitutional history men too poor to retain counsel had been put on trial in many States without the assistance of an attorney, even men charged with serious, albeit not capital, crimes. The constitutionality of the practice had been sustained in numerous cases.[4] Since *Gideon v. Wainwright*[5]— a story celebrated in Anthony Lewis' fascinating Book *Gideon's Trumpet*—indigents must be supplied with counsel at public expense in all serious criminal cases. The same rule applies to the provision of transcripts[6] and lawyers for appeal.[7]

No longer may a State Court follow the prevailing and apparently well-settled practice of allowing the police to use evidence obtained by an unlawful arrest or by entering a house without a warrant.[8] The requirements for obtaining arrest warrants and search warrants have been stiffened.[9] In other cases the Court, again overruling a long line of precedents, extended to State prosecutions the same privilege against self-incrimination that prevails in the federal courts, including freedom from comment upon the accused's failure to testify in his own defense.[10] The law of confessions has been rewritten.[11] A start has been made upon developing standards governing the admission and exclusion of evidence obtained by wiretapping and other forms of electronic surveillance.[12] There has been far closer scrutiny of the observance of constitutional standards relating to: conduct of the prosecutor in using, revealing, or withholding evidence;[13] selection of the jury;[14] the privilege of confronting adverse witnesses;[15] and the right to compulsory process in order to obtain witnesses for the defense.[16] Another

---

[4] See, e.g., Betts v. Brady, 316 U.S. 455 (1942).
[5] Gideon v. Wainwright, 372 U.S. 335 (1963).
[6] Griffin v. Illinois, 351 U.S. 12 (1956).
[7] Douglas v. California, 372 U.S. 353 (1963).
[8] Mapp v. Ohio, 367 U.S. 643 (1961).
[9] Aguilar v. Texas, 378 U.S. 108 (1964).
[10] Griffin v. California, 380 U.S. 609 (1965).
[11] Escobedo v. Illinois, 378 U.S. 478 (1964); Miranda v. Arizona, 384 U.S. 436 (1966).
[12] Osborn v. United States, 385 U.S. 323 (1966); Berger v. New York, 388 U.S. 41 (1967).
[13] Brady v. Maryland, 373 U.S. 83 (1963); Giles v. Maryland, 386 U.S. 66 (1967).
[14] Arnold v. North Carolina, 376 U.S. 773 (1964); Coleman v. Alabama, 377 U.S. 129 (1964).
[15] Douglas v. Alabama, 380 U.S. 415 (1965); Pointer v. Texas, 380 U.S. 400 (1965).
[16] Washington v. Texas, 388 U.S. 14 (1967).

precedent-breaking decision put proceedings against juveniles under many of the safeguards applicable to ordinary criminal cases.[17]

Never has there been such a thorough-going reform of criminal procedure within so short a time. Nearly all the changes benefit the accused. To discuss them in detail is not feasible. Two deserve attention: the problem of electronic eavesdropping, because of its intrinsic interest, and the law of confessions, because it epitomizes the trend.

III

Constitutional law about wiretapping begins with the era of prohibition. In the *Olmstead* case[18] a five-man majority led by Chief Justice Taft held that the Fourth Amendment's guarantee of the "right of the people to be secure in their persons, houses, papers, and effects, against unreasonable searches and seizures" was not violated by federal officials tapping telephone wires in order to obtain evidence of rum-running, because listening to telephone conversations involved no physical trespass to the premises or property of the defendants. The same principle would permit the police to eavesdrop by "bugs" put upon the outer wall of a room, or by a parabolic microphone which can pick up a conversation hundreds of feet away, or by wiring an informer for sound and sending him to talk with suspected criminals while a hidden recorder takes down the conversation and a tiny transmitter, likewise concealed, broadcasts it to the waiting receivers of government agents. The application of the *Olmstead* principle to these practices was sustained in later cases.[19]

The first limitations upon Olmstead were imposed under the Federal Communications Act. Section 605 provides that "no person . . . shall intercept any [wire] communication and divulge or publish the existence, contents, purport, effect or meaning . . . ." *Nardone v. United States*[20] held that Section 605 applies to federal officials and requires the reversal of any criminal conviction based upon evidence which is the fruit of a violation. There are three important limitations, however, upon the scope of the ruling. First, since it rests upon the Communications Act, it applies only to the interception of wire communications and leaves all other forms of eavesdropping unrestricted. Second, even as applied to wire communications, it was interpreted by Attorney General Robert H. Jackson to forbid only interception *and* divulgence; there is no divulgence and therefore no illegality, he said, in federal agents' tapping telephone conversations and reporting the contents within the executive departments. The opinion of the Attorney General was given under the pressures of wartime fears of espionage

---

[17] In re Gault, 387 U.S. 1 (1967).
[18] Olmstead v. United States, 277 U.S. 438 (1928).
[19] See, e.g., Goldman v. United States, 316 U.S. 129 (1942).
[20] 302 U.S. 379 (1937).

and subversion, but it laid the foundation for the recent controversial eavesdropping in investigations of organized crime. Third, the *Nardone* ruling did not necessarily bar the use of wiretap evidence in the State courts.

The result was inconsistency, immorality, and intolerable confusion. Under a dubious interpretation of the Communications Act the federal government engaged in wiretapping of which it was ashamed as dirty business. The interpretation made legality depend upon shrouding the practice in secrecy; yet it is secrecy that creates the greatest fears of abuse if not the actual abuses. State officials practiced wiretapping, often in ways regularized and sanctioned by State law, and they used the evidence in court. Federal prosecutors could hardly prosecute them for thus discovering proof of crime, even though their conduct plainly violated the Communications Act, for it was substantially similar to federal practices authorized by the Attorney General. Meanwhile, individual opinions written by Supreme Court justices criticizing eavesdropping made it doubtful whether *Olmstead* continued to command a majority of the Court.

Bringing order into this confusion will require a combination of federal legislation and constitutional interpretation. Three cases suggest that at least the broad outlines of the constitutional position have begun to emerge.

In the first place, it is probably constitutional to use tape and wire recordings to verify the oral testimony of a witness concerning a conversation in which he openly participated. In *Lopez v. United States*[21] a taxpayer under investigation by the Internal Revenue Service invited the agent to his office in a manner suggesting that he would seek to bribe the agent. The agent reported to his superiors and then accepted the invitation equipped with a concealed recorder. At a subsequent trial for attempted bribery, the agent testified and the recording was introduced in evidence over the taxpayer's objection that its use violated his constitutional rights. The jury returned a verdict of guilty. The Supreme Court affirmed the conviction over the dissents of Justices Douglas, Brennan, and Goldberg. The decision seems likely to stand. As the Chief Justice said in a special concurrence, the only purpose the recording serves in such circumstances is to protect the credibility of a witness against that of a man who, if the recording be believed, was seeking to corrupt the witness in the performance of a public trust. Presumably the doctrine goes beyond attempts at bribery. No man should have a constitutional right to the assurance that, if he denies what other participants in a conversation disclose, none shall produce an accurate record of the words.

The second case arose out of the prosecution of James Hoffa in Nashville, Tennessee. An investigator hired by Osborn, Hoffa's attorney, reported to an agent of the Department of Justice that when he told Osborn of his close acquaintance with three prospective jurors, Osborn proposed that he arrange a bribe. The information was presented in a sworn affidavit to two federal judges who then gave instructions to have the investigator carry a concealed recorder at

[21] 373 U.S. 427 (1963).

later meetings with Osborn. Subsequently the recordings were used to corroborate the investigator's testimony at Osborn's trial. The evidence was damning. Osborn was convicted. The Supreme Court ultimately held that the recording was properly admitted in evidence.[22] The opinion noted that its use was sanctioned by the *Lopez* case but put the decision upon the narrower ground that the central requirement of the Fourth Amendment—authorization for the search by an independent magistrate upon a showing of justification—was satisfied by the submission of a "detailed factual affidavit alleging the commission of a specific criminal offense" and by the district judges' authorization of use of the recorder "for the narrow and particularized purpose of ascertaining the truth of the affidavit's allegations." Only Justice Douglas dissented.

The third case, *Berger v. New York*,[23] makes explicit the inference that could be drawn from the *Osborn* opinion—that the Court had resolved to assimilate secret electronic surveillance of private conversations to the trespassory searches and seizures in terms of which the Framers wrote the Fourth Amendment. A New York statute empowered State judges to enter *ex parte* orders authorizing secret surveillance and recording of conversations upon application of a district attorney or ranking police officer supported by an affidavit that "there is reasonable ground to believe that evidence of crime may be thus obtained." The district attorney's office followed this procedure in an investigation of the New York State Liquor Authority and obtained evidence leading to prosecution of Berger for conspiracy to bribe the chairman. Berger was convicted largely upon the evidence of the recordings, some of which were obtained by bugging the private offices of other conspirators. Berger appealed, claiming violation of the Fourth and Fifth Amendments. The Supreme Court reversed his conviction by a vote of 6–3. The contrariety of views is evidenced by six different opinions, three in the majority and three in dissent. Three points deserve attention.

First, the Court held that secret surveillance of private conversations is prohibited by the Fourth Amendment, if the electronic device is secreted inside the defendant's dwelling or office during a trespass. Most of the discussion would be equally applicable to a case in which there was no trespass. Justice Black alone stood on the *Olmstead* case, arguing that the Fourth Amendment bars only "searches and seizures" and protects only "houses, papers, and effects."[24] One does not "search" or "seize" a conversation, he said, and a conversation is not a house, paper, or effect. The opinion is a tribute to the Justice's consistency in giving effect to the belief that the Constitution must be applied as it was written and judges have no authority to keep it up to date by deviating from the literal meaning of the words even to apply it to modern devices unknown to the Framers. In my opinion the other justices had the better of the argument. The government's use of electronic bugs to penetrate the secrecy of the home or office is, in all significant respects, the same kind of official intrusion into privacy

[22] Osborn v. United States, 385 U.S. 323 (1966).
[23] 388 U.S. 41 (1967).
[24] Id. at 70, 81.

in search of evidence of wrongdoing as the Framers sought to outlaw by the Fourth Amendment. The interpretation of an on-going instrument that custom bars rewriting ought not to be limited to the specific applications with which the draftsmen were familiar, in disregard of the principle that lies behind them.

Second, the Court held that obtaining evidence by secret electronic surveillance of conversations would be constitutional provided that the government adhered to the search-warrant procedure contemplated by the Fourth Amendment. On this point, only Justice Douglas disagreed. With the full support of precedent he took the view that the Fourth Amendment bars all searches for mere evidence and limits the government to seizing contraband and the weapons or fruits of crime. This doctrine would have blocked any police use of electronic intrusions, assuming the Fourth Amendment to be applicable, because the only uses of a recording are to supply or lead one to evidence. The weight of professional opinion appears to be that, despite the precedents, the majority espoused the wiser rule. The old distinction contained more than a little hypocrisy. Frequently, the government's interest in the thing seized was purely technical, and the only purpose was to use it as evidence of guilt. Nor is there any interest save that of acquitting the guilty to be served by putting known, physical evidence of guilt beyond the government's power to procure.

The third branch of the *Berger* opinion reversed the conviction on the ground that the New York statute did not conform to the procedural requirements of the Fourth Amendment. The Court found it defective because it failed to require the officers "to describe with particularity the conversation sought" and thus authorized them "to seize any and all conversations." An application describing only the person whose conversations were to be recorded was thought too general to satisfy the amendment. The opinion also criticized the statute for failure to require prompt execution of the warrant and cessation of the surveillance "once the conversation sought is seized"; the order authorizing surveillance was good for two months, 24 hours a day, and the time could be extended in the public interest. The Court's final objection was that the statute had "no requirement for notice as do conventional warrants nor does it overcome this defect by requiring some showing of special facts."

This branch of the *Berger* opinion has many extraordinary aspects—not the least of which is that its author was the father of an Attorney General who was even then engaged in sharp political controversy upon the same subject. There is no explanation of the Court's determination to judge the constitutionality of the New York statute on its face—a step theretofore reserved for restrictions upon freedom of expression. The normal course is to see whether what was done in the case at bar violated the constitutional rights of the defendant. Again, the *Berger* opinion leaves obscure the criteria it states for measuring the constitutionality of particular instances of electronic surveillance. Much of the language suggests that the order, which constitutes the search warrant, must limit the police to overhearing or recording a particular conversation. Since that can be done only when the police are able to identify the time, place, and participants in an expected conversation, and also to turn on their device for just the period necessary to hear it, the restriction would virtually eliminate the use of electronic devices in the detection of crime. Again, the suggestion that the statute was defective because there was no provision for notice of the execution of the warrant leaves several ambiguities. Must the notice be given in advance or after surveillance has ended? What "special facts" will excuse the omission of notice? Notice in advance is obviously self-defeating, and even in arrears it would alert the members of criminal rings to the closing in of police investigation.

Under the strictest interpretation it would be difficult to draw a statute satisfying the Court's reading of the requirements of the Fourth Amendment. Justice Clark's response was, "If that be true then the fruits of eavesdropping devices are barred under the Amendment." The answer seems inadequate. If the justices may interpret some of the words of the Fourth Amendment freely in order to protect those whose privacy may be invaded by scientific devices which the literal meaning does not prohibit, then the Court cannot consistently insist on reading other words literally in order to escape deciding the questions of policy involved in bringing the search-warrant procedure into line with modern conditions.

The *Berger* case, although technically susceptible of limitation to situations in which there was a trespass, now sets the stage for congressional action. There is some reason to believe that F.B.I. Director Hoover previously placed such value upon uncontrolled discretion to use electronic devices in cases "involving the national security"—one wonders how broadly the term was defined—under the Jackson ruling that he opposed any new legislation. Since the *Berger* ruling seems to imply that any electronic surveillance is unconstitutional without a warrant, if there is time to secure one, continuation of the past practice will be of questionable constitutionality until a bill is enacted establishing a warrant procedure. Mr. Hoover's support would greatly improve the prospects for legislation.

In framing legislation it is easier to identify the considerations than to evaluate their relative importance. Electronic surveillance of conversations, on the telephone or otherwise, is a major invasion of privacy affecting not only the suspect but many wholly innocent persons who converse with him about unrelated matters. On the other hand, such surveillance unquestionably has some value in law enforcement. No one denies this in instances affecting national security. How much value it has in other cases is obscure because those who are offended by the invasions of privacy tell us there is none and those who wish to legalize the practice testify to its great worth. Scarcely anyone seems to have found the truth coldly, as a matter of fact, because few detached observers have substantial information.

Under the best of circumstances it would be hard to know where to strike the balance or how to arrange an accommodation. The one clear point seems to be that the present situation is intolerable. Perhaps the best that can be done is to frame a temporary measure designed to strike a passable accommodation by

The Reform of the Criminal Process

effectively outlawing the clear abuses and regularizing the eavesdropping made permissible in such a way as to provide a factual foundation for subsequent reevaluation. Such a measure might embody these points:

1. The Jackson ruling should be repudiated. The most worrisome invasions of privacy are in the eavesdropping and accumulation of materials in government files. If it is ever right to engage in the surveillance, it is no less right to use the information in the prosecution of wrongdoers.

2. Electronic eavesdropping without a warrant, when there is time to procure one, should be prohibited. Under the *Berger* ruling this would seem to be a constitutional necessity, even in cases affecting the national security. The Department of Justice's cagily phrased abandonment of electronic eavesdropping "for prosecutional purposes" is not enough to conform to the Fourth Amendment. Furthermore, requiring warrants is essential to removing the cloak of executive secrecy and bringing the practice under control.

3. Authority to apply for warrants should be limited to the Attorney General and the Assistant Attorney General in charge of the Criminal Division and their State counterparts.

4. "Warrants" should be obtainable only in connection with offenses against national security, organized racketeering, and other major crimes.

5. Provision should be made for reports covering all instances of surveillance and the use of any information obtained. The problem, of course, is to obtain an accurate picture of the value and dangers of the practice without identifying the people affected.

Upon such a record of experience subsequent measures might be devised with considerably more understanding and less emotion than is possible today.

IV

The constitutional standards governing the use of confessions in criminal cases have been under debate and revision for nearly three decades. In 1966, in *Miranda v. Arizona*,[25] the Court endeavored to promulgate definitive rules.

Miranda had been arrested at his home and taken to the police station under suspicion of kidnapping and rape. He was questioned by two police officers. He was not told that he was entitled to have an attorney present, but at some point he apparently was informed that he need not make a statement and that anything he said might be used against him. After two hours of questioning, without threats or coercion, he signed a written statement confessing his guilt. The confession was admitted as evidence at the trial, and Miranda was convicted. The Supreme Court reversed upon the ground that the questioning and subsequent

[25] 384 U.S. 436 (1966).

use of the confession as evidence violated the privilege against self-incrimination. Laying down broad rules for the guidance of the police and lower courts, the Supreme Court said that the prosecution may not use as evidence in a criminal case a statement resulting from police interrogation of a person in custody unless he has been warned of his right not to be questioned, of the danger that any statement may be used against him, and of his right to have an attorney present, either of his own retainer or appointed at public expense. The rights, moreover, even though waived initially, can be invoked at any time.

The *Miranda* decision has evoked both praise and criticism in roughly equal proportions, but I am more concerned here with what went into the decision than with its consequences. The ruling can hardly be explained by the words of the Constitution. The Fifth Amendment provides only that no person "shall be compelled in any criminal case to be a witness against himself." For more than a century and a half those words had never been held to require the presence of a lawyer during stationhouse interrogation. Some of the reasons for overturning the consistent line of precedents are in the Court's opinion. The rest can fairly be guessed.

In the first place, the Court was obviously troubled by fear that confessions were still being widely obtained by physical violence, threats, trickery, and other forms of overreaching the defendant's will. Beginning in the 1930's the Court reversed a long series of convictions where confessions had been obtained by torture, beatings, interrogation to the point of physical or psychological exhaustion, and isolation from lawyers, family, and friends.[26] New cases involving the same old police abuses continued to arise. Since relatively few such cases go to trial, the visible examples suggested that the secrecy of the stationhouse cloaked many other instances of the third degree in which the defendant was too poor or too cowed to make a defense, or in which the jury, figuring that a man would not confess if he were innocent, chose to believe the policemen's testimony rather than the defendant's account of the manner in which the police obtained his confession. If the third degree or subtler forms of coercing a confession were still prevalent after thirty or forty years of attempts to eliminate them by inquiry into the fact of coercion, case by case, had not the time come to establish a broader prophylactic rule that would bar all evidence of a confession unless some circumstance, such as the presence of the defendant's lawyer, gave assurance that the confession was voluntary?

A second factor in the thinking of some justices may have been the feeling that the time had come to eliminate some of the hypocrisy of our criminal procedure. We have long boasted that, in Anglo-American courts, every defendant is entitled to a lawyer to assist him in his defense; and that no man accused of crime need take the witness stand and subject himself to interrogation. At the same time we allowed prosecutors and police to interrogate defendants in the

---

[26] Brown v. Mississippi, 297 U.S. 278 (1936); Ashcraft v. Tennessee, 322 U.S. 143 (1944); Spano v. New York, 360 U.S. 315 (1959); Haynes v. Washington, 373 U.S. 503 (1963).

stationhouse in the presence of a stenographer, without the aid of a lawyer or the restraining influence of a judge. Police interrogators were trained in psychological devices for obtaining confessions from reluctant suspects. Later, if a man confessed, the prosecutor would read into evidence at the trial either a transcript of the questioning or the narrative statement to which the answers were reduced. The boast that no man is required to testify against himself rings hollow next to the practice. If interrogation in the courtroom is different in any material respect from questioning in the stationhouse, read into evidence at the trial, the distinction lies in the fact that the stationhouse questioning is more susceptible of abuse.

A third element behind the *Miranda* ruling appears to be the egalitarianism that has become a dominant force in the evolution of our constitutional law. The broad egalitarianism stirred by the civil rights revolution had already found expression in criminal law in decisions requiring the State to offset inequalities of wealth by paying for a lawyer for the defendant[27] and furnishing a stenographic transcript for appeal.[28] Who were the defendants who were led into giving confessions in police stations? Not the well-to-do, who could procure a lawyer immediately. Not the experienced criminal, who knew enough to keep silent until his mouthpiece arrived. More often than not those who confessed in the police station would be the poor and ignorant, the friendless and frightened, or the young and weak. Should not society be required to do what it could to put them on an equality with the more fortunate, or at least to stop taking advantage of their situation?

Broader forces undoubtedly contributed to the *Miranda* decision, as they have influenced the general trend of constitutional development in criminal law. The law is feeling the impact of the newer sciences. . . . The doubts which psychologists raise concerning freedom of the will breed skepticism of the very notions of guilt and punishment. Much of our criminal law is based upon the premise that antisocial conduct can be deterred by fear of punishment, but many observers have come to question the predicate in the face of the social, economic, and psychological causes of crime. Most prison systems appear to breed more criminals than they cure. One wonders whether respect for, and therefore observance of, law is better secured by the tough cop and frequent convictions, however obtained, or by requiring law enforcement officials to observe practices earning respect for their fairness. We are woefully ignorant upon all such questions, as we are about the anatomy of crime. I do not mean to imply that the majority of the Court is committed to any view, but the doubts arising from awareness of ignorance, when they replace once accepted verities, are likely to influence the course of decision.

The active intervention of the Warren Court into the administration of criminal justice followed State defaults, both legislative and judicial. It would have been better if the States had themselves reformed their criminal procedure

[27] Gideon v. Wainwright, 372 U.S. 335 (1963).
[28] Griffin v. Illinois, 351 U.S. 12 (1956).

by providing counsel for all indigent defendants at public expense, but the simple fact is that a minority of States failed to act despite a long period of warning. For years it was plain that State and local police often resorted to unlawful searches and seizures, but the local courts continued to offer incentives for misconduct by receiving the fruits of the illegality as evidence without adopting other measures to restrain the officials from invading constitutional rights. The problem of coerced confessions is another example. Of course, not all the business of government is constitutional law, but if one arm of government cannot or will not solve an insistent problem, the pressure falls upon another. This has been a major factor in the Supreme Court's activity in the field of criminal law.

V

If one may measure "activism" by the overruling of settled precedents and the establishment of new constitutional doctrines, the Warren Court has been extraordinarily "activist" in the field of criminal procedure. If Winston Churchill was right in saying that "the quality of a nation's civilization can be largely measured by the methods it uses in the enforcement of its criminal law," then the activism of the Warren Court has enabled our civilization to give a vastly better account of itself. There is room for honest debate as to whether such decisions as *Miranda* go too far in correcting the acknowledged evil. A number of dissenting opinions and even some opinions of the Court seem to slide off into sentimentality or run libertarian dogma into the ground at the expense of the substance of liberty, as happened when the Court held that search warrants must be obtained for routine fire or health inspections but then watered down the showing required for a warrant until the requirement would be little more than red tape.[29] Despite occasional excesses the net effect has been extraordinarily important reform in the administration of criminal justice, in the States where reform was most needed, within an unusually short span of time.

Nor should the consequences be measured solely in terms of legal doctrine. The establishment of a constitutional requirement for the appointment of counsel in all criminal cases, for example, set in motion countless local reforms because the activity of counsel brought to the attention of judges practices that had escaped their notice or which they had let slide, such as confining offenders for long periods without arraignment or advice about their legal rights. The spirit engendered by the decisions supplied much of the stimulus for broader undertakings such as the Attorney General's Conference on Bail, the Attorney General's Conference on the Provision of Legal Services to the Indigent, and the work of the President's Commission on Law Enforcement and the Administration of Justice.

[29] Camara v. Municipal Court of the City and County of San Francisco, 387 U.S. 523 (1967).

The Reform of the Criminal Process

The costs of the Court's activism must be reckoned in long-range institutional terms. The rapidity of the doctrinal changes and the readiness of a bare numerical majority of the justices to overturn recent precedents immediately upon a change in the membership of the Court do no service to the ideal of law as something distinct from the arbitrary preferences of individuals. Yet misgivings on this score should be tempered by the realization that many of the changes have roots in prior decisions. The constitutional rights of the defendant in a federal trial are stated with some degree of specificity, and the Court had long been evolving the doctrines necessary for their implementation. By the doctrine of selective incorporation those guarantees have now been applied to the States. The decisions brought sharp changes in some States, for they had applied much looser standards, but the rationale is necessarily self-limiting. Once the federal rights are carried over to the States the pace of change may be slowed.

The gravest questions are raised by the radical revision of the structure of government that results from shifting the ultimate judicial responsibility for the administration of criminal justice from the States to the Nation—a point the majority refuses to discuss despite Justice Harlan's dissents.[30] Under the older view of due process a criminal prosecution seldom raised questions of constitutional law. Today constitutional law affects innumerable aspects of criminal cases from investigation to sentence, and recent decisions suggest that the Court is ready to deal with more and more details.[31] The judgments of the State courts of last resort are thus subject not only to reversal by the Supreme Court of the United States on certiorari but also, under the rule allowing the use of federal habeas corpus to review constitutional questions, to scrutiny by a federal district judge, the federal court of appeals, and again the Supreme Court. Even if the possibility of injustice makes so much judicial review a wise allocation of resources, one wonders about the consequences of the delay in reaching a truly final decision in the case of defendants with the funds and perseverance to exhaust every conceivable remedy. Moreover, men of ability may find that positions on State courts of last resort become less attractive if they are reduced to way stations on the route to ultimate constitutional review; and the State judges may feel less and less inclined to exercise responsibility for continuing improvement in the administration of criminal justice. It is far from clear that we can wisely look to the impulse of constitutional adjudication for continuing reform.

In the New York eavesdropping case Justice Harlan protested his colleagues' new contrivance of constitutional rights "without apparent concern for the empirical process that goes with legislative reform." [32] If the apparent lack of concern is real, then the institutional changes associated with reform by constitutional adjudication could indeed tend to freeze a particular set of preconceptions into permanence at a time when the public concern about crime in the streets and the work of the President's Commission may stimulate new investigations

---

[30] Miranda v. Arizona, 384 U.S. 436, 504 (1966); In re Gault, 387 U.S. 1, 65 (1967).
[31] See, e.g., In re Gault, 387 U.S. 1 (1967); United States v. Wade, 388 U.S. 218 (1967).
[32] Berger v. New York, 388 U.S. 41, 89 (1967).

enormously increasingly our understanding of the practical impact of sundry rules of criminal procedure. I am more inclined to believe that the Court is simply filling a void, and that the present use of constitutional law will not bar careful legislation in the future. Generally speaking, the administration of criminal justice has thus far been the special responsibility of the judicial branch on both the State and federal level. The Supreme Court, in imposing changes, has not yet disturbed the processes of representative self-government.

Perhaps we may glean some hint of the future from a passage in the Chief Justice's opinion in the *Miranda* case where he carefully left room for movement by emphasizing that the procedural safeguards the opinion requires are applicable "unless other fully effective means are devised to inform accused persons of their right of silence and to assure a continuous opportunity to exercise it." Later he declared that "Congress and the States are free to develop their own safeguards" for the privilege against self-incrimination during questioning by the police.[33]

The Constitution bars some changes in criminal procedure, however fair and however soundly based on empirical investigation they may be. The right to jury trial, for example, limits the functions that can be delegated to a board of experts, and the privilege against self-incrimination bars accusatorial investigation. The Court would doubtless give short shrift to legislative attempts to authorize the very same police practices which it has recently proscribed unless the legislation was based upon new data. Within such limits, however, nothing in the Court's opinions is inhospitable to legislative action rooted in careful investigation, even if it involves some qualification of the doctrines announced in recent cases. Indeed, one of the chief benefits flowing from the recent decisions may be the stimulus they have given to more empirical channels of study and reform.

▢ Curbing the Union

ALEXANDER M. BICKEL

This engagingly ominous title, suggested to me by Professor Karl W. Deutsch ..., is a fair comment on three states' rights constitutional amendments put forward in December, 1962, by the Council of State Governments. Two of these

FROM Alexander M. Bickel, *Politics and the Warren Court* (New York: Harper & Row, 1965), pp. 146–61. Copyright © 1955, 1956, 1958, 1960, 1961, 1962, 1963, 1964, 1965 by Alexander M. Bickel. Reprinted by permission of Harper & Row, Publishers, Inc.

[33] 384 U.S. 436, 467, 490 (1966).

proposed amendments were approved by thirteen state legislatures, a fact that subsequently brought considerable notoriety to all three. It is not too much to say, indeed, that the amendments caused widespread alarm. They are interesting, however, not so much because of any danger they still represent to the existing constitutional structure (although there is about them something of the menace of the unexploded bomb) but because they bespeak a certain discontent, a certain mood and certain grievances that stir a substantial and perfectly respectable body of opinion.

Briefly (I shall give the full text presently[1]) the first of the proposed amendments would alter the Amending Clause itself. It would enable two thirds of the state legislatures to initiate a constitutional amendment without action by Congress, or by a national convention, or, indeed, in any national forum whatever. The second would overrule *Baker v. Carr*, the famous legislative apportionment case of 1962, and the decisions that followed it. The third would create a Court of the Union, consisting of the chief justices of the fifty states, as a more supreme Supreme Court, empowered to overrule the decisions of the present Supreme Court in certain circumstances.

Discussion must begin by placing these proposals in context. The Supreme Court, possessing, in the famous Hamiltonian phrase, neither the sword nor the purse, but relying only on its place in the hearts of its countrymen and on their law-abiding habits, is engaged in a continuous colloquy with the nation. Over time, the Court proposes and the nation disposes. This relationship breaks up roughly into recurring cycles. The Court proposes major ideas—they are relatively few in number—and a period of vigorous debate follows, during which the Court's proposed principles are far from stable. Eventually, and for a time, consensus is arrived at, which may or may not coincide in this or that degree with the principles initially broached by the Court. There follows a period during which the Court consolidates the position on the basis of the consensus, and this is normally a period of relatively placid acceptance of the Court's work. Then, before long, the Court tackles some other subject, or an old one once more, and the cycle begins again. Of course, I oversimplify. This is a model. Real life is not so neat. Yet, schematically, this is how things operate, and since 1954, when the *School Segregation Cases* were first decided, we have been in a cycle of debate and turmoil. If there is anything unusual about this particular cycle, it is only that the Court has not waited as long as may have been usual in the past to consolidate its gains from its first enterprise—the segregation decision—before floating one or two other major principles.

It is characteristic of the debating portion of the cycle that constitutional amendments are proposed by the bushel. Like various legislative proposals aimed at reforming the Court or overruling its work—"curbing the Court," in a phrase popularized by former Justice James F. Byrnes in the spring of 1956[2]—proposed

---
[1] The text is most conveniently available in 36 *State Government* 10 (1963).
[2] J. F. Byrnes, "The Supreme Court Must Be Curbed," *U. S. News & World Report*, May 18, 1956, p. 50.

amendments serve as convenient summations, rallying cries, or slogans, and they constitute quite an accustomed feature of the debate. They have been with us during the decade since the decision in the *School Segregation Cases,* as the most casual survey of the Congressional Record will readily reveal. They have always been with us. I am about to touch on a recently suggested amendment which would empower Congress to override any constitutional decision by a two-thirds vote. Senator LaFollette made the same proposal in the course of his third-party presidential campaign in 1924. In those years also, Felix Frankfurter favored repealing the Due Process Clauses of the Fifth and Fourteenth Amendments.[3] And there is good reason to believe that so—privately—did Justice Brandeis.

I offer—chiefly for the edification of the collector of curios—a sampling of proposals for constitutional amendment culled from the Congressional Record from 1954 to date. It turns out, to begin with, that the first of the proposals put forward by the Council of State Governments, the one to amend the Amending Clause, is nothing new. It is, moreover, comparatively conservative. In 1955 a Joint Resolution was introduced in the House to amend the Constitution so as to provide that the legislatures of any twelve states could submit an amendment directly for ratification, without the intervention of any Congressional action.[4] Nor is the proposal to overrule *Baker v. Carr* new. Thirteen House Resolutions proposing constitutional amendments to overrule *Baker v. Carr* were introduced in the first year or so following decision of the case. In June, 1964, the Court extended the holding of *Baker v. Carr* in a series of new decisions, and a second rash of proposed amendments immediately broke out, including one—relatively moderate—that was endorsed by the Republican platform of 1964, and is sponsored by the Republican leadership in Congress.[5] Going further afield and listing draft amendments in a vague descending order of importance and generality of application, one finds: A series of proposals to restrict the Supreme Court's power to reverse its own precedents—which the Court, of course, did in the *School Segregation Cases,*[6] another series, similar to the LaFollette proposal already mentioned, seeking to empower Congress to overrule the Court's constitutional decisions;[7] a proposal—which might seem too outlandish to mention even in this context were it not that its author was the recently retired dean of the House, the powerful Carl Vinson of Georgia—in effect to reverse John Marshall's decision in *McCulloch v. Maryland* (1819) and to enforce a reading of the Constitution as granting to the federal government only those powers which are *expressly*

---

[3] See F. Frankfurter, *Law and Politics* 10–16 (E. Prichard and A. MacLeish, eds., Capricorn edition 1962).
[4] H.J. Res. 200, 84th Cong., 1st Sess. (1955).
[5] H.J. Res. 678, 683, 686, 687, and 704, 87th Cong., 2nd Sess. (1962); H.J. Res. 30, 34, 162, 178, 223, 300, and 349, 88th Cong., 1st Sess. (1963); S.J. Res. 2, 89th Cong., 1st Sess. (1965); see *New York Times,* Feb. 9, 1965, p. 31, col. 2.
[6] E.g., H.J. Res. 201, 86th Cong., 1st Sess. (1959).
[7] E.g., H.J. Res. 476, 85th Cong., 2nd Sess. (1958); H.J. Res. 790, 87th Cong., 2nd Sess. (1962).

mentioned, to the exclusion of any implied powers;[8] a proposal to reverse the gradual process by which portions of the first eight Amendments—the Bill of Rights—have been made applicable to the states, and to free the states of any further embarrassment from those Amendments;[9] an ample and continuing series of proposals to reverse not only the *School Segregation Cases* but all other racial decisions, and to leave the states entirely to their own devices in regulating the relations between the races;[10] and finally, an equally ample and continuing series of draft amendments that would make structural changes in the Court, such as requiring unanimity before a state statute could be declared unconstitutional, or changing the lifetime tenure of the justices to a term of years, or prescribing new qualifications for appointment, including one that would allow only sitting members of state Supreme Courts to be appointed to the federal Supreme Court.[11]

All these attempts to reform the Supreme Court and to correct its work are by way of attempted constitutional amendments. I have yet to offer even a sampling of proposed *legislation* aimed at the Court and at its recent controversial decisions. Legislative efforts are of course much more dangerous. It is not easily forgotten how close some of the notorious Jenner-Butler bills of 1957 and 1958 came to enactment. These bills would have removed from Supreme Court jurisdiction —and though they were of somewhat doubtful constitutionality, they would nevertheless in some degree have been successful in removing—all cases (a) affecting the conduct of Congressional committees, (b) relating to security dismissals of government employees, and (c) having to do with state antisubversive legislation.[12] Nor should the famous H.R. 3 be forgotten, which would have materially, if somewhat unpredictably, altered the Court's function in reconciling concurrent or conflicting federal and state statutes under the Supremacy Clause.[13] But there is also a large variety of other proposals that have never been heard of. There have been a number attacking the Court's jurisdiction in racial cases.[14] And there have been legislative attempts, quite possibly valid if enacted, to hamper the appointing power by imposing a set of qualifications for prospective justices, although the Constitution now mentions none.[15]

The point of this parade of horribles is that in such a period as this such horribles are always with us. There is, therefore, nothing particularly startling in themselves about the three proposals put forward by the Council of State Governments. They simply take their place in the parade. If there is anything not-

---

[8] H.J. Res. 495, 84th Cong., 2nd Sess. (1956).
[9] S.J. Res. 176, 87th Cong., 2nd Sess. (1962).
[10] E.g., H.J. Res. 532, 83d Cong., 2nd Sess. (1954); H.J. Res. 587, 87th Cong., 1st Sess. (1961).
[11] E.g., H.R. 13857, 85th Cong., 2nd Sess. (1958); H.J. Res. 91, 83rd Cong., 1st Sess. (1953); H.R. 11374, 84th Cong., 2nd Sess. (1956); H.J. Res. 453, 86th Cong., 1st Sess. (1959).
[12] S. 2646, 85th Cong., 1st Sess. (1957); S. 3386, 85th Cong., 2nd Sess. (1958).
[13] H.R. 3, 85th Cong., 1st Sess. (1957).
[14] E.g., H.R. 1228, 85th Cong., 1st Sess. (1957).
[15] E.g., S. 3759, 84th Cong., 2nd Sess. (1956); H.R. 4020, 88th Cong., 1st Sess. (1963).

able about them, anything at all extraordinary, justifying the brouhaha they have provoked, it is not in their nature or timing, nor in their adoption by a baker's dozen of state legislatures, but in their sponsorship. Thirteen state legislatures—that is not really an alarming number, no more alarming than the number of voices that can be summoned against the Court in a Congressional debate. You can probably get a dozen legislatures to come out in favor of almost anything that they do not themselves have the power to do and that they do not really believe in their heart of hearts will ever be done. Nor do I, for one, find confirmation here of the wisdom of *Baker v. Carr*. The short, silent, and then arrested progress of these amendments through thirteen state legislatures seems to me to illustrate not so much that our legislatures are unrepresentative bodies as that they are secret places. The notable thing about these amendments is that they were sponsored by the Sixteenth General Assembly of the States, held under the auspices of the Council of State Governments.

The Council of State Governments is an admirable organization, dedicated to high and worthwhile purposes, of which regrettably little is known. Perhaps this unfortunate circumstance is owing to the kind of subject matter that is generally grist to the organization's mill. It is a subject matter worthy in the extreme, but not as a rule highly charged. The Council of State Governments may be a relatively secret place for much the same reason that a state legislature is. In December, 1958, for example, the Council's General Assembly of the States, which four years later was to propose the constitutional amendments I am discussing, passed resolutions recommending study of problems of atomic energy, water development, flood insurance, mental retardation, the aging, and highway safety. These matters were to be studied. The only subjects on which the Assembly chose to commit itself flatly were statehood for Hawaii, which it was for, and the use of virulent hog cholera virus for vaccination purposes, which it was against and recommended prohibiting. Meaning no disrespect either way, the Council of State Governments reminds one of nothing so much as the Council of Europe—not any of the institutions of the Common Market or the Coal and Steel Community, but the Council of Europe, with its little Parliament of Man —or perhaps one or another of the technical agencies affiliated with the UN. The Council of State Governments normally labors earnestly and thanklessly in distant vineyards, has some influence, and can show some beneficial results, but is utterly without power and suffers not a little from a sense of frustration.

The Council originated in private initiative, and with an attachment to the Department of Political Science at the University of Chicago in the 1930's. As now organized, it is supported and recognized by state legislatures, which create local councils, called Commissions of Interstate Cooperation and consisting typically of ten members of the legislature and five administrative officials. The central Council is essentially a research organization, governed by a Board of Delegates drawn from the state councils. Information is exchanged, there are publications of common interest, there is a staff and an executive director, and secretariat services are provided for such bodies as the Governor's Conference, the Conference of State Chief Justices, the National Association of State Attorneys General, the National Association of State Budget Officers, the National Legislative Conference, the National Association of State Purchasing Officials, the Parole and Probation Compact Administrators Association, the Association of Juvenile Compact Administrators, and the National Conference of Court Administrative Officers. Biennially there is a General Assembly of the States, a little parliament to which the local councils appoint delegates, who are mostly state legislators. The states vote as units in the Assembly, each having one vote. The Sixteenth General Assembly of the States, which met in December, 1962, and proposed the amendments we are discussing, was attended by more than 300 people comprising delegations from 47 states. In the past, so far as I can discover, the Council of State Governments and its General Assembly of the States seem to have irritated or alarmed no one but the far-right fringe, which they have now, no doubt, delighted. A writer in the *American Mercury* for January, 1960, accused the Council of engaging in a "uniform mail-order law movement," of proposing "half-baked experiments in weird [sic!] fields, such as urban renewal demolition and mental health legislation," and, in culmination, of being "part of a linkage that leads into Red Russia." [16]

That from such an innocuous and well-meaning source should come proposals to stand the constitutional system on its head—this, I think, is what was startling and alarming. This was what separated these proposed amendments out of the common run to which in such a time as this we are fairly accustomed. Here, then, are the amendments.

The first would amend Article V of the Constitution, the Amending Clause, to read in its entirety as follows:

> The Congress, whenever two-thirds of both Houses shall deem it necessary, or, on the application of the Legislatures of two-thirds of the several states, shall propose amendments to this Constitution, which shall be valid to all intents and purposes, as part of this Constitution, when ratified by the Legislatures of three-fourths of the several states. Whenever application from the Legislatures of two-thirds of the total number of states of the United States shall contain identical texts of an amendment to be proposed, the President of the Senate and the Speaker of the House of Representatives shall so certify, and the amendment as contained in the application shall be deemed to have been proposed, without further action by Congress. No state, without its consent, shall be deprived of its equal suffrage in the Senate.

Under Article V as it now stands, amendments can be proposed by a two-thirds vote of both Houses of Congress or by a "Convention for proposing Amendments," which is to be called by Congress on the application of the legislatures of two thirds of the states. The convention method, never heretofore em-

---

[16] B. Hindman, "1313's Mail-Order Laws," *American Mercury,* Jan. 1960, pp. 33, 35, 37, 39. For information on the structure and functions of the Council of State Governments, see 32 *State Government* 162 (1959); *The Book of the States* (1960).

ployed, is, incidentally, the method by which the Council of State Governments proposes that its three amendments, including this one, be submitted for ratification. The Council's proposals are all directed to the state legislatures, which are to transmit them to Congress in the form of a request to call a convention for proposing amendments, which, in turn, would then submit them to ratification. That is all that the dozen or so state legislatures that have acted on these amendments have done—they have transmitted them to Congress which, when two thirds of the legislatures of the states have made exactly the same transmittals, is to call a convention, which in turn may or may not submit these amendments for ratification by three fourths of the states.

This unprecedented, although allowable, procedure itself raises some interesting questions.[17] The proposed amendment to Article V, at any rate, while hoping to get itself enacted by this procedure, would then abolish it, and substitute direct proposing power on the part of two thirds of the state legislatures. Thus a method would be made available for proposing amendments without the need for discussion in any national forum. And there is another change, this time in the ratification rather than in the proposal process. As Article V now stands, Congress has the option to submit amendments, no matter how proposed, for ratification by three fourths of the states either through their legislatures or in special conventions, called in each of the states as Congress may provide. It is proposed to abolish the ratifying conventions as an option, and that is something of a change, although they are an option that Congress has exercised but once. Such are the proposed changes in Article V. The provision that no state may without its consent be deprived of its equal vote in the Senate is old.

The flaw in the proposal is obvious. When we come to changing the law under which we live as a nation we ought to discuss it as a nation in a national forum. The sum of discussions in fifty legislatures is not a national discussion, it is not national consideration in a national forum such as Congress or a convention for proposing amendments. Eliminating the option of ratification by state conventions is also objectionable because it would remove an element of flexibility, which, although it may not in the past have been of much use, cannot by the same token be pointed to as the source of any evil. If the question is, shall we or shall we not retain an element of flexibility which cannot be shown to have ever hurt anyone, the sensible position, proceeding from simple general principles, is to favor retention.

The second of the proposed amendments is as follows:

Section 1. No provision of this Constitution, or any amendment thereto, shall restrict or limit any state in the apportionment of representation in its legislature.

Section 2. The Judicial power of the United States shall not extend to any suit in law or equity, or to any controversy, relating to apportionment of representation in a state legislature.

[17] See C. L. Black, Jr., "The Proposed Amendment of Article V: A Threatened Disaster," 72 *Yale Law Journal* 957 (1963).

This is the attempt to overrule *Baker v. Carr* and the other apportionment decisions, but only in their application to state legislatures. It does not touch these decisions as they may apply—and some lower courts have already so applied them—to representative bodies in the political subdivisions of the states, such as city councils. I expect that this was an inadvertent omission, rather characteristic, incidentally, of the drafting of all three of these proposals. Nor does this amendment touch the application of *Baker v. Carr* to Congressional apportionment. This, I expect, was an intentional omission, for it indicates the single-minded, almost obsessive motivation behind the proposals. These are not the usual Court-hating or even Court-curbing proposals, nor were they put forward in a blind and indiscriminate rage against federal authority as a whole. The purpose is the enhancement of state authority, the resumption by the institutions of the states of a place in the center of affairs, the return to them of competence in matters of importance, and thus also more generally of dignity and influence. There is behind these amendments something not unlike the Gaullist hankering after the old exalted place in the sun, the old power and the glory, a hankering which carries with it a bit of haughty indifference toward the arrangements *others* may make for *themselves*. And so let Congress and the Supreme Court decide between themselves who shall decide how *Congress* is to be apportioned.

Now, the reaction to *Baker v. Carr,* and even to the cases that followed it, has been on the whole favorable. Still there are those—both professional observers and others—who are troubled. From the point of view of those, then, like myself, who have misgivings about the decision, what is wrong with the proposed amendment? If we think the decision was wrong, must it not follow that the amendment is right? The answer is no, for two reasons. First, to borrow a phrase of Paul A. Freund, the misgivings come at retail, the amendment at wholesale. I do not object, for example, to having the Court strike down an utterly obsolete apportionment, such as the sixty-year-old Tennessee apportionment that was involved in *Baker v. Carr* itself; I object only to having the Court lay down, as it did in the later cases, its own standards for valid apportionments. I do not object, in other words, to having the Court tell a legislature that it must act; I object only to having the Court tell it, in these circumstances, how it must act. Others may qualify their objections in other ways. The proposed amendment makes no such discriminations. Moreover, in a case such as the famous Tuskegee gerrymander case,[18] where it can be objectively demonstrated that the sole purpose of a so-called apportionment is to disadvantage or invidiously segregate voters of a given race, purely on the ground of race, I do not object to having the Court strike down the legislative action, no matter how recent, and many other people who have misgivings about *Baker v. Carr* would also distinguish between that case and the situation just described. Again, the proposed amendment does not. To change the figure, it is cheerfully ready to throw out the baby with the bath. That is most frequently the case with proposed constitutional amendments. They are

---

[18] Gomillion v. Lightfoot, 364 U.S. 339 (1960).

not often closely tailored to a limited purpose about which a consensus may be said to exist. Constitution-writing seems to have become a lost art.

The second, and in itself equally conclusive argument, against overruling *Baker v. Carr* by constitutional amendment is that to do so is both unnecessary and pernicious. If there exists the sort of consensus against the decision which would be necessary to get an amendment enacted, the decision is doomed— wholly and totally doomed—without the need to amend the Constitution. It is, in that event, only a matter of time before the Court itself abandons the path on which it set its foot in *Baker v. Carr;* the apportionment problem occurs regularly with every census, and can be freshly attacked after 1970. And so amendment is unnecessary. It is pernicious, because the practice of hastening or confirming in this fashion the demise of unwanted judicial doctrines would lead to a pestilence of amendment that would destroy the value of our Constitution as a symbol and as a cohesive force in society. "We must never forget," was John Marshall's famous admonition, "that it is a *constitution* we are expounding." Nor can we forget that it is a *Constitution* we are proposing to amend, and that if, in another phrase of Marshall's, it should come to "partake of the prolixity of a legal code," it will seem false and alien to the people, who are expected to pour into it their sense of union and common purpose, regardless of the ways and byways, the trial and error of judicial construction. When something has gone wrong, it is useful that we should know it was the Court, and not our Constitution.

There have been 24 amendments in nearly two centuries. I put aside the first 12, the last of which became effective in 1804, as part of the process of the original framing, although the eleventh was necessary to correct an error of drafting that a Supreme Court decision had uncovered. I put aside also the three Civil War amendments, which constituted the treaty of peace. Finally, I put aside the Seventeenth, Nineteenth, Twentieth, Twenty-second, Twenty-third and Twenty-fourth. Four of these dealt with organizational matters covered by very precise original provisions and not conceivably changeable otherwise than by an amendment; one, the Nineteenth, dealt with a broad principle—woman suffrage— fully appropriate in every sense for constitutional statement; and one, the Twenty-fourth, which outlawed the poll tax in federal elections, was also, though not so unavoidably, a fitting constitutional statement. That leaves three, and the two prohibition amendments, the Eighteenth and its repealer, can safely be passed in silence. The Sixteenth, the income tax amendment, is thus the only modern one comparable to the proposed *Baker v. Carr* amendment. It was enacted to overrule the Supreme Court's decision in *Pollock v. Farmer's Trust Company*.[19] But there can be little doubt that had Congress acted by new legislation, reaffirming the income tax act that the Court had declared unconstitutional, as Congress at the very time when it proposed the amendment at least half intended to do, the Court would have reversed itself. And there is no doubt that had the word "in-

---

[19] 157 U.S. 429 (1895).

come" never been written into the Constitution, as under the circumstances I project it would not need to have been written in, we would have been better off, for we would have been spared some unedifying interpretive decisions made possible by the new constitutional term "income." The Sixteenth Amendment is an illustration of the paradox that language added to the Constitution in order to overrule the Court will generally enlarge as much as restrict the Court's function. This is equally illustrated by the Eleventh Amendment, and by the first sentence of the Fourteenth, which was intended to overrule the *Dred Scott* case. Constitutional language is the fuel on which the Court's engine runs. New words in the Constitution are a source of new power, even when their primary meaning was to diminish existing power.

The third and last of the proposed amendments is the most complex:

Section 1. Upon demand of the legislatures of five states, no two of which shall share any common boundary, made within two years after the rendition of any judgment of the Supreme Court relating to the rights reserved to the states or to the people by this Constitution, such judgment shall be reviewed by a Court composed of the Chief Justices of the highest courts of the several states to be known as the Court of the Union. The sole issue before the Court of the Union shall be whether the power or jurisdiction sought to be exercised on the part of the United States is a power granted to it under this Constitution.

Section 2. Three-fourths of the justices of the Court of the Union shall constitute a quorum, but it shall require concurrence of a majority of the entire Court to reverse a decision of the Supreme Court. . . .

Section 3. On the first Monday of the third calendar month following the ratification of this amendment, the chief justices . . . shall convene at the national capital, at which time the Court of the Union shall be organized. . . .

Section 4. Decisions of the Court of the Union upon matters within its jurisdiction shall be final and shall not thereafter be overruled by any court and may be changed only by an amendment of this Constitution.

Section 5. The Congress shall make provision for the housing of the Court of the Union and the expenses of its operation.

It is hard to escape the feeling, as one reads this extraordinary prose, that the provisions for seating the Court of the Union in the national capital and for requiring Congress to house and pay for it are subtle compromises of the principles of the framers of the amendment. Nor is it possible to avoid feeling that the last-mentioned provision adds some insult to the injury it inflicts on federal supremacy. Beyond this, one can only say with Dean Fordham of the Pennsylvania University Law School, that "there is so much wrong with this proposal that one hardly knows where to begin in discussing it." [20] Such a court would be institu-

---

[20] J. Fordham, "The States in the Federal System—Vital Role or Limbo?", 49 *Va. L. Rev.* 666, 672–73 (1963).

tionally incapable of acting as a court. It would either surrender its authority to committees (to be called panels, no doubt) or act like a legislature, seeing issues in the large, without application to immediate facts, and pursuing political rather than judicial methods, including logrolling and other forms of give-and-take. Or it would do both. What is not unrelated and at least equally important, such a court would be incapable of taking a national view. It would arrive in Washington to render its nationally applicable decisions only occasionally, and it would see the issues before it from the vantage point of the local experience and local dependence of each of its members. This is intended, of course, but it is disastrous. A composite of local vantage points is not a national point of view, and national issues deserve to be decided on considerations that have national relevance. And so ultimately, and quite aside from everything else, this proposal is objectionable on essentially the grounds that make the first of these draft amendments, the amending amendment, inadmissible.

We need not idly guess at the parochialism and lack of constitutional sophistication of a pride of state chief justices in convention assembled. A conference of state chief justices exists as a going concern, and in December of 1958 it adopted, 36 to 8, a report of its Committee on Federal–State Relationships as Affected by Judicial Decisions.[21] This is an illuminating if depressing document, to which I shall return briefly in my conclusion. It deplores the making of social and economic policy, as opposed to the strict application of legal rules, by the Supreme Court, and the threatening fact that we are becoming a government of men more than of laws—and is thus not a little simple-minded. It tends to deplore also the use of the federal spending power—the very use of it, as in the social security program and various grants-in-aid, not merely the manner of its use—and is thus somewhat fatuous. And it criticizes various applications of the Fourteenth Amendment to the states, chiefly in matters of free speech and of criminal procedure, quite indiscriminately and without giving evidence of any organizing principle about the proper function of the Supreme Court of the United States, other than a generalized desire to be let alone.

Whatever might be said about the draftsmanship of the other two proposed amendments, the draftsmanship of this one is, in its indefiniteness, atrocious beyond belief. What is meant by a right reserved to the states or to the people under the Constitution? If Congress says something is interstate rather than intrastate commerce and the Supreme Court agrees, does that relate to a right reserved to the states or to the people? Suppose the Court holds that a private home may not be searched without a warrant? Does that so relate? Everything does or nothing does. The Tenth Amendment, which speaks in somewhat similar, although by comparison infinitely more precise terms, has been held, naturally enough, to be tautological and nugatory. Then, again, what is meant by the question whether the power of jurisdiction sought to be exercised on the part of the United States is a power granted to it under this Constitution? Who must

---

[21] See 32 *State Government* 60 (1959).

seek to exercise power on the part of the United States in order to come within this formulation? Will the jurisdiction of the Court of the Union attach only when Congress has acted, or does the Supreme Court itself, construing the Constitution directly without the benefit of federal legislation, seek to exercise power on the part of the United States? What happens when the Supreme Court declares an act of Congress unconstitutional? Who then is exercising power on behalf of the United States?

These are the proposed amendments. It should, in justice, be remarked that the amendments are not all recommended by the General Assembly of the States with equal force. The first passed that Assembly by a vote of 37 to 4, four states abstaining. The second gathered 26 votes against 10, with ten states abstaining. The third barely squeaked by, 21 to 20, five delegations abstaining. Of the state legislatures that have acted, thirteen each completed action approving the first two, and only five adhered to the third.[22]

But it is not enough—it is neither fair nor in the long run wise—simply to dismiss these amendments as utterly improbable and of course unacceptable. Nor is it enough simply to think of them as speeches, like the flood of amendments, to which I have referred, that gets introduced in Congress—lines spoken in the continual and accustomed dialogue between the Court and the country. We deal here with a symptom of something more pervasive and more fundamental than displeasure and debate over this or that decision, more pervasive and fundamental than the endurance of this or that Supreme Court decision as a constitutional principle. We ought to pause and look past the symptom. Having joined in condemning Theodore Roosevelt's endorsement of the popular recall of judges in 1912, Felix Frankfurter went on to pinpoint what should be heeded about proposals such as these. "The policy of a specific remedy may be crushingly exposed," he said, "but we cannot whistle down the wind a widespread, insistent, and well-vouched feeling of dissatisfaction."[23] That, as I have indicated, is what we are dealing with here. It was evident in the ill-advised report of the Conference of State Chief Justices. "We believe," the chief justices said,

that strong state and local governments are essential to the effective functioning of the American system of federal government; that they should not be sacrificed needlessly to leveling, and sometimes deadening, uniformity; and that in the interest of active citizen participation in self-government—the foundation of our democracy—they should be sustained and strengthened.

Many people will agree wholeheartedly with this statement, and more should than will. Similarly, the committee that reported these proposed amendments to the Sixteenth General Assembly of the States, said:

[22] See F. Shanahan, "Proposed Constitutional Amendments," 49 *American Bar Association Journal* 631, 636, n. 4 (1963).
[23] Frankfurter, *op. cit.*

It is the ultimate of political ingenuity to achieve a vigorous federal system in which dynamic states combine with a responsible central government for the good of the people. Your committee is dedicated to this objective.

Again, many people share dedication to this objective. It is clear that the objective is in danger of being lost sight of in many quarters in Washington, not excluding the chambers of some Supreme Court justices.

This is not the place to discuss acts of commission and omission that are necessary to strengthen state government in this country. Moreover, most of these acts are not within the competence of the Supreme Court of the United States, and most past and present sins in this respect are not chargeable to the Supreme Court but to the other branches of our government, the two other federal branches, and to the states themselves. But the record of the Supreme Court is also not without blemish. I would call attention chiefly to decisions by the Court under the Supremacy Clause, especially in the field of labor relations, but in other areas of federal regulation as well, some of which have unnecessarily hampered or struck down concurrent state programs that were not really in conflict with federal policy. And I would note that not everyone is required to be entirely happy with the recent extension of federal supervision over the administration of criminal justice, rendering uniform—and not necessarily always more humane or liberal—the law as to the admissibility in evidence in criminal trials of the products of police searches and seizures.[24]

There is nothing more to be deprecated, wrote Holmes in 1921, than the use of the Fourteenth Amendment

to prevent the making of social experiments that an important part of the community desires, in the insulated chambers afforded by the several States, even though the experiments may seem futile or even noxious to me and to those whose judgment I most respect.[25]

And Brandeis, a decade later:

It is one of the happy incidents of the federal system that a single courageous State may, if its citizens choose, serve as a laboratory; and try novel social and economic experiments without risk to the rest of the country.[26]

The bright and hopeful idea of federalism carries the seed of change, of improvement, and of truly meaningful democracy. But you could not tell it by looking at our states today. We are, of course, a nation, and as a nation we carry responsibilities not only for defense and for general welfare but moral responsibilities. One cannot concede to the "insulated chambers" of the states experiments

---

[24] See Ker v. California, 374 U.S. 23 (1963).
[25] Truax v. Corrigan, 257 U.S. 312, 344 (1921).
[26] New State Ice Co. v. Liebmann, 285 U.S. 262, 311 (1932).

that are morally abhorrent to the nation, or the *fainéant* maintenance of islands of poverty and misery, rather than the "courageous" pursuit of a "novel" social or economic policy. Nor can we concede effective withdrawal from the pursuit of nationally adopted policies, any more than withdrawal from behind the nation's defense shield would be tolerated or is desired. But we might, nevertheless, heed the admonitions of Holmes and Brandeis. We might have a care that we do not exaggerate the requirements of uniformity inhering in national policy. And we might be more slow to regard our every value, or even every national consensus, as a moral imperative that can brook no deviation. The lines we are thus required to draw are extremely difficult and uncertain, and they may be disagreeable. But the system demands that they be drawn, even though we all tend to forget it when our particular ox happens to be badly gored. In their clumsy, improbable way, the three constitutional amendments put forward by the Council of State Governments mean to remind us.

SUGGESTIONS FOR FURTHER READING

There are a number of good general treatments of the Supreme Court as an institution; especially fine are Paul A. Freund, *The Supreme Court of the United States* (Cleveland, Ohio: World, 1961), John P. Frank, *The Marble Palace* (New York: Knopf, 1958), and Robert G. McCloskey, *The American Supreme Court* (Chicago: University of Chicago Press, 1960). Perhaps the best history of the Court presently available is Charles Warren, *The Supreme Court in United States History,* 2 vols. (Boston: Little, Brown, 1922).

On the development and consequences of the practice of judicial review, see Alan F. Westin's introduction to Charles A. Beard, *The Supreme Court and the Constitution* (Englewood Cliffs, N. J.: Prentice-Hall, 1962); Learned Hand, *The Bill of Rights* (Cambridge, Mass.: Harvard University Press, 1958); and Alexander M. Bickel, *The Least Dangerous Branch: The Supreme Court at the Bar of Politics* (Indianapolis, Ind.: Bobbs-Merrill, 1962).

Excellent work is now being done on the political setting of the Court. Representative of the best traditional research are Walter Murphy's *Congress and the Court* (Chicago: University of Chicago Press, 1962) and *Elements of Judicial Strategy* (Chicago: University of Chicago Press, 1964). Representative of the new quantitive work are the papers presented at the Shambaugh Conference on Judicial Research held at the University of Iowa in October 1967 and published under the editorship of Joel B. Grossman and Joseph Tanenhaus as *Frontiers of Judicial Research* (New York: Wiley, 1968).

Two further works on the Warren Court are also of interest: John P. Frank, *The Warren Court* (New York: Macmillan, 1964), and Alexander M. Bickel, *The Supreme Court and the Idea of Progress* (New York: Harper & Row, 1969).

For particular issues in constitutional law, see Harry Kalven, Jr., *The Negro and the First Amendment* (Chicago: University of Chicago Press, 1966), Martin Shapiro, *Law and Politics in the Supreme Court* (New York: Free Press, 1964), John P. Roche, *The Quest for the Dream: The Development of Civil Rights and Human Relations in Modern America* (New York: Macmillan, 1963), Leonard G. Miller, *Double Jeopardy and the Federal System* (Chicago: University of Chicago Press, 1968), and Bryce Rucker, *The First Freedom* (Carbondale, Ill.: Southern Illinois University Press, 1968).

A fine historical study of the political setting of the Court is Raoul Berger, *Congress versus the Supreme Court, 1957–1960* (Cambridge, Mass.: Harvard University Press, 1969). More wide-ranging recent works are Charles L. Black, Jr., *Structure and Relationship in Constitutional Law* (Baton Rouge, La.: Louisiana State University Press, 1969), and Edwin Lemert, *Social Action and Legal Change* (Chicago: Aldine, 1970).

An excellent source for articles on aspects of the Court's work is the annual *Supreme Court Review,* edited by Philip B. Kurland (Chicago: University of Chicago Press, 1960–69). Also useful is the review of the Court's work in the preceding term that appears each year in the November issue of the *Harvard Law Review.*

10 Intergovernmental relations

IN AN ESSAY PUBLISHED IN 1955,[1] which has since become a minor classic of political science literature, David B. Truman argued that the division of formal governmental responsibilities between the federal government and the states has been a powerful cause of the decentralization of our informal political structures. Thus, it is difficult to speak of national political parties in the United States; such as they are, they must be painfully recreated every four years for a presidential campaign. Because so many of the governmental services that immediately affect the people (such as police, schools, and sanitation) have traditionally been provided at the city and county levels, the tightest party organization has tended to form there, robbing state and national leadership of influence and power. Likewise, interest groups, which possess multiple points of access to national, state, and local governmental powers, have proliferated at all levels. Federalism and a multifarious, uncoordinated structure of political power are mutually reinforcing.

But, supposing our view of this relationship to be correct, what happens when one element begins to change? Certainly, changes in the distribution of formal governmental power have been taking place. Some have been incremental and almost unnoticed; others have been swift and highly visible.

The gradual changes have come about as a result of the increasing

[1] David B. Truman, "Federalism and the Party System," in Arthur MacMahon, ed., *Federalism Mature and Emergent* (Garden City, N.Y.: Doubleday, 1955).

incapacity of small governmental units to function effectively. Two hundred million of us have sprawled over the landscape with no regard for municipal or county or even state lines and jurisdictions. We have, as we have compacted and multiplied in great conurbations, developed needs for social services that simply cannot be provided on a small scale. For instance, we demand the most modern medical care, which can be made economical only by centralizing hospital facilities for the service of large populations. Obviously, a number of small community hospitals cannot provide the range of services and equipment that a lavishly funded central facility can afford. Many small operations do not, given the state of American technology, add up to one large operation. Also, the tax bases of small governmental units (usually the property tax) are spotty. One jurisdiction will have a lot of nice rateables but few people; another will have legions of families with three children but few industrial properties to contribute heavily to municipal coffers. Inevitably, demands come to be focused on the levels of government that have the constitutional authority to tax and regulate across large social and geographical sectors—that is, on states[2] and, especially, on the federal government. Problems are identified and described in nationwide terms, and national responses have come to be expected.

Over the years, cooperative arrangements have been worked out among federal, state, and local suppliers of social services in an effort to offset the increasing impracticality of the small operations. Morton Grodzins' essay in this chapter on the informal nationalization of police services is an excellent description of the process.

The more rapid and visible changes in the pattern of intergovernmental relations have resulted from our two most difficult domestic problems, poverty and race relations. The Economic Opportunity Act of 1964, for instance, provided for direct federal implementation of certain programs, bypassing existing state and municipal bureaucracies.[3] The traditional grant-in-aid approach (with federal funds administered by the states) was consciously eschewed in favor of new structures created at the request of the federal government.

In the area of race relations, the failure of state and local governments to meet their moral and legal responsibilities toward Negroes has resulted in an increasing willingness on the part of federal judges, politicians, and students of federalism to ignore long-standing assumptions concerning the scope of federal power. Such departures have been paralleled by reexaminations of the conventional constitutional wisdom regarding the extent to which states must be left free to conduct their own affairs. The second selection in this chapter, by Mark DeWolfe Howe, is a spirited argument for an alteration in the accepted understanding of federalism that would

---

[2] See James E. Connor and Richard E. Morgan, "The Governor and the Executive Establishment," in Chapter 11.
[3] See Roger H. Davidson, "The War on Poverty: Experiment in Federalism," *The Annals of the American Academy of Political and Social Sciences*, Vol. 385 (September 1969), pp. 1–13.

allow for more central power and less provincial autonomy. It is an argument that, as Howe correctly estimates, courts are finding more and more persuasive.

Whether these present and prospective changes in the distribution of formal power are of sufficient magnitude to produce changes in the informal structures (for example, stronger national political parties) is still unclear, but we are more than justified to be on the watch for them.

Sharing of Functions: The "National" Police System

MORTON GRODZINS

Police work is often considered an example *par excellence* of a "purely local" function. The evidence is quite the contrary. Here as elsewhere there exists the most intimate federal–state–local collaboration. Primary responsibilities over a wide range of police functions remain in state–local hands. But the federal government has carved out an extensive area of police activities. More fundamentally, there is hardly a local police force, however small and parochial it may be, that does not depend upon federal assistance in its day-to-day activities; and hardly a federal police activity that is not dependent upon local aid.

• • •

1. BACKGROUND FOR POLICE COOPERATION

Root causes for collaborative police activities are found in the nature of the American federal system. The individual criminal has become mobile. He may flee or fly across state boundaries, and he can plan a robbery in one state, execute it in another, dispose of his loot in a third, and look for sanctuary in a fourth. Criminal activities, moreover, tend like other forms of endeavor to evolve through handicraft to industrialized stages. Crime becomes organized into

FROM Morton Grodzins, "Sharing of Functions: The 'National' Police System," in Daniel J. Elazar, ed., *The American System*, pp. 89, 93–113, 121–24. © 1966 Rand McNally & Company, Chicago. Seventy-two footnotes have been deleted by permission of the publisher.

larger units, "mobs" or "syndicates" dividing territories into quasi-monopolistic units for the provision of prostitution, bootleg whiskey, gambling, narcotics, and stolen goods. Customers for such services exist everywhere, and the larger the population concentration, the greater the supply of consumption units. Where a natural market does not exist, the underworld, especially when organized and disciplined, can supply an artificial market. Here are found the more or less pure rackets: "protection" for restaurants, laundries, and garages; "leadership" for bogus unions; "services" to truckers, manufacturers, and others—all forms of blackmail to prevent threatened violence. Industrialized vice and industrialized racketeering readily and ordinarily cross state lines. The telephone, telegraph, and other modern modes of communication and transportation make control from central points feasible and easy. Operating members of the mobs, including specialists in violence, are moved from place to place as a measure of efficiency. Stolen goods, prostitutes, or narcotics can be produced on order from widely scattered places.

Many Law Enforcement Agencies

The response of the American governments to these and other crime control problems has been characteristically piecemeal. Local law enforcement units, as the Kestnbaum Commissions Advisory Committee on Law Enforcement remarked, are so numerous and so difficult to classify or describe that they cannot even be counted exactly. The total number of state and local police units is "approximately 39,000." They differ enormously in size and professionalization. More than 3,000 counties have elected sheriffs. Their offices may not even contain a typewriter; on the other hand, a sheriff's establishment may include a large staff and a considerable laboratory, and it may display a high degree of professional sophistication. The more or less independent police agencies include one-man constabularies (most of whom are part-time employees) in many of the nation's 20,000 townships. At the other extreme, the police department of New York City had (as of 1958) a budget exceeding $160 million and more than 23,000 employees, a force roughly equal to the entire field staffs of all federal law enforcement agencies. Each of the 50 states except Hawaii maintains a police unit, and they too vary widely in size, technical training, and the limits of their jurisdiction. In the majority of states, the state police are principally concerned with highway patrol even when formal jurisdiction extends over the full police power. Some states—New York and Texas, for example—assign state officers to a wide range of crime problems, maintain effective criminal identification laboratories, and carry on extensive training activities for local police forces.

There is a corresponding lack of neatness in the organization of police work within the national government. Enforcement responsibilities for criminal statutes are widely dispersed: there are at least 34 investigative and enforcement agencies in the federal government organized under 16 separate departments, commissions, and agencies. Since the Revenue Cutter Service was established in 1790 to control smuggling and to aid in the collection of taxes, federal law enforcement agencies have been characterized by limited jurisdiction. The separate agencies possess strong traditions of independence, and there is no federal mechanism to focus the activities of federal agencies (to say nothing of state and local ones) on general problems of law enforcement.

The Federal Bureau of Investigation is the largest national agency concerned with the enforcement of criminal laws and the one with the widest jurisdiction. In addition to responsibilities for enforcing the espionage, sabotage, and treason statutes, it is charged with maintaining more than 150 other federal criminal laws, including those covering kidnaping, bank robberies, extortion, and automobile thefts. Its "investigative jurisdiction" indeed extends to all matters in which the United States is, or may be, a party, but in practice it has simplified its work by not giving attention to matters specifically assigned by Congress to other agencies. A group of five Treasury Department agencies covers a wide and overlapping field of criminal law enforcement. (1) The Intelligence Unit of the Bureau of Internal Revenue has numerous responsibilities but specializes in the investigation of income tax frauds. (2) The Enforcement Division of the Alcohol Tax Unit is concerned with violations of several national firearms acts as well as liquor tax laws. (3) The Division of Investigation and Patrol of the Bureau of Customs has primary responsibility over illegal imports and exports (the Treasury's Coast Guard shares some of these responsibilities). (4) The Secret Service Division enforces counterfeiting and forgery laws, as well as a number of banking and related statutes, and also has the task of protecting the President and his family. (5) Finally, and of first importance, the Bureau of Narcotics is charged with enforcing all federal statutes aimed at controlling the use of narcotics and other harmful drugs.

Still other federal agencies have important law enforcement responsibilities. The inspection service of the Post Office is concerned with mail theft, fraudulent use of the mails, forgery of money and postal savings certificates, mailing of obscene matter, and other criminal acts related to the mails. The Border Patrol of the Immigration and Naturalization Service (Department of Justice) has as its duty prevention of unlawful entry of aliens and the apprehension of persons who are illegally resident in the country. Other agencies concerned with criminal law enforcement include the various branches of the Military Police, whose concern extends to military personnel off duty as well as to deserters and those "absent without leave"; the Food and Drug Administration of the Department of Health, Education, and Welfare, whose work centers on preventing the sale of misrepresented or poisonous materials; and branches of the Department of Agriculture concerned with plant and animal diseases, meat inspection, and pest control. Many other federal agencies have police authority that shades off from other regulatory or service functions.

Many Laws

The many law enforcement agencies must cope with a "spectacular increase in the number and types of functions delegated to American systems of criminal justice."

When Congress determined that kidnaping was a federal crime, a federal agency (the FBI) was assigned the task of enforcing the statute, and a new link of federal-state-local police collaboration was forged. If Congress had not made the determination, there would be one fewer item of interaction. If there were no state or local prohibition or alcoholic tax laws, there would be no moonshiners or bootleggers. The total increase in the work load of police forces is even more the consequence of state laws and local ordinances than it is of federal legislation. Roscoe Pound referred to this total development when he said that "of one hundred thousand persons arrested in Chicago in 1912, more than one-half were held for violation of legal precepts which did not exist twenty-five years before." A more recent estimate holds that ". . . the number of crimes for which one may be prosecuted has at least doubled since the turn of the century." The development of the national police system has in part been the consequence of the sheer increase in criminal law legislation.

Federal Criminal Legislation

The main body of criminal law is state law, and the administration of justice is largely in the hands of the state courts. The Constitution on its face provides limited crime control powers for the central government. They relate to treason and counterfeiting; piracy and felony on the high seas; and the law of nations. In addition, the Thirteenth Amendment gave Congress authority to enforce the prohibition of slavery; the Eighteenth Amendment provided concurrent authority to Congress for prohibiting "the manufacture, sale, or transportation of intoxicating liquors," and the Twenty-first Amendment left the national government with responsibility for aiding in the enforcement of prohibition in states with prohibition laws. In addition to these specific provisions, the national government is also authorized "to make all laws which shall be necessary and proper for carrying into execution" the powers granted to it, and this general authorization is the source of the largest fraction by far of federal criminal law. Thus Congress has made it a criminal offense to rob, destroy, or obstruct the mail (from the power "to establish post offices and post roads"); to evade taxes (from the power "to lay and collect taxes"); to obstruct interstate commerce by robbery or violence (from the power "to regulate commerce"). Federal criminal statutes are in some cases built upon a pyramiding of implied powers:

thus the Federal Bank Robbery Act of 1934 rests upon the national power to charter banks which in turn is implied from the power to regulate the currency.

Many federal criminal statutes, based upon the necessary and proper clause, are in fact aimed at aiding states in their police functions or substituting federal penalties in cases where state action has been ineffective. As early as 1890 a statute was aimed at assisting states to enforce their own prohibition laws. In 1900 Congress provided criminal penalties for anyone transporting in interstate commerce game killed in violation of a state law. In 1910 federal penalties were provided for those transporting a woman for immoral purposes in interstate or foreign commerce, and in 1919 for those transporting a stolen automobile across state lines.

Legislation of this nature reached a high point in the 1930's as a reaction to prohibition and its aftermath, the sensational kidnaping and murder of Charles A. Lindbergh, Jr., a series of spectacular bank robberies, and a gang massacre. (There was considerable debate over the possibility of a national police force to combat crime which, it was said, could not be dealt with by the states alone.) Federal criminal laws provided penalties for those using interstate commerce for kidnaping, bank robbery, stolen property, and extortion. Subsequent years saw this list further extended to such items as gambling devices and racketeering. Federal taxes, and penalties for their nonpayment, were utilized to control narcotics, firearms, and certain gambling operations.

Perhaps the most significant federal laws in direct aid of state and local police work are those covering fugitive felons and witnesses, and persons attempting to avoid custody or confinement after conviction. These statutes, among other things, make it a federal offense if a person crosses a state line ("to move or travel in interstate commerce") to avoid prosecution under state laws for murder, kidnaping, burglary, robbery, mayhem, rape, assault with a dangerous weapon, or extortion. Penalties range up to five years in prison and a $5,000 fine. No initial federal offense need be involved. The federal offense is simply the act of attempting to avoid state prosecution. This legislation was passed at the request of state and local law enforcement officers who have subsequently (1950) unsuccessfully attempted to have the statute broadened to cover all felonies.

The participation of the federal government in criminal law enforcement thus rests upon status (1) to punish antisocial conduct of distinctive federal concern, as in the case of treason; (2) to secure compliance with federal regulatory and tax programs; and (3) to supply penalties for specified criminal activities. In the last field, federal laws compensate for the ineffectiveness of, and bring aid to, state–local law enforcement efforts. To steal an automobile is to break a state law; to transport the stolen automobile across state lines is to break a federal law. This illustrates the complementary quality of federal and state criminal legislation. Their complete overlapping is illustrated in the case of robbery of a bank with federally insured deposits: here the single act is subject to both state and federal penalties. Whether complementary or overlapping, the mixture of laws inevitably leads to close collaboration among law enforcement officers. Collaboration, however, is by no means limited to those cases involving clear complementary or overlapping statutes. The mutual help relationship among federal, state, and local enforcement officers extends over the total area of their activity. There are in practice no "pure" federal or state or local fields of police work.

The states themselves have tried to overcome the disadvantages of limited geographical jurisdictions through interstate compacts and uniform laws. For example, the interstate compact for the supervision of parolees and probationers, enacted by all states except Alaska, facilitates capture of criminals who have violated the terms of their freedom and crossed state lines; the compact also encourages rehabilitation by permitting the supervised interstate movement of parolees and probationers. As the historians of the compact movement have remarked, "One of the most prominent uses to which the interstate compact has been put is crime control." Both the number of compacts, and the number of signatories, increase yearly. Uniform state statutes in the crime control field are even more numerous than compacts. Two organizations—The National Conference of Commissioners and Uniform State Law and the Drafting Committee of The Council of State Governments—are the chief avenues by which uniform crime control statutes are brought to state attention. The National Conference has recommended legislation since 1892; among crime control measures, its statute on securing attendance of out-of-state witnesses has been adopted by 48 jurisdictions; on narcotic control by 50; on criminal extradition by 45. The Drafting Committee of the Council of State Governments works closely with the National Conference, frequently recommending the latter's statutes, and itself develops texts of model acts and suggested interstate compacts. The efforts to achieve interstate cooperation or uniformity seem, on their surface, not to involve the federal government. In fact, federal crime control agencies often are the source of suggested uniform laws, and federal officials work in many drafting sessions of both the National Conference and the Drafting Committee. The federal government's involvement in interstate compacts is even more direct. Compacts require federal approval before becoming effective. In 1934 Congress gave a blanket advance approval to interstate compacts directed at the control of crime.

Uniform laws and interstate compacts work toward a national uniformity of criminal law procedures. Decisions of the Supreme Court have tended in the same direction. Since its 1932 decision in *Powell* v. *Alabama* the Court has scrutinized under the due process clause of the Fourteenth Amendment a continuously enlarging area of state criminal procedures. The Powell case held that due process was abrogated when illiterate defendants in a murder trial were denied the right to secure their own counsel. Due process has been abrogated in state criminal proceedings, according to subsequent Court decisions, in cases where police have physically coerced confessions, or where defendants have been unduly detained, confined incommunicado, moved from place to place during interrogation, or questioned for prolonged periods. Court decisions have also put limits on police search and seizures and, utilizing the equal protection clause, have invalidated criminal convictions when racial discrimination was evident in the selection of juries. Other manifestations of unfair trial have also been condemned.

The net effect of the Supreme Court's decisions on day-to-day police practices is difficult to gauge. A Court decision invalidating a coerced confession does not end police brutality. Yet some direct impact of Supreme Court rulings can certainly be found at the local scene; and indirect effects follow state statutes which are at least partially the consequence of Court decisions. The impact of the Court is by no means uniform with respect to states or to areas of police activity. And the major portion of criminal law administration remains relatively unaffected, either because of the slowness of states and localities to respond to Court decisions, or because of the deference of the Court to state authority, or because criminal procedures have been untested—and are perhaps untestable—under prevailing Court doctrine and practice. Nevertheless, the Supreme Court's decisions are clearly another nationalizing force in police work and criminal law administration.

The principal fabric of the national police system is not to be found in Supreme Court decisions or interstate compacts or uniform state legislation. It is not to be found in occasional sensational local clean-up campaigns or congressional investigations. The national police system is principally found in the support given each other by federal, state, and local officers who in common do the nation's job of law enforcement.

2. LOCAL DEPENDENCE ON NATIONAL SERVICES

Services-In-Aid

Local police units maintain their most continuous and important federal relationships with the FBI. The FBI national fingerprint file—containing in 1960 the classified prints of more than 150 million people—is the prime point of contact. Virtually every police force, as a matter of course, fingerprints all persons suspected of more than trivial offenses. The fingerprinting is done according to FBI instructions on FBI forms, and sets are routinely mailed to the FBI laboratory, using franked FBI envelopes. The FBI gives rapid service to localities in making identifications from the fingerprint records. Fingerprint identification in turn supplies to local police dossiers of a suspect's criminal career. Nothing is more satisfying to a local police officer than this service. It provides a quick means for establishing the existence of criminal history, confounding or confirming a given suspect's statements of prior lawfulness. Where only fingerprints are available at the local scene, the FBI service can supply descriptions of the persons concerned, their characteristic modes of work, places of residence, and, in many cases, their photographs.

The FBI also maintains extensive records of the handwriting specimens of known forgers and "cold check" passers, and a skilled staff for identifying new samples of forged and bad checks. Local police forces use this service continuously and as a matter of course; next to the fingerprint service it is perhaps the federal service-in-aid most frequently used by local units. The national FBI laboratory has special resources for the analysis and identification of many other sorts of evidence: these include ash from wood and other materials; restored printed matter from burned paper; blood and other stains; casts of shoe prints, heelprints, and tire treads; typewriting, printed matter, paper, watermarks on paper, and erasures and obliterations on paper; gunpowder stains; soil, toolmarks; wood, hair, and fibers; metal fragments; poisons; and bullets and cartridge cases. Through FBI publications and public relations programs, most local police officers know about the existence and utility of these services for the identification of criminal evidence. And through police training programs, largely directed or influenced by the FBI, there is widespread knowledge about the detection and preservation of evidence for transmittal to the FBI. Not only are the services widely known; the skills to make use of them are also widely dispersed.

Most large cities maintain their own criminal evidence laboratories and are less dependent upon national facilities than are smaller communities. Even the largest city nevertheless often finds records or data in Washington—for example, the extensive FBI file of tire treads—that are not available on the local scene. Private and university laboratories are also used by local police forces. Proximity gives them an advantage. But usually they demand a fee which local police are reluctant to pay in the light of the free services supplied by the FBI. A number of state police forces, whose leading personnel is likely to be composed of ex-FBI agents or those trained at the National Police Academy, also maintain fingerprint files and laboratory identification facilities. California, Massachusetts, Georgia, Texas, and Michigan have such establishments. Local officers, as a matter of state pride or speed, or out of friendship, often use these rather than national facilities. FBI services will still be used when the states' prove inadequate.[1] Despite overlapping and partially competing services, the FBI facilities are of utmost importance to local forces. They make possible a level of police work that, in the words of one local chief, would be "absolutely impossible with our own resources."

Local use of Washington Laboratory facilities is only one aspect of the

---

[1] The FBI, rather than state, criminal identification services may also be preferred merely for purposes of sheer window-dressing. Issues of greater efficiency need not be involved. A state prosecutor, for example, told an interviewer: "In a difficult case, it is nice to have an FBI rather than a state-police witness, and FBI rather than state exhibits." They would show exactly the same thing, he explained, "but the FBI label is impressive to a jury, and we need every bit of advantage that we can get." . . .

local dependence on federal services. On the local scene, whatever the size of the community or the particular criminal problems facing it, important local–federal relationships are almost certain to exist. For example, the police department of a rural area of Oklahoma or Arkansas may find that bootlegging and moonshining are among its most difficult police problems. If local police believe that whiskey is being illegally distilled, they will ask a Treasury Department investigator to look into the matter. (In a small town local officers may be so well known that they cannot do this sort of investigation.) The national officers will in many cases turn over their evidence to the local police chief. Where substantial amounts of illegal liquor are concerned, local and federal officers will collaborate in their investigation. Joint "raids" are commonplace.

The extent and kind of local–federal collaboration is largely dependent upon the sorts of problems facing local enforcement officers. Stolen cars in transit or for sale may plague an Ohio or California highway town, and this will lead to close, daily contacts with the FBI. Communities close to military installations find it necessary to work out detailed arrangements with military police units. It may be agreed, for example, that all drunks picked up by the Military Police will be turned over to the local police for detention and punishment; local police in return aid in tracking down deserters and those AWOL and will hold them in the local jail (even though no state laws are involved) until they can be transferred to the appropriate military installation. In other areas, special aid will be received from and given to the Border Patrol, or the Customs Service, or the Post Office inspector's office.

Crimes, like other aspects of life, follow fads and fashions, and a given community may find itself facing a "wave" of bank robberies or filling station holdups. The first sort of case almost certainly involves federal laws; the second does not. The significant point is that local and federal officers will work in common on both sorts of problems. Evidence against a bank robber may be developed by the local police and the suspect incarcerated by local officers. But the prisoner will be interrogated by a joint team of FBI agents and local officers, and an amiable agreement will be reached between state and federal prosecuting attorneys concerning the best jurisdiction in which to try the suspect. Despite the absence of federal legislation with respect to filling station robberies, the FBI will supply all sorts of technical aids to the local police, including descriptions of characteristic work habits of known filling station thieves. FBI personnel will be alerted to apprehend suspected persons.

In the event that the local police believe that a suspect has left the state (thus becoming a fugitive felon), the nationwide resources of the FBI are brought directly into play. The fleeing person is subject to arrest by federal agents throughout the country.[2] The fugitive felon warrant also results in the

---

[2] Though the suspect may be tried in a federal court for attempting to avoid arrest, he is usually returned to the state from which he fled, to be tried in a state court. If he is acquitted in this court for the felony originally suspected, federal prosecutors can get a "second crack" at him on the fugitive charge.

suspect's picture and description being distributed throughout the country to FBI agents, post offices, and local and state police forces. From the point of view of local police officers, the fugitive felon law makes their effective jurisdiction nationwide, "transforming all FBI agents in fact into a part of our local force," as one chief told an interviewer.

One way to summarize the interaction of local–federal police forces, and particularly the extent of local dependence on federal services, is by looking more closely at a single local police department. The chief of police in a midwestern city of approximately 50,000 population recently outlined the federal contacts of his force in the following terms: (1) The local force used the FBI fingerprint file daily. Prints of all persons arrested on criminal charges (and of all who applied for local police jobs) were sent routinely to Washington for reports. (2) On from ten to 15 occasions a month, cases involving bad checks and forgery made it advisable to send handwriting specimens for analysis to the FBI laboratories in Washington. (3) In the preceding 12 months, evidence on "from eight to a dozen cases" was sent for analysis and identification to the FBI laboratory. Evidence transmitted included casts of tires and shoes, and a blood-stained automobile seat. (4) FBI men visited the local police department two or three times a week "collecting information for their own uses." (5) Exchange of information on matters of mutual concern—with respect to narcotics, bootlegging, stolen mail, and stolen cars, for example—was "continuous" (6) Investigative work collaboratively carried on within the city was not uncommon, "but there is not much occasion for it here." ("We haven't had a bank robbery in many years.") (7) When crimes occurred in neighboring towns, outside the area of the local police radio system, the FBI notified the local police "as a matter of routine courtesy." (8) The relationship with local FBI activities was particularly close because one of the resident agents had formerly been a member of the local force, and "we're good friends." (Two members of the state police force were ex-officers of the local force, and this made for excellent state–local collaboration.) (9) The chief and his assistant were graduates of the (FBI) National Police Academy. (10) One local officer had recently been graduated from a special school operated by the Department's Bureau of Narcotics. (11) A number of local officers had attended a state-sponsored police training school, directed by an ex FBI agent. (12) Professional and social contacts with national police were also maintained through the state and international associations of chiefs of police. ("We don't only get speeches. At a recent state meeting, two Bureau men gave a demonstration of how to take a couple of bank robbers who had barricaded themselves in a home with a hostage.") (13) When the chief and several of his associates in neighboring towns established a special joint squad for vice and narcotics work, they were advised on matters of organization and technique by both FBI and Narcotics Bureau personnel.

This picture of continuous local–federal collaboration in police matters is duplicated in all parts of the country. In rural areas and in cities of fewer than 50,000 population dependence upon federal services from Washington is greater than it is for larger places. On the other hand, the larger the local unit, the more frequent the federal–local collaboration in actual investigative work on the local scene, and the more often do the local police use the federal fugitive warrant. In big cases—a bank robbery or kidnaping—police of all governments strive to organize their work as if they were a single unit, though interagency and interlevel conflicts over evidence and publicity may also occur. Where state police agencies are active and organized, exactly the same sort of close federal collaboration occurs.

• • •

3. LOCAL AID TO NATIONAL POLICE AGENCIES

Police collaboration, as we have indicated, does not go only in one direction. Dependence of national police agencies on local forces is as great as local dependence on national forces. The sheer preponderance of manpower resources at the local level largely accounts for this. There are an estimated 250,000 officers in local police forces; all the national enforcement personnel in the field do not total one-tenth this number. In a large city like Chicago, to take one example, federal enforcement agents must look to local officers for information and manpower assistance of all kinds. The Federal Bureau of Narcotics in 1955 had a total of 22 agents to cover the three states of Illinois, Wisconsin, and Indiana; at this time the Chicago police force alone had 60 persons detailed to narcotics work. Federal agents daily examined files in the Chicago bureau, looked to Chicago police officers for detailed reports on narcotics sales and consumption (the sort of information available only to those with intimate knowledge of the local situation), and heavily depended upon local personnel in raids and arrests.

With respect to such matters as stolen automobiles in interstate commerce, federal officers (in this case from the FBI) must rely even more heavily on local police. Full-time federal officers assigned to the recovery of stolen cars are few in number. In contrast, big city police forces maintain specialized, stolen car details and, in fact, the total personnel of local forces is involved in the recovery of stolen cars. The stolen auto division of a local department routinely receives from the FBI descriptions of automobiles stolen in other states. This information is logged as a part of the local record system while, simultaneously, advice is also received on every automobile involved in every recorded local crime. In the nature of the situation, the preponderant number of stolen automobiles that are recovered, including those that have moved in interstate commerce, are turned up by local police. If the individuals apprehended with stolen interstate automobiles cannot be charged with more serious crimes, they are turned over to federal authorities for prosecution under United States law for transporting the cars across state lines. In any case, a stolen car in interstate traffic can be labeled "recovered." As one former FBI agent remarked, "The statistics of FBI recoveries of stolen automobiles in interstate traffic are largely statistics testifying to local assistance given to the federal agency in this matter."

In a very similar manner, federal law enforcement officers must look for local aid in the control of prostitution, bootlegging, counterfeiting, mail thefts, illegal immigration, and other matters. A concomitant of the local force's larger personnel is an intimate knowledge of local conditions. In a big city, for example, a local officer in a prostitution detail "can tell pretty rapidly when new girls are being imported into the city—because he knows all the local prostitutes pretty well." Frequently rotated federal officers rarely have this sort of insider's view of local conditions. As for smaller places, a single FBI agent may be the only federal law enforcement officer on the scene and he may have to "cover" a half-dozen communities. He will drop by the local police station once or twice a week. His dependence upon local police for information concerning federal crimes is well nigh complete.

· · ·

The flow of information from local to federal agencies covers matters over which local police have no concurrent jurisdiction. The FBI, for example, has extensive responsibilities for enforcing statutes with respect to espionage and sabotage and for the collection of loyalty-security dossiers on government workers as well as workers in defense-related industries. Precise information concerning investigations of this type is not readily available. Yet local police forces are obviously a prime source of information for individuals under investigation by the FBI. Some local officers complain about the fraction of their time taken by FBI agents asking questions and searching for records about individuals who, as far as the local police are concerned, are "clean" and in some cases outstanding citizens. One chief in a small town estimated that the FBI agent who visited him regularly about such matters "must spend at least half of his time in this town—and must collect more than half of the information he gets here—right in my office." Considerations of jurisdictional niceties have little place in the national police system.

4. THE SYSTEM IN OPERATION

The national police system is not adequately described in terms of mutual aid rendered by local and federal officers in discharge of others' duties. In actual practice, when the law enforcement agents work together, they do so virtually as if there were no distinctions among them. Unified by a common task, they work in unity. The area of narcotics control provides a convenient example.

Narcotics Control

All states, as well as the federal government, provide criminal penalties for the unauthorized possession or sale of narcotics. In addition, a number of state laws and local ordinances make it illegal to be "under the influence" of narcotics. Great publicity has been given the detrimental effects of narcotic addiction and the criminal acts performed by addicts seeking money to buy narcotics. Peddlers have become a prime target of congressional investigation and public distaste, especially for their alleged distribution of the drugs to persons of high school age. There exists throughout the country a high public and police interest in the control of narcotics.

Many branches of government act in concert, though not always without friction, to control the sale of narcotics and narcotics addiction. Collaboration exists at the minor points of the control system, as well as at the most important ones. To take an example involving governmental units not usually considered in the network of control, federal customs officers, patrolling a section of the Mexican border, wished to concentrate their efforts on persons attempting to smuggle narcotics into the United States. The federal agents could not deal adequately with addicts "under the influence of" narcotics, people who in effect were internally transporting narcotics across the border. On the advice of the federal officers, the California county in which the principal United States–Mexican border station was located passed an ordinance imposing severe penalties for those under the influence of narcotics. Subsequently, federal customs officials simply turned over to the county sheriff all persons returning from Mexico under the influence of narcotics. "Many persons have been so prosecuted and sentenced to jail for their violations." The arrangement allowed the customs officers to concentrate their full attention on searching for narcotics peddlers.

Those centrally concerned with narcotics control, the Federal Bureau of Narcotics and the local police departments, also collaborate closely and in the process bring other agencies into the scheme of control. In Seattle, Washington, the chief of police said that "members of the . . . Police Department Narcotics Squad and the Federal Bureau of Narcotics work very closely together . . . the main objective being to make cases against these people (addicts and peddlers) regardless of who initiates them, and in most cases both (federal and state officers) work on them." The Seattle district office of the Food and Drug Administration, the state Board of Pharmacy, and the local Board of Health were also involved in enforcing narcotics statutes. An effective liaison and division of labor were achieved. At the request of the district supervisor of the Federal Bureau of Narcotics, for example, the state Pharmacy Board had "taken over almost all investigations which involve drugstores, hospitals, nursing homes, forged prescriptions. . . . This leaves more of . . . [the federal] men free to investigate illegal imports and actual peddlers." The cooperation and especially the exchange of information proved "invaluable to both departments." The same sort of relationship was worked out with the federal Food and Drug Administration in the control of barbiturates. "Cases which involve only Washington state laws have been turned over to us by the Food and Drug Administration, and those cases which involve interstate shipments have been referred by us to them."

The United States Commissioner of Narcotics has for some years encouraged and aided local police departments of larger cities in establishing special units for the control of narcotics. More than two dozen cities have adopted this suggestion, including Chicago, which established a Narcotics Bureau in 1950. By 1955 the Bureau had grown to a force of 60 men (New York's force numbered 200). Specialized squads of this sort maximize points of collaboration between local and equally specialized federal officers. The officer in charge of the Chicago Narcotics Bureau has testified that "The United States Bureau of Narcotics and the Narcotics Bureau of the Chicago Police Department have worked in close cooperation on many investigations, arrests, and prosecutions and, in particular, on cases involving major violators." The District Supervisor of the Bureau of Narcotics has echoed this statement: "The cooperation between [the Chicago Narcotics Bureau] and the Federal Bureau of Narcotics has been 100 per cent. We work on most cases together and if he (Lt. Healy, in charge of the Chicago squad) runs into an interstate trafficker, before he even investigates he will call our office and we will figure out ways and means in which to build up a better and stronger case against the alleged violator." The Chicago police provide the federal bureau with records of every local narcotics arrest. Contacts between the two groups are continuous and intimate. Local and federal officers frequently act together in making raids. Federal funds are often used by the local police to make "buys" of narcotics in the process of building up evidence for an arrest. If the local police inadvertently arrest an addict who turns out to be a paid informer for the federal agency, the local police turn him over to their federal colleagues (whether or not a federal offense is immediately involved), mark the case "closed," and do not concern themselves with what dispositions the federal agency makes of the prisoner.

· · ·

6. CONCLUSION

Strains in the federal–state–local police system—whether within or among governments—are strains of propinquity. They are products of closeness, not of distance. They arise out of many groups working together. They are publicized because they are departures from expected, usual standards. They are evidences of rivalry, ill-will, and cross-purposes within vastly more important and more pervasive evidences of amity and collaboration.

Modern technologies produce criminal activities that in no way correspond to the jurisdictional boundaries of the many local, state, and federal law enforcement units. Moreover, criminal activities do not correspond to the specialized tasks assigned to a particular unit: a narcotics addict may rob a bank, a bank robber may murder, and a murderer may also be a confidence artist. The task of the many enforcement agencies is to produce a total system of law enforcement surmounting jurisdictional boundaries as well as the non-geographical boundaries of specialized missions. The task is one of enforcing laws that grow more and more numerous and that continuously add to the kinds of acts labeled "criminal." Finally, it is the task of surmounting the parochialism, jealousies, and suspicions of workers at all "levels" and in different units of government.

We have seen the police of the many American governments attempt to accomplish these tasks through a well institutionalized system of mutual help. The total network of police relationships produces nationwide standards of professionalization—of conduct and effectiveness. It produces friendships that easily bridge the accidental fact that officers draw salaries from different "levels' of government. Widely accepted professional standards, the easy working together of colleagues, and the sharing of information and problems among friends are both evidence and cause of the national police system. They are often symbolized in the bare offices of local police chiefs: the most notable objects are frequently an autographed photograph of J. Edgar Hoover and a diploma certifying graduation from the National Police Academy.

National agencies are undoubtedly responsible for establishing standards of organization and conduct. They are dominant in training programs and in scientific crime detection. National standards exist for everything from state laws to the desirable public relations activities of a local chief. The Bureau of Narcotics defines heroin addiction and the FBI's *Law Enforcement Bulletin* (circulated "confidentially" to some 8,000 state and local forces) offers authoritative advice on the proper organization of police files. National standards are recognized for all phases of criminal investigation, and FBI forms and categories produce whatever uniformity there exists for reporting and publishing criminal statistics. It may even be said that national agencies provide many effective definitions of crime itself. Within the wide ambit of what the statutes define as criminal behavior (and the statutes themselves are crucially affected by professional opinion), police emphasis winnows out the effective definition: that behavior which is in fact punished. Mr. Hoover, for example, has great resources—through speeches, magazine and newspaper articles, radio and television appearances, congressional testimony, and training programs—to influence police forces throughout the country so that they will give greater attention to, say, the sale of narcotics than to highway homicides, to juvenile delinquency than to homosexuality.

If the cues for police action come from national bureaus and national leaders, action on most criminal law fronts remains in the hands of locally selected police. They possess the widest jurisdiction in law, and they possess the preponderant manpower. Local officers are not unaware of their dependence on national agencies. Neither are they unaware of their own independent status. One police chief said: "I use the FBI every day. But only at my own initiation. J. Edgar Hoover is a great cop. But he has no control over me. If he came into this office tomorrow and asked me to do something I did not want to do, there would be nothing to prevent me from booting the great Edgar out the door." This independence exists in law. In fact, however, over most of the country, police standards of the national bureau have become nationally accepted standards. A local officer follows the edicts of Mr. Hoover not because he has been told to—certainly not because in law he has to—but because Mr. Hoover's standards are almost always his own.

Universal adoption of common professional standards is handicapped by a number of factors, principally that some communities will not tolerate complete law enforcement and many local police forces are small, unspecialized, and financially underprivileged. Officers in some small towns still utilize the published roster of National Academy graduates (and of the Association of Former Special Agents of the FBI) before asking aid of other local forces whose members are unknown. "If I can find someone on the roster," one chief explained, "I know that I can get competent help and that the crook I am chasing won't be tipped off by some dishonest cop." This procedure, however, is rarely necessary in most parts of the country.

The "single bad egg in the case" can be more prejudicial to police work than to most other administrative operations; yet an officer in one community can with increasing confidence expect a professional response to his request from other localities. The training programs in Washington and in the field, with their secondary and tertiary consequences of students becoming teachers, are one strong factor in the direction of molding a single group of professionals. The routine of frequently working together on cases, and of exchanging information, has the same effect, and the easy transferability of personnel also cements unity: an FBI agent will have previously worked on a local police force; or the local chief will have had experience in one of the federal agencies. All this not only establishes the standards of law enforcement as such. It also produces definitions of what a "proper" policeman should be, personally and technically, and it ties the police forces of the country together into a single group, some sharing a common alma mater but a far larger number sharing definitions of the desirable and the proper.

Professional ties are cemented through an elaborate and extensive network of police organizations. The group of top local leaders—the International Association of Chiefs of Police—usually has J. Edgar Hoover as the principal speaker at its annual meetings. State organizations of chiefs and groups such as the Fraternal Order of Police are meeting places for the exchange of ideas without regard for whether they come from local, state, or federal officers. Such meetings produce a camaraderie that transcends allegiances to a particular "level" of government. The range of such contacts is enormous. Federal officers will take a prominent role in the horseshoe pitching match at the annual fish fry sponsored by the local Fraternal Order of Police in a small midwestern town. Communion breakfasts provide a different sort of tie in a large New England city. The Attorney General's occasional Crime Control Conference and other meetings sponsored by federal agencies bring together leaders of all police systems for sociability as well as consideration of professional problems.

The evidence suggests that professional contacts often lead to personal ones. Despite inevitable points of tension, the very character of police work leads police officers of all governments to regard themselves generally as friends, as well as colleagues. Local and federal officers may habitually lunch or dine with each other. They may play bridge and poker and go fishing together. They and their wives may see each other at parties. In this milieu collaboration in professional matters is easy and natural, not even subject to special consideration. Local officers, on matters of particular federal interest, and federal officers, even where no national laws are involved, work together because, as one former FBI agent said, "We all work on the same side of the street, and we all know and like each other pretty well."

Federalism and Civil Rights

MARK DE WOLFE HOWE

Ninety-four years ago the junior Senator from Indiana addressed the conscience of the Nation when he discussed the course which untamed violence had recently taken in the South:

It is a reproach to the Republic and a confession of its failure as a Government, that such things may occur, not once or occasionally, as might happen under the best Government, but habitually and for months in succession.... Where, today, in any government laying claim to be a civilized one, are such outrages enacted with impunity as are borne to us on every breeze which comes from the South?[1]

FROM Mark DeWolfe Howe, "Federalism and Civil Rights," in Archibald Cox, Mark DeWolfe Howe, and J. R. Wiggins, *Civil Rights, the Constitution, and the Courts* (Cambridge, Mass.: Harvard University Press, 1967), pp. 31–55. Copyright, 1967, by the Massachusetts Historical Society. Reprinted by permission of the publishers.
[1] Remarks of Senator Pratt, April 6, 1871, *Congressional Globe,* 42nd Cong., 1 Sess., p. 504.

The southerlies are still blowing. They have told us of the killing of Medgar Evers, William Moore, James Reeb, Andrew Goodman, James Chaney, Michael Schwerner, Lemuel Penn, Viola Liuzzo, and Jonathan Daniels. They brought us the names of others, but those others we have forgotten because they were merely four little children at church in Birmingham. The breezes from the South have told us these ugly tales, but they have not spoken of convictions of the guilty. They tell us, instead, of murders, acquittals, mistrials, and local pride.

My purpose here is not to arouse your indignation. The task which I have set myself is that of identifying and comprehending the concept which, above all others, has served to incapacitate the Nation's conscience. I mean, in other words, to look rather closely at certain aspects of American federalism—at elements in constitutional history that seem to me to have been overlooked. The inquiry, I fear, will lead me into that forest which frightens and repels so many Americans—even American historians—the dark woodlands of American legal history. I cannot, however, conceal my conviction that the shape of our moral expectations, like the structure of our political capacities, has been much affected by the legal setting in which the expectations were born and bred.

The story that concerns me begins with the familiar pronouncement of Lord Mansfield, uttered on the King's Bench in 1772: "The state of slavery . . . is so odious, that nothing can be suffered to support it, but positive law."[2] This emancipating dictum was, of course, woven into a confused pattern of contradictory traditions and practices. One tradition (or was it merely a slogan?) asserted that "England was too pure an air for slaves to breath in."[3] Yet imperial Britain was quite willing to encourage the slave trade between Africa and her American plantations, and English courts of common law were quite ready to respect the positive law of any colony that chose to establish or to uphold slavery. Surely it is not surprising that the American heirs of such a confused tradition could in southern plantations maintain, and in northern colonies disclaim, the institutions of slavery. In these matters, as in many other aspects of our social order, it is important to remember that in the house of Anglo-American law there have been many mansions. At the close of the eighteenth century, English and American lawyers found nothing strange in a pronouncement that while the common law of England and the law of nature condemn slavery, positive law and the law of nations sustain it.

This pluralistic character of the laws of England was not unimportant to the Justices of the Supreme Judicial Court of Massachusetts when they came in 1783 to consider the status of slavery in the Commonwealth. Much has been written on the Quock Walker case, and of the charge delivered to the jury by Chief Justice Cushing.[4] Acknowledging that slavery had been countenanced

---

[2] The Case of James Sommersett, 20 How State Trials 2, 82 (1772).

[3] Quoted in Catterall, *Judicial Cases concerning American Slavery and the Negro* (Washington, 1926), I, 1.

[4] See, e.g., John D. Cushing, "The Cushing Court and the Abolition of Slavery in Massachusetts," *American Journal of Legal History*, 5 (1961), 118.

by provincial statute, Cushing emphasized that it had never been expressly brought into being by legislative action and that it had no firmer sanction than that of usage. Whether or not the Chief Justice thought that custom and usage constituted "positive law" within the meaning of that phrase as Lord Mansfield had used it, we do not know. In any case, the Chief Justice was unwilling to let the institution survive under a Constitution that proclaimed equality and promised liberty. I might add that Wendell Phillips and Lemuel Shaw seem to me to have spoken quite accurately when they asserted that Lord Mansfield's dictum with respect to the dependency of slavery upon positive law made usage and custom no less effective instruments for sustaining the infamous institution than did statutes.[5]

This pluralistic inheritance has, I believe, a greater significance in American constitutional history than has commonly been recognized. Statesmen and scholars have often called our attention to the awkward and embarrassed circumlocutions by which the framers of the Federal Constitution made reference to the ugly fact of slavery. An anonymous pamphleteer in 1819 wrote of "that policy of virtuous shame which sought to shadow our internal condition in a constitution destined for the study and admiration of the world." [6] What the commentator had in mind, of course, were those coward's clauses that dared not speak of slaves but spoke instead of persons "held to service or labor" and, with something less than candor, contrasted "free persons," not with Negro slaves, but with "all other persons." [7] I have no doubt that the desire to shadow our shame from European inspection played some part in these evasions. I think that it is clear, however, that they were also designed by the lawyers to fit the law of the Constitution to the law that Lord Mansfield has so recently proclaimed. If slavery gets its life from positive law—from constitution, statute, custom, or usage—it was important to those who longed for the institution's early end that the Constitution should say nothing that would give it "positive" endorsement. It was no less unlikely that the foes of slavery would accept a document that provided explicit sanctions for safeguarding and preserving the institution than that South Carolina and Georgia would ratify a Constitution that contemplated its outlawry by national authority. What the Nation needed, accordingly, was what the Nation had inherited—a British pluralism in law if not in morals—a tolerance sufficiently generous to allow slavery in the South and permit abolition in the North.

One word more is needed, I fear, if I am to set the scene for the later events of our constitutional history. You will remember that English aphorisms with respect to freedom have, in one form or another, reiterated the principle that the common law of England is so permeated by the spirit of liberty as to

---

[5] Phillips, *Review of Lysander Spooner's Essay on the Unconstitutionality of Slavery* (Boston, 1847), pp. 84–85; Shaw, C. J., in Commonwealth v. Aves, 18 Pick. 193, 212 (1836).
[6] *Free Remarks on the Spirit of the Federal Constitution, the Practice of the Federal Government, and the Obligations of the Union Respecting the Exclusion of Slavery from the Territories and New States by a Philadelphian* (Philadelphia, 1819), p. 20.
[7] Art. IV, Sec. 2, paragraph 3; Art. I, Sec. 2, paragraph 3.

make slavery intolerable. If that common law is our inheritance, as the founding patriots constantly asserted it to be, how can the Nation's government at once preserve the inheritance and the slavery? The classic answer, being technical, is not wholly satisfying, but it must, I fear, be accepted. It consists in the reminder that there is no common law of the United States. The law of the Nation contains no other elements than those provided by the Constitution and by the statutes enacted by the Congress. This classic principle is important for my present purpose, because it underlines the fact that if the Constitution and statutes of the Nation before the Civil War preserved a deep and silent neutrality with respect to slavery, there was no other law of the Nation that could speak to the issue that divided the minds and the hearts of the American people.

This analysis suggests that the shame that shadowed our condition was the by-product of British pluralism—the consequence of a system of law ingeniously designed to allow the survival of an institution that the King's justices in some circumstances sustained, but in all circumstances branded a violation of the law of nature and intolerable by the standards of the common law. While our federalism embraced enough of this disorder in principle to permit South Carolina to have her slavery and Massachusetts her freedom, our Federal judges were denied the consoling jurisdiction of the common law—the capacity occasionally to circumvent a positive law of servitude by enforcing a common law of freedom. This Nation's commitment to silence on the largest issue that confronted the American people was at once a distinctive and a startling contribution to the art of government. Though war, constitutional amendments, and economic revolution have vastly altered the structure and the content of American law, the old commitment to national silence and national disability still serves to make American federalism a significant impediment to the fulfillment of civil rights.

In what I have said of the constitutional commitment to incapacity I am afraid that I have given too much attention to the role of judges. The decision of the framers of the Constitution that the domestic destiny of slavery was to be in the hands of the States and not in those of the Nation meant, of course, that the Congress should not by positive law sustain slavery, or by negative law end it. I have sometimes wondered whether the framers might not most accurately have expressed their determination to keep the congressional hands off all problems of slavery by adopting a provision modeled upon the neutralities of the First Amendment—a provision stating, in effect, that "Congress shall make no law establishing slavery or prohibiting the enslavement of Negroes." Some such prohibition as that would, I believe, have made explicit the tacit negations of the Constitution. It would have served to accentuate the conviction of the framers that if the Nation should seek to deal either sympathetically or antagonistically with the institution of slavery the frail bonds of union would burst apart.

May I pause in my hurried passage through time to call your attention to the peculiar brand of federalism which these silences and disabilities brought into being? We generally suppose that the central problems of federalism concern the relationships that prevail between the Nation and the States— that the crucial issues in making the constitution of a Federal society effective relate to defining the scope of national and State power. Classic examples of such issues I should take to be the determination of the range and significance of congressional power to regulate commerce among the several States, and the definition of the limits of the States to tax instrumentalities of the Federal government. To cite those examples is to dramatize the very different character of the issue of federalism as it related to the institution of slavery. Starting with the dominant presupposition that the Nation had no power of any sort to touch the institution of domestic slavery, the American courts soon discovered that problems of federalism as they bore on slavery did not concern the relationships of States to Nation but the relationships of States to one another. Could South Carolina imprison free Negroes serving as seamen on Massachusetts vessels in Charleston?[8] Could Massachusetts give freedom to slaves who were brought by their masters from Louisiana to enjoy a cool summer in the Bay Commonwealth?[9] There being no Federal common law of freedom and no congressional positivism establishing slavery, there was simply a conflict of laws to be resolved in the courts of the several States, and a conflict of principles to be resolved by the churches throughout the land. The Nation's judges, the Nation's legislators were powerless to resolve either of those conflicts.

Doubtless the learned minds of some of my readers are troubled by my failure, so far, to say anything of the implications in those evasive phrases in Article Four that dealt with fugitive slaves. This ingenious circumlocution of the framers deserves quotation: 'No person held to service or labor in one State, under the laws thereof, escaping into another, shall, in consequence of any law or regulation therein, be discharged from such service or labor, but shall be delivered up on claim of the party to whom such service or labor may be due." If you look behind the shadows cast by those shamefaced words you will see the commitment that came to outrage the abolitionists—the assurance that the United States Constitution saw masters of men as owners of property. If we ask ourselves whether the constitutional assurance with respect to fugitive slaves provided that sort of recognition of slavery by positive law which Mansfield said sufficed to sustain it, our answer, I fear, will depend upon our moral presuppositions. On its face the provision seems to reflect one supposition— the assumption that issues with respect to the rendition of fugitive slaves must be resolved by interstate arrangements. Nothing in the language of the provision quoted from Article Four suggests that the Congress was empowered to impose duties upon the custodian of the fugitive to restore him to his master. Every

---

[8] See Elkison v. Deliesseline, 1 Brunner 431; Fed. Cas. No. 4366 (1823).
[9] Commonwealth v. Aves, 18 Pick. 193 (1836).

settled principle of interpretation supports the thesis of Charles Sumner and Chancellor Walworth that the fugitive-slave clause of the Constitution, in the eyes of the framers, was to find its enforcement in the good faith of the States and not in the strong arm of the Nation.[10] The provision, in other words, reflected the basic constitutional assumption that I have emphasized—the supposition that the destiny of slavery within and between the States was to be determined by their law and not by the laws of the United States.

The Congress in 1793 and the Supreme Court in 1842 rejected the constitutional thesis that Sumner urged in his day and that I once more support as well-grounded. The Second Congress in February, 1793, adopted An Act Respecting Fugitives from Justice and [Respecting] Persons Escaping from the Service of Their Masters[11]—a statute which had a somewhat surprising and tragic career when it came into the hands of the judges. The statute's first sections—those which dealt with fugitives from justice—were held by Chief Justice Taney to subject the officials in the state of refuge to no other than moral obligations to surrender the fugitive.[12] Yet a majority of the Court, with Taney concurring, held in *Prigg* v. *Pennsylvania* that the sections of the statute that dealt with fugitive slaves not only were constitutional but subjected those persons who sheltered fugitive slaves to a legal obligation to restore them to their owners.[13]

I will not put your patience to the strain of following the details of an argument that seems to me to sustain Sumner's thesis that the congressional effort to require the rendition of fugitive slaves was unconstitutional. Lawful or unlawful, the power was exercised and it was sustained. In that exercise of power the Congress broke the silence which the framers had endeavored to guarantee. A positive law sustaining one aspect of slavery had been enacted by the Congress and had been so interpreted by the Court as to involve the planting of the seeds of a new nationalism. From that first and almost casual endorsement of slavery there grew, of course, the searing controversies of the 1840's and '50's with respect to the rendition of Anthony Burns, Thomas Sims, and all the other refugees from slavery.

One element in this chapter from the history of the relationships between federalism and civil rights deserves special emphasis. I have suggested that the constitutional offense which the Congress committed in 1793—and which the Court endorsed in 1842—was its creation of a Federal obligation to fulfill a responsibility which the Constitution had left in the exclusive jurisdiction of the States. Let me remind you once more of certain language in the section of Article Four that deals with fugitive slaves. "No person held to service . . .

---

[10] Charles Sumner, "Freedom National; Slavery Sectional," *Works of Sumner* (Boston, 1871), III, 95, 147 *et seq.*; Walworth, C., in Jack v. Martin, 14 Wendell 507, 524, 525–528 (1835).
[11] 1 Stat. 302.
[12] Kentucky v. Dennison, 24 How. 66 (1861).
[13] Prigg v. Pennsylvania, 16 Peters 539 (1842).

in one State, . . . escaping into another, shall, *in consequence of any law or regulation therein,* be discharged from such service." No one who is willing to accept the supremacy of the Federal Constitution over State law could, I take it, seriously question the unconstitutionality under this provision of any State statute that purported to emancipate fugitive slaves. Using the language of today's constitutional law one can accurately assert that the provision in Article Four that I have quoted deals with and prohibits State action. Despite that fact, when the Second Congress in 1793 adopted its statute on fugitive slaves, it showed no hesitation to impose criminal liability upon private persons who hindered the rendition of fugitives. In *Prigg* v. *Pennsylvania* the Supreme Court found no great difficulty in legitimating the congressional control of private action that served to frustrate claims of slaveholders and prevent the State of refuge from fulfilling its constitutional responsibilities.[14]

The Court's determination in the Prigg case that nothing in the Federal structure of our government precludes the Congress from fully safeguarding private rights derived from the Constitution seems to me wholly unexceptionable. To say that, however, is not to endorse the Court's accompanying decision that the Congress was empowered to enact positive law in support of slavery. The recognition of that power constituted, in my judgment, the repudiation of a studied and elaborate effort of the framers to produce a national authority that on one matter should be voiceless. Perhaps Justice Story and his associates had come to believe that the effort of the framers had been born in innocence and had been nurtured in false hope and, therefore, could no longer be permitted to govern the Nation's destiny. The decision, however, that slavery henceforth would be sustained not merely by interstate comity but by national authority brought an end to the old federalism—the close of the era of silence and disability.

If constitutional law had terminated with *Prigg* v. *Pennsylvania,* scholars and lawyers could confidently assert that there is nothing in the nature of American federalism that disables the Congress from controlling private conduct affecting the civil rights of others. Yet after a Civil War that preserved the Union, after constitutional amendments that abolished slavery, promised equal protection of the laws to Negroes, and specifically empowered Congress to make the assurances of the amendments effective, we find ourselves somehow committed to the doctrine that American federalism outlaws congressional legislation directed against private acts of violence that are designed, through terror, to frustrate the fulfillment of the Nation's promise. Let me now try to trace a few neglected strands in the unhappy progression from pre-War power to post-War impotence.

When the Congress proposed and the States ratified the Thirteenth Amend-

---

[14] Daniel Webster, in 1850, expressed doubts concerning the Court's willingness to find constitutional justification for congressional control of private action in a prohibition of State action. See *Works of Daniel Webster* (Boston, 1856), V, 354.

ment, the people announced their decision that slavery should no longer exist in the United States.[15] Experience had taught us that a nation cannot avoid the responsibility of decision—that the dream of the framers that somehow the United States need make no commitment for or against slavery was shattered. It seemed wise, therefore, not only that there should be a constitutional outlawry of slavery, but that Congress should be explicitly empowered to make the outlawry totally effective. The second section of the Thirteenth Amendment provided, accordingly, that the Congress should have power to enforce the constitutional prohibition.

Within a few months after the amendment became effective, the Congress, exercising the powers thus newly conferred upon it, adopted the Civil Rights Act of 1866.[16] The statute, passed over the veto of Andrew Johnson, was written by men who were thoroughly familiar with the old problems of law to which I have directed your attention—the problems, that is, that Lord Mansfield had endeavored to resolve in 1772 and that American judges had wrestled with for nearly a century. Had the slavery that was now being overthrown been born of common law, of international law, of custom, or of usage? Whatever its sources might have been the Congress wanted to make sure that the institution and the badges of inferiority with which it had degraded the Negro should be wholly eradicated. Accordingly the equality act of 1866 in its first section decreed that Negro citizens of the United States should henceforth be entitled to the same rights with respect to property, contracts, and inheritance that were enjoyed by white citizens. This assurance was explicitly to be made effective notwithstanding "any law, statute, ordinance, regulation, or custom to the contrary." The second section of the statute went on to make it a criminal offense for any person "under color of any law, statute, regulation, or custom" to deprive anyone of the rights of equality guaranteed by the first section.

Read in the context of the pluralism that I have described, the meaning of these statutory prohibitions takes on, I believe, a very different significance from that which they have generally been given. The Congress was not, I suggest, seeking to make it a Federal offense for State officials to deny equality of rights to Negro citizens. Instead, it was seeking to make it a crime for private persons, acting under the aura of a system outlawed by the Thirteenth Amendment, to persist in their discriminatory ways. Before emancipation no one who held Negroes in slavery had been able, with confidence, to say whether or not the holding was by virtue of law or by virtue of custom. A Congress that was anxious to prohibit the anticipated effort of white Southerners to keep alive their old advantages quite naturally supposed that it could undercut that effort by saying that those who denied equality under color of local laws or local

---

[15] "Section 1. Neither slavery nor involuntary servitude, except as a punishment for crime whereof the party shall have been duly convicted, shall exist within the United States, or any place subject to their jurisdiction." "Section 2. Congress shall have power to enforce this article by appropriate legislation."

[16] 14 Stat. 27.

customs that the Nation had now, in its new positivism, repudiated would be guilty of crime.

Many of you will remember that Andrew Johnson's unsuccessful veto of the equality act of 1866 stimulated some persons in the Congress to make their own confidence in its constitutionality doubly sure by proposing an additional amendment to the Constitution—that which became the Fourteenth. That amendment, you will recall, prohibited the States from impairing the privilege of citizenship, from depriving persons of life, liberty, or property without due process of law, and from denying persons the equal protection of the laws.

I have sometimes played with the paradoxical thought that this effort to assure Negro citizens that what they had been promised by the Thirteenth Amendment and the act of 1866 would really and truly be theirs was ultimately the source of their undoing. The paradox has this much truth. When the bits and pieces that constituted the Fourteenth Amendment were put together it included a prohibition of State denials of equal protection of the laws. The provision seems, on its face, to legitimate the equality act of 1866. What no one seems to have contemplated, however, at the time of reinforcement, was that the meaning of the statute might acquire a very different shading from the sweeping prohibitions of the Fourteenth Amendment than from the more specific interdictions of the Thirteenth. Remember that whereas the latter secures a few rights against the whole world, the Fourteenth Amendment safeguards an almost unlimited number of rights primarily against a very few persons—those who represent the State. The statutory condemnation of discriminations under color of law or usage, read in the context of the Thirteenth Amendment, seems to outlaw all conduct, public and private, designed to keep alive the degradations that were rooted in the laws and customs of slavery. The same condemnation, read in the context of the Fourteenth Amendment, may seem to reach no other discriminations than those enforced by officials exercising the State's powers. In 1870 the Congress transposed the equality act of 1866 into the center of a new Civil Rights Act that afforded protection for rights conferred by the Fourteenth and Fifteenth Amendments.[17] That transfer, not surprisingly, led courts and lawyers to forget the statute's Thirteenth Amendment paternity and to see it as the fruit of the powers conferred on Congress by the Fourteenth Amendment. Thus there came into being the assumption that the presuppositions of the Fourteenth Amendment confined the reach of the equality act to official denials of equality.

Where has this search for meaning taken me? What the story suggests is that the framers of the Thirteenth Amendment and the draftsmen of the act of 1866 were willing to have the Congress outlaw any private discriminations against Negroes that were traceable to the institutions of slavery. It does not seem to me surprising that a generation which recalled the frustrations of a federalism that had endeavored to sanctify national disability should consider

---

[17] Sections 16 and 17 of the Civil Rights Act of May 31, 1870, 16 Stat. 140, 144.

it time for a national government to be established. I have not seen any evidence that when the Fourteenth Amendment was adopted its framers intended to take back any of the congressional authority which the Thirteenth Amendment had created—the authority, that is, to deal with private efforts to perpetuate the inequalities born of slavery. Nor is there, in my judgment, persuasive evidence to suggest that the congressional power specifically granted in the Fourteenth Amendment to enforce its prohibitions of State action was intended merely to authorize legislative condemnations of practices that the amendment's own prohibitions outlawed. I see very little reason, in other words, to believe that the Fourteenth Amendment denied Congress the power to condemn private action designed either to impair the privileges of the colored citizens of the United States or to prevent the States from safeguarding the liberty and equality of Negroes.

Before I briefly consider the paradoxical fallout from the liberating promises of the Fourteenth Amendment, I must pause to ask what contribution the Civil War amendments made to the progress of American federalism. If I am right in my suggestion that the Nation's pre-War constitutional commitment to silence and disability was not the reflection of a general philosophy with respect to federalism but the consequence of our pluralistic inheritance with respect to slavery, then it would seem that the Thirteenth Amendment's breaking of silence—its resounding renunciation of the old neutrality—should have served to release the Nation's powers so that they might be applied to outlaw the indecencies of racial discrimination. Of course the general principles of federalism would still operate to make inadvisable—perhaps even unconstitutional—the needles or abusive exercise of national power over matters of primarily local concern. But the restraints derived from such general principles as those are surely less disabling than those that had been born of the old specific commitment to incapacity with respect to slavery. In 1866 any prophet other than a visionary cynic would have assumed that if, in the old period of promised silence and neutrality, the Federal government could effectuate the rendition of fugitive slaves, in the new period of affirmation and commitment, it could take charge of their emancipation. Yet within twenty years after the War it became clear that the post-War Congress could do less to assure freedom than the pre-War Congress had done to safeguard slavery.

To uncover the forces that encouraged the revival of national disability would require an analysis of logic, law, and politics beyond my competence hastily to develop. I shall not, accordingly, seek to perform that task here. All that I can do is suggest that a crucial element in the resurrection of the old federalism was the almost unlimited sweep of the language of the Fourteenth Amendment. We know that its draftsmen were predominantly, if not wholly, concerned with assuring the total fulfillment of the promises of the Thirteenth Amendment and of the equality act of 1866. Yet the words that they selected to embrace this assurance made so many promises to so many persons that a cautious judiciary was not entirely wrongheaded, when the time for interpretation came, in seeking restrictive elements in the American tradition which could be used to confine the reach of national power.[18] If the Court had read the Fourteenth Amendment to authorize congressional protection of the lives, liberties, properties, and equalities of all persons against private injury, it would have given its blessing to a revolution much more radical than even abolitionists had demanded.

Had the Fourteenth Amendment specifically confined its prohibitions to racial discriminations, the Court might have been more tolerant of congressional control of private action. It might, accordingly, have acknowledged that Congress could make social discriminations in places of public accommodation unlawful in any State that did not fulfill its constitutional duty to outlaw them. The fear that under the Fourteenth Amendment, as it was in fact adopted, the Congress might not only seek to enact such legitimate laws as that but might endeavor to assure all persons security of person and property was not entirely unreasonable. In any case the fear contributed to the Court's determination that the reach of the amendment should be confined to those injuries that were done under the authority, real or apparent, of the State. From that determination derives today's uncertainty whether the Nation has power to punish those persons who killed our neighbors to prevent them from being our equals.

Does this return to my starting place bring me back with nothing more useful than indignation? I hope not. It seems to me that if the suggestions that I have offered have merit, they indicate that with a somewhat fuller consideration of the roots of our asserted disability its extent diminishes. It would indicate, in the first place, that the Congress is still vested with the power conferred upon it by the Thirteenth Amendment—the power, that is, to extirpate the vestiges of slavery. It indicates, furthermore, that the Congress should be permitted to seek the fulfillment of the predominant promise of the three Civil War amendments. That promise was that henceforth the Nation's authority would so be exercised as to subdue law's inhumanity to man. From the lesson of our first era of national disability we learned that a neutral government is a participant in the inhumanities of its citizens. Surely today it takes no stretch of constitutional power to exercise the Nation's authority over acts of racial terror and violence in communities that have rejected the supreme law of the land and encouraged hatred to go at large.

SUGGESTIONS FOR FURTHER READING

Perhaps the best short work on American federalism is Daniel Elazar, *American Federalism: A View from the States* (New York: Crowell, 1966). Another

---

[18] Probably the cases that did most to discover restrictive traditions were the Slaughterhouse Cases, 16 Wall. 36 (1873) and The Civil Rights Cases, 109 U.S. 3 (1883).

useful source is Aaron Wildavsky, ed., *American Federalism in Perspective* (Boston: Little, Brown, 1962).

Other valuable works are William H. Riker, *Federalism: Origin, Operation, Significance* (Boston: Little, Brown, 1964); W. Brooke Graves, *American Intergovernmental Relations* (New York: Scribner's, 1964); and William Anderson, *The Nation and the States, Rivals or Partners?* (Minneapolis, Minn.: University of Minnesota Press, 1955).

A fine historical study is Daniel J. Elazar, *The American Partnership* (Chicago: University of Chicago Press, 1962).

A good collection of readings is Daniel J. Elazar, R. Bruce Carroll, E. Lester Levine, and Douglas St. Angelo, eds., *Cooperation and Conflict: Readings in American Federalism* (New York: Peacock, 1969).

Perhaps the most interesting recent work is James L. Sundquist, *Making Federalism Work: A Study of Program Coordination at the Community Level* (Washington, D. C.: Brookings Institution, 1969). See also Deil S. Wright, *Federal Grants-in-Aid: Perspectives and Alternatives* (Washington, D. C.: American Enterprise Institute for Public Policy Research, 1968), and V. O. Key, Jr.'s classic *The Administration of Federal Grants to the States* (Washington, D. C.: Public Administration Service, 1939).

An especially rich source of materials on the operations of American federalism are the reports of the Advisory Commission on Intergovernmental Relations. The commission, a permanent federal agency, has responsibility for continuing research and periodic recommendations in the area of intergovernmental relations.

11 Local and state governments

IT IS ONE OF THE ANOMALIES of contemporary political science that local and state governments have been neglected subjects of study. This gap in our knowledge has been reduced somewhat by the recent concern with the problems of the cities (see Chapter 12, "The Urban Crisis"). But non-urban municipal governments and the state capitals are still sadly under-observed.

Perhaps the most important area of local government in America today is the suburbs, and this is precisely the area social scientists know the least about; there is more information available on country towns. The causes and consequences of the suburban "revolution" are just beginning to be understood. The movement from the American countryside since World War II has not substantially increased the populations of most central cities; rather, it has created new concentrations of single-family dwellings surrounding our cities in great belts across the land. These belts have become the characteristic environment of the American middle classes, which have forsaken both the countryside and the teeming central city.

On reflection, of course, we begin to see that this migration was perfectly predictable. The social and cultural factors that have pressed Americans toward the split-level ranch-style home are basic and powerful ones. Despite their increasing tendency to identify with national symbols and to expose themselves to national news media, Americans still respond strongly to an ideal of the country life. The young and ambitious have moved to centers of manufacturing and communication when changes in the patterns of production and distribution made it necessary, but they have made every effort to preserve their life styles and their "friend and neighbor" institutions—neighborhood schools, village police forces, and occcasionally even town meetings. Old-stock Americans, drawn into the central cities, have tended to think of themselves as transients, and have resolved the contradiction between their desire for the economic advantages of the city and their psychological need for a detached single-family residence by heading out along the new parkways and the old commuter railroads. Moreover, this trend has been encouraged by federal law. Soft loans, mortgage insurance, and tax deductibility of interest payments all make it easy for those "sojourning" in central cities to follow their anti-urban instincts.

As with old-stock Americans, so with foreign migrants to the cities. In successive waves they moved into the cheap housing of the central city; then, as they gradually achieved middle-class status, they began to work their way out—sometimes leapfrogging to newly constructed Levittowns, but more often replacing (in such areas as Queens in New York) a previous middle-class group that was moving farther out. As Edward C. Banfield put it in *The Unheavenly City*,[1]

If there is any check on outward expansion, it is probably the limited supply of vacant land. This supply will be used up faster than ever, not only because more people will be able to afford land, but also because they will be able to afford larger lots. (In the New York metropolitan region, for example, the next six million people to move into new homes in the outlying suburbs are expected to take as much land as the previous sixteen million took. Two-thirds of the land in these suburbs is now zoned for single-family houses on lots of a half acre or more.) It will be many years before the frontier of vacant land is reached, however.

To some observers, the persistence of a multiplicity of small suburban governmental units around all our cities, large and small, is a very troubling phenomenon. There is no more sensitive student and critic of suburban political patterns than Robert C. Wood, the former Secretary of Housing and Urban Development. Even though his *Suburbia* is now more than twelve years old, it is still one of the best books in the literature. While regretting the dilution of public authority that results from the perpetuation of small governmental units, Wood relates their strength to a deeply rooted and not unattractive aspect of American culture—the passion for what he calls the American miniature. His analysis of this "miniature" is the first selection in this chapter.

If anything, state governments have fared worse than local governments at the hands of scholars. Only recently have works of high analytical quality begun to replace the sterile administrative guidebooks that, with a few exceptions, had been all there was on the shelf.[2] However, most of the good new literature is concerned with what might be called comparative

---

[1] (Boston: Little, Brown, 1970), p. 37.
[2] Excellent older studies are V. O. Key, Jr., *Southern Politics* (New York: Knopf, 1949), and Duane Lockhard, *New England State Politics* (Princeton, N. J.: Princeton University Press, 1959).

state politics—it explores why one state political system developed in one way and another in a different way. There are few works dealing with the quite crucial question of the future of state governments in the larger American political system.

The editors have resolved this difficulty rather egotistically by including a brief essay of their own. This essay was prepared for a symposium that preceded the 1967 convention for revision of the Constitution of the State of New York.[3] Although the specific recommendations contained in the piece were directed at the situation in New York several years ago, they are of general applicability, and the comments on the future of state government still seem correct.

After World War II, state governments—at least those of the more populous states—entered a period of modernization. By "modernization" we mean not merely the increased size of the state bureaucracies, but the increased degree to which the agencies of state government are centralized under the governor's control and the increased dependence on the governor for policy innovation within the state. The question in every case should be whether the governor is becoming the mainspring of the state system, as the President clearly is at the federal level. As this centralization takes place, state legislatures can be expected to meet for longer periods to handle the greater volume of business (New York's now sits for almost half the year), and state legislators can be expected to become more professional.

It is likely that the 1970's will see more experiments in regional and in metropolitan (both city and suburban) governmental arrangements. State governments have a great advantage over such new units, however, in that states already exist and possess the power to revise their own constitutions to allow for structural changes required by new programs. The states need not be painfully and laboriously brought into existence one by one, with their every added power grudgingly surrendered by existing units. The states, or some of them, will almost certainly develop as centers of pragmatic innovation, especially if the Nixon administration should institute a tax-sharing arrangement whereby part of the federal income stream is diverted to state capitals.

[3] The new charter that emerged from that convention was defeated by the voters, after much controversy, in November of 1967.

◘ The American Miniature

ROBERT C. WOOD

... Against the broad wave of mass culture, mass values, and mass society, there is at least one stubborn holdout. While residential suburban living and individual suburbanites may represent modern character and behavior, their suburban governments do not. They join the other suburban political units around our large cities in clinging persistently to the independence they received when they were isolated villages and hamlets in a rustic countryside. If the suburb is a brand new development taking the place of forest or potato farm, the inhabitants insist on creating governments modeled after their older autonomous neighbors. These rural neighbors, far from acquiescing to the cult of size, turn their backs on progress and resist the influences of modernity. Though they accept the homes of the organization man, they insist on retaining the legal form and the public institutions which are relics of a bygone age.

This superimposition of provincial government on cosmopolitan people provides a strange pattern of incongruity. Within the single economic and social complex we have come to call a metropolitan area, hundreds and hundreds of local governments jostle one another about. Counties overlie school districts, which overlie municipalities, which overlie sanitary and water districts, which sometimes overlie townships and villages. Except for the special-purpose "districts," each suburban government maintains its own police force, its fire station, its health department, its library, its welfare service. Each retains its authority to enact ordinances, hold elections, zone land, raise taxes, grant building licenses, borrow money, and fix speed limits.

The spectacle of these ancient jurisdictions careening merrily on their way is often amusing and more frequently disturbing. By ordinary standards of effective, responsible public services, the mosaic of suburban principalities creates governmental havoc. Across a typical suburban terrain, twenty or thirty or fifty volunteer fire departments buy equipment and, with varying degrees of efficiency, put out fires. A welter of semi-professional police forces, usually poorly equipped and inadequately staffed, jealously compete or lackadaisically cooperate, uncertain of the limits of their jurisdiction. Independent school systems build costly plants, some crammed to capacity, others with excess space. In one municipality the water table dips perilously low; in another, foresighted or fortunate enough to have access to a reservoir, sprinklers turn all summer

FROM Robert C. Wood, *Suburbia* (Boston: Houghton Mifflin, 1958), pp. 9–28. Copyright © 1958 by Robert C. Wood. Reprinted by permission of the publisher, Houghton Mifflin Company.

long. And, always, for suburban governments taken together, there is the extra and apparently unnecessary cost of doing individually what might be done collectively: the additional expense of making separate purchases without benefit of quantity discounts, of administrative and political overhead, of holding local elections and hiring city managers, of reporting, accounting, and auditing these separate activities.

The anachronisms of suburban governments have long been apparent and long decried. For almost half a century, the conditions of inefficiency, confusion, duplication, overlapping and waste have been under fire. For at least twenty-five years, reform movement after reform movement has moved against the antiquated political structures, proposing their consolidation, advancing one scheme after another to bring together their conflicting activities. Again and again the call has rung out for a king-sized government to fit the king-sized metropolitan community. Some critics emphasize the inequities of tax burdens and public services among the suburbs, some point to their incapacity to solve common problems of water supply and mass transportation, some underscore the absence of a responsible region-wide political process and system of representation. All condemn the compounding of confusion which the array of municipalities, boroughs, and districts brings about as they play hob with the orderly provision of municipal services and public finance.

Yet with extraordinarily few exceptions the ranks of suburban governments hold fast. They cling to their independence, stand successfully against the demands for efficiency and economy, and resist the lure of the big organization. More numerous than at any time in our history, their boundaries bursting with new inhabitants, their administrative and tax structure apparently strained to capacity or beyond, suburban political institutions remain adamant. They reject the prospect of consolidation with the larger society; they continue to hold out when every other influence in modern life calls for their absorption.

The paradox which suburban government presents to suburban society sharply limits the theory of suburbia as the looking glass and suburbanites as the advance guard of the new America. A social order apparently built upon a commitment to the virtues of large organizations, indoctrinated to the advantages of size and scale, still tolerates tiny, ineffective governments which seem almost willfully bent on producing chaos, and which are still multiplying. As political entities, suburbs represent an order unwilling to join in the change going on about them; they flout the modern ideology attributed to suburban man.

They flout this ideology, moreover, by raising an ancient and honorable standard straight out of American political folklore. The justification of suburban legal independence rests on the classic belief in grassroots democracy, our long-standing conviction that small political units represent the purest expression of popular rule, that the government closest to home is best. The defense of suburban autonomy is that no voter is a faceless member in a political rally, but an individual citizen who knows his elected officials, can judge their performance personally and hold them accountable.

In the suburb, according to the folklore, the school board is likely to be composed of neighbors or friends, or at least friends of friends or neighbors of neighbors. Its members do not come from another part of a large city; they are available and accessible. So are the mayor, the county clerk, the commissioners, the councilmen, and selectmen. So are the chief of police, the water superintendent, the plumbing inspector, and the health officers. In this way, elected officials, bureaucrats, party leaders—the entire apparatus of democratic politics—are exposed to view, recognized and approached as they never are in a great metropolis. In politics, the suburb dwellers hold fast to a conviction that the small organization, run by a group of relatively few individuals, provides the best management of public affairs that is possible.

The strength of this conviction has been powerful enough, at least to date, to blunt the edge of all the reform efforts to bring suburban governments into the twentieth century. In spite of statistics indicating that the metropolitan area in which suburbia exists is actually a single community, in spite of the obvious organizational chaos brought on by this political multiplicity, even the most ardent efficiency expert hesitates to deny the values small governments represent. Instead of recommending outright abolition of suburban jurisdictions, he presents one ingenious scheme after another—federations, special authorities, new systems of representation, new complexities of local government—designed to provide some measure of administrative rationality while still maintaining suburban autonomy. At rock bottom he accepts the value of small size and he works to preserve the suburb as a legal entity even if its powers must be reduced in the face of the realities of the modern world.

So, as yet there is little sign that this array of small municipalities merely represents a cultural lag. On the contrary, the statistics point in exactly the opposite direction, for every census report shows more—and smaller—and more self-consciously independent suburban governments than existed ten years earlier. And those which the looking-glass theory selects as the best examples of the home of modern man are also the ones which exhibit the most independent political institutions.

There are also signs that this renaissance of small-scale autonomy is not confined to suburban governments alone. Even the most confirmed advocate of the New American Character still finds signs of small town behavior throughout the suburbs he studies. So William H. Whyte, Jr., in investigating the organization man at home, discovers two sides to every coin he examines, notes something old as well as something new, remains ambivalent in his judgment of the suburb in a way which contrasts sharply with his indictment of the organizational world in general.

Whyte's residents are, of course, transients, newcomers to the town in which they live, and they are soon to move on to other, better suburbs. Nonetheless, they try to put down roots and they succeed to some degree; even though the roots are shallow. To Whyte there is something admirable in the vigor with which they respond to the advertisements that call their suburb a friendly small town, as contrasted to the lonely big city, and in the way they work to make the advertisement a reality. The suburbanite penchant for joining his neighbors to agitate against the town hall indifference and the developer may be participation for participation's sake, but it also may express citizenship of the highest sort. Small roots are better than none, civic spirit is to be preferred to apathy, and the chance to "chew on real problems" in public affairs is desirable, for it creates allegiances that have purpose.

Whyte does not scorn community affairs then. He approves of the suburbanite's self-conscious efforts to guide his town's future, even though he is only passing through and cannot stay to enjoy it. It is still an indication of older values, however sugar-coated in new jargon, and so is the classlessness of his suburbia. The melting-pot analogy is, after all, another cherished American ideal. It seems a laudable fact that the suburb often promotes better understanding among inhabitants with different ethnic origins, religions, and backgrounds, even though they are all within the middle class, that it helps prevent the emergence of classes and furthers the ideal of equality. It is to be preferred to the jarring hostility of groups wrangling among themselves in the large cities and it is a sign of small town life as it has always been known.

The pattern of inconspicuous consumption, the web of friendship, and the outgoing life that Whyte describes also have something of the flavor of a renaissance. Although "keeping down with the Joneses" may indicate group tyranny, it is still better than keeping up with them. At least it displays disapproval of overt snobbishness and obvious symptoms of city superciliousness; it harks back once again to the frontier spirit of equality. While suburbanites should probably manage their budgets more prudently than they do, at least their desire for improvement and progress is a sturdy American trait. Even suburban friendships have their admirable qualities so far as the observers are concerned. They may be largely determined by the location of play areas, the placement of driveways and lawns, and the size of the living room, and they may impose a surveillance that makes privacy clandestine and the way of the introvert hard. But here are old-time qualities of warmth, helpfulness, and service to others. While Whyte finds pressures for benevolent conformity, he also discovers brotherhood. He sees that the church may have sacrificed theology for acceptance and the school may stress adjustment at the expense of the liberal arts, but he sees also that it is good to have churches and schools. These provide a sense of community, institutions that are socially useful, and it is not surprising that in the end Whyte speaks of his suburbanites as pioneers.

Even more impressive than the fragments of small town culture still persisting in the suburb is the ideal that every analyst of suburbia seems to cherish of what suburbia ought to be. There is a special temper in the rage which the looking-glass philosopher expresses when he uncovers the organization man at home, for to him there is a special irony and incongruity in making the suburb synonymous with modern life.

John Keats sketches the idealized suburb most clearly. Following Mary and

John Drone through their weary succession of inadequate, overpriced homes in suburbs inhabited by directionless people who do not know they are unhappy, he is angry not at suburbia but at what has been done to it. He objects not a whit to the popular demand for space, for relatively small neighborhoods, for private homes, for roots, however temporary. He protests only against the degradation of these aspirations by greedy, selfish contractors and by the foolish, undisciplined residents themselves. He describes developments, and he wants communities.

Keats' prescription is not to tear suburbia apart, but to build it better. He wants homes arranged so that the illusions of privacy and aesthetics can be cultivated in small space. He wants suburbanites to join together to build libraries and swimming pools, where truly useful and common purposes are served. He would encourage the flight from the city so long as it is properly done, with taste and recognition of family budgetary limits and with awareness of the public problems to be faced. He would surround with regulations and controls the builder who remains the sturdy nineteenth century individualist and is responsible for the damage suburbs do. What suburbia ought to be, for Keats, is a carefully designed constellation of small towns, each with its own community center, each self-contained, each controlling its local affairs at the local level with polite regard for the larger region to which it belongs.

The small town, the small community, this is what seems good about the suburb to most observers, what needs to be preserved, and what the large organization should not be permitted to despoil. Spontaneous collaboration, voluntary neighborliness, purposeful participation, these are the goals of real suburbanites. And all of the observers seem to cherish the hope that in the suburbs we can re-create the small communities we have lost in our industrial sprawl since the Civil War. The irony they find is that our suburbanites do not discriminate between the type of association a small town can give and that which Madison Avenue promotes. The ambivalence of Whyte is genuine; to him suburban virtues lie in the degree to which the suburb approximates the small town, and vices lie in deviation from this ideal. The image of the small community shines through the condemnation of modern life. If it is faithful to this ideal, the suburb may save us all from the artificial group without reestablishing the unpalatable culture of the rugged individualist.

Even the harshest critic of our modern suburb is not insensitive to this appeal. Although the great organization seems essential to contemporary society, and the pressures of mass society appear overwhelming, no analysis counsels surrender. For the most pessimistic there is, it seems, still a chance for an individual to fight the organization, even if he has to cheat. And the best way to fight is on home ground where the suburbanite can try to fuse the political ideology of the small government with the social mores of the small community.

Thus, while the looking-glass theory protests the onrush of modern culture, it takes comfort in the hope that suburbia can somehow hold out against it. It is encouraged by the possibility that the suburbs may break up the sprawling metropolitan area into discrete units distributing here an industrial area, here a low-income neighborhood, here a retail center, here an exclusive residential area, but everywhere permitting a closer communion within the small localities. It applauds newspaper editorials which warn against making governments and communities "so big that no one counts" and speaks out for "the concept of people working together in identifiable units in a community with a cohesive past and future . . . of which the individual can feel a part and for the life of which he can feel a sense of participation and responsibility."

These hopes are imperfectly realized today, of course; modern circumstances always threaten them and frequently combine to subvert them. But the vision is powerful; it helps move the ordinary citizen to suburbia, the sociologist to protect it, and the political scientist to preserve it. The ancient symbol of the "republic in miniature" persists, and the suburb is its contemporary expression. For all our changes in culture and behavior, for all the heavy price we pay in inadequate local public services, nonexistent metropolitan services, and high taxes, the good life and the good government still come for us in small packages. Although minimum adjustments to the demands of urban life must be made, it seems the job of the suburb, either by social resistance or political compromise, to ensure the preservation of these values.

Suburbia, defined as an ideology, a faith in communities of limited size and a belief in the conditions of intimacy, is quite real. The dominance of the old values explains more about the people and the politics of the suburbs than any other interpretation. Fundamentally, it explains the nature of the American metropolis. It indicates why our large urban complexes are built as they are, why their inhabitants live the way they do, and why public programs are carried out the way they are. If these values were not dominant it would be quite possible to conceive of a single gigantic metropolitan region under one government and socially conscious of itself as one community. The new social ethic, the rise of the large organization, would lead us to expect this development as a natural one. The automobile, the subway, the telephone, the power line certainly make it technically possible; they even push us in this direction.

But the American metropolis is not constructed in such a way; it sets its face directly against modernity. Those who wish to rebuild the American city, who protest the shapeless urban sprawl, who find some value in the organizational skills of modern society must recognize the potency of the ideology. Until these beliefs have been accommodated reform will not come in the metropolitan areas nor will men buckle down to the task of directing, in a manner consonant with freedom, the great political and social organizations on which the nation's strength depends. A theory of community and a theory of local government are at odds with the prerequisites of contemporary life and, so far, theory has been the crucial force that preserves the suburb. There is no economic reason for its existence and there is no technological basis for its support. There is only the stubborn conviction of the majority of suburbanites that it ought to exist, even though it plays havoc with both the life and government of our urban age.

If a belief in small government and small society helps explain why the modern suburb exists in an age of bigness, the suburban renaissance should not be surprising. The conviction that provincial life is best has been with us for a long time and it has endured in the face of greater attacks than the ones contemporary America presents. We show our instinctive commitment to the ideology by the fact that we rarely examine its assumptions critically. We show our conscious allegiance by the oratorical homage we pay to the ideal of small neighborhoods, single homes, and political jurisdictions of limited size.

It is difficult to overestimate the vigor and pervasiveness of the belief. Three centuries stand behind the heritage—a full two hundred years of spectacular success and one hundred years of abject failure. The first period endowed the American cult of localism with its basic articles of faith: an assertion that local communities should maintain their own identity and manage their own affairs, and a justification for that assertion by the claim that the small society is the natural home of democracy. The last hundred years added endurance and stubbornness to the ideal by the very adversity which the reality of the urban world inflicted upon it. But whether made confident by success or contentious by disaster, the creed has remained to shape the American metropolis and make it what it is today.

Not the least of the reasons for the strength of the ideology is in its natural partiality to the American habitat. Grassroots life existed in fact in the United States long before the justification for its existence was ever articulated. The first settlements on the new continent were by necessity small and relatively isolated, and the characteristics usually associated with small town life developed spontaneously. Colonial conditions led to a similarity of interests, and a sharing of customs, aims, and ambitions. Some degree of economic interdependence and equality, a constant recognition of a vast, unexplored land beyond the frontier outposts, close daily contact, bred early a conscious sense of community identity.

Under these social circumstances, nothing was more natural than the independence in fact, if not in legal theory, of local political institutions. Technically speaking, the first New England towns relied on grants of power from the Massachusetts Bay Company and later from the colonial legislature. Early settlements in the other colonies used the medieval corporation as the model for their authority. But in actual fact, colonial towns exercised independently the essential powers of police and taxation, and were, from the beginning, self-governing. They were independent because there was no other alternative; local authority stemmed from "the exercise of English common sense combined with the circumstance of the place."

Not only were the towns possessed with self-conscious identity, but by any standard of seventeenth century life, their political institutions seemed democratic. Small groups of people, barely sustaining themselves economically and faced with constant dangers, congregated without forethought to discuss common affairs. They elected their own officials, and these officials knew they were accountable to the citizens. In Lane Lancaster's words:

The original government of the New England town was that of a pure democracy. We may well admit that it was inquisitive and gossipy, that it gave too liberal rein to the crank, the bore, the windbag and the troublemaker, that it put a premium upon talk, and that it was tolerant of somnolent administration. But in spite of these defects, it had the sovereign merit of bringing the rulers and the ruled together, it made easy the ventilation of grievances, it encouraged an intelligent and disinterested attitude toward public questions, and it fostered at its best a keen sense of the reality of the community.

This state of affairs usually contrasted sharply with contemporary conditions in the Old World, though the forms of local social organization and government appeared similar and scholars later sought to trace the principal of local autonomy back to the rights accorded English boroughs and before them to Teutonic and ecclesiastical sources. Yet no European locality, however consciously a community, exhibited the autonomy and democracy of its American counterpart.

Even in England the parish of the seventeenth century, that mixture of church and secular authority, could not parallel the colonial experience. Theoretically, all members of the parish had their say in civic management, but actually only the "most substantial" exercised authority. Nor was the second unit of English local organization, the manor, a truer expression of the local will. In this jurisdiction the eminent landlord of the area presided aristocratically as justice of the peace and principal officer of the countryside. At the county level, no pretense of local autonomy or democracy was maintained: the lord lieutenant, the high sheriff, and the justice of the peace were appointed by the king from among the county gentry. While the American localities moved toward increasing autonomy, comparable English governments remained oligarchies, organs of "local obligation," "thoroughly undemocratic and thoroughly responsible."

From the middle of the seventeenth century to well into the nineteenth, local communities in America ran their own affairs, by and large, and ran them by a popular political process. Along the entire Atlantic seaboard, counties, cities, towns, and villages tackled energetically the problems of land disposition, the regulation of commerce, public health, law enforcement, fire protection, building control, and education. The manageable size of even the largest colonial city and its relative isolation allowed the town fathers to behave both decisively and responsibly; the New England selectmen might seem to have "the broad finality of dictatorship in local matters," but "the spirit of their service resembles the humblest agent . . . thoroughly and publicly checked."

Even the Revolution and the subsequent establishment of state authority by the Constitution did not seriously affect these prerogatives. Although the states were granted legal control over public activities below the national level, their authority existed mainly in the law books. The exercise of government, in fact, depended on the town and county. It was the local unit which, almost to the Civil War, collected the taxes, established the schools, cared for the poor, maintained the roads—in short, which exercised the responsibility for prime community endeavors. Practice and habit kept local democracy strong, even when legal independence was denied.

Of course, neither perfect autonomy nor pure democracy, even of the character sanctioned by the times, was ever completely realized. So far as political institutions were concerned, the structures which were later to define suburbia were sometimes hobbled at the very start. In the case of Charlestown, for example, the colonial government interfered so continually and so closely in local affairs that genuine self-government never developed and the legacy of legislative dominance continues in South Carolina to this day. For the larger cities, the medieval corporation was everywhere an imperfect model and never provided all the powers needed properly to direct municipal growth.

So far as popular control was concerned, both formally and informally there were limitations on democracy. Almost immediately after settlement the ministry and the merchants exercised disproportionate influence, and property restrictions limited participation. In New England there was a distinction between the freeman and the inhabitant in the early town meeting, and in other colonies the voting electorate was even more narrowly defined. There was also, throughout the colonies, class conflict—accusations that social position rather than numbers was decisive in the management of town affairs. A tendency toward tight political dominance by a few, a forerunner of city machines, could be discerned in Boston, New York, Philadelphia, and Charlestown by 1700, and editors and ministers could thunder against cliques and individual misuse of public authority generations before the Constitution.

These aberrations were real enough, and not to be discounted in painting an accurate picture of colonial life in the United States. The fact remains, however, that the predominant tendency was toward autonomy and democracy, and in sufficient measure so that when men came to rationalize these institutions the characteristics they recognized were distinctively these two. The schoolboy's conception of the American miniature republic is right, by and large, when applied to our early history.

When the abstractions about localism began to appear, then, there was historical precedent and a tradition of actual practice on which to rest the case. And the eloquence and distinction of the men who chose to advance its cause added luster to the theory. Jefferson before the Revolution, Tocqueville afterward—what better advocates could be imagined to hand on the faith to coming generations?

It was Jefferson who first proclaimed the superiority of the New England town and urged the rest of the nation to follow this example. "Those wards," he wrote,

called townships in New England, are vital principles of their governments, and have proved themselves the wisest inventions ever devised by the wit of man for the perfect exercise of self-government. Each ward would be a small republic within itself and every man in the State would thus become an active member of the common government, transacting in person a great portion of its rights and duties, subordinate indeed, yet important and entirely within his competence.

No contemporary disputed Jefferson's opinion. The founding fathers found the local governments in being when they met to organize the nation. In drafting the new state constitutions, sometimes the legal authorities of the large municipalities were revised. The new doctrine of the separation of powers was occasionally extended downward, apparently stimulated as much by a desire to carry logic to its ultimate conclusion as to correct deficiencies. But the new Congress showed its approval of the basic pattern of local government in the Northwest Ordinance of 1789, when it established the township as the basic unit in the new territory and decreed its universality.

Forty years later Tocqueville found the image flourishing. He was in error when he asserted that American political authority originated in the township and that municipal independence was a natural consequence of the sovereignty of the people. But in actual practice, he was close to the truth—close enough, at any rate, so that his generalizations sounded right to his generation and to ours. His unbounded enthusiasm reinforced and extended Jefferson's early claims. To Tocqueville, the careful deference paid to local autonomy within the federal system was the secret of American political success. On the one hand, it permitted a centralized government of sufficient power to face world problems. On the other, it required decentralized administration, which precluded usurpation.

But even more important than institutional checks and balances, this pattern of government set benign influences to work upon the people and their social life. The dissemination of power, Tocqueville was certain, created a town spirit which civilized all who felt its touch, stimulating affection rather than ambition and reason in place of emotion. To him,

the township, at the center of the ordinary relations of life, serves as a field for the desire of public esteem, the want of exciting interest, and the taste for authority and popularity; and the passions which commonly embroil society change their character, when they find a vent so near the domestic hearth and family circle.

Thus "provincial" institutions became the best protection against despotism or the license of mob, for otherwise, "How can a populace, unaccustomed to freedom in small concerns, learn to use it temperately in great affairs?" In short, vigorous small governments enhanced the influence of small communities, and small communities, by their very nature, brought out the best in man, the qualities of reason and good will on which a Lockian commonwealth was based.

So the image crystallized. Small communities apparently experienced the sense of self-identity, the compactness, the self-sufficiency necessary to produce interdependence and equality and the sharing of common values and objectives. Given these circumstances, their governments should be independent, positive and aggressive, asserting their claim to all the powers and prerogatives they could possibly exercise, with a minimum of supervision and restraint.

Small towns deserved their autonomy because they were the natural home of democracy. Only in small governments could each man participate effectively, not in selfish pursuit of his own interests but with the capacity to understand the problems his community faced and thus further the common good. Independent local governments had legitimate claims to power because they were closest to home. And in the early days of the nation, the concept of home, of distinct social groupings, discrete social systems, was real and tangible. Small town life was the American way because there was, beyond the seaports, literally no other method to organize communal existence.

In this way the miniature republic was established, beginning as an institution and rationalized brilliantly as a theory of how government and society actually did operate and should operate in America. Because initially it worked, and worked well, and because it was sanctioned by illustrious native philosophers and distinguished foreign observers, it has been, like all beliefs so established, a powerful force. Since its logic was simple, consisting of only two parts, easily grasped and instinctively felt by every man, its force expanded exponentially. With no other better way at hand for organizing government, the prospects for serious criticism of its propositions diminished, also exponentially. With the passing of the years, the conditions under which the working principles of autonomy and direct democracy were first established became obscure and hardly recognized; only the principles themselves remained in view. In this way, the image became a legacy, and like all legacies, was accepted as something precious and therefore useful for each generation.

When men receive legacies under new conditions of society, they are more prone to try to adjust their circumstances so that the bequest may be applied than to abandon their inheritance. This has been done in many areas of American government and social life; our founding fathers were so successful that they have often inhibited our own search for success. It was true with a vengeance in the case of Jefferson's miniature republic. . . .

▣ The Governor
and the Executive Establishment

JAMES E. CONNOR AND RICHARD E. MORGAN

When proposals are advanced for revising a state constitution one can be sure that lurking behind them is a set of assumptions about state government, its "proper" role and its anticipated course of development. At the present time, however, there seems to be considerable confusion about what role the states should play over the next few decades; some even question whether states any longer have a part to play in the modern governmental process. Because of this confusion and doubt, political scientists who would recommend constitutional changes for New York are obliged to make their perceptions of the desired or anticipated "future" of the state as explicit as possible.

Divining the evolution of state governments has recently become a favorite indoor sport of politically sophisticated individuals. Their predictions generally fall into one of two broad categories: the future of bypass and decay, and the future of programmatic innovation and integration.

The former prediction sees the effective political relationships of tomorrow developing between the federal and local governments. American political history since the start of the New Deal has been the story of expanded federal authority and increased local problems. Despite a post–World War II revival, state capitals are destined to become stagnant political backwaters. Their failure to cope with crucial contemporary problems condemns them to a future of performing certain residual functions such as motor vehicle regulation and alcoholic beverage control, and they will have little part in the adventures in human welfare and environmental improvement which are on the domestic agenda for the last third of the twentieth century. Those who hold this view see the Economic Opportunity Act of 1964, which directly linked federal power to local needs, as a portent of things to come. For adherents of this position, the only satisfactory revisions of state constitutions are those that will render state governments innocuous enough to keep them from being too great a drag on the rest of the system.

The second prediction takes full account of the present infirmities of the states but considers them as temporary rather than permanent maladies. Pro-

FROM James E. Connor and Richard E. Morgan, "The Governor and the Executive Establishment," reprinted with permission from the *Proceedings of the Academy of Political Science*, Vol. 28, No. 3 (January 1967), "Modernizing State Government: The New York Constitutional Convention of 1967," pp. 173–82.

ponents of this view are quick to point out that the fatal flaw in federal–local relationships is the narrow jurisdiction of local governments. The problems of today spill over local boundaries. The solutions thus far advanced—special school, sanitation, and water districts—have only contributed to the process of governmental proliferation; they have not produced particularly effective results in terms of administrative coordination. Metropolitan organization, that is, the creation of great supercities with the legal and fiscal powers needed to achieve governmental integration, has been suggested. But the various groups that might be integrated into such communities have been notably unenthusiastic about the prospect. For all its administrative desirability, metro-government seems politically unfeasible.

State governments, however, are already in being, and they can be used as coordinating mechanisms. Their jurisdictions are by no means wholly congruent with population clusters or with critical ganglia of transportation, but nevertheless they possess the inestimable advantage of being able to redefine their own powers without going to a higher authority, and they can operate along a much broader front than any local government. The states, in short, are in a good position to integrate complex and comprehensive programs; the localities are not. This being the case, federal architects will turn increasingly to the states as a valuable mid-range mechanism for policy implementation. For those who see this future, the purpose of constitutional revision in New York is essentially to render the state's government better able to confront the tasks that await it.

The limited compass of this paper precludes arguing the respective cases in more detail. We think that the future will conform much more closely to the second than to the first prediction. The state government and its chief executive are going to play an important integrative and innovative role over the next thirty years. The governor will have little choice but to be an activist; he is chosen by the people of the state to lead it, and is unquestionably *the* legitimate policy innovator. He will have to lobby for funds in Washington, and then strive to ensure that federal dollars entering his state are spent in accord with his goals and conceptions of how the state should develop. He will be required to complement federal lobbying activity with pressures on his own legislature for the authority and the money needed to support his programs. Finally, he will have to mediate between localities and coordinate their actions.

Most of these gubernatorial activities are, however, decidedly unglamorous. Governors will continue to spend much of their time on extremely important matters about which the people in the state neither know nor care. This phenomenon has already been described by V. O. Key, Jr., who argued that because of it "state politics is peculiarly the politics of administration." By this he meant that, unlike Washington, the state capitals are rarely affected by widespread public sentiment or concern over issues. The governor may, on occasion, find such public apathy a blessing, but he will frequently miss being able to use public pressures to achieve his ends vis-à-vis other participants in the state political process. In lieu of "public" political resources, the governor must be provided with sharper administrative tools with which to work in his bureaucratic environment. Obviously, the nature of that environment is of crucial importance in determining his ability to initiate, coordinate, and implement policy.

Before going further, we should point out that there never has been a single "ideal," "neutral," or "correct" form of administration that would suffice for any government at any time. It was the grand illusion of the Progressives that there existed autonomous, eternally valid goals of efficiency, honesty, or "sound business practice," which dictated organizational forms independent of specific public policy goals. A given administrative system invariably favors some of the participants at the expense of others with other goals. Rearranging this structure may reverse the advantages; it may increase the power of the latter and make political life difficult or impossible for the former. Decisions on governmental structure, therefore, are in very real ways decisions on program.

One of the easiest ways to aid the governor in mastering his bureaucratic environment is to increase his capacity to shape and reshape it. Americans are in the bad habit of thinking about their public administrative structures as immutable. Although such opinions are understandable in bureaucrats, they should not clutter the minds of citizens. Bureaucracies have not existed from time out of mind; they were established in response to particular needs at particular times. Some may adapt to changing circumstances, some may not; but if unchecked almost all tend to go on indefinitely, becoming perhaps a bit bigger and a bit more complex. Organizations, it should be realized, may outlive the problems they were designed to meet. It may become apparent that the solutions they have learned to apply may have ceased to be relevant to the problems they confront. One need only look to the record of state and local welfare agencies for empirical support of the last proposition.

When a governor is confronted by an unresponsive or inadequate bureaucratic structure, he must squander many of his most valuable political resources on overcoming its resistance. His policies are rendered less effective because they must pass through channels which were not designed to accommodate them. Decisions to redefine a bureaucracy's purpose or to rearrange its structure are not solemn, once-in-a-lifetime steps that need to be deliberated for years on end; they are merely the necessary corollaries of decisions on policy. The election of a governor or the passage of a bill indicates that the basic decisions have already been made. Given the pace of social change and the domestic revolution of rising expectations, there is a great need to equip the governor of New York with a flexible, and at times disposable, bureaucracy.

We are not advocating that the governor be given the power to rule by decree. His program, especially its funding, would remain subject to the normal, agonizing legislative struggle. We are proposing an arrangement similar to the federal Executive Reorganization Act of 1949. Under the terms of such an act the legislature would be in a position to veto any particular gubernatorial administrative innovation within a specified time after its announcement. This would improve significantly the flexibility of administrative arrangements and enhance the governor's capacity for purposeful action. It would enable him to design the instruments needed to implement his programs. Such a proposal sacrifices no substantial democratic value or guarantee of minority rights, but it does ensure that the governor will be able to compete effectively in the "politics of administration."

Closely allied to the problem of administrative structure is the problem of staffing. As we have seen, the governor is not merely a president writ small. Nor should all the powers possessed by, or desired for, that latter official be vested analogously in the occupant of the gubernatorial mansion. Nonetheless, students of the politics of the presidency, such as Richard E. Neustadt, can be consulted with profit by those interested in encouraging activist governors. Again and again in *Presidential Power*, Neustadt stresses the importance to the man on top of having his "own men," lieutenants in administration, who share, to a high degree, his goals and his risks. *Equally important to determining the content of programs is determining who is going to manage them.* The greater the formal independence of the bureaucrats, the more difficult is the job of bending the administrative apparatus to executive purpose. It is a commonplace of political science that tenured bureaucrats are natural enemies of innovative political executives. How can the governor redirect the efforts of an agency and redefine its operative goals if he cannot appoint, cannot fire, and cannot transfer? How can the governor's "own men" be placed in the critical positions? What steps might be taken to reduce the capacity of hidebound agencies to block the political executive, to sabotage his program, to ally with narrow interest group constituencies, or simply to bleed a new program to death through elaborate and rigid procedures?

The issue of staffing can be attacked at various levels. Of primary importance in the New York context is the problem of executive departments whose heads are not chosen by the governor. This is true today of four of the nineteen departments, and these are critical ones: the Departments of Education, Social Welfare, Audit and Control, and Law.

In the first two cases it would be an adequate reform simply to vest selection in the governor, but we also advise abolishing the cumbersome panels, the Board of Regents and the Board of Social Welfare, which presently appoint the commissioners. These boards are textbook examples of structure outliving function. At one time, perhaps, it was advisable to overcome the low visibility of education issues and apathy toward welfare by creating "public" interest group representatives, but that day is long past. There is no longer any real reason to retain them. In this day of highly vocal and influential private sector spokesmen, it is unnecessary to represent various geographic and ethnic interests on formal boards which share and dilute executive responsibility and control. The political environment is already dangerous enough for governors and commissioners without building in more problems.

The Department of Law and the Department of Audit and Control present slightly different problems. Their heads, the attorney general and the state comptroller, are elected independently by statewide constituencies and thus are formally free from gubernatorial control. Most of the duties of these two officials can be described as typically executive, although they possess some other powers, such as the ability to propose legislation and render opinions, which distinguish them from other department heads. The rationale behind independent legal and financial officials springs from the notion that election will somehow ensure "honesty" in these important areas. This rationale strikes us as unconvincing. It first of all assumes that the governor is not a particularly honest man, an unflattering and erroneous assumption in the mid-twentieth century. Secondly, it suggests that a number of independently elected executives sharing power and scrutinizing each other will be an encouragement to honesty. It seems to us equally plausible that they might combine their nefarious talents in a spirit of cheerful bipartisanship. In our day there are no easy guarantees of official probity. Election is just as likely to produce corrupt office-holders as appointment. In fact, as the unfortunate case of a recent Illinois state auditor indicates, electing officials below the governor may be a risky business. Several political scientists have pointed out that a combination of weak state parties and low candidate visibility has bestowed public office on ingenious thieves.

Both positions should be brought into line with other departments and with federal arrangements. The state attorney general, like his federal counterpart, should be made an executive appointee. The numerous duties of the comptroller might be distributed between two separate officials, a more powerful state treasurer, who would supervise accounting and pre-audit functions, and a comptroller general, appointed by the governor for an extended term but responsible to the legislature, who would carry on the important task of post-audit evaluation of the bureaucracy. The comptroller's role as trustee of the State Retirement System would revert to the governor. His other duties, such as audit of localities, might be performed by either of the two new officials. Once again the absence of formal independence would not be sorely missed and the resulting increase in gubernatorial authority and effectiveness would be significant.

The civil service system, the mechanism by which the state's rank and file administrators are selected and maintained in power, is pivotal in terms of gubernatorial control. The provision of the present constitution for selection solely on the basis of examination is dangerously rigid. The time has come in New York to reexamine the assumptions which underlie the system and to consider certain changes in its operation.

Rarely has the tyranny of words over thought been more vividly demonstrated than in the phrase "merit system." It is as if some abstract or mechanical notion of individual (or relative) "merit" qualifies a person for a position, regardless of whether he has the disposition or the desire to carry out the mission associated with it. Only in metaphysical or theological terms could such an argument have validity. In a world where personal relationships are necessarily intertwined with policy preferences, that is, in the world of political administration, such distinctions cannot be drawn. If an individual is hostile or even indifferent to the goals of his superior, there is a very good chance that these goals will be less than fully realized. Anyone who has had the opportunity to look at the relationships between policy-makers and bureaucrats in business or academic life, as well as in politics, should be able to recall occasions on which executive will was frustrated by dilatory tactics or other more subtle methods. When this happens the process of policy-making in a democracy is rendered nugatory.

As presently constituted, the civil service system in New York seems to breed resistance to executive control. Only with difficulty can the governor rid himself of those who either consciously or unconsciously thwart his aims. Moreover, by placing a premium on competent mediocrity and seniority on the job, the system has made it increasingly difficult to attract the best college graduates to careers in state administration. For many years the state has been living off the talents of a number of highly qualified people who entered its service during the thirties, when few jobs were available. As this group nears retirement age, are equally qualified replacements on hand? Given the jobs that are now open to college graduates in federal agencies, in business, and in academic life, the answer is, No. Unless certain changes in the system are instituted rather quickly, the state can only look forward to a decline in the caliber of its civil servants.

The changes we propose for the civil service are of two sorts: increased gubernatorial power in determining appointments at certain levels, and increased opportunity for "unconventional" careers in state government.

We would like to see the creation of a division of personnel within the executive department. Like the Division of the Budget, the new division would act as the governor's personal agent in dealing with the other departments. It would be empowered to handle appointments to the more important "policy-sensitive" positions in the bureaucracy. The head of the division would have to be personally loyal to the governor. He must not have institutional interests in potential conflict with the governor, and he must agree with his superior on policy issues. It would be an extraordinarily sensitive position, requiring tact as well as courage, and it probably would not produce rewards in public prestige. But such an official would be of incalculable value to governors of New York in the years to come.

A category of policy-making and top-level administrative appointments would be created along the lines of the new federal Executive Assignment System. These special positions would be managed from within by the personnel division. The division would also be in a position to develop, for the governor and legislature, a comprehensive revision of the Civil Service Law which at least would do the following: (1) Provide greater opportunity for the transfer of officials below the executive level. (This might be accomplished by establishing fewer and more general categories of classification and by allowing transfers within these broad categories at the order of the personnel division.) (2) Lower the retirement age to sixty, with extension at the behest of the Civil Service Commission for most jobs and of the personnel division for high-grade positions.

(3) Create a super-internship program, which would place new entrants on rapid-acceleration tracks. Only when high-quality university products know that they can expect to reach important positions relatively early in life will careers in state civil service appeal to them. (4) Remove a few non-crucial jobs from the civil service system in order to increase the governor's patronage. In a political system where formal power is as diffused as it is in ours, the manipulation of patronage becomes, within bounds, a legitimate and necessary way to centralize power and provide political bases for innovation.

Do these proposals add up to the creation of a gubernatorial tyranny or a return to the massive corruption of the spoils system? By limiting the domain of the civil service are we selling the hard-won reforms of our grandfathers for a few flashy programs of public spending and social innovation? In our opinion an affirmative answer to either question would not only be wrong, but would miss the point of our proposals.

The notion that the governor will become unstoppable after being accorded a bit more capacity to fit administrative arrangements to his needs is a bogeyman designed to frighten people who already tend to believe that politics and politicians are evil. The countervailing forces that operate throughout the State of New York will continue to ensure that the governor will not go on a rampage. The difficulties of building legislative coalitions, the fragmented nature of political parties, the array of skilled interest groups, and the eagerness of journalists to expose "political scandals" and improper behavior will not be affected by our proposals to increase the governor's ability to control and change his bureaucracy.

The situation of our state and nation has changed remarkably since the time of the Progressive reformers. Their paramount objective was to reduce corruption and to keep stealing on the part of public officials to a minimum. Because the role of government was then so limited, they were prepared to accept considerable paralysis in policy innovation in return for a modicum of honesty. One can make it very difficult to corrupt or to be corrupted, but by doing so one makes it equally difficult to do anything at all. We have suggested that in the future state governments will be called on increasingly to provide a high level of public services and to perform the integrative and innovative functions to support such services. A modest pruning of Progressive reforms is necessary if these goals are to be achieved. If we keep in mind the risks that our altered political culture and compulsive scrutiny by mass media create for the larcenous politico, we should realize that it is absurd to be frightened by ritualistic invocations of the image of Tweed.

SUGGESTIONS FOR FURTHER READING

The literature on local politics was given an important lift by the interest of political scientists and sociologists during the 1950's and 1960's in describing the power structures of communities. Such research began with the study of Muncie, Indiana, by Robert and Helen Lynd, published as *Middletown* (New York: Harcourt Brace Jovanovich, 1929), but the work that really triggered the movement was Floyd Hunter's *Community Power Structure* (Chapel Hill, N. C.: University of North Carolina Press, 1953), a study of Atlanta, Georgia. Both Hunter's research method (asking people who they thought was powerful in Atlanta) and his conclusion (that Atlanta was run by an oligarchy of rich men) came under heavy attack. In 1961 Professor Robert Dahl, of Yale, published *Who Governs? Democracy and Power in an American City* (New Haven, Conn.: Yale University Press, 1961). In this study of New Haven, Connecticut, Dahl analyzed selected civic decisions to determine who had, in fact, participated in the decision-making process. The result was a power map of the community showing a number of different élites operating in different issue areas. This sort of "map" is generally described as pluralistic. The debate over methods and conclusions has raged for a decade, and a good, if calculatedly one-sided, collection of materials is William E. Connolly, ed., *The Bias of Pluralism* (New York: Atherton, 1969). As an antidote see Nelson W. Polsby's *Community Power and Political Theory* (New Haven, Conn.: Yale University Press, 1963), and to finish the lesson see Peter Bachrach and Morton S. Boratz's *Power and Poverty: Theory and Practice* (New York: Oxford University Press, 1970).

A seminal work in comparative state politics is Herbert Jacob and Kenneth N. Vines, eds., *Politics in the American States: A Comparative Analysis* (Boston: Little, Brown, 1965). This was followed by James W. Fesler's collection, *The Fifty States and Their Local Governments* (New York: Knopf, 1967), and such works as Thomas Dye's, *Politics, Economics and the Public: Policy Outcomes in the American States* (Chicago: Rand McNally, 1966); Wayne L. Francis' *A Comparative Analysis of Legislative Issues in the Fifty States* (Chicago: Rand McNally, 1968); and Ira Sharkansky's, *Regionalism in American Politics* (Indianapolis, Ind.: Bobbs-Merrill, 1969).

A few works on particular states are helpful; see especially Leon Epstein, *Politics in Wisconsin* (Madison, Wis.: University of Wisconsin Press, 1958), and Joseph Huthmacher, *Massachusetts People and Politics* (Cambridge, Mass.: Harvard University Press, 1959).

For basic data on state politics see *The Book of the States*, published annually by the Council of State Governments.

12 The urban crisis

IN THE PRECEDING CHAPTERS we have presented selections dealing with the major components of our political process—with political culture, with political ideas, and with institutions, formal and informal. In most cases we have been concerned with the likely directions of change or with persistent continuities. But we can learn about possible directions of change by studying political issues as well as by examining the components of the system.

The selections by Mark DeWolfe Howe in Chapter 10 and by Alexander M. Bickel in Chapter 9 suggested ways in which the struggle for racial equality is forcing the modification of important American political institutions and assumptions. Without a doubt the racial issue is the toughest domestic problem facing the system and an important precipitant of change. There are, however, three other discrete sets of issues that have become the occasion of intense concern and that are likely to be change-producing: the so-called crisis of the cities, the eruption of political violence, and the struggle over the direction of U. S. foreign policy. Because these three crucial areas have not been treated directly in previous chapters, it is appropriate to conclude this volume with brief chapters on each.

The old centers of America's largest cities are vexed by increasingly painful problems. This much seems beyond dispute. Deterioration in law enforcement, lack of housing for middle- and low-income groups, failing transportation facilities, inadequate education, sanitation, and pollution controls—these form the base of what many publicists are teaching us to call the "urban crisis." These very visible problems are compounded, so the argument usually goes, by the removal of industrial production plants and distribution centers from the cities since the end of World War II. In addition to all this, there is the persistent refusal of whites, once they have achieved middle-class status, to remain in the cities. Thus the central-city tax bases have shrunk, and what is left is a network of ghettos, gilt-edged business districts, and posh apartment-restaurant-theater districts servicing traveling businessmen as well as those few highly paid professionals who prefer to live close to their work and to high culture.

The specter is raised of a future in which poor black centers are surrounded by white suburban sprawl. This would be disastrous, not only because of the unattended sufferings of the urban poor that would result, but also because the low-density suburbs offer an inferior style of life to those who think they are escaping into a bucolic paradise. High culture requires high compaction; libraries, art galleries, and concert halls must have large populations close at hand to support them. The city provides experience with diversity and change that is absent in the monotonous suburbs. The city is the natural seat of civilization, and if the city is "dying" the implications for civilization are obvious. Even more disturbing, it has been suggested, is the fact that the census figures show we are a nation of cities, and thus their death would crucially affect us all. Surely, we are told, this should be identified and dealt with as a national crisis.

The two selections in this chapter are intended to qualify some of the assertions of the "crisis analysis" of our urban situation. Daniel J. Elazar explores the notion of America as a nation of cities, and James Q. Wilson analyzes the dilemma in which big-city mayors find themselves as a result, in part, of the rhetoric of crisis.

There are, it appears, a number of difficulties with the crisis analysis. First, there is the question, Just how many Americans are actually touched by the problems of the large central city? Second, how accurate is the contention that the middle classes have forsaken the large cities? Part of the difficulty with the "crisis" argument lies in the failure to insist upon the distinction between the central city and the city as a governmental unit. It is important to remember that 80 per cent of the population of New York City lives outside of Manhattan; that most of the cities, whose slums have supplied the data for generalizations about crisis, have within their borders vast tracts or areas that might be called "internal suburbs"; and that few major cities are likely to have poor black majorities in the near future. Another difficulty arises from the failure to distinguish clearly between the middle classes and the working classes. While it is true that middle-class groups have been deserting the central cities, this has not been as true of working-class populations, and these latter urbanites do not perceive their interests as coinciding with those of the poor and the black. To the extent that crisis analysis focuses exclusively on Negro problems, it invites serious political conflict with the working classes. We are not suggesting (and neither does Elazar or Wilson) that the cities do not urgently need attention, but only that more is required in defining urban problems than is usually embodied in the crisis analysis.

Finally, it is not easy to discern what effects the new concern for cities and the quality of urban life will have on the processes of centralization or decentralization of political power within the national political system. But to the extent that the communications media have succeeded in defining urban problems as requiring action on a national scale, it is likely that the federal government's role in funding and ultimately managing various aspects of urban life will increase. Despite calls for decentralization as a tactic for coping with urban ills, and suggestions of regional and metropolitan governmental units, "crises" tend to invite federalization.

Are We a Nation of Cities?

DANIEL J. ELAZAR

It is generally agreed that the United States is now "a nation of cities"—to use a phrase popularized by Lyndon B. Johnson—and that this has given rise to a unique and dramatic "urban problem." When a proposition of this kind receives general assent, however, it may be just the right moment to look at it critically and skeptically.

The difficulty of understanding the "cities problem" in America is heightened by the existence of numerous mythical assessments of urban reality; particularly since the prevalent urban myths have given rise to all sorts of mythical models for urban improvement. Perhaps the central myth is the one that adheres to the very notion of "a nation of cities"—a notion which conjures up a vision of nearly 200 million Americans living shoulder to shoulder along crowded streets, seeking their pleasures in theaters or poolrooms and suffering the pains of living under conditions of heavy congestion. The foundation of this central myth is the "fact" that over 70 per cent of all Americans now live in urban places. This "fact," however, must be considered in the context of the United States Census Bureau's definition of "urban place": any settlement of 2,500 population or more. Only when cities are thus defined, is the United States a nation of cities. But, of course, a town of 2,500—or even 25,000—is not likely to conform to the foregoing vision which most of us share when we speak of cities.

The 1960 population distribution by city size reveals that *58.3 per cent of the nation's total population lived in rural areas or in cities of under 50,000 people (which means approximately 15,000 families)*—and that only 9.8 per cent lived in cities of over one million population. Of the more than 6,000 legally consti-

FROM Daniel J. Elazar, "Are We a Nation of Cities?" *The Public Interest,* No. 4 (Summer 1966), pp. 42–58. © National Affairs, Inc., 1966. Reprinted by permission of the author.

tuted cities in the nation, only five have a population of over one million, and only 51 have populations of over 250,000.

Furthermore, while the rural population has continued its decline, *the percentage of population in urban places of less than 50,000 has actually increased by 50 per cent since 1920. In the same period, the percentage of the national population living in cities of over 500,000 barely increased at all.* At least since 1920, the class of cities with the largest single segment of the nation's urban population (and it is also the fastest growing segment) has been that of the 10,000 to 50,000 group. Most Americans would agree that cities of that size hardly deserve to be considered cities at all, in common-sense usage.

Proponents of the current myths may argue that most small city growth has taken place within the nation's metropolitan areas. While they are technically correct, they are wrong to assume that "the metropolitan area" is just some kind of bigger city, lacking only a single government to formalize reality. The independent suburban townships and smaller cities exist for real reasons, not by historical accident. In fact, the larger the metropolitan area, the more likely the small cities within it are to value their autonomy and their separate identities. Moreover, while the rise of small cities originally created the contemporary metropolitan pattern, their continued growth—together with the stagnation of the central city—is now working to replace that pattern with one which dilutes the supposed "extended city" character of metropolitanism, replacing it with a pattern of extended urban settlement based on a whole ménage of cities of varying sizes and degrees of inter-relationship.

The non-urban character (in common-sense usage) of American urban settlement (in Census Bureau usage), even in metropolitan areas, is shown in the relatively low density of population in the "nation of cities." The accepted minimum measure of an urban environment is a population density of 1,000 or more per square mile; the measure of suburbanization is a population density of 500 per square mile. *Seventeen states do not have even one county—not a single county—with a population density of 500 per square mile.* Only five of the small Northeastern states have more than 30 per cent of their counties in the suburban-density category. Less than half the states—24 to be exact—have even one county with an urban-density of 1,000 or more. *Population density in the Northeastern "megalopolis" exceeds the suburbanization level only in the biggest cities.* Furthermore, three-fourths of all Standard Metropolitan Statistical Areas contain fewer than 500,000 people, *even when central cities and suburbs are combined.* This usually means that the central city population is less than 250,000, and may even be less than 100,000. In short, what is developing in the United States is the spread of a relatively low-density population engaged in urban economic pursuits; many of these American-style city dwellers actually live on plots of land that would look large to a Chinese or Indian farmer.

American urban living is further complicated by the vast difference in the life-styles of residents of American cities, depending on each city's size and location. It should not be difficult to visualize the differences between cities of

20,000 on the fringes of Boston and those of the same population in the heart of the Rockies, between a Philadelphia of two million people in the shadow of New York and a Denver of half a million which serves as the "capital" of a region that ranges five hundred or more miles in any direction. Yet the picture of urbanized America that is implicit in most contemporary discussion depicts all urbanized Americans as living in the same kind of environment and facing the same, or at least very similar, problems. Thus, the national news media convey pictures of traffic jams in New York and talk about the American city being crushed by the automobile. This may be as true of New Rochelle (pop. 77,000) as it is of Manhattan, but it is hardly true of Minneapolis or even Philadelphia, where rush-hour delays hardly add fifteen minutes to the total travel time of motorists who drive to the peripheries of the commuting belt. The media show pictures of miles of slum or small tract houses on both sides of the Hudson River and complain that the American urban population is miserably housed and has destroyed its open spaces. These may become problems in Atlanta or Los Angeles, but neither slums nor sprawl have hindered a very comfortable lifestyle in either place as yet. The media show pictures of violent crime in the nation's capital and describe the American city as a place where people cannot go out on the streets after dark. While the crime rate is rising in most parts of the country, in Peoria or Indianapolis women still consider the streets sufficiently safe for evening movement. Whatever the national spread of traffic jams, water pollution, and violent crime—and these problems are certainly present nationwide—any well-traveled person can vouch for the differences in magnitude of all three from community to community and from region to region, differences which reflect different meanings of "urbanization" from place to place.

MYTHICAL PROBLEMS, MYTHICAL SOLUTIONS

On a slightly different plane, American cities are typified in the contemporary mythology as places where people wish to live anonymously, and where they make every effort to seek the variegated activities cities are supposed to offer. From this, one is led to draw a picture of an urbanized population that is also urbane, except insofar as its urbanity is frustrated by the "crisis of the city." Thus, according to the myth, we face a newly urbane population frustrated because it cannot easily get to the concert halls, the art museums, and the theaters; a population that is forced, against its will, to live in sprawling suburbs; forced to depend upon the family automobile; forced to maintain lawns, raise flowers, and rake leaves. The *Life* double-issue of December, 1965, devoted to "The City," provides the most recent comprehensive example of this myth, presented in its most universally accepted form.

An honest look at the evidence belies this whole picture for all but a small portion of the urban population, located in a few of the largest cities. Wherever the choice has been offered, Americans have worked to cultivate their identities among neighbors, whether through "togetherness" or through neighborhood associations; have sought activities that are by no means citified in character, whether through "Little Leagues" and "do-it-yourself activities" or through outdoor barbecues and camping; and have clearly sought the suburban conditions of living with lawns and automobiles—often within the great cities themselves. Philadelphia, for example, in the heart of the great eastern megalopolis, boasts that 70 per cent of its dwellings are owner-occupied and that there are over 6 million trees within its limits—an average of three per person.

This composite of myths about American urban reality has led to the conclusion that our cities have failed us and that we face an urban crisis. This, in turn, has led to the development of certain models for urban improvement which are based on another set of myths, derived from the classic European stereotype of the city, either directly or as translated into modern terms by social scientists. The most obvious of these is the notion that fragmentation of governmental responses to the urban situation represents a frustration of the will of the people. This argument is used whether the critics of the present situation speak of fragmentation of programs or fragmentation of governmental jurisdictions. Their position is that "rational consolidation" of these programs and jurisdictions will solve the urban problem.

Below the surface of the "fragmentation" argument, however, lies a particular kind of commitment as to the direction in which the American city should develop. Most of those who articulate such solutions for urban problems start with the hidden assumption that there is a public interest in favor of the radical "citification" of the United States, i.e., that the people would like nothing better than to make their cities modern versions of Florence or Rome or Paris, and that they are frustrated in their efforts to do so by fragmentation, by tradition, or by the politicians.

But there is a great deal of evidence to indicate that most of the models of improvement proposed for the American city are nothing more than projections of the desires of certain articulate minorities in American society today. Whatever the dissatisfactions that stir the American people regarding the urbanized world in which they live, they are not the dissatisfactions pointed to by the spokesmen for "the city in crisis." Traffic jams and urban sprawl are not high on the agenda of complaints of the American people—because those are not great problems to most of the people who are defined as "urban dwellers" in the United States today. The blighting of old neighborhoods does not appear to concern the overwhelming majority of Americans, most of whom have never seen a slum. Governmental fragmentation has been ratified time and again when the issue has been presented to the voters; and, indeed, support for fragmentation of one kind or another is so great that the issue has rarely reached the stage of formal voting.

Whatever changes the American people seem to be seeking, they are not directed toward the enhancement of the facilities that lead to an urbane or citified life, but rather to the introduction into the city of qualities associated with the rural life—whether trees, cleaner air and water, larger parks, or new family-style dwellings to reduce the overall density of population. The most recent Gallup Poll on the subject, published in March, 1966, shows that only 22 per cent of the American people desire to live in cities, while 49 per cent would prefer to live in small towns or on farms, with the remainder (28 per cent) opting for the suburbs, probably as a small-town surrogate. This attitude of wistful longing for the rural life is fully as prevalent among younger adults (ages 21-29) as among their elders. (In contrast, two out of three Negroes say they would live in a city or suburban area, if they could live anywhere they chose.) No doubt this response also reflects a mythology—but it is a mythology that must be considered when we seek to understand American attitudes toward the city. The historical record confirms this American desire to gain the economic benefits of urbanization while resisting the way of life usually associated with living in cities. It might be said that the American people persist in maintaining an implicit distinction between urbanization and citification, willingly accepting the former while seeking to avoid the latter.

THE THREE FACTORS AFFECTING AMERICAN CITIES

In understanding the reasons for the rejection of citification we can understand the real character of the American city and of the "American way of urbanization." *The American urban place is preeminently an "anti-city,"* implicitly developed to reflect a basic American life-style which has repeatedly emphasized agrarian elements from the days of the first colonists to our own. The underlying character of the American urban place is shaped by three basic phenomena: agrarianism, metropolitanism, and nomadism.

AGRARIANISM

Since the nation's founding, American values have been rooted in a vision of a commonwealth that supports and encourages the agrarian virtues of individual self-reliance and family solidarity, within a cooperating community of freeholding property-owners where class distinctions are minimal. This agrarian ideal has held the qualities of urbanity, sophistication, and cosmopolitanism to be seriously suspect, despite their undeniable attractiveness.

Nobody conversant with American history need be reminded of the rural roots of American civilization. Articulate Americans consistently viewed the rural life as the good life, or, indeed, the best life, where the vices inherent in man by virtue of Adam's fall would be least likely to flourish. Until the middle of the 19th century, this doctrinal position was reinforced by an agrarian economic system and a pattern of political organization that rested on individual agricultural freeholders. Furthermore, social equality—always a basic, if abstract, element in the American ideal system—found its closest approximation in the middle-class agricultural society of early America (at least in the North and West), a fact which was not lost upon those who seriously concerned themselves with the problems of creating the good society.

From an ideology which looked upon rural living (either in separated farms or in agricultural villages) as the best way to limit individual sin, the agrarian doctrine was translated into positive terms to become part of the world view of the 18th-century enlightenment. Thomas Jefferson, the best-known spokesman for positive agrarianism, articulated the new view as one which saw the agrarian life as the life best suited to bringing out the natural virtues of individual men and most likely to prevent the social evils always possible in society. The city was seen as the source of social corruption even more than individual corruption; the city was to be avoided as a source of inequality, class distinction, and social disorganization that could lead to tyranny in one form or another.

Both the positive and the negative views of "agrarian virtue" versus "urban corruption" became part of the mainstream of American thought, articulated by intellectuals from Thoreau to Frank Lloyd Wright, and made the basis of political movements from Jeffersonian Democracy, through Populism and the New Deal, to the "new conservatism" of the 1960's. The city was and continues to be viewed by many as a breeder of crime, corruption, social disorganization, and *anomie*, not really fit to be lived in, even when valuable for its economic utility. While it is now fashionable in many quarters to attack this kind of thinking as a ridiculously naive relic of the nation's unsophisticated past, there is at least enough probable truth in many of its conclusions to give those who do not otherwise wish to foster citification ample justification for their position.

AGRARIAN IDEALS IN URBAN SETTINGS

Even when the agrarian myth was in full flower, Americans had begun to flock to the cities, primarily to gain economic advantage; and the cities had become the pace-setters in American life. But, while they desired to gain economically and socially by exploiting the benefits of urban concentration, the new city-dwellers rejected the classically urban styles of living (as developed in Old World cities). Accepting the necessity and even the value of urbanization for certain purposes, in particular, economic ones, Americans have characteristically tried to have their cake and eat it, too, by bringing the old agrarian ideals into the urban setting and by reinterpreting them through the establishment of a modified pattern of "rural"-style living within an urban context. The result has been the conversion of *urban* settlements into *metropolitan* ones, whose very expansiveness provides the physical means for combining something like rural and urban life-styles into a new pattern which better suits the American taste. It was hoped that this pattern would combine the advantages of an urban environment with the maintenance of the essence of the traditional American "agrarian" virtues and pleasures, to preserve as much as possible of what is conceived to be the traditional "American way of life."

As part of this effort, sets of institutions and symbolic actions have been developed, partially by design, which are meant to evoke rural and small-town America and its traditional way of life. Limited and fragmented local government is one of these. The creation of many smaller cities—the *bête noire* of most professional city-planners—in place of a single large metropolis reflects this desire for maintenance of the small community, both as an abstract principle and in order to control such crucial local functions as zoning and police, which in a direct or derivative sense embody the traditions of local control. We see this in the continued emphasis on political autonomy for suburban communities, and in their resistance to any efforts, real or imagined, to absorb them into the political sphere of the central city.

Moreover, in many parts of the nation there is a hesitancy among suburbanites to use government for local services, for fear that the addition of more local services will increase the urban character of the environment. Even in the fringe areas of cities, large numbers of people resist sidewalks because sidewalks represent "the city." Street lights are often frowned upon, sewer systems resisted, and the maintenance of the neighborhood school is an article of faith, all for the same reasons.

It is generally known by now that suburbia has become the equal of small-town America as the symbol of the country's "grass-roots" and as the fountainhead of what is distinctive about "the American way of life." This is so regardless of whether suburbia is praised or condemned for its role. (The Chicago *Tribune*, traditional champion of the agrarian virtues as it perceives them, now features suburban settings for its "rural virtue" cartoons.) The popular literature defending suburbia and that attacking it are both strongly reminiscent of the popular literature devoted to small-town America two to four generations ago. If some see virtue in the small community—whether it is typified by a predominantly small-town society or a predominantly suburban society—others see ignorance, provincialism, decadence, and even corruption in the same locale. If the latter speak loudly with words, the former are speaking louder with their feet.

Yet another manifestation of neo-agrarianism is the physical structure characteristic of American cities. The American city sharply separates its commercial and residential areas, creating a "town and country" pattern within its boundaries. Outside of its central core, it emphasizes low-density construction set along wide, easily accessible, tree-lined streets that fade into the countryside without sharp distinctions. At its best, the American urban place further reflects an effort to merge city and country through the development of large, unmanicured public parks which thrust the country into the city and which, in turn, merge into private lawns to further that penetration by creating an overall natural setting that is not subordinated to the buildings. Still another manifestation of Americans' agragrian outlook is the continued emphasis on home ownership, and the complex of activities and symbols which surround it. Owner-occupied, free-standing homes, each with its lawn and garden, represent a major voluntary expenditure of energy and resources in contemporary American society. Virtually every American urban area embodies these neo-agrarian features in some way. Outstanding examples in every section easily come to mind: the greater part of Connecticut in the Northeast, Miami and Nashville in the South, Cleveland and St. Paul in the Middle West, Denver and Seattle in the Far West, to name only a few of the largest and best.

A HOME IS A HOUSE

While urbanization and metropolitanization in other nations have led to the development of official policies to encourage high-density living, federal, state, and even local policies (other than the property tax) in the United States are heavily weighted in favor of the homeowner and low-density development. Mortgage guarantees, home financing funds, homestead exemptions, zoning regulations, and many other specific devices have been enacted into law to encourage widespread home ownership. The foundations for today's widespread home ownership were laid during the 1930's by the New Deal, as part of the New Dealers' overall efforts to translate the ideals and values of traditional American agrarianism into terms appropriate to the new urban setting. The percentage of owner-occupied homes has been increasing rapidly since 1940, when only 43.6 per cent of the nation's housing units were owner-occupied. By 1950, 55 per cent were owner-occupied, a figure which rose to 61.9 per cent by 1960. This figure compares well with the 64.4 per cent of owner-occupied *farm* housing units in 1900.

The trend to owner-occupied housing has revived such symbolically rural occupations as gardening and "do-it-yourself" home maintenance. The public response to these activities—state and county fairs (not to mention home and garden shows) outdraw art galleries in annual attendance *even in the largest cities,* and the greater share of adult education courses deal with home-related activities—indicates that they are, in effect, an urban recrudescence of a significant "vernacular" cultural tradition long associated with rural and small-town life. The importance of this vernacular tradition in American life is generally overlooked in discussions of American culture since those who are generally deemed to be the custodians of the civilized arts in this country tend to be products of the more urbane traditions of Western civilization which originated in Europe.

Similarly, the impact that private maintenance of lawns and gardens has on the maintenance of the aesthetic qualities of American urban areas has generally been ignored by students of urbanization. In the days of "Great Society" beautification programs it would serve us well to recall that the private expenditure for lawn and garden maintenance far exceeds the public expenditures for parks, tree plantings, and similar efforts at urban beautification. It represents an important contribution to the "public good" that would be prohibitively expensive if charged against the public purse and sorely missed if eliminated.

The near-universal American concern with promoting home ownership as the solution to the problems of urbanization and metropolitanization is in itself a strong reflection of the strength of underlying agrarian ideals. Except for New York and Chicago, apartment living remains the domain of unmarried young adults, newly married couples, and the retired. The recent spurt in apartment construction is apparently designed to meet the needs of those groups rather than to replace the single-family home. Curiously enough, much of the so-called apartment "boom" is a suburban phenomenon, one which is reinforcing the developing self-sufficiency of the suburbs by providing indigenous housing for those who are likely to live in apartments, thus helping to transform many suburbs from dormitories for the central city into smaller but self-sufficient cities (American-style) in their own right.

METROPOLITANISM

Excepting only the 19th-century factory towns, founded specifically to bring together enough population to serve industry, the American city was not created for its own sake or to be internally self-contained, but to serve as the center of a larger area—a hinterland tributary to it in some way. From the first, the American city was really part of a larger geographic entity rather than a self-centered community, even in its economic purposes. In contrast, the great cities of Europe, though each may be the metropolis of its particular country, have always offered their residents a self-contained way of life, one that is separated from that of the rest of the country in profound ways. In the United States, this is not true even of New York. The only American cities that even approach such a self-centered separation are San Francisco and New Orleans. In America, cities have thrived only by cultivating their hinterlands, whether it is New York serving as the nation's empire city, Minneapolis playing an imperial role in the Northwest, Pasadena serving the San Gabriel Valley in California, or Charlottesville serving its metropolitan region in central Virginia.

Metropolitanism of settlement, as well as metropolitanism of commerce, began with the very birth of cities in the United States. Urbanization and suburbanization went hand in hand. Even as the rate of urban growth began to accelerate after the War of 1812, a counter, almost anti-urban, trend began to develop alongside it. As fast as some Americans moved to the city, others who were able to do so moved out, while maintaining their ties with it. The process of suburbanization can be traced throughout the 19th century. After 1820, the nation's largest cities, such as New York, Boston, Philadelphia, Baltimore, and New Orleans, began to experience an out-migration to newly created suburban areas. Though most of these early suburbs were later annexed by their central cities, the suburbanization process continued after each set of annexations, gaining new impetus as new means of transportation were developed and made possible movement out of the city for people who worked in the city. First the railroad, then the electric trolley, and finally the automobile stimulated suburbanization past the "horse and buggy" stage.

By 1920, over half the nation lived in "urban places," and nearly a third lived in cities of over 100,000. However, no sooner did the big city become the apparent embodiment of the American style of life, than it began to be replaced by a less citified style in turn. *The upward trend in the growth of big cities came to an end during the depression,* then gave way to the development of medium- and smaller-size cities on the fringes of the big cities themselves. The decline of the big cities began when the problems of population density and congestion seriously cut into the possibilities for maintaining an agrarian-influenced life-style within them. So long as city life was able to offer most of the amenities of rural-style living as well as the economic, social, and cultural advantages of the city to those who were in a position to determine the cities' growth, the expansion of cities as cities continued. Newly settled suburbs and smaller cities were annexed to already large cities because their residents, or at least those who made the decisions locally, felt reasonably confident that their suburban style of life would be maintained, even within the city limits. When this became no longer possible, metropolitanism then became firmly fixed as suburbanization, with the semi-city becoming more important than the city as the locus of growth in area after area.

NOMADISM

This trend is additionally encouraged by the penchant toward nomadism which has always characterized Americans. With a population that is so highly mobile that one family in five moves every year, the older European notion of the city as a stable, self-perpetuating community could not apply in the New World. This penchant has been characteristic of Americans from the very first; *the actual percentage of families that have migrated from one state to another has not changed appreciably in the last century.* Consequently, the city, like every other local governmental subdivision, has become a politically defined entity populated to a great extent by different groups in every generation, with a relatively low level of continuity among groups from one generation to another.

This, in turn, significantly alters the meaning of moving from farm to city, and from central city to suburb, in the United States. In other countries, the great move from a fixed rural location to a fixed urban one has represented a major uprooting that is unique in the life experience of each family, perhaps for generations. In the United States the similar movement, for most people and their families, has been no more than one of a continual series that originally propelled European immigrants across the seas; then, as Americans, westward and into cities; and now from city to suburb or city to city.

The emergence of the "megalopolis" is a perfect reflection of the new nomadism. People escaping the cities of the Eastern seaboard, and now the cities of the interior and West Coast as well, settled first in the interstices between them wherever possible, first forming the traditional suburban circle and then a more or less continuous belt of urban-related settlement as the circles merged and overlapped. Now they have begun to move from place to place within each belt or its segments, preserving a nomadic way of life that is urban without being permanently attached to any particular icty, or even to citified living. Traditionally these migrating Americans have been brought into the political realm as individuals through the possibilities of involvement in local communities, thus preventing them from becoming members of an anomic mass.

THE REVIVAL OF THE BIBLICAL CITY

The American urban place, then, is a very different phenomenon from the city which is usually used for the model against which it is measured. The classic city is a product of Greece and Rome, of medieval and modern Europe. This is the city of the *civitas*, the city which was the center of the political order of the ancient European world and the focal point for the founding of modern republicanism in later European experience. The exemplars of this classic city—Athens, Rome, Florence, Hamburg, Paris—remain today the symbols of urbanity, cosmopolitanism, and sophistication. They became the centers of their world to the point that people not involved with them were excluded from a share in the inner life of that world. Within their respective worlds, they brooked no competition. Men were citizens of those cities until the rise of the nation-state and, for many men, national ties have become synonymous with ties to the central city of their nation. In such cities, the city government was generally equivalent to the central government. That is to say, it was a national as well as a local government. As such, it was internally centralized as well, with all local functions concentrated under the leadership of the general governing body.

The American city, on the other hand, has its classic antecedent in the pattern of Israelite city-building described in the Bible, as befits the cities of an agrarian republic produced by the heirs of the Bible-inspired Reformation. Like the cities of ancient Israel, the American city is located within territorial political jurisdictions that take precedence over it—in its case, the state rather than the tribe, and in both cases, the nation above that. Thus, the city in this country, as in ancient Israel, developed not as the equivalent of the State, but to serve certain functions for an existing civil society which could best be served by bringing men together in relatively dense population groups where they could interact socially and commercially.

Three particular elements in the general structure of the American city bring it into close parallel with its Biblical predecessor. Unlike the Classical city, which, in effect, first established its limits, and then developed its various functions within those limits, the American and Biblical cities grew almost haphazardly from a central point, the "tower" in Biblical parlance. In the ancient Biblical city, the tower was often a fortress, a temple, or perhaps a granary which attracted people who did not seek the city *per se,* but settled around it to make use of the special facilities it offered. In the United States, the equivalent was often the governmental center for the local territorial jurisdiction; the city hall, or, more frequently, the county courthouse. Sometimes it was the general-store–post-office combination or railroad station which centralized communications with the outside world. More recently, Americans have regarded the skyscraper, which rises from the midst of low-density settlement, to be a very real power as a new focal point for the city. In each and every case, the city grew around some function which touched the lives of all the residents of the city and served as a focal point for them in some important way.

Unlike the more or less self-contained Classical city, the American and Biblical cities have developed economically through a relationship with their hinterlands in a special pattern of suburbanization which can be considered unique and characteristic. In both cases, the urban center has been surrounded by satellites—villages or cities—that stand in what we would call a metropolitan relationship to the center. Though the relationship between the tower center and its peripheries is a symbiotic one, in both cases the centers are more dependent on their hinterlands than in the European metropolitan tradition. Both the American and Biblical cities were designed to serve an agrarian ideal. This means, in particular, that the life of the city has been subordinated to the values of the society rather than being given a free hand to shape those values along "sophisticated" lines. In the second place, both kinds of cities have served mobile populations; the Biblical city served an agricultural population that migrated with its flocks within the city's hinterland along set patterns, while the American city increasingly serves a population that migrates from center to peripheries and back, or from section to section within the metropolitan area, with the average resident changing location several times during his life.

The particular structural-functional pattern of the classic Biblical-American city has had direct and observable effects on the character of urbanization. Two examples will illustrate this.

A major complaint among professional urbanists today is that marketing has become decentralized—through shopping centers, etc.—because of metropolitanization. Taking their cues from European city patterns, they argue that marketing must be recentralized if the city is to survive. In fact, the decentralization of the marketing function is characteristic of the Biblical-American city. Marketing has always been a central function in the classical European city, one with important public elements, because it is preeminently a social act, involving daily give-and-take in a manner conducive to the development of latent functions of sociability as well as the manifest functions of buying and selling. In the Biblical-American city, marketing tends to be much more a private affair, conducted in the most efficient possible way by people who do not use it as a social outlet. Thus, in ancient Israel most marketing was done at the "gates of the city," where farmers could come and meet city people for the purposes of commerce. The contemporary American city, with its shopping centers located in such a way as to attract both suburban and urban people without regard to their relationship to the city's center, is simply a contemporary expression of the same pattern. Americans wish *private* convenience in shopping, first and foremost; hence the failure of downtown enthusiasts to recentralize that function. At best, "downtown" has become another regional shopping center in the metropolis.

Similarly, the common complaint about the lack of centralized government at the local level falls on deaf ears, because it is based on European notions of the city. The political structure and functions of the American and Biblical cities have been markedly distinct from those of the classical cities of Europe. The limited role played by a city that is simply one focal point among many in a larger civil society lends itself both to a reduction in the importance of the city's government and to the possibility of the separation of its governing institutions along functional lines without undue inconvenience.

THE PRINCIPLE OF LOCAL CONTROL

While Americans have an ideological predilection for emphasizing the primacy of local government, in fact they have not hesitated to utilize the powers of government at all levels—federal, state, and local—to secure their political ends. At the same time, they have continued to emphasize the principle of local control over all government activities within the community, regardless of the official point of origin of these activities. What this means is that every local community is inextricably bound up in a three-way partnership with the federal and state government, one in which virtually every activity in which it is involved is shared intergovernmentally. Not only is this true today, but to a significant degree it has always been true, changing only to the extent that the increase in the total velocity of government at all levels has intensified the amount of shared activity.

The existence of this partnership, with its emphasis on the national government's role as stimulator of better public services, coupled with maximum local control over actual implementation of specific programs, has certain consequences that up to now have operated to reinforce the classical patterns of American urbanization. First of all, and most obviously, it reduces the desire of the local people to give up their local autonomy. Within the federal system, all local governments act as acquirers of federal and state aid; as adapters of national or state programs to local conditions, needs, and values; as initiators of new programs at the state and national, as well as the local, level; and as experimenters in the development of new services. Most important, for every local community or communal interest, possession of its own local government gives it a seat in the great game of American politics. Governmental organization is, in effect, a form of "paying the ante" that gives the community as a whole, or the specific interest, access to a political system that is highly amenable to local influence properly managed. Relinquishment of structural autonomy, on the other hand, substantially weakens the position of the community, or interest, in its all-important dealings with the state and federal governments. This militates against any local government—whether the general-purpose government of a city or township or the special-purpose governments such as school, library, or park districts—willingly giving up its existence unless its constituents cease to desire a special seat at the political table.

This basic tendency is reinforced by the role of the states in the federal system. Because the states are able to "run interference" for those of their cities that wish them to do so, they enable the smaller urban places to benefit from the nation's overall system of local assistance to a degree that would be impossible if those cities had to confront Washington alone. Lacking the expertise or the political influence necessary to capitalize on all the benefits offered by the federal government in its efforts to improve the caliber of public services in the country as a whole, the smaller cities can use the expertise and influence of the state governments and congressional delegations to their advantage.

Of course, the nation's largest cities, the great metropolitan centers, do not feel the need for this kind of service, nor are they willing to pay the various surcharges which the states quite naturally demand for doing the job; hence their desire to obtain federal aid directly. But the suburbs and smaller cities find no particular advantage in sharing the big cities' desire.

The present system also robs the "metropolitan consolidationists" of one of their primary arguments: that the creation of larger, supposedly more viable cities, i.e., ones with metropolitan-wide general governments, will lessen the federal role in local affairs. The entire thrust of American history militates against this idea. Since virtually all governmental activities are invariably shared by all levels of government whether the local levels act energetically or not, restructuring local government is not likely to alter the federal role in any appreciable way. A metropolitan area is no more likely to be financially and economically self-sufficient than the largest states are today, and we know that no state is presently willing or able to give up federal assistance, particulary since none feels the need to do so to maintain reasonable local autonomy.

What would happen under "metropolitan consolidation" is that the present system—whereby the national administrators can speak for the ostensible interests of the larger public, while the local governments can speak for the most specific interests of the local publics, so that together they can strike a balance—would be replaced by one in which national and local officials would tend to speak for much the same interests, leaving legitimate local interests in a far weaker position in their efforts to be heard. In more than one community, had local consolidation taken effect, there would be fewer owner-occupied homes, tree-lined streets, and locally responsive schools. Americans are not about to give up any of these.

MESSIANISM AND URBANISM

Only the existence of an otherwise unmanageable and authentic urban crisis would lead Americans to seek to alter the present situation, or would persuade those who value the present semi-urban way of life available to most people in this country that they ought to alter their life-style. Most vocal urbanists today argue that such a crisis does indeed exist. But, given the value preferences of the great majority of Americans, that argument seems hollow. As long as Americans prefer private homes to ease of access to work, trees and lawns to easy access to theaters and museums, private shopping to public marketing, and the quiet of the suburbs to the bustle of the city, solution of the problems usually packaged together as "the crisis of the cities" becomes much less important.

This is not to say that there are no important problems generated by the urbanization of the United States. There are indeed great ones which must be tackled—most especially in the dozen or so largest cities. But they do not call for an "overresponse" based on a crisis psychology. Unquestionably the solutions to these urban problems must be pursued by governments at all levels. Since most Americans would very likely argue that, with all its problems, the American pattern of semi-urbanization is the freest and most comfortable yet created, there is every reason to believe that the preservation of that pattern is a desirable goal for the governments of this country to pursue.

In one respect, at least, the idea of "the city in crisis," while generally based on false premises, represents a characteristically American response to problems of the environment. Perceiving some real problems in the urban environment, the bulk of the vocal reformers in our midst began to generate steam (for themselves and for others) to meet those problems, first by portraying them in apocalyptic terms, and then by prescribing messianic solutions which not only ignore but denigrate political and social realities. Up to a generation ago, this messianic urge sought to reverse the process of urbanization by returning the American people to the soil. That vision was clearly unattainable even then. Nor was it desired by most Americans. It has given way, in turn, to a vision that calls for the transformation of an urbanized America into a citified one, hallowing the city as the only key to the civilized life, much as the early agrarians hallowed ruralism as the only key to a moral life. This new messianic view is no more likely to be accepted than its predecessor.

It is a mistake to assume that urbanization in America stands apart from the other influential movements uniquely important in the American experience, or that Americans view the proper ends of urbanization apart from their larger view of the proper ends of life—their overall set of values. Unless urbanization and the responses to it are considered in relation to, if not in the context of, such values as federalism, freedom to make choices about life-styles, the agrarian spirit, and the concern for "the American way of life," we fall prey to mythical assessments of urban reality and to the building of mythical models of urban improvement.

In fact, the American urban place is a non-city because Americans wish it to be just that. Our age has been the first in history even to glimpse the possibility of having the economic advantages of the city while rejecting the previously inevitable conditions of citified living, and Americans apparently intend to take full advantage of the opportunity. If we wish to make a realistic approach to our real urban problems, we would be wise to begin with that fact of American life.

The Mayors vs. the Cities

JAMES Q. WILSON

So accustomed have we become to the daily dispatches from the urban battlefront —reports of perpetual crisis, the descriptions of mayors struggling in vain against seemingly hopeless odds, the ominous warnings of growing frustrations and anger —that we are in danger of taking for granted, as though they were part of the natural order, some rather remarkable developments. By the standards of any other era, what is happening today—or more precisely, what is *not* happening— needs to be explained.

Consider: Despite the fact that ghetto riots have torn scores of cities and that rising rates of violent crime have afflicted even more, and despite the fact that George Wallace revealed by his campaign that there are millions of Americans ready for a hard-line, get-tough policy on civil disorder, there are few big-city

FROM James Q. Wilson, "The Mayors vs. the Cities," *The Public Interest*, No. 16 (Summer 1969), pp. 25–37. © National Affairs, Inc., 1969. Reprinted by permission of the author.

mayors—Los Angeles in this, as in other respects, is an exception—who publicly endorse this approach or who act as if they thought there was any political mileage in it. In New York, Boston, Detroit, San Francisco, Atlanta, and many other cities, the mayors, far from trying to put together a political base out of white "law-and-order" sentiments, are repudiating this strategy and continuing to argue for meliorative measures designed to better the lot of the poor and the black. Though every public opinion poll shows Americans, especially but not wholly white Americans, to be deeply troubled and angered by crime and disorder, and though every group of organized police officers [is] demanding that the mayors "unleash" them; and though there is usually a primary opponent in the wings, waiting to run against "crime in the streets"—nevertheless the standard reply of the mayors has been to deplore violence, to call for renewed efforts to eliminate its causes, and to attack overzealousness about this issue as a form of disguised racism. Finally, a "law-and-order" candidate in office rarely maintains the "hard line" that got him there; Sam Yorty, since reelection, has been speaking far more softly and sociologically than he campaigned. So, it can be predicted, will Marchi or Procaccino, if either of these gentlemen is elected Mayor of New York.

Consider also: Whenever a clear choice confronts a mayor, he tends (again, especially in the big cities) to side with the liberal (though rarely the radical) side even when the liberal side appears to be widely unpopular. John Lindsay favored a civilian review board for the police, though any sounding of opinion would have shown that the vast majority of New York voters were strongly opposed to the board. Joseph Aliota became, as mayor, a backer of the police–community relations unit of the San Francisco police department even though the unit was detested by many, probably most, San Francisco officers and criticized by many civilians for allegedly "siding with the criminals" against the police. The response of Jerome Cavanagh to the fearful riot in Detroit was to appoint and actively support a "New Detroit Committee" that consulted with (though did not satisfy) the most militant blacks and urged programs and patience rather than tanks and toughness. And he did this though he was facing an organized campaign among white voters to recall him from office for alleged failures to curb rising crime (by which the petitioners meant, of course, rising *Negro* crime).

Consider finally: Though municipal tax rates have been steadily rising and though the "revolt of the taxpayers" is often predicted and indeed sometimes occurs, the "new breed" mayors are rarely, if ever, fiscal conservatives. Instead, they launch new programs and raise property and other taxes to new highs, despite the fact that one reason they defeated their predecessor may have been that he seemed to be responsible for a tax level the voters found unacceptable. Of course, many of the subsequent increases result from forces over which no mayor has any control—legislatively mandated pay raises for city workers, for example—but some substantial part of the boost is caused by the fact the mayor is innovative and program-oriented rather than single-mindedly tax-conscious.

FINDING EXPLANATIONS

One possible explanation for these apparent paradoxes is that acting other than as the mayors do would be politically risky. A tough law-and-order posture would alienate Negro voters and a failure to improve services (even at the cost of higher taxes) would alienate white homeowners. But in many of these cities with the most conspicuously "new breed" mayors—Boston, New York, San Francisco—the black vote is but a small fraction of the total (in Boston, for example, it is probably less than 10 per cent of the whole and in New York and San Francisco, it could not be much more). And in some of these cities, as well as in cities (such as Detroit) where Negroes are a much larger fraction of the population, persons get elected to the city councils on the basis of much more conservative images, even though they run at large and thus have exactly the same constituencies as does the mayor.

Nor can it be said that the present strategy of the more progressive mayors confers any obvious political rewards. At this writing, the probability of Lindsay's reelection hardly seems overwhelming. The common complaint of (white) New York voters seems to be that he "gives too much to the Negroes" (though, naturally, Negroes may feel that they have in fact received very little). And Cavanagh in Detroit did not appear to enhance his shaky political position with the steps he took after the riot—indeed, for many voters he probably worsened it. By contrast, Mayor Richard Daley in Chicago won a great deal of support by his tough line during and after the police clashes with demonstrators at the Democratic National Convention.

Of course, chance may play some part in deciding who gets to be mayor. After all, Louise Day Hicks campaigned in Boston in a way that attracted strong support from the police, from opponents of measures designed to further school integration, and from many victims of the city's chronically high tax rate. She led the field in the preliminary election and ran a quite respectable second in the elimination round. If she had not been a woman and if some campaign breaks had gone her way, she might well be the mayor of Boston. But what is striking is not that she lost, but that Kevin White, who won, did not operate the mayor's office in a way obviously calculated to win over to him the voters who opposed him. One of his first acts was an effort (aborted by premature publicity) to replace the police commissioner; subsequently, he announced some of the largest tax increases any Boston mayor has ever had to take responsibility for. And other measures intended to help the lot of Boston Negroes have earned for him, in certain neighborhoods, the unflattering nickname of "Mayor Black."

To some persons, finding explanations for why mayors act as they do is unnecessary, or rather the explanation is obvious—these officials are courageous, right-thinking persons who deeply believe in what they are doing and are willing to take the blame for having done it. There is no doubt a good deal of truth in this view, but it does not seem adequate. These mayors are also intelligent, and they would have little to lose by deciding that discretion is the better part of valor. Given the heavy law-and-order majorities in many cities, one would expect even the most forward-looking chief executive to at least talk tough if only to win breathing space for himself and perhaps some consent for the programs he seeks to carry out. Most liberal mayors face no threat from the left (the Negroes have no realistic alternative), but they do face serious threats from the right. Yet the center-seeking tendencies of state and national candidates seems not to be duplicated at the big-city level. Hubert Humphrey as well as Richard Nixon found it important to have firm law-and-order (or "order-and-justice") positions; anybody running against Ronald Reagan in California would be foolish indeed to assume that he would improve his chances of election by departing radically from Reagan's position on student unrest, welfare programs, or crime in the streets. The best he could hope for would be to display a difference in emphasis sufficient to acquire votes on the left while keeping his losses in the center and on the right to a minimum.

A NEW ERA IN CITY POLITICS?

I would suggest that there is a general, structural reason for the behavior of many big-city mayors, a reason that, if correct, implies the arrival of a new era in city politics, one unlike either the era of the political machine or that of conventional political reform. For many mayors today, and perhaps for some time to come, their *audience* is increasingly different from their *constituency*. By "audience" I mean those persons whose favorable attitudes and responses the mayor is most interested in, those persons from whom he receives his most welcome applause and his most needed resources and opportunities. By "constituency" I mean those people who can vote for or against him in an election.

At one time, audience and constituency were very nearly the same thing. The mayor was reelected if he pleased his party and the city's voters, or at least a substantial number of the wards and factions making up these voters. The only resources he needed (money to finance his campaign and taxes with which to run the city) were available from city interests. The only help he needed was from party workers who not only staffed his campaign but his government as well. From time to time, the highly partisan, machine-style mayor would be replaced by a nonpartisan or reform mayor, but for him, too, audience and constituency were similar. His constituents were those voters (temporarily a majority) who were disgusted by scandal or bored by sameness; his audiences were essentially *local* reformers—business groups, good government or "municipal research bureau" organizations, and crusading big-city newspapers.

With the decline of the urban political party and with the decline in the vitality and money resources of the central city, postwar mayors began to look to new sources for both support and issues. Many found them in urban redevelopment. Business and planning groups were concerned about the fate of the downtown business district and willing to back mayors who promised to do something. But many, if not most, of these supporters had themselves moved outside the city limits, and a large part of the bill for the new improvements was to be paid by the federal government with grants directly to the cities (and not, as with traditional programs, funnelled through the states). In this period, the separation between audience and constituency began. The mayor was elected by city residents, but he campaigned through the help of—and in part with the intention of influencing—businessmen, planners, and federal agencies.

In the 1960's, the primarily physical emphasis of the urban renewal program fell under strong criticism, and new needs, chiefly involving problems of poverty and racial isolation, came to the fore. The new concerns were nonbusiness, and to a degree antibusiness, though businessmen later joined in some of the programs created, especially those having to do with employment. But this shift in substantive focus to social issues was not so much a reassertion of the concerns of constituents as it was a change in the composition of the audience. To be sure, the riots were chiefly the acts of a certain group of constituents, but these disturbances, though they imparted a special sense of urgency to urban concerns, did not create them. The model cities program, the war on poverty, most civil rights bills, the aid of education programs, and the various pilot projects of both the government and private foundations were largely devised, promoted, and staffed by groups who were becoming the mayor's audience though they were not among his constituents.

This audience consists principally of various federal agencies, especially those that give grants directly to cities; the large foundations, and in particular the Ford Foundation, that can favor the mayor with grants, advice, and future prospects; the mass media, or at least that part of the media—national news magazines and network television—that can give the mayor access to the suburbs, the state, and the nation as a whole; and the affluent (and often liberal) suburban voters who will pass on the mayor's fitness for higher office.

No mayor can afford to cater to this audience to the exclusion of constituency interests nor is the audience always in agreement as to what it will applaud. But to a growing degree, the audience is the source of important cues and rewards that tend, however much they may conflict in detail, to be on the whole consistent. First of all, the audience sets the tone and provides much of the rhetoric for the discussion of urban issues. Indeed, it often decides what *is* an urban issue. At one time, taxes and the fate of the central business district were the issues; then housing became more important; juvenile delinquency enjoyed a brief vogue and now seems to be coming back for an encore; poverty and race have been the most recent issues, though while the "race problem" was once thought to require removing the barriers to integration, it is now more likely to be seen in terms of "community control" and "neighborhood action" (neither of which will do much at all for integration). "Talking the language" of the audience is an important way for a mayor to win esteem and to become a state or even national figure.

THE AUDIENCE HAS POWER

But more than esteem is at stake. The audience also controls much of the free resources that a mayor needs so urgently, given his pinched tax base, the rising demand for services, and the shortage of able people to staff city hall. The great bulk of any city's budget is, in effect, a fixed charge the mayor is powerless to alter more than trivially. He must pay the policemen, firemen, and sanitation workers; he must service the municipal debt; and he must meet his share of welfare and educational costs. After he does these things, there is not much left over to play around with. If he is to be "innovative," or even if he is to respond to any new demands, he must find new money and, equally important, more staff people. The federal government is obviously one source of new money, but is not always available—at least in large amounts—just for the asking. If the mayor wants his city to be a "model city" or if he wants a generously funded poverty program, it helps if he is thought, by the relevant agency, to be a "good mayor" with "ideas" and the "right approach." Such decisions are not made so much in traditional political terms—Congress, for example, may have little collective influence on these allocations though substantial influence in particular cases involving particular members—but in terms of bureaucratic politics in which most of the persons involved do not think of themselves as politicians at all. Undersecretaries and assistant secretaries and bureau administrators and (often of greatest importance) the personal assistants to department heads decide whom among the mayors they can "talk to."

Nor is the money always used wholly for the stated purposes. Cities such as Boston and New Haven that had vigorous urban renewal programs had them in part to get federal funds for the city but also in part to create within the city, but outside the normal departmental structure, a large staff of professional talent that could be used for any number of purposes. The best local renewal authorities become generalized sources of innovation and policy staffing, and their directors become in effect deputy mayors (and sometimes more than that).

Foundations and private organizations can also provide free resources that, though small in amount compared to federal largesse, can often make the difference between running an "ordinary" administration and running one that is newsworthy, exciting, or "different." The Ford Foundation "Gray Areas" program was for a while a systematic effort at serving, however unintentionally, just this function. (Many mayors later decided that what they really wanted was the attention that came from *announcing* the program, not the often less flattering attention that came from trying to *run* it. The ideal "pilot project" from the mayor's point of view is one that puts some money into the city treasury, gets some good headlines, provides a few more staff assistants, and then promptly vanishes without a trace before anyone can start quarreling about what purpose it is to serve or who should control it.)

The audience is just as important as a source of skills. For all the talk about cities being "where it's at," very few able administrators seek out employment in the low-prestige, low-paying jobs that city hall has to offer. There are such people, but they are small in number and young in age. To get the best of them, or even to get any at all, every big-city mayor is in competition with every other one. The mayor that runs (however well advised) a "business-as-usual" administration is at a profound disadvantage in this competition. Indeed, the would-be mayor must often start seeking them out when he decides to run for office so that they can give him the speeches, the position papers, and the "task force reports" that increasingly are the hallmark of a campaign that wins the sympathy of the media. The process of tuning the mayor to be responsive to the audience begins, therefore, even before he becomes mayor. And if he should ever entertain any thoughts about taking a "tough line" or going after the "backlash vote" (however rational such a strategy might be), he would immediately face a rebellion among his young campaign and staff assistants.

THE NEW UPWARD MOBILITY

Finally, the audience is increasingly able to reward and thus shape the career aspirations of the big-city mayor. There was a time when being mayor was a dead-end street, and in terms of advancing to higher elective office, it may still be. Cavanagh could not win his own party's nomination, to say nothing of the Senate seat, even when he was still enjoying the unstinting praise of the media and the tranquility of preriot Detroit. Kevin White of Boston appears eager to run for governor in 1970, but many are skeptical that he can get either the nomination or the office. (His predecessor, John Collins, tried for the Democratic nomination for United States Senator but in the primary election failed even to carry his own city, Boston.) This may be changing, however, as more public attention is focused on cities, and if the mayor is adroit enough to get out of city hall and into a safer office before criticisms begin to mount up.

But higher elective office is no longer the only place for an ex-mayor to go. Today he can reasonably hope—*if* he is in good standing with the audience—to be offered an important Washington assignment, to join a private organization or foundation working in the urban field, or at least to acquire some sort of professorship that will sustain him, offer him a chance to gather his thoughts, and provide a base from which he can seek consulting opportunities (and fees). If he had his choice, of course, almost any mayor would prefer public office to the relative obscurity of private action; one must have a powerful love of politics even to think seriously of running for mayor in the first place. But whereas former mayors once had a choice among higher elective office (sometimes shabby), idleness, or at best a low-paying judgeship or post as recorder of deeds, now they can be fairly sure that they can join the board of a corporation doing business in cities or the ranks of the nonprofit (but not necessarily unrewarding) foundations, alliances, coalitions, institutes, and centers. Sure, that is, if their credentials are in order with the audience that has created and sustains such enterprises.

OPPOSED PERSPECTIVES

It is important not to overstate the point. "New-style" mayors are no more engaged in the single-minded pursuit of audience acclaim than "old-style" mayors were preoccupied with winning constituency votes. The former clearly need votes, too, and the latter were at least partially concerned with "respectability." And in either case, no one theory can possibly explain all the actions undertaken at city hall—every mayor of any style responds to a complex set of external pressures and personal judgments that cannot be summarized as mere self-interest, however conceived.

Furthermore, the behavior rewarded by the audience changes from time to time. Once, urban renewal was the favored policy, but that is no longer the case. Today, influential parts of the audience are concerned about neighborhood representation, community control, and governmental decentralization. Many mayors are hoping that there is now a substantial overlap between audience concerns and constituency interests and accordingly are betting heavily on "little city halls," neighborhood service centers, and school decentralization. The audience is now reacting against the excesses of urban renewal—its orientation to the central business district and to land clearance—and is developing a concern for neighborhood integrity and local public services that can reinforce the obvious interest constituents have in just such matters.

The congruence of interest may be real; at the very least, it tends to obscure the differences, described in exaggerated terms earlier in this article, between audience and constituency. Obscures, but does not eliminate, for the two groups act out of fundamentally different motives and with quite opposed perspectives on what a "neighborhood orientation" is supposed to achieve. The audience, though it may give lip service to neighborhood benefits and decentralization in general, is primarily interested in such things for the poor and the black, especially the latter; the constituency, or at least its white majority, sees a neighborhood orientation as meaning getting help from city hall to hold down taxes, provide more police, and keep black children from being "forcibly" (i.e., by busing or redistricting) brought into their schools. "Community control" to many elements of the audience means Negro control; to many central-city white constituents, it means anti-Negro control. In the reaction against the disadvantages of the era of mayor-backed urban renewal and highway projects, some of the compensating advantages of a city-wide perspective were lost sight of. Taking influence over decisions away from neighborhoods meant preventing them from acquiring governmental power to use against one another, admittedly at a price in decreased responsiveness to local interests.

Managing a city government so that it is receptive to legitimate neighborhood concerns and unreceptive to illegitimate ones is difficult under the best of circumstances, but especially trying when the consensus as to what is legitimate has begun to disintegrate. In New York City, Jewish voters, who are normally warm supporters of any mayor who seems forward-looking, liberal, and honest, have been plunged into a state hovering between confusion and fury by the discovery that school decentralization seemed to mean allowing black militants to harass Jewish teachers and a Jewish-led teachers' union. As a result, a part of the audience that might ordinarily think decentralization is a good idea has defected from its ranks. (It is interesting to speculate what their attitude might have been if community control had come first to the police instead of the schools. They might have regarded it—as they did the civilian review board—as a threat to "law and order" or they might have ignored it as a threat only to Irish police and an Irish policeman's union.)

In short, though present mayors seem to be neighborhood-oriented and thus constituency-oriented, the style and to a degree the substance of that orientation is heavily influenced by audience rather than constituency concerns: it favors social experimentation and innovation, it gives special attention to the interests of black citizens, and it treats gingerly (if at all) local demands for a strong law-enforcement policy. It does not follow, of course, that the supposed beneficiaries of this policy, the blacks, see themselves as having benefited. They are no doubt likely to give strong political support to the present mayors in New York, Boston, and elsewhere, but many of their leaders feel that the neighborhood orientation, though in general desirable, has delivered rather little in the way of concrete gains and that it may in fact have raised neighborhood expectations unrealistically.

BENEFITS AND COSTS

The advantages of the growing influence of the mayor's audience should not be underestimated. The reasons for the importance of the audience—its control of important resources in money and talent—are directly related to the needs of the cities. At a time when new funds are hard to find and able people hard to entice, one is prepared to look kindly on almost any strategy that will provide more of either. Indeed, the role of the audience may be important in getting some men to run for mayor in the first place. When city hall seems to be both a political dead end and an institutionalized nightmare, audience support and interest may be critical as an inducement for attracting at least certain kinds of talent to mayoral elections. (I do not wish to exaggerate this point. With no audience interest whatsoever, there would still be a surprising number of candidates for the special purgatory that is city hall. Ambition has probably led to the ruination of more men than lust.)

Above all, the audience has played a critical role in preventing (or since history is yet to run its course, slowing) the emergence of an urban nativism that would exploit base emotions and encourage vindictive sentiments. Without the increase in the number of big-city Negro voters as well as the increased salience of a liberal, city-oriented audience, there would surely have been a large number of candidates and officials making racist (in the strict sense) appeals to white voters.

But the advantages should not blind us to the costs of audience involvement. Its members, because they rarely have anything personally at stake in big-city politics, attach rather little value to stability and order and a high value to experimentation and change. Furthermore, because they have little direct experience with the results of programs, they are likely to be relatively uncritical of what is new (newness suggests initiative, concern, action) but highly critical of what exists (oldness suggests the status quo, passivity, and indifference). And since few members of audience need take (in the usual case) responsibility for any programs, the audience as a whole is generally unaware of, or unconcerned with, the failure of earlier ideas it had once endorsed. If a bold new program falls flat on its face, that fact is either unremarked or taken as a sign that what is needed next time is a program that is even newer and bolder.

There is also a tendency for the mayors, in responding to audience concerns, to accelerate the rate of increase in unrealizable expectations. The new mayors are under considerable pressure to out-promise each other (at least initially), but, because they can rarely deliver on these promises, they may leave a legacy of frustration and cynicism. This would be true, of course, even if the audience did not exist—candidates always tell voters what they want to hear, even if what they want is utterly impossible. But the audience exacerbates this tendency. By making mayors rival claimants for media attention and federal largesse, it induces a mayor to bid against mayors in other cities as well as opponents in his own. Mayors must now not only out-promise challengers with respect to what the constituents want, but out-promise them with respect to what the audience wants as well.

To be sure, the audience-oriented mayors occasionally succeed. A riot may (apparently) be prevented, or a public agency usefully reorganized, or a new service installed. When that happens, it is often as much the result of luck and particular circumstances as of style and skill. But a success in one place, and for reasons unique to that place, encourages others to believe that similar successes are possible in other places. The audience generalizes the example of the single mayor and makes him the model for all mayors. Everywhere, one hears of persons who are running or acting in the "Lindsay style" as if that style were both an unqualified blessing and an exportable commodity. Television commentators, who are especially prone to conceptualize public events in stylistic terms, owing in great part to their own needs to attract audience interest with one- or two-minute film clips, are particularly likely to seize on a "good style" (good, they believe, for both their entertainment needs as well as for public problems) and measure other persons by that standard.

One group of mayors may be exempt from the dilemmas of pleasing both constituency and audience. The black mayors, at least for the time being, enjoy a guaranteed audience with instinctively favorable reactions. Being black, they attract the sympathetic attention of the media, the foundations, the federal agencies, and most liberal voters. Grants for special purposes and designations as "model cities" are likely to come fairly easily for such mayors. To the extent they can take audience support for granted, they are free to turn their attention to constituency problems, and, in dealing with these constituents, can afford to promise less. (Partially offsetting their freedom is the greater criticism from white voters and the higher expectations of black ones within their cities.)

DEMOGRAPHY AND AUTHORITY

All the foregoing is said, not in criticism of mayors, but in sympathy for their plight. The audience, after all, is almost as ready as the constituency to criticize a mayor who fails to conform to their expectations. When a man is elected with an audience-acclaimed style and then, within a few weeks, begins speaking prosaically about the tax rate and the demands of the organized city employees, he begins to disenchant his audience who thought that he was somehow "above that sort of thing." And he, in turn, can be pardoned for becoming exasperated at the unreasonable demands of his vicarious voters, the unfranchised audience.

At the root of his difficulties are demography and authority: the liberal voters have moved out of the city without relinquishing their claim to share in its governance, and the process of governing has been made immeasurably more difficult by the inability of the mayor to acquire enough power to manage an increasingly intense conflict. There has been a simultaneous growth in the problems of central cities and a decline in the authority of the mayor to handle those problems. Among the many crises, real and imagined, that are the lot of cities these days, should be numbered the crisis of authority.

The mayor is increasingly unable to control his own bureaucracy owing to the growth both in its size and in the strength of its protective devices (civil service and employee organizations). He increasingly finds that there are no political parties capable of producing stable governing majorities on the city councils. And he increasingly confronts issues that are of such fundamental importance or laden with such symbolic significance that they cannot be resolved by the normal processes of bargaining and modest revenue reallocations—crime, racial conflict, and civil disorder. It is not surprising that, faced with these difficulties, he should seek allies and help wherever he can find them. Thus, when a national commission blames urban riots on "white racism," the mayors of the cities where those riots occurred hastened to agree with this diagnosis—partly because they may think it is right, but more importantly because they see the acceptance of this verdict as a useful means for placing a moral obligation on the federal government to send more financial aid to the cities.

The situation that results is inherently unstable. If the resources to govern can only be obtained by the mayor joining his audience in characterizing white big-city voters in terms the latter reject as untrue and unfair, these constituents are likely quickly to lose patience. If, on the other hand, no resources are to be had from any source, black voters are also likely to lose patience. Newsworthy "happenings," theatrical events, and walking tours of the slums may divert attention from these dilemmas, but they are unlikely to resolve them. (There is something to be said for even a diversion, of course. The vitriolic mayorality campaign in Boston in 1967 was less divisive than otherwise owing, I believe, to the preoccupation of the voters with the dramatic Red Sox pennant race, and the tense Detroit summer of 1968 did not become explosive partly because the Tigers, by winning the pennant and the World Series, were a unifying influence. Unfortunately, only two teams can win pennants each year.)

There is little comfort and even less guidance to be drawn from these somber reflections. If there were a better way to do things, no doubt some mayor would by now have found it. What seems clear, however, is that the "new breed" mayors —of whom John Lindsay is perhaps the archetype—are new in more senses than one. They are not simply new personalities or new styles, they are responses to important underlying shifts in the distribution of influence in American urban politics—shifts that have brought new sources of power to bear on cities as, indeed, they have brought such sources to bear on the country generally. Urban politics have become, in significant degree, nationalized.

SUGGESTIONS FOR FURTHER READING

The rennaisance of interest in the politics of American cities has stimulated a number of good books, and among the distinguished ones are Wallace Sayre and Herbert Kaufman, *Governing New York City* (New York: Russell Sage, 1960), and Theodore Lowi, *At the Pleasure of the Mayor* (New York: Free Press, 1964).

In the spate of new writing on the problems of the central cities two other names stand out: Edward C. Banfield and James Q. Wilson. Banfield's *Political Influence* (New York: Free Press, 1961) helped return to fashion the study of urban politics in American universities, and Banfield and Wilson's *City Politics*

(Cambridge, Mass.: Harvard University Press, 1963) has already achieved the status of a minor classic. Two Wilson collections, *The Metropolitan Enigma: Inquiries into the Nature and Dimensions of America's Urban Crisis* (Cambridge, Mass.: Harvard University Press, 1968; and Doubleday Anchor Books, 1970), and *City Politics and Public Policy* (New York: Wiley, 1968) are also valuable. Another helpful collection is Lawrence H. Fuchs, ed., *American Ethnic Politics* (New York: Harper Torchbooks, 1968).

On housing patterns see Seymour Toll, *Zoned American* (New York: Grossman, 1969), and Rose Helper, *Racial Policies and Practices of Real Estate Brokers* (Minneapolis, Minn.: University of Minnesota Press, 1969). On crime see Richard Harris, *The Fear of Crime* (New York: Praeger, 1969), and William Ryan, *Distress in the City: Essays on the Design and Administration of Urban Mental Health Services* (Cleveland: Case Western Reserve University Press, 1969).

13 The eruption of violence

ANOTHER DEVELOPMENT THAT MAY PERMANENTLY ALTER THE PATTERNS of American politics is the increasing resort to the tactics of demonstration, confrontation, and violence by militant groups. It is clear that these are three distinct tactics, but it is also clear that after the demonstrations in the early 1960's proved successful, they were quickly followed by the more disruptive tactics of confrontation and violence. There is at least presumptive evidence for a connection among all three techniques of "direct action." The exaggerating, tub-thumping rhetoric that is always necessary in urging large numbers of normally unpolitical people to the direct action of a demonstration seems to create expectations of immediate and total success. When these overheated expectations are frustrated, bitterness and cynicism and rage are provoked, furnishing an atmosphere for confrontation and, ultimately, for violence. This is not to characterize the process as "bad," but only to set the stage for a discussion of the pros and cons of direct action, and to suggest that we would do well to welcome and encourage one kind of direct action—demonstrations—while taking care to avoid, so far as possible, its "natural" degeneration into confrontation and violence.

For a considerable period before 1962, there was little direct action in American politics; power was sought not in the streets but in corridors, in conference rooms, and in traditional, highly stylized electoral campaigns. There was some violence during the labor disputes of the 1930's, but this was isolated within the industrial community—with activity in and around the plants rather than in downtown streets or in parks. One must reach back to the second half of the nineteenth century to find examples of truly violent tactics at the center stage of American politics. The images that come to mind are of the Civil War with its bloody battles and draft riots, the street fights in raw mining towns, the Haymarket affair, the Pinkerton men and the Molly Maguires, and the building of armories in major cities during the 1870's and 1880's.[1] In addition, until 1900 there was a western frontier, with its unstable new communities and vigilante law enforcement. America's history is replete with political violence; but, and this is the important point, America's recent history is not. The conventional interpretation is that the frequency of "direct action" in the late nineteenth century was a function of America's social, economic, and political immaturity. Social change (industrialization, the moving frontier, immigration) was taking place so rapidly that it was impossible for the existing agencies charged with handling conflicts (town government, the courts, political organizations) to adjust and contain clashes of interest.

An appreciation of civility and compromise was not widely shared in the underdeveloped political culture of the nineteenth century. The amplification of violence in the twentieth century (chronicled in living color on the six o'clock news) has called conventional analysis into question. If violence is actually a mark of political immaturity (a few serious analysts doubt that it is), then the United States is not as "advanced" a polity as, from the comfortable perspective of the 1950's, we had thought. Putting it another way, it seems that there are seriously underdeveloped components of our society that, until quite recently, had been successfully ignored, contained, and denied meaningful participation in the political process. The most obviously subordinated components are adolescents and black people.

In the first selection of this chapter, Edward C. Banfield reflects on the causes of recent urban violence and warns against overreacting to riots. In the second selection, an abbreviation of one of the reports commissioned by the National Commission on the Causes and Prevention of Violence, Richard Maxwell Brown recalls the extent of the vigilante movement in America and speculates on the possibility of its revival as a response to the activities of contemporary militants.

[1] See Philip Taft and Philip Ross, "American Labor Violence," in Hugh Davis Graham and Ted Robert Gurr, eds., *Violence in America: Historical and Comparative Perspectives,* a report to the National Commission on the Causes and Prevention of Violence, June 1969, Signet edition, Chapter 8.

◻ Rioting Mainly for Fun and Profit

EDWARD C. BANFIELD

> "Picketing and marching ain't getting us anywhere, man," said Byron Washington, a 16-year-old 11th-grader who was arrested during this week's riots for having a rock in his hand.
> "The whites got to face it, man, this is a new generation. We aren't going to stand for the stuff our mamas and fathers stood for.
> "Look at me, I've got a B average, but I can't get a summer job. And if you don't work, you can't afford to go to college."
>
> —*New York Times* report from Waterloo, Iowa, July 14, 1967

In the law of most states a riot is a lawless act engaged in by three or more persons and accompanied by violence or breach of the public peace. If the rioters are Negroes it is usually taken for granted that the riot is in some sense racial. Probably the most widespread view is that Negroes riot because they can no longer contain their pent-up fury at the mistreatment they receive from whites. The Watts riot, we are told "was a manifestation of a general sense of deep outrage, outrage at every aspect of the lives Negroes are forced to live, outrage at every element of the white community for forcing (or permitting) Negroes to live such lives."[1]

On this view it follows that the way to end rioting—the *only* way to end it—is to stop mistreating the Negro and, so far as possible, to repair the damage already done him. "Doing such things as punishing police misconduct, providing decent housing and schooling, ending job discrimination and so forth are essential, but the problem goes deeper than that. The ghetto itself, with all the shameful economic, social, political, and psychological deprivation it causes, must be done away with once and for all. The riots have 'let America know' that this is what must be done. Now America must do it."[2]

This is not the view that will be taken here. The assumption that if Negroes riot it must be *because* they are Negroes is naïve. If one rejects this as a starting place and looks at the facts instead, one sees that race (and, inciden-

---
FROM Edward C. Banfield, *The Unheavenly City* (Boston: Little, Brown, 1970), pp. 185–209. Copyright © 1968, 1970 by Edward C. Banfield.

[1] Report of the Task Force on Assessment of the President's Committee on Law Enforcement and Administration of Justice, *Crime and Its Impact—An Assessment* (Washington, D. C.: U. S. Government Printing Office, 1967), p. 121.
[2] Ibid., p. 122.

tally, poverty as well) was not *the* cause of any of the Negro riots and that it had very little to do with many of the lesser ones. Indeed, it is probably not too much to say that some of the riots would have occurred even if (other things being the same) the people in the riot areas had all been white and even if they had all had incomes above the poverty line. The implication of this view is, of course, that punishing police misconduct, providing decent housing, and so on will not significantly affect the amount of Negro rioting. The causes of rioting, it will be argued, will continue to operate for another twenty years or so no matter what is done. But although more and possibly worse riots are to be expected, rioting will not destroy the cities. Dr. Kenneth B. Clark's warning that "The dark ghettoes now represent a nuclear stock-pile which can annihilate the very foundations of America,"[3] need not be taken very seriously if his metaphors refer to rioting of the sort that has occurred in recent years.

(1) Two thousand juveniles break windows after an amusement park closes early, leaving them without transportation.
(2) A gang of hoodlums robs a clothing store and smashes the display windows of three other stores, stealing watches, cameras, and rings.
(3) A young man has been shot and killed by the police during a burglary, and a crowd, shouting "This is for Willie," pelts the police with rocks, bottles, and fire bombs.
(4) Following an inflammatory speech by a racist politician, a mob overturns automobiles and assaults motorists.

To that strict behaviorist, the man on the moon, all four of these events probably look alike: all are "riots" and, if the rioters are Negro, presumably "racial." But to an observer able and willing to take motives into account (that is, to take note of the meaning of an act to the actor) the events are very different and some are not in any sense racial. The first is a rampage by frustrated teen-agers who happen to be black. The second is a foray for pillage by young toughs who find "taking" things the easiest way of getting them. In this case, too, race is not a motive and is in fact irrelevant to behavior: the toughs are Negro, but they could as well be white. The third event is an outburst of righteous indignation on the part of people who have witnessed what they think is an act of gross injustice. The young man who was killed was black and the policeman who killed him was white, but it is possible that the indignation the crowd feels is mainly or even entirely against the police rather than against whites as such. (In September 1962, Negroes in the all-Negro village of Kinlock, Missouri, rioted when a Negro policeman shot a Negro youth.) Indeed, some members of the crowd may be indignant at whites, others at the police, and still others at both whites and the police, and so it might be impossible to say whether or not the riot was "mainly racial," even if one had full knowledge

---

[3] Kenneth B. Clark, "The Wonder Is There Have Been So Few Riots," *New York Times Magazine*, September 5, 1965, p. 10.

of the subjective states of all rioters. In the final case, the event is a demonstration carried on for the express purpose of calling attention to a political position; since the position is a racist one, the riot can easily be called racial.

Each of these four motivations implies a corresponding type of riot. (This is not to say that a certain type of riot is *caused* by a certain type of motive; as will be explained later, it is more useful to look elsewhere for causes.) The four types are as follows:

The Rampage. This is an outbreak of animal—usually young, male animal—spirits. Young men are naturally restless, in search of excitement, thrills, "action." Also, as David Matza has explained, they are apt to feel "pushed around"; one who is caught in this mood of fatalism (as Matza calls it) wants dramatic reassurance that he can "make things happen," and breaking the law is one of the few actions open to him that immediately and demonstrably makes things happen.[4] Rioting (which Matza does not mention) is a way of making them happen on a wholesale scale. "These young people, to whom a voter registration campaign, a picket line, or an economic boycott mean very little, have found that they can stun an entire community by engaging in rioting. They can mobilize entire police forces and National Guard companies, keep mayors at their desks through the night, and bring representatives of the news media from all over the country."[5]

A rampage may start either with an incident—for example, an argument or an arrest—or "out of the blue." If it starts with an incident, the incident is more in the nature of a pretext than (as in a riot of the outburst of indignation type) a provocation; that is, the rampage begins not because the incident made the rampagers angry (although they may pretend that) but because they were looking for an excuse (signal?) to rampage. There is no pattern to the violence once it starts: it involves destruction for the sake of destruction and fighting for the sake of fighting. The police are frequently attacked by rampagers; this is not because they are hated (although they may be) but because they are at hand and will put up a good fight. Rampaging by teen-agers has always been a problem in the cities. From the very earliest times, harassing the watch, vandalism, and arson have been favorite pastimes of the young.[6] In Pittsburgh in 1809 an editor proposed satirically that the city establish a "conflagration fund" from which to buy twelve houses, one to be burned each month in a civil celebration.[7] Until the middle of the last century fire companies in the large cities

[4] David Matza, *Delinquency and Drift* (New York: Wiley, 1964), pp. 189–90.
[5] Fred Powledge in *New York Times,* August 6, 1964.
[6] See Richard C. Wade, *The Urban Frontier* (Chicago: University of Chicago Press [Phoenix Books], 1964), p. 90; and Howard O. Sprogle, *The Philadelphia Police, Past and Present* (Philadelphia, 1887), p. 50.
[7] Wade, *The Urban Frontier,* p. 92. In Boston one house a month would not have been nearly enough; more than fifty buildings were fired by incendiaries in 1844 (Arthur Wellington Brayley, *A Complete History of the Boston Fire Department* [Boston, 1889], p. 207). In Philadelphia thirty-four boys aged five to fifteen were arrested in three summer months of 1862 for starting fires. (Sprogle, *The Philadelphia Police,* p. 318).

were manned by volunteers, mostly boys and young men, and were in many cases what today would be called conflict gangs. Whether they put out more fires than they started is a question. In Philadelphia, for example, firemen used to riot almost every Sunday, using bricks, stones, and firearms, apparently with intent to kill.[8] In the slums of the large cities there were also street gangs, some claiming more than a thousand members, which fought each other and the police almost constantly.[9] Usually the authorities did not try very hard to interfere with these activities, which were regarded as in the nature of sporting events.[10]

Youth rampages occur today not only in the slums but elsewhere. Thousands of college boys rioted at Hampton Beach, New Hampshire, and at Seaside, Oregon, in 1964, the year the inner-city riots began, and there have been large rampages of white boys on the Sunset Strip of Los Angeles, in Atlantic City, and elsewhere since. It is not only American boys who behave this way, but boys almost everywhere. In Stockholm, for example, hordes of teen-agers hang around the subway stations committing acts of vandalism and harassing the police. "The police say that if a constable has to arrest a drunk who is disturbing the peace, the youngsters will often set upon the policeman, and a major riot looms before reinforcements can be called." [11] Probably many of the student "political demonstrations" reported in this and other countries are actually rampages.

In the upper classes the norms of culture tend to restrain the restlessness of youth and to encourage its sublimation. In the lower classes, on the other hand, cultural norms reinforce feelings of restlessness and the "mood of fatalism." Accordingly, lower-class youths are more apt than others to be caught up in frenzies of mob activity, and even adults of the lower class are, by comparison with those of the other classes, highly susceptible to the same influences.

The Foray for Pillage. Here the motive is theft, and here also boys and young adults of the lower class are the principal offenders. Stealing is ordinarily most conveniently done in private, of course, but when disasters—earthquakes, fires, floods, power failures, blizzards, enemy invasions, police strikes—interrupt law enforcement it may be done as well or better in public. On these occasions, when "Everyone is doing it" and "If I don't take the stuff it will just go to waste," upper-working- and middle-class adults who, under normal circumstances, would not steal, are likely to join the looters. (In 1711 the selectmen of Boston passed an act to punish persons "taking advantage of such confusion and calamities [as fire] to rob, plunder, embezzle, convey away and conceal the goods and effects

---

[8] Sprogle, *The Philadelphia Police*, pp. 90, 106. See also Eli K. Price, *The History of the Consolidation of the City of Philadelphia* (Philadelphia: Lippincott, 1873), pp. 118–19.
[9] Cf. Richard O'Connor, *Hell's Kitchen* (Philadelphia: Lippincott, 1958). See also Herbert Asbury, *The Gangs of New York* (New York: Knopf, 1927).
[10] Roger Lane, *Policing the City, Boston 1822–1885* (Cambridge, Mass.: Harvard University Press, 1967), p. 29.
[11] *New York Times*, September 16, 1965.

of their distressed neighbours."[12]) From the star[...] lower-class adult who makes a practice of stealing, [...] have a riot every day. Riots are seldom started by thieves [...] stealing, however. One reason is that the culture of the lower class [...] incapable of the planning and organization that would ordinarily be necess[...] to start a riot by design. Another and perhaps more important one is that although all thieves would benefit from a riot, no one thief would benefit enough from it to justify his taking the trouble and running the risks of starting it. (As an economist would put it, the riot is, from the standpoint of the thieves, a "collective good.")[13] But if thieves rarely start riots, they are always quick to join ones that are under way, and their presence in sufficient number may transform one from, say, a rampage to a foray for pillage. "I really know of no instance of a riot occurring in New York, or in any other large city, during which robbery did not play a prominent part," New York's Police Chief Walling wrote toward the end of the last century.[14]

The Outburst of Righteous Indignation. Here the rioters are moved by indignation at what they regard, rightly or wrongly, as injustice or violation of the mores that is likely to go unpunished. Their indignation is partly at the wrongfulness of the act and partly at the wrongfulness of its going unpunished. A riot of this type is always spontaneous—people do not become indignant according to plan. Indignation is aroused by an incident of some sort (which may, of course, have been contrived by someone for the purpose), and in the nature of the case, the indignant people are without leaders. The incident itself may help to make up for this lack by serving a coordinating function; as Thomas C. Schelling has pointed out, "Without something like an incident, it may be difficult to get action at all, since immunity requires that all know when to act together."[15]

A righteously indignant mob usually consists mainly of working-class people. The lower-class individual is too alienated to be capable of much indignation, especially in a matter that he thinks does not affect him personally and directly; middle- and upper-class people are usually confident of their ability to get wrongs righted by making appeals through proper channels, and, besides, they abhor violence. The working class is not under any of these limitations: it has a capacity for righteous indignation, distrusts lawyers, public relations people, and "channels" generally, and does not greatly mind—indeed, sometimes very much enjoys—a good brawl and the spilling of some blood.

[12] Brayley, *Boston Fire Department*, pp. 15, 31.
[13] See Mancur Olson, Jr., *The Logic of Collective Action* (Cambridge, Mass.: Harvard University Press, 1965). The theory as applied to small groups is particularly relevant here; it is summarized on pp. 33–36.
[14] George W. Walling, *Recollections of a New York Chief of Police* (New York: Caxton Book Concern, 1887), p. 85.
[15] Thomas C. Schelling, *The Strategy of Conflict* (Cambridge, Mass.: Harvard University Press, 1960), p. 90.

...orable circumstances, that is, where the working class is large and consists of people who have enough in common so that they will respond with indignation to the same provocation, an outburst of righteous indignation may involve a great many people—far more, certainly, than a rampage or a foray, both of which by their nature ordinarily draw upon relatively small "constituencies." All the large riots of the nineteenth century were mainly outbursts of righteous indignation. Some of them were very large indeed. For example, the Boston riot of 1837 (a native-American working-class attack on Irish immigrants) is supposed to have involved more than 15,000 persons, roughly one-sixth of the city's population.

In an outburst of righteous indignation the pattern of violence and destruction reflects the mob's wish to end, and also to redress or avenge, the wrong that aroused its indignation. As Rudé says in his account of popular disturbances in preindustrial France and England, the mob imposes a conception of "natural justice": "Strikers tended to destroy machinery or 'pull down' their employers' houses; food rioters to invade markets and bakers' shops and enforce a popular price control or *taxation populaire;* rural rioters to destroy fences and turnpikes or threshing machines and workhouses, or to set fire to the farmer's or landlord's stacks; and city rioters to 'pull down' dissenters' meeting houses and chapels, to destroy their victims' houses and property, and to burn their political enemies in effigy."[16]

The Demonstration. Here the motive is to advance a political principle or ideology or to contribute to the maintenance of an organization. The riot is not a spontaneous, angry response to an incident. Rather, it is the result of prearrangement by persons who are organized, have leaders, and who see it as a means to some end. The word "demonstration" is descriptive, for the event is a kind of show staged to influence opinion. Those who put it on are usually middle or upper class, these being the classes from which the people who run organizations and espouse political causes are mostly drawn. Demonstrations characteristically involve breach of the public peace rather than violence (if they involve neither they are by definition not riots); the middle- and upper-class cultural style favors the use of mock violence (for example, the spraying of slogans with paint and the throwing of steer's blood), "happenings" (for example, halting traffic with police whistles), and behavior calculated to make the demonstrator the object, or the apparent object, of violence inflicted either by himself (as when he chains himself to something) or by the authorities (as when he "goes limp"). The middle and upper classes' abhorrence of violence is so great that techniques like these, which trade upon it without requiring the demonstrator to hurt anyone but himself (and usually not himself either), are often effective as a means of putting "the other side" at a moral disadvantage in the eyes of the middle- and upper-class television viewers for whose benefit the demonstration is staged.

[16] George Rudé, *The Crowd in History* (New York: Wiley, 1964), p. 238.

These four types of riots are presented as analytical models. Some concrete riots very closely approximate a "pure" type, but most riots—and probably all large ones—are compounds of two or more of the types. The New York Draft Riot of 1863, for example, was a compound of at least three. It was a rampage of young toughs from the slums (three-fourths of those actively engaged in violence were boys and men under twenty years of age who were not subject to the draft, a *Times* writer estimated; it was a foray for pillage (houses and places of business were ransacked all along Eleventh Avenue); and it was also —and perhaps mainly—an outburst of righteous indignation on the part of the Irish working class at the prospect of having to compete with freed Negroes for jobs and against the alleged injustices of the draft law.[17] Large riots tend to be compound, if for no other reason, simply because they attract looters. But it is likely that the fact of their being compound also tends to make them larger: that is, that interaction among types of rioters tends to reinforce the motives and heighten the activity of each type. For example, the looters and rampagers in the Draft Riot no doubt got some moral support from having all about them rioters motivated by righteous indignation; at the same time, the presence of the looters and rampagers, most of whom were not clearly identifiable as such, must have added to the general sense of confusion and frenzy and by so doing must have helped sustain the fury of the righteously indignant. That these latter had *two* objects of indignation—Negroes and the draft law—must also have increased the interaction. One may conjecture that the greater the variety of motivational elements appealed to, the larger the number of rioters who will be recruited and—what is more important—the more interaction tending to sustain and escalate the riot there will be among the rioters.

Looking from this perspective at the recent series of inner-city riots, one is struck by the fact that for twenty years prior to July 18, 1964, there had been very few riots by Negroes, and that these few, with only one exception, had been protests against racial injustice. In 1961, for example, white mobs in six cities attacked Negroes, but there were no riots by Negroes. In 1962 there were four Negro riots—one was a demonstration by Black Muslims, two seem to have been outbursts of righteous indignation provoked by incidents of alleged police brutality, and the fourth, the exception, was a rampage by high school students after a football game in the District of Columbia stadium. In 1963 and the first half of 1964 there were eleven Negro riots, all apparently outbursts of righteous indignation and all but three occurring in the South. In none of these years was there a major Negro riot—one involving several hundred rioters and lasting more than a day.[18]

On July 18, 1964, a riot began in Harlem that proved to be a turning point. Two days before, an off-duty white police lieutenant had shot and killed a fif-

---

[17] See E. C. Banfield, "Roots of the Draft Riots," *New York Magazine,* July 29, 1968.
[18] This section depends heavily upon a chronology compiled by the Legislative Reference Service of the Library of Congress. It appears in the *Congressional Quarterly* Special Report on Urban Problems and Civil Disorder, No. 36, September 8, 1967, pp. 1708–12.

teen-year-old Negro youth whom he said had attacked him with a knife. The incident created widespread anger, and there was a protest march on the precinct police station the next day. The following evening (July 18) a second group of marchers refused to disperse; instead, it began throwing bottles and stones at the police station and was soon joined in this by a band of black nationalists who had been meeting nearby. The riot, which lasted in Harlem for three days, spread to the Bedford-Stuyvesant district of Brooklyn and six days later, for no apparent reason, to Rochester.[19] (The incident—an attempt by a policeman to arrest a drunk and disorderly adolescent at a street dance—seems to have been a pretext rather than a provocation.) A few days later the rioting spread, also for no apparent reason, to three New Jersey cities, an industrial suburb of Chicago, and Philadelphia.

In Harlem, when it first broke out, the rioting was mainly an outburst of righteous indignation at the police. There was little looting; the mob was chiefly occupied in bitter fighting with the police. As the rioting continued and moved to other cities, however, its nature changed. Looting and rock throwing became the mob's principal activities, with attacks on the police sporadic and incidental. In Rochester, the city manager said later, the riot had "racial overtones" but was not actually a race riot.[20] In Philadelphia, the first policeman attacked was a Negro. Nowhere did a Negro mob invade a white neighborhood or assault whites as such.

Opinion leaders and publicists did not at this time see the riots as manifestations of deep unrest or anger on the part of Negroes. At the end of the summer, J. Edgar Hoover, whose views were probably close to one end of the spectrum, reported to the President that although racial tensions had been a factor, none of the disorders—not even the Harlem one—was a race riot in the accepted meaning of the term (that is, race against race); they were, he said, "purposeless attacks" in which youths were responsible for most of the violence, and he classed them with the college-boy riots that occurred about the same time.[21] Others made similar assessments. Most civil rights leaders dismissed the idea that the riots were conscious protests; that was not merely an after-the-fact rationalization, Kenneth B. Clark said, it was an "independent of the fact" one.[22] Bayard Rustin was applauded by an audience of New York planners when he explained that the violence was caused by "merely a few confuesd Negro boys throwing stones in windows or a Molotov cocktail at a cop who was perfectly capable of ducking."[23] The police commissioner of New York said in effect that they were rampages and forays. "They riot either out of sheer cussedness or for criminal reasons, and in some instances because mob action seems to be taking

[19] The Harlem and Bedford-Stuyvesant riots are described in Fred C. Shapiro and James W. Sullivan, *Race Riots, New York 1964* (New York: Crowell, 1964).
[20] *New York Times,* November 7, 1964.
[21] *New York Times,* September 27, 1964.
[22] *New York Times,* September 11, 1964.
[23] New York City Planning Commission, "The Future by Design," October 14–16, 1964, transcript, p. 55.

on the aspects of a fad. . . . Bedevil the police, strip stores, shout and yell, crush anyone who opposes you . . . and if the police try to stop it, just yell 'brutality.' This is the pattern. . . ."[24]

The view that riots did not manifest feelings of outrage widespread among Negroes was consistent with the findings of an elaborate survey of Negro opinion made late in 1964 by Gary T. Marx. It showed that most Negroes were neither sunk in hopelessness nor consumed with anger. Only about a third were in any sense militant, and the proportion of Negroes who were strongly anti-white was much smaller. Most thought that things were getting better for the Negro (81 per cent of a sample in non-Southern metropolitan areas thought this), that America was worth fighting for (87 per cent), that a day would come when whites would fully accept Negroes (70 per cent), and that the police treated Negroes either fairly well or very well (59 per cent). "The overwhelming majority of those questioned," Marx concluded, "felt that progress is being made and that integration is being pushed by the government at the right speed and were optimistic about the future."[25] That most Negroes held these opinions does not necessarily mean that the rioters held them, of course; in fact, however, there is some reason to suppose that most of them did.[26]

The 1964 riot pattern was repeated the following August in the Watts district of Los Angeles. This area was not a slum in the usual sense (it was an area of single-family, detached houses, most of which were in good condition), and Los Angeles was a city in which the Negro fared better than in most places (the Urban League rated it first among sixty-eight cities on the basis of a "statistical portrait" drawn in 1964). In this case, too, the incident that supposedly set off the riot could hardly have aroused a great deal of righteous indignation (a drunken Negro motorist had been arrested in what seems to have been a proper manner). Apparently, the incident was mainly important as a pretext for a rampage by teen-age Negro boys and young men who began throwing whiskey and beer bottles and pieces of asphalt and cement at motorists on Avalon Boulevard.[27] Two hours after the incident the mob, which then numbered about fifteen hundred, consisted mostly of these boys and young men. There was nothing "racial" about what they were doing. "One thing that impressed me was that these Negroes who were hurling stones were throwing them right into their own people. That's why I believe this didn't start out to

[24] *New York Times,* October 7, 1964.
[25] Gary T. Marx, *Protest and Prejudice* (New York: Harper & Row, 1967), p. 39. See also the survey reported in the special issue of *Fortune,* December 1967.
[26] Comparing a sample of Negro males arrested during the Detroit riot of 1967 with a control group chosen from the area most affected by the riot, Luby found that the arrestees had no more grievances than the controls, that both arrestees and controls felt that they had made substantial progress in the past five years, and that both were remarkably optimistic about the future. Eliot D. Luby, M.D., "A Comparison Between Negro Riot Arrestees and a Riot Area Control Sample," Paper presented at the annual meeting of the American Political Science Association, 1968.
[27] Jerry Cohen and William S. Murphy, *Burn, Baby, Burn!* (New York: Avon Books, 1966), pp. 62–63.

be a race riot. These were just young hoodlums working off their frustrations. They were out to do destruction. They just wanted to hurt anybody, black or white."[28]

The statistics on arrests at Watts provide some slight basis for inferences about the motives of the rioters. About 15 per cent of those arrested were juveniles. (The percentage would have been much higher, it has been suggested, were it not for the fact that the police, being short-handed, arrested the people who were easiest to catch.) Of the 3,438 adults arrested, nearly one-third had been convicted of major crimes (that is, crimes for which they had received sentences of more than ninety days) and fully one-third had minor records (that is, arrest or conviction with a sentence of ninety days or less).[29] Since the police may be quicker to arrest Negroes than whites, it is hard to say what significance should be attached to the proportion having minor records. It is more noteworthy that one-third had never been arrested.

Although the Watts riot followed the pattern that had been set the year before, Negro spokesmen at once proclaimed that it was politically motivated —it was, they insisted, a revolt, not a riot. Bayard Rustin wrote that it was carried on for an "express purpose" and was "the first major rebellion."[30] No one gave a very clear or convincing account of what the rioters were revolting against, however. The facts did not support the view that they were expressing hatred for the white man; even Rustin said the rebellion was against the Negro's "own masochism." Nor did the facts support very well the view that the rioters were asserting that (in Rustin's words) they "would no longer quietly submit to the deprivation of slum life"; after all, most Watts people lived comfortably in fairly good housing. It was somewhat more plausible to claim that they were angry about mistreatment by the police, but even this view did not fit the facts entirely, for the rioters had shown themselves more interested in burning and looting than in fighting the police.

However unjustifiably, Watts was regarded by many Negroes as something to be proud of—a kind of black Bunker Hill. This definition tended to make the rioting of the year before appear in retrospect as a kind of black Concord and Lexington and to establish a moral basis for any battles that might yet be fought in a black revolution. As one would expect, the frequency of rioting increased after Watts. In 1966, there were eleven major (that is, two-day or more) and thirty-two minor riots, and in 1967 there were twenty-five major and thirty minor riots. In most instances, the rioting began either without any precipitating incident, boys and young men simply smashing windows, starting fires, and assaulting passers-by for no apparent reason, or with an incident that was a pretext rather than a provocation. Only two of the major riots in 1966

---

[28] Newspaperman Don Cormier, quoted in *Burn, Baby, Burn!*, p. 71.
[29] Governor's Commission on the Los Angeles Riots, *Violence in the City—An End or a Beginning?*, Los Angeles, December 2, 1965, p. 24.
[30] Bayard Rustin, "The Watts 'Manifesto' and the McCone Report," *Commentary*, March 1966, p. 30.

(those in Jacksonville, Florida, and San Francisco) seem to have started from a provocation and only eight (six of which were in Southern cities) of those in 1967 seem to have started from provocations.

The Detroit riot of 1967, although vastly more destructive, was in many ways typical. Like Los Angeles, Detroit was a city of relative prosperity and opportunity for the Negro; it had no real "ghetto" and its police had for several years been under very enlightened and determined leadership. The incident with which the riot started seems to have been a pretext rather than a provocation: when the police raided a speakeasy early one Sunday morning, a crowd began pelting the policemen with stones. This might not have led to a riot were it not for the fact that at that particular time very few policemen could be mustered. (Early Sunday morning was a "low crime" period and the stronger daytime shift was not scheduled to report for duty at precinct stations until 8 A.M.) For several critical hours the police were conspicuous by their absence. It was well known, too, that the police would not use their guns except in the most extreme circumstances. For five or six hours after the speakeasy raid Negroes and whites mingled on the streets and looted amicably side by side. On the second day of the riot Governor Romney said that it was "not primarily a civil rights disturbance but rather lawlessness and hoodlumism by Negroes and whites," an opinion with which Mayor Cavanagh agreed.[31] Almost all the arrests made were for looting, and of those arrested nearly half were aged nineteen through twenty-four. The pattern of destruction was what one would expect in a foray for pillage. Stores having things that could be consumed directly—liquor, cigarettes, drugs, clothing, television sets, appliances, furniture—were looted no matter who owned them. Stores having things that would have to be "fenced"—jewelry—were usually left untouched, as were all buildings symbolic of the "white power structure"—banks, public offices, and schools. As one of the rioters, a child, explained, "There was nothing to steal in the school. Who wants a book or a desk?"[32]

It would appear, then, that what requires explanation is not so much rebellion by Negroes (whether against the whites, the slum, their "own masochism," the police, or something else) as it is outbreaks of animal spirits and of stealing by slum dwellers, mostly boys and young men and mostly Negro. (A few non-Negroes participated, mostly as looters, in the Detroit riot and possibly in some of the others, and one major riot, a rampage-foray for which

[31] *New York Times*, July 24, 1967. John Howard, a sociologist who observed the Detroit riot, later wrote that poor whites played a major role in it. He found the Detroit (and also the Newark) riot to be a "lower-class, rather than racial, revolt." William McCord et al., *Life Styles in the Black Ghetto* (New York: Norton, 1969), p. 273.

[32] Quoted in *Education News*, October 16, 1967, p. 16. Luby's study (see note 26) of a sample of Detroit arrestees and a control group also found the arrestees to be younger than the controls, less often married, more often raised in the urban North, more often raised in a family in which the father was not present during the first 11 years, less affiliated with organizations, less conscious of political leadership, and no more unemployed.

there seems to have been no precipitating incident, was carried on entirely by Puerto Rican youths in Perth Amboy, New Jersey, at the end of July 1966.) That racial injustice may have had less to do with the riots than is generally supposed is strongly suggested by the fact that a major riot (two men were killed and scores injured, and an estimated $5 million in damage was done by looting, vandalism, and arson to some 175 stores, hotels, and office buildings) occurred in Montreal in October 1969 during a sixteen-hour wildcat strike of policemen.

In framing an explanation, it will be useful to begin by listing certain events ("accelerating causes"), each of which independently increased the probability of such riots occurring. This listing will be followed by a description of a set of states ("background causes"), the concurrent existence of which established *some* probability of their occurring.[33]

Accelerating Causes. Without attempting to pass on their relative importance, several such causes may be listed.

1. Sensational television coverage of the riots recruited rampagers and pillagers. As the mayor of Plainfield, New Jersey, explained, "The sensational coverage of the Newark riot showed persons looting stores while the police took no action to halt them. This view of looting appealed directly to the criminal and susceptible element." [34] Prior to the advent of television, it would have been very difficult for the authorities to have brought the possibilities for fun and profit in rioting to the attention of the lower class even if they had wanted to do so. Lower-class people do not read newspapers, but nearly all of them have at least one television set.

2. By carrying vivid accounts of rioting to cities all over the country, television not only eliminated the necessity that would otherwise have existed for the independent discovery of certain techniques of rioting (for example, the use of fire bombs) but also, and especially, it established the *possibility* of it. That by throwing rocks, smashing windows, and setting fires one can throw a great city into turmoil is something that the ordinary person does not recognize until it happens. Once the possibility of an action has been established, the probability of someone's taking it is very much increased. "Some cats come in the bar and talk about how they are going to start burning again next month— down about Broadway. Mostly, it is just talk, but they know that they could do it." [35] The main point here is that, thanks to television, knowledge that "they could do it" was widely disseminated to people who otherwise would have been slow to discover it for themselves. In 1935 and 1943 Harlem had riots, but for lack of television coverage these did not provide a model that was known and imitated in cities all over the United States.

[33] For the distinction between "accelerating" and "background" causes, the writer is grateful to Bruce Jacobs.
[34] *New York Times,* December 7, 1967.
[35] *New York Times,* November 7, 1965.

3. The rioters knew that they had little or nothing to fear from the police and the courts. Under the pressure of the civil rights movement and of court decisions and as the result of the growing "professionalism" of police administrators (these developments, in turn, being consequences of "middle-class-ification" of the population), the patrolman's discretion in the use of force declined rapidly after the war. At the same time courts were lenient with juvenile offenders. "Tough kids" had always attacked policemen when they got the chance, but by the 1960's the amount of toughness required was not very great, for in most cities it became more and more apparent that a policeman who shot a boy would be in serious trouble. Not being able to use force, the police could not effectively use the *threat* of it. It was not uncommon for a gang of boys to disarm and beat a policeman who, following orders, would not use his gun against them. During a riot, the police were especially ineffective—because their offenses were not very serious, most rioters could not be successfully threatened; the only thing that could be done with them was to take them into custody, and this was something the police were seldom numerous enough to do. Sometimes the police had to stand by and allow looting to go on before their eyes. This, of course, increased the tempo of the rioting.

"Those first hours, when the cops pulled out, were just like a holiday," recalls one young man who joined in the looting of shops on 12th Street that morning. "All the kids wandered around sayin', real amazed like, 'The fuzz is scared; they ain't goin' to do nothin'.' I remember one day me and another kid, we was locked in the school and there wasn't any teachers around and we had a ball, we did all the things we'd been wantin' to do for a long time. We set some fires in the baskets and we emptied the teachers' desks and we stuck a whole mess of toiletpaper in the principal's mailbox. Well, that's what it was like out on the Street." [36]

4. The probability of rioting was increased by several factors that tended to give it legitimacy in the eyes of potential rioters. One was an outpouring of vivid television and newspaper portrayals of outrages against Negroes and civil rights workers in the South; perhaps Sheriff "Bull" Connor of Alabama created much of the indignation that was discharged in Harlem against the officer who shot the boy in July 1964. Another was a barrage of statements by leaders of both races that represented the Negro's problems as entirely, or almost entirely, the result of racial injustice, implying that only white racism stood between the Negro and affluence. Another was the discovery that rioting was possible; as David Matza points out with reference to juveniles, learning through experience that an infraction *can* be done leads, by an illogic characteristic of childish thought, to the conclusion that it *may* be done.[37] Another factor was the spread of the rioting to several cities; the knowledge that "everybody is doing it" tended,

---

[36] J. Anthony Lukas, "Postscript on Detroit: 'Whitey Hasn't Got the Message,'" *New York Times Magazine,* August 27, 1967, p. 44.
[37] Matza, *Delinquency and Drift,* p. 184.

by more childish illogic, to the conclusion that doing it could not be very wrong. "If they can do it in Detroit, we can do it here," Milwaukee teen-agers cried as they began smashing store windows. But what probably did most to make rioting seem legitimate was acceptance of the claim that the Watts riot was a "revolt" and that the rioting everywhere had some political purpose. Byron Washington, the Waterloo, Iowa, youth whose words appear at the head of this chapter, doubtless threw his stone with the strength of ten because he knew (having heard it over television perhaps) that he was not a boy out raising hell but a victim of injustice fighting for a college education. Whether correct or not, explanations that find the cause of rioting in the rioters' environment are bound to be taken as justifications, or at any rate extenuations, of their behavior and therefore tend to reinforce the irresponsibility that is characteristic of the age and class culture from which rioters are largely drawn.[38] Rustin may have been right in saying that the looters were "members of a deprived group who seized a chance to possess things that all the dinning affluence of Los Angeles has never given them."[39] But, right or wrong, the effect of such statements is to make it easier for the potential rioter to justify his behavior, and therefore the statements are themselves a contributing cause of rioting. One can see this process clearly enough in something a twenty-year-old Watts rioter said to a reporter: "The white power structure looks on us as hoodlums when actually we are deprived people."[40]

If explaining the riots tended to justify them, so did predicting them. One who said that if drastic measures were not taken to end injustice riots could be expected might be correct, but correct or not his words would help form an impression in the public mind that rioting is a natural and perhaps even laudable response to the continuance of an injustice. From the very beginning of the civil rights movement its leaders have been wont to predict that violence will occur if reforms are not accepted at a faster pace; the riots, of course, made these predictions much more credible and therefore gave the civil rights leaders

---

[38] Ibid., p. 95.

> Modern guides written for those who work with juveniles stress the importance of supporting the child. Whenever supporting the child leads to statements excusing or understanding his behavior, as they occasionally must, the precepts of subcultural delinquency are also supported. . . .
> Statements reinforcing the delinquent's conception of irresponsibility are an integral part of an ideology of child welfare shared by social work, psychoanalysis, and criminology. This ideology presents a causal theory of delinquency which, when it attributes fault, directs it to parent, community, society, or even to the victims of crime.

[39] Rustin, "The Watts 'Manifesto,'" p. 30. Vice President Humphrey helped to extenuate the rioting when he said in New Orleans that if he lived in a slum tenement with rats and with no place to go swimming, "You'd have more trouble than you have already, because I've got enough spark left in me to lead a mighty good revolt [sic] under those conditions." *New York Times,* July 19, 1966.

[40] *New York Times,* November 7, 1965.

more incentive than ever to make them.[41] At the end of 1966, Dr. Martin Luther King, Jr., after acknowledging that "a prediction of violence can sometimes be an invitation to it," went on to predict that "failure to pursue justice" would result in more riots.[42] Rustin, at about the same time, told a Senate subcommittee that if the President asked for only a small increase in funds for the poverty program, the Negro leadership "can no longer be responsible for what happens"; and Senator Robert Kennedy said that unless "major steps" were taken "we will reap a whirlwind that will be completely uncontrollable."[43] Even if these predictions had been based on actual knowledge, and even if by making them—and *only* by making them—it had been possible to secure the needed reforms, one would have to say that making the predictions increased the probability of there being riots; obviously, it was impossible for the reforms to achieve their effect in time to prevent what was being predicted. Realistically, however, those who made the predictions could not be at all sure that the measures they were proposing, some of which—for example, "pursue justice"—were so vague as to be almost meaningless, would have any tendency to prevent rioting; moreover, they had little or no reason to believe that their making the prediction would bring about the adoption of the measures they advocated. Rustin, for example, could not have supposed that his words to the Senate subcommittee would cause the President to ask for a larger increase in the poverty program. The one thing the predictions *were* likely to do was to make rioting appear more natural, normal, and hence justifiable.[44]

Background Causes. For there to be *any* probability of rioting of the kind here under discussion, several conditions had to exist concurrently.

1. Without a large supply of boys and young men of the lower classes to draw on, major rampages and forays would be impossible. In the 1920's and 1930's . . . the number of such people in the inner cities was very much reduced from what it had been in the previous century because of the aging of the immigrant population and the movement of the relatively well-off to

---

[41] There is a striking parallel between the rhetorical strategy of the civil rights leaders in the early 1960's and that of James Mill prior to the passage of the Reform Bill of 1832. See Joseph Hamburger, *James Mill and the Art of Revolution* (New Haven: Yale University Press, 1963).

[42] *New York Times,* December 16, 1966.

[43] *New York Times,* December 7, 1966.

[44] In March 1968, the process of explanation and, by implication, justification reached its apogee with the publication of the report of the National Advisory Commission on Civil Disorders (the Kerner Commission), which found that "white racism," poverty, and powerlessness were mainly responsible for the riots. The next month there were riots in several cities following the assassination of the Rev. Martin Luther King, Jr. These riots followed the familiar pattern of looting, burning, and vandalism, and it was apparent that despite all that had been done to give a political character to these events, most rioters were not there in order to protest. "It wasn't vengeance," a Chicago poverty worker said, "just material gain." *Wall Street Journal,* April 10, 1968. See also *New York Times,* April 12, 1968.

outlying neighborhoods and suburbs. During the Depression it looked for a while as if the inner-city slums and semislums might be permanently depopulated. During and after the war, however, these districts were filled or nearly filled once again by a new migration, this one from the rural South (and, in New York, from Puerto Rico). Being a young population with a very high birthrate, the newcomers quickly put more boys and young men on the streets than had been there before. The new (black) generation of inner-city youth may be somewhat more prone to violence than the earlier (white) ones. (Southerners, both white and black, tend to be violent as compared to other Americans.) But if so, the difference is not great. Lower-class youth in every generation and in every ethnic and racial group are extremely violent as compared to middle- and upper-middle-class adults.

2. The lower- and lower-working-class people who now comprise much of the inner-city residential population are largely cut off from participation in institutions that in times past regulated and restrained the behavior of people whose class culture and situation were similar to theirs. Racial discrimination, although obviously a factor, is not the main thing that cuts them off from these institutions; rather, what cuts them off is the changes that have occurred in the nature of the institutions because of the "middle-class-ification" of the population of this country. In the last century, for example, the volunteer fire company gave boys and young men of the lower classes opportunities to express animal spirits under conditions that were to some degree controlled: the firemen fought *each other,* usually for the "honor" of their companies. Today, of course, fire departments are run on a professional basis and are open only to mature men who have placed well in an examination. More or less the same thing has happened in politics. Not so long ago party machines labored to establish claims on even the lowest of the low; the trading of jobs and favors in return for loyalty tended to create some sort of bond between the individual and the government. Now that the machine, precinct captain, and corner saloon have been replaced by the welfare bureaucracy, the nonpartisan election, and the candidate who makes his appeal on educational television, the lower classes no longer participate in politics at all and are therefore no longer held by any of the old ties. Even in criminal activities there has been the same trend. Like fire-fighting and politics, the money-making kinds of crime (as opposed to "kid stuff") are organized in such a way as to exclude—and therefore to exert no discipline upon —the unskilled and incapable.

This exclusion from institutions of those who are not able or willing to participate on the terms set by the now predominant middle class has the effect of reducing the influence within the lower classes of those persons who, although not able to perform according to the standard set by the middle class, could nevertheless lead and set an example for—and thus place some restraint upon —less able members of their class. The situation is strikingly like that which, when it occurs in prisons, is said to cause riots. "It is the cohesively-oriented prisoner committed to the values of inmate loyalty, generosity, endurance, and the curbing of frictions who does much to maintain the prison's equilibrium. When the custodians strip him of his power—when the custodians destroy the system of illicit privileges, of preferential treatment and laxity which has functioned to increase the influence of the cohesively-oriented prisoner who stands for the value of keeping things quiet—the unstable elements in the inmate population have an opportunity to capitalize on the tensions of prison life and to rise into dominance. The stage has been set for insurrection."[45]

3. A considerable number of upper-working-class, middle-class, and upper-class people who have made large income and status gains in recent years and are impatient to make even larger gains live in the inner city in close physical proximity to the lower classes. Upwardly mobile members of earlier slum populations very quickly left not only the slum but the inner city as well, and usually the neighborhoods they vacated were occupied by some different newly arrived ethnic group. In the case of the Negro, the outward movement has been rather slow, partly because of job and housing discrimination and partly because of a preference Negroes have for living near other Negroes; moreover, in the case of the Negro, the places of those who *have* moved away have usually been taken by newly arriving Negroes. Upwardly mobile Negroes who for one reason or another live in or near the slum tend, of course, to be very sensitive to the dangers and unpleasantnesses of slum life and to blame them not on conditions common to the white and the Negro (for example, lower-class culture, low income, and so on) but on racial injustice past and present, real and imaginary. If, like the upwardly mobile members of earlier groups, these Negroes lived in suburbs far from the inner-city slums, they would not be available physically (and perhaps psychologically) for participation in riots. As it is they do not participate in them actively in large numbers. They do provide enough politically motivated rioters, however, to make possible the interaction effect that, it was argued earlier, tends to escalate a rampage-foray into a major riot. Even those who do not participate in the rioting tend to help legitimate it in the eyes of potential rioters by putting forward or concurring in the claim that it has a political purpose.

Several conclusions bearing on policy may be drawn from this analysis. One is that there is likely to be more rioting for many years to come, and this no matter what is done to prevent it. So long as there are large concentrations of boys and young men of the lower classes on the streets, rampages and forays are to be expected. Without some support from righteously indignant members of the working class and from politically minded members of the middle and upper classes, such outbreaks probably will not reach the scale that was reached in Los Angeles, Newark, and Detroit, but even so some of them will probably be well beyond the ability of local police forces to deal with. Eventually, much of the inner-city population will move to the suburbs; this change, which is

---

[45] Gresham M. Sykes, *The Society of Captives* (Princeton, N. J.: Princeton University Press, 1958), p. 126.

already under way, will reduce the potential for very large riots by physically separating the lower class from the working class and the working class from the middle and upper classes and thus (1) curtailing the number of persons available in any one place as recruits for a riot and (2) making interaction between rioters of different motivational types (for example, rampagers and demonstrators) less likely. For at least another twenty years, however, there will be enough potential rioters of all types in the inner cities to produce frequent rampage-forays and some major riots.

It is naïve to think that efforts to end racial injustice and to eliminate poverty, slums, and unemployment will have an appreciable effect upon the amount of rioting that will be done in the next decade or two. These efforts are not likely to be very serious or, if they are, very successful. But even if they are both serious and successful they will not significantly affect the factors that produce riots. Boys and young men of the lower classes will not cease to "raise hell" once they have adequate job opportunities, housing, schools, and so on. Indeed, by the standards of any former time, they have these things now. It may be that in the very long run good opportunities and a high standard of living will bring about the assimilation of the lower classes into the middle and by so doing will make them less violent. But this will happen over the long run—say, from one generation to the next—if it happens at all, and, besides, even middle- and upper-class boys riot sometimes. As for the upwardly mobile and politically minded Negro who has a potential for outbursts of righteous indignation and for demonstrations, even serious and successful efforts at reform are likely to leave him more rather than less angry. The faster and farther the Negro rises the more impatient he is likely to be with whatever he thinks prevents his rising still faster and still farther. As the HARYOU manual, "Youth in the Ghetto," remarks: "The closer the Negro community gets to the attainment of its goals—the closer it gets to the removal of the determinants and manifestations of racial exploitation and powerlessness—the more impatient individual Negroes will become for total equality." [46]

It is not only the Negro who will become more disaffected as his situation improves. The process of "middle-" and "upper-class-ification" is making the whole society more sensitive to departures, both real and imaginary, from the ideal, inherently unrealizable, of how things ought to be. As the economy becomes more productive and social arrangements more decent, the well-off—and among them youth especially—become more restless and more intolerant of the continued failure to achieve social perfection. Demonstrations, confrontations, protests, dialogues, and so forth, are bound to be more frequent as the middle and upper classes grow and more and more people have the leisure to act upon what the Judeo-Puritan tradition tells them is a positive obligation to make society over. Paul Goodman, who, it seems likely, is a portent of things to come,

[46] Harlem Youth Opportunities Unlimited, Inc., "Youth in the Ghetto" (New York: multilithed, 1964), p. 20.

says that he looks forward to a "conflictual community" that will "combat the emptiness of technological life."[47] No doubt most of the blood spilled by the middle and upper classes will be steer's blood carried for the purpose in plastic containers. The effect on the lower classes of this sort of behavior by the upper classes may be serious, however.

Although the underlying factors making for riots will not change for quite some time, there may be changes in accelerating factors. Television coverage of riots may be less provocative; if so, one force feeding the growth and spread of riots will be reduced. (This will not, however, undo the main damage already done: the discovery that burning and looting on a wholesale scale is possible will not be forgotten.) The ability of the police to bring incipient riots under control may be improved by the introduction of better methods and equipment; of importance, perhaps, is the chemical Mace, which, if it proves to be both effective and acceptable to public opinion, may change the situation significantly by giving police the upper hand in dealing with juveniles and other offenders whom it would be wrong to shoot. On the other hand, one accelerating factor will doubtless gain in strength. This is the opinion that rioting is a way of protesting injustice and is therefore in large degree justified. As was remarked earlier, the spread of this opinion has made each successive wave of rioting somewhat more ideological than the last. Now that the rationale of rioting has been well worked out, future riots may be mainly for protest rather than for fun and profit.

Insofar as the motives of the past few years predominate in the future, however, it is safe to say that none of the following will make riots less likely: the election of Negro mayors, a mayor's courageous strolling in the slums, the elimination of police brutality and the improvement of police manners, efforts to placate, co-opt, or restrain Negro extremist leaders, the measurement of the "grievance level" of the Negro community, and the provision of jobs for the "hard-core" unemployed. Politically motivated persons may perhaps be influenced by such things, but looters and youthful rampagers will not be.

There is no intention here to extenuate the crime of rioting. It is easy, however, to exaggerate the harm that riots of the kind that have occurred since 1964 have done and are likely to do. In the first place, not many people were killed or seriously injured by the rioters; in all of the more than one hundred riots from 1964 through 1967, apparently no more than about twenty persons were killed by rioters.[48] It is angry or panicky policemen who do most of the killing and maiming, and when the police are equipped with nonlethal weapons

---

[47] Paul Goodman, "Utopian Thinking," *Commentary*, July 1961, p. 26.
[48] Some deaths were undoubtedly accidental. That the rioters deliberately killed so few may be regarded as additional evidence that they were not motivated by hatred for whites. On the other hand, there have been many riots which unquestionably were outbursts of righteous indignation and in which the rioters, although furious, did not kill. See Rudé, *The Crowd in History*, p. 225.

there will probably be much less of this. Because "routine" crime sometimes ceases or is much reduced during a major riot, there may even be some net saving of life and limb by virtue of riots.

The property losses are not as staggering as may be supposed either. In the majority of the recent riots the damage consisted mainly of smashed windows, the theft of liquor, and the burning of some not very valuable buildings. It would not take a very heavy snowfall to cost a city and its people more than an average-sized riot costs them. Major riots are another story, of course, but even they do not cause destruction very different in kind or amount from what would be caused by a sizable urban renewal program. Wasteful as it is to destroy useful structures in either way, the costs of doing so are well within the ability of a very affluent society to bear. In the course of time, too, property losses will be cut as people adapt to the likelihood of rioting by changing the location of structures or the design of them. In Europe, heavy metal shutters are used to protect store windows; doubtless the same thing will be done here (in the worst slums it long has been, of course) when the danger to windows becomes great enough. (On the other hand, if, as seems likely, the government compels insurance companies to insure properties in high-risk areas at normal premium rates, incentives to make such adaptations will be removed.)

The danger that a riot will so disrupt essential services—sewage disposal and water supply, for example—as to create a major public health hazard is very small. To inflict serious damage of this kind would require a considerable degree of expertise and organization. If anything of this sort is to be feared, it is to be feared from a highly disciplined band of political zealots, not from a mob—least of all from a mob of rampagers and looters.

There are those who think that up to now, at least, the riots have been a good thing on the whole because (the Negro view) they have impressed white society with the necessity of drastic action to improve the Negro's conditions of life or (the white view) because they have helped to instill in the Negro a sense of pride. According to the executive secretary of the Milwaukee Teachers Education Association, "There is a certain amount of Negro pride which resulted from the riot. The pride factor is evident when you walk or drive down the street. Caucasians are sensitized to Negroes; they are aware that they exist. Before, they could psychologically dismiss them as inferior. . . . The Negroes feel this focus on them. And when they are in school, they are going to expect something to happen. Frankly, I think it's great." [49]

Such claims are impossible to evaluate and yet they cannot be ignored.[50] Very probably, the immediate effects of the burning, looting, and killing are

---

[49] *Education News*, October 16, 1967, p. 16.
[50] A claim that might be expected but does not seem to have been made is that the rioting has produced some natural leaders of the slum neighborhoods. That such leaders have not been produced (and there is no reason to believe that they have) is perhaps further evidence of the essentially nonpolitical character of the rioting. In any case, it is interesting that, according to Rudé (*The Crowd in History*, p. 251) very few of the leaders who were produced by the preindustrial riots were ever heard from again once the riots were over.

of little importance as compared to the enduring changes in attitudes, feelings, and opinions that have been brought about by the rioting. No one now can have the least idea of the nature of these changes, however, and even in retrospect the cause-and-effect relations will remain unclear. The rioting may have given Negroes a new pride (that the facts do not justify it is of course beside the point), and this may do more for the lower-class Negro than all the compensatory education, public housing, job training, and community organization that could be provided with a dozen Freedom Budgets. It may also have impressed whites as nothing else would with the need for immediate and far-reaching reforms, and this may—although there is no reason for confidence—lead to much good and little or no harm. If one could be certain that these effects were indeed produced by the rioting, one would be tempted to conclude that it was a good thing in spite of its cost in life and property. But one cannot be certain. Moreover, even if these effects were produced, others that are disastrous may also have been. A racial myth may be very helpful to the Negro lower class and very harmful to the society as a whole. It may be that the principal effect of the rioting has been on white opinion, that it has checked a growing disposition on the part of the working and lower-middle classes to accept reforms, and that it has established as something beyond question for everyone the mistaken notion that the "problem" is mainly one of race rather than, as has been maintained here, of class. Explaining as "racial" behavior what can as well or better be explained in other terms would seem to be a dangerous game even when played with the best of motives.

The American Vigilante Tradition

RICHARD MAXWELL BROWN

The vigilante tradition, in the classic sense, refers to organized, extralegal movements which take the law into their own hands. The first vigilante movement in American history occurred in 1767. From then until about 1900, vigilante activity was an almost constant factor in American life. Far from being a phenomenon only of the far western frontier, there was much vigilan-

FROM Richard Maxwell Brown, "The American Vigilante Tradition," in Hugh Davis Graham and Ted Robert Gurr, eds., *Violence in America: Historical and Comparative Perspectives*, a report to the National Commission on the Causes and Prevention of Violence, June 1969, Signet edition, pp. 144–206.

tism in the Eastern half of the United States. . . . Although the first vigilante movement occurred in Piedmont, S. C., in 1767–69, most of the Atlantic Seaboard States were without significant vigilante activity. But beyond the Appalachians there were few states that did not have vigilante movements. There may have been as many as 500 movements, but at the present only 326 are known.

American vigilantism is indigenous. There were "regulators" in early-18th-century London who formed a short-lived official supplement to London's regular system of law enforcement, but there was no connection between London's legal regulators and South Carolina's back country "Regulators" of 1767 who constituted America's first vigilante movement. From time to time in European history there appeared movements or institutions (such as the *Vehmgericht* of Germany and *Halifax law,* of the British Isles) which bear resemblances to American vigilantism, but these phenomena did not give rise to a vigilante tradition either on the Continent or in the British Isles. European expansion in other areas of the world has, similarly, failed to produce anything like the American vigilante tradition. Perhaps the closest thing to it was the *commando system* (against marauding *kaffirs*) of the Boer settlers in South Africa; the *commandos,* however, were more like the Indian-fighting rangers of the American frontier than the vigilantes.

Vigilantism arose as a response to a typical American problem: the absence of effective law and order in a frontier region. It was a problem that occurred again and again beyond the Appalachian Mountains. It stimulated the formation of hundreds of frontier vigilante movements. On the frontier the normal foundations of a stable, orderly society—churches, schools, cohesive community life—were either absent or present only in rough, immature forms. The regular, legal system of law enforcement often proved to be woefully inadequate for the needs of the settlers.

Fundamentally, the pioneers took the law into their own hands for the purpose of establishing order and stability in newly settled areas. In the older settled areas the prime values of person and property were dominant and secure, but the move to the frontier meant that it was necessary to start all over. Upright and ambitious frontiersmen wished to reestablish the values of a property holder's society. The hurtful presence of outlaws and marginal types in a context of weak and ineffectual law enforcement created the spectre and, often, the fact of social chaos. The solution hit upon was vigilantism. A vigilante roundup of ne'er-do-wells and outlaws followed by the flogging, expulsion, or killing of them not only solved the problem of disorder but had crucial symbolic value as well. Vigilante action was a clear warning to disorderly inhabitants that the newness of settlement would provide no opportunity for eroding the established values of civilization. Vigilantism was a violent sanctification of the deeply cherished values of life and property.

Because the main thrust of vigilantism was to reestablish in each newly settled area the conservative values of life, property, and law and order, vigilante movements were usually led by the frontier elite. This was true of the greatest American vigilante movement—the San Francisco Vigilance Committee of 1856—which was dominated lock, stock, and barrel by the leading merchants of the city. Again and again it was the most eminent local community leaders who headed vigilante movements.

"Vigilance Committee" or "Committee of Vigilance" was the common name of the organization, but originally—and far into the 19th century—vigilantes were known by the now obsolete term of "regulators." Variant names for vigilante groups were "slickers," "stranglers," "committees of safety," and, in central Texas, simply, "mobs." (In this study "vigilante" will be used as a generic term to cover all phases of the general phenomenon of vigilantism.) The duration of vigilante movements varied greatly, but movements which lasted as long as a year were long lived. More commonly they finished their business in a period of months or weeks. Vigilante movements (as distinguished from ephemeral lynch mobs) are thus identifiable by the two main characteristics of (1) regular (though illegal) organization and (2) existence for a definite (though possibly short) period of time.

· · ·

VIGILANTISM AS A PARALLEL STRUCTURE

Vigilantism characteristically appeared in two types of situations: (1) where the regular system of law and order was absent or ineffective, and (2) where the regular system was functioning satisfactorily. The first case found vigilantism filling a void. The second case revealed vigilantism functioning as an extralegal structure of justice that paralleled the regular system.

Why did vigilantes desire to erect a parallel structure when the regular one was adequate? There were a number of reasons. By usurping the functions of regular law enforcement and justice or, at times, duplicating them, the cost of local government was greatly reduced. As taxpayers the vigilante leaders and the rank and file benefited from the reduction in public costs. Second, the process of community reconstruction through the re-creation of social structure and values could be carried on more dramatically by a vigilante movement than was possible through the regular functioning of the law. A vigilante hanging was a graphic warning to all potentially disruptive elements that community values and structure were to be upheld.

The sort of impression that vigilantes wanted to make was that received by young Malcolm Campbell who arrived in Cheyenne, Wyoming, in 1868 at the age of 28. No sooner had he arrived than there were four vigilante hangings. "So in rapid succession," he recalled, "came before my eyes instances which demonstrated the strength of law [as carried out by vigilantes], and the impotence of the criminal. Undoubtedly, these incidents went far in shaping my future life and in guiding my feet properly in those trails of danger where I was later to apprehend some of the most dangerous outlaws of the plains." (Campbell later became a leading Wyoming sheriff.)

Finally, the vigilante movement sometimes existed for reasons that were essentially unrelated to the traditional problems of crime and disorder. The San Francisco vigilance committee of 1856 is one of the best examples of the vigilante movement as a parallel structure. The San Francisco vigilantes spoke of a crime problem, but examination of the evidence does not reveal a significant upsurge of crime in 1855–56. The regular authorities had San Francisco crime well under control. Fundamentally, the San Francisco vigilantes were concerned with local political and fiscal reform. They wished to capture control of the government from the dominant faction of Irish Catholic Democrats. The vigilantes actually left the routine enforcement of law to the regular police and intervened only in a few major cases. The parallel structure of the vigilante movement was utilized to organize a reform political party (the People's Party) and to shatter the Irish Catholic Democratic faction by exiling some of its leading operatives.

Sometimes the regular and parallel structures were intertwined. Law enforcement officials often connived with vigilantes. Here a sheriff or police chief was not taken by surprise when a vigilante force bent on a lynching converged upon his jail, for he had helped plan the whole affair. Appearances were preserved, usually, by a token resistance on the part of the law officer, but it was well known in the community that he had shared in the vigilante plot.

Why would men violate their oaths and subvert their own functions as officers of the law? For some men the reason was that they were little more than hirelings of the local vigilante elite to whom they were beholden for office. Other officers were of higher social status but, as large landholders or businessmen themselves, they shared the vigilante desire to keep down governmental costs. Little interested in legal niceties, the vigilante-minded law officers were happy to have a nefarious bad man disposed of quickly, cheaply, and permanently by a lynching.

• • •

AN EVALUATION OF AMERICAN VIGILANTISM

In shortrun practical terms, the vigilante movement was a positive facet of the American experience. Many a new frontier community gained order and stability as the result of vigilantism which reconstructed the community structure and values of the old settled areas while dealing effectively with a problem of crime and disorder.

The American Vigilante Tradition

From a longer perspective, the negative aspects of vigilantism appear. Although the era of classic vigilantism came to an end in the 1890's, the tradition lived on. In fact, it was extended into areas of American life where it was wholly inappropriate. Thus arose the latter day phenomenon of neovigilantism.

Neovigilantism grew mainly after the Civil War and was largely a response to the problems of an emerging urban, industrial, racially and ethnically diverse America. The transition from the old to the new vigilantism was heralded by the San Francisco Vigilance Committee of 1856. The latter represented a blending of the methods of the old vigilantism with the victims of the new. Virtually all the features of neovigilantism were present in the San Francisco movement of 1856. Neovigilantism was to be frequently urban rather than rural, and that was the case in San Francisco. The old vigilantism had been directed mainly at horsethieves, counterfeiters, outlaws, bad men, and lower people. Neovigilantism found its chief victims among Catholics, Jews, immigrants, Negroes, laboring men and labor leaders, political radicals, and proponents of civil liberties. The actions and overtones of the San Francisco movement were strongly imbued with the passions and prejudices that came to feature the neovigilantism.

The San Franciscan vigilantes were ethnically biased; their ire focused on one group: the Irish. The vigilantes were anti-Catholic; their hero and martyr was the anti-Romanist editor, James King of William, and most of their victims of 1856 were Catholics. Although their ranks included laborers and mechanics, there was a distinct class tinge to the 1856 movement: middle and upper class merchants were aligned against the lower class adherents of the San Francisco Democratic machine. Last but not least was a disregard for civil liberties. Angered by the arguments of John Nugent of the San Francisco *Herald* in favor of regular justice, the merchant vigilantes of '56 quickly organized an advertising boycott that transformed the *Herald* overnight from the strongest to the weakest of the city's major dailies.

Allegedly concerned with a crime problem, the San Francisco vigilantes of 1856 were in actuality motivated by a desire to seize control of the municipal government from the Democratic political machine that found the nucleus of its support among the lower class Irish Catholic workers of the city. Basic to the vigilante movement was the desire to establish a business-oriented local government which would reduce expenditures, deprive the Irish Catholic Democrats of access to municipal revenues, and lower taxes. To a considerable extent, the San Francisco vigilante episode of 1856 represented a struggle for power between two blocs of opposed religious, class, and ethnic characteristics. Thus, the vigilante leadership of upper and middle class, old American, Protestant merchants was aligned against a political faction based upon Irish Catholic lower class laborers. Such were the social and economic tensions that typically enlisted the violence of neovigilantism.

The protean character of neovigilantism precludes an extensive discussion of it at this time. Only significant tendencies may be noted. Negroes have been the targets of three distinct Ku Klux Klan movements over a 100-year period

THE ERUPTION OF VIOLENCE 432

going back to 1867. Catholics and Jews were singled out for verbal attack by the second Ku Klux Klan (of the 1920's), but the bulk of Klan violence in the 1920's seems to have been leveled against ne'er-do-well white Anglo-Saxon Protestants who did not measure up to the puritanical Klan moral standards and was similar to the White Cap movement which violently regulated the immoral and shiftless from 1888 on into the 20th century. Immigrants were repeatedly the victims of neovigilantism. One of the most spectacular instances was the lynching of 11 Sicilians in New Orleans in 1891. Laboring men and labor union organizers (many of whom were immigrants) were frequently the subjects of vigilante violence when on strike or attempting to organize.

Political radicals have often undergone vigilante harassment; one of the most striking examples was the arrest of thousands of Communists and radicals in the "Red raids" of January 1, 1920. The raids were carried out under the color of law, but the whole action resembled nothing so much as a giant vigilante roundup. Proponents of civil liberties have at times fallen afoul of a quasi-vigilante spirit manifested in such waves of intolerance as the "McCarthyism" of the early 1950's. In contrast to the old vigilantism not even a pragmatic justification can be made for neovigilantism, whose efforts have been wholly pernicious. As an index of the tensions of America in an age of transition, neovigilantism is revealing, but as an attempt to apply vigilante methods to the solution of the complex social problems of urban, industrial, diverse America it has been a massive failure.

Neovigilantism is one phase of a larger American failing to which vigilantism has significantly contributed—the spirit of lawlessness. Americans have long felt that intolerable conditions justify defiance of law and its extension, revolution. In large part the spirit of American lawlessness (equal in importance to the spirit of lawfulness) goes back to the American Revolution where Americans learned a lesson that has never been forgotten: that it is sometimes good and proper to rebel and that rebellion succeeds.

Powerfully nurturing American lawlessness has been the vigilante tradition. A part of the historical heritage of hundreds of American communities from the Piedmont to the Pacific, vigilantism—like the American Revolution—has taught the lesson that defiance of law pays. The typical vigilante took the law into his own hands sincerely (but paradoxically) in the interest of law and order. He desired social stability and got it. But was it purchased at too high a cost?

Yes, said the principled opponents of vigilantism who hammered home a philosophy of antivigilantism that went as far back as the opposition to the original South Carolina movement of 1767-69. From the very beginning antivigilante theorists cogently argued that due process of law was a precious Anglo-American legacy, that true law and order meant observing the law's letter as well as its spirit, and, finally, that the only way to obtain real and lasting law and order was to pour all one's energies and substance into making the regular system work.

One trenchant opponent of the San Francisco Vigilance Committee of 1856 noted that "if the same energy which prompted the formation of the Committee and organized the armed force that assaulted the jail had been directed to strengthen the regular course of justice as public opinion can do it, there would have been no need for the [vigilante] outbreak." "The precedent is bad, the law of passion cannot be trusted, and the slow process of reform in the administration of justice is more safe to rely on than the action of any revolutionary committee, no matter how great may be the apparent necessity," he continued. "Better to endure the evil of escape of criminals than to inaugurate a reign of terror which to-day may punish one guilty head, and tomorrow wreak its mistaken vengeance on many innocent lives," he concluded.

Aside from the danger of vigilante action veering off into extremism, the critics of vigilantism were upset by its fundamentally subversive character. A southern Illinois opponent of the Regulator movement in Pope, Johnson, and Massac Counties, Richard S. Nelson, charged in 1847 that by attacking citizens and taking their property the Regulators had violated "those great principles of civil liberty" upon which the Illinois State constitution was based. Nelson also turned the vigilante justification of popular sovereignty against them by noting that in forcing elected county officials to leave the county or surrender their offices the Regulators had "made a direct attack upon the sovereignty of the people." There is no doubt, however, that, for all the plausibility of Nelson's invocation of popular sovereignty against vigilantism, the appeal to popular sovereignty was made much more often by vigilantes than by their opponents.

Occasionally, vigilante opponents got at the sociological causes of the crime and turbulence which led to vigilantism. The Reverend William Anderson Scott was a courageous opponent of the powerful San Francisco vigilantes of 1856. In a sermon entitled "Education, and not Punishment, the True Remedy for the Wrong-Doings and Disorders of Society," Scott called for industrial education for the lower classes and for urban eleemosynary institutions as means of eradicating the root sources of crime. "You may depend upon it," he insisted, "the stream of blood will never be staid [sic] while men take the law into their own hands."

Americans have for generations been ambiguous in their attitude to law. In one sense, Americans are a law-abiding people of exemplary character. But the many organized movements in our history which have openly flouted and ignored the law (Revolutionary Whigs, Northern abolitionists, Southern filibusters, regulators, vigilantes, Ku Klux Klansmen, White Caps, lynch mobs, etc.) are in indication that lawlessness has been rife. In 1837, the young Abraham Lincoln delivered an address on "The Perpetuation of Our Political Institutions" and found that the chief threat came from "the increasing disregard for law which pervades the country—the growing disposition to substitute the wild and furious passions in lieu of the sober judgment of courts, and the worse than savage mobs for the executive ministers of justice."

Basic to American lawlessness has been our proclivity to pick and choose the laws we would obey, respecting those which we approve and defying those with which we disagree. Our arbitrary attitude toward law reflects a fundamental and deep-seated disrespect for law, or, to put it another way, reveals only a superficial allegiance to law. Perhaps the most important result of vigilantism has not been its social-stabilizing effect but the subtle way in which it persistently undermined our respect for law by its repeated insistence that there are times when we may choose to obey the law or not.

EPILOGUE

Vigilantism of the 1960's

The middle and late 1960's have produced a new upsurge of vigilantism. The following movements (to be listed chronologically and then analyzed) differ from classic vigilantism in the sense that, apparently, they have not yet taken the law into their own hands; they have restricted themselves to patrol activity and to assisting the police. In another sense, however, these movements are in the authentic vigilante tradition, for they are movements in which citizens join together for self-protection under conditions of disorder and lawlessness. Moreover, these movements have commonly been viewed as "vigilante" movements by their members, the police and the authorities, and by society at large.

1964

1. May 1964 (through the summer of 1966 and perhaps later): The "Maccabees," a neighborhood patrol organization, is formed in the Crown Heights area, Brooklyn, New York. Nightly radio-car patrols are established for the purpose of spotting and reporting criminal actions. Predominantly Hasidic Jewish in its membership (but with some white Christians and Negroes) of 250, it was formed after a mass meeting of 500 Jewish neighborhood leaders and led by Rabbi Samuel Shrage. The crime problem was mostly by teenage Negroes coming into Crown Heights from adjacent areas. By March 1966, the *New York Times* reported that crime had fallen in the Crown Heights area and that the Maccabees were patrolling at a reduced rate. In June 1966, Rabbi Shrage was appointed assistant executive director of the Youth Board of New York City, and since that time the Maccabees have dropped out of the news, suggesting that they are either inactive or no longer considered newsworthy.

2. December 1964: Apartment dwellers in the Delano Village complex of North Harlem, New York City, establish interracial anticrime foot patrols equipped

with walkie-talkies. In one apartment building there had been 14 assaults on residents in one month.

3. December 1964: Apartment dwellers in buildings on Manhattan's West Side in New York City in the vicinity of West End Avenue, Riverside Drive, and 103d Street form a patrol organization similar to the one in Delano Village. The problem is an increase in crime stemming from a recent rise in the price of heroin, many addicts resorting to robbery and burglary to support their expensive habit.

4. December 1964: Twenty-four citizens of Port Chester, New York (near the Connecticut State line), form a "vigilante group" to deal with rowdy youngsters from Connecticut who came to Port Chester to take advantage of New York's law allowing 18-year-olds to drink. Patrol action was apparently contemplated by the "vigilante group."

1965

5. March 1965: The Midland Beach Progressive Association, a civic organization of Staten Island, New York, forms a system of nightly unarmed radio-car patrols to protect Midland Beach women who have been the victims of recent assaults. The patrol cooperates with police.

6. April 1965: On April 1, 100 Negroes in the Bedford-Stuyvesant area of Brooklyn, New York, establish automobile and foot patrols (the latter with big dogs) to prevent and discourage crime. Modeled on the Maccabees of Crown Heights and cooperating with police, the organization was an outgrowth of a meeting of the Fulton Park Community Council. Note that this was a Negro organization established to deal with a Negro crime problem.

7. May 1965 (through 1966 and perhaps later): Deacons for Defense and Justice, a Negro self-protection organization, founded in Jonesboro and Bogalusa, Louisiana, in May 1965. An armed patrol-car system was set up to protect civil rights workers (some of whom were white) and Negro residents against violence and harassment by Ku Klux Klansmen, white rowdies, and the police. The tough, dynamic leader of the Deacons in violent, racially troubled Bogalusa was Charlie Sims, a non-middle-class Negro. Wholly successful in Jonesboro and Bogalusa, by May 1966, the Deacons claimed 7,000 members in Louisiana and 60 loosely federated chapters in Mississippi, Alabama, Florida, and the Carolinas, and were attempting to gain a foothold in Chicago. The Deacons have not been mentioned lately, suggesting that they have become inactive or that their activities are no longer considered newsworthy.

1966

8. March 1966: A radio-car citizens' patrol of 15 members is established to prevent, discourage, and report crime in Bushwick, Brooklyn, New York. A recent robbery-killing and a rape precipitated the organization of the group which, however, had been in the planning stages for several months. Headed by a Lutheran minister, the Reverend Samuel L. Hoard, the group had the support of an organization of 12 Protestant and Catholic churches in the area. It was modeled on the Maccabees of Crown Heights and was cooperating with the police.

1967

9. January 1967: The People's Civic Association of the East New York, Brownsville, and Flatbush areas of Brooklyn, launched a radio-equipped vigilante patrol of 350 members with five automobiles. Operating mainly around East 98th Street in order to spot and discourage criminal activity, it cooperated with the police.

10. March 3, 1967: Thirty-five tenants (mostly women) form a "temporary vigilante committee" to patrol a large apartment building at 441 East 20th Street in Peter Cooper Village, Manhattan. The committee was an outgrowth of a mass meeting of building inhabitants called in response to a wave of rapings and muggings. Neither the police nor Metropolitan Life (the owner of the building) were able to supply adequate police protection. An irony in the situation was that New York Police Commissioner Howard R. Leary lived in an adjacent building.

11. June 1967: A force of about 50 private security guards (called "vigilantes" by *Time*) armed with shotguns is formed in Houston, Texas, by three drycleaning chains and six other businesses for the purpose of protecting their premises against robbery which had recently reached a crisis level. Another reason cited for the hiring of the vigilantes was Houston's extremely low police-citizenry ratio. Mayor Louie Welch gave the organization his approval.

12. Summer of 1967 through 1968 and presumably still in existence: The North Ward Citizens' Committee of Newark, New Jersey, was organized to conduct nightly radio patrols for the dual purpose of spotting and discouraging criminal activity and repelling, should the need arise, an incursion of Negro rioters and looters from the adjacent Central Ward of Newark. Headed by its dynamic founder, Anthony Imperiale, the North Ward Citizens' Committee was an outgrowth of the racial confrontation in Newark stemming from the

tremendous Negro riots of June 1967. The members of the committee are primarily Italians and thus reflect the ethnic composition of the North Ward. The North Ward Citizens' Committee has been one of the most publicized vigilante organizations of the 1960's. Its founder, Anthony Imperiale, was elected to the Newark city council in November 1968, largely upon the basis of popularity gained through his Committee leadership.

13. October 1967: Operation Interruption, an "armed police militia" was founded in Harlem (New York City) by the Reverend Oberia D. Dempsey, pastor of the Upper Park Avenue Baptist Church and the unofficial "mayor" of Harlem. A Negro organization of 2,600 members, of whom 200 armed and active members formed a core, it was formed to combat "criminalization" in Harlem stemming from drug addiction and centering on 125th Street. The members maintained themselves in readiness to stop crimes, patrol areas, escort citizens, and work as informants for the city police, FBI, and the Federal Narcotics Bureau. Capt. William J. O'Rourke of the 25th Precinct police station, conceding the lack of an adequate number of police, worked closely with the Reverend Dempsey and Operation Interruption. Note that this, too, was a Negro organization against Negro crime.

1968

14. June–July 1968: Self-proclaimed vigilantes of West Hollywood, Florida, consist of 12 businessmen who patrol nightly in prowl cars and are armed with shotguns. Their announced purpose was to protect their shops and stores against robbery, charging Sheriff Allen B. Michell of Broward County with negligence.

15. July–September 1968: White vigilantes are said to be active in various areas of Cleveland, Ohio. They are mainly anti-Negro and are a response to Negro turbulence in the Hough section, a Negro "ghetto" area of Cleveland. The unsolved killings of two Negroes may have been the result of vigilante action.

16. July–September 1968: "Night riders" in Irasburg, Vermont, harass the Reverend David L. Johnson, a Negro accused of adultery with a white woman. The charge against Johnson was later dismissed in court.

17. Summer of 1968: Fight Back, an anti-Negro organization in Warren, Michigan, is apparently similar in character to the North Ward Citizens' Committee of Newark.

18. Summer of 1968: The Home Defense Association of Oakland, California, is an anti-Negro organization apparently similar in character to the North Ward Citizens' Committee of Newark.

19. October 1968: Negroes form unarmed "vigilante units" in Pittsburgh, Pennsylvania, for nightly walking patrols in response, apparently, to crime and, especially, to Negro–white racial tensions. The Negroes had intended to have armed patrols but were discouraged from doing so by the Public Safety Director of Pittsburgh.

20. December 1968: The *New York Times* reports the existence in New York City of various citizens' anticrime operations, including private and volunteer guards in apartment-house lobbies, guards in public housing projects, and neighborhood block guards.

1969

21. January 1969: The Community Patrol Corps in the Negro ghetto of Detroit, is an unarmed street patrol of 15–20 young Negro men in semimilitary dress. The patrol was formed for the dual purpose of curbing Negro criminality and white police brutality and was aided by a $50,000 grant from the New Detroit Committee, Detroit's local Urban Coalition group.

(Related to the "vigilante" movements recounted above has been the Crime-Stop movement. Chicago's Police Superintendent, O. W. Wilson, originated Crime-Stop in that city in April 1964. The idea was for citizens to telephone in reports of crimes or suspicious activities to a special police number. In 1967 *Parade* reported that more than a million Chicagoans had pledged to cooperate with Crime-Stop and that the movement had spread to 111 cities [including Boston and Los Angeles] in 34 states.)

The survey above indicates that there are three vigilante-prone segments of the population today: (1) Negro enclaves, South and North, which feel the need of self-protective organizations against white violence and harassment. The Deacons for Defense and Justice are the best example of a vigilante response in this situation. (2) White urban and suburban neighborhoods in the North which feel threatened by a possible incursion of Negro rioters and looters. The North Ward Citizens' Committee of Newark is the leading example of the vigilante response in this situation. (3) Urban neighborhoods beset by crime. The Maccabees of Crown Heights, Brooklyn, have served as the model for the vigilante response to this situation.

Both the white versus Negro and the Negro versus white vigilante-type organizations are heavily freighted with neovigilantism in that racial fear and animosity is a major motivating factor in the vigilante activity. The most typical vigilante organization thus far in the 1960's is, however, the pure anticrime combination exemplified by the Maccabees of Crown Heights, Brooklyn. Thus the typical vigilante organization arises in urban neighborhoods among residents who feel that there is a severe crime problem. The leadership of the organization—like the vigilantes of old—is indigenous, often consisting of neighborhood religious leaders (e.g., Rabbi Shrage of the Maccabees, the Reverend Hoard of the Bushwick, Brooklyn, movement of 1966, and the Reverend Dempsey of Operation Interruption in Harlem). Combination is a spontaneous act of the people but is often an outgrowth of an existing organization.

In contrast to the classic vigilantism of the 19th century, vigilantes of the 1960's do not take the law into their own hands nor do they kill. Instead their main activity is patrol action in radio-equipped automobiles (linked to a central headquarters) for the purpose of spotting, reporting, and discouraging criminal acts. Characteristically these modern vigilantes cooperate with the police, although the latter have occasionally worried that the vigilantes would get out of hand. To a considerable extent the vigilantes of the 1960's resemble the antihorsethief societies (late 18th century to early 20th century) who restricted themselves to the pursuit and detention of malefactors and did not ordinarily take the law into their own hands. Both the earlier antihorsethief societies and the current vigilantes supplemented but did not substitute for regular law enforcement.

The next stage—that of contemporary vigilantes taking the law into their own hands—may not come. That it may, however, was the recent warning of a spokesman for crime-ridden Harlem Negroes, Mr. Vincent S. Baker, chairman of the anticrime committee of the New York City branch of the NAACP. Invoking the vigilante tradition, Mr. Baker noted that "in towns of the Old West where there was no law, people paid gunslingers to protect them from the depredations of marauding outlaws." "There is an embryonic vigilante movement in this community," he declared. "It's cropping up all over. Tenant groups are arming themselves." Baker called for more police in Harlem and harsher penalties for criminals as a minimum program if the community was "to escape the reign of criminal terror without resorting to vigilantism." "Asserting that the Harlem situation was no better than Dodge City, Abilene, or other towns of the Old West," Mr. Baker attacked vigilantism as being "inherently undemocratic, antisocial and unsound," but contended "that it might be generated by a feeling of 'anarchy and complete helplessness against marauding hoodlums.'"

Whether or not the crime rate is really rising or declining is currently being debated by experts, but in one way the question is beside the point. Most urban Americans, particularly in the largest cities, are firm in their belief that there is too much crime, that their persons or property are in danger, and that regular law enforcement is not coping with the problem. The same feelings in earlier times led Americans to resort to vigilantism.

SUGGESTIONS FOR FURTHER READING

Serious writing about "political violence" has not caught up with the recent surge of interest in the subject. In fact, we have yet to see any work that successfully distinguishes political violence from other, presumably more common and less troubling, sorts.

Perhaps the best available book is Ted Robert Gurr's *Why Men Rebel* (Princeton, N. J.: Princeton University Press, 1969), which argues, elegantly if not surprisingly, that there is a strong relationship between the resort to violence and the perception of unfair treatment on the part of those who rebel.

Hannah Arendt has contributed a characteristically sensitive essay *On Violence* (New York: Harcourt Brace Jovanovich, 1970), which suggests some of the dangers involved in advocating violence as a way of forcing social change. A number of contributions to the report of the National Commission on the Causes and Prevention of Violence are worth consulting; see Hugh Davis Graham and Ted Robert Gurr, eds., *The History of Violence in America: Historical and Comparative Perspectives* (New York: Praeger, 1969).

Other useful works are Tom Rose, ed., *Violence in America: A Historical and Contemporary Reader* (New York: Random House, 1969), and Richard E. Rubenstein, *Rebels in Eden: Mass Political Violence in the United States* (Boston: Little, Brown, 1970).

Two journals—*The Public Interest* and *The Journal of Conflict Resolution*—are rich sources of articles dealing with political violence.

14 The battle over foreign policy

THE PAST DECADE SAW two rather searching congressional examinations of the procedures by which foreign and military policy are made in America. In the early years of the decade, the Subcommittee on National Security Policy Machinery—a subcommittee of the Government Operations Committee chaired by Senator Henry M. Jackson of Washington—conducted a lengthy and well-publicized review of the practices of the Eisenhower administration. At the end of the decade, the Vietnam war prompted the Senate Foreign Relations Committee, under Senator J. William Fulbright of Arkansas, to launch a less systematic but more impassioned examination of the practices of the Kennedy and Johnson administrations. United States involvement in a land war in Asia also raised serious questions concerning the substance of American policy—the assumptions that have guided American decision-makers since World War II.

The period immediately after World War II saw the development of a fundamental conception of America's role in the world that came to be called containment. The Marshall Plan in Europe, the Truman Doctrine (which provided aid to Greece and Turkey), the response to the North Korean thrust across the 38th parallel, and the development of NATO as a shield against Soviet initiatives in Europe all rested on the assumption that it was the proper business of the United States to frustrate the development of Marxist-Leninist political systems by the deployment of its economic and military resources around the world.

The development of thermonuclear weapons and intercontinental delivery systems in the 1950's added a new dimension to containment. For almost a decade, under Dwight D. Eisenhower and John Foster Dulles, the United States followed a policy of "massive retaliation" whereby Soviet aggression might be "punished" by an American nuclear strike. While it is possible to argue that this gambit made sense in the early 1950's, when America possessed a virtual monopoly on nuclear weapons, its effectiveness was quickly undermined by the Soviet development of an impressive strategic capacity. The policy of massive retaliation gave way to a notion of mutual deterrence in which each nuclear power guaranteed its own security by maintaining sufficient military capacity to wreak havoc after having absorbed the fiercest first blow the initiator could deliver.

Thus containment became subordinated to the delicate balance of terror, and attention gradually shifted from the possibility of head-on collision between the superpowers to secondary and tertiary theaters of operation—usually in the underdeveloped nations of the "third world." Here were unstable political situations which the superpowers sought to stabilize in ways that would, over the long haul, improve their respective international positions. The Congo, Cuba, the Dominican Republic, Lebanon, Laos, and Vietnam became the places most prominent in the news. This picture was further complicated in the early 1960's by the rise of China as a superpower *manqué*.

As foreign policy proceeded along these axes, a continuing struggle took place within the executive branch to adjust military policy to correspond to the changing emphases in foreign policy. A major plan for rearmament was debated in 1948; the early 1950's saw a concentration on the nuclear punch of the Strategic Air Command, the late 1950's a preoccupation with strategic parity, and the early 1960's a concern for the development of forces for limited conventional and guerrilla warfare. This continuing struggle over the "fit" between foreign and military policy has been brilliantly chronicled by Samuel P. Huntington in his *The Common Defense*.[1]

Throughout this twenty-year period the executive branch in general and the President in particular assumed primacy in the process of policy formation. In military policy, for instance, defense appropriation requests for new weapons systems and the maintenance of troop strengths have been worked out within the executive branch among the President's office, the Bureau of the Budget, and the Department of Defense. The congressional role in the process has been largely restricted to alteration of domestically significant details (deciding where a new plant will be built, for example) and occasional attempts to increase appropriations for particular projects. Congressional efforts to limit spending, eliminate or phase out weapons systems, or flatly deny funding for certain projects, have almost always failed. The closest Congress has come to reversal of a major military policy advocated by the executive branch was the battle in 1969 over the Safeguard Anti-Ballistic Missile System. After that effort failed, the former pattern of congressional approval, with tinkering at the margins, reasserted itself.

In the area of foreign policy proper, the Senate prerogative of concur-

[1] (New York: Columbia University Press, 1961).

ring in treaties was progressively eroded during the 1950's and 1960's by an increased presidential reliance on the executive agreement as a way of doing international business. The very idea of the Senate defying a President of the United States in a major international negotiation has become so frightening that few on Capitol Hill are prepared to entertain it. We have come a long way from Wilson's defeat in the Senate over the Treaty of Versailles. Foreign service appointments—ambassadors, ministers, and consuls—must also be approved by the Senate. From time to time objections are raised, as in the battles over the confirmation of Charles Bohlen as ambassador to the Soviet Union in 1953 and Mrs. Clare Boothe Luce as ambassador to Brazil in 1959. The general disposition of the Senate, however, has been to let the President enjoy a free hand in deploying American diplomats around the world.

Thus, in considering the future of American foreign policy, the first issue that presents itself is the extent of congressional participation in the process by which policy is determined. The first two selections in this chapter are addressed to the question of policy formulation. Roger Hilsman, a former Assistant Secretary of State for East Asian Affairs, argues that foreign policy is generally made in a narrow arena, within the executive branch, with outside interests considered but taking no active part themselves. This, he suggests, is the necessary consequence of the types of decisions being made. Foreign-policy initiatives must be decided on quickly and require high levels of information and specialization. The Congress, of course, should have a role in setting the very broad guidelines of policy and in criticizing and policing its implementation, but the President must remain the only nonspecialist—or, perhaps better, the only political generalist—directly and continually involved in deciding on particular American initiatives in the world. He must have the power to commit the nation, and his responsibility for doing so is fixed not only by the expectations of other nations but also by the Constitution, which, as interpreted by the Supreme Court, makes him not only Commander in Chief, but Chief Diplomat. In short, Hilsman is saying that the way foreign policy has been made is the way it *must* be made, and that the process is sufficiently responsive to the anticipated reactions of nonparticipants to render it democratic. Paired with the selection from Hilsman is a selection from a recent report of the Senate Foreign Relations Committee. The committee, under the leadership of Senator Fulbright, argues that the "narrow arena" procedures described by Hilsman represent an illegitimate modification of American constitutional practice, and that the Congress (or at least the Senate) must be involved as at least a fifty-fifty partner in the process of foreign-policy making.

The second and related issue involves the substance of U. S. policy. Should we continue selectively to deploy American forces around the world in efforts to stabilize volatile situations in ways that we hope will contribute to our security, or should we retrench and adopt a more passive policy, intervening only in the case of a direct physical threat to America? We hasten to add that these are not the only options; there are a variety of shadings in between. It is useful, however, to have the polar positions stated forcefully, and this is the purpose of the second pair of selections. John P. Roche, political scientist and former Special Consultant to President Johnson, presents the case for the pre-Vietnam policy of flexible response, and Ronald Steel, author and critic of American policy, presents the case for severely limiting U. S. commitments and interventions around the world.

▢ Improving the Policy "Machinery"

ROGER HILSMAN

Foreign policy is politics, and politics is a "slow boring of hard boards." There is probably no quick or easy way of making improvements. Certainly tinkering with the organizational "machinery" is not going to help very much. The debate about how to "organize for national security" that preceded the Kennedy administration reached the conclusion . . . that the problems of national security policy were not going to be solved by reorganizing the government. "Super-staffs and super-secretaries" were no way out, it was clear, and neither was strengthening the National Security Council or creating a "vice-president for foreign affairs." And certainly nothing happened in the Kennedy administration that would alter that conclusion. In fact, the major recommendation that came out of the debate about organizing for national security—that the prime voice and co-ordinating power should center in the Department of State—in practice only proved the validity of the conclusion that reorganizing was no solution. Merely assigning power to the State Department did not guarantee that the Secretary and the Department would use it.

All this, of course, does not mean that changes in organization do not affect policy. Organizational changes usually follow a shift in power, as, for example, the changes in the way intelligence problems were handled in the State Department followed CIA's loss of power in the aftermath of the Bay of Pigs. But changes in organization can in themselves bring about an increase or decrease of power and alter the weight that one set of considerations will have over another in policy deliberations. But whether the result is better or worse policy depends on your point of view, on whose interests are being given addi-

FROM Roger Hilsman, *To Move a Nation*, pp. 565–76. Copyright © 1964, 1967 by Roger Hilsman. Reprinted by permission of Doubleday & Company, Inc., and Robert Lantz–Candida Donadio Literary Agency, Inc.

tional weight. What is an "improvement" in this sense to one person may not be to another.

Some improvements are undoubtedly possible in organizational structure that everyone would agree were improvements. Ways might be found, for example, to make the communications process among participants in the making of policy quicker and easier. There might also be organizational changes that could bring more precision in assigning the flow of work, or in the effectiveness of applying the proper expertise at the proper stage. But these are not of fundamental importance and would result in only marginal improvement in the foreign policies that came out the other end.

PREDICTION AND KNOWLEDGE

Effective foreign policy depends on the capacity to predict events in the social affairs of men, and a better capacity to predict would mean better and more effective foreign policy. But more is required than simple factual information. Predicting the outcome of alternative policies requires knowledge in the sense of an ability to identify and weight the different factors bearing on the particular situation and an understanding of the dynamism by which those different factors interact. In the Middle Ages, for example, no one foresaw the Black Death, the great plague that swept Europe, or knew what to do about it after it came. Yet when men learned that germs cause disease and the means by which germs are transmitted, they could not only treat individual cases of the plague, but could foresee that an increase in filth in the cities and the rats that live on it would create the conditions for an outbreak of the plague and indicate the measures needed to head it off.

There is no doubt that knowledge in this sense of the ability to make sound predictions is the crux of the matter. The debate in the Kennedy administration over Vietnam policy, for example, revolved around rival analyses about the nature of guerrilla warfare and predictions about the effects of alternative ways of dealing with it. In China policy, the debate centered on the analysis of the nature of Chinese Communism, its capacity to change Chinese society, and whether or not it was a "passing phase" as well as on predictions about the effects of the rival policies of "isolating" Communist China or maintaining an "open door" for a lessening of hostility and eventual accommodation. And so it was through all the other cases—the Cuban missile crisis, the Congo, Laos, and Indonesia. The crux of the debate in each instance turned on an analysis of the factors bearing on the problem and on predictions about the consequences of alternative ways of dealing with it.

More and better knowledge of the kind that permits accurate prediction is undoubtedly the most important single thing that is needed for the improvement of foreign policy. But here again, there is no quick or easy solution. If there was a wide and obvious gap between the pool of basic knowledge available in the universities, say, and what was actually used in informing governmental decisions, something dramatic might be done. But this particular gap, the gap between the knowledge of experts in government and experts outside, is infinitesimal. Take, for example, the field of "Sovietology." The great body of what is known about the Soviet Union and the workings of Soviet society is shared—and subscribed to—by Soviet specialists within and outside the government. By and large, in fact, the personnel themselves are interchangeable and frequently do shift back and forth. What disagreements there are in the field of "Sovietology" are not between government experts and academic experts but between one group of specialists cutting across both government and academia and another, also cutting across both government and academia. And what is really remarkable is how small the area of disagreement is, how accurate are their judgments about Soviet reactions and behavior, and how few are their failures at prediction—no matter how harshly their role in the Cuban missile crisis is judged.

New and better knowledge is needed, but how can it be developed? Certainly the attempts to institutionalize the effort within government have not been very fruitful. It was this need for knowledge and foresight, according to Dean Acheson, that led General Marshall when he was Secretary of State to establish in 1947 the Policy Planning Staff, a group of about a dozen top-level specialists under an assistant secretary. But in practice, the Policy Planning Staff did not work out to be the panacea some had hoped for. It proved to be a useful pool of talent that could be tapped in time of crisis—as its second chief, Paul Nitze, for example, was pulled out for the negotiations after Mossadegh and his government nationalized oil in Iran. Its members have also contributed "think-piece" memoranda, which have been neither better nor worse, on the average, than similar thoughtful memoranda written in the action bureaus, in the intelligence agencies, or by outside scholars and writers. But none of this, no mater how well done, fulfills the concept of a "planning" staff, and yet beyond this the Policy Planning Staff has done very little.

What is "planning"? Men building a dam or a bridge can plan in a long-range and very precise sense. They can predict the forces that the dam or bridge must withstand and determine with great accuracy the materials and strength needed for each part of the structure. In building a dam or a bridge, men can also draw blueprints and develop a schedule for the work to be done that will permit them to specify months in advance the exact dates on which cement, for example, should be ordered and delivered. Some military planning is also of this nature, such as providing port facilities and hospitals and stockpiles of ammunition and so on. But beyond the field of logistics, military planning is limited—for the fundamental reason that there is an enemy who has some choice in the matter too. In war, the only long-range "planning" that can be done apart from logistics is the making of very broad strategic choices.

Long-range planning in foreign affairs is more similar to this kind of military planning than it is to either logistics planning or the kind of planning used to build a dam or a bridge. It is, essentially, analyzing the nature of the problem and making broad strategic choices for dealing with it. Secretary Dulles' . . . 1957 speech about Communist China, for example, which argued for a strategy of isolating the Chinese Communists, was one strategic choice. The "open door" speech of 1963, which argued for an alternative strategy of "firmness and flexibility" leading toward an eventual accommodation, was another strategic choice. The choice in dealing with Indonesia and Sukarno was the United States posture toward the "new nationalism," whether it could be brought into constructive channels or would respond only to firmness. In Vietnam, the problem was how to treat guerrilla warfare, as we have said—as fundamentally a political problem or as fundamentally a war.

Short-range planning in foreign affairs is working out the moves and countermoves in the midst of an ongoing situation, of developing instructions for an ambassador or orders for the fleet. Should the United States move troops into Thailand in response to the Communists' violation of the cease-fire in Laos, and if so what will the Communists then do? Should the United States use an air strike to take out the Soviet missiles in Cuba, confine its action to diplomatic moves, or begin with a blockade? In China policy, should the United States lift travel restrictions on Americans, push for Chinese participation in disarmament talks, and recognize Mongolia, and if so, what will be the Chinese response?

But both the making of broad strategic choices in foreign affairs and this shorter-range form of making contingency calculations of move and countermove are at the political heart of policy-making. Consequently, the truth of the matter is that both of these kinds of "planning" are done at several places at once—by the advocates of the rival policies and their allies. In the Laos crisis of 1962, for example, one set of "plans" of what the United States should do if the Communist side continued to violate the cease-fire in spite of our having put troops in Thailand was prepared in the Pentagon and another was prepared by the Bureau of Far Eastern Affairs and their allies in the State Department's Intelligence Bureau. In the struggle over Vietnam policy, one strategic concept for fighting the guerrillas was developed out of the work of Thompson in Saigon, people in the Intelligence Bureau at the State Department and in the White House, and military people at the Special Forces center at Fort Bragg— but all this "planning" was overridden by the "planning" for traditional warfare that took place in the military headquarters at Saigon. In the Congo crisis, "planning" took place most of the time in the Bureau of African Affairs, but every now and again it was done elsewhere—in the bureau responsible for UN affairs, in the Intelligence Bureau, and occasionally, to be completely accurate, in the office of Senator Dodd.

At one time or another, the Policy Planning Staff "planned" in this sense as the ally of one or another set of advocates, but it succeeded in being the *principal* advocate and planner in very few cases. The Multilateral Force for NATO and the earlier Developmental Loan Fund are two outstanding examples, and it is instructive of the politics of statecraft that both of these problems were bureaucratic orphans, matters that cut across the regular responsibilities of both the regional and the functional offices of the State Department.

Policy is made in a political process for good and sufficient reasons, and so long as these basic reasons persist, attempts at institutionalizing "planning" or "foresight" or "wisdom" are likely to fail. Some improvements, of course, can be made. A climate of receptivity to new ideas and knowledge can be created rather easily, for example, and creating such a climate of receptivity can have important consequences as people are encouraged to experiment with new ideas and to put them forward. Although it was partly nullified in the State Department by the attitude at the top, President Kennedy established this climate of receptivity at the beginning of his administration very quickly. His actions showed that he was reading people's memos, and he called up "little" men on the phone, all of which created an excitement that the bureaucracy had not known for many years. Government can also do more to encourage research and the development of new knowledge in political and social affairs. The Defense Department, for example, spends billions of dollars supporting research in the physical sciences, but it was not until the Kennedy administration that the State Department obtained money for supporting research in foreign affairs, and as it was, Congress appropriated less than one hundred thousand dollars for the purpose. Something might also be done to direct research and the work of increasing basic knowledge to questions that are more immediately relevant to the issues of foreign policy. Much of the work in the universities on social, political, and economic matters, for example, would benefit a better understanding of the issues as the policymaker must view them. Not only would the results be of more utility to governmental decisions, but the research itself would benefit in a purely scholarly sense by a sharpening of its perspectives.

But important though the results of these kinds of effort might be in the long run, the immediate results would not be any very dramatic improvement in United States foreign policy. The making of foreign policy is a groping effort at understanding the nature of the evolving world around us. It is a painful sorting out of our own goals and purposes. It is a tentative, incremental experimentation with various means for achieving these purposes. It is an unremitting argument and debate among various constituencies about all of these questions and an attempt to build a consensus on how the United States as the United States should decide on these questions and what action it should take. And none of these several activities is the kind that will yield to organizational or institutional gimmicks.

PERSONNEL

One other possible area for improvement in United States foreign policy is people. Other things being equal, good people make good foreign policy and better people make better foreign policy.

There is a wide variety of people who make foreign policy, as we have seen—the press, interest groups, attentive publics, congressmen—but within the Executive Branch itself, where something concrete could be done, the "people who make foreign policy" fall into two general groups. One group is made up of career officials in the foreign service, the civil service, and the military services. The other group are presidential appointees and the people they bring with them—the group of officials who make up an "administration."

There was a time when the quality and training of people in the career group were undoubtedly not as good as they should have been. But much has been done in the years since World War II, not only to broaden the foreign service and the career civil service, but to improve the knowledge and training of everyone concerned with foreign affairs and national security, civilian and military. Pay, retirement, and other benefits have made a government career more attractive. Qualifications have been raised. Mid-career training is provided, not only at the Foreign Service Institute and the service war colleges, but also by new legislation that permits agencies to send officials to private universities for special training. The task of maintaining high standards in the career services and of seeking new ways to improve training is never completely ended, but by and large the United States can be proud of its career services, both civilian and military. The people in them are able, well trained, and dedicated professionals, and although there are things that can be done to help them and to maintain the present high standards, none will bring any marked improvement in the quality of foreign policy.

THE FRONT MEN

As far as the second group of people are concerned—the group of people who make up an "administration"—the thing to mark down first is the function they perform. One aspect of their function is to be the President's man, the representative of the administration. If he is in a staff job in the White House, this is the total of the presidential appointee's function. He is expected to jab and prod and push all the different bureaucracies. He must make sure they produce the data, the recommendations, and so on that the President should have to make decisions. And he must follow up decisions to make sure the bureaucracies take timely and effective action to carry them out once they are made.

The presidential appointee who heads a department, agency, or bureau or serves in a line job in one of them—a secretary or director or assistant secretary —is expected to shape and mold the bureaucracy to the President's needs. He must represent political management, represent the top level of the administration in the form either of the President or the cabinet member in whose department he serves. But if the presidential appointee in the line job is the President's man with the careerists, he should also be the careerists' man with the

President and the top levels of the administration. He should represent the specialists' view to the President and his cabinet officers and be the vehicle for their expertise. He must be the judge of whether what they have to say should be laid before the highest councils, but when he does decide that their views should be heard, he ought to be their unrelenting champion. The head of a department or bureau or agency and the presidential appointees who serve in them *should* run interference for their organization and its careerists. Otherwise, in a political process of decision-making, their expertise will go unheard.

All this applies to the cabinet member—the secretary heading a department or the director of an independent agency. It also applies in general to lower-ranking presidential appointees. Some of these, in fact, may have a relationship to the President almost exactly similar to that of a cabinet member. In the Kennedy administration, for example, Mennen Williams enjoyed this status as Assistant Secretary for African Affairs. The President was deeply interested in the problems of Africa, and Mennen Williams was a public figure in his own right. The result was that Williams had a special status and a special relationship to both the President and the Secretary of State. The position of the Assistant Secretary for Middle Eastern Affairs, held by Phillips Talbot, on the other hand, was less independent, more closely tied to the position of the Secretary of State than to the President.

Inevitably, most presidential appointees come to identify with the organizations they head and to represent the men and women who make up these organizations, whether they represent them well or badly. This is one source of the tension between presidents and cabinet ministers, which has been so often remarked upon. It is also a reason that presidents must go consensus-building in the Executive Branch as well as in the wider rings of policy-making.

Another source of the tensions between presidents and their appointees is the fact that presidents so often seek their men precisely because they represent an outside, public constituency. President Kennedy chose Mennen Williams for the Africa post because he represented liberal opinion in the United States—which was also the reason he preferred Adlai Stevenson at the UN. He chose John McCone—an Irish Catholic, a Republican, and a millionaire shipbuilding tycoon—to head the CIA precisely to make the conservatives in business, in industry, the military, and Congress feel that they and their foreign and defense policy interests would be represented. Having chosen men because of their affiliations with particular constituencies, a president can hardly be surprised if they speak for that constituency in the internal policy debate.

The function of these men, in sum, is to be the advocates of policy and to represent the different bureaucratic constituencies inside the government and the public constituencies of special interests and attentive publics outside of government. It is their function to force an issue up to decision, to try to make the government face up to an emerging problem. It is their function to put forward an alternative policy and to become identified with it. They are the "front men." They are the men who will become public figures if they are not already.

A "front man" need not be a specialist in a particular subject, but if he lasts he is or will become a specialist in using specialists, in knowing when the specialists are right and should be backed, and when they are caught up in their own parochialism. It is the front man who pushes for a particular policy at different places inside the government and outside, with higher officials and lower, with other agencies, in congressional hearings, in backgrounders with the press, in public speeches, and in endless struggles over countless pieces of paper. It is the front man who is the leader of a constituency, the sponsor of a policy, and the builder of a consensus for it. Career men down the line may push a particular policy with unrelenting passion; they may be advocates to the core fiber of their being, but it is this front man who is *the* advocate. The *function* of advocacy is his. He is the man who runs interference by the nature of his job. Out in front, as he is, he is the one who first feels the blast of political heat. And above all, in consequence, the front man is expendable.

THE FRONT MAN AS AN "IN-AND-OUTER"

It is the high expendability of the front men—as well as the fact of their identification with a particular president and his administration, which are, after all, impermanent—that accounts for their being dubbed the "in-and-outers." Unlike J. Edgar Hoover, who has headed the FBI for over forty years, there is no example of someone who was always "in" the foreign affairs field in the sense of holding high office. But the term "in-an-outers" does have some misleading connotations, especially the implication that there is a ladder and that men come in and out to gradually increasing responsibilities and experience. Many do. Dean Acheson started as Assistant Secretary of the Treasury under Roosevelt. He went out in a disagreement over fiscal policy, then came back as Assistant Secretary for Economic Affairs in the State Department. He was then Assistant Secretary for Congressional Relations, then Under Secretary, and out again. Finally, he came back as Secretary of State under President Truman. W. Averell Harriman started very near the top, but he gained in experience by serving in every Democratic administration since Roosevelt's, being out of the foreign affairs area of government only during the Eisenhower years. Dean Rusk was Assistant Secretary for UN Affairs in the Truman administration, Deputy Under Secretary, and Assistant Secretary for Far Eastern Affairs. He went out to head the Rockefeller Foundation, and then came back again to be Secretary of State. Other, completely random examples are the following: Henry L. Stimson, Chester Bowles, Allen Dulles, Paul Nitze, Adolf Berle, George W. Ball, McGeorge Bundy, Arthur H. Dean, Robert A. Lovett, Douglas Dillon, J. Kenneth Galbraith, John J. McCloy, and John McCone.

Some front men come in only once. Henry A. Wallace, for example, held three positions the first time in—Secretary of Agriculture, Vice-President, and

Secretary of Commerce—but he never came back once he went out. Eisenhower's Secretary of Agriculture, Ezra Taft Benson, and his Secretary of Defense, Charles E. Wilson, had never held government posts before their appointments as cabinet members. Neither had Kennedy's Secretary of Defense, Robert S. McNamara.

Where do the front men come from? Many have come from Wall Street—Henry L. Stimson, James V. Forrestal, Paul Nitze, Douglas Dillon. Some from politics—G. Mennen Williams and James F. Byrnes. Some came from the law—Dean Acheson, George W. Ball, and Arthur H. Dean. Some came from a combination of law and politics—Adlai E. Stevenson. Some have come from business and industry—Charles E. Wilson, and Averell Harriman and Chester Bowles, the last two having an interim period in politics. Some have come from academia and the foundation world—Dean Rusk, McGeorge Bundy, Adolf Berle, Philip C. Jessup, and J. Kenneth Galbraith. Some have come from the career service—Robert Murphy, who went pretty steadily up and went out only on retirement. Coming from the career service, Murphy was an "up-and-outer" rather than an "in-and-outer." And George F. Kennan was both. He rose to prominence as Ambassador to the Soviet Union and head of the Policy Planning Staff, left for an academic post, and returned as Ambassador to Yugoslavia. Some of the front men are really "up-and-backers" or "up-and-one-siders"—Charles E. Bohlen, for example, who was at the heart of policy-making in the Truman years, sat out the Eisenhower administration as Ambassador to Manila, and returned to the heart of policy-making in the Kennedy administration. There are also the "in-and-outers" and "up-and-backers" from the military—Maxwell Taylor, James Gavin, Walter Bedell Smith, George C. Marshall, Lucius Clay—all of whom held high civilian office after reaching prominent military positions.

These "front men," as we have said, are key in making foreign policy *effective*. They are the ones who kick and push and shove to get the government to recognize a problem and face up to the policy choices rather than drift in indecision. They are the ones who sponsor policy alternatives, who do the work of enlisting support, arguing, selling, persuading, and building a consensus around a particular course of action. It is their leadership or lack of it that determines whether a decision will be vigorously or indifferently carried out.

The effectiveness of foreign policy depends peculiarly on the front men. If their quality, training, and progressive experience can be improved, so will foreign policy. The nation should clearly pay careful attention to their upbringing, care, and feeding.

But here again there is no simple solution. To an American, for example, the British parliamentary system seems to provide a neat solution to the problem of providing an obvious ladder, early selection, and progressive experience for policy leaders. There is an opportunity to start early. Men may run for parliament from any district without residence requirements, and an able man may get a seat while still very young. There is opportunity to work up. The member sits on the back benches and learns, eventually earning a position as parliamentary undersecretary where he can work from inside the great departments. If he is an apt pupil with sufficient luck, sooner or later he will get a cabinet post. And there is provision for the "out" period that permits him to develop and work in the field of his major interest. When his party is out of power he still has a seat in parliament from which he can participate, study, and follow developments in his special field. Most importantly of all, there is the clear expectation on his part, by his constituency, his colleagues, and his adversaries that he will in fact be back.

To an American all this seems a marvelous system for the upbringing of "front men." But to an Englishman, on the other hand, it does not always look quite so wonderful. To him, the system sometimes seems to ensure that there will never be any new blood. Responsibility for policymaking alternates between two small groups of familiar people in a tight procedure that works against any possibility of new faces and fresh ideas. More than one Englishman has commented on how difficult it would be for a new British government to bring into high and influential posts such a glittering array of new, young, and vigorous people full of verve and fresh ideas that the Kennedy administration assembled. The old, familiar "shadow cabinet," they complain, merely replaces the old, familiar cabinet—and back and forth in a dull minuet. Once in a while a single new face can be brought in, but only by the ponderous device of forcing a resignation in a safe seat and holding a by-election or by having the man elevated to the peerage and given a seat in the House of Lords.

In the United States there are a few things that might be done to improve matters. The attractions of going "in" or "up" can be increased, and the risks of having no place to go "out" or "back" can be reduced. Perhaps other measures can be taken to ease the lot and improve the incentive of the "front men." But it is difficult to conceive of any very radical changes in their recruitment, training, or conditions of servitude. And so here again, the somewhat pessimistic conclusion seems inescapable—that there is no easy route to dramatic improvement.

And so it goes. Knowledge can and should be increased and made available at all levels of participation, inside and outside the government and among the attentive publics—but the improvement in foreign policy will be slow. Communications and the flow of information among all participants at all levels can and should be improved—and the results will be good but not dramatic. Policy is made in a political process involving debate among rival advocates before a variety of constituencies, and the wisest course is probably to concentrate on trying to maximize the strengths of the system rather than changing it. Secrecy should in general be mistrusted, although it is sometimes necessary. Expertise should be given a full hearing, but experts themselves should be watched, at least for the narrowness of their interest. Deliberate heed should be paid to the role of the process itself, the need for debate and the involvement of all those who have a legitimate interest or contribution. The best way to improve policy, in a word, is probably to conduct it with an eye—but a highly discriminating eye—to the political realities of the process by which it is made.

"DEMOCRACY" IN THE MAKING OF FOREIGN POLICY

One final word should be added. All these considerations have been about the "effectiveness" of foreign policy, not whether it was "good" or "bad." Whether foreign policy is "effective" turns on whether or not the government recognizes an emerging problem and faces up to it; whether or not the policy adopted is in fact the alternative most likely to achieve the desired goal; and whether or not the decision is vigorously and efficiently carried out. The results, however, can be either "good" or "bad" depending on one's particular goals and interests —which is why the making of foreign policy is a political matter. And this involvement of the values and interests of the different segments of society in turn raises the question of "democracy" in the making of foreign policy.

The relative openness of the process of policy-making as we have seen it in the particular cases related in this book, the variety of constituencies, and the strain toward consensus provide at least for the possibility that different views of what is "good" and what is "bad" will be heard. By and large the very existence of these different constituencies—including the constituency of the press with its peculiar interest in conflict and disagreement—ensures that most of the major foreign policies will continue to be decided in the relatively open process of "conflict and consensus-building" and that the full range of different views will be represented even when the number of participants is restricted for reasons of security. But this still permits an occasional decision to be made in an inner circle that excludes major constituencies and major bodies of knowledge and expertise—as the Bay of Pigs so vividly illustrates. President Kennedy used to say, as mentioned earlier, that a domestic failure would hurt the country, but that a failure in foreign affairs could kill it. Yet it is in foreign affairs that "closed" decisions like the Bay of Pigs are most possible, for the President's power to take independent action is far greater in the field of foreign affairs than it is in domestic matters.

Once burned by the Bay of Pigs, President Kennedy made sure that his decisions in the Cuban missile crisis, in sending troops to Thailand in the Laos crisis, and so on, were taken only with the full range of both the interested constituencies and the relevant expertise, even though secrecy demanded that the decision be "closed" in a public sense. But an egocentric president, a man who saw himself as infallible and whose thirst for power had excluded independent-minded men from his administration or muted their voices, could make a particular decision without considering the range of constituencies at any time and could succeed in making the process itself much less open than it normally is—at least for a time.

And once more there is no simple or easy solution. No constitutional amendment will give this guarantee, and neither will reorganizing and strengthening the National Security Council. And any other alternative—such as giving Congress a more direct role—would probably make it impossible to move quickly and effectively in time of crisis. The Cuban missile crisis, for example, could not have been effectively handled by a congressional committee. As a practical matter, the nearest thing we have to a guarantee that foreign policy will continue to be made in this relatively open, "democratic" process of "conflict and consensus-building" is the way that men get to be President of the United States. And that, in fact, may be guarantee enough, at least for normal circumstances. A man who can last through the long, hard climb up the ladder of American politics to the pinnacle of the presidency must have an urge to power. But it is also unlikely that a man could come within reach of the presidency who did not have at the center of his character a sympathy for the range of values among Americans and a natural instinct for the political process of "consensus-building." For there is nothing quite like the buffeting and merciless public scrutiny of political life in America to expose the weaknesses of human character.

For an Increased Congressional Role in Foreign Policy Making

THE SENATE FOREIGN RELATIONS COMMITTEE

Our country has come far toward the concentration in its national executive of unchecked power over foreign relations, particularly over the disposition and use of the armed forces. So far has this process advanced that, in the committee's view, it is no longer accurate to characterize our government, in matters of foreign relations, as one of separated powers checked and balanced against each other. The executive has acquired virtual supremacy over the making as well as the conduct of the foreign relations of the United States.

The principal cause of the constitutional imbalance has been the circumstance of American involvement and responsibility in a violent and unstable world.

FROM Report #797, issued on November 20, 1967, to accompany Senate Resolution 187, relating to United States commitments to foreign powers.

THE BATTLE OVER FOREIGN POLICY

Since its entry into World War II the United States has been deeply, and to a great extent involuntarily, involved in a series of crises which have revolutionized and are continuing to revolutionize the world of the 20th century. There is no end in sight to these global commotions; there is no end in sight to deep American involvement in them.

The committee believes that changed conditions, though the principal cause of the present constitutional imbalance, are not its sole cause. It believes that events have been aided and abetted by what Justice Frankfurter called the "generative force of unchecked disregard of the restrictions that fence in even the most disinterested assertion of authority." Both the executive and the Congress have been periodically unmindful of constitutional requirements and proscriptions, the executive by its incursions upon Congressional preorgative at moments when action seemed more important than the means of its initiation, the Congress by its uncritical and sometimes unconscious acquiescence in these incursions. If blame is to be apportioned, the greater share probably belongs to the Congress. It is understandable, though not acceptable, that in times of real or seeming emergency the executive will be tempted to take shortcuts around constitutional procedure. It is less understandable that the Congress should acquiesce in these shortcuts, giving away that which is not its to give, notably the war power, which the framers of the Constitution vested not in the executive but, deliberately and almost exclusively, in the Congress.

Since 1940 crisis has been chronic and, coming as something new in our experience, has given rise to a tendency toward anxious expediency in our response to it. The natural expedient— natural because of the real or seeming need for speed—has been executive action. In instances such as the undeclared naval war we fought with Germany prior to the formal declaration of war in December 1941, the Korean war, the intervention in Lebanon, the two crises over Cuba, the Dominican intervention and the Vietnamese war, we have not deliberately overriden our constitutional processes; rather, we have been unmindful of them. Perceiving, and sometimes exaggerating, the need for prompt action, and lacking traditional guidelines for the making of decisions in an emergency, we have tended to think principally of what needed to be done and little, if at all, of the means of doing it.

Entering our second quarter century as an active world power, we should by now be sufficiently acquainted with crisis and world involvement to be able to restore our decision making to institutional foundations. The effort to do so might, conceivably, reveal that the war power of the Congress, and perhaps the very system of checks and balances, are obsolete, in which event it would be necessary to amend the Constiution—by one of the procedures for doing so set forth in the Constitution. A constitutional amendment giving the President plenary powers in foreign policy would, in the view of the committee, be dangerous to American liberties; it could, however, be justified if our system of separated powers, checked and balanced against each other, were to prove so incapable of meeting foreign emergencies as to undermine national security. What cannot be justified is the alteration of the Constitution by expediency and inadvertency. Precedent and practice, long established, can acquire the force of law, but change is not its own justification; the mere exercise of a power does not legitimize it and, under our system of law, bad precedents can be reversed.

The committee believes that the division of powers spelled out in the Constitution is in fact compatible with our country's role as a world power. The principal purpose of that division, as Justice Brandeis noted, is liberty rather than efficiency, but, unless speed is equated with efficiency and deliberation held to be an obstacle to it, there is no reason why we cannot have under our system of government a foreign policy which is efficient as well as democratically made. Indeed, it can be argued that the division and limitation of powers are indispensable to American foreign policy.

For these reasons the committee believes that the restoration of constitutional balance in the making of foreign commitments is not only compatible with the requirements of efficiency but essential to the purpose of democracy. The committee does not share Mr. Katzenbach's[1] view the demarcation of authority between President and Congress can and should be left to be settled "by the instinct of the nation and its leaders for political responsibility."

There is no uncertainty or ambiguity about the intent of the framers of the Constitution with respect to the war power. Greatly dismayed by the power of the British Crown to commit Great Britain—and with it the American colonies—to war, fearful of the possible development of monarchical tendencies in their new republic, and fearful as well of the dangers of large standing armies and military defiance of civilian authority, they vested the power to commit the United States to war exclusively in Congress. This power was not, like certain others, divided between the executive and legislature; it was conferred upon Congress and Congress alone.

It was understood by the framers—and subsequent usage confirmed their understanding—that the President in his capacity as commander in chief of the armed forces would have the right, indeed the duty, to use the armed forces to repel sudden attacks on the United States, even in advance of Congressional authorization to do so. It was further understood that he would direct and lead the armed forces and put them to any use specified by Congress but that this did not extend to the initiation of hostilities.

It should be remembered that the Congress was not expected to be in session for more than 1 month a year and it was thought that it would be dangerous to leave the country defenseless during the long adjournment. Were the matter being considered now, in our age of long Congressional sessions, rapid transportation, and instantaneous communication, one may wonder whether it would be thought necessary to concede the executive any authority at all in this field. In

[1] [Attorney General Nicholas de B. Katzenbach had presented the Johnson administration's position to the Committee.—Ed.]

any case it was authority to repel sudden attacks—that and nothing more—that the framers conceded to the President.

The evidence is abundant that the framers did not intend the executive to have the power to initiate war. In a letter to Madison in 1789 Thomas Jefferson wrote:

"We have already given in example one effectual check to the Dog of war by transferring the power of letting him loose from the Executive to the Legislative body, from those who are to spend to those who are to pay."

The early Presidents carefully respected Congress' authority to initiate war. President Adams took action to protect American ships from French attacks on the Atlantic only to the extent that Congress authorized him to do so; even in the case of this "limited war" between the United States and revolutionary France the President did not regard himself as free to use the armed forces without authorization by Congress.

Early in his term of office President Jefferson sent a naval squadron to the Mediterranean to protect American commerce against piracy, but it was not permitted to engage in offensive action against the Barbary pirates. Later such action was taken after having been authorized by Congress.

The Monroe Doctrine is often cited as an instance and precedent for making of foreign commitments by executive action. In fact a distinction was made at the time between a statement of policy and its implementation, the latter being regarded as falling within the province of Congress.

In 1846 President Polk sent American forces into the disputed territory between Corpus Christi and the Rio Grande River, precipitating the clash which began the Mexican War. The constitutionality of this act is uncertain but Abraham Lincoln, then a Congressman from Illinois, was certain that it was unconstitutional.

During the 19th century American armed forces were used by the President on his own authority for such purposes as suppressing piracy, suppressing the slave trade by American ships, "hot pursuit" of criminals across frontiers, and protecting American lives and property in backward areas or areas where government had broken down. Such limited uses of force without authorization by Congress, not involving the initiation of hostilities against governments, came to be accepted practice, sanctioned by usage though not explicity by the Constitution.

Some Presidents, notably Polk, Grant, and McKinley, interpreted their powers as commander in chief broadly, while others, such as the early Presidents and Buchanan and Cleveland, were scrupulously deferential to the war power of Congress.

The use of the armed forces against sovereign nations without authorization by Congress became common practice in the 20th century. President Theodore Roosevelt used the Navy to prevent Colombian forces from suppressing insurrection in their province of Panama and intervened militarily in Cuba and the Dominican Republic. Presidents Taft and Wilson also sent armed forces to the

Caribbean and Central America without Congressional authorization. In Haiti, the Dominican Republic, and Nicaragua these interventions resulted in the establishment of American military governments.

President Wilson seized the Mexican port of Vera Cruz in 1914 as an act of reprisal, in order, he said, to "enforce respect" for the government of the United States. The two Houses of Congress adopted separate resolutions in support of President Wilson's action but the Senate did not complete action on its resolution until after the seizure of Vera Cruz. After the Mexican bandit Pancho Villa raided the town of Columbus, N. Mex., in 1916, President Wilson sent a force under General Pershing into Mexico in "hot pursuit" of the bandits; the expedition turned into a prolonged intervention of nearly 2 years and almost brought about war with Mexico. The Senate adopted a resolution supporting the President after General Pershing's force had entered Mexico; this resolution was never reported out of the Foreign Affairs Committee of the House of Representatives.

The military powers which had been acquired by Presidents in the 19th century—for purposes of "hot pursuit" and the protection of American lives and property, and under treaties which confered rights and obligations on the United States—were not serious infringements on Congress' war power because they had been used for the most part against individuals or bands of pirates or bandits and not against sovereign states. Roosevelt, Taft, and Wilson used these powers to engage in military action against sovereign states, thereby greatly expanding the scope of executive power over the use of the armed forces and setting precedents for the greater expansions of executive power which were to follow. The Congress of that era did not see fit to resist or oppose these incursions of their constitutional authority; indeed, as we have noted, one or both Houses of Congress gave retroactive approval to President Wilson's unauthorized interventions in Mexico.

Roosevelt, Taft, and Wilson asserted no general or "inherent" Presidential power to make war. Indeed, when it came to full-scale conflict with Germany, President Wilson explicitly acknowledged the war power of the Congress. Advising Congress to declare war on Germany in his war message of April 2, 1917, the President said:

"I have called the Congress into extraordinary session because there are serious, very serious, choices of policy to be made, and made immediately, which it is neither right nor constitutionally permissible that I should assume the responsibility of making."

President Franklin Roosevelt expanded executive power over the use of the armed forces to an unprecedented degree. The exchange of overaged American destroyers for British bases in the Western Hemisphere was accomplished by executive agreement, in violation of the Senate's treaty power, and was also a violation of the international law of neutrality, giving Germany legal cause, had she chosen to take it, to declare war on the United States. The transaction was an emergency use of Presidential power, taken in the belief that it might be essential to save Great Britain from invasion.

In 1941 President Roosevelt, on his own authority, committed American forces to the defense of Greenland and Iceland and authorized American naval vessels to escort convoys to Iceland provided that at least one ship in each convoy flew the American or Icelandic flag. When the American destroyer *Greer* was fired on by a German submarine, after having radioed the submarine's position to the British who then sent planes to attack it, President Roosevelt utilized the occasion to announce that thereafter American naval vessels would shoot on sight German and Italian ships west of the 26th meridian. By the time Germany and Italy declared war on the United States, in the wake of the Japanese attack on Pearl Harbor, the United States had already been committed by its President, acting on his own authority, to an undeclared naval war in the Atlantic. Roosevelt, however, achieved his objective without asserting a general or "inherent" Presidential power to commit the armed forces abroad.

The trend initiated by Theodore Roosevelt, Taft, and Wilson, and accelerated by Franklin Roosevelt, continued at a rapid rate under Presidents Truman, Eisenhower, Kennedy, and Johnson, bringing the country to the point at which the real power to commit the country to war is now in the hands of the President. The trend which began in the early 20th century has been consummated and the intent of the framers of the Constitution as to the war power substantially negated.

By the late 1940's there had developed a kind of ambivalence as to the war power in the minds of officials in the executive branch, Members of Congress and, presumably, the country at large. On the one hand, it was and still is said that Congress alone has the power to declare war; on the other hand it was widely believed, or at least conceded, that the President in his capacity as commander in chief had the authority to use the armed forces in any way he saw fit. Noting that the President has in fact exercised power over the armed forces, we have come to assume that he is entitled to do so. The actual possession of a power has given rise to a belief in its constitutional legitimacy.

The fact that Congress has acquiesced in, or at the very least has failed to challenge, the tranfer of the war power from itself to the executive, is probably the most important single fact accounting for the speed and virtual completeness of the transfer. Why has Congress agreed to this rearrangement of powers which is without constitutional justification, and at its own expense?

To some degree, it seems to be the result of the unfamiliarity of the United States with its new role as a world power. Lacking guidelines of experience for the accommodation of our constitutional system to the new demands that have been made upon it, Congress has acquiesced in the resort to expedients in foreign policy making which we have already noted. In addition, the fact that so many of the great policy decisions of the postwar era have been made in an atmosphere of real or contrived urgency has put tremendous pressure on Members of Congress to set aside apprehensions as to the exercise of power by the executive lest they cause some fatal delay or mission in the nation's foreign policy.

Another possible factor in Congressional passivity is that Congress may have permitted itself to be overawed by the cult of executive expertise. Like the newly rich who go beyond the bounds of good taste in material display, the newly powerful may go beyond the bounds of good judgment in their intellectual display. A veritable army of foreign policy experts has sprung up in government and in the universities in recent years, contributing greatly to our knowledge and skill in foreign relations but also purveying the belief that foreign policy is an occult science which ordinary citizens, including Members of Congress, are simply too stupid to grasp.

There may also be a historical memory at work in Congress' acceptance of executive predominance in foreign relations. The Senate, it has long been widely agreed, acted with disastrous irresponsibility in its rejection of the Covenant of the League of Nations in 1919. Since at least 1945, when the Senate ratified the United Nations Charter with virtually no debate, Congress has been doing a kind of penance for its prewar isolationism, and that penance has sometimes taken the form of overly hasty acquiescence in proposals for the acceptance of one form or another of international responsibility. Congress, it seems clear, was deficient in vision during the 1920's and 1930's, but so were Presidents Harding, Coolidge, Hoover, and—prior to 1938—Roosevelt. Just as no one has a monopoly on vision, no one has a monopoly on myopia either. In its deference to the executive in foreign affairs, Congress has conceded him, and the experts around him, a kind of infallibility which the wisest among them would readily acknowledge they do not have. Versailles, like Munich, has conveyed more lessons than were in it; its only lesson, as far as the workings of the American government are concerned, is the need not of Congressional diffidence but of Congressional responsibility. . . .

Can a Free Society Fight a Limited War?

JOHN P. ROCHE

In the spring of 1966, the President asked me to go to Vietnam to get the "feel" of the place and some sense of the possibilities for the development of representative institutions. Since that time (despite rumors in the New York *Times* that I

FROM John P. Roche, "Can a Free Society Fight a Limited War?" Reprinted with permission from *The New Leader*, October 21, 1968, pp. 6–11. Copyright © The American Labor Conference on International Affairs, Inc.

was playing therapist to disaffected intellectuals), I have lived day in, day out, week in, week out, with the problems of Vietnam. And I have watched, impotent and heartsick, while the War has eroded the position of the Johnson Administration.

As an old fashioned liberal cold warrior, I have seen and still see nothing immoral about fighting to contain aggressive totalitarianism. Suppressing my human fears, I was prepared to go to the brink with John Kennedy over Berlin and Cuba, and last year I was equally prepared to support the Israelis to the hilt had the Soviets intervened to rescue their incompetent Arab clients. In sum, just to get the record clear at the outset, I take for granted the vital role that the United States must play in helping to achieve a stable world, and I believe that South and Southeast Asia present a major challenge to stability in our generation. I may be wrong—I have never been able to attain the witless certainty of the True Believer, and have lost a lot of sleep as a result. But right or wrong, this is what I believe. The unfortunate thing about this world is that one always has to make a 100 per cent action commitment on the basis of inadequate evidence. If you wait for all the precincts to report, you do not make history—you write it.

On occasion, I have reacted bitterly to criticism and have been particularly hard on the communications media. But bitterness destroys the analytical capacity—and the hard fact in my judgment is that (whatever the distortions of the media and the critics may have been) Vietnam has poisoned our political atmosphere for a far more fundamental reason than a failure of communication between the Johnson Administration and the people.

The basic issue in Vietnam is this: Can a free society fight a limited war? That is, a strategic war, a war without hate, a war without massive popular involvement. To put it differently, the war in Vietnam is being fought for an abstraction: American national interest in a non-totalitarian Asian future. And it is being fought by a new set of rules, rules which began to emerge during the Korean War but were forgotten in the subsequent years. It is very difficult to tell a young soldier, "Go out there and fight, perhaps die, for a good bargaining position." It is almost impossible to explain to Congressmen that Vietnam is a crucial testing ground—on one side for a brilliantly mounted "war of liberation"; on the other, for our capability to cope with (and in the future deter) such liberators. What sense, moreover, can the average American make of our offer of future economic assistance to a nonaggressive Hanoi? What, in short, has happened to the concept of "the enemy"?

As one of the early advocates of flexible response and limited war, I have watched the defection of the liberal intellectuals with somber anguish. The record is perfectly clear: Limited war was conceived of *by liberals* as *the liberal* alternative to massive retaliation and/or isolationism. It was the liberal answer to John Foster Dulles that was to find classic formulation in the speeches of President John F. Kennedy and in Robert McNamara's spectacular reorganization of the Department of Defense. At root, the theory asserted that instead of relying on apocalyptic nuclear power to deter aggression, the United States would be capable of a flexible, measured response to the forces deployed on the other side of the hill—enough force, and no more than was necessary, to frustrate aggression. Kennedy and McNamara realized that the very character of nuclear war made any other response an all or nothing proposition; one either pushed the button or capitulated.

John Foster Dulles managed to combine verbal brinkmanship with *de facto* isolationism (the Siamese twins of Republican defense policy to this day), but to many of us liberals it seemed that American power under Eisenhower and Dulles was undergoing the death of a thousand cuts. So we assailed Dulles, called for an active foreign policy, and beat the drums for flexible response: the defense posture that did not leave the United States with the two crisis options of nuclear weapons or appeasement. Indeed, in November 1962, the *New Republic* editorially took an unblinking view of the possibilities of a land war in Asia—and chose it as preferable to another nuclear confrontation on the Cuban model.

We assumed, naively as it turned out, that the knowledge that the U.S. could transport 100,000 men 12,000 miles in 47 hours and 32 minutes (or some such logistical triumph) would itself act as a deterrent. Discussions of military strategy began to sound more and more like seminars in game theory. There was a kind of antiseptic quality permeating the atmosphere; one often had the feeling he was attending a chess match.

This, in part, was the source of many later problems. An expert chess player can at a certain point confidently tell his opponent "mate in 12 moves." Normally the opponent, if he is worth playing with, concedes and starts a new game. The atmosphere made those of us who come from the harsh training of poker decidedly uneasy. We knew that nobody has ever folded a full-house because he suspected another player of holding four of a kind. Education in these matters always costs money. In international relations it costs more than money—human lives are involved.

Vietnam has provided an agonizing education on the limitations of our theory of limited war. The worst of it is that what I believe to be the real "lessons of Vietnam" have been largely ignored on the political circuit this fall. The hustings are full of politicians solemnly intoning "No More Vietnams." But try to find out what this means. The late Senator Robert Kennedy was relatively clear. In his lexicon it merely meant "Don't support losers." (If one changed a few words in Kennedy's major address on the subject and travelled back 30 years in time, his speech becomes a devastating case against anti-Franco intervention in the Spanish Civil War. Franco did, after all, become the very model of a polycentric fascist, a nationalist "Tito" in Hitler's New Order.) Assuming the winner is identifiable from the outset, this advice can be helpful.

But what is one to make of Senator Eugene McCarthy's gloss on "No More Vietnams"? It was a bit murky, but the gist of his admonition seemed to be that we should only help *good* nations. Even weak ones, for he specifically mentioned India.

Now ever since I took seriously President Kennedy's statement that we are "the watchmen on the walls of world freedom"—only to learn later from reading Arthur Schlesinger's *Bitter Heritage* that Kennedy did not really mean it—I have been reading the small print rather carefully. So when I came upon McCarthy's nomination of India as a possible substitute for Vitenam, I was, to say the least, startled. The small country of South Vietnam has swallowed up half a million American troops. Can one conceive the magnitude of the troop commitment that would be necessary to bolster India's feeble defenses? Or of the bill for the military hardware that would come due if the Indian Army were to be equipped properly?

Since I take McCarthy's intelligence for granted, his statement could only make sense if (1) he had an ironclad promise from Peking that India will not again be invaded; or (2) he was silently and surreptitiously returning to the Dulles strategy of nuclear containment. If the latter is the case, McCarthy's "No More Vietnams" formula involves the abandonment of limited war and a rejuvenation of the nuclear strike. Thus militant "liberals" are in the odd position of embracing the H-bomb as the key instrument of American policy.

The Republican position is quite simple. Richard Nixon will, of course, submit that the Democrats get the country into wars they cannot *end*—citing Korea. This is shorthand for the proposition that the Republicans know how to deal with Communists, that President Eisenhower ended the Korean War by threatening to use nuclear weapons on the sanctuary, that limited war is a "no win" policy and a gross misuse of our incredible national power.

I believe today as I believed in 1956—that this nuclear strategy would in the long run be disastrous for the United States. But it has the enormous political advantage of being abstract. In October 1962, we lived through the most perilous week in the history of mankind, but there was no blood on the TV screens. The "dirty little war" in Vietnam, on the other hand, is infinitely and, with TV, intimately bloody. While one can argue that fewer Americans have died there in the last six years than die annually in the United States from drunken driving, that one MIRV would destroy more people than have been killed in all of Vietnam in 20 years, he can expect no sympathetic response. Vietnam is *war*—nuclear holocaust is a remote fantasy.

Paradoxically, the marginal character of the war in Vietnam has contributed to its political liabilities. It is not a big war; it is not, comparatively speaking, costing much—3-4 per cent of the Gross National Product compared with roughly 11 per cent for Korea—but it has no built-in support in the electorate. The President could have drummed up support by hitting the traditional chord of messianic anti-Communism, by engaging in old-style McCarthyism. There were some in Washington, in fact, who advised him three years ago that he could not fight an invisible war, that unless he provided the American people with a vivid "enemy," he would face massive defections.

But Lyndon Johnson flatly refused to whoop up yahoo chauvinism. At least half a dozen times, I have heard him say that he remembered the anti-German hysteria of World War I and the consequences of Joe McCarthy in the '50s; that he was not going to be the President "who got Americans hating." The historical irony of this is that by prohibiting a return to the old reactionary McCarthyism, he generated the new liberal McCarthyism, which has loosed more hate in the United States than "old Joe" could ever have dreamed of.

The rhetoric of limited war is in itself a major problem. Johnson was carved up by his critics for telling the troops at Camranh Bay to "bring home that coonskin." Perhaps the figure of speech could have been improved upon, but what American commander-in-chief could address his troops in the field and urge them to die, if necessary, for a stalemate? The British in the 19th century could play strategic chess with their regulars and mercenaries—invading such unlikely places as Tibet, Ethiopia, Zululand, and Afghanistan—with no repercussions at home unless (as in the First Afghan War) they lost. Once they achieved their usually limited objectives, a treaty was forthcoming and the troops pulled out. Individual families would mourn a sergeant killed in the Sixth River War, or a sepoy butchered at Kabul, but except for disasters these wars were fought outside the forum of British public opinion.

If Ho Chi Minh had permitted the war in Vietnam to remain invisible—with only professional soldiers involved—the pattern of the 19th century might have been retained. But Ho Chi Minh has always been a problem. While we may be fighting a limited war against him, he has declared total war against us—and he has played his hand brilliantly. His central goal (learned from his experience with the French and from the lessons of Algeria) was to escalate the war in Vietnam to the point where it became *politically* unjustifiable in the United States. Put differently, he would not permit Johnson to fight an invisible war and—knowing the major tenets of the doctrine of limited war—he proceeded in 1965–68 to utilize his assets to the maximum. To be specific, the United States had foresworn any direct attacks upon the legitimacy of the Hanoi government, had barred the use of nuclear weapons, had—in short—recognized Ho's *political* sanctuary.

True, we denied him military sanctuary by bombing the North, but he obviously wrote off bombing as a painful harassment and countered at our weakest point: ground control in the South. Over the DMZ, and in from Laos and Cambodia, came the regulars of the North Vietnamese Army to buttress the guerrillas already on the ground. The infiltration began well before the decision to bomb the North and—with a great deal of coming and going across unmarked frontiers—has probably exposed over 200,000 North Vietnamese troops to combat in the South.

This commitment of PAVN (Hanoi's regulars) was a death blow to the concept of the invisible war. Airpower enthusiasts to the contrary, there is only one way to fight infantry—with other infantry. Air power provides mobile artillery, but nobody ever pacified a province with an F-4. In 1965 and 1966—for reasons we will explore subsequently—there was suddenly an acute shortage of riflemen in the Republic of Vietnam.

THE BATTLE OVER FOREIGN POLICY 466

So far, we have been cutting across time and history with a certain amount of recklessness in the interest of exploring the various consequences of our commitment to limited war in Indochina. Let us now proceed in a more orderly historical fashion. What we tend to forget is that in the years of the Kennedy Administration, Vietnam was not center-stage—the real crises were in Berlin, Cuba, and, of all places, Laos. The Soviet willingness to make a Laotian deal, which appeared to be completely ignored by Hanoi, suggested that perhaps the big powers could bilaterally close down Indochina as a source of instability by simply getting the children out of the game.

The difficulty was that the Soviets either could not, or did not choose to, go through with their end of the bargain. (In my judgment, their efforts were simply spiked by Hanoi's intransigence; Khrushchev overestimated his influence on the Viet Minh hardliners and was probably later incensed by their effrontery in disregarding the Geneva Agreement of 1962.) Thus, instead of Laos returning to its status as a kingdom with a thousand years on LSD, the Pathet Lao guerrillas, aided as in South Vietnam by PAVN regulars, took over the task of protecting the Zone of Communication: the Ho Chi Minh trail.

The significance of this double-cross cannot be underestimated. What the Laos agreement of 1962 represented was a willingness by the United States and the Soviets to respect a genuine neutralization of that country, to achieve a "political solution." This had been a liberal demand in the United States for years. I, for example, had supported it vigorously at various conventions of Americans for Democratic Action, and liberal spokesmen had been unsparing in their attacks on Kennedy, and Eisenhower before him, for supporting a Right-wing military junta in Laos. Now the authentic, 24-karat "neutralist" Souvanna Phouma was brought back to Vientiane and given our blessing to opt his nation out of the Asian cold war. Had he been successful, we hoped to follow the same pattern in all Indochina.

The Laotian agreement was a horse dead at the post, however, a complete non-starter. And all the evidence that I have seen indicates that President Kennedy, who had a cold eye, realized this—and realized that Laos was, with the possible exception of Bhutan, the worst place in the world to try to match Communist military pressure. So, writing Laos off as tactically hopeless, Kennedy turned his attention to Vietnam where the situation was very different, particularly in terms of accessibility. His reply to Hanoi's repudiation of the Laotian settlement was to reinforce the defenses of the Republic of Vietnam.

There have been a number of accounts by associates of the late President Kennedy to the effect that he wanted out of Vietnam too. Regrettably, these lack empirical foundation—and quoting the dead is an ancient form of historical fraud, immune to either proof or disproof. The fundamental evidence—notably his support of Secretary of State Dean Rusk and McNamara—suggests that he was unhappy about the situation in Vietnam (as who with any knowledge of the place was not?), but felt the line had to be drawn and enforced in that nation. On this basis Kennedy made the quantum jump: Disregarding the Geneva

Accord of 1954 (which we had unofficially respected but never signed), he increased the number of American "advisors" from roughly 750 (as authorized at Geneva) to over 16,000. In addition, "Green Berets" were bootlegged into Vietnam under covert auspices.

This is no place to investigate the internal affairs of the Saigon government. Suffice it to say that the Diem regime, after a seemingly amazing start in the 1950s, was in deep trouble in 1962–63. Objectively viewed, Diem was in an impossible enfilade: The Americans would not let him run an efficient dictatorship (like the one in Hanoi), and he was incapable of building effective representative government. Confronted by the chaos in Saigon, which became much worse after the fall of the Diem government in November 1963, the Americans gradually made—without really recognizing its import—a critical decision: to fight the war independently.

The basic premise, which I do not believe I have ever seen clearly articulated, was that the United States, with its massive technological assets, would directly force the Hanoi leaders to pull back their troops. We would, in other words, "punish" the Democratic Republic of Vietnam (DRV). Once Ho and his chief strategist, General Giap, knew what they were up against, they would agree "mate in 12 moves" and give up the game. This shortcut had two admirable arguments in its favor: First, we could effectively ignore the condition of the Saigon government; second, we could employ our air power assets with a relatively slight loss of American lives. The unfortunate consequence was that the South Vietnamese Armed Forces (ARVN) were treated as orphans and given essentially a spectator role in the U. S.-Hanoi competition.

Unfortunately, too, Ho and Giap were never programmed by the Pentagon's game-theorists. They were determined to prevent the United States from fighting a cut-rate war. Down the Ho Chi Minh trail came the trained regiments of the PAVN with the mission, not of defeating the United States on the ground, but of forcing the Americans to fight a ground war in full, costly visibility. To a considerable extent these soldiers were on a suicide mission, but when one appreciates that their goals were *political* rather than military the "kill-ratio" loses much of its impact. North Vietnamese Premier Pham Van Dong had announced the scenario as far back as 1962 when he told the late Bernard Fall: "Americans do not like long inconclusive wars—and this is going to be a long inconclusive war."

President Kennedy presided over the transformation of American strategic theory from massive retaliation to flexible response, but at the time of his murder (less than a month after Diem fell) the United States had only put this doctrine into action in the Cuban missile crisis. Lyndon Johnson, then, inherited from Kennedy a strategy, a Cabinet, and a seemingly trivial conflict in Vietnam. As he went on to election in his own right in 1964, Vietnam was still on the back pages—but there was great stirring in Hanoi and PAVN engineers and support troops were busy building base camps in the Central Highlands of South

Vietnam. Indeed, communications with the Vietcong were being developed to the point where, in the remarkably short period of six months, the guerrillas were rearmed with the 7.62 weapons family, most notably the AK-47 automatic rifle. (Not only was the AK-47 incomparably superior to the Garands and M-1s of ARVN, but no American rifle before the M-16 could match it. In fact, I have seen Marines up in I Corps who carry the AK-47 in preference to the M-16.)

There is no need to recapitulate in detail the events of the next few years. President Johnson, who was only alerted to the full gravity of the Vietnamese crisis in the fall and winter of 1964–65, has been savagely assaulted for deserting the Kennedy doctrine for a "military solution." Nothing could be further from the truth: Johnson committed American air power and then, in the summer of 1965, ground forces to frustrate a "military solution," a Hanoi victory. (Lincoln did not want a "military solution" to the Secession Crisis of 1861, but despite his wishes half a million Americans died. Like Ho and Giap, Jefferson Davis and Robert E. Lee were most uncooperative.)

In 1964–65, the Americans began looking for trained Vietnamese soldiers to meet Ho Chi Minh's challenge on the ground in the South; they found a poorly trained, miserably equipped, dispirited ARVN. Despite our experience in Korea, where in 1950–51 American divisions had scouts out on their flanks to make sure the ROKS were still there—although five years later South Korea had probably the finest army in Asia—ARVN had remained a stepchild. So American soldiers and Marines, instead of providing a steel frame for the training of ARVN, had to take the field themselves. There simply was no time for the necessary training (the lead time in Korea had been a good year and a half). The "Americanization" of the ground war was thus a consequence of military necessity.

Yet military necessity, while an explanation for what has occurred over the past three years, is not an excuse. Why did President Kennedy and Johnson and Secretary McNamara consistently neglect ARVN? One can suggest a number of partial answers: The American officers in the field obviously felt that nothing short of a drastic purge of the officer corps would do any good—and such a purge was politically impossible in Saigon; the Pentagon's budget experts, faced with the need to cut, would patently give higher priority to the needs of an American service than to ARVN; and Congress *in 1962–63*—the key years—would clearly have taken a dim view of a massive and expensive rearmament and training program. Vietnam was a kind of low-level infection which they hoped would go away. (And had the President endorsed such a program, the organized liberal community in the United States—with me in the forefront in my capacity as National Chairman of Americans for Democratic Action—would have denounced him to the rafters for supporting the "reactionary, unrepresentative Diem clique.")

But these are partial answers. I think the real key to ARVN's neglect was the Pentagon game-theorists' belief in their own press releases; they believed that pressure on Hanoi, "turning the screw," would lead Ho to make the logical calculation that he had more to lose than gain by continuing the conflict. Unfortunately, this was based on a complete misreading of the mind and character of a dedicated and ruthless Leninist—one who, in Koestler's phrase, is prepared to sacrifice one generation in the interest of its successor.

What Ho Chi Minh has done, to return to the main theme, is to hit the doctrine of limited war at its weakest point: domestic opinion. The Johnson Administration, hit by ground war on a scale never anticipated and by the accompanying casualty lists, tried to maintain the ground-rules of limited war. What this often amounted to was simply "hunkering up like a mule in a hailstorm" as the apocalyptics of the Left- and Right-wing spokesmen for national frustration raged throughout the land. The crux of the matter is that while any two-bit demagogue can make the eagle scream in a nice, neat "us or them" confrontation, explaining the rationale of limited war is incredibly difficult.

Adding to the burden was the disaffection of the young, notably the college elite who compensated for their deferment—with the noxious psychic compound of safety and guilt it provided—by a torrent of abuse of the President and the Administration worthy of a 16th century lunatic sectarian. Though this in aggregate probably influenced relatively few young people—who are as leery of religious extremism as the rest of us—the cold fact is that American youth has a genuine grievance. Never in our history has a war been fought with so little involvement by the society as a whole. Which is another way of saying that Vietnam really has been an adult's war and a young man's fight.

Who has been hurt? The economy roars along, the Dow-Jones creeps up, unemployment is down, incomes are at a record high, corporate profits are pushing the roof. The answer is that nobody except the young men directly at war—and indirectly their families—has been hurt. In existential terms, the young have been left alone with the war. When I was in Danang last year, a Marine major put it to me. "Oddly enough in the light of all the agitation," he said, "I have never seen Marines with such good *political morale*. Not even in World War II, and certainly not in Korea. Can't the Administration get the people to take this war seriously? Couldn't Johnson at least ration tires so they would know there is a war on?"

These are the things we never thought of when, with all the zeal of innocence, we liberals advanced our doctrine of limited war. Now in 1968 those who have stayed the course, who have had the courage of their consequences, stand appalled by the revival of isolationism—and its identical twin, nuclear deterrence. They stand appalled, too, by the fact that a great President, Lyndon Johnson, has gone into political limbo because of his indomitable commitment to a sound but unpopular policy, flexible response and limited war.

Johnson can look with confidence to the judgment of future historians, but the immediate problem remains. If the "lesson of Vietnam" is that a free, democratic society cannot fight a limited war, what strategic options are still open?

Must we revert to the balance of terror? Or, as some notable liberals today seem to think, can we build affluence in one country and somehow escape the broils of the outside world?

I confess that, battered as I am, I still believe that flexible response is not only a sound but a *liberal* alternative to the only other strategies I see on the horizon. And I would suggest that those who are busy leaping up and down about Vietnam take a brief pause in their exercise to inform us precisely *how* they plan to employ American power in the interest of international stability and world order.

Except for the pacifists (and those who are pro-Hanoi), I have yet to find a critic who—when pushed back on his premises—did not end up embracing some variety of isolationism. There is nothing wicked or un-American about being an isolationist, but it is a doctrine that American liberals outgrew a quarter of a century ago. It would be tragic if a united front of Nixonites and followers of Eugene McCarthy, playing up to the understandable frustrations of the American people, undermined our commitment to limited war and returned us to the Age of Dulles. Perhaps we should recall that while limited war is nasty, for most of us resurrection would be a precondition for appreciating the strategic virtue of nuclear retaliation.

The Case for Retrenchment

RONALD STEEL

Richard Nixon comes to the Presidency with a good deal of experience in foreign affairs and an avowed commitment to hammer out a new diplomacy geared to the demands of today's world. While the mandate for change is clear enough, that is a big promise. Without questioning the new President's sincerity or ability, it is reasonable to ask whether it is likely to be fulfilled. There are, in fact, two questions at issue: First, is Richard Nixon's approach to foreign affairs substantively different from that of Lyndon B. Johnson or John F. Kennedy? Second, is it possible, with the best intentions in the world, substantially to change the basic outlines of American diplomacy?

The President's scope for initiative is as sweeping as it is ill defined. Rarely has the need for change been more obvious or more urgent. Rarely has it been felt at so many layers of society: not simply among intellectuals and the tiny

FROM Ronald Steel, "The Case for Retrenchment." Reprinted with permission from *The New Leader*, February 17, 1969, pp. 9–14. Copyright © The American Labor Conference on International Affairs, Inc.

minority that concerns itself with foreign affairs, but even among those who normally have been content to leave such matters to professionals. The nation is ready, indeed eager, for a new look at America's involvements—at Vietnam, at NATO and the Alliance for Progress, at the quarantine of China and the old arguments for foreign aid, at the assumptions of nuclear deterrence and the policies of détente, at the relics of cold war and the unexamined premises of America's global role.

The situation is reminiscent of 1952, when Dwight D. Eisenhower was swept into office on a vague promise to end the Korean War and bring the nation back to some semblance of "normalcy." In that election, too, there was the feeling that the Democrats had been in power too long, that they had involved the nation in commitments that could not be honored at a price the people were willing to pay, that deep fissures within the society had grown unmanageable and dangerous. Yet Eisenhower's foreign policy proved to be not much different than Harry S. Truman's. He did, as promised, end the Korean War. But Truman had already begun the negotiations, even though it might have been politically difficult for him to carry them through without incurring the wrath of Republican fundamentalists. The major outlines of Eisenhower's foreign policy—NATO, the Truman Doctrine, foreign aid—were laid down by his predecessor. Eisenhower simply pursued them with a somewhat different style. Still, he did make possible a political truce that finished off Senator Joseph McCarthy, and, for all the sanctimony of Dulles' inflated rhetoric, managed to keep the nation at peace for eight years. His was an Administration of consolidation and, in some senses, of retrenchment—precisely what the country needed and wanted in 1952.

By one of the ironies of history, Eisenhower's Vice President finds himself, perhaps somewhat to his own surprise, now head of state. And the problems he faces are not unlike those of his former chief. By the same token, his approach to the great issues of foreign policy is as similar to that of Johnson as Eisenhower's was to that of Truman. He inherits a war whose purpose and methods he has never disavowed. Indeed, in 1954 (which, admittedly, was a long time ago when many people felt very differently) he argued in favor of United States military intervention on the side of the French to "save" Indochina. He is a firm supporter of NATO and of "Atlantic interdependence"; a convert to détente, though insisting on "negotiation from strength"; a believer in foreign aid and mutual defense treaties. He offers no new foreign policy, but rather an improved performance of the old one, resting on increased cooperation with allies. "What I call for is not a new isolationism," he said during the campaign. "It is a new internationalism in which America enlists its allies and its friends around the world in those struggles in which their interest is as great as is ours."

There is, at least on the surface, little here to give heart to the apostles of retrenchment and withdrawal. Nixon is a confirmed internationalist, or, as the critics would have it, an interventionist. During his campaign for election, however, he could hardly have failed to catch the popular mood of disenchantment, doubt and impatience engendered by the Vietnam war—a mood that has spread to much of our foreign policy. Vietnam was not a major debating issue in the campaign. But this meant neither indifference, nor wide-scale public acceptance of the war. Rather it indicated that the war had become as politically undefinable as it has been militarily unwinnable. Hubert H. Humphrey could not attack a war he had spent most of his term as Vice President defending, nor did he make any serious attempt to justify it on grounds of national interest. Nixon, of course, did not defend the war, but neither could he attack it, since it was fought on premises he largely agrees with. The war had become an albatross. Yet the alternatives were so ambiguous and threatening to established positions that none of the major candidates could articulate, let alone propose, any. Nonetheless, these alternatives lurked in the background and everyone was aware of them.

It was assumed by the electorate, and by the candidates themselves, that the war had to be wound up early in the term of the next President. Otherwise he would find himself in Johnson's predicament: neglecting the nation's domestic crisis, incapable of governing effectively, and no doubt unable to run for reelection. Since the war cannot be won militarily, even by destroying North Vietnam, a political settlement, whatever its disguise, will in the long run be little more than a face-saving compromise. What is remarkable is that this has been generally accepted—not because it is desirable, but because it is unavoidable. The crusade in Asia has now come to be viewed, even by such ardent former crusaders as McGeorge Bundy and Robert S. McNamara, as a disastrous misadventure which ought to be concluded as quickly and unobtrusively as possible. Further, Nixon must not only end the war, but, as a corollary, he must conduct his foreign policy in such a way as to insure that there will be no more Vietnams. That is the great lesson of a foreign policy that has been exhausted and must now be entirely rethought.

By force of circumstances, Nixon will have to evolve a diplomacy based upon the supposition that the American people will simply not tolerate another Vietnam. This does not mean, as the Vietnam hawks would have it, that the nation would then be driven into isolationism. Nixon does not believe in it, and relatively few Americans consider it desirable or necessary. The most pacific doves favor some kind of intervention when it involves the survival of Israel or the tragedy of Biafra. The "taste for intervention," in Charles de Gaulle's uncharitable phrase, has become so elemental a part of America's attitude to the outside world during the past quarter-century that it is unlikely any President would—or could—completely reverse it. Certainly Nixon would not want to. For he is an interventionist by conviction, a member of the generation that grew up in World War II, when isolationism became a dirty word, and which in the early years of the cold war discovered how exhilarating and morally satisfying the exercise of international power could be. These are the people who, be they liberal Republicans or liberal Democrats, McGeorge Bundy or Walt Rostow, have held positions of high responsibility under both parties

—the people who launched the Bay of Pigs, the occupation of the Dominican Republic, and the Vietnam war.

NARROW MARGIN FOR MANEUVER

Thus Nixon is not going to revolutionize the nation's foreign policy because, given his view of the world, he does not think any revolution is necessary. He will be Johnson with a little less arrogance and, hopefully, a little less adventurism. Moreover, his margin for maneuver is not nearly so great as critics of our present diplomacy like to believe. The basic outlines were drawn more than 20 years ago and are not going to be erased overnight. During that time the vast majority of Americans became convinced not only that it was necessary for the United States to intervene throughout the world politically, economically, and when need be, militarily, but also that there was a moral imperative for doing so. The "American Empire," to use a somewhat abused descriptive phrase, rests upon the conviction of most Americans that the world role of the United States is a beneficent one. In fact, without this conviction it would have been extremely difficult, if not virtually impossible, for the last four Presidents to have carried out their interventionist policies. "What America has done, and what America is doing now around the world," Johnson declared in all sincerity shortly before he ordered the bombing of North Vietnam, "draws from deep and flowing springs of moral duty, and let none underestimate the depth of flow of those wellsprings of American purpose." The verbiage may be sticky, but it describes a true sentiment, and let no one who seeks to alter American foreign policy underestimate it.

The mood, to be sure, is changing. While isolationism is not rife in the land, the number of Americans questioning the wisdom, if not the sincerity, of "what America is doing now around the world" has grown to serious proportions. This could not have occurred without the Vietnam war, and particularly if the war had not turned into such a costly stalemate. A good deal of sanctimony went down the drain in Vietnam, and even those who accept the premises of the war are touched by the stigma of its failure. Faith has been shaken, but not destroyed. The nation is ready for a new assessment of its purpose, a new definition of its responsibilities. This can be fairly basic—the McCarthy campaign indicated how willing perfectly average, unradical Americans are to contemplate rather "heretical" ideas about our foreign policy. These ideas simply must not be, or seem to be, revolutionary. That would raise fundamental questions about international responsibility and the morality of the nation-state that few citizens or politicians are willing to contemplate. Foreign policy needs an element of continuity, and the new scaffolding has to stand, unavoidably, on the old foundation.

What is viable in the foreign policy the new Administration has inherited?

Everything, according to some; nothing, according to others. The truth, for once, may lie somewhere in between.

Nixon inherits, first of all, nearly three-quarters of a million soldiers stationed in 30 countries, four regional defense alliances, mutual defense treaties with 42 nations, membership in 53 international organizations, and military or economic aid programs to nearly 100 nations. Put it all together and it leaves us, in James Reston's words, with "commitments the like of which no sovereign nation ever took on in the history of the world." In addition, of course, the new Administration has to cope with a war which the mightiest military machine in the world has been unable to win and which so far has eluded an acceptable political solution.

The war, it goes without saying, is not viable—that is precisely why Johnson was put in a position where he dared not run for reelection, and why Nixon is President of the United States today. Since the Republicans cannot win the war either, they have no alternative but to end it on whatever decent terms they can get, and turn to other pressing, neglected matters. Primary among these, obviously, is the deteriorating condition of the nation's cities and the nation's psyche: the mounting insecurity and disaffection that expresses itself in racial fears, in anxiety over property, in suspicion and hatred of young people who refuse to play the game. Perhaps the Republicans cannot heal this wound, perhaps no one can. But unless it is healed, or at least some effort in that direction is made soon, prospects for the American Dream—what is left of it—are bleak indeed.

The new Administration inherits an attitude toward American responsibility and American power that was a necessary corrective to the old excessive isolationism, but now has become encumbering and dangerous itself. It takes over a sense of mission about the uses of American power, the idea that the world would be a better place if it conformed to an American conception of virtue. Many nations succumb to a similar temptation. But the extraordinary power of America has transformed its sense of mission from a vision into a program, although an ill-defined and only half-recognized one. The power of this nation, to a degree not fully realized even by those in whose name it is employed, has been turned into an instrument for the pursuit of an American ideology. That ideology is not merely the defense of the nation, but something far more sweeping: the establishment of a world order on the American model. Its instruments are defense pacts and military bases, foreign aid and defense support, the economic power of the government and American business, and where other measures fail, American combat troops and American bombers.

ASSUMING GLOBAL RESPONSIBILITIES

The new Administration inherits, in short, a commitment to intervention as an operative concept of American foreign policy. Within certain limits, inter-

The Case for Retrenchment

vention is, of course, perfectly proper and necessary. It was right for the United States to intervene in World War II to save Europe from Nazi domination, just as it was right to intervene after the War to protect and help rebuild the demoralized nations of Western Europe. But this intervention for the military containment of a hostile great power was expanded, in the Truman Doctrine of 1947 and the policies that flowed from it, to a commitment to defend governments everywhere against direct or indirect aggression. In other words, what was a limited responsibility expanded into a global policy that could neither be defined nor restricted in terms of American interests. From the looseness of the Truman Doctrine there emerged a variety of carelessly conceived, dubiously valid pacts and pledges, glossing over the difference between Communism as an ideology and Communism as an instrument of Soviet power. These came to be treated as though they were virtually identical, thereby confounding the attempt to make a rational assessment of American security interests.

The United States has intervened deeply in the affairs of countries where our national interest was only remotely involved. This has been done in the name of freedom and the struggle against Communism. But we have not intervened in a number of countries where freedom is a mockery, such as Saudi Arabia and Haiti; or where it is confined to a privileged few, as in Rhodesia and South Africa; or even where there was open Communist aggression, as in Tibet, Hungary and Czechoslovakia. In some cases we did not intervene because Communists were not involved; and where Communists were very much involved, as in Central Europe, we did not intervene because we feared the danger of igniting a third world war. In practice what this comes down to is not intervention against injustice, but intervention against Communism—where Russian power and national interests are not directly threatened.

That is not a particularly noble policy, especially when one considers the rhetoric in which it is usually framed. But it could be thought of as a necessary or practical one under certain conditions. Unfortunately, those conditions assume that the Communist bloc is a unified conspiracy directed from the Kremlin and intent upon world domination by, if need be, military means. Whether such assumptions were ever valid (and some, such as George Kennan, have argued that they were not valid even in the critical area of Central Europe), they are little more than a historical anachronism today. The Communist world has been dramatically split, first by the Russo-Chinese rivalry, and then by the mounting assertions of nationalism in Eastern Europe and in the Communist nations of Cuba, North Korea and North Vietnam. What is important is not the label a regime chooses to pin on itself, but the policies it follows. Small Communist nations are no threat to the United States nor, as we should have learned from experience, are they likely to remain satellites of Moscow or Peking for very long. We coexist very well with totalitarian governments of the Right. We can learn to coexist with totalitarian governments of the Left as well, and let the Russians and the Chinese worry about the purity of their ideology.

We have defined stability as anti-Communism, and thus we have been drawn into the suppression of progressive forces simply because Communists have been involved. Although it has not been our stated intention to preserve the status quo, this has been the impact of our policy. So long as we are mesmerized by Communism as an ideology, it will be extremely difficult for us both to accept the fact that even violent changes in the status quo need not be hostile to our interests, and to restrain our urge to suppress violent or even undemocratic movements of social transformation. In some instances violent or undemocratic change is the only way that the modernization we incessantly advocate is likely to take place. Regimes which have lost the support of their own population, which cannot wrench them free from the bondage of feudalism, which find their *raison d'être* in the protection of the privileged minority, cannot be saved even by the wold's mightiest military power. That is the lesson of Vietnam, and we have had to learn it the hard way.

Now that the lesson has presumably been learned, it is up to the new Administration to apply it with intelligence and dispatch. Intelligence because it must be discriminating, dispatch because it would be exceedingly dangerous to drift along with reflex commitments that are no longer intellectually supportable. One of Johnson's great mistakes was that he did not get rid of Kennedy's foreign policy advisers. It would be more than unfortunate if Nixon made the same mistake, for if ever a policy was bankrupt, it is the one he is now inheriting.

REASSESSING NATO

Some elements are worth salvaging: the alliance with Western Europe; the effort, halfhearted though it may be, to aid the underdeveloped world; the limitation on nuclear proliferation; the détente with the Soviet Union. Yet even these worthy objectives are becoming outmoded, or are in a bad state of disrepair. NATO is clearly on its last legs and needs to be succeeded by some less antiquated conception of America's relations with Western Europe. Since neither the United States nor its allies have shown any serious desire to transform NATO into an "Atlantic federation," it has to relinquish some of its more pretentious ambitions and come to terms with the realities of a fragmented, increasingly nationalistic Europe. This means that it must be turned into a more equitable partnership, with the Europeans assuming a continually greater share of the burden of their own defense, or else it must give way to a simple mutual guarantee pact, with the United States pledging itself to defend Western Europe against Soviet attack by whatever methods seem most appropriate.

The latter alternative is not nearly so attractive to the Europeans as the present situation, in which the United States provides both the nuclear deterrent and a powerful land army in West Germany. But American patience is likely to give out even before the balance of payments requires a massive reduction of troop forces in Europe. When that day comes—and it has already been postponed too long—the Europeans will either have to pool their resources in some meaningful way to provide for their own defense, or rely on an American nuclear guarantee that is not supported by American hostages on the Continent. The smaller European countries are not ready to pull out of NATO, for they prefer American leadership to French or German dominance. But the usefulness of the alliance to the United States is diminishing, and the fact that the Atlantic Treaty is now 20 years old offers the new Administration an opportunity to conduct a long-overdue reassessment.

The Soviet occupation of Czechoslovakia has, for the time being, infused a bit of oxygen into NATO. This is particularly true among the Europeans, many of whom were deeply shocked and alarmed by the August 1968 invasion. Where the Americans took it as regrettable but hardly disastrous—the ultimate in nonchalance being Dean Rusk's remark that no pity should be lost on the Czechs and Slovaks since they were the fourth largest supplier of arms to North Vietnam—the West Europeans were made brutally aware of how fragile their defense forces really are. Without the American deterrent, and the willingness of Washington at least to threaten its use, they would be unable to hold back any determined Russian attack. It had been assumed for years in Western Europe that the Soviet Union had no intention of attacking and, in certain circles, the alliance with America was considered a tiresome insurance policy that could eventually be allowed to lapse. De Gaulle's vision of France (perhaps Western Europe?) as a mediator between the "two hegemonies" was based on precisely this view. It was shattered by the invasion, and even France has been notably cooperative in the councils of NATO in recent months.

This might seem like the happy harbinger of the rejuvenation of NATO. But unless the Russians extend their bellicosity westward, rather than confine it to their own restive empire, this new-found unity will be hard to maintain. The Atlantic alliance is based upon an identity of interests basically limited to the military field. The United States is determined that Western Europe be kept out of Soviet hands. Once that is assured, it is possible to reach various economic, political and even military agreements that are not necessarily identical with the common interests of the European allies. The Europeans, however, have more than their defense to worry about. They are concerned about the "American challenge" in business and industry, the attempt to achieve economic and political integration, the eventual reunification of the Continent, and Europe's place between two great but unstable empires.

CONTINUED COOPERATION WITH THE USSR

While seeking to maintain the old ties with Western Europe, the new Administration is eager to expand the détente with the Soviet Union. Washington allies have a vested interest in the détente; they also fear that it may be sustained at the price of the indefinite partition of Europe. The superpowers, though, are motivated by the internal mechanics of their own imperial positions, and are learning that cooperation is the price of survival. The hands-off policy toward one another's aggressions (Czechoslovakia, Dominican Republic), the nuclear nonproliferation treaty, the attempt, albeit feeble, to keep the arms race from getting totally out of control—all these are essential if the two relatively satiated superpowers are not to destroy one another. We can expect the new Administration to be driven by circumstances into continued cooperation with the Soviet Union.

There is always the danger, naturally, that the Kremlin leadership, which has lately shown certain signs of instability (as, for that matter, has the entire American political system), will try to upset the present political balance by some sudden act of *force majeure,* that it will provoke reckless moves by its wards in the Middle East or elsewhere, that it will invade Yugoslavia (an act of provocation, as distinguished from a family settling of accounts, as in Czechoslovakia, or even Rumania), or that there will be a rapprochement with China. Any of these would imperil, if not destroy, the détente and the whole policy responsible for it. Yet, until such an eventuality, the wiser course, the only viable one, is to proceed on the assumption that cooperation with the Soviet Union is possible and desirable.

Just as there is a danger that the Russians may upset the present balance— whether from an exuberant belligerence or from an alarmed defensiveness— there is as great a danger that the United States may do the same. If the new Administration proves incapable of keeping in check what an inspired Eisenhower speech writer referred to as the "military-industrial complex," if it tries to press for the kind of absolute military superiority that Nixon sometimes referred to in his campaign speeches, if it falls victim to the same bloated rhetoric and liberal self-delusion that haunted the Kennedy and Johnson Administrations, if it fails to understand that the cold war with Russia is over and that from here on in even the most advanced industrial societies will be preoccupied with the effort to hold themselves together, then we are in for serious trouble.

It is questionable whether the Nixon Administration is up to the task. The foreign policy it carries out, like the policies of its predecessors, will almost certainly be imperialistic. It would be virtually impossible for the United States, with its present economic, political and social structure, to carry out any other kind of foreign policy. But the Republicans may not delude themselves into believing that their imperialism is necessarily good for everyone it affects. And in this case skepticism may be the first step toward restraint. If the new Administration can provide a breathing space between the wars of intervention against Communism abroad and the coming guerrilla wars against racism and exploitation within America itself, it will have served a useful function. If it addresses itself to the root causes of the domestic crisis, it could even pave the way for a government, for a concept of community responsibility, that might

The Case for Retrenchment 479

blunt the edge of domestic guerrilla warfare, and perhaps make it unnecessary. What is ultimately at stake is not simply a change in policy, but a change in direction. This must be so fundamental that it is difficult to see how it can be accomplished without a drastic reform of the nation's social structure and charismatic leadership of the kind few societies ever enjoy or long tolerate. The nation must right the social imbalance that still concentrates power in the hands of the very rich at the expense of the poor, some of whom do not even realize the degree of their exploitation; launch a determined assault on racism that will uproot traditional attitudes and even the structure of our society; find a quality (though not a policy) of leadership similar to that exercised by de Gaulle when he assumed power in a country shaken by revolt; and give conscious recognition of the degree to which much of our foreign policy is rooted in economic and military imperialism. Without recognition there can be no change, and without enlightened leadership there is unlikely to be adequate recognition.

An enlightened foreign policy would require an attitude of tolerance, rather than hostility, toward violent revolutions—even where Communists are actively involved or in the vanguard. A few American corporations will suffer, vestigial attitudes about Communism will be shaken, but the national interest of the United States is unlikely to be harmed even if revolutionary governments come to power in much of Latin America—as happened in Mexico more than 50 years ago. Revolution in backward countries is no threat to the United States. The attempt to suppress revolution, as we should have learned from the Dominican Republic and Vietnam, involves a threat to the survival of American democracy. The willingness to tolerate progressive-minded revolutionary regimes—however unsympathetic we may find their methods or their political rhetoric—means coming to terms with the whole problem of development in the Third World. It means recognizing that the development process will be nasty, brutish and long, that democracy may be a political luxury for many such countries, and that the rich nations are going to have to return, in the form of development assistance, some of the booty they have extracted from the nonindustrialized ones.

The great problems of foreign policy for the 1970s will not be those of the 1960s—the restructuring of NATO, the containment of Communism, the effort to achieve nuclear superiority. The problems of the next decade will be those of seeking withdrawal from dangerously overextended positions without succumbing to the mentality of isolationism; of learning to live with revolution in the Third World; of narrowing the dangerous gap between the privileged minority in the Northern Hemisphere and the exploited majority in the underdeveloped nations; of controlling nuclear weapons; of achieving new methods of international cooperation going beyond the war-inducing confines of the nation-state; of accepting a relationship with the Soviet Union and other major powers based on limited cooperation and continued antagonism over a wide range of issues; and of liberating ourselves from the deep-rooted social and political anxieties that are expressed in an emotional hatred of Communism and an instinctual fear of revolution.

The hardest, but perhaps the most important, task of the new Administration will be to create a climate that will permit a retrenchment from the self-deluding fantasies of global intervention, while making it possible to attack the fundamental causes of disorder and disaffection at home. On the success of this task hangs not only the fate of the Nixon Administration but of the nation itself.

SUGGESTIONS FOR FURTHER READING

Careful studies of the process of foreign-policy making are few. Several volumes of papers submitted to Senator Jackson's Subcommittee on National Policy Making are available in paperback; see *The National Security Council* and *The Secretary of State and the Ambassador* (New York: Praeger, 1965 and 1964). There are some excellent case studies, such as Richard E. Neustadt's *Alliance Politics* (New York: Columbia University Press, 1970), and first-person accounts, such as Dean Acheson's *Present at the Creation: My Years in the State Department* (New York: Norton, 1969).

Tracts, polemics, and pleas for new departures in the substance of foreign policy abound. An excellent example is David Halberstam's *The Making of a Quagmire* (New York: Random House, 1965). This account of American blundering in Vietnam in 1963 draws on Halberstam's Pulitzer Prize-winning dispatches to the *New York Times*.

Among histories of recent American foreign policy, H. Bradford Westerfield's *The Instruments of America's Foreign Policy* (New York: Crowell, 1963) is useful, as in John Spanier's briefer *American Foreign Policy since World War Two* (New York: Praeger, 1968). And for revisionist analyses see J. F. Flemming, *The Cold War and Its Origins*, 2 vols. (Garden City, N. Y.: Doubleday, 1961), and Gar Alperovitz, *Atomic Diplomacy: 1965* (Garden City, N. Y.: Doubleday, 1969).

Preeminent among works on military policy is Samuel P. Huntington's *The Common Defenses: Strategic Programs in National Politics* (New York: Columbia University Press, 1961). Also useful are Warner R. Schilling, Paul Y. Hammond, and Glenn H. Snyder, *Strategy, Politics and Defense Budgets* (New York: Columbia University Press, 1962). On our European deployment, see Alistair Buchan, *NATO in the Nineteen Sixties: The Implications of Interdependence* (New York: Praeger, 1963). Harold Stein, ed., *American Civil-Military Decisions* (University, Ala.: University of Alabama Press, 1963), is a valuable collection of case studies.

Good work on strategic intelligence is extremely scarce. Serious scholars need data, and for obvious reasons not much information is available. Sherman Kent's *Strategic Intelligence for American World Policy* (Princeton, N. J.:

Princeton University Press, 1951) is dated but still useful, and Roberta Wohlstetter's *Pearl Harbor: Warning and Decision* (Stanford, Calif.: Stanford University Press, 1962) is a first-rate study of the interrelation of intelligence and policy. There are a number of sensationalistic books by journalists on intelligence gathering; quite good, however, is David Wise and Thomas B. Ross, *The Invisible Government* (New York: Random House, 1964).

Useful periodicals in this area are *Foreign Affairs, World Politics*, and *International Affairs*.

Finally, a very helpful tool, which should be on the desk of every undergraduate major in political science, is Richard L. Merritt and Gloria J. Pyszka, *The Student Political Scientist's Handbook* (New York: Harper & Row, 1969).

1-102

Date Due